DEIXIS IN NARRATIVE
A Cognitive Science Perspective

D1340348

DEIXIS IN NARRATIVE
A Cognitive Science Perspective

Edited by

**Judith F. Duchan
Gail A. Bruder
Lynne E. Hewitt**
State University of New York at Buffalo

Routledge
Taylor & Francis Group

NEW YORK AND LONDON

First Published by

Lawrence Erlbaum Associates, Inc., Publishers
10 Industrial Avenue
Mahwah, New Jersey 07430

Transferred to Digital Printing 2009 by Routledge
270 Madison Ave, New York NY 10016
2 Park Square, Milton Park, Abingdon, Oxon, OX14 4RN

Cover design by Kate Dusza

Library of Congress Cataloging-in-Publication Data

Deixis in narrative : a cognitive science perspective / editors,
   Judith F. Duchan, Gail A. Bruder, Lynne E. Hewitt
        p.   cm.
    Includes bibliographical references and index.
    ISBN 0-8058-1462-0. — ISBN 0-8058-1463-9
    1. Discourse analysis, Narrative. 2. Grammar, Comparative and
general—Deixis. 3. Cognitive science. I. Duchan, Judith F.
II. Bruder, Gail A.   III. Hewitt, Lynne E.
P302.7.D45   1995
401′41—dc20   94-2713
                                                    CIP

Publisher's Note
The publisher has gone to great lengths to ensure the quality of this
reprint but points out that some imperfections in the original may be apparent.

To our spouses:

Alan I. Duchan
Bernard Greenblatt
Shashi S. Singh

CONTENTS

Preface   **xi**

Prologue: A Simple Exercise in Narrative Understanding   **xvii**
Judith F. Duchan, Gail A. Bruder, and Lynne E. Hewitt

Part I   Deictic Theory

1   Narrative Comprehension and the Role of
        Deictic Shift Theory   **3**
        Erwin M. Segal

2   Deictic Shift Theory and the Poetics of
        Involvement in Narrative   **19**
        Mary Galbraith

3   A Cognitive-Phenomenological Theory of Fictional Narrative   **61**
        Erwin M. Segal

4   An Introduction to a Computational Reader of Narratives   **79**
        Stuart C. Shapiro and William J. Rapaport

5   Cognition and Fiction   **107**
        William J. Rapaport and Stuart C. Shapiro

6 The Deictic Center: A Theory of Deixis in Narrative   **129**
     David A. Zubin and Lynne E. Hewitt

Part II Deictic Tracking in Narrative

7 Time in Narratives   **159**
     Michael J. Almeida

8 Computational Representation of Space   **191**
     Albert Hanyong Yuhan and Stuart C. Shapiro

9 Preschool Children's Introduction of Characters into
     Their Oral Stories: Evidence for Deictic Organization of
     First Narratives   **227**
     Judith F. Duchan

10 Psychological Evidence That Linguistic Devices Are Used
      by Readers to Understand Spatial Deixis in Narrative Text   **243**
      Gail A. Bruder

Part III Subjectivity in Narrative

11 References in Narrative Text   **263**
      Janyce M. Wiebe

12 Discourse Continuity and Perspective Taking   **287**
      Naicong Li and David A. Zubin

13 Experiential Versus Agentive Constructions in
      Korean Narrative   **309**
      Soon Ae Chun and David A. Zubin

14 Anaphor in Subjective Contexts in Narrative Fiction   **325**
      Lynne E. Hewitt

15 Recognizing Subjectivity and Identifying Subjective
      Characters in Third-Person Fictional Narrative   **341**
      Gail A. Bruder and Janyce M. Wiebe

Part IV Extensions of Deictic Theory

16 Expanding the Traditional Category of Deictic Elements:
      Interjections as Deictics   **359**
      David P. Wilkins

17 Wayfinding Directions as Discourse: Verbal Directions in
English and Spanish 387
David M. Mark and Michael D. Gould

18 Deixis in Persuasive Texts Written by Bilinguals of
Differing Degrees of Expertise 407
*Carol Hosenfeld, Judith F. Duchan, and
Jeffery Higginbotham*

19 Narrative Structure in a Cognitive Framework 421
Leonard Talmy

20 A Structural Analysis of a Fictional Narrative:
"A Free Night," by Anne Maury Costello 461
*Anne M. Costello, Gail A. Bruder, Carol Hosenfeld,
and Judith F. Duchan*

References 487

Author Index 507

Subject Index 513

PREFACE

INTRODUCTION TO THE NARRATIVE GROUP

The work presented in this volume emerged from a unique interdisciplinary association among the contributors. Almost all of the authors in this book are, or were at one time, members of a research group formerly known as the Graduate Group in Cognitive Science, at the State University of New York at Buffalo. The erstwhile Graduate Group has now become one of several nuclei that form the Center for Cognitive Science at the university. Its research focus has broadened over the years, and it is currently known as the Discourse and Narrative Research Group, a forum for interdisciplinary discussion of issues related to all aspects of language in context. The present volume encapsulates the period of time during which all members of the group were primarily concerned with issues related to narrative fiction. The majority of the core members of this group are represented among the authors of this book.

In discussing our past, we find ourselves unable to devise an agreed-upon story line; this is as it should be, given the unique importance we give to the subjective nature of story world experience in our theoretical discussions. Certain facts are clear, however: The group has always been composed of faculty and graduate students working from different disciplines and methodologies. Fields represented include artificial intelligence, philosophy, linguistics, psychology, communicative disorders, education, English, and geography. We have even had a bona fide writer of fiction in our midst for some time. The work we present here coalesced around issues common to research problems we tackle separately in our disparate fields. People came to the group with questions something like these:

- How can we make an artificial intelligence comprehend stories?
- How do human intelligences comprehend stories?
- How do children learn to understand and tell stories?
- How do people use language to construct a representation of space?
- What is the ontological status of fictive versus real-world information?
- What is the nature of fictional language—how is it structured, and what are its unique properties?
- What is the best model for analyzing the representation of experience in fiction?

Of course, parts of answers to these questions can be found working within the boundaries of a single discipline. Just as obviously, a comprehensive search of the literature related to any one of them will turn up references from fields as far divided as literary criticism and natural language processing. We found that talking to each other stimulated our individual research programs, sending us in new directions. And it considerably simplified the task of navigating in alien paradigms. This, for us, is what cognitive science is: not a methodology arising from any one discipline, but rather, an ongoing conversation among researchers interested in understanding the mind.

The group applied for and received a grant from the National Science Foundation (1987–1989, IRI–8610517) to pursue its interdisciplinary research. In addition, the State University of New York at Buffalo, under the auspices of the graduate school's program for graduate groups, provided support for several years prior to the group's incorporation into the Center for Cognitive Science. The center presently supports the group's activities. The group has a close association with the Semantic Network Processing System Research Group (SNeRG) under the auspices of Stuart C. Shapiro and William J. Rapaport.

ORGANIZATION

In the Prologue, we present a simple constructed text used in the early days of the group as a starting point for discussion. This exercise presents an interesting contrast to chapter 20, by Costello, Bruder, Hosenfeld, and Duchan, in which a complex short story is analyzed using some of the concepts explored in this book, and also goes beyond those to expand in new directions. In between, we have grouped the chapters into sections on deictic theory, deictic tracking in narrative, subjectivity in narrative, and deixis within a broader theory of narrative.

The six chapters grouped under the heading Deictic Theory present the theories from philosophy, literary criticism, and linguistics that form the basis for our deictic approach to narrative. In chapter 1, Segal discusses the genesis of this project, emphasizing its roots in cognitive science. He positions us as proponents of a broad view of cognitive science, and traces the theoretical background of the models of production and comprehension of language on which we all have drawn. He introduces the model of narrative structuring used by the group, terming it *deictic shift theory.*

In chapter 2, Galbraith presents some literary critics' theories of narrative, describing how a phenomenology of narrative offers insight into the reader's experience of stories. She argues for the importance of subjectivity in narrative, and uses evidence from analyses of classic texts to support her position. Galbraith's work can profitably be read in conjunction with the chapters in part III, Subjectivity in Narrative, in which computational, cross-linguistic, and quantitative linguistic analyses of subjectivity in fiction are presented. Wiebe's computational work was ongoing at the same time as Galbraith's literary analyses, and there was much cross-fertilization of ideas between their separate projects. In such associations can be seen the benefit of a broad approach to cognitive science; the rigors of Wiebe's computational methodology force decision-making that the analyses of literary criticism are not constrained to make. This rigor, in turn, drives new theorizing. Alternatively, the scope of a literary approach may include aspects that are not computationally tractable at this time, thus allowing it to present a big picture with fuzzy edges.

In Segal's second contribution to this section, chapter 3, he blocks out one of the essential aspects of a deictic center approach to fiction: the concept of the story world, and its mimetic relation to the real world. The model proposed by Segal is presupposed by most contributors to this book.

In chapters 4 and 5, Rapaport and Shapiro cover ground that is more traditionally cognitive science in emphasis. They present the SNePS knowledge representation and reasoning system used to implement a natural language understanding program, and discuss its utility in modeling beliefs, and hence, fiction. In addition, Rapaport provides philosophical support for the model of fiction they implement, taking a Meinongian tack to explain the epistemological ontology of fictional entities.

Chapter 6 is a transition from the theories of part I to the implementations of those theories in part II. Zubin and Hewitt outline a linguistically derived theory of the deictic shift model of fiction. They discuss the mechanics of deictic centering in narrative, offering a taxonomy of deictic operations, and substantiate it with numerous examples derived from literary texts.

Part II, Deictic Tracking in Narrative, brings together studies whose methods are disparate, including computational approaches and psycholinguistic methods. Again, this variety of approaches reflects our belief in the benefits of coming at a problem from a number of different angles. The chapter by Almeida and the one by Yuhan and Shapiro outline computational theories of time and space in narrative, respectively, and develop functioning computer programs that implement those theories in SNePS. Duchan undertakes a psycholinguistic investigation of children's acquisition of deictic terms and their ability to organize their narratives deictically. She found that children as young as 2 years of age are sensitive to deictic centering in stories. Bruder offers yet a third perspective on deictic tracking in narrative, reviewing the psycholinguistic literature on spatial tracking in narrative, and describing a series of experiments studying the effect of spatial terms on readers' comprehension of narrative text.

Part III, Subjectivity in Narrative, offers a collection of papers representing a sea change in our thinking about fiction. Influenced by the work of narrative theorists such as Banfield, Hamburger, and Kuroda, Wiebe and Galbraith presented to the group a new perspective on narrative—the representation of subjective experience in fictional narrative. Many of us came to believe that one of the pleasures, and hence one of the purposes, of reading fiction is to enable us to experience vicariously another person's phenomenal world. This led to a wide-ranging exploration of the nature of the language used to represent subjectivity in narratives. In the first chapter in this section (chap. 11), Wiebe describes the philosophical background underlying her approach to referring expressions in subjective contexts. She also describes aspects of the algorithm she used to implement computational processing of subjective contexts.

Cross-linguistic work by Li and Zubin in Mandarin (chap. 12) and Chun and Zubin in Korean (chap. 13) offers evidence for the influence of subjectivity on the language of narrative texts. These two chapters show that reflexive pronominals are clear markers of subjective context and that the challenge of representing subjective experience linguistically is met by specialized uses of linguistic structures that are used differently in oral language.

Hewitt (chap. 14) offers further evidence for the importance of subjectivity in structuring the language of narrative fiction. Using a quantitative text linguistic approach, she investigates anaphoric referencing in subjective contexts. Hewitt uses her results to argue for a model of psychological processing of text in which the subjective character is the most activated, and hence, most available for reduced anaphoric evocation.

Bruder and Wiebe (chap. 15) describe a series of psycholinguistic experiments investigating readers' tracking of subjective characters in fiction, using categories from Wiebe's algorithm (described in chap. 11). They offer experimental evidence supporting Wiebe's model.

In part IV are collected papers in which deictic theory is expanded in a number of ways. Some of the papers look at deixis in genres other than narrative. In chapter 16, Wilkins argues for the deictic nature of interjections, and offers evidence from literary texts for their deictic functioning in subjective contexts. His extension of deixis to a linguistic category not traditionally analyzed as deictic offers further support for our deictically centered approach, in that deixis operates in genres other than narrative. Mark and Gould, in chapter 17, look at deictic references in the discourse of people giving wayfinding directions, analyzing the differences between speakers of English and Spanish. Their examples show that, when giving directions, many speakers assume a type of fictive deictic center from which their discourse is grounded, influencing their use of terms such as *go* and *come*.

Deictic centering in yet another genre is examined by Hosenfeld, Duchan, and Higginbotham in chapter 18, in an analysis of the deictic nature of persuasive texts written by bilinguals. They found systematic linguistic consequences of the difference in genre, relating to the goal of the discourse. The theory of deixis in narrative proffered by other contributors to this volume is centered in assumptions about the goal of reading fiction. Persuasive texts are intended to be taken differently. In contrast to fiction, for example, sentences of persuasive text are taken by the reader to be subjective or objective not just because of their linguistic coding, but rather depending on the degree to which the text has succeeded in persuading him or her.

Chapters 19 and 20 differ from the others in this section in that they, like most of the chapters in the rest of the book, deal with narrative fiction, but they also touch on aspects of fiction not covered by deictic theory. Talmy's chapter is, in some sense, a response to his experience as a latecomer to the Narrative Group and his feeling that there was a need to block out all the applicable parameters in analysis of fiction beyond deixis. Talmy's approach is a strong contrast with that of most of the other contributors. Most of us used the questions raised by the special character of deixis in fictional language to build up analyses with foundational implications for all of narrative. Talmy has approached the question from the other end, seeking to describe the foundations for the entire domain of narrative as a prologue to analysis. The impact of Talmy's ideas on some members of the group can be seen in chapter 20, in which Costello, Bruder, Hosenfeld, and Duchan use ideas from deictic shift theory, as well as categories that Talmy has sketched out, in order to analyze a short story. The story is presented in its entirety, and its author's perspective on the challenges of writing it is included in the analysis. This is a fitting conclusion for this volume, as it shows the scope of our ambition broadening from limited, constructed texts, to complex literary fiction, from the reader's ability to process text to the author's view of the process of creating text, and ultimately, the range of our theory extending to meet new challenges in fitting into a complete theory of narrative fiction.

ACKNOWLEDGMENTS

We wish to acknowledge the State University of New York at Buffalo—the program of Graduate Groups, the Offices of the Dean of Social Sciences and the Dean of Natural Sciences and Mathematics—and the National Science Foundation

(IRI-8610517, 1987–1989), which provided financial support for much of the work reported in this book.

We also wish to acknowledge the following publishers for granting permission to reprint, in part or in whole, the original or modified versions of the following articles.

Chapter 4, "An Introduction to a Computational Reader of Narratives," by Stuart C. Shapiro and William J. Rapaport and chapter 5, "Cognition and Fiction," by William J. Rapaport and Stuart C. Shapiro are revisions of "Predication, Fiction, and Artificial Intelligence" by William J. Rapaport (1991), *Topoi, 10*, 79–111, copyright 1991 Kluwer Academic Publishers, printed in the Netherlands. Reprinted by permission of Kluwer Academic Publishers.

Study 5 reported in chapter 10, "Psychological Evidence That Linguistic Devices Are Used by Readers to Understand Spatial Deixis in Narrative Text," was published as: J. Daniels (1986), "A Psychological Investigation into the Diectic Center," *Proceedings of the 8th Annual Conference of the Cognitive Science Society*, published by Lawrence Erlbaum Associates.

Chapter 11, "References in Narrative Text," by Janyce M. Wiebe was previously printed as "References in Narrative Text" by Janyce M. Wiebe (1991), *Nous, 25*(4), 457–486. Permission to reprint this article was granted by Blackwell Publishers (Cambridge, MA).

Chapter 12, "Discourse Continuity and Perspective Taking," by Naicong Li and David A. Zubin previously appeared as "Perspective Taking and Discourse Continuity" in *The Proceedings of the Chicago Linguistics Society* (Vol. 26). Permission to reprint this paper was granted by the Chicago Linguistics Society.

Chapter 13, "Experiential vs. Agentive Constructions in Korean Narrative," by Soon Ae Chun and David A. Zubin previously appeared as "Experiential vs. Agentive Constructions in Korean Narrative" in Kira Hall et al. (Eds.), *Proceedings of the Sixteenth Annual Meeting of the Berkeley Linguistics Society*. Permission to reprint this paper was granted by Berkeley Linguistics Society (Berkeley, CA).

Chapter 16, "Expanding the Traditional Category of Deictic Elements: Interjections as Deictics," by David P. Wilkins is a modified version of "Interjections as Decitics" by D. P. Wilkins (1992), *Journal of Pragmatics, 18*, 119–158. Permission to reprint this article was granted by Elsevier Science Publishers B.V.

Chapter 17, "Wayfinding Directions as Discourse: Verbal Directions in English and Spanish," by David M. Mark and Michael D. Gould was previously published as "Wayfinding Directions as Discourse: A Comparison of Verbal Directions in English and Spanish" by David M. Mark and Michael D. Gould (1992), *Multilingua, 11*(3), 267–291. Permission to reprint this article was granted by Mouton de Gruyter.

Judith F. Duchan
Gail A. Bruder
Lynne E. Hewitt

PROLOGUE:
A SIMPLE EXERCISE IN
NARRATIVE UNDERSTANDING

Judith F. Duchan
Gail A. Bruder
Lynne E. Hewitt
State University of New York at Buffalo

HISTORY AND RATIONALE FOR THE EXERCISE

In the early 1980s, the Narrative Research Group, whose work is represented in this volume, developed a graduate course, "Introduction to Cognitive Science." A number of faculty—Bruder, Duchan, Rapaport, Segal, and Shapiro—shared the responsibility of teaching this course for a period of several years. One approach we took was to introduce students to the various methodologies of communicative disorders and sciences, computer science/artificial intelligence, linguistics, philosophy, and psychology. We used as our content language understanding in general, and narrative understanding in particular. As our focus, we explored our emerging theory of the deictic center, which will be described in some detail in this volume.

One year, Stu Shapiro took the major responsibility for managing the course and used a narrative comprehension exercise to sensitize graduate students to the issues of deixis and comprehension of narrative. He asked Joyce Daniels, the graduate assistant for our research group, to write a short narrative to be used as an exercise for the first class session. Graduate students were separated into groups and were asked to read the narrative, discuss a series of questions relating to their understanding, and report back to the class at large. The exercise was successful in raising issues of deixis—how we know where and when events are taking place, and who is participating in them.

We now offer a similar exercise to the reader of this volume. We present the short story and a series of questions relating to the tracking of events and inferences about characters and events. For those not familiar with us, this will provide a first glimpse into our work.

THE STORY AND QUESTIONS ABOUT THE STORY

An Approach to Serenity, or The Doctor Will See You Now
by Joyce H. Daniels

Lorna had a toothache. She was in agony. When she called the dentist's office, the receptionist said to come right over. Lorna ran down the stairs to her garage and raced to the dentist's office. She happily sat down thinking that her misery was soon to be over. However, she sat in the waiting room for forty-five minutes before she asked the receptionist how much longer it would be before she saw the dentist. Smilingly, the receptionist informed her that she needed to wait only a few more minutes. The minutes dragged by. Finally, the dentist called Lorna's name and escorted her to the dental chair. He swiftly diagnosed the problem and remedied the situation. He then charged Lorna the $150.00 fee that he normally charged for emergency visits.

QUESTIONS FOR THE READER

1. When Lorna called the dentist's office, did she still have a toothache? How do you know?
2. Who is "the receptionist"? What justifies the use of the definite article "the"?
3. Where are you after "the receptionist said to come right over"? Note that the receptionist is at the dentist's office. Are you? If we are with Lorna at her house, why does the sentence above use "come" rather than "go"?
4. After "Lorna ran down the stairs to the garage," are you with Lorna, or did you stay in the house?
5. When Lorna "ran down the stairs to her garage," did she reach the garage? How do you know? When do you know?
6. What mode of transportation did Lorna use to get to the dentist's office? How do you know?
7. When do you know that Lorna reached the dentist's office? After "raced to the office"? Or, after "she sat down"?
8. How long was it between the telephone call and Lorna's arrival at the dentist's office? Why do we keep using "long" to refer to intervals of time?
9. Who is the "she" who "happily sat down"? How do you know?

10. Is the receptionist a man or a woman? The dentist?

11. Where are you when the dentist appears in "finally, the dentist appeared"? And where is the dentist?

12. How long was it between Lorna's talking to the receptionist and the dentist's calling her name?

13. Did the dentist ever come into the waiting room? When? How do you know?

14. Why is it natural to use "come" in the previous question, rather than, for example, "go"?

15. Where did Lorna end up after "escorted her to the dental chair"? Where did you go?

16. Did Lorna ever leave the waiting room? When? How do you know? Do you feel that you as reader also left the waiting room at that time?

SUMMARY

As is evident from the questions just listed, our issues involve understanding how readers interpret deictic terms, as well as how they locate events in time and space when that information is not explicitly provided. To cite just a few examples from the many possible ones:

1. *Reference.* The use of *the* when a character has not previously been mentioned. Is the receptionist instantiated as part of the dentist office script? And what about the use of pronouns—how do we decide to whom they refer?

2. *Movement of time* (when). At the end of a sentence, is the action completed or not? Have we moved on to the next time interval?

3. *Movement of characters* (where). How do the deictic verbs, such as *come* and *go* influence where we think characters are, or whose perspective is being taken?

These and similar questions were a starting point. The chapters of this book are a record of where some of us ended up in our pursuit of answers.

DEICTIC THEORY

1

NARRATIVE COMPREHENSION AND THE ROLE OF DEICTIC SHIFT THEORY

Erwin M. Segal
State University of New York at Buffalo

This book represents the collaborative work of a group of students and faculty at the State University of New York at Buffalo. We have our homes in various disciplines, including communicative disorders, computer science, education, English, geography, linguistics, philosophy, and psychology, but most of us think of ourselves as practicing cognitive scientists. As cognitive scientists, we are able to consider a far larger set of concepts and methods than are normally available within each of the individual disciplines. Moreover, by seriously interacting with one another on a regular basis, we attempt to keep our ideas coherent with positive inputs from all of the disciplines.

The idea of cognitive science is one that is beginning to have greater favor within the walls of academe. The path to truth is not defined by a single discipline nor by a single methodology. Cognitive science takes its topic—cognition—and tries to understand it from a variety of knowledge bases and basic methodologies.

As illustrated in Fig. 1.1, we assume that different disciplines, using different methods, have each developed an accepted database or shared set of beliefs which can contribute to the understanding of cognition. The science of cognition is informed by all of the disciplines. Cognitive scientists presume that two pieces of information must be consistent with each other if they are to be considered valid. The researchers in cognitive science have the task of using knowledge from each of the disciplines to help sharpen and clarify the claims of the others. Conceptual inconsistencies across methodologies or disciplines are viewed by cognitive scientists as problems to be solved. The output of such an approach

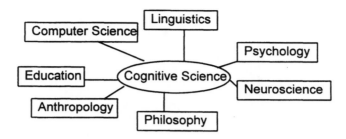

FIG. 1.1. Some of the disciplines that supply concepts and methods to the field of cognitive science.

should be a solid database and a theory that is conceptually coherent with the best of each of the separate disciplines.

The research represented in this book is focused on the process of interpretation of narrative text and the mental representation that might result from this process. We do not directly investigate perceptual or motor processes or the differences between oral and written text. Therefore, unless otherwise specified, telling, writing, hearing and reading, all refer to language activity generalized across modality.

The ultimate goals of our research program include (a) identifying the knowledge that a reader must bring to a text in order to understand it, and (b) that a writer must have brought to a text in order to have produced it, (c) describing the abstract structure of the knowledge needed for (a) and (b), (d) characterizing the processes by which a representation in memory is modified as a text is being read, and (e) by which a representation in memory is accessed as a text is being produced, (f) describing the new representations, (g) constructing a (computational) model of this process and representation, and (h) showing that the model understands the text by having it pass a Turing test by answering questions about it.

In addition to having the above goals, some of us are concerned with other questions concerning narrative. What is a story? Why are some stories or storytellers "better" than others? What does one gain by reading, viewing, or listening to a story? Why do people tell stories? Why do they listen to them? Why are these popular activities in virtually all cultures?

This anthology represents some of the work we have done so far. Much of this work has been in the development and articulation of the process by which certain information representing the spatial, temporal, and character structure implicit in the narrative is produced and understood.

In this chapter, we review some ideas relating to discourse comprehension and production and narrative interpretation that have influenced our research. We then present a brief overview of Deictic Shift Theory, which underlies the research of most of the contributors to this volume.

APPROACHES TO NARRATIVE COMPREHENSION AND PRODUCTION

Different researchers, theories, and disciplines emphasize different aspects of cognition and communication, and thus explicitly or implicitly impose different sets of constraints on how narrative comprehension and production is to be understood. In this section some of these different approaches are described. We learn from and are influenced by each of them.

Communication Theory

Communication theory originated in an analysis of communication from the perspective of people sending and receiving messages over communication systems such as telegraph and radio (Shannon & Weaver, 1949). Such physical systems support the conduit metaphor, which is a popular metaphor for communication and language comprehension (Reddy, 1979). This view holds that a message is transported from a sender to a receiver within the symbols of the communication system. The metaphor is quite explicit in general language use— "He delivered the message to me" "I acted upon the message as soon as I received it"—and is implicit in several language and narrative theories.

In some sense, the mathematical theory of communication (Shannon & Weaver, 1949) formalizes the conduit metaphor. It is designed to evaluate the success of the transfer of a message from the source (e.g., speaker) to a destination (e.g., hearer). The theory emphasizes the properties of the code. We learn from communication theory that a communication system such as language contains a small number of basic elements (e.g., phonemes), and that these are combined to produce larger more meaningful elements (e.g., words). Still larger units of communication are possible, but are not usually studied. By implication, the message to be communicated is hidden within the coded message. The speaker sends a message by encoding it into transmittable units, and the hearer understands the message by decoding the coded sequence of units received. Communication may fail if some of the codified elements get distorted in transit or there are encoding or decoding errors. Certain, but not all, interpretations of classic communication theory (Shannon & Weaver, 1949) are consistent with the conduit metaphor. Those interpretations argue that in order to communicate, the source starts with an identifiable unit of information to be communicated (a message), puts it into a form in which it can travel, and sends it toward its destination. When the encoded message arrives at the destination, it can be decoded —that is, put back into its original form.

Meaning Extraction Theories

Meaning extraction theories focus on the structure of the language rather than on the communication process, but the implicit constraints of the conduit metaphor remain. Communication theory relies heavily on the mathematics of probability applied to the likelihood that linguistic units will succeed one another.

The formal and computational linguists who presume a meaning extraction theory agree that ideas are expressed by sequences of units, but in order to produce or understand a text, a language user must apply a sequence of syntactic and semantic rules to the idea to be communicated or to the presented text. This process goes far beyond decoding and concatenating a string of elements.

It became clear many years ago (Katz & Fodor, 1963; Lashley, 1951) that concatenations of word meanings alone cannot explain comprehension. One needs to recognize the specific relationships among meanings. "Man bites dog" does not mean the same thing as "dog bites man." Although the tasks of comprehension and production became much more complicated with the addition of complex syntactic rules marking the semantic relations, the major premise of the conduit metaphor remained unsullied. Language still works because writers write sentences which contain meanings, and readers understand text by unpacking the meanings contained in the sentences.

Meaning extraction theories, which require a literal linguistic approach to comprehension, have been implied or held by many researchers (Chomsky, 1965; Davidson, 1967; Fodor, 1975, 1983; Pinker, 1984). They presume that language is a very complicated system. In order to be able to speak and understand linguistic utterances, one must know the rules of the language. Rules are manifested in implicit structural relations between elements within sentences, and these rules must be known by both speaker and hearer. Thus, problems such as, "What has to be known in order to comprehend the sentences of a language?" and, "How is the knowledge of that language acquired?" are important to study. This approach, which underlies the study of generative grammar, has some very important theoretical constraints, including the presumption that the first stages of language processing are dependent solely upon formal properties of the language, and are strongly circumscribed. Thus, language researchers can confine their study to properties of the linguistic system. They do not have to deal with general knowledge, nor the physical, social, and intentional context of utterances.

One difficulty that these theories face is the complexity of some of the proposed rules. Linguistic rules, which are needed to uncover the meaning conveyed by the text often seem so complex that their learnability is doubted. If rules necessary for comprehension and production are too complex to be learned, they must be innately given. Many linguists lean toward nativism because of such problems (Chomsky, 1965; Pinker, 1984), because regardless of the complexity of the rules, they hold that whatever meaning a sentence contains must reside within it, and the meaning must be recoverable by a competent hearer.

In meaning extraction theories, the comprehension process requires parsing the incoming sentences using lexical and syntactic information, retrieving the appropriate lexical meanings, identifying the logical relations among them, and building the semantic structure(s) implicit in the sequence of sentences. These tasks may be difficult or even impossible to learn, but they clearly constrain the domain of analysis. Comprehension is a linguistic problem; it does not require knowing where the sentence was said, who said it, what knowledge the hearer has about the subject, nor why the speaker said what he or she did. Production can also be seen as a linguistic problem; one starts with the semantic representation of a sentence to be communicated. By successive transduction of forms from the original idea unit (probably stored as a semantic representation), to its lexical and syntactic representations, to its phonological and phonetic representations, the speaker gradually converts the idea to a form that can be spoken. From a meaning extraction theory perspective, language comprehension and production take place in an encapsulated linguistic module in the brain that receives an input of linguistic strings and produces as output their conveyed meanings (Chomsky, 1965; Fodor, 1983).

Meaning extraction theories presume the conduit metaphor. The meanings of the messages are contained in the linguistic strings. When interlocutors communicate, they send each other messages encrypted within the uttered sentences. Receivers of messages must use their powerful decoding apparatuses, that is, knowledge of the language, to recover the meanings of the sentences received.

Theories of Structured Representation

Most of the research and analyses done by proponents of meaning extraction theories focused on the analysis of linguistic units, usually no larger than single sentences. Their analyses tended to be of the sentences considered in isolation and out of context. In the 1960s, after a period of several decades during which it was neglected, empirical scientists again began to study narrative and discourse (Freedle, 1977, 1979; Pompi & Lachman, 1967). It did not take researchers long to realize that the syntax and semantics of expressed sentences do not contain all of the information that is conveyed. Much of what is needed to understand a text has to come from elsewhere. There was a growing amount of empirical evidence to support such a claim. A great deal of information not directly contained in a text is often implied by it (Brewer, 1977; Pompi & Lachman, 1967; Schank & Abelson, 1977), and text often cannot be understood if taken out of context (Bransford & Johnson, 1972; Dooling & Lachman, 1971).

Meaning extraction theorists could argue that one must separate the comprehension process from what is concluded from the text. Other researchers, however, argued that comprehension cannot be separated from interpretation (Minsky, 1981; Rumelhart, 1975; Schank & Abelson, 1977). Whatever the explanation, much of the information necessary to understand the event or situation under discussion is often missing in the sentences of the text. Consider, for example, the following sentence: "Smith hit a sharp grounder to short, but he was so fast that he beat Miller's throw by two steps." Important issues concerning the mechanisms and processes of comprehension are, "What is necessary for understanding this passage?" and, "When is it understood?"

One understands the previous example only after activating a memorial structure containing knowledge about baseball. The baseball "frame" has in it information about the rules of baseball, and the expected sequence of events that occur during episodes within a game. Understanding the sentence given earlier requires understanding that Smith hit a baseball thrown to him by a pitcher, that he hit the ball with a baseball bat, that it was picked up off the ground by Miller (a shortstop), that Miller threw the ball to the first baseman who caught it, that Smith ran quickly from the batter's box next to home plate toward first base, that he stepped on first base and ran beyond it before the first baseman caught the ball. The reader would also know (and therefore would not have to be told) that Smith would remain on first base for the time being, that his next immediate goal was to get to second base, that the pitcher would next throw the ball to someone else, and so on.

Structured representation approaches to comprehension take the position that a major data source of the intended message resides in hearers and is not delivered by the text (Adams & Collins, 1979). Moreover, these approaches presume that one cannot theoretically isolate a context-free component of the comprehension process. Hearers and speakers have within themselves different conceptual structures containing the information needed for comprehension and production. Bartlett (1932) introduced the idea of structured representations in his seminal work, *Remembering*. He said that readers create a schema in their minds based on previous knowledge and experience to help them remember the text that was read. The current view is that the appropriate structure needs to be selected, activated, and updated in order for the message to be completed. Several efforts characterize such approaches (Bobrow & Winograd, 1977; Minsky, 1981; Schank & Abelson, 1977). These approaches use different labels for the data structures enabling comprehension or production; some of these labels are *schemas* (Bartlett, 1932), *frames* (Minsky, 1981), *story grammars* (Rumelhart, 1975) and *scripts* (Schank & Abelson, 1977).

According to Minsky (1981), frames can be adapted to fit a given linguistic or perceptual event. The frame contains different kinds of information represented by a network of nodes and relations. Some of the nodes and relations are abstract and unchangeable; others are more specific and modifiable as a function of incoming information. The frame includes principles of interpretation and modification. It can also contain expectancies implemented as conditional updating rules, such that incoming information at one time would be interpreted in relation to a particular node in the frame, and information received at another time would be interpreted in relation to a different node. At the lower levels, a frame often contains default values as well as empty slots. A default value is a detail that is tied to the frame and understood as being the case unless it is explicitly dislodged on the basis of new information (Minsky, 1981).

Frame theory, as do all structured representation theories, assumes there is a large top-down component in understanding. These theories may disagree about how much bottom-up processing there is. Somehow the frame which represents the type of situation currently encountered is activated. As the text is read, the asserted components are understood in relation to assigned loci within the frame, rather than as self-contained propositions. The structured relations within the frame also supply unasserted relations, as needed, among the textual elements. From the previous baseball example, we see that once the baseball frame is activated: Smith fills the role of batter, "grounder" is a particular way that a baseball traverses a path, the ball is hit toward fielders, and "short" is often an abbreviation of "shortstop." The frame would contain the information that after a batter hits the ball on the ground, his next goal is to reach first base before the ball gets there, and if a fielder retrieves the ball after it has touched the ground, his next goal is to try to get the ball to the first baseman before the batter reaches the base.

Another kind of structured representation that has received considerable attention in narrative comprehension is that of a *story grammar* (Mandler & Johnson, 1977; Rumelhart, 1975; Stein & Glenn, 1979). Story grammars make sense of, and integrate, the sequence of sentences in stories. A story grammar was originally defined in terms of a set of rewrite rules that would generate a story structure (Rumelhart, 1975), although the formal properties of rewrite rules were not usually developed. Most story grammarians tried to identify the elements of a story, and the standard occurrence sequence of these elements with implied meaning relations among them. Different story grammars do not all contain the same categories, but a typical grammar would include such elements as setting, initiating event, internal response, attempt, direct consequence, and reaction (Stein & Glenn, 1979). Story grammars are like the other structured representation theories in that readers and authors must know the structure ahead of time, and the knowledge of the structure allows them to give meaning and a structural role to the sentences in the text.

According to Schank and Abelson (1977), all mentally competent people in the world have specific knowledge about many societally relevant standard situations or event sequences which they call scripts. In the United States, these could include such scripts as eating at a restaurant, riding a bus, football games, and birthday parties. A participant in a script, or a reader of a story which contains a script, makes use of that knowledge and interprets particular events or expressions against that knowledge background. He or she needs to be told about only the specific variations of the particular situation. The script fills in where the variants belong and how to interpret them.

Structured representation theorists have as their goal the representation of the meaning of the text, but they do not fully accept the conduit metaphor. They presume that much of the conveyed meaning is implicit, and is not inherent in the conventional linguistic meanings of the sentences written. It follows that the process of language interpretation cannot be linguistically encapsulated. The reader must use contextual and world knowledge to understand and represent the text as intended by the writer.

One criticism, at least for many implementations of structured representation theories, is that they require most of the relations conveyed by a text to be known prior to its being heard. To control comprehension, they require a well-defined a priori set of structural relations (Schank & Abelson, 1977). Most stories or events worthy of discussion, however, attain that status by deviating from the stereotypic situation (Burke, 1969; Lucariello, 1990), and therefore, do not fit easily into a frame. Frame theories do not have mechanisms to handle the deviations.

Situational Semantics and Deixis

Situational semantics theory, like structural representation theories, requires information not conveyed by the text for interpretation—it focuses on the nonlinguistic context of the discourse (cf. Barwise & Perry, 1983). Much of the interpretation of a sentence depends upon this context. The most obvious need for context is in the interpretation of *deictic* terms. Such terms, which directly implicate the context, include *I*, *now*, and *here*. These refer to the person, time, and place of the speech act. Consider the sentence, "I am here now." Used in context, this statement would normally inform hearers of the whereabouts of a particular person. However, considered as an independent sentence free of context, the sentence has no meaningful content.

There are many deictic terms. These terms include semantic content based on the situation of use with more context free semantic content. *Today, yesterday, this morning*, and *ago*, are dependent upon the time of the utterance in conjunction with the semantics of temporal relation. To identify *Aunt Mary* and *Mother*, deictic knowledge of the utterer in conjunction with the semantics of kinship terms are often required. Verbs, such as *come* and *arrive*, and present, future and past tenses, are often dependent on the time and place of the utterance as well as the semantics of space and time. Definite descriptors (e.g., *the book*) and even proper names are frequently subject to the speech situation for interpretation. Careful study of sentence tokens continues to uncover new deictic phenomena (Wilkins, this volume).

Rather than considering deixis as something added to normal language use, situation semantics makes context dependence the basis of semantics. According to Barwise and Perry (1983):

> One of the simplest facts about human language . . . [is the fact that] an utterance must be made by someone, someplace, and sometime. That is, an utterance always takes place in a discourse situation, and so the facts about the discourse situation can always be exploited to get from the meaning of the expression used to whatever information is to be conveyed. (pp. 32–33)

Barwise and Perry also suggested that the speech situation is naturally and automatically included as a component of the interpretation of a sentence. They presented what they called the relation theory of meaning. For them, "meaning . . . is a relation between situations" (p. 6); and the interpretation of an utterance has three components: the situation of the utterance, the content of the utterance, and the facts concerning the described situation.

Situation semantics is based on a set of important insights. However, it seems to be most directly applicable to face-to-face conversation. There are discourse genres in which the speech situation cannot directly play the role Barwise and Perry indicated for them.

Context and Contextualization

Fillmore (1975, 1981) noticed that some sentences imply important information about their context of use. He called this *contextualization of a* sentence. He identified two kinds of contextualization: external and internal. *External contextualization* is what the sentence form and content imply about the situation in which it is expressed. For example, if someone says, "I need a box about yea big," the addressee must be in visual contact with the hearer in order for the message to be fully understood. External contextualization is subtly different from situation semantics in terms of its emphasis. Whereas situation semantics implies that one only understands sentences by being in the context, external contextualization holds that certain sentences found outside of appropriate contexts cannot be interpreted.

Internal contextualization concerns what the speaker and hearer must presume about the context of the situation in order to understand it correctly. Consider the following example: "The door of Henry's lunchroom opened and two men came in" (Hemingway, 1938/1953, p. 279). In this sentence, the internal contextualization suggests that the sentence was expressed from inside Henry's lunchroom. We know that to be the case even though we ourselves are not inside the lunchroom when we read it.

How a sentence is processed and interpreted depends upon the physical and conceptual context within which it appears. A sentence is not processed, and then related to its context; rather, sentences are often first understood in relation to their context. There are several psycholinguistic experiments that show that, without an appropriate conceptual context, some passages are not understood (Bransford & Johnson, 1972; Bransford & McCarrell, 1974; Dooling and Lachman, 1971). Also, there is evidence that some components of a sentence are tied to the context and given an interpretation based on that context, before other parts are interpreted (Greenspan & Segal, 1984).

Cooperative Principle

Grice (1975) identified the *cooperative principle* to be a pragmatic constraint on the interpretation of conversation. The principle states that normally, language is a cooperative venture between the interlocutors. In this cooperative spirit, speakers give to hearers information that they need for their intended purpose;

they don't mislead them by giving them misinformation, or information that is irrelevant to their goals. In addition, the cooperative speaker does not assert things that the hearer is expected to know. These principles not only make communication more efficient, it makes it pragmatically possible. Grice applied the principle directly to face-to-face conversation, but he implied that it applies to all genres of language and human action.

Because of the cooperative principle, asserted information can be incomplete, and hearers tend to accept the propositions of the speakers. Since the cooperative principle is normative, surface deviations from expected expressions may lead the reader to look for a cooperative interpretation of the expression (Grice, 1975; Searle, 1975a).

Speech Act Theory

The idea that people do different kinds of things when they talk, write, read, and listen is very important for understanding narrative comprehension and production. Austin (1962), Grice (1975), Searle (1969, 1975c), and Wittgenstein (1958) first pointed out the importance of these issues. Austin and Searle tried to place on a firm theoretical footing the idea that people do different things with language.

Austin first identified three levels of analysis for a linguistic act:

1. Locutionary act—the execution of the intention to utter a sentence in a language. By uttering a sentence, the locutionary act is carried out.

2. Illocutionary act—the execution of the intended purpose of the expression. If A intends to tell B proposition S, A asserts S in B's presence. By asserting S in B's presence, A executes the illocutionary act of telling B something. There are many illocutionary acts. Many of these acts are identified by an illocutionary verb such as *telling, asking, promising, affirming, beseeching*, and *advising*. According to Austin (1962), there are over 1,000 illocutionary verbs in English which, he suggested, might be categorized in five more global categories.

3. Perlocutionary act—the intentional effect of the expression on the audience. The perlocutionary act differs from the illocutionary act in that it requires the audience to understand the intention. *Persuade* and *entertain* are two examples of perlocutionary verbs. A can attempt to persuade B by uttering S, but if B doesn't agree, he or she fails.

Searle (1975c) attempted to create a taxonomy of speech acts and identified five major categories. These are: (a) representatives—basically, statements about the world, (b) directives—requests and questions, (c) commissives—promises and threats, (d) expressives—statements about or implications of one's own psychological state, including greetings and exclamations, and (e) declarations—statements that create institutional facts (e.g., marrying, christening). Searle argued that this taxonomy encompasses all uses of language. He argued elsewhere

(Searle, 1975b) that there were no special narrative or story speech acts. Sentences in fictional narrative are purported to be primarily representatives. Other analyses, however, imply that there are speech acts applicable to narrative that do not fit easily into the Searle taxonomic classes (cf. Bruner, 1986; Clark & Carlson, 1982).

Clark and Carlson (1982) proposed that there is a speech act category they called *informative*. It is designed to inform hearers, other than the person directly addressed, of the content of the message. Speakers can intentionally create messages to have different perlocutionary effects upon different hearers. Brewer and Lichtenstein (1982) argued that certain narratives have the particular intention to entertain. This leads to a different set of criteria from those of informatives, or any of the Searle set. Deictic Shift Theory (Segal, 1990) implies that, in addition to the author's speech acts, the pragmatics of narrative generation and interpretation have important parameters that need exploration. These are discussed in chapter 3, and they are implied in several other chapters.

Narrative Theory

The role of narrative theory in this taxonomy is not as clearly defined as are the theories described in the previous sections. Whereas all of the other theories are directly involved with cognitive issues of competence and performance, narrative theory is not. Narrative theorists are interested in describing and characterizing the content and structure of narratives. What makes something a narrative? What are the components of narratives and what are their properties? How is the relevant information represented? (Chatman, 1978; Genette, 1980; Prince, 1982; Todorov, 1977). From a cognitive perspective, narrative theorists are scholars whose task is to identify the properties of the input stimulus (cf. Gibson, 1966), and to imply what kind of information needs to be extracted from it (cf. Bruner, 1986).

Analysis of narrative has a long tradition, beginning with Plato's *Republic* and Aristotle's *Poetics*. It developed into quite a crescendo in recent decades. Interestingly, few of the researchers cited in the previous sections acknowledged any insights derived from this body of scholarship. One exception is Rumelhart's proposal of a story grammar, that derives from Propp's analysis of Russian folk tales (1975).

There is no universal agreement as to the nature of narrative text (Banfield, 1982; Genette, 1988; McHale, 1983) and there are different genres of narrative, but most narratives share some properties. (For a fuller discussion of these similarities and differences, see Galbraith, this volume). Narratives contain *existents* (e.g., characters, objects, settings), and *events* (e.g., happenings, actions). These existents and events are assumed to be temporally and spatially related to one another. That is, they exist in the same world (Chatman, 1978; Pavel, 1986). Existents and events possess particular attributes which are either expressly granted by the text, or else are implied by more general properties of the narrative genre, although much modern fiction challenges these presumptions.

Fictional narrative is often presented by a text in a natural language. The sentences are sequential, but their sequence is not necessarily isomorphic with the sequence of events in the story world. In other words, the reader does not necessarily learn of events in the temporal order in which they purportedly occur (Genette, 1980, 1988). The language of the text can directly imply that the sentences are generated by a witness to the events (a fictional narrator), and sometimes does not (Banfield, 1982; Chatman, 1978; Cohn, 1978). Often, the language in fictional narrative text has properties that one is unlikely to find in other genres (Banfield, 1982, Cohn, 1978; Galbraith, this volume; Segal, this volume).

Narrative theory helps to identify a domain within which cognition occurs. In order to understand or to produce decent fictional narrative, the reader and writer must have cognitive states and processes that accommodate the properties of the text. We cannot understand what the cognitive system does when it produces or interprets narrative if we do not know what it needs to do (Marr, 1982). Narrative theory helps us to learn that.

DEICTIC SHIFT THEORY

The theoretical approach adopted in this volume is identified by a cognitive act. Readers and writers of narratives sometimes imagine themselves to be in a world that is not literally present. They interpret narrative text as if they were experiencing it from a position within the world of the narrative. This act of imagination was commented on over 2,000 years ago by Aristotle in his *Poetics*. He pointed out that poetry (tragedy, comedy, epic) was a mimetic art; its primary mode was to represent actions. The Greek word, *mimesis*, refers to imitation, or representation, or experience of that which is not literally present. Many modern scholars touch on at least some aspects of this experiential process in their work (e.g., Auerbach, 1953; Bruner, 1986; Walton, 1990). We found that this act of imagination, this deictic shift, has important interpretive and computational consequences. It gave us a way to approach narrative text that seems to be experientially and cognitively sound. Without the idea of a deictic shift, it is difficult to account for much of the detail of narrative text. Many researchers circumvent that problem by making up their own text, or giving global interpretations of actual text. We think that much of the detail of text is only understandable from a position somewhere within the narrative world requiring a deictic shift (e.g., Li, 1990). Our approach allows us to grapple with subtleties of naturally occurring narrative text. The deictic shift approach is consistent with phenomenological experience. When reading fictional text, most readers feel they are in the middle of the story, and they eagerly or hesitantly wait to see what will happen next.

Readers get inside of stories and vicariously experience them. They feel happy when good things occur, worry when characters are in danger, feel sad, and may even cry, when misfortune strikes. While in the middle of a story, they are likely to use past tense verbs for events that have already occurred, and future tense for those that have not.

The Deictic Shift Theory (DST) argues that the metaphor of the reader getting inside of a story is cognitively valid. The reader often takes a cognitive stance within the world of the narrative and interprets the text from that perspective. We show that there is much data to support this idea, and we attempt to specify some mechanisms and computational processes that could implement it. DST claims that how a text is interpreted depends on the cognitive stance of the reader.

We have not seen the DST elsewhere in the cognitive psychology literature, but there are near analogues. Many studies in psychology attempt to manipulate intentions or set when they make instructions to subjects an independent variable (cf. Graesser, 1993), and these manipulations can have a major effect on performance (e.g., Hyde & Jenkins, 1973). In DST, the properties of the set of the reader or writer is simply generalized and more explicitly specified. The phrase *cognitive stance* is more self-explanatory than is set. We suggest that when one reads a narrative as it is meant to be read, he or she is often required to take a cognitive stance within the world of the narrative. A location within the world of the narrative serves as the center from which the sentences are to be interpreted. In particular, deictic terms such as *here* and *now* refer to this conceptual location. It is thus the *deictic center*. DST is a theory that states that the deictic center often shifts from the environmental situation in which the text is encountered, to a locus within a mental model representing the world of the discourse.

The Deictic Center

In ordinary usage, deictic terms are interpreted from the speaker's and hearer's environmental situation (Barwise & Perry, 1983). Buhler (1982) identified three deictic components of this situation—temporal, spatial, and person. At the center, or origo, are *here*, *now*, and *I*. Something that is *here* may be *this*. *That* is not *here* but *there*. I address *you*, and refer to *him* or *her*. Both temporal adverbs (e.g., *then*, *soon*) and tense (*present, past, future*) mark the temporal relation to the origo. The center from which the deictic terms derive is more than just the point of origin for the deictic terms. This deictic center (DC) contains all of the elements of the here and now, or the phenomenal present for the user of the deictic terms. Deictic Shift Theory states that in fictional narrative, readers and authors shift their deictic center from the real-world situation to an image of themselves at a location within the story world. This location is represented as a cognitive structure often containing the elements of a particular time and place within the fictional world, or even within the subjective space of a fictional character.

The DC is a structure which lends coherence to a text when that coherence is not directly represented in the syntax or lexicon. Events and other aspects of a story are often described without explicit mention of where, when, or to whom they belong. We all know that these interpretations are constrained by context. If a DC has been established, the reader can correctly localize those story aspects where they belong. The DC does not remain static within the story, but shifts as the story unfolds. Major research problems of the DST are to identify the properties of DCs and the principles by which a DC may be created, identified, and shifted. Several of the following chapters are involved with these issues.

Some Properties of the Deictic Shift Approach

The research reviewed in the previous sections helped us to shape our position. Some of the guidelines we tend to follow are outlined and are compared to the theories reviewed previously.

Detailed Analysis of Form and Content of Text. Most cognitive scientists use self-generated, short examples in their research. Real text, however, almost always has properties that one is not likely to find among sentences generated in order to illustrate or evaluate some a priori hypothesis. Successful writers present textual material that is enjoyed by readers and understood at several levels. Some of the specific devices they use to communicate their narrative intentions include sentence and paragraph structure, tense, intersentential connectives, lexical choice, pronominalization, and other textual details. In addition, writers may use such paralinguistic devices as white space, font, punctuation, chapter breaks, and headings. Speakers may use voice quality, gestures, and even orientation of the body to convey parts of the message. Much information about mechanisms underlying generation and comprehension of narrative can be gleaned from the details of the form and content of narrative text.

Presumption of an Open Text. The comprehension of a narrative goes far beyond the information retrievable from a linguistic analysis of the sentences in the text. Much of what is conveyed to the reader is not directly expressed in the sentences read. What a sentence means depends, in part, on its sequence of words, but it also depends on the specific linguistic and nonlinguistic context within which it appears, and the intentions of the writer. Readers must use general knowledge, logical and pragmatic constraints, and special stances toward the text to experience and interpret it correctly.

Speaker–Hearer Model Is Not Presumed. The speaker–hearer communication model accounts for a small percentage of the sentences in narratives. The author uses the language to exploit many different intentions. The syntactic form of a sentence does not often conform to one in which the author is addressing a reader. Much of the text is mimetic or representational rather than asserted. Both author and reader often take a cognitive stance other than their literal physical positions. None of this eliminates the need of the author to consider the effect of his or her words on readers, but rather, it opens up the possibilities of varied pragmatic goals presented by various means.

Primary Epistemology of Narrative Is Not That of Assertion. In most discourse, it is assumed that a speaker asserts sentences or propositions. One of the tasks of the hearer is to evaluate whether the speaker can justify the claims that he or she makes. If the claims are justified, then it is epistemologically legitimate to accept the claims made, otherwise they may be challenged. Such is not the case in fictional narrative. Objective sentences in fiction must be accepted as true, even when known to be false (Wiebe, 1990b). If propositions are to be justified at all, the justification would be for reasons of aesthetics or verisimilitude. Sentences that are not objective or in propositional form serve other interpretive or experiential functions.

A Mental Model Is Constructed. Almost all cognitive science projects attempt to generate a structured representation that contains the specific information needed for its purposes. Our approach is not different. Currently we assume that the reader constructs a model representing the fictional world from the text as it is encountered. Much of our research concerns the properties of the model. How is the model constructed? What categories of narratives should be represented? How shall they be related to one another? How does currently encountered text get represented in the incomplete model?

Most Events Occur in a Deictic Center. The story tends to be constructed locally. Although there are many temporal and spatial shifts in the presentation of a text (Genette, 1980, 1988) the reader tends to witness most events as they seem to happen (Almeida, 1987, this volume; Wiebe, 1990b, this volume). The events tend to occur within the mental model at the active space-time location to which the reader has been directed by the syntax and semantics of the text (Segal, 1990, this volume). The Deictic Shift Theory is our explanation of this shift to a deictic center in the model.

Deictic and Other Referring Expressions Primarily Refer to People, Places, Things, Events, and Relations Within the Story World. The situation necessary for the interpretation of text is the conceptual situation of the story world. This is necessary in order to be able to give the text a close reading and make sense of the terms and tenses encountered there. Once the existents and events of the story world are created by the text, they exist in relation to one another. Deictic terms, proper names, definite descriptions, pronouns, and other referring expressions almost invariably refer to these existents and events.

Deictic Shift Theory is by no means a complete theory, but it provides a means of approaching narrative text that has many possibilities. Many of these are explored in the following chapters.

2

DEICTIC SHIFT THEORY
AND THE POETICS OF INVOLVEMENT
IN NARRATIVE

Mary Galbraith

SUBJECTIVITY IN NARRATIVE

What about the role of subjectivity in the language-act? Phenomenology links language not only to the objective referent in the world, but also to the subjectivity which is speaking. The phenomenologist Serge Doubrovsky explains it most succinctly: "Whenever something is said, someone must be saying it." Or if we use Ricoeur's formulation, "the display of a world and the positioning of an ego are symmetrical and reciprocal." Though Ricoeur, pressured by the opposition of the structuralists, has a more complex definition of the self–world relation than did the generation of phenomenologists preceding him, the basic formula of Merleau-Ponty still applies: for the phenomenologist, meaning (in and through language) arises from the action, or more precisely the interaction, between self and world. Meaning is densest and richest in literary discourse. This is so because literary language can best "embody" (a favorite metaphor of Merleau-Ponty) non-conceptual as well as conceptual intentionality. Intentionality is by its very nature unique to the *Lebenswelt* of the individual speaker, since each person's self–world relations are unique. It is through the intentionality unique to any given author, and present in the language of that author, that he is present in his literary work. In fact, language does not only embody intentionality—language is an extension of the author's intentional field. Language becomes a vital theater of exchange through which the author interacts with world. (Magliola, 1973, pp. 238–239)

Recent approaches to fiction in the humanities and social sciences have made problematic the twin issues of referentiality and subjectivity in narrative. There has been an overall recoil from the naivete of literary analysis built on simplistic equations between the subjectivity of the author and the intentionality found in his or her work, or between literary and historical worlds. New Criticism demanded that the analysis of literature be grounded in "the work itself," whereas structuralism simply bracketed questions of subjectivity and referentiality as irrelevant.

Poststructuralist theory has been more actively hostile to traditional notions of subjectivity and reference. It calls into question the whole notion of a real world and a transcendent subject, finding instead that referentiality and subjectivity are effects of language. As Carroll (1982) states, "the subject remains only as a skeleton of its former self, as a function of language" (p. 15), and, "this . . . anti-subject . . . consists of *the rules of the game,* the laws which govern the 'generation' of a text" (p. 17).

Two theoretical approaches that work for a critical but positive and subtle rendition of the role of subjectivity in narrative are hermeneutics and the phenomenology of reading. These concentrate on the subjectivity or intersubjectivity of the author/reader or reader/text relationship.

Finally, narrative theorists have argued about the status of fictional subjectivity and its relationship to narrative techniques. Most of them assume an a priori model of fictional subjectivity that sets a narrator as mediating subject between the reader and the characters.

In what follows, I approach the issue of subjectivity in narrative using a linguistically based tradition largely rejected or ignored by narrative theorists. I combine this tradition with that of Merleau-Ponty's phenomenology of language in the manner called for by Ricoeur (1974), to create a poetics of involvement, that is, a poetics that profits from structuralist (and poststructuralist) insights while nevertheless asserting that the primary purpose of reading novels continues to be entering into and living the experience of the self–worlds of fictional beings.

Deixis

The key to this intersection between the linguistics of subjectivity and the phenomenology of language is the term *deixis.*

When philosophers, linguists, and narrative theorists attempt to understand the role of subjectivity in language and conversely, the role of language in subjectivity, they invariably notice a certain aspect of language which seems to depend on extralinguistic, subjective, occasion-specific considerations. Theorists have variously named this aspect of language *egocentric particulars* (Russell), *shifters* (Jespersen, Jakobson), *indexicals* (Peirce), *token-reflexives* (Reichenbach), *occasional terms* (Husserl), or *deictics* (Bühler). By these terms, they designate those words and aspects of language that can only be understood with reference to a NOW, a HERE, and an I. For some, the irreducible deictic word is THIS, which can refer to anything at all, depending on the particulars of the speech situation. "This time" is NOW, "this place" is HERE, and "this person" is I.

Deixis (adjectival form, *deictic*) is a psycholinguistic term for those aspects of meaning associated with self–world orientation. Deixis is a language universal (Hockett, 1963) that orients the use of language with respect to a particular time, place, and person. Karl Bühler, the Austrian psychologist and semiotician, was the first person to employ the term in its modern sense. He distinguished the deictic field (*Zeigfeld*) of language from its symbolic field, and named the orientational axes of the deictic field the *Origo of Here/Now/I*:

> Two intersecting perpendicular strokes on the page can serve as a coordinate system for us with O as the origo, the point of origin for the coordinates:

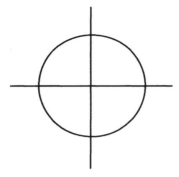

> I maintain that three deictic words must be put at the place of O, if this scheme is to represent the deictic field of human language, namely the deictic words *here, now,* and *I.* These lexical items, so simple in their sound structure, might induce the language theorist into philosophical abysses or to respectful silence, when challenged to determine their function. Rather, he should simply acknowledge that it is certainly very peculiar, but nevertheless precisely statable, how they function in a concrete utterance. . . . In the sound form, in the phonetic pattern of the words *now, here, I,* there is nothing conspicuous; it is only peculiar that they ask, each in turn: look at me as a sound phenomenon, take me as a moment marker, as a place marker, as a sender marker (sender characteristic).
>
> And this the naive speech partner has learned, and does take them in this way. . . . Only the logician is baffled. . . . But it is hoped that we can ease his deliberations via our coordinate concept; because the "setting up" of a coordinate system always has a specific function, as the logician knows. In our case, it is just the coordinate system of "subjective orientation," to which all parties in verbal exchange are and remain attached. (Jarvella & Klein, 1982, pp. 13–14)

Deixis is not limited to a few selected words such as *I, you,* and *this.* It is also, as defined by Peirce (Buchler, 1955) in his description of the same phenomenon, the function that connects all language use to situations.

[A] symbol, in itself, is a mere dream; it does not show what it is talking about. It needs to be connected with its object. For that purpose, an index is indispensable. No other kind of sign will answer the purpose. That a word cannot in strictness of speech be an index is evident from this, that a word is general—it occurs often, and every time it occurs, it is the same word, and if it has any meaning *as a word,* it has the same meaning every time it occurs; while an index is essentially an affair of here and now, its office being to bring the thought to a particular experience, or series of experiences connected by dynamical relations. (p. 56)

Deixis has long been associated with the gestural dimension of language. Peirce's definition of the index as anything that focuses the attention or anything that startles us applies both to the spatial gesture of pointing and to the phonic gesture of shouting (Buchler, 1955). Revzin (1974), in an essay on the possible origins of language, called deixis "the primordial function of gesture" (p. 18) and found in deictic signals "the concepts conveyed in modern language by words of the type 'here,' 'there,' 'near,' 'distant,' and by different grammatical categories" (p. 18). Atkinson (1979), in a study of children's first utterances, asserted that "if we interpret 'basicness' as having implications for ontogenesis, one particular nonpropositional function is more fundamental [than the propositional function] to the development of language" (p. 230). This most fundamental function is the deictic function of calling attention to a situated particular. This function, which can be performed gesturally by pointing and shouting, can also be performed verbally by a "single deictic particle [whose] function is to draw attention to some feature of the situation, . . . normally accompanied by some paralinguistic movement of the head or hands. . . . We may think of the deictic as meaning 'look!' or 'there!' " (Lyons, 1975, p. 645).

The deictic function is not only a phylogenetic or ontogenetic stage in the development of language, but the continuing prerequisite for all reference (Lyons, 1975). All language use depends on some felt relevance to situation, on the attention of participants, and their ability to lift out the topic. Gale (1967) pointed out that the efforts of some analytic philosophers to produce a language devoid of deixis are in vain, because without it, "we could not know, for example, that some event is now happening, simultaneous with this token [instance of speech]" (p. 152). If such cues were removed from verbal articulation, they would have to be supplied by inference or other contextual cues. Like zero in mathematics and the dark space in the theater, deixis orients us within a situation without calling attention to itself.

The concerns of Merleau-Ponty with language are largely with its deictic functioning. Again and again, Merleau-Ponty (1962) makes the point that language has a bodily, oriented dimension which gives it life: "[Language] presents or rather is the subject's taking up of a position in the world of his meanings" (p. 193), and, "I reach back for the word as my hand reaches towards the part of my body which is being pricked; the word has a certain location in my linguistic world, and is part of my equipment" (p. 180).

Deixis and Subjectivity

Deixis governs such grammatical and epistemological categories as topicalization (Buchler, 1955), orientational mapping (Buchler, 1955), unique reference (Gale, 1967), narrativity (Bruder, Duchan, Rapaport, Segal, Shapiro, & Zubin, 1986), and induction (Apel, 1980). In the present work, the most important aspect of deixis is its relationship to subjectivity: "expressions which we group as 'deictic' introduce an explicitly subjective orientation into linguistic classification" (Wales, 1986, p. 401). Ricoeur's (1974) comments on indicators are addressed to this issue:

> These signs do not connote a class of objects but designate the present occurrence of discourse; they do not name but indicate the *I*, the *here*, the *now*, the *this*, in short, the relation of a speaking subject to an audience and a situation. What is admirable is that "language is organized in such a way that it allows each speaker to appropriate the entire language by designating himself as the '*I*.' " (Benveniste, 1971, p. 226 [internal quote]; Ricoeur, 1974, p. 255)

Benveniste (1971) found in the word "I" the source of our ability to adopt language as our own, and therefore the source of subjectivity, rather than vice versa. Ricoeur (1974) used Benveniste's arguments but dissented from his conclusion, arguing with Merleau-Ponty that language is necessarily and originally embodied and that, although subjectivity is performed through language, subjectivity originates in our bodily interactions with the world:

> Speech is itself the reanimation of a certain linguistic knowledge which comes from the previous words of other men, words which are deposited, "sedimented," "instituted," so as to become this available *credit* by which I can now endow with verbal flesh this oriented void in me (which is signifying intention) when I want to speak. (p. 249)

Ricoeur's phrase, this oriented void, recalls Merleau-Ponty's (1962) position that:

> The word "here" applied to my body does not refer to a determinate position in relation to other positions or to external co-ordinates, but the laying down of the first co-ordinates, the anchoring of the active body in an object, the situation of the body in face of its tasks. (p. 100)

The Deictic Field and Its Functioning in Narrative

The first theorist to consider the role of deixis in narrative was Karl Bühler, the Austrian psychologist. He noticed that what he called the *Zeigfeld*, the deictic field, operates in three different modes. The first, which he called *ad oculos*, operates in the here-and-now of the speaker's sensible environment. Thus, when the speaker points at an object and says "this," those who share his or her sensible environment perceive what he or she is indicating. The second, which he called *anaphora,* operates on the context of discourse itself considered as a structured environment. When a speaker or writer uses the word "this" to refer to something in his or her own discourse, those who are following the speaker's words can easily understand what is being referred to. The third mode in which the deictic field can operate is that of imagination and long-term memory, which Bühler called *deixis at phantasma*:

> If someone wants to show something to someone else, then both of them, the one who is doing the leading and the one who is being led, must have a sufficient degree of harmonious orientation. . . . [But] [h]e who is led by phantasma cannot follow the arrow of the speaker's outstretched arm and pointed finger with his gaze to find the something out *there*; he cannot use the spatial origin quality of the voice's sound, to find the place of a speaker who says *here*; the voice character of an absent speaker saying I also does not belong to written language. And still, a rich variety of these and other deictic words are offered to one in vivid accounts of absent objects and by absent narrators. A look at any travel report or novel will essentially confirm this on the first page. (Bühler in Jarvella & Klein, 1982, pp. 22–23)

Bühler attempted to describe the psychological and physical process whereby the live deictic field of our own bodily orientation and experience can be transposed into an imaginative construction. In his model, the body–feeling representation, or *Korpertastbild* (what psychologists would probably now call the body schema), becomes loosened from its involvement with the HERE/NOW/I deictic coordinates of waking life in our immediate environment, and becomes available to translation into an environment we construct both conceptually and orientationally. (Bühler used the word "loosened" to indicate that in this process, the normal subject never really forgets where he or she is in the physical world, but rather backgrounds this knowledge to allow for imaginative travel.) The deictic coordinate system, which Bühler called the *Origo of HERE/NOW/I* (Jarvella & Klein, 1982), is then used in the constructed environment to orient ourselves within "the somewhere-realm of pure imagination and the there-and-there in memory" (p. 23). This is what Merleau-Ponty (1962) called "summoning," the body's freedom from immediacy:

> In order to enjoy the use of [my body] as the mood takes me, in order to describe in the air a movement formulated only verbally or in terms of moral requirements, I must reverse the natural relationship in which the body stands to its environment, and a human productive power must reveal itself through the density of being. (p. 112)

Though he mentioned the "rich variety of . . . deictic words" (p. 23) in narration, Bühler did not go into the specifics of how deictic words are used in literature. This job was taken up by Käte Hamburger, a German narrative theorist, in her major work, *Die Logik der Dichtung* (1957, translated and revised in English as *The Logic of Literature,* 1973). Hamburger argued that there are two realms of language act: reality statement and fiction. What distinguishes these two realms is the different logic they call into play. Reality statement derives its logic from the fact that it calls into play a speaker and a world which is independent of the speaker: reality statements are by someone (Hamburger called this the statement–subject or I–Origo, after Bühler) and about something (the statement–object). This corresponds to Doubrovsky's statement, "whenever something is said, someone must be saying it" (quoted in Magliola, 1973, pp. 238–239). Acts of fictional narration, on the other hand, transfer their referentiality from the actuality of the historical world to the entertained reality of the fictive world, and transfer the subjectivity of the speaker to the subjectivity of story world characters. Thus the fictional Origo is not the "speaker" of the text but the experiencing character within the story world. Hamburger made much of two facts which demonstrate this transfer: that deictic adverbs which indicate "presentness," such as "here," "today," and "now," are often found in past-tense narration; and that psychological verbs such as "think" or "feel" are used with third-person subjects in fictional narration. For example, the sentence "She felt sad now" is not anomalous in a novel, although it would be deictically contradictory in conversation or even in historical narration. This is because conversation and historical narration, both of which fall into Hamburger's category of reality statement, take their deictic anchorage from the act of communication, which provides the basis for verb tenses, deictic adverbs, and other markers that derive their meaning from the position of the SPEAKER and ADDRESSEE. In addition, historical statements are constrained by common-sense epistemological assumptions, such as that only the speaker can state the reality of "feeling sad." In fictional narration, the tense of verbs is not keyed to the author's act of writing or the reader's act of reading (although it may be keyed to a fictive act of narrating, such as is the case with explicit first-person narrative). Moreover, the subject of lived experience, the person who constitutes the Origo of the deictic field in fiction, is not the SPEAKER "I" (real I–Origo, author, narrator) but, paradigmatically, a third-person character. In short, the notions of HERE, NOW, and SELF are constituted in fiction on the plane of the story rather than in the act of narrating. Hamburger summed up her argument as follows:

> We have both specified and endeavored to account for those phenomena—or better those symptqms—which in themselves reveal that fictional narration is of a categorically different nature and structure from [reality] statement . . . : the use of verbs of inner action with reference to the third-person, . . . the disappearance of the narrative preterite's significance of designating past-ness [with respect to the time of narration], and the possibility (not the necessity) created by this of its combination with deictic temporal, particularly future, adverbs. These are not symptoms which as such are isolated; they mutually condition one another. They alone are elements which make fictional narration recognizable as a special verbal–gram-

matical phenomenon . . . [T]he symptoms pointed out thus far are linked with the transferral of the real spatio-temporal system onto the fictive persons or I–Origines, which at the same time implies the disappearance of a real I–Origo, i.e., of a statement–subject. (1973, p. 134)

This "dislocation of the 'I–origin' from speaking self to silent other," as Cohn (1989, p. 8) summarized Hamburger's thesis, is the basis of the Deictic Shift model of fictional narration that this chapter develops and presents.

Any theory that seeks to distinguish fictional narration from other uses of language must find distinctions on two axes: the narrational and the fictional. There are nonfictional uses of narration and there are ways of presenting stories other than through literary representation. It seems to me that Hamburger elegantly distinguished fictional narration from both of these cousins in her analysis of the I–Origo. In nonfictional narration, one may find evidence of a transfer of spatio-temporal deixis (e.g., use of the "historical present," deictic adverbs such as "here" and "now" keyed to narrated time), but one will not find third-person verbs of inner action. If one does, one will begin to take the narrative as partially fictionalized, as in Truman Capote's (1965) *In Cold Blood*. Similarly, in fictional forms that are not narrated, third-person consciousness cannot be directly presented, but must be conveyed symptomatically through observable behavior such as gesture, dialogue, monologue, or expressive enactment. We have no more access to another person's consciousness in a play or a history book than we do in ordinary life. Only in fictional narration is the lived, unexternalized experience of a person directly representable. Hamburger summed up the uniqueness of fictional narration with the statement that *"Epic* [i.e. narrative] fiction *is the sole epistemological instance where the I–originarity or (subjectivity) of a third-person* qua *third-person can be portrayed"* (1973, p. 83, emphasis in original).

In Hamburger's theory of fiction, first-person narrative has a different status from that of third-person fictional narrative, because the former linguistically observes the epistemological constraints of the statement system of language: tying the deictic field to the act of "utterance," and denying access to third-person subjectivity. Hamburger called first-person narrative *feigned reality statement.*

In 1973, the linguist S.-Y. Kuroda took the next step in the development of a linguistically informed theory of subjectivity in narrative in his ground-breaking article, "Where Epistemology, Style, and Grammar Meet: A Case Study from Japanese." Like Hamburger, Kuroda based his argument on the relationship of epistemology to linguistic markers, including deictics. Also like Hamburger, he based his argument on examples from natural narratives, but he supplemented this with the generative grammar method of inventing and comparing "minimal pair"-type acceptable and unacceptable sentences. The oddity that struck Kuroda is the distinction, in Japanese, between ways of attributing sensation depending on epistemological perspective.

Different markers are used in Japanese to indicate the source of knowledge of a sensation. If a sensation is known through being experienced or lived, it is marked as an adjective, whereas if the sensation is inferred from observed behavior, it is marked as a verb. Kuroda noticed that in Japanese fictional narratives of a particular type, the adjectival form was used with third-person subjects, contrary to conversational usage. The type of narrative which used this form was the type commonly called "omniscient narration," that is, narration in which there is no overt first-person narrator, and in which information about third-person characters' thoughts and feelings is given without any epistemological qualification—"he was sad," rather than "he seemed to be sad" or "he appeared sad."

Kuroda outlined two ways of structurally conceiving this fictional presentation: the traditional conception and his own alternative conception (which closely parallels Hamburger's). In the traditional conception, omniscient narration is set up as the allseeing mind of an omnipresent narrator, speaking to us as readers about the truths of the story world. This conception is predicated on the theory of language use that says there must always be a speaker and an addressee for every artifact of language. This truism assumes that all language use adheres to the communicative paradigm, which Hamburger called the *statement function* of language: to say something to someone about something. Kuroda's alternate conception is that there are two modes of language use in narrative: reportive and nonreportive. Reportive language use is referable to and thereby framed by a narrator's epistemology, and nonreportive language use is the direct narration of a character's subjectivity. In place of the omniscient narration theory, Kuroda proposed the *multiconsciousness theory*, in which characters' consciousness can be directly represented by the text without need of an intermediary narrator. He argued that this latter theory is more empirically adequate to the different grammars evinced by reportive versus nonreportive narration, as exemplified by the use of sensation adjectives and reflexives in Japanese.

Meanwhile, literary theorist and linguist Ann Banfield was writing articles about represented speech and thought that would later be consummated in *Unspeakable Sentences: Narration and Representation in the Language of Fiction,* published in 1982. The theory of narration contained in this book both corroborates and extends the work of Hamburger and Kuroda. Banfield asserted in her introduction that "[Kuroda's] distinction between the reportive and nonreportive styles does exist in the grammar of English.... It manifests itself ... in the grammar of reported speech" (p. 12). Banfield went on to show that the syntax of the literary style known variously as free indirect discourse, *erlebte Rede* (lived speech), or *represented speech and thought* (Banfield's term) is disallowed in nonnarrative contexts. For example, a typical specimen of represented thought might be:

How happy she felt!

where the SELF whose emotion is expressed by the exclamation is that of "she" rather than that of a reporting "I." Banfield found a number of linguistic elements that cannot be expressed by someone other than their experiencer. That is, they cannot be contained in indirect discourse, in which a subject reports on something someone else said. The previous example cannot be embedded in indirect discourse:

* He said that how happy she felt!

Similarly, questions, incomplete sentences, and direct address cannot appear in indirect discourse. Because such expressive elements are referable only to their experiencers, they cannot be subordinated to another SELF's discourse. The presence of these elements in narration is evidence that the deictic field of narration is anchored not in the SELF of an omniscient SPEAKER who can report on the experiences of others, but in the SELF of characters whose experience can be directly represented by the text.

Banfield argued that Benveniste's (1971) distinction between *histoire* and *discours* was misinterpreted by later narrative theorists, who included fictional narrative in the category of *discours* (see especially Genette, 1980). Benveniste asserted that there are two distinct uses of language: *discours*, which is grounded in the act of utterance, and *histoire*, which excludes references to the act of utterance and hence presents itself as without a speaker. In French, the distinction between these two language uses is exemplified by the presence of two past-tense systems, the aorist and the imperfect. The aorist is barred from use in sentences containing first and second-person pronouns (though Banfield found a limited exception to the bar on first-person pronouns), or deictic adverbs such as "yesterday" or "now." Benveniste was not clear how or even whether fictional narrative fits into the category of *histoire*; he explicitly included it in some of his generalizations, but the bulk of his argument was based on historical narrative.

In contrast to *histoire*, *discours* is anchored in the I/YOU of communication, and its references to the past or future are in relation to the act of speaking/hearing or writing/reading. Thus, the aorist is barred from *discours*.

Banfield noted that Benveniste never took up the problem addressed by Hamburger, that of the use of deictics in narrative that are anchored not in an act of communication between author and reader, but in the experience–field of characters on the plane of the story. But she believed that Benveniste's identification of the sentence of *histoire* also carries great significance for a theory of fictional narration. Fictional narrative in French often contains mixtures of aorist and imperfect. Banfield found that the imperfect is used in sentences that express or represent the SELF or subjectivity of characters in the story world, whereas the aorist is used for *pure narration*, in which story world reality is directly represented without any mediating SELF/subjectivity, either of a character or a narrator.

With Hamburger, then, Banfield believed that one of the distinguishing marks of fictional narrative is its representation of third-person consciousness (though unlike Hamburger, she included certain first-person narratives in this definition), but Banfield considered the essence of narration to be the sentence of pure narration, in which there is no deixis because there is no SELF. This is, in fact, quite consistent with Hamburger's view that the sentence of narration does not belong to the statement system of language, in which assertions are made by a statement–subject about statement–objects, but to the logic of narrative fiction, in which what is narrated is thereby created. In both subjective and objective sentences of fictional narration, the I/YOU of communication is excluded. Thus, narrative does not belong to *discours* using Benveniste's schema.

Banfield did not adopt Hamburger's or Benveniste's terms for her own theory of narration, although she used their terms and arguments to build her own case. Instead, she preferred to talk in terms of communicative and narrative uses of language.

Kuroda's (1973) article was written with only a cursory knowledge of Hamburger's book and without knowledge of the work of Banfield. In 1976, Kuroda wrote a more general theoretical article, "Reflections on the Foundations of Narrative Theory from a Linguistic Point of View," in which he joined forces with Hamburger and Banfield in their refutation of the so-called "communication model" of narrative.

Because the view that all language is communicative seems virtually tautological, the questioning of this view needs explanation. Like Hamburger, Kuroda insisted there are two fields of language use, one the "statement system" or "field of communication," and the other, the narrational system, in which language is not structured as a communication, but as a creation. I try to illustrate this difference by way of an analogy from *case grammar* (Fillmore, 1968).

The sentence, "Van Gogh painted a house" may have three different meanings, according to the case relation perceived between "painted" and "house." In the first instance, Van Gogh is perceived to have used a bucket of paint to apply paint to an already existing house. This is what Fillmore (1968) called the *object relation* between predicate and noun. In the second instance, Van Gogh paints a representational picture of a particular house. This second sense is analogous to Hamburger's notion of *statement,* insofar as the painting is a statement about a particular, real house. In the third instance, which Fillmore called *factive,* Van Gogh paints a picture of a house which thereby exists as a particular house only through his painting of it. This relation is analogous to Hamburger and Kuroda's notion of the creative function of narration:

> Epic fiction, the product of narration, is not an object with respect to the narrative act. Its fictivity, that is, its non-reality, signifies that it does not exist independently of the act of narration, but rather that it only *is* by virtue of its being narrated, i.e., by virtue of its being a product of the narrative act. One may also say that the act of narration is a function, through which the narrated persons, things, events, etc. are created: the narrative function, which the narrative poet manipulates as, for example, the painter wields his colors and brushes. That is, the narrative poet is

not a statement–subject. He does not narrate about persons and things, but rather he narrates these persons and things; the persons in a novel are narrated persons, just as the figures of a painting are painted figures. *Between the narrating and the narrated there exists not a subject–object relation, ie., a statement structure, but rather a functional correspondence.* This is the logical structure of epic fiction, which categorically distinguishes it from that of the reality statement. (Hamburger, 1973, p. 136; emphasis in original)

Kuroda pointed out that first-person as much as third-person fiction is created through a narrative act. For Kuroda, the linguistic oddities of third-person fiction call attention to an epistemology peculiar to all fiction, and it is the epistemology, rather than the linguistics, that creates the essence of fictionality. In first-person as in third-person narration, the sentences of narration create the reality of the story world. Thus, he claimed that even if there were no linguistic evidence of the epistemological divide between the communicative or statement function and narrative acts, this divide nevertheless exists. Kuroda's argument was phenomenological: he took his cues from linguistic evidence, but was not bound by linguistics. Kuroda's standpoint is the one most closely related to the standpoint assumed here.

Because all narrative meaning is only realized by being read, one may object that, by definition, all narrative is communicative, but Hamburger and Kuroda (as well as Banfield) mean by communication or statement system the Jakobsonian model, in which all language use is structured by an "addressor > message > addressee" paradigm (Jakobson, 1960, p. 353). The consequences of this model are that every sentence of language must be implicitly framed as follows: "I [the addressor or narrator] do assert to you [the addressee or reader] that. . . ." Kuroda (1976) commented on the way this model has been extended to models of fictional language:

Taken seriously, or literally, then, a theory of narration based on the notion of narrator (the narrator theory of narration) must claim that each sentence of a story—for the time being let us exclude direct quotations—is a message communicated by the narrator; each sentence is the product of an act of judging in the narrator's consciousness. (p. 206)

Hamburger, Kuroda, and Banfield all argued in their own ways that in the canonical language of written fictional narrative, there is no addressor and no addressee—no I/YOU—and that paradigmatically, language in narrative is structured either by the model "subject of consciousness > representation of consciousness," or "objective narration > representation of the story world." The former of these models gives us the shift of the deictic field from the spoken or written I/YOU/HERE/NOW of communication to the moment of a character's consciousness within a story world, where the character is experiencing modes of consciousness that may or may not have communicative intent, but that certainly do not "intend" toward the reader (except, fictionally, in some of the deliberate transgressions of postmodern fiction). And, as Kuroda (1976) pointed out, even narrative that is structured as a communicative act is premised on the same epistemological shift:

> Thanks to the faculty of imagination, one can imagine a communicational setting and materialize a sentence which is imagined to be materialized in that imaginary communicational setting. The sentence then represents the content of a mental act in some imaginary consciousness, that of the narrator. (p. 223)

But the conclusive empirical evidence for this shift comes from the language of nonnarrated stories, that differs in particular ways from communicative language in German, Japanese, English, and French, as Hamburger, Kuroda, and Banfield pointed out. This model does not deny the pragmatic reality of the author and the reader, but it asserts that the language of fictional narration is not deictically grounded in this reality, as it is in the language of I/YOU communication.

Hamburger, Kuroda, and Banfield's challenge to the Jakobsonian model is not deconstructive in the sense of challenging the notion of subjectivity, or in the sense of claiming that subjectivity is an artifact of language. Instead, they each saw language as capable of being used in two radically different ways for subjects. Assumed by their theories is a phenomenological subject who takes language in different ways. Language taken as historical statement has one kind of intentional logic; language taken as fictional narration has another. The conventions of language instruct us to take particular texts one way or the other, but we can also choose to contextualize sentences as historical statement or as fictional narration for purposes of play, perversity, or philosophical thought experiment. For example, I can read the following sentence as if it were part of a spy novel or a scientific observation: "The door opened slowly." Note, however, that if I recontextualize a sentence that is linguistically marked as historical (e.g., "I saw the man walk in") as fictional, I must treat it as a feigned reality statement, and if I recontextualize a sentence that is marked as fictional ("How stupid she had been!") as historical, I must construct a SPEAKER to whom to attribute the expressiveness instead of referring it to the SELF of "she."

The notion of two different modes of narration is, of course, not new. Beginning with Aristotle and Plato, there have been theories of the difference between speaking in one's own person and fictional narrating. But Hamburger, Kuroda, and Banfield pinpointed specific epistemological and syntactic differences between I/YOU communication and narration that set their ideas apart from those of other narrative theorists: third-person subjectivity, the transfer of the deictic field, the exclusion of the second person, the possibility of objective contexts (that is, contexts without a SPEAKER or even a SELF). Each of these three theorists found a link between the language of narrative and its logical status. Unlike other theorists, they claimed that there are not only pragmatic differences between fictional and nonfictional sentences, but linguistic–syntactic differences, as well.

In light of the arguments of Hamburger, Kuroda and Banfield, the Magliola epigraph that heads this chapter takes on new meaning. The two quotations Magliola cites as roughly equivalent (Doubrovsky's "whenever something is said, someone must be saying it" [1966, p. 36], and Ricoeur's "the display of a world and the positioning of an ego are symmetrical and reciprocal" [1969, p. 85]) can be seen, in fiction, to be quite different assertions. In fiction, many things are said without anyone (fictionally) saying them, and the display of a world may reveal an ego that is not a sayer's. From inside the fiction, worlds may also be displayed without positioning an ego—in objective contexts. None of this contradicts Magliola's own assertion that "It is through the intentionality unique to any given author, and present in the language of that author, that he is present in his literary work" (p. 239). The rich perceptions of being-in-the-world that we form and inhabit from an author's language owe their life to the freedom of fictional epistemology, that offers the author and reader new ways of representing and conceiving self–world relations.

The Deictic Shift Model

The term *Deictic Shift model* is used here to refer to the Hamburger–Banfield–Kuroda thesis that the deictic field is constituted on a different basis in fictional narrative than it is in conversation and other language situations, as this thesis is being used and developed by an interdisciplinary group of researchers at the State University of New York at Buffalo, including the contributors to this volume. The Deictic Shift model has implications for the study of narrative comprehension in the disciplines of linguistics, communicative disorders, psychology, and artificial intelligence, as well as literary theory. The notion that the deictic field in narrative is constituted at the level of the story world rather than in the act of utterance, or moment of communication between author and reader, opens up many research questions. What is the linguistic and psychological evidence for this assertion, and what are the consequences of this thesis for theories of language use and narrative understanding? For example, some of the consequences of accepting the Deictic Shift model are:

1. Real readers conceive of canonical fictional language (that is, narrative without a narrator) as self-constituting rather than emanating from a fictional teller.
2. The Gricean Cooperative Principle functions in a different way in narrative than it does in conversation (for example, a novel may begin *in media res* without apology).
3. Narrative acts qua fictional acts do not belong to the category of speech acts.

4. Such linguistic indicators as definite and indefinite reference, verb tense and aspect, sentence modality and logical connectives must, in subjective context, be understood with respect to the epistemology of the subjective character rather than with respect to author/reader communication.

A number of projects being pursued by the group in Buffalo are discussed in other chapters of this book. These projects reflect a variety of philosophies and methodologies, but they share a rejection of the communication model and subscription to the notions of subjective and objective contexts.

Other Models of Fictional Language Relevant to the Deictic Shift Model—the "No Linguistic Difference" View and the "Dual Voice" View

The "No Linguistic Difference" View. It is often claimed that there is no language specific to fiction, but that fiction uses all languages. For example, Searle (1975b) suggested that the difference between fictional and "serious" discourse is that fiction pretends to execute speech acts, whereas serious discourse actually executes these speech acts. But the examples he gave of fictional and nonfictional language are obviously different with regard to those elements foregrounded by the Deictic Shift model. His example of a serious speech act is taken from *The New York Times* of December 15, 1972:

> Washington, Dec. 14—A group of federal, state, and local government officials rejected today President Nixon's idea that the federal government provide the financial aid that would permit local governments to reduce property taxes. (quoted in 1975b, p. 321)

His example of a fictional speech act is taken from Murdoch's *The Red and the Green*:

> Ten more glorious days without horses! So thought Second Lieutenant Andrew Chase-White recently commissioned in the distinguished regiment of King Edwards Horse, as he pottered contentedly in a garden on the outskirts of Dublin on a sunny Sunday afternoon in April nineteen-sixteen. (quoted in 1975b, p. 322)

The latter example has the following distinguishing elements of narrative fiction, as defined by Banfield, Kuroda, and Hamburger: exclamation without quotation referable to a third-person character, parenthetical noncommunicative psychological verb, reversed verb–object word order ("so thought"), and, less conclusively, a situational verb (Hamburger's term for verbs which designate mundane physical acts such as eating or sitting—in this case, "pottered") paired with a full calendar date. The example of fiction which Searle used to demonstrate his own theory of fiction as pretended speech act is precisely the kind of narrative act for which there is no speech act counterpart: the narration of third-person consciousness. Dorrit Cohn remarked that narrative theorists who take their model of fiction from its resemblance to speech acts

> disregard the moments in third-person fiction that cannot be accommodated in their model: notably those moments—in some instances extended over the entire length of a long novel—that narrate life as experienced in the privacy of a character's consciousness. Clearly there is a crying need for a different model, one that is better suited to account for our pervasive mindreading experience in third-person novels, that awakens our sense of wonder at this singular experience and raises our theoretical consciousness of its uniqueness. (1989, p. 7)

Cohn went on to endorse Hamburger's work as such a model (she did not see Banfield as a successor to Hamburger).

Another philosopher, Hector Castañeda, not only ignored syntactic differences between fictional and nonfictional texts in his discussion of fictional versus nonfictional objects (Castañeda, 1989), but concocted the two examples by which he showed how similar the two kinds of reference can be. His example of nonfictional text, which is presented tongue-in-cheek as a "startling case" of similarity with a fictional text, is supposedly taken from the *Martinsville News*:

> Pamela, now 45 years old, had rented again the old bungalow at 123 Oak Street. She had it decorated and furnished exactly as she had done 20 years before. Her bed had the same pale blue sheets and pillowcases it had that afternoon when she strangled her companion Randolph Reilly. She still loved and hated him both with equal passion. (pp. 176–177)

This "example" of "nonfictional" language use, which is almost identical to Castañeda's equally concocted example of fictional language use, has at least four of the features of fictionality mentioned by Hamburger, Kuroda, and Banfield. When I read the example that purported to be nonfictional, I immediately felt that it read like fiction. That a respected philosopher would consider it harmless fun to invent his examples of fictional versus nonfictional text (and to do so in such unconvincing fashion) in a serious article on the nature of fictional reference shows that the linguistics of fictional narrative is an invisible issue even for some scholars studying the nature of fictionality.

Certainly narrative can be written that deliberately blurs the boundaries between the fictional and nonfictional epistemology. Journalism which uses fictional devices has become known as new journalism in the past few decades, and biographies have always borrowed fictional devices to flesh in their subjects. Conversely, fictional narrative has been masquerading as historical statement for centuries, in the form of epistolary novels, first-person narratives, and other documentary forms of fiction. Hamburger called this type of narrative feigned reality statement, because such narratives, unlike third-person fiction, have to argue for the validity of their propositions by linking their evidence to the experience-field of the narrator (I was there, I saw it, these letters have been preserved). The linguistic differences between text in the two modes of narrative is not merely stylistic, then, but reflects adherence to an epistemological divide. In nonfictional epistemology, the SELF must always be I, the NOW must always be the present moment, and HERE must always be the place where I am now. In fictional epistemology, the SELF can be anyone (including a fictional first person), the NOW can be any time, and the HERE can be anywhere. The designations "fictional" and "nonfictional" refer to sets of linguistic and referential differences.

Depending on how linguistic structure aligns with referential differences, there are four possible results: (a) fictional linguistic structure with fictional referentiality (third-person fiction), (b) nonfictional linguistic structure with fictional referentiality (first-person fiction), (c) nonfictional linguistic structure with nonfictional referentiality (reality statement), or (d) fictional linguistic structure with differing degrees of nonfictional referentiality (novelized history or journalism). Of these, (b) and (d) are complicated by their mix of epistemological cues. The feigned reality statement is text that follows nonfictional epistemological constraints in its language, but lacks a real, independent referent for both its SPEAKER and its propositions. The new journalism or historical novel style is text that follows fictional epistemological rules in its language, but whose unqualified attributions of third-person subjectivity, central facts, and events are more or less supported by real, independent evidence such as interviews, observations, and historical records. The difference between these two hybrid forms is that, whereas feigned reality statement is just as fictional as third-person fiction, the representation of third-person consciousness in historical text necessarily indicates a shift to fictional epistemology, because this is not possible nonfictionally (with one exception—text which shifts the author's SELF to the third person, such as Norman Mailer's *Armies of the Night*).

The Dual-Voice Position.   On the other side of the spectrum from those who consider literary style irrelevant to the issue of fictional epistemology are literary theorists who find Banfield's theory in particular lacking literary adequacy. The most pointed criticism of Banfield's theory came from poetician Brian McHale (1983), who found her approach doctrinaire and empirically unsound. McHale faulted Banfield on three major grounds: (a) her use of sentences as the units of narration, (b) her insistence that each expression (which normally corresponds to a sentence) is limited to one SELF, and (c) her "horizontal" model of meaning (that is, she sees sentences as having a single syntactically correct frame of reference within which they either express the subjectivity of a particular SELF or designate narrative reality).

Each of these objections raises important issues for a narrative theory that seeks to be more than formally coherent. Banfield answered these objections in her own way (see especially chapter 5 of Banfield, 1982, pp. 183–223), but because the Deictic Shift model being advanced in this chapter has a somewhat different analysis of these issues, I propose answers that incorporate a good deal of Banfield's own arguments with some modification and difference in emphasis.

The Issue of the Basic Unit of Narrative Analysis. Banfield (1982) used sentences as her basic unit of meaning, limiting herself to the syntactic unit used in transformational grammar. But she used sentences in a way that does not contradict a discourse-based theory. Like Fillmore, Banfield looked at sentences for their contextualizability within some situation. Janyce Wiebe and William Rapaport (1988) expanded Banfield's notion of subjective and objective sentences into subjective and objective contexts and found that this expanded notion is easily built upon Banfield's basic schema. In fact, Banfield's theory of discrete subjective and objective units works better at the discourse level because it explains how sentences that, when isolated, look like objective sentences or psychonarration (a category that mixes subjective content with objective propositional form, and thus is subjective but not expressive), can actually be subjective and/or expressive when they are part of a subjective context that pulls them in. An example provided by Banfield: "She felt the man standing, watching them go with dislike. He disliked women and despised them. He was merely stupid" (Lawrence, 1978, p. 26; quoted by Banfield, 1982, p. 263). The second sentence of this excerpt, which by itself looks like a psychological report of his (Parkin's) subjectivity, must be read in context as a representation of her (Constance Chatterley's) subjectivity, and thus fallible. Wiebe and Rapaport (1988) revised Banfield as follows:

> Subjective sentences that are not marked as such, or that do not indicate who the subjective character is, usually appear in the midst of other subjective sentences attributed to the same subjective character. That is, once a clearly marked subjective sentence appears for which the subjective character can be determined, unmarked subjective sentences attributed to the same subjective character often follow. Thus, to recognize subjective sentences in general, we need to consider subjectivity at the level of the discourse. For this reason, we extend the notions of subjective and objective sentences to the notions of subjective and objective *contexts,* which consist of one or more subjective sentences attributed to the same subjective character, or one or more objective sentences, respectively. (p. 131)

The Problem of SPEAKER, SELF, and Voice. McHale asserted that the point of view expressed in individual sentences can be read at several levels, and that Banfield's rule of "1 Expression/1 SELF" ignores the complexity of levels found in many narratives. The examples given by McHale (1983) to refute Banfield's "1 Expression/1 SELF" rule fall into four categories:

1. One character parodies another character's expression (numbers before literary examples are McHale's):

Banfield writes: "In 'Yes, she could hear his poor child crying now,' the *yes* cannot be the expression of 'her' point of view and *poor* of 'his' " (94). But as a matter of fact it is relatively easy to construct a context for this sentence which would encourage the reader to interpret *yes* and *poor* as expressing different points of view:

(16) She was about fed up with both of them, father and daughter. Above all, she was sick and tired of hearing him moan about his poor child. His poor child this, his poor child that: enough already! Yes, she could hear his poor child crying now.

The contextualizing sentences prepare the way for a dual-voice reading of the sentences in question by compelling the reader to reconstruct a hierarchy of voices. The dominant voice is "hers," and "she" in turn quotes "his" voice with ironic intention. "He," we understand, habitually uses the phrase "my poor child," which "she" here recontextualizes within "her" own speech. Thus, we read *yes* in the final sentence of (16) as expressing "her" point of view alone, but *poor* as expressing two superimposed points of view—"his" being travestied by "her." (1983, pp. 35–36)

2. Gradual shift from one character SELF to another character SELF with unclear boundary between, as in the "Nausicaa" section of *Ulysses*:

(15) He was leaning back against the rock behind. Leopold Bloom (for it is he) stands silent, with bowed head before those young guileless eyes. What a brute he had been! At it again? A fair unsullied soul had called to him and, wretch that he was, how had he answered? An utter cad he had been. He of all men! But there was an infinite store of mercy in those eyes, for him too a word of pardon even though he had erred and sinned and wandered. Should a girl tell? No, a thousand times no. (Joyce, 1973, p. 367; quoted by McHale, 1983, p. 33)

3. One character's "voice" is used to represent another character's SELF (diverging of "voice" and "perspective," also found in "Nausicaa" example, [15] above).

4. A character SELF is described using a "voice" alien to the character SELF's own mental or linguistic process, conjuring up "someone 'behind' or 'above' him—a narrator, in fact" (McHale, 1983, p. 37), as in McHale's "Eumaeus" example from *Ulysses*:

Preparatory to anything else Mr. Bloom brushed off the greater bulk of the shavings and handed Stephen the hat and ashplant and bucked him up generally in orthodox Samaritan fashion, which he very badly needed. His (Stephen's) mind was not exactly what you would call wandering but a bit unsteady and on his expressed desire for some beverage to drink Mr. Bloom, in view of the hour it was and there being no pumps of Vartry water available for their ablutions, let alone drinking purposes, hit upon an expedient by suggesting, off the reel, the propriety of the cabman's shelter, as it was called, hardly a stones-throw away near Butt Bridge, where they might hit upon some drinkables in the shape of a milk and soda or a

mineral. But how to get there was the rub. For the nonce he was rather nonplussed.
. . . (Joyce, 1973, p. 533; quoted by McHale, 1983, p. 37)

Before going further to analyze McHale's point, I dwell at some length on the terms germane to this discussion. Of particular importance are SELF, "voice," SPEAKER, and "point of view." SELF is Banfield's epistemological and deictic term for the subjectivity whose experience is being lived in the NOW of a particular sentence. This is commonly summarized in narrative theory by the question, "Who sees?", the verb "see" standing for all perceptual and other experience. "Voice" is a widely and casually used term for those stylistic attributes of a linguistic expression which conjure up attributes of a speaker. This aspect of a text is often summarized as, "Who speaks?," but for a reason I give shortly, I think this catch phrase is an inappropriate synonym for "voice." Banfield rejected the term "voice" for the language of narration, reserving it for representations of oral performance. Similarly, she rejected the term "speech" for the language of narration, which she found to be a separate kind of performance, writing, with its own characteristics. SPEAKER is Banfield's deictic term for the subject of discourse in the sense of the "I" who speaks, in other words, Hamburger's statement–subject. There is no SPEAKER or statement–subject in canonical narration as defined by Banfield and Hamburger. The word "speaker" as used by most other narrative theorists includes a priori the narrator presumed to be "speaking" all the words of every narrative text. Finally, the term "point of view" is used to refer to a multitude of different aspects of a text, including SELF, voice, speaker, opinion or ideology, and spatio-temporal perspective. (For attempts at sorting through these, see Uspensky, 1973; also Chatman, 1986.) In Banfield's statement quoted by McHale, and in McHale's own usage in the previous passage, point of view was used in two different ways. For Banfield, point of view meant SELF (i.e., the subjectivity whose experience is being lived in the NOW of a particular sentence). In McHale's reading of Banfield, point of view meant the source of the words being used, or the "voice" conjured by the words. Since the words "poor child" in his made-up example were originally used by the fictional "him" (let's call him George), they retain George's "voice" even when he is not using them. Thus, Banfield would find one SELF in the expression, even as contextualized by McHale, whereas McHale found two voices. This kind of confusion is rife in all discussion using these basic terms, and I try to cut down on some of this confusion by defining and being consistent in my own usage. The capitalized and deictic terms SELF and SPEAKER as used here always connote Banfield's usage, and "voice," enclosed in quotes where I have a reluctant relationship to the term as used, will be given its common usage from mainstream narrative theory. Likewise, "speaker" (without capitalization) denotes the source of a "voice," without arguing that the speaker is the SELF of a particular passage. I avoid the confusing term "point of view."

As can be gathered from the "poor child" example given earlier, the definition of terms is especially important to the argument between the dual voice theory and Banfield's "1 Expression/1 SELF" rule. Some clarity can be brought to both sides by borrowing some further terms from phenomenology. The phenomenologist and psychologist Wilhelm Dilthey introduced the term *Erlebnis* to denote the lived quality of experience as opposed to its behavioral aspects. In Dilthey's scheme, *Erlebnis* or lived experience gives rise to *Ausdruck,* expression, that both objectifies experience and creates further lived experience for the subject. Because expressions are both objective and subjective, they are available for interpretation by others even as they are lived by oneself (Dilthey, 1977). SELF is Banfield's term for the subject of *Erlebnis,* and SPEAKER is her term for the subject of Aus*druck* in the NOW of speaking. The generic terms "voice" and "speaker" do not discriminate between the objective and subjective aspects of expression, nor do they limit their meaning to THIS act of speaking—the act of speaking that is taking place in the NOW of the narrative. It is possible for a single expression to reverberate with many voices and to conjure up many speakers, as in the "heteroglossic" texts pointed out by Bakhtin. But the questions "Who sees?" and "Who speaks?," commonly used as synonymous with the terms "point of view" and "voice" or "speaker," *do* limit their force to THIS act of experiencing (e.g., seeing) and THIS act of speaking, or, in Banfield's term, this consciousness-in-the-NOW. The answer to "Who thinks?" in McHale's example must be the person who thinks in the NOW of that particular sentence, namely "her." This is not the same as asking whose voices reverberate in the sentence. Thus McHale's interpretation of "1 Expression/1 SELF" as "1 sentence/1 voice" was not sensitive to Banfield's own arguments, based as they were on the principle of a deictic field and an ORIGO at the level of the story world.

The first three kinds of "dual voice" pointed out by McHale all involve the mixing aspects of two characters in a single expression. In the first, one character mimics another; in the second, SELF shifts without a clear signal; in the third, textual elements of a single expression are associated with two different characters.

Mimicry certainly involves two voices—one to be mimicked, and one to do the mimicking. Unlike straight quoting, mimicking expresses an attitude toward the words (and thus the person) quoted. When a character mimics another's speech, he or she "takes over" the language of that other to make a point of her own. But this is not the same as two different SELVES expressing themselves through the same expression. In example (16), the passage is clearly a subjective context attributable to "her," not to "him." His habitual expression is used, but it is used here by her. His attitude is alluded to, but his subjectivity is not the epistemological source of the passage. Speech is a behavior that others may observe and reproduce (or distort) for their own purposes. Thus, even if one were to grant that there are two voices in this passage, there is only one SELF.

The second kind of example occurs often in the writings of Virginia Woolf. Before recognizing from overt cues that a shift in perspective is occurring, the reader will recognize from the "mind-style" of a passage that there has been a disjuncture with the mind-style of a preceding passage:

For he was gone, she thought—gone, as he threatened, to kill himself—to throw himself under a cart! But no; there he was; still sitting alone on the seat, in his shabby overcoat, his legs crossed, staring, talking aloud.

Men must not cut down trees. There is a God. (He noted such revelations on the backs of envelopes.) Change the world. No one kills from hatred. Make it known (he wrote it down). He waited. He listened. A sparrow perched on the railing opposite chirped Septimus, Septimus, four or five times over and went on, drawing its notes out, to sing freshly and piercingly in Greek words how there is no crime and, joined by another sparrow, they sang in voices prolonged and peircing in Greek words, from trees in the meadow of life beyond a river where the dead walk, how there is no death. (Woolf, 1963, p. 28)

In this passage, the subjective processes of Rezia and Septimus Smith are represented. It is clear to the reader who is following the novel that the beginning of the passage ("she thought") is Rezia's subjective context and that the end is Septimus', but the boundary between one SELF and the other is hard to identify. The paragraph break represents a potential change (cf. Wiebe, 1990b, 1994) from Rezia to either another character or to an objective context. But the ending of the earlier paragraph—"there he was; . . . talking aloud"—primes the reader to think that what follows may be a representation of what Rezia heard Septimus saying when he was talking aloud, and so a continuation of Rezia's subjective context. What follows could be either a representation of Septimus' own subjectivity or Rezia's observation and representation of his behavior. The verbs "waited" and "listened" are more strongly suggestive that this must be Septimus' subjectivity, because both verbs denote his intentionality in addition to his behavior. But both are conceivably an inference by Rezia. Finally, the sentence beginning "A sparrow perched on the railing" conclusively puts us into Septimus' SELF since it describes Septimus' perception of the bird as chirping Septimus' name and singing in Greek. We know from earlier context that Septimus lives in a world in which everything he notices has ultimate significance directed at him personally. The "sparrow" sentence is conclusively Septimus' because it describes without amazement happenings that to Rezia are utterly impossible (a bird calling someone's name and singing in Greek); once we decide that the perception expressed in the sentence is that of Septimus', we must attribute the SELF of the sentence to him, because Rezia does not have access what he hears, as she does to what he says or writes.

If my reconstruction of my first reading of this passage is accurate, I had to double back several times to figure out whose consciousness was being represented. This doubling back, which occurred many times in my reading of *Mrs. Dalloway,* had its own stylistic effect, and the fuzziness of the boundaries between subjective contexts inevitably saturated the feel of the novel as a world. Any reading of the novel that only considered the correct attribution of SELF in each subjective context would be inadequate. The epistemology of Woolf's novel as life-world is enacted in this stylistic effect: People living in the same place and the same time are steeped in each other's subjectivity, but paradoxically, know almost nothing about each other. The boundaries are there, but they are not.

At the same time, I do not think the fuzziness of boundaries between characters' subjective contexts constitutes a case of dual voice, let alone double SELF. In each case, the reader makes an effort to find the right SELF to whom to attribute a subjective context. Even in the "Nausicaa" example used by Banfield and McHale, which combines boundary fuzziness with a divergence between voice and SELF, McHale cites "the point . . . where the perspective shifts from Gertie to Bloom" (1983, p. 36). The reader's realization that there is or has been a shift of SELF must take place at some moment in time, even though different readers may make this shift at different moments in the text depending on a number of factors, both psychological and linguistic, such as familiarity with the text, involvement in the text, and the strength of the cues. Prolonged confusion about whose consciousness is being followed does not constitute proof that more than one consciousness is being followed at the same time. Rather, at these moments of ambiguity, a SELF exists but is not identifiable.

The third case, divergence of "voice" and "perspective" (SELF) between two characters, is rather rare, I believe. In the example used by McHale, the linguistic style associated with Gertie McDowell was used to represent Leopold Bloom's consciousness. Since Gertie cannot know at this moment what is going on in Bloom's consciousness, there is something impossible about this passage if "her style" is construed as "her subjective context." Narration of one character's private states by another character is a violation of epistemological realism, which does not allow characters on the same ontological level to "live" each other's subjectivity unless such telepathy is asserted as possible in a particular story world, as in some science fiction or magical realism. But her style need not be construed as her subjective context, unless there are specific markers that indicate this is the case. It may be a kind of metonymy between her presence and the style of the text, rather like the theme of Peter in "Peter and the Wolf." Still, the passage is an expressive one in the style of represented thought ("At it again?"), so it must be someone's subjective context. And the epistemological content of the text, according to McHale, points inexorably to Bloom.

What is one to make of this? McHale naturalized this passage as the "divergence of voice and perspective" (p. 37), but surely he cannot mean that the consciousness-in-the-NOW represented here is Bloom's, but the style of the consciousness is the narrator's. Either we must attribute the expressive force of a thought such as "At it again?" to a narrator, or we must attribute it to Bloom (or Gertie). If it is attributable to a narrator, what is the passage then saying about Bloom's own consciousness at this moment in the story? That he is thinking something like this but in his own style that isn't represented here? Such a reading requires epistemological gymnastics that I cannot summon. The most likely epistemology I can offer for this passage, as a nonexpert, is that Bloom may be projecting what Gertie would think if she knew what he knows. This, of course, does not constitute Bloom having access to her consciousness, but Bloom being able to guess what she might think and the style in which she would think it. That is, all the knowledge in this reading would originate with his consciousness.

Another possible reading is that Joyce is here being more the trickster than the epistemologist, flaunting the logic of possible worlds. I do not claim that all narrative must make epistemological sense; only that unless we can make some sort of epistemological sense out of a narrative, we cannot enter into it as a world. In short, I call this case an undecidable stylistic effect and ask for more examples.

Finally, we come to the heart of the controversy over the speaker: the ever-present narrator controversy. Many narrative theorists have argued that the necessary difference between a character's subjectivity (SELF) and the words used to contextualize and articulate this subjectivity ("voice") constitutes irrefutable evidence for a narrator whose consciousness has merged with or diverged from the character's consciousness, thus creating, in Pascal's term (1977), a *dual voice*. As Pascal argued, "the narrator must provide a language for matters that, for the character, resist verbal formulation" (p. 112).

These theorists argue that such necessary aspects of narrative as the arrangement of episodes, descriptive passages, and even such additions as "he said" are signs of a narrator's presence. Typical statements of this position: "there is always a teller in the tale, at least in the sense that any utterance or record of an utterance presupposes someone who has uttered it" (Rimmon-Kenan, 1983, p. 88); "we might conceive of narrative discourse most minimally and most generally as verbal acts consisting of *someone telling someone else that something happened*" (Herrnstein-Smith, 1980, p. 231). Other theorists, such as Chatman, Cohn, and Tamir, are not committed to a particular stand or are inconsistent on the existence of narrators for all narrative texts, and use the concept when it seems useful.

This controversy is important for the discussion of the Deictic Shift model of narration as it is being described here, because the dual voice theory is an affirmation of the communication model of narration that the Deictic Shift model explicitly rejects. If there is always, as a cognitive necessity, an a priori SPEAKER (in the case of fiction, a narrator) structured into our understanding of every instance of language, then the deictic field of a narrative must be structured in relation to this SPEAKER, and the language of every narrative text must be understood as being an utterance on the same model as conversation, with an attending discourse structure, whether or not it actually exhibits such a structure.

I believe a great deal of the misunderstanding and confusion about these two views of narration has to do with the difference between our experience of narrative as fiction and our experience of narrative as a multilevel construction that includes both fictional and nonfictional meaning. Pragmatically speaking, a work of fiction is always the work of someone—the author—who arranges the words, articulates the subjectivities of characters, and expresses attitudes through the language of the narrative. I venture to say—indeed, I hope—all readers of fiction form dynamic concepts of the author as they read. These concepts may include a psychological profile and beliefs about what the author intends and what moral stance he or she takes within the fictional world and toward the real political world in which he or she writes.

In addition, the ontologies represented by the existence of a novel are at least two: the historical world of the author and the fictional world of the characters. Attitudes expressed by the text that we may at first take to sincerely represent the author's own ideology may be at any time preempted by a superior level of knowledge that scoffs at these attitudes and places them figuratively or literally in quotation marks, distancing them from the author's own subjectivity. Bakhtin (1981) referred to this aspect of narrative as the degree of refraction of the author's intentionality. But this refraction is not dependent on the existence of a narrator; the languages used to capture characters' experience commonly reflect a hierarchy of evaluation, but this evaluation may be objective (i.e., absolutely true within the fiction) or it may represent the attitudes of social groups or characters at the story level.

In the "necessary narrator" theory of narrative, the reader must always construct a fictional narrator who is the source of the "telling" of the narrative. That is, this theory posits that there must be a fictional level between the character and the author, a level with a fictional SPEAKER. When this SPEAKER is not linguistically identifiable, this theory calls the narrator a "third-person narrator," an "omniscient narrator," the overall "voice" of the narrative. Thus we are back to Searle's "fiction as pretended speech act" model of language use in fiction. If there is always a fictional narrator "speaking" the story, then it is this narrator who is producing all the speech acts of the text and to whose epistemology we refer for justification of assertions. And what epistemological justification can there be for a narrator's knowledge of third-person consciousness? Omniscience.

As Cohn (1978) pointed out, early novelists felt constrained to either avoid representing characters' subjectivity, or to externalize it through such devices as thinking aloud, so that the author could justify his or her knowledge of another's thoughts. This pressure to make the epistemology of fictional exposition conform to the epistemology of real-world experience reminds me of a dreamer clinging to a wall in a dream, not realizing that in a dream one can fly at will. Because in reality we do not have direct access to another person's thoughts, many early novelists either avoided representing a character's experience or resorted to the dramatic technique of having characters declaim their thoughts in monologue. But such epistemological timidity soon fell away as readers and writers learned to accept the representation of subjectivity as just as plausibly mimetic as representations of landscapes. Modern novels that give epistemological justification for their representations of characters' consciousness do so either playfully or in the interest of specific stylistic effects.

Although writers and readers have moved on to explore the freedom of representation allowed by fiction, critics have been slow to drop the model in which there must always be some naturalistic justification of knowledge represented in a text. When there is no overt sign of a narrator, they speak of narrators who "merge" with characters in order to express what is going on in their minds, or of narrators who merely report the story. Of course, merging with other subjectivities is not possible in real-world epistemology, but evidently this is more plausible than simply dropping the core epistemological assumption—that there must be a narrator who is the source of knowledge and language in the text. The thought of dispensing with the narrator is considered "counter-intuitive" (McHale, 1983, p. 21) and even "dizzying" (Toolan, 1988, p. 130).

In the work of sensitive critics who do not distinguish clearly between authors and narrators, the distinction between works with and without fictional narrators comes through in their choice of terms in particular instances: for example, each time Booth (1961/1983) made a point about stories that seem to be unmediated by a narrator, he called the narrator who "must" be there the author. Booth confused the fictional epistemology of the novel with the real situation of the novel's creation. The author is not a fictional part of the novel; he or she is its creator. There is no need to justify how the propositions in a novel came to be known, because they are fictional propositions, and therefore, as Hamburger argued, simply the case by virtue of being narrated. We do not have to ask ourselves, as we read the fictional sentence "John felt bad," how the SPEAKER or WRITER of this sentence came by this knowledge, any more than we have to ask the same question of the fictional sentence "John walked down the street." We do not have to picture an author divining into the character's mind because the character's mind is a creation of the author's mind, and the author's mind belongs to a whole different realm from the fiction. Instead, we enter into the fiction and take its propositions as the reality that simply exists in this story world, without any need of a mediating SPEAKER. Questions about the author's knowledge, motives or intentions are not out of bounds, but they are outside of the fiction qua fiction. Here Genette (1988) agreed: "In pure fiction [the term omniscience] is, literally, absurd (the author has nothing to 'know,' since he invents everything) . . ." (p. 74). But elsewhere, he dismissed the distinction between fictional and nonfictional as unworthy of separate categories of narrator:

> There is an enunciating instance—the narrating—with its narrator and its narratee, *fictive or not, represented or not,* silent or chatty, but always present in what is indeed for me, I fear, an act of communication. (1988, p. 101)

Genette's sarcasm was directed at Banfield, but since the substance of his argument is against those who insist on banishing the author from a work of fiction, I fear his sarcasm is misdirected. Banfield did not deny the reality of authors, only of fictional SPEAKERS in the absence of positive signs of their existence. Like Booth, Genette referred to authors and narrators without having a model that distinguishes the fictional from the nonfictional act of narrating. When he argued that "Narrative without a narrator, the utterance without an uttering, seem to me pure illusion and, as such, 'unfalsifiable' " (1988, p. 101), he missed the key point of Banfield's argument: Fiction is just such an illusion. And he compounded the confusion by continuing that if he were to meet a narrative without a narrator:

> I would flee as quickly as my legs could carry me: when I open a book, whether it is a narrative or not, I do so to have the author *speak to me*. And since I am not yet either deaf or dumb, sometimes I even happen to answer him. (1988, pp. 101–102)

The refreshing humanist attitude expressed here, which I gladly second, has nothing to do with the presence or absence of fictional narrators.

Booth said of *Portrait of the Artist as a Young Man* (Joyce, 1976), that "We accept, by convention, the claim that what is reported as going on in Stephen's mind really goes on there, or in other words, that Joyce knows how Stephen's mind works" (1961/1983, p. 163). The first clause of this quotation from Booth uses the model of fiction espoused in this chapter: the model in which fiction is accepted as the manifestation of a world, without need of epistemological recourse to a narrator unless one is specifically posited, or to an author unless we change realms to ask historical questions. The second clause makes the error being argued against here, of thinking that a realistic epistemological justification such as a SPEAKER, author, narrator, or teller is required to back up the fictional propositions found in a narrative. Joyce doesn't know how Stephen's mind works in the manner of a subject knowing an object; he lives Stephen's mind as its creator. We as readers don't know how Stephen's mind works in the manner of a subject knowing an object; we live his mind as we construct it and inhabit it for ourselves as we read. The "mistake" Booth attributes to the "inexperienced reader" who thinks that "the story comes to him unmediated" (p. 152) is precisely the essential fictional effect created by that story: the mistake we happily collude in when we enter into a fictional world. This is not to say that there are not countless "disguised helps" (Booth, 1983, p. 163) from the author, but that these helps remain successfully disguised for the immersed reader, and need only be called attention to when we "pull out" to see how a particular effect was made possible.

For several years, mention of the author has been somewhat taboo in narrative theory. Banfield pointed out that the concept of the omnipresent narrator has filled the empty place of the author in mainstream narrative theory as the epistemological source of the text. Whereas nonstructuralist, independent narrative theorists such as Lubbock, Bakhtin, Cohn, and Booth (and, as illustrated previously, the "structuralist" but incorrigible Genette) used the term "author" freely and almost interchangeably with the term "narrator," most current narrative theorists are careful to speak only of a narrator even as they attribute powers to the narrator that were formerly considered to be those of the flesh-and-blood author alone, such as "organizer and guarantor of meaningfulness" (McHale, 1978, p.

281), "subject of this enunciation which a book represents" (Todorov, 1966, p. 146; quoted in Banfield, 1982, p. 184), and even the agent who inserts chapter breaks, chapter numbers, and headings (Toolan, 1988)! The theory of narrative espoused by Hamburger, Kuroda, and Banfield does not deny the existence of narrators, but it does require specific linguistic evidence of one.

The Deictic Shift model of fiction, then, bases its notion of the presence or lack of a SPEAKER or narrator on specific deictic indicators in a text, rather than on an a priori argument based on an analogy with ordinary human experience.

Verticality and the Deictic Shift Model. Returning, then, to the issue of verticality raised by McHale, what does the Deictic Shift model of narration have to say about the different levels of reading that are admittedly necessary to a competent reading of literary language?

According to the Deictic Shift model, fictional narration requires the reader to imagine deictic fields in which HERE, NOW, and SELF coordinates are transposed from their usual anchorage in the "I" into an anchorage in the narrative text. This fictional deictic field is constructed (and lived) according to the linguistic specifications of the text, as a world-to-word *direction of fit* (Searle, 1983). These specifications include verb tense and aspect (Rapaport et al., 1989), deictic pronouns, verbs and adverbs (Fillmore, 1974), expressive elements (Banfield, 1982), experiential verbs, modals, argument structure (Wiebe, 1990b), and presentative structure. All fictional narratives contain a multitude of such clues. By following them, the reader is able to move with the fictional situation as it emerges with each new sentence.

The hypothesis of the Deictic Shift model is that a deictic field is created by a fictional narrative through these particular clues as they are instantiated in particular texts and "picked up" by particular readers. There is no story world deictic field until it is established by the text and by the reader following the text. Similarly, there is no deictic field at the level of narration unless one is specifically called for by the text. Without a story world deictic field, there can be no story, but there can be narration without a fictional narration-level deictic field. Unless a fictional SPEAKER or WRITER who exists on a deictic plane separate from that of the characters is specifically signalled by the text, the reader need not constitute a separate fictional deictic field at the level of narration. Of course, the reader has an idea of a real author who wrote the text at some real historical time and place. The very existence of the text is pragmatic testament to the reality of the author or authors. But narrators as fictional beings must be created by the text. They do not spring automatically to life as part of the reader's fixed cognitive model of fictional structure.

Perhaps many narrative theorists would grant this as true in the abstract, but would claim that fiction cannot be written without providing clues to a narrator's existence. The difference of opinion seems to be centered on the question of what constitutes a clue to a fictional narrator's existence. The only constellation of clues that is uncontroversial is the presence of a first person who uses the present tense in a narrative whose basic story world deictic field is designated by the past tense. According to arguments by Hamburger and Banfield, the use of the past tense for story world time does not by itself imply a narrational NOW in the present tense. In fact, as noted previously, Hamburger defined fiction by its use of the "epic preterite" tense combined with a deictic NOW anchored in this tense rather than in the present (Hamburger, 1973, p. 66). Use of the first person for an experiencing SELF in a narrative does not by itself imply a first person SPEAKER who views the story world from a different vantage point (Banfield, 1982). Other clues often used to argue for the existence of a narrator—descriptive passages that are not in a character's experience (Rimmon-Kenan, 1983), reports that articulate a character's experience in ways superior or alien to a character's own verbal ability and style, and reports of a character's behavior or private states such as "he got up" or "he thought" (Rimmon-Kenan, 1983)—are all representations of story-level reality, whether subjective or objective, and thus do not require the construction of a second fictional deictic plane.

This is not to say that fiction is not typically multilevelled and hierarchically ordered. This truism is recognized in all narrative theories. A story (or a reader) can always potentially change frames in one of two directions. One may emerge from one deictic plane to a higher or more basic-ontological-level deictic plane, as in awakening from a dream or looking up from reading. Borrowing a computer science term, I call this process *POPping*. Conversely, one may submerge from a basic level to a less available deictic plane, such as episodic memory (known as "flashback" in fiction), fictional story world (this may be a fiction within the fiction), or fantasy. I call this submersion a *PUSH*, the term paired with POP in computer science. There is theoretically no limit to the number of POPs and PUSHes possible in a fictional narrative. The most common PUSHes are probably flashbacks and dream sequences, and the most common POPs (other than coming back from flashbacks and dreams) are irony and narrator commentary.

There is a basic level of story epistemology and ontology to which one normally expects to return from these POPs and PUSHes; that is, if a character dreams, we expect him or her to awaken, or if a narrator makes a remark that reveals that he or she knows how a story will turn out, we expect him or her to go back to story time rather than just revealing what he or she knows and spoiling the story. This basic story level is usually activated throughout the narrative and becomes part of the reader's construction of the narrative as a whole, even when it is put on hold, so to speak, for a textually cued POP or PUSH. Other levels which are not as basic will, I hypothesize, gradually decay as reader constructions, and will eventually be dropped if they are not activated by use in the text. I think this is what happens with vestigial narrators who are used briefly at the beginning of a story to introduce a situation and who then disappear for the remainder of the narrative. Hamburger mentions this pattern as typical of a stage in the history of the novel when consistency of perspective was not as scrupulously observed as it came to be later. An author would begin with a narrator who is the fictional source of the knowledge in a story, and then "forget" about the narrator as the story became more and more "fictionalized," that is, as its pretense of being the statement of a historical subject was dropped in favor of third-person fiction.

Thus, even the creation of an overt narrator does not necessarily mean that this narrator exists for the reader behind those parts of the narrative that do not evoke this presence. If the narrator is not continually activated by signs in the text, and if his or her presence is not of importance to the overall meaning of the work, then it is hypothesized here that his or her telling of the story will decay and eventually drop from the reader's construction.

The opposite case is also possible, but very rare, I believe. A text that has shown no sign of a narrator may suddenly acquire one, and this appearance may require the reader to change, in retrospect, the meaning of all that has gone before. Genette mentioned an example of a surprise POP at the end of a narrative, *Portnoy's Complaint* (Roth, 1969), that retrospectively frames the whole narrative as being a monologue addressed to a psychoanalyst. But this occurs in a first-person narrative; it is the other person's voice, not the narrator's, that is the surprise. Genette's claim that "every narrative is, explicitly or not, 'in the first person' since at any moment its narrator may use that pronoun to designate himself" (1988, p. 96) is a claim that readers always have a mental construction of a fictional "I" who may appear at any time. But as I mentioned, any number of fictional POPs or PUSHes may be signalled by a narrative, and readers are able to construct each new level on the spot, as called for by the text. This does not mean that readers must keep in mind a permanent schema of all possible levels and bring this schema to all texts, whether or not these levels are activated by a particular narrative. I submit that in a novel such as *To the Lighthouse* (Woolf, 1955), a POP to a narrator would be not only a surprise, but a felt violation.

What McHale meant by the term "verticality," I believe, is our ability as readers to understand the language of narrative on many different levels. Each level adds richness of meaning to our understanding of literature. On this point, there is no quarrel. For example, when Jane refers to Mrs. Reed as the "mama" of the three Reed children at the beginning of *Jane Eyre* (Brontë, 1973), this reference resonates from its most direct meaning as evoking the relationship between the children and Mrs. Reed, to Jane's own lack of someone to call Mama, to her jealousy of the Reed children for their favored place, to her superior distance from their dependence on a mama. Thus, a single reference resonates with Jane's projective identification with the other children, her own neediness, and her defense against this neediness—her lofty distance. Jane's feelings as evoked cannot be neatly divided between Jane the young child and Jane the first-person adult narrator. One may go further to bring in the author's relation to the word Mama or one's own feelings about Mamas. This is not to say one should or shouldn't bring in these levels; this is to say that one often does. All of these associations may be brought to a single word. But as with the concept "voice," the levels of resonation here do not alter the attribution of SELF in the particular NOW of the sentence in which it appears.

Banfield mentioned that irony is a way of reading rather than a linguistic (read syntactic) phenomenon. There is nothing syntactic in a sentence such as "torture is fun" to tell the reader that the sentence is to be taken ironically. Rather, a reader accumulates a sense of the values that underlie a literary work, and if some story statement contradicts these values, the reader will either attribute the values expressed to a currently foregrounded character whose values match those of the statement, or he or she will POP out of the story world to search for other motivation for this contradiction. Although dual-voice theorists argue that there is always a narrator, I argue that there is always an author, whose attitudes and subjectivity saturate the text, albeit from another realm. The reader may always POP to consider how to take a given passage by comparing its values with a mental representation of the author's intentions. This kind of consideration is a necessary part of the task of reading.

To summarize: At any moment of reading a narrative, a reader may attentionally occupy one of several deictic fields—for example, a character's subjectivity within the story world, or the author's wry commentary on some historical phenomenon. The same sentence read from different levels has different self–world significance and, hence, a different meaning. There are textual, logical, psychological, and accidental factors that influence our choice of level at any moment of reading.

The Fictional Status of the Language of Narration, and the Attribution of Style. In a fictional narrative without a narrator, the language of narration is not itself part of the fiction, except where it represents the verbal expressions of characters or other story-level language, such as words painted on a wall. Rather, the language of narration is the mode of being of the fiction. Fictional people, events, experiences and verbal expressions are all represented and come to life through the language of the text, and the style of the language makes each fiction a different kind of experience, a different texture, a different self–world relation. Style that is not fictionally attributed to a narrator's or character's verbal expression in a NOW is not itself fictional. There need not be anyone in a fictional world responsible for the words of narration.

In terms of different techniques for representing subjectivity, the language of narration plays a different role according to the linguisticality of the subjectivity being represented. In first-person "feigned reality statement" narration, all the language of narration exists fictionally, because the "I" is purported to be writing or telling the narrative. In narration without a narrator, the representation of subjectivity may be more or less fictionally linguistic as its referent is more or less linguistic. For example, in the directly quoted speech of characters, the referring expression and the referent are both made of the "same stuff": language.

Similarly, Cohn (1978) has pointed out that stream-of-consciousness monologues, by purporting to convey not only the content of a character's thoughts but the verbal style in which it is thought, implies a highly verbal consciousness on the part of characters. The language of narration in such a style is part of the fictional world because the language of the text represents the language of the character's thought processes. As one moves away from mimesis of linguistic forms of subjectivity, there is more controversy about the status of the language of narration. What about language that represents perception, or unconscious desires, or the simple experiencing of a character? In the usual context of a sentence such as "She felt sad," what is the relationship of the language of narration to the subjectivity of the character? Borrowing the terminology of Gendlin (1980), I say that the language of narration *explicates* the character's subjectivity, but without the language being expressive of such, because the words are not part of the character's experience. The language explicates the character's SELF without itself being part of that fictional SELF. Thus, the language is objective: it is not part of a fictional being's consciousness in the NOW. At the same time, the language captures the subjectivity of a character's consciousness in the NOW. The language is objective, but it captures a SELF.

The most pointed style question is raised about situations in which the experiencing of a verbally limited character is explicated and captured using a distinctive and sophisticated style. The consciousness being represented and the sophistication of its representation may seem too far apart to call the latter simply "explication." One may feel it necessary in such cases to conjure a fictional mediating being who speaks for the character. My own attitude in such a case is that style belongs to the author, not to a fictional being, unless fictionally ascribed to one. When Cohn (1978) commented on what may be the paradigmatic case of this splitting, *What Maisie Knew,* she referred the sophistication of the style to James, not to a fictional narrator speaking for Maisie:

> Occasionally James will make a half-hearted attempt to color his psycho-narration with child-language, as when he mentions Maisie's "tucked-in and kissed-for-good-night feeling" for Miss Wix (p. 36). But these phrases always stand in sentences of typically complex Jamesian syntax. (p. 278)

When a reader is immersed in the story world, style constitutes the feel of the story world without itself becoming the fictional object of judgment. (Of course, readers often POP to consider the role of style, and particularly with "difficult" authors, style may be so dense as to retard the reader's attempt at total immersion.) But it is also often the case that the language of a text is called into question by the text itself and becomes an object for the reader's judgment. McHale argued that in *Ulysses* (Joyce, 1973), a separation is created between style and central consciousness by such passages as the "Nausicaa" example and the "Oxen of the Sun" chapter:

I am thinking especially of the notorious "Oxen of the Sun" chapter, whose language successively parodies some thirty historical styles of English writing. The central consciousness of "Oxen of the Sun" is presumably Bloom, although this is far from clear, and Stephen, too, is on the scene. Neither Bloom nor Stephen, however, seems a plausible source for the parodic styles. Ultimately, of course, it is the author who is responsible for "Oxen of the Sun"—for the selection of styles to be parodied, for the arrangement of the parodies, for the parodic intention and means. But each style gives rise, in turn to a distinct image of a speaker, a "particular personality" in Banfield's phrase—a Latinate speaker, an Anglo-Saxon speaker, an Elizabethan, Miltonic, Pepsyian, Swiftian, Dickensian, or Carlylean speaker, and so on. A narrator, in short, who is separable on the one hand from the author ("organizer and guarantor of meaningfulness") and on the other hand from the characters. (1983, p. 38)

McHale raises the interesting case of the unattributed use of various literary and social languages, or *heteroglossia*, as it is termed by Bakhtin. Briefly, I point to McHale's own seeming preference to attribute a point of view to an existing character rather than to a narrator whose existence has not been established. In the section of *Ulysses* he referred to here, he found it implausible to attribute the epistemological source of the many distinctive styles to the characters on the scene, and because the author's own parodying of the styles points up his own distance from them, he feels forced to conjure a narrator to whom to attribute each of these styles. This may be the case—that when a reader cannot plausibly attribute an idiosyncratic language in the text to a character, he or she constructs a narrator to whom this language may be attributed. But Bakhtin, whose own use of the term narrator is ambiguous with "author," does not interpret heteroglossia as the discourse of a narrator in the following passage:

Incorporated into the novel are a multiplicity of "language" and verbal-ideological belief systems—generic, professional, class-and-interest-group (the language of the nobleman, the farmer, the merchant, the peasant); tendentious, everyday (the languages of rumour, of society chatter, servants' language) and so forth, but these languages are, it is true, kept primarily within the limits of the literary written and conversational language; at the same time these languages are not, in most cases, consolidated into fixed persons (heroes, storytellers) but rather are incorporated in an impersonal form "from the author," alternating (while ignoring precise formal boundaries) with direct authorial discourse. (1981, p. 311)

POPping Out of the Fiction.   So far, I have mentioned only intrafictional levels. But a fictional narrative necessarily has a relation to extrafictional worlds as well. A reader not only constructs and inhabits the fictional story world; he or she also constructs an idea of the actual author and the relations between the author and the story world, and the relations between the story world and the historical world. These, too, are a part of the meaning of a novel. One measure of the quality of a work of fiction is the degree to which it challenges a reader to modify or expand his or her conception of reality. I do not dwell on this very difficult question, but make the point that irony, which many theorists argue is proof of a dual voice in narrative, is primarily a phenomenon of the perceived relations between the created fictional world and the author's real intentionality. For example, there is a presence behind Huck Finn's (Twain, 1981) narration. The ironic commentary provided by this presence is derived not from any single linguistic element that one could point to, nor any epistemological source within the fiction, but from the implications we draw from certain contradictions in the text between what people profess and how they behave. These contradictions are called attention to by strategic juxtaposition, hyperbole, and other rhetorical devices. This use of rhetoric, and the values it implies, will be referred by the reader (according to the Deictic Shift model) to the real author, not to a fictional narrator who is behind the fictional narrator Huck.

Objective Contexts and Contexts of Nonreflective Consciousness.   According-ing to the Deictic Shift model, objective context is text with no SELF, that is, text whose fictional epistemology does not originate in a consciousness. This contradicts common sense normal epistemology, but then, this is the essence of fiction: Its "reality" is established by fiat, not by consensus and corroboration. Again, I emphasize that the lack of a SELF is a fictional phenomenon. The subjectivity of the author at the time of writing is not doubted by this model, nor is it found to be irrelevant or uninteresting—it is just a topic that awaits development within the context of this model.

The characterization of a passage as objective is never absolute in real-time immersed reading. There are absolute linguistic cues, such as exclamations and curses, that a context is not objective, but a sentence that has none of these cues may nevertheless turn out, in retrospect, to be part of a subjective context if a later sentence recontextualizes the objective context within the consciousness of a SELF:

> The ship sailed at midnight. And for two hours her husband stayed with her, while the child was put to bed, and the passengers came on board. It was a black night, the Hudson swayed with heavy blackness, shaken over with spilled dribbles of light. She leaned on the rail, and looking down thought: This is the sea; it is deeper than one imagines, and fuller of memories. (Lawrence, 1976, p. 528)

In this example, the first sentence does not have any indications of subjectivity. But the following sentences establish that the first sentence, rather than being an objective statement of something that happened, is actually a prospective thought of the woman: The ship is to sail at midnight, and the actions and thoughts of the following sentences take place before midnight, as the woman prepares to leave. The entire passage is a subjective context within the woman's consciousness.

In an objective context, story settings, events, and characters are narrated directly, without mediation by a consciousness. To the questions "who sees?" and "who speaks?" the answer is, "no one." As with most written stage directions in a script or most camera shots in film, fictional reality in objective contexts is designated without being spoken or seen by a fictional subject. There may be a spatio-temporal orientation in an objective context, but there is no fictional subject occupying this orientation.

The fictional status of the text in an objective context is that of total referentiality. What it says, is, and its saying disappears. The story world is constructed to fit the words of the text. This does not mean that style is unimportant; the text's referentiality lies not only in what it describes, but in its syntax, its sociolinguistic register, its case grammar, and all the other concomitants of style. These produce the texture and felt reality of the story world.

This aspect of objective context is also true of contexts of nonreflective consciousness, a kind of objective "capture" of nonreflective subjective states. The sentence of nonreflective consciousness faithfully captures the lived experience of a character without implying that the character knows, understands, or would agree with the language used to capture this experience. The narration of childhood subjectivity must use a vocabulary far beyond that of a child in order to capture the child's perception and lived experience. The same is also true of other beings who are conscious without being linguistically adept. In the following short text, for example, a cat's lived experience is captured:

> With glad meows he sprang from the couch. As soon as the door opened, Socks was outside, his forepaws against Mrs. Bricker's thigh, stretching to be petted. A light breeze ruffled his fur, and spring sunshine drew the fragrance from the lemon blossoms. Life was good again. (Cleary, 1973, p. 41)

In this passage, the first two sentences can be read as either objective or subjective, whereas the third sentence is probably subjective, and the fourth, "Life was good again," is definitely subjective. (In its full context, the entire passage—the entire book—is solidly established as Socks' subjective context.) It is certain within the logic of the book's story world that Socks the cat does not know the names of common objects such as "door" or "couch," nor does he know Mrs. Bricker's name. The words of this passage explicate the relationship between directly felt referents in Socks' lived experience, not his linguistic or cognitive representations of them.

Objective contexts and sentences capturing lived experience share this in common: They are the direct representation of the "raw material" of fictional reality, in one case the *noumena*, or things-in-themselves, and in the other, the phenomenal experience of a subject. In neither case does the linguisticality of the text imply that the reality described is itself linguistic.

In Bakhtin's (1984) typology of discourse in Dostoevsky, objective context is one kind of "direct unmediated discourse directed exclusively toward its referential object, as an expression of the speaker's ultimate semantic authority" (p. 199) (Bakhtin's "speaker" is the author). According to Bakhtin, this kind of discourse is "not possible in every epoch . . . —for [it] presupposes the presence of authoritative perspectives and authoritative, stabilized ideological value judgments" (p. 192). In other words, objective context is warranted by social consensus and certainty about the nature of reality. But by using the argument that the authority to designate reality comes from conventionalized norms, Bakhtin missed the creative power of objective contexts to command new ways of portraying existence. Fictional objective contexts need not buckle under the strain of their difference from historical normality, nor apologize for the strangeness of the worlds they portray. Indeed, they may establish existents (as in science fiction) or ways of presenting reality (as in the Nouveau Roman) at great odds with normal orthodoxy without arguing for the right to do so.

Conclusion

The Deictic Shift model of narrative subscribes to Banfield's dictum 1 EXPERIENCER/1 SELF. One may not be able to determine, from isolated narrative sentences or expressions, the epistemological source of the knowledge or experience represented therein. But there will always be only one fictional SELF as the Origo of any fictional expression. As to "voice," I argue that "voice" is a poor synonym for SELF, because a voice is a public behavior that may be referred to the SELF or Origo of a HEARER as easily as to a SPEAKER. A mimic's use of another's voice is based, not on his or her merging with the other's subjectivity, but on his or her ability to hear and reproduce. A double voice does not equal a double SELF. I also argue that the so-called merging of a narrator with a character can be more adequately described as the absence of a narrator. Finally, the difference between the characters' own use of language and the language of the narrative does not ipso facto conjure a fictional narrator, because the language of fiction (the "narrating") may be simply fiction-creating, rather than being an object of fiction itself.

The Deictic Shift model also subscribes to Banfield's division of narrative into subjective and objective sentences, with Wiebe's additional notions of subjective and objective contexts and with some elaboration on the status of psychological reports.

Some issues of paramount importance to Banfield are not battle lines for me here. One such issue, which is proclaimed in the name of her book (1982), is that sentences of pure narration and represented subjectivity are not speakable. Although I find her arguments on this score historically and intuitively plausible, I do not see any principled reason why oral narrative should exclude these types of sentences. Just as the author is not part of the story world, so an oral storyteller can efface his or her own discourse and allow the shift of deictic plane to take place.

Mark Clarke stated that conversational narratives may represent an "altered state of consciousness" compared to ordinary conversational interaction: "to the extent that the storyteller becomes absorbed in the narration, this [story]world becomes separated from the conversation" (1986, p. 324). Where such a story is nonfictional, the deictic field may separate from the speaker's SELF-in-the-NOW and become centered in a past SELF whose experience is relived. Where the story is fictional, the speaker may live the experience of the story world as an imaginatively constructed deictic field, just as a reader or listener does. The reality of the speaker does not necessitate a fictional SPEAKER whose consciousness anchors the deictic field.

On a similar issue, I do not object to the idea that signs of pronunciation can appear in represented speech. McHale pointed to many examples of signs of pronunciation both in represented speech and in sentences of the syntactic form of indirect speech. Apparently, Dos Passos and other "proletarian novelists" made a point of mixing direct and indirect forms, perhaps as a way of drawing attention to and breaking through the concealed authority and pretension of objectivity that unmarkedness allows in the indirect forms. The shock value of the result decreases as one reads more of this type of sentence: "She shook her head but when he mentioned a thousand she began to brighten up and to admit that que voulez vous it was la vie" (Dos Passos, 1937, in *Nineteen Nineteen*, p. 382; quoted by McHale, 1978, p. 255 and Banfield, 1982, p. 115). Banfield argued strongly that signs of pronunciation are signs of communication, but I do not see a necessary connection between the voice and communication. I do not subscribe to Banfield's statement that "the oral . . . cannot free itself from the I–you relation" (1982, p. 242). In some psychotherapies, for example, one may have the freedom to express oneself without addressing anyone. Fictional narrative and therapeutic self-expression have this in common: They are a form of revelation, bringing something out into the open before (potential) witnesses, without being bound by norms of politeness and decorum that permeate and constrain language in direct address. Clarke pointed out that the talk of the mentally ill is paradigmatically not organized with regard to an addressee, and that the narratives of young children are often found "faulty" in this regard. He contended that there is often a double bind tension in the role of storyteller, in that the teller may be more interested in living an experience than in the communicative needs of his or her listeners (1986, p. 333).

I also find that SELF and voice are separable issues, and that although a voice comes from a person, this person is not necessarily the SELF. I even find that, on occasion, there are passages with many voices but no SELF.

In the first case, where the voice in a passage does not belong to the SELF, the SELF is a HEARER rather than a SPEAKER. A positive sign that this is the case is that there are ellipses in direct speech, indicating that the SELF is impaired and cannot hear all that is said. A HEARER may also be the epistemological source of represented speech. Further, a first-person SELF who has heard another character's speech may later represent that speech in the form of represented speech. In this case also, represented speech is referred to the epistemology of the HEARER, the first person. Neumann (1988) gives several cases of this type from the eighteenth-century epistolary novel *Sir Charles Grandison* (Austen, 1980). In the following example, each paragraph break signals a change in speaker in a first-person report of a conversation:

> We can't be all of one mind, replied I. I shall be wiser in time.
> Where was poor Lord G. gone?
> *Poor* Lord G. is gone to seek his fortune, I believe.
> What did I mean?
> I told them the airs he had given himself; and that he was gone without leave, or notice of return.
> He had served me right, *ab-* solutely right, Lord L. said.

Neumann believed that represented speech and thought (she used the term *free indirect discourse*, or *FID*, and defined this more loosely than Banfield's term) may have originated in everyday speech, noting that characters in eighteenth-century novels often use untagged, shifted reports of another's speech that retain the original speaker's evaluative elements, suggesting that this is a mimesis of everyday conversational usage. But the examples she used are from fictional letters, that feign written rather than oral usage. Still, the usage is nonfictional, suggesting that FID as a style (at least in English) may have originated as an entertaining way of recounting conversations in letters.

Once again, the epistemological divide between speech and thought is important. Speech is just as much an experience for the hearer as for the speaker, so represented speech may be referred to a SELF other than the speaker, namely a HEARER. Thought, perception, and other forms of private experience, on the other hand, can only be referred to the subject of consciousness who experienced them.

My second point, that a text may contain voices without SELF, diverges from Banfield in that it asserts that expressive elements may be found in an objective context. This is my contention about unattributed heteroglossia, in which bits and pieces of voices are used to create a milieu, but these voices are not speaking in a NOW. Instead, these voices are used to conjure up a typified social context:

> In the towns, on the edges of the towns, in fields, in vacant lots, the used-car yards, the wreckers' yards, the garages with blazoned signs—Used Cars, Good Used Cars. Cheap transportation, three trailers. '27 Ford, clean. Checked cars, guaranteed cars. Free radio. Car with 100 gallons of gas free. Come in and look. Used Cars. No overhead.
> A lot and a house large enough for a desk and chair and a blue book. Sheaf of contracts, dog-eared, held with paper clips, and a neat pile of unused contracts. Pen—keep it full, keep it working. A sale's been lost 'cause a pen didn't work.
> Those sons-of-bitches over there ain't buying. Every yard gets 'em. They're lookers. Spend all their time looking. Don't want to buy no cars; take up your time. Don't give a damn for your time. Over there, them two people—no, with the kids. Get 'em in a car. Start 'em at two hundred and work down. They look good for one and a quarter. Get time.

> Owners with rolled-up sleeves. Salesmen, neat, deadly, small intent eyes watch-
> ing for weaknesses.
>   Watch the woman's face. If the woman likes it we can screw the old man.
> (Steinbeck, 1966, p. 53)

This passage is part of an entire chapter that evokes a number of voices in order
to establish a milieu. The voices do not belong to people speaking in the NOW
of a narrative; rather, they paint a picture of what a place is like without enacting
any narrative story-line. The voices illustrate a general atmosphere rather than a
particular event. Thus they are an example of the *they say . . . relation* between
language and world.

Finally, I believe with Kuroda that it is to phenomenology and epistemology
rather than to linguistics that the final appeal must be made for the Deictic Shift
model, although it is linguistic structures that call our attention to the need for
this model. Although I admire Banfield's (1982) linguistic argumentation, and I
find her rigor of great use to my own understanding of what happens in fiction,
I think that her own perceptiveness goes considerably beyond the linguistic
devices she finds. In her other work, such as "The Empty Centre: Describing
the Unobserved" (1987), she demonstrates her own knowledge of and reliance
on phenomenological and epistemological categories, even as she continues to
try to find falsifiable ways of making her claims.

Many of the assertions made here on behalf of the Deictic Shift model are
subject to testing. As of now, I subscribe to the truth of these assertions because
they seem more faithful to my own experience of reading than the alternative.
It may be that those who have been trained to believe that there is always a
narrator really do construct this extra mediating level as they read, regardless of
whether one is called for by the text. Similarly, now that I am used to the
no-narrator-unless-marked notion, I may have dropped a mediating level that I
had before. If so, I believe I have thereby gained new narrative effects that are
not possible using the old model, effects that some authors are specifically striving
to achieve. Consider the following quotations, for example, from Sartre (1965):

> Since we were *situated,* the only novels we could dream of were novels of *situation,*
> without internal narrators or all-knowing witnesses. In short if we wished to give
> an account of our age, we had to make the technique of the novel shift from
> Newtonian mechanics to generalized relativity; we had to people our books with
> minds that were half lucid and half overcast, some of which we might consider
> with more sympathy than others, but none of which would have a privileged point
> of view either upon the event or upon himself. (p. 224)

> Thus, our technical problem is to find an orchestration of consciousnesses which
> may permit us to render the multidimensionality of the event. Moreover, in giving
> up the fiction of the omniscient narrator, we have assumed the obligation of
> suppressing the intermediaries between the reader and the subjectivities—the
> viewpoints of our characters. It is a matter of having him enter into their minds

as into a windmill. He must even coincide successively with each one of them. We have learned from Joyce to look for a second kind of realism, the raw realism of subjectivity without mediation or distance. (p. 228)

[Our predecessors] thought that they were justifying, at least apparently, the foolish business of storytelling by ceaselessly bringing to the reader's attention, explicitly or by allusion, the existence of an author. We hope that our books remain in the air all by themselves and that their words, instead of pointing backwards toward the one who has designed them, will be toboggans, forgotten, unnoticed, and solitary, which will hurl the reader into the midst of a universe where there are no witnesses; in short, that our books may exist in the manner of things, of plants, of events, and not at first like products of man. (p. 229)

From this viewpoint, absolute objectivity, that is, the story in the third person which presents characters solely by their conduct and words without explanation or incursion into their inner life, while preserving strict chronological order, is rigorously equivalent to absolute subjectivity. Logically, to be sure, it might be claimed that there is at least a witnessing consciousness, that of the reader. But the fact is that the reader forgets to see himself while he looks and the story retains for him the innocence of a virgin forest whose trees grow far from sight. (p. 229)

If there is always a fictional SPEAKER whose voice is heard by the reader as he or she reads, then a particular kind of aloneness can never be represented in a narrative. Virginia Woolf, in particular, wrote often about an aloneness for which there is no one to speak, and I think this effect is much more strongly conveyed when the text is not conceptualized as being relayed by a fictional SPEAKER. Consider, for example, the following passage from the "Time Passes" section of *To the Lighthouse* (Woolf, 1955):

So with the house empty and the doors locked and the mattresses rolled round, those stray airs, advance guards of great armies, blustered in, brushed bare boards, nibbled and fanned, met nothing in bedroom or drawing-room that wholly resisted them but only hangings that flapped, wood that creaked, the bare legs of tables, saucepans and china already furred, tarnished, cracked. (p. 194)

In this passage, I think it is important that there is not only no one who sees what is depicted here, but also that no one speaks. The fictional subjectivity of the passage belongs only to the airs.

Finally, I comment on the relationship (or lack of one) between the Deictic Shift model and structuralist and deconstructive views of subjectivity. A great deal of the passion that greeted Banfield's theory of unspeakable sentences came from a perception that she was trying to destroy the last human presence in literary analysis, the narrator. Because we were deprived of the author by the New Critics and the structuralists, the narrator was a last bastion of human attribution for the beauties and complexities of the novel. The deconstructionists and the Lacanians argued that subjectivity was an illusion structured by language, and that all of this concern about personhood was nostalgia. From another angle, linguists were claiming that all literary meaning could be scientifically explained, which sounded a lot like "drained." Humanist literary study was besieged on all sides.

But my own reading of Banfield, Hamburger, and Kuroda is that they are restoring the real author (in partnership with the real reader) as the creator of the text, and are asking us to look at the different ways subjectivity can be represented fictionally. They are not denying the reality of subjectivity; they are celebrating its complexity and the unique ways it can be represented in fiction.

3

A COGNITIVE–PHENOMENOLOGICAL THEORY OF FICTIONAL NARRATIVE

Erwin M. Segal
State University of New York at Buffalo

THE ROLE OF NARRATIVE IN SOCIETY

Narrative is concerned with storytelling. We are interested in the cognitive processes involved in creating, telling, interpreting, and understanding narrative. An obvious, but limited way to approach this domain is: A narrator utters or writes a text and the audience or reader successively processes each sentence and builds a meaningful representation of the text. This model, with amplification, identifies many of the studies of narrative by cognitive scientists (see Segal, this volume). From a pragmatic perspective, the model seems ill-conceived. Much narrative is fictive. Even so, probably all societies have narrative and storytelling, and many encourage it. Why should so many societies develop and encourage narrative if what it involves is simply committing to memory the propositions in fictional texts? Why would so many people willingly do so? There must be reasons other than committing propositions to memory.

Storytelling can be manifested in many different ways and in many different media. Narrators or storytellers orally tell stories to audiences. Authors write novels and short stories that are published and read by readers. Playwrights write plays that are performed on stages by actors using props. Screenwriters write screenplays that are implemented by producers, directors and actors, and are then filmed. Choreographers and composers choreograph and compose ballets that are danced on stages, often with costumes and props. Composers compose operas that are also performed with costumes and props. Even cartoonists draw sequences of cartoon boxes that tell stories. Although different media present very different aesthetic and emotional experiences, using a variety of linguistic and nonlinguistic tools, each of them can be used to present a story.

Why is narrative production such a large industry? What does it do for the reader or audience? Narrative allows us to vicariously experience phenomena that would be too dangerous or costly to experience directly. Narrative allows us to emotionally experience exciting and even tragic events without suffering the consequences, and it allows us to vicariously visit and understand diverse peoples within our culture, and in other cultures. Narrative is a good way to learn; we learn better using narrative than expository forms (Freedle & Hale, 1979). Most of us have cognitive operations that allow us to make reasonable inferences about which aspects of fictional narrative are pure fiction, and which ones are likely to be valid in the real world (cf. Rapaport & Shapiro, this volume). Experiencing the interplay of events presented by narrative is emotionally involving, structurally appealing, and educational. No wonder narrative is so popular.

Narrative is part of our daily lives. When we talk about what we have seen, read, or heard—which we often do—fictional narrative is treated the same as any other experience. One can talk about the experience of reading a book or watching a movie, crossing between real and fictional events as if they were of the same cloth. One can easily move in conversation from a discussion of the physical context of a movie house to images on a film, to experiences of the actors in making the movie, to the fictive events portrayed in the story, without any specific change of terminology. People easily shift from one "mental space" to another (cf. Fauconnier, 1985). We need a conceptualization of narrative and of the cognitive processes associated with narrative that is consistent with its worth. This chapter attempts to identify some of the properties of such a theory.

THE STRUCTURE OF NARRATIVE

Story and Discourse

Structural analyses of narratives led to several important logical distinctions. One such distinction is that between the sentences in the text and the story that the sentences express.[1] This distinction, between discourse and story, was made by many narrative theorists (Bal, 1985; Chatman, 1978; Genette, 1980; Rimmon-Kenan, 1983; Toolan, 1988) and was even implied in Aristotle's *Poetics*.

Chatman argued that one can present the same story through various means. Sometimes a story that originated in one medium is transformed into a different medium. Many novels and short stories have been presented as movies, (e.g., *Gone with the Wind* (Mitchel, 1936), "The Killers" (Hemingway, 1938/1953),

---

[1]This is a variant of model theory; one structure is determined by the sequence of presentation, and the other by the relations among meanings.

Jurassic Park (Crichton, 1990). I recall that as a child, I read many a classic novel in comic book form. The story of Othello is a play by Shakespeare, an opera by Verdi, and an opera by Rossini. Sometimes a story is redone in the same medium, for example, the various remakes of the movie, *A Star is Born* (Wellman, 1937; Cukor, 1954; Pierson, 1976). In order for it to be possible to present the same story in different media, or with different texts, the story must be something other than the form and the medium of the presentation.

Othello is about a Moor in Venice, who had a wife who loved him and a servant who didn't. The narrative discourse, whether it is in the form of a play or an opera, presents the story of these people and their situation. The story then, consists of the Moor and the relations between him, his wife, his servant, and their relations to other people and situations. In a play about this story, the discourse is comprised of the dialogue and the associated props; in an opera, the words and music with associated props form the discourse; in a movie, the discourse includes all the material on the film and sound track. This distinction between story and discourse allows for the possibility that a given story can be presented through various media.

There are some problems with the definition of what constitutes the same story, that cannot be resolved in this chapter. Different presentations of the same story often deviate from each other. The set of events in a comic book are not entirely equivalent to the events in the novels so illustrated. Nor are the events represented in an opera exactly like those represented in a play. Remakes vary dialogue and even venues for stories. What it is that creates equivalence between two presentations of the same story has not been clarified. Nevertheless, one can present essentially the same story using widely different media. Thus, stories (that is, the sequences of events and the objects involved in them) are conceptually distinct from the sentences of a narrative about them.

If the distinction between story and discourse is to be considered valid we must find cognitive processes and mechanisms that can account for it. We suggest that when we enjoy a narrative, we activate or create a mental model which represents the story. In the Deictic Shift Theory we propose, readers and authors represent themselves at a spacetime location within the mental model, and from there they vicariously witness the events of the story. Although participants sense and feel different discourses and different media, these sensory and emotional experiences occur in the context of the objects and events they create and witness in the story.

Narrative discourse and story differ in the kind of units they contain, and in the relationships between the units. The elements of a discourse combine and produce linguistic units such as noun phrases, sentences, and preposition phrases. The relations among these units are largely syntactic and concatenative. The units of a story are nonlinguistic entities such as people, objects, events, places, and times. The relations among these are largely spatio-temporal and causal. There is a partial correspondence between many of the linguistic units within the text and many of the story units. Noun phrases are often interpreted as referring expressions which map onto persons or objects. Sentences may be interpreted as propositions which map onto events, and preposition phrases may map onto temporal or spatial relations, times or places.

One of the tasks of the author or performer is to present the discourse in such a manner that the reader or audience can understand and represent the story's temporal and spatial relations. Extending Austin (1962) and Grice (1975; Segal, this volume), we can think of the presentation of a story as an illocutionary act. Authors, playwrights, composers, actors, and narrators present the discourse with the intention of creating the experience of a sequence of events identifiable as a story in the reader or audience. The readers or audience are expected to recognize the presenter's intentions and act appropriately if they wish to experience the story.[2]

Story Worlds[3]

Although many of the units of the discourse map onto units of the story, the two systems are not isomorphic. The relations among the discourse units are sequential, usually left–right, whereas the relations among the story units are temporal and spatial. Contiguous discourse units do not always represent spatially and temporally contiguous story objects and events. In fact, places and times contiguous to those referred to in the text often are not mentioned in text, and may play no direct role in the story. However, such places and times are potentially available to the author and reader and give the story coherence. The story thus is seen to be embedded in a larger structure, a *story world* which surrounds the events in the story (Pavel, 1986; Walton, 1990; Young, 1987). Story worlds are possible worlds, hypothesized to have properties analogous to those of the real world. For instance, story worlds have a timeline (Almeida, this volume; Reichenbach, 1947; Segal, 1990) and a spatial structure, and each story world contains locations, persons, places, things, and events. A story is a (proper) subset of a story world. Its events are ordered according to the temporal, spatial, and causal relations of the story world. The story world contains some events not mentioned in the story, so that the objects and events that are mentioned can be coherently interrelated. This coherence is preserved in a story regardless of when the story units are referred to in the discourse. Whatever their order of presentation in the discourse, events that occur earlier in the story precede events that occur later; people and objects in the story are located in relation to one another in the story world's spacetime.

Discourse and Story Revisited

The discourse is directly presented to a reader, whereas the story must be created by him or her. But the reader often is interested primarily in the story, using the

---

[2] The focus of this book is on linguistic narratives and narrative text, so I will hereafter generally limit the discussion to these. Similar discussions can be made for other media.

[3] In this chapter, I use "story world" in order to discuss a kind of world. This parallels "real world." I use "storyworld" to refer to an instantiation of such a world.

discourse as a means toward an end.[4] The reader experiences the events of the story and often becomes emotionally involved with them. He or she is likely to worry about the potential dangers and disappointments of the characters and may feel their pains and share their happinesses. He or she wants to know what happens to them, how it happens, what the characters think about it, and why. The reader explores, interprets and experiences the story through sequential encounters with the linguistic units of the discourse.

The reader may experience the events in the story, but it is the author who has the task of presenting the discourse so that the reader can have the appropriate experiences. The author uses different devices to give the reader what he or she considers the right information at the right time. He or she chooses which aspects of the story to highlight, and as noted previously, might present events in an order other than that of the story. Thus, later occurring story events may be witnessed by the reader prior to earlier occurring ones. By selecting both the sequence in which to present events and which aspects to emphasize, he or she can affect the emotional and aesthetic reactions of the reader to the story (cf. Burroway, 1982). The divergence from the timeline of the story is necessary for certain narrative genres, such as mysteries and detective stories. The events that lead up to a murder early in the time within the story are often not revealed in the discourse until near the end of the story.

The mental model of the story must, either implicitly or explicitly (Bobrow, 1975), represent the temporal order of events as they occur in the story, not as they are referred to in the discourse. Otherwise, the causal and temporal relations in the story would not be available to the reader. Almeida (this volume) presents one of our attempts at computationally representing the timeline of the story through an analysis of temporal indicators in the discourse.

Narration

Narrative is more a temporal than a spatial art. A narrative is not presented to a reader all at once. Whatever experience readers have in response to a narrative occurs over time. *Narration* is used here to signify the process of moving temporally through a narrative.

Readers and authors live in real time, read and write texts in real time, and experience the story in real time. But reading time is not isomorphic with story time; a story which may be read in an hour, a day, or a week, may encompass many years in storytime. *Jane Eyre* (Brontë, 1847/1985), for example, begins when she is 10 years old, and ends some time after her marriage, the last few paragraphs encompassing several years. Genette (1980) pointed out that *Eugenie Grandet* (Balzac, 1833/1967) covered 44 years in 172 pages.

---

[4]Readers may be interested in many aspects of a narrative: linguistic style, literary allusions, thematic structure, character representations. These are not the topic of this chapter.

Let us explore a metaphor (cf. Lakoff, 1987): Reading can be depicted as going on a journey. We can think of narrative discourse as being a component of a real physical object such as a book, through which the reader travels via his or her eyes. We use such expressions as "I'm getting to a good part here," and, "I'm almost through the second chapter." If a narrative is presented orally, we can think of the audience and the narrator travelling through the text as it is being told. Other forms of storytelling can also be envisioned as a trip: through an opera, a film, a play. Because each of these media have a discourse that is presented and experienced over time, we can think of ourselves as travelling through them as they unwind.

The story presents a similar metaphor. The narration guides the reader through a story world. The reader presupposes that the storyworld exists with its own spacetime. Narration is used to place the reader at a particular location within the preexisting storyworld. However, a trip through a story world is not entirely similar to a trip through the real world. We normally think of time as a dimension we can move through in only one direction and at only one rate. And we usually think of space as a three-dimensional continuum through which we can pass in different directions and at several different rates; but in the real world, all points along the direction of movement are traversed. As readers, our passage through stories does not necessarily abide by these real-world guidelines. Although narration generally moves us consistently through story time (cf. Rapaport et al., 1989), we have the possibility of direct access to many spacetime locations within the story world. In "Lorna had a toothache," presented in the prolog, we see how the narration transports the reader directly from Lorna's living quarters to the dentist's office. The reader does not traverse the intervening space. The narration applies to how the reader gets around in the storyworld, not how the characters do. We assume that, although we did not witness it, in the storyworld Lorna used physical transportation to get from her home to the dentist's office.

The reader relates linguistic elements within the discourse to the objects and events of the story according to a complex set of principles. The mapping between the discourse and story elements is not 1:1, nor is it simple. Some discourse elements do not map onto any story elements, and different discourse elements often map onto the same story element. Some story elements may occur fleetingly, and not even be identified directly by any discourse elements, whereas others may persist for a long time in the story, and be identified many times and in many ways by the discourse. For example, major characters recur many times in the story, and are often referred to by different discourse elements.

The journey metaphor within the story helps us understand how multiple references to the same object can be followed so easily. The reader finds himself or herself cognitively within the story. He or she is located at the Deictic Center, the moving spacetime location from which the sentences are interpreted. The recurring characters usually move with the Deictic Center, or reappear within it. Any reference to the character is, by the context of the reference, marked for its spacetime location. This theory accounts for the lack of confusion if there are changes in the properties of the characters or objects during the course of the story. Narration is the process by which the reader is guided to a particular place at a particular time within the storyworld.

In summary, our model identifies two logically different structures, discourse and story, through which the reader simultaneously travels by the process of narration. While the reader is moving through the pages of a book, he or she is also moving in a more erratic manner through the world of the story. The author presents the story from a location within the story world and the reader interprets the story from the same location. The possibility of such a deictic shift gives narrative great power. The power of narrative discourse is such that (a) the author and reader can each use it to transport themselves from the spacetime location from which the narrative is written or read, to a place where they observe and experience physical and mental events they might not be able to witness in the real world (Banfield, 1982; Cohn, 1978; Wiebe, 1990b; see also Galbraith, this volume); and (b) the reader can understand and keep track of the relations between objects and events and the changes in recurring objects.[5]

MIMESIS

Narrative scholars since Plato and Aristotle identified narrative as a mimetic art. That is, they described narrative as being imitative of a possible reality (cf. Auerbach, 1953; Walton, 1990). The mimetic view of these scholars differs from the view presumed by most communication and semantic representation theorists, who proposed that narrative text contains a sequence of propositions composed by an author or narrator to be represented by a reader (cf. Searle, 1975b; Segal, this volume). In most narrative discourse, the story's phenomena are contextualized and presented from a particular perspective within the story world (Fillmore, 1981; Segal, this volume). A reader in a mimetic mode is thus led to experience the story phenomena as events happening around him or her, with people to identify with and to feel emotional about.

The view that narrative is a mimetic art leads some of us to the conclusion that different genres, such as narrative and expository text, are likely to have different sets of pragmatic presuppositions and modes of processing (cf. Banfield, 1982; Bruner, 1986).[6] In narrative, events are often shown and not asserted. Reading narrative as intended by the author requires that the reader mentally

---

[5]The sensitivity of the contexts to the properties of objects and events directly follow computationally from the CASSIE implementations of SNePS (see Almeida; Rapaport & Shapiro; Shapiro & Rapaport; Wiebe; and Yuhan, this volume.)

[6]McHale (1983) and Genette (1988) did not accept this conclusion. Although they acknowledged some expressive aspects of narrative text that others take to be mimetic, they claimed they were foundationally communications between authors and readers.

construct a semblance of reality to experience (Bruner, 1986; Hamburger, 1973) from a particular perspective. Rather than authors telling readers about the objects and events in the story, both the author and the reader witness it from that perspective (Segal, 1990).

There is much evidence to support the claim that large portions of narratives are mimetic. Many sentences in narrative text do not have the form of assertions (Banfield, 1982). One finds in narrative text exclamations, slang, expressive repetitions, incomplete sentences, nonstandard forms, and other expressive elements. The following example has several such elements:

> The friendliness of it, the—the—Just to prove how happy she was, just to show the tall fellow how at home she felt, and how she despised stupid conventions, Laura took a big bite of her bread-and-butter as she stared at the drawing. (Mansfield, 1937/1992, p. 536)

These elements represent a mental state of the character to whom they belong. They show the reader what is seen, heard, or thought. It is our hypothesis that the way this is achieved cognitively is by situating the reader at a location where he or she can perceive the source of the expression. In this example, the reader must be close enough to Laura to perceive her thoughts directly (Cohn, 1978).[7]

One aspect of narrative experience that directly relates to the locus of the reader in the story, is that the reader often is presented a view of the narrative world from the point of view of a character. Thus, the reader may become aware of an event at the same time a subject does, and may even see it through the subject's eyes. Almost all narrative scholars are aware of this presentation of a character's subjectivity. We propose, which most of them do not, that this can occur by the reader cognitively situating him or herself in or near the mind of the character in order to interpret the text (Bruder & Wiebe, this volume; Galbraith, this volume; Wiebe, 1990b).

Let us consider dialogue. It is a patently mimetic form found in narrative discourse and seldom found in expository text. In expository text, if a direct quote occurs, a speaker has to be identified prior to the quote (e.g., John said, ". . ."; or more likely, The President said, ". . ."). In narrative discourse, the identification of the speaker often follows the utterance. Dialogues in narrative are seldom asserted by the author, nor addressed to the reader, but they directly represent conversations between characters that happen to be overheard by the reader. The character speaking is often, but not always, directly identified; usually the speaker is identified primarily to direct the reader's attention to the source of the utterance, as in the following example:

> . . . Mitch directed the driver to an empty slot near the building.
> "Ain't you getting out?" the driver asked.

---

[7]Cohn (1978) pointed out how, in narrative fiction, the minds of characters seem to be transparent, because the reader can look inside them.

"No. Keep the meter running."
"Man, this is strange."
"You'll get paid."
"You got that right." (Grisham, 1991, p. 206)

Authors present dialogue to let readers witness a conversation taking place. When a narrator orally tells a story, he or she often varies voice quality and even direction of gaze and posture to simulate different speakers of a dialogue. This emphasizes the mimetic aspects of the discourse. Obviously, the narrator is showing the utterances to the audience and not telling about them. When reading dialogue, a reader can imagine different qualities of voice and direction of gaze in duplication of a narrator's performance.

Mimesis and a Fictional Narrator

The standard structuralist view of narrative discourse views narrative as a communication that requires, even "presupposes two parties, a sender and a receiver" (Chatman, 1978, p. 28). Ultimately, the sender is the author, and the receiver is the reader (Chatman, 1978). There are seldom, however, direct assertions by the author to the reader. The criteria for such assertions are not met by the narrative discourse. Assertions require certain situational and epistemological presuppositions (cf. Searle, 1975c) that are not met in most narrative discourse (Galbraith, 1990; this volume), and assertions have a particular grammatical structure one often does not see in narrative text (Banfield, 1982).

If one holds to the communication model, an assertion must be epistemologically justified by its speaker. But many of the sentences of a fictional narrative describe events that have never occurred. The author, who lives in the real world, cannot justify them. Most narrative theorists resolved this dilemma by arguing that the author creates a fictional narrator to tell the fictional story (Booth, 1961/1983; Chatman, 1978; Genette, 1988; Rimmon-Kenan, 1983). The fictional narrator is the person who witnessed the events of the story.

The fictional narrator model of narrative text, however, neither satisfies the implicit constraints of communication theory, nor is generally supported by the language of the text. There is no existing fictional narrator who can communicate with the reader, so such a narrator cannot play any direct role in an assertion. From a cognitive perspective, one has to explain how an author can speak through a fictional narrator, rather than how a fictional narrator can talk about fictional events.

Authors can, and often do, invent characters through whom to tell a story. There are many first-person narratives in which a character in the story is identified by "I" or "me" in many of its sentences. These are not written from the author's perspective, but rather from the perspective of a character in the fictional world. In order to write such text and make it linguistically and deictically correct, the author must take the perspective of the narrator. That is, he or she must make a deictic shift into the fictional world and the mind of a character who observes the events in that world to imitate what the character would write if he or she were to write a story about his or her experiences. For example, Melville wrote: "Call me Ishmael. Some years ago—never mind how long precisely—having little or no money in my purse . . ." (Melville, 1851/1967, p. 11).

First-person narration, however, does not require that the fictional narrator tell the story as a sequence of assertions. Rather, even the fictional narrator can make a deictic shift into the time of the events he or she is describing. The author makes a deictic shift into the mind of the fictional narrator and views the story world from his or her perspective. The narrator, in telling the story, represents the phenomena that he or she is describing mimetically. This requires the narrator to make a deictic shift to the time of the event being reported. The description of the events in this situation requires a double shift for the author. The first shift constrains the author to remember events as constrained by the presumed knowledge of the narrator, and the second shift adds to that the perception of the events from a perspective at the deictic center where they occur. This analysis, if it has any validity, suggests that rather than supporting a communication model of fiction, a first-person narrative supports a mimetic or representational view of fictional discourse. The following example, also from *Moby Dick* (Melville, 1851/1967), is centered in the Spouter Inn prior to dinner, and not at the time several years later from which the opening sentence, cited previously, was presented: "But the fare was of the most substantial kind—not only meat and potatoes, but dumplings; good heavens! dumplings for supper!" (p. 22).

In terms of the cognitive or computational structure of this mimetic enterprise, the author pushes to the mind of a narrator, and then the narrator pushes into the events being described mimetically. Thus, the author can constrain his description according to the knowledge he or she has imparted to the narrator.[8]

STORY WORLDS REVISITED

Stories are objects. As objects, they should be coherent and consistent. The sequences of events must be meaningfully related to one another. Our analysis, shared by others (Bruner, 1986; Pavel, 1986), is that the events of a story primarily take place within a single spacetime continuum which we identify as a story world. The story world contains people, places, objects and events that exist in spatial, temporal and causal relationship with one another. Whatever the ontology of a story world,[9] it functions to constrain the properties and relations of the entities identified in the story, and to give the reader the phenomenological feeling of coherence.

---

[8]SNePS is a representational system that is designed to easily maneuver through such a hierarchy of representations while observing the constraints (cf. Shapiro & Rapaport, this volume).

[9]It may be representations within the mental model, it may be a system of constraints learned by the author and reader, or it may have properties of both.

The world we live in, the real world, is the one most of us think of when we think of time, space, people, objects, events. But there are times and spaces we are well aware of that do not belong in our world. Many stories begin with existential claims such as the following: Once upon a time there were three little pigs. When were there three little pigs? Last year? A thousand years ago? Where were they? In Texas? In South America? There is no answer! They exist on a fictional time which is not temporally related to our time and in a fictional place not related to our space. Whatever story worlds are, they are not necessarily deictically related to the world in which we live.

The primary constituents of stories are events. According to Prince (1982), a minimal story consists of two events. For example: John ate and Mary ate. What makes them a story is that the events are related to each other. Event A must precede event B, follow B, or occur at the same time as B. Two events, however, cannot be temporally related to each other if they do not occur within the same world. A story world is a conceptual domain that is temporally and spatially coherent. It exists so that different events of a story have a time and a place where they can occur in relation to one another (Pavel, 1986). Thus, each story world has a timeline (Reichenbach, 1947), a spatial frame, and its own set of people, places, events and existents. In a story world, it is usually the case that story time is similar to real time, and story space is similar to real space. Story events and existents are logically confined to the world in which they appear, and all events that occur in the story world are temporally and spatially related to one another. Events that do not occur in that world are not related in this way.

Verisimilitude and Storyworld Logic

As a first approximation, the events and objects in a story world are intensionally of the same kind as those found in the real world experienced by the author and the reader. Thus, the events have the character of having verisimilitude, of being "true to life." Verisimilitude refers to the suggestion that the objects in the story world have properties there that similar objects would have in the outside world experienced by the author and reader. To the extent that a story world has verisimilitude, temporal and spatial relations are the same as one would be likely to find in the real world. Characters' interests, expectations, perceptions and beliefs would also be similar to those of people in the real world. And the events that occur in the story would not be discriminable by their properties, from real world events. Many story worlds are as verisimilar as possible. This should hold true for purportedly true narratives and realistic fiction.

Whereas having verisimilitude in the story world as a first approximation is extremely important in constructing and experiencing a story (Todorov, 1977), many stories deviate from having verisimilitude as the sole arbiter of events. Fantasy and science fiction may introduce objects with properties they do not have in the real world. Historical fiction and other genres may have constraints that are different from those of the author or reader. The reader and author may not even share the same set of cultural and physical conditions. However, many of the relationships among the events in a story are not explicitly stated; if readers are to understand them, they must be able to infer what the implied relationships are. They must have knowledge of the principles which guide these relationships. They must understand the storyworld logic.

Every story world has a set of implicit constraints, rules, or principles which dictate what can or cannot be the case within that world. These constraints serve as a *storyworld logic*, that specifies what the possible properties of objects are and what relations can exist among them. Knowledge of the storyworld logic constrains the interpretation and experience of the story. Because no story can completely specify all of the constraints that are implicit in the relationships among its events, the reader must have some way of inferring what they are. The default condition is verisimilitude. If there are no reasons to believe otherwise, the reader presumes the relationships are what they would be in the real world. If verisimilitude is not followed completely, the reader will try to infer the variations from it by striving to conserve coherence in the storyworld. As a genre develops and becomes established, the particular storyworld logic for the genre becomes established and can serve as the basis for story comprehension. Todorov (1977) generalized the concept of verisimilitude to include genre regularities. As a reader becomes more familiar with a genre, he or she is likely to learn the storyworld logic; the genre's constraints become its verisimilitude, so new stories from the same genre may be comprehended and followed more easily.

Nonrealistic fictions tend to introduce variants from verisimilitude somewhat slowly. Animals might talk, mythological creatures may be introduced, or people might live on other planets, but most of the relationships expressed can still occur in the real world. Verisimilitude, with the addition of a few particular deviations from real world phenomena, serves to constrain the interpretation of fiction in a way analogous to how Grice's conversational postulates (1975) constrain the interpretation of conversation. The more verisimilar the story and the more explicit the deviation, the easier the narrative should be to understand.

The reader approaches a new story presupposing that it has a storyworld logic to help structure the incoming text. His or her understanding of the logic may be modified as he or she progresses through the text. Although the logic constrains events within the story world, the constraints, especially those which are not verisimilar, have to be learned by the reader. If the genre is new, he or she may not be able to make all of the expected inferences and connections between events. This is one reason why two readers may differ in how they interpret a text.[10] It suggests that one value of reading a text more than once is that the

---

[10]Many of the places in the text where inferences have to be made are not totally constrained by the storyworld logic. Thus, even well-versed readers can construct and experience different worlds from the same text.

logic of the storyworld, which was slow in developing can, on later readings, be available for interpreting the early parts of the text. Some postmodern fiction can be quite difficult to understand because the author has intentionally interfered with some of the premises of a coherent spacetime that is one of the major contributions of verisimilitude to storyworld logic. Attempting to figure out what is going on may be part of the value in reading and rereading a text, although it can have other experiential values.

THE REAL WORLD AND STORY WORLDS

The theoretical perspective supported by this volume presumes there are at least two worlds relevant to the experience of narrative: the reader's world and the story world. In fictional narrative, these two worlds are deictically independent of each other (Segal, 1990). Fictional events occur neither before nor after real events (Buhler, 1982). Nonfictional narrative contains the same two spacetime continua for reading and phenomenal experience, but the story world represents events that can be related deictically to the reader. The two worlds share the same timeline and spatial structure. From my physical location in time and space, I can claim that historical and all past real events occurred prior to the present time. Some events, such as my typing this sentence, and the current session of Congress, are occurring at the present time. And I can anticipate that certain events, such as my meeting a class tomorrow, will occur in the future. I can point to their temporal relationship to me. But fictional events are in a different world, with its own timeline and its own space. I cannot point from my physical situation to when or where they occurred or will occur.

The isolation of fictional events from real events requires careful analysis. Much fiction is conceptually related to real places and times. *A Tale of Two Cities* (Dickens, 1859/1980) is about London and Paris after the French Revolution. Some of us may think that we can point to when and where the events of the novel are supposed to have fictionally occurred, but we cannot point to the events themselves. The setting of the novel allows us to conceptually ground the setting. We can use our knowledge of 18th-century Europe to help understand the story events and their interrelationships. But because the events are fictional, they are not referentially identifiable in real spacetime.[11] We find them only in a fictional world, regardless of how many properties the two worlds have in common.

---

[11]The logic of the deictic location of historical fiction requires study. It may be the case that although many events in historical fiction are false in the real world, they may be true in some possible worlds accessible to certain historical states of affairs (cf. Hughes & Cresswell, 1968). In such a case, we might want to claim that the historical fiction is at least indirectly "pointatable" from a real situation.

Because the real world and fictional story worlds are deictically independent of each other, a reader cannot move from one world to the other. The magic of fiction is that a person, in the blink of an eye, can shift from being cognitively in one world to being cognitively in another. We do not doubt that readers can shift their deictic center to a spacetime location within the story world. It is a cognitive move that is analogous to everyday phenomenal experiences such as dreaming, daydreaming, and playing games with imaginary objects and people. Even children as young as 2 do it (Walton, 1990). We just need to identify some of the cues that guide this move.

Boundaries and Edgework

The world has been defined by physicists as an unbounded, finite object that exists in spacetime. The fact that it is unbounded means that no one can escape from its spacetime. Story worlds share with the real world the possibility of being unbounded objects; there are no logical reasons they cannot be indefinitely extended. Because the spacetimes of storyworlds exist outside those of the real world, no one can physically move from the real world to a story world, or vice versa (unless they are with Mary Poppins or someone else equally magical). In order to get from one world to another, a person has to make a conceptual leap. In narratives, that conceptual leap is usually a deictic shift.[12]

All discourse, including narrative discourse, exists in the real world. Books, film, and performances are all real (cf. Goffman, 1974). Some of this discourse is designed to represent storyworld phenomena and some is not. Boundaries can and do exist between these two categories of discourse. Authors and performers who produce discourse are likely to know which parts of it are storyworld related. It is their responsibility to mark in the discourse its relevant boundaries. Young (1987) investigated some of the boundaries between these different realms in oral narrative discourse. She called the signs that mark these boundaries *edgework*.

Authors and producers of discourse have the responsibility to mark the boundaries between different categories of discourse, and many, but not all, do so. Most readers know many of the conventional cues that mark boundaries. When a boundary is cued, the reader is invited to switch his or her deictic center to a location within a storyworld. For the reader, edgework includes identifying the cognitive domain in which the storyworld is to be experienced, and instantiating it with its initial content and the values for its spacetime dimensions. A default constraint system consisting of the expected storyworld logic based on verisimilitude and previous experience with the genre of the story must also be attached.

---

[12]As long as the domain is conceptual, the deictic shift readers make is not really magical. The computational equivalent to such a move is a push. Polanyi and Scha (1984) showed how discourse analysis requires such pops and pushes. Goffman (1974) and Young (1987) identified levels of coherence that frame other levels, easily modelled with such devices.

Edgework

In order to enter a storyworld, the reader must have, located in a mental space (Fauconnier, 1985), a cognitive representation of the phenomena that he or she is to experience. When the first sentence of the first chapter of a novel or short story is being read (or the curtain opens on a play, or the words "feature presentation" are replaced by a scene at the movies), a reader usually responds by anticipating that what comes next will represent a new entity. The objects and events represented by the discourse following the boundary are to be instantiated in the space made available. Later narrative discourse may lead to the instantiation of new objects and events in spatial, temporal, and causal relationship to the first events as dictated by the storyworld logic.[13] There is no attempt to deictically relate any of these events to the reader's real situation.

I have around me several books. On the white cover of one it says "NARRATIVE DISCOURSE," and in slightly smaller print, "*An Essay in Method*," and in still smaller print, "BY GERARD GENETTE." Another book has a purple cover with large gold print proclaiming "ALICE HOFFMAN" and "Turtle Moon." It also has a picture on the cover and another just inside. The point here is that most readers would know before they begin reading that Genette's (1980) book is an expository text and Hoffman's (1992) is fiction. There are also cues (titles, text arrangement and blank space, different fonts, pagination) that tell readers what the particular function of each different part of the text is, so that they may read each part according to a different set of interpretation criteria, or possibly not read some at all. Generally readers know from the context and cues what the role of a particular sentence is at the time it is encountered.

There are many different cues that can be identified which mark boundaries around narrative text. In *Turtle Moon*, the type of paperback book, the color of the cover, and the size and color of the print of the author and title imply that this book contains fictional narrative text. Inside the cover, the pages before the title page are presumed to be prior to the narrative text. The same holds true for blank pages after the title page. When, however, we get to a page that in this case centers the words, "Chapter One," followed by a continuous text in the same smaller font, we know the narrative begins there. Everything from the beginning through "Chapter One" are all to be read as assertions addressed to the reader. These are assigned to different categories with different evaluative and interpretation criteria. The next sentence, "The last major crime in Verity was in 1958, when one of the Platts shot his brother in an argument over a Chevy Nomad they had bought together on time," (Hoffman, 1992, p. 1) is to be instantiated in the storyworld. The reader is to put himself or herself into a storyworld at a place called Verity, at a time somewhat later than 1958. He or she

---

[13]Rapaport and Shapiro (this volume) explain how SNePS and CASSIE create and expand mental spaces based on the reception of narrative text.

will look around and get a feel for the place as he or she comes into contact with more of the properties of the place by reading the following sentences. The default category of the succeeding sentences is to represent and to experience them within the storyworld.

The first sentence of a fiction is often treated differently from the subsequent sentences. The reader may presume that the first sentence does not relate deictically to anything that he or she knows. This may be marked in the text. "Once upon a time," or another indefinite beginning, informs the reader that what is coming cannot be spatially or temporally tied to the real world. It also implies that the storyworld that follows is to be deictically isolated from all other story worlds. At other times, a fictional text may imply that a spacetime location is deictically tied to the reader, such as with a heading like "London, June 1939." But if the external props, such as the book jacket, identify the text as fiction, the reader is likely to initiate processes to create a unique storyworld for the objects and characters mentioned. The heading informs the reader that the world created will use properties of the historical location identified, but the entities instantiated would be extentionally different from their real world counterparts.[14]

Other Boundaries and Edgework

Within narrative discourse there are boundaries between different locations within the story world. These boundaries are often marked by lexical, syntactic and other structural cues, like paragraph breaks (cf. Bruder, this volume; Rapaport et al., 1989; Zubin & Hewitt, this volume). The reader uses such cues in the discourse to direct the shift of his or her deictic center from one location to another. There are also more powerful discourse cues, such as chapter breaks and blank lines, that serve the same purpose. An author may use different cues to mark greater implied distances between different storyworld events.

In addition to movements from one location to another at the same level within a storyworld, there are boundaries between discourse that refers to "real" events in the storyworld, and discourse that refers to "subjective" events—thoughts and perceptions of characters in the world. Subjective sentences play an important role in much narrative fiction. Wiebe (1990b) and the chapters by Chun and Zubin, Li and Zubin, Bruder and Wiebe, and Zubin and Hewitt in this volume, identify some of the devices that cue the reader to push or pop out of a subjective level.

Quite often, a reader of fictional narrative needs to enter the same storyworld more than once. When a novel or other long narrative discourse is read, it is expected that the reader will not read it in its entirety at a single sitting. The reader has the ability to return to a storyworld that he or she previously visited.

---

[14]Rapaport (1991; Rapaport & Shapiro, this volume) discussed factors involved in establishing real-world validity to storyworld content and vice versa.

The mental space which contains the storyworld has to be stored in memory for reactivation, so that the reader can revisit some of the events previously experienced and continue his or her journey through the storyworld.

There are many storyworlds that contain more than one story. Doyle wrote at least 37 short stories and a novel which take place in Sherlock Holmes' Victorian storyworld. Among his many publications, Asimov wrote 14 books containing short stories and novels that, together, are a partial history of a single "future" storyworld.

Some narrative texts include discourse that is not contextualized from the storyworld. If the boundaries are well marked, the reader is likely to pop out of the storyworld and read it as if the author directed the sentences to him or her, and then push back in. However, M. Galbraith and I, after considering passages such as the following, hypothesized that authors prefer to present information from the deictic center within the storyworld, rather than by popping out:

> Tandy got up and went to the mirror. The magic lantern brightened as she approached, so that she could see herself. She was nineteen years old, but she looked like a child in her nightie and lady-slippers, her brown trusses mussed from constant squirming, her blue eyes peering out worriedly. (Anthony, 1982, p. 2)

This passage is telling the reader what Tandy looks like, but it is presented from her subjective perspective as she sees herself in a mirror. We see it with her. Anthony could have described her using a distant voice, but it was more natural not to.

There are times when the boundaries between real world and storyworld discourse is not clearly marked, as there are times when the location of the deictic center is not clearly marked (Zubin & Hewitt, this volume). In these cases, the reader reaches a point of confusion where he or she may attempt to shift his or her deictic center midstream, and try to reinterpret some of what has preceded it in the text. Examples of such discourse are not rare. Some authors seem to thrive on engendering feelings of not knowing and bewilderment in their readers.

In summary, a single source of connected discourse encompasses text that is often designed to do different things—such as to inform readers, and to represent phenomena for them to experience. The boundary between these pieces of discourse are usually, but not always, clearly cued. One task for the writer or discourse presenter is to select boundary cues that can be identified by readers; the readers have the task of identifying the cues and implementing the appropriate cognitive activity.

CONCLUSION

Narrative, even fiction, plays an important role in society. This chapter presents a general cognitive–phenomenological theory of narrative. In it, I attempt to show how the deictic shift account of narrative processing that is central to this volume can satisfy pragmatic, computational, and phenomenological aspects of narrative interpretation. These are three major requirements for any theory of narrative.

The theory outlined in this chapter at times extrapolates beyond the data available. Many of the claims made here need theoretical clarification, empirical validation, or both. Although there is much left to do, the chapters in this volume show how far we have come in our goal of designing and testing a cognitively coherent, pragmatically realistic, and phenomenologically satisfactory theory of fictional narrative.

4

An Introduction to a Computational Reader of Narratives

Stuart C. Shapiro
William J. Rapaport
State University of New York at Buffalo

In this chapter, we describe the SNePS knowledge-representation and reasoning system. We look at how SNePS is used for cognitive modeling and natural language competence. SNePS has proven particularly useful in our investigations of narrative understanding. Several other chapters in this book (Almeida; Rapaport & Shapiro; Yuhan & Shapiro) use SNePS to discuss specific issues in areas relevant to narrative understanding.

SNePS

SNePS is an intensional, propositional, semantic-network knowledge-representation and reasoning system that is used for research in artificial intelligence (AI) and in cognitive science. "Knowledge" representation is the study of the representation of information in an AI system (because the information need not be true, a more accurate name would be "belief" representation; cf. Rapaport, 1992).

SNePS (Shapiro, 1971, 1979; Shapiro & Rapaport, 1987, 1992) is a programming language whose primary data structure is a semantic network (a labeled, directed graph), with commands for building such networks and finding nodes in such a network given arbitrary descriptions (including partial descriptions). The particular kind of semantic network SNePS builds is *propositional*. Furthermore, the particular kind of propositional semantic network that we believe is appropriate for cognitive modeling and natural-language competence is one that is *fully intensional*. Both of these notions will be clarified later (cf. Maida & Shapiro, 1982; Shapiro & Rapaport, 1987, 1991).

In addition to being able to build and find networks, the SNePS Inference Package (SNIP) permits *node-based reasoning, path-based reasoning,* and *belief revision.* Node-based reasoning can be thought of as conscious reasoning following explicit rules stated in the form of networks. These "rules" are really axioms or nonlogical postulates, not rules of inference. The rules of inference are not explicitly represented, but are implemented in the "inference engine"— SNIP. Path-based reasoning can be thought of as subconsious reasoning; it is a generalization of the notion of inheritance found in many other semantic-network systems (cf. Shapiro, 1978, 1991; Srihari, 1981). A belief revision system is a facility for detecting and removing inconsistent beliefs; the SNePS version is based on a form of relevance logic (cf. Martins & Shapiro, 1988).

Finally, in addition to using the SNePS User Language (a programming language written in Lisp) to build, find, and deduce information directly, one can also interact with SNePS in natural language, using a generalized augmented-transition-network parser-generator (Shapiro, 1982). This makes it especially appropriate for use in our project of understanding narrative text.

PROPOSITIONAL SEMANTIC NETWORKS

A Brief Introduction to Semantic Networks

A semantic network is usually thought of as a labeled, directed graph, whose nodes represent entities and whose arcs represent binary relations between the entities. In the stereotypical semantic network found in most AI texts, there are arcs with such labels as "ISA" and "A-KIND-OF," corresponding, roughly, to set membership and the subset relation. When these labels prove insufficient, labels such as "PROPERTY" are sometimes used, corresponding to the relation of having-as-a-property.

Such networks, which can be thought of as descendents of the medieval Porphyrian tree, are essentially taxonomic and "object-oriented": The nodes represent individuals, classes, or other objects, as well as their properties. One important feature of such networks is the property of *inheritance*: Information stored about an object represented by some node need not be stored (redundantly) at all the nodes that are related to it by ISA or A-KIND-OF. For example, if a dog ISA mammal, and mammal is A-KIND-OF animal, then a dog ISA animal; and if animal has as a PROPERTY mortal, then dog has as a PROPERTY mortal; that is, if a dog is a mammal, mammals are animals, and animals are mortal, then a dog inherits being an animal and being mortal. There are, of course, much more sophisticated varieties of such taxonomic inheritance hierarchies (such as the KL–ONE family of systems), and their logical properties have been extensively investigated (for surveys, see Brachman & Levesque, 1985; Lehmann, 1992; Sowa, 1991, 1992).

Representing Propositions

In a *propositional* semantic network, by contrast, the nodes can represent propositions in addition to objects, classes, and properties. To see how this can be done, consider the network in Fig. 4.1. Suppose that the `Plato` node represents Plato, the `philosopher` node represents the class of philosophers, and the `isa` arc represents the relationship that holds between Plato and the class of philosophers. Now suppose that one wanted to deny that Plato was a philosopher. How would negation be represented? One couldn't, using only graph-theoretical techniques, easily or simply negate the `Plato` node or the `philosopher` node. The former option would presumably mean that not-Plato is a philosopher, but what is a "not-Plato"? The latter option would presumably mean that Plato is a not-philosopher, but what is a "not-philosopher"? Nor could one negate the `isa` arc without violating the conventions of graph theory.

The SNePS solution is to "split" the arc in two. There are several ways this can be done, one of which is shown in Fig. 4.2. The `Plato` node can still represent Plato, and the `philosopher` node can still represent the class of philosophers. But now there is a third node, arbitrarily labeled `M1`, that can represent the *proposition* that Plato is a philosopher. This node is "structured": It represents the proposition as explicitly consisting of an object (Plato), and a class (of philosophers). The class membership relation represented by the arcs is implicit.

Suppose, however, that we wanted to make the relation that holds between Plato and the class of philosophers explicit, so that we could talk about it (in SNePS, one can only talk about nodes, not arcs). There are several ways this could be done; one way is shown in Fig. 4.3. Here, the `Plato` and `philosopher` nodes can be interpreted as before, as can node `M1`. The new `ISA` node represents the class membership relation itself. The arc labels reflect the new structure of this proposition. In this network, the `ISA` relation is explicit, but the higher order `rel/object-1/object-2` ternary relation is implicit.

Case frames (cf. Fillmore, 1968) such as `rel/object-1/object-2` can also be thought of along the lines of Davidson's analysis of events (Davidson, 1967): The proposition that Plato is a philosopher is represented by the network of Fig. 4.3 as being structured as follows:

$$\exists p[\texttt{rel}(p, \texttt{ISA})\ \&\ \texttt{object-1}(p, \texttt{Plato})\ \&$$
$$\texttt{object-2}(p, \texttt{philosopher})],$$

with `M1` being thought of as the value of p or (better) as a Skolem constant. (For more details on the nature of the case frames in SNePS, cf. Shapiro & Rapaport,

FIG. 4.1. An ISA network representation.

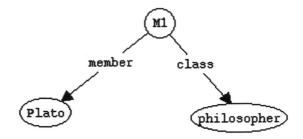

FIG. 4.2. One possible SNePS representation.

1987; Shapiro, 1991. For a view of proposition nodes as functional terms, cf. Shapiro, 1993. In using SNePS for cognitive modeling, we use both the implicit case frame of Fig. 4.2 and the explicit case frame of Fig. 4.3, as discussed later.)

Advantages of Propositional Semantic Networks

Representing Beliefs.   To see the advantage of propositional semantic networks over object-oriented ones, consider how we would represent the proposition:

Mary believes that John is rich, but he isn't.

One way of representing this in SNePS is shown in Fig. 4.4. Nodes that are marked with an exclamation point are said to be *asserted*; they represent "beliefs" of the system. Node M2 ! represents the system's belief that an agent, Mary, performs the mental act of believing, directed (in a Meinongian sense) to the object M1 (cf. Rapaport, 1978). Node M1 represents the proposition that John is rich; thus, M2 ! represents the system's belief that Mary believes that John is rich. Node M3 ! represents the system's belief that it is not the case that M1; thus, M3 ! represents the "but he isn't" part of the proposition. (The min/ max/arg case frame is used to represent the proposition that at least min and at most max of the propositions pointed to by argument arcs are true; here,

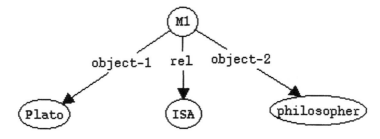

FIG. 4.3. Another possible SNePS representation.

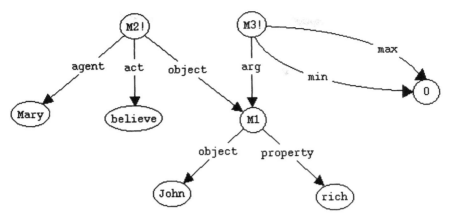

FIG. 4.4. One SNePS representation of: Mary believes that John is rich, but he isn't.

between 0 and 0 of the single argument M1 are true—that is, M1 is false. For details, cf. Shapiro, 1979; Shapiro & Rapaport, 1987.)

For ease of exposition, we will let [[n]] represent the denotation of node n—what n represents. For example, referring again to Fig. 4.4, we could say that [[M2!]] is the proposition that [[Mary]] believes the proposition [[M1]], and [[M1]] is the proposition that [[John]] has the property [[rich]].

Actually, the network of Fig. 4.4 is vastly oversimplified. It fails to take into account the difference between *de re* and *de dicto* belief reports, for one thing. A more accurate representation of Mary's mistaken belief that John is rich is shown in Fig. 4.5. Node M9! represents the system's belief that an agent named "Mary" believes that something (represented by B2) is rich. In particular, [[M2!]] is the proposition that [[B1]] has the propername [[M1]], expressed in English by the lexical item "Mary." Node M8 represents the object of Mary's belief, namely, that [[B2]] is an object with the property [[M7]], which is expressed in English by "rich." Node M6! represents the system's belief that Mary believes that [[B2]]—the rich object—is named "John." So, taken together, M6! and M9! represent the system's belief that Mary believes *de dicto* that John is rich. Finally, M10! represents the system's belief that it is not the case that John is rich. Consider the agent/act/object case frames whose act is [[M3]]. The subnetworks at the heads of the object arcs form the "belief space" of the agent. They represent the system's beliefs about the agent's beliefs.[1]

---

[1]Details of the representation of belief reports and belief spaces is given in Rapaport, 1986a; Rapaport, Shapiro, & Wiebe, 1986; and Wiebe & Rapaport, 1986. A discussion of what the nodes in such belief spaces represent can be found in Shapiro, 1993, and Shapiro & Rapaport, 1991. Recent papers by Crimmins and Perry seem to be consistent with the ontology behind SNePS networks. Their *beliefs, ideas,* and *notions* seem to correspond precisely to SNePS propositional nodes, property nodes, and individual nodes, respectively (cf. Crimmins, 1989; Crimmins & Perry, 1989).

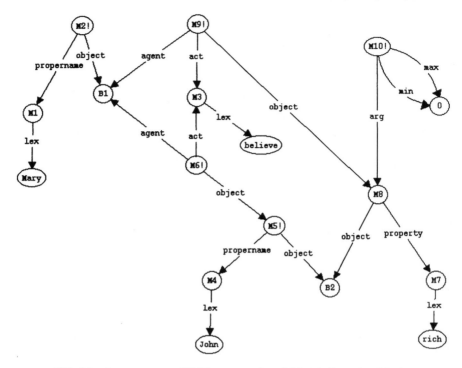

FIG. 4.5. A more accurate SNePS representation of: Mary believes that John is rich, but he isn't.

Node-Based Reasoning. Another advantage of propositional semantic networks is their use in node-based reasoning. Rules can be represented as propositions in the same knowledge base as the propositions to which the rules are intended to apply. This differs from the architecture of the typical production system used to implement an expert system. In such architectures, the rules are in long-term memory separate from the working memory containing the propositions the rules manipulate.

SNIP interprets certain propositional nodes as being rules and performs forward- and backward-inference using them. For instance, the proposition:

$$\forall v1[\text{human}(v1) \rightarrow \text{mortal}(v1)]$$

might be represented by node M1! in Fig. 4.6. It has a universal quantifier arc (forall) pointing to a variable node, V1; an antecedent arc pointing to node P1; and a consequent arc pointing to node P2. Nodes P1 and P2 can be thought of as propositional functions in Russell's sense; they are called *pattern* nodes in SNePS. Node P1 represents the propositional function that [[V1]] is human; node P2 represents the propositional function that [[V1]] is mortal.

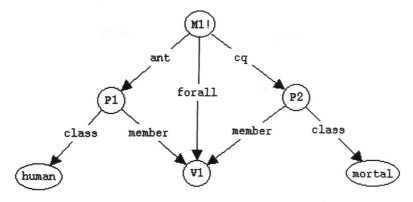

FIG. 4.6.   A SNePS representation of $\forall v1[\text{human}(v1) \rightarrow \text{mortal}(v1)]$.

Suppose that the system is told that Socrates is human, resulting in node M2!
being asserted (see Fig. 4.7). Note that the human node is shared by nodes M2!
and P1; this is a result of the *uniqueness principle*: Every node represents some
entity in the domain of discourse, and no two nodes represent the same entity
(cf. Maida & Shapiro, 1982; Shapiro & Rapaport, 1987). Next, suppose that the
system is asked who is mortal. If the question is phrased in such a way that the
system is merely being asked to *find* asserted nodes representing propositions of
the form "*x* is mortal," it will find none. However, if the question is phrased in
such a way that the system is asked to *deduce* whether anyone is mortal, it will
behave as follows: Imagine that it has been asked to find or to build asserted
propositional nodes matching (i.e., with the structure of) the pattern node P2.

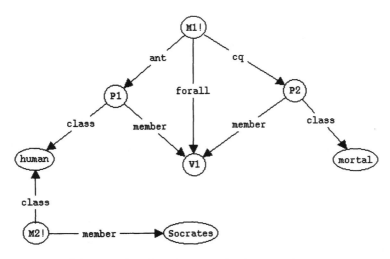

FIG. 4.7.   After telling the system that Socrates is human.

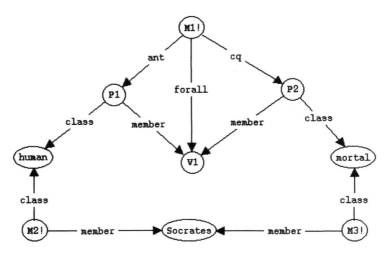

FIG. 4.8.   After inferring that Socrates is mortal.

Finding none (because there aren't any), it will backchain and seek asserted propositional nodes matching P1. It will find M2!, which matches P1 if the Socrates node is bound to V1. This information is used to assert a new node, M3!, matching P2, with V1 bound to the Socrates node. Node M3! is the conclusion of the inference. The network has now grown, to look like Fig. 4.8.

INTENSIONAL KNOWLEDGE REPRESENTATION

SNePS is an intensional knowledge-representation system; that is, it supports multiple representations of what could be one physical object.[2] We argued in earlier papers that the nodes of a semantic network not only can, but ought to, represent intensional entities (Maida & Shapiro, 1982; Rapaport, 1985a, in press; Shapiro & Rapaport, 1987, 1991). By *intensional entity*, we have in mind things like Fregean senses (Frege, 1892), Meinongian objects (Meinong, 1904), Castañedian guises (Castañeda, 1972), and Routleyan items (Routley, 1979). There does not seem to be a clear characterization in the literature of what these things are, but they seem to satisfy the following:

1. They are nonsubstitutable in intensional contexts, even if they are "the same" (i.e., they can be equivalent without being identical). The morning star and the evening star are examples.

---

[2] We owe this way of putting the matter to Susan Haller.

2. They can be indeterminate. That is, they can be "incomplete", as in the case of fictional entities. (Did Sherlock Holmes have a mole on his left arm or not?)
3. They need not exist. The nonexisting golden mountain is an example.
4. They need not be possible. The round square is an example.
5. They can be distinguished even if necessarily identical. For example, *the sum of 2 and 2* and *the sum of 3 and 1* are distinct objects of thought.

We claim that to model a mind, a knowledge-representation and reasoning system must model only intensional entities. There are two main arguments for this. The first may be called *The Argument From Fine-Grained Representation* and is summarized as follows: Inten*T*ional entities (i.e., objects of thought) are inten*S*ional. That is, one can have two objects of thought that correspond to only one extensional object (as in the familiar examples of the morning star and the evening star). The second argument may be called *The Argument From Displacement*, summarized thus: We can think and talk about nonexistent objects—fictional ones, impossible ones, etc.—thus, we need to be able to represent and reason about them, especially if we are interested in using the system for understanding works of fiction.

As an example of how intensional objects can be represented in SNePS, consider Fig. 4.9. It shows one of the possible networks that can represent "The Morning Star has the property of being a planet." Node M2! represents the proposition that intensional entity [[B1]] is the Morning Star. The proposition is structured as follows: [[B1]] is an object whose propername is [[M1]], and [[M1]] is expressed in English by the lexical item "The Morning Star." (This is neither the only or even the best way to represent this proposition, but it will suffice.) Node M4! represents the proposition that [[B1]] is a planet. This proposition is structured as follows: [[B1]] is an object that has the property

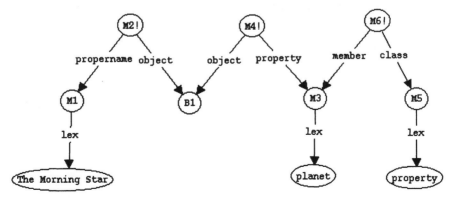

FIG. 4.9. A possible SNePS representation of: The Morning Star has the property of being a planet.

[[M3]], which is expressed in English by the lexical item "planet." The network described thus far represents "The Morning Star is a planet." To make it explicit that being a planet is a property, we use node M6!, whose structure is that [[M3]] is a member of the class [[M5]], expressed in English by "property."

Note that *being the Morning Star* is predicated of [[B1]], and that [[B1]] can be considered as a bare particular (cf. Allaire, 1963, 1965; Landman, 1986). Similarly, *being a planet* is predicated of [[B1]]. Finally, *being a property* is predicated of [[M3]] (though [[M3]] is not quite bare; it has structure, as do [[M1]] and [[M5]], all of which are structured objects).

If the system is next told, "The Morning Star is the Evening Star," the structure shown in Fig. 4.10 will be added. Here, [[B2]] is the intensional entity *The Evening Star*, which is distinct from [[B1]]. (Proposition [[M8!]] asserts that [[B2]] is named "The Evening Star.") Node M9! represents the proposition that [[B1]] and [[B2]] are equivalent, that is, the Morning Star is the Evening Star. There is no node that represents the extensional entity that is both the Morning and Evening Stars. (You might think that it would be a node representing an entity named "Venus," but that would just be a third intensional entity, equivalent to the other two. For a very different way of representing intensionality in SNePS, see Wyatt, 1989, 1990, 1993.)

PUTTING IT ALL TOGETHER: CASSIE READS A NARRATIVE

We have been talking about the system as if it were (merely) an AI program. It is that, of course, but it is, in particular, a program in the area of AI called *cognitive modeling*. We are constructing a model of a cognitive agent who can reason, solve

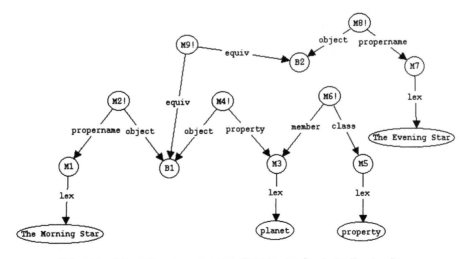

FIG. 4.10.   After telling the system that: The Morning Star is the Evening Star.

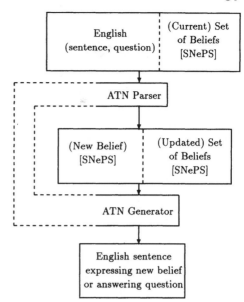

FIG. 4.11. Communicating with Cassie.

problems, and read and converse in natural language. We argued elsewhere that such a model of a cognitive agent *is* a cognitive agent (or, more modestly, that such a model will be such an agent when all of the problems of cognitive modeling will have been solved; cf. Rapaport, 1986b, 1988a, 1988b; Shapiro & Rapaport, 1991).

We call our cognitive agent *Cassie* (the *C*ognitive *A*gent of the *S*NePS *S*ystem—an *I*ntelligent *E*ntity). SNePS nodes represent the objects of Cassie's thoughts. In addition, we can give a fully intensional semantic interpretation for the nodes in terms of a Meinongian Theory of Objects without recourse to possible worlds—which are neither needed or wanted, because we want to be able to deal with impossible objects (cf. Rapaport, 1985a, in press; Shapiro & Rapaport, 1987).

Cassie can read a narrative in (a fragment of) English, as indicated in Fig. 4.11. Cassie has a set of background or current beliefs, represented in SNePS, and reads or is asked something in English. The English statement or question is interpreted by the parser fragment of a generalized augmented-transition-network parser-generator (Shapiro, 1982), which outputs a SNePS node. This node might be an already-existing node in Cassie's "mind" (cf. Rapaport, 1988a) or a new node asserted as the result of an inference (as described previously). The result is a possibly updated set of beliefs in Cassie's mind (her mind may, literally, have changed). The node that was found or asserted is then expressed in English by the generator fragment of the generalized augmented-transition-network parser-generator. Figure 4.12 shows Cassie reading a short narrative, and occasionally being asked questions to test her understanding. The sentence on the first line of each interaction, following the ":" prompt, is either a sentence of the narrative or a question posed to Cassie. Cassie's response begins on the subsequent line.

```
1: John petted a yellow cat.
I understand that John petted a yellow cat.
Time (sec.): 0.617

2: The cat is a manx.
I understand that the yellow cat is a manx.
Time (sec.): 0.25

3: What did John pet?
John petted a yellow cat.
Time (sec.): 0.7

4: The dog is a mammal.
I understand that dogs are mammals.
Time (sec.): 0.283

5: Every dog is owned by a boy.
I understand that every dog is owned by a boy.
Time (sec.): 0.35

6: Young Lucy petted a yellow dog.
I understand that young Lucy petted a yellow dog.
Time (sec.): 1.017

7: The boy saw her.
I understand that the boy saw young Lucy.
Time (sec.): 0.6
```

FIG. 4.12. A conversation with Cassie.

Before she began reading, Cassie's mind contained one explicit belief (node M1! in Fig. 4.13), some implicit beliefs for path-based reasoning, and some other, deictic, information. The implicit beliefs allow certain kinds of inheritance, for instance, that a path consisting of a SUPERCLASS arc followed by zero or more pairs of converse-SUBCLASS/SUPERCLASS arcs can itself be considered as a ("virtual") SUPERCLASS arc; no more will be said of them here. The deictic information consists of a "now"-pointer pointing to node B1, representing the current time, and an "I"-pointer pointing to node B2, representing Cassie's "self-concept." The now-pointer–mechanism is a fairly primitive way of representing time and tense; it was superseded by the more sophisticated facility described in Almeida (1987). The I-pointer–mechanism was described more fully in Rapaport, Shapiro, and Wiebe (1986).

Node M1! represents Cassie's belief that:

$$(\forall v1,v2,v3)[\text{if } v1 \text{ is a } v2 \text{ \& } v2 \text{ is a } v3, \text{ then } v1 \text{ is a } v3].$$

But note that this is represented, not as the transitivity of "is a", but using three different propositions. Node P1 represents the proposition that V1 is a V2 in the sense of class membership; node P2 represents the proposition that V2 is a V3

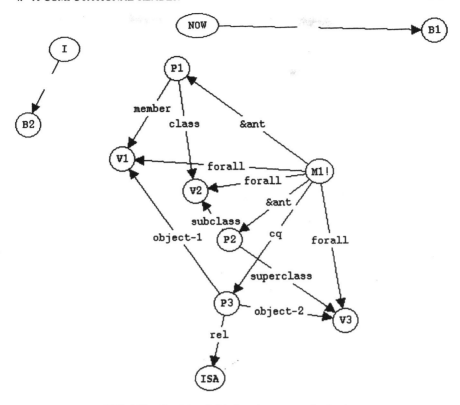

FIG. 4.13. Cassie's mind before the conversation begins.

in the sense of the SUBCLASS/SUPERCLASS relation; and node P3 represents the proposition that V1 is a V3 using the ISA relation of taxonomic semantic networks. Why the variety? The choices for P1 and P2 should be apparent. Class membership is not used for P3 for the following reason: We use class membership to represent the relation obtaining between an individual and the basic-level category to which it belongs (in the sense of Rosch, 1978). We use the SUB-CLASS/SUPERCLASS relation to represent the relation obtaining between a basic-level category and its superordinate-level category. And we use the ISA relation to represent the relation obtaining between an individual and any non-basic-level categories (subordinate or superordinate). One advantage of this for the purposes of natural-language competence is the ability to get Cassie to converse more normally. (For a more complete explanation of this representation, see Peters & Shapiro, 1987a, 1987b; Peters, Shapiro, & Rapaport, 1988.)

When Cassie reads that John petted a yellow cat, nodes M3!, M7!, M8!, M9!, M10!, and M11! are asserted, changing her mind to look like Fig. 4.14. Node M3! "says" that [[B3]] is named "John"; node M7! says that [[B4]] is a cat (*cat*

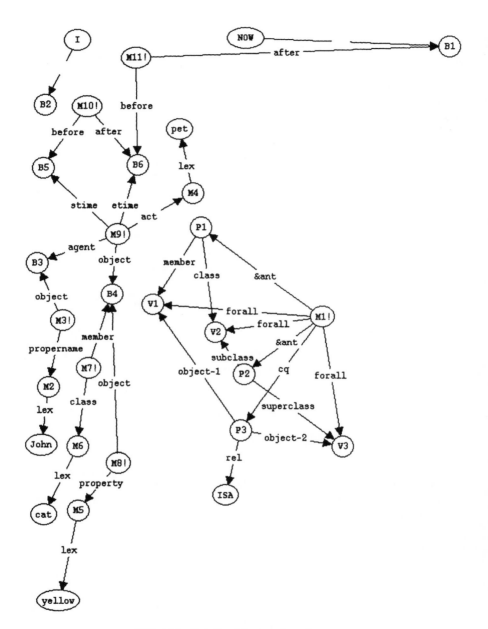

FIG. 4.14. [[M9!]] = John petted a yellow cat.

92

is a basic-level category); node M8! says that [[B4]] (the cat) is yellow; and node M9! says that [[B3]] petted [[B4]]. The past tense "petted" is represented by indicating that the ACT of petting had a StartTIME represented by B5 and an EndTIME represented by B6, that [[B5]] is before [[B6]] (this is asserted by M10!), and that [[B6]] is before "now" (asserted by M11!).

Cassie then reads that *the* cat is a manx. Which cat? Since she only has beliefs about one cat (the one petted by John), she decides that it is the cat that is a manx. Her mind grows to include node M13!, which represents that the cat ([[B4]]) ISA manx (*manx* is a subordinate-level category). Note, too, that Cassie's way of expressing [[M13!]] in English shows us that she understands that the cat that is a manx is the yellow cat that John petted. When we ask Cassie (in order to test her understanding of the narrative that she is reading) what John petted, she responds that he petted a yellow cat rather than that he petted a yellow manx. This might not seem remarkable, but had we not distinguished between the propositions—*being a cat* is represented by class membership, *being a manx* is represented by ISA—Cassie might have replied (and, in an earlier implementation, did reply) that John petted a yellow manx, a decidedly unidiomatic way of putting things in this context. Cassie's mind now looks like Fig. 4.15.

Next, Cassie reads that the dog is a mammal. Which dog? Since there have been none in the narrative thus far, Cassie assumes that this is to be interpreted as a generic sentence, that is, as "dogs are mammals," and node M16! is built. Note that at this point, there are two disconnected subnetworks: That dogs are mammals is entirely irrelevant to Cassie's beliefs about John, the cat, manxes, petting, and being yellow. Well, almost entirely: Cassie does believe that if an individual is a member of a basic-level category that is a subclass of a superordinate-level category, then the individual stands in the ISA relation to the superordinate-level category; because *dog* is a basic-level category that is a subclass of the superordinate-level category *mammal*, there is an implicit connection between the two subnetworks. Cassie's mind now looks like Fig. 4.16.

Cassie then reads that every dog is owned by a boy, and her mental model of the conversation changes to reflect this new piece of information. Node M19!, which represents this rule, has a structure similar to the rule:

$$\forall v8[dog(v8) \rightarrow \exists y[boy(y) \ \& \ owns(y, v8)]].$$

However, the current implementation of SNePS does not have an existential quantifier, so, instead, we use the Skolemized version:

$$\forall v8[dog(v8) \rightarrow [boy(b7(v8)) \wedge owns(b7(v8), v8)]]$$

where b7 is the Skolem function. Specifically, the structure of M19! is: There is a universally quantified variable-node, V8. The ANTecedent of M19! is node P10, which says that [[V8]] is a dog (thus linking up to the previously constructed, isolated subnetwork dominated by node M16!). The ConseQuents of M19! are nodes P12 and P13, both of which refer to P11, which is the result of applying

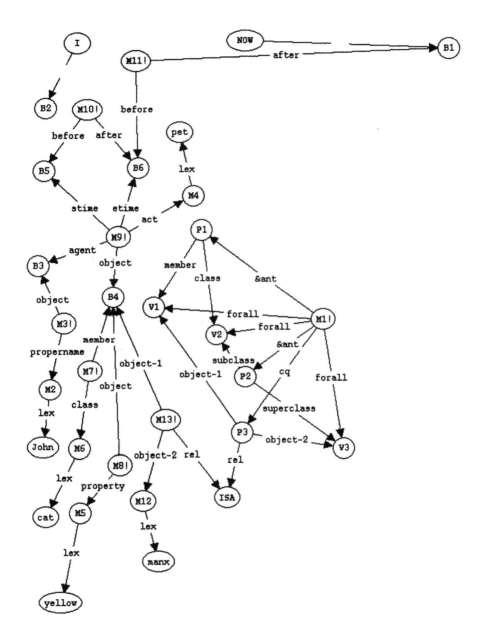

FIG. 4.15. [[M13!]] = The cat is a manx.

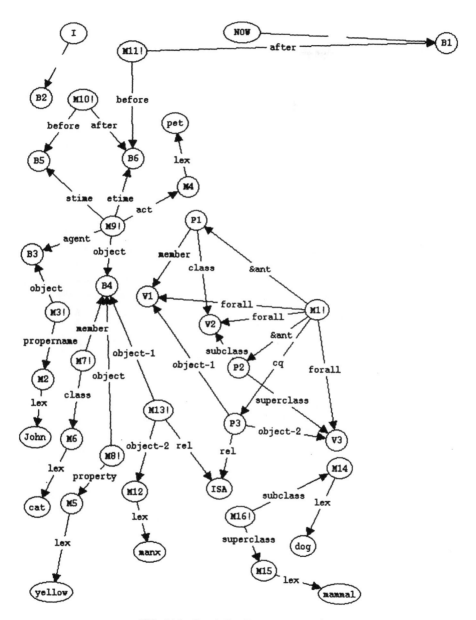

FIG. 4.16. [[M16!]] = Dogs are mammals.

the Skolem function B7 to V8. Node P12 says that [[P11]] is a boy; node P13 says that he owns [[V8]]. The present tense of "owns" is represented by having the StartTIME, B8, be before "now", and the EndTIME, B9, be after "now." Cassie's mind now looks like Fig. 4.17.

Next, Cassie reads that young Lucy petted a yellow dog. The first thing that Cassie understands is that someone ([[B10]]) is named "Lucy" and that Lucy is young (nodes M24! and M25!). Then she understands that there is a dog, [[B11]]. So, [[B10]] is young Lucy, and [[B11]] is a dog. Cassie's mind now looks like Fig. 4.18.

However, Cassie already believes that every dog is owned by a boy. So she conceives of an individual, [[M27]], which results from instantiating P11 by substituting B11 for V8, and infers the proposition that this individual is a boy ([[M28!]]). (Cassie's mind now looks like Fig. 4.19.) Then, Cassie infers that this boy owns the dog ([[M29!]]). Cassie's mind now looks like Fig. 4.20.

There are other rules that Cassie believes, namely, that dogs are mammals and that if something is a dog, then it is a mammal (rule [[M1!]]); so she infers that [[B11]] ISA mammal ([[M31!]]). Cassie's mind now looks like Fig. 4.21.

All of this occurs while she is in the process of understanding that young Lucy petted a yellow dog. What she understands of this sentence so far is that someone is named "Lucy," that that someone is young, and that something else is a dog. She has then inferred that the dog is a mammal and that it is owned by a boy. Now she comes to understand that the dog is yellow ([[M32!]]). Cassie's mind now looks like Fig. 4.22. Subsequently, she comes to understand that young Lucy petted the yellow dog ([[M33!]]), and that this event occurred after "now" ([[M35!]]). Now all previously disconnected subnetworks are linked, and Cassie's mind has grown to look like Fig. 4.23.

Finally, Cassie reads that *the* boy saw her. Which boy? Well, no boys were explicitly talked about, but she has inferred the existence of a boy, so he must be the boy who saw her. Her? Who? An anaphoric-pronoun–resolution system determines that it was young Lucy whom the boy saw (Li, 1986). The result is the set of nodes M37!, M38!, and M39!. Cassie's mind now looks like Fig. 4.24.

The narrative is now complete (actually, this is a fragment of a much longer narrative, but by now you should see how things work). Cassie's mind at the end of the narrative is shown in Fig. 4.24; this is what she came to believe while reading. It is also her mental model of the story of John and Lucy.

SUMMARY

We provided an introduction to the SNePS knowledge-representation and reasoning system, and to Cassie, a computational agent that can read natural language texts and form an understanding of those texts in terms of beliefs represented in

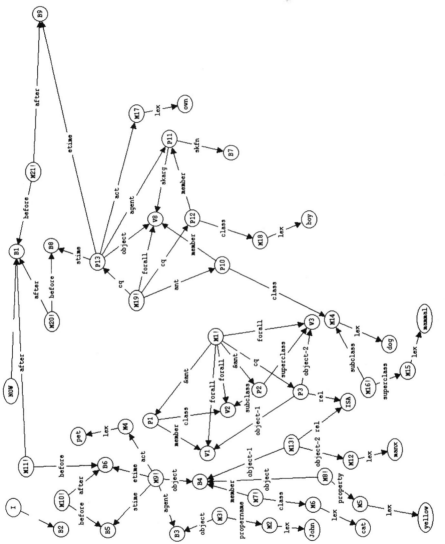

FIG. 4.17. [[M19!]] = Every dog is owned by a boy.

97

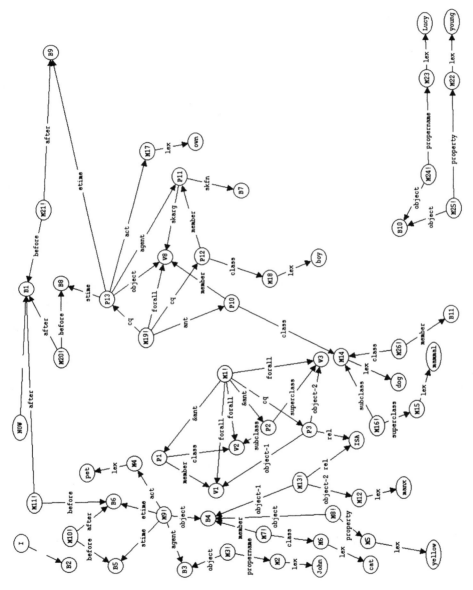

FIG. 4.18. [[B5]] = young Lucy. [[B11]] = a dog.

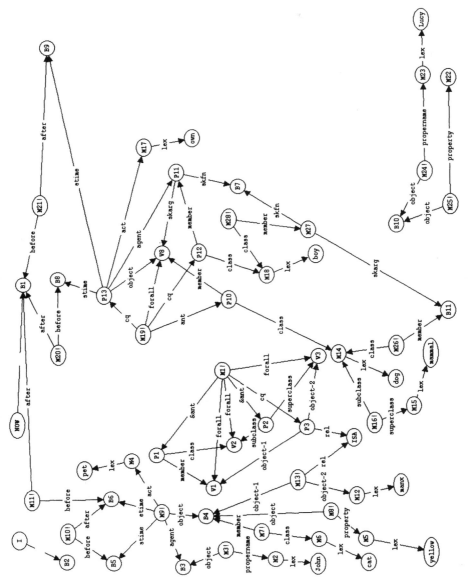

FIG. 4.19. [[M27]] = the boy.

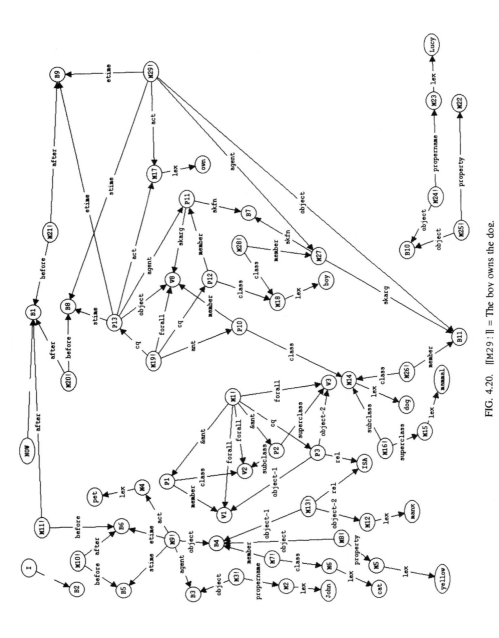

FIG. 4.20. ‖M29!‖ = The boy owns the dog.

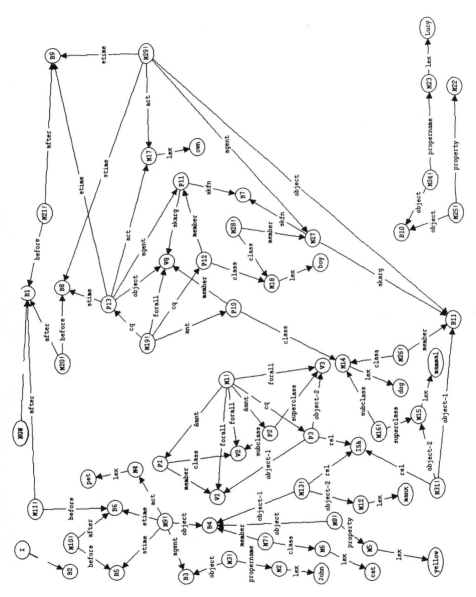

FIG. 4.21. [[M31!]] = The dog is a mammal.

101

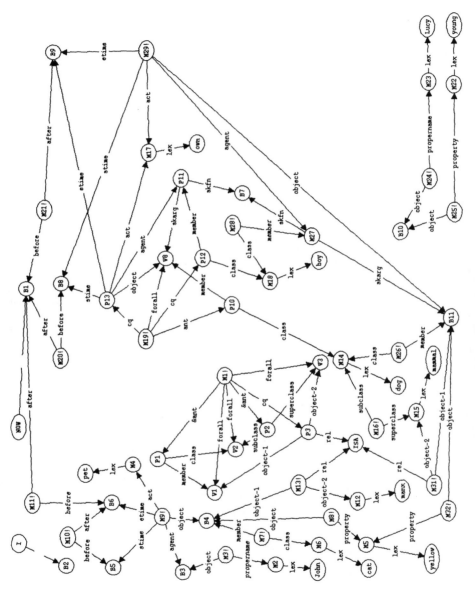

FIG. 4.22. ⟦M32!⟧ = The dog is yellow.

102

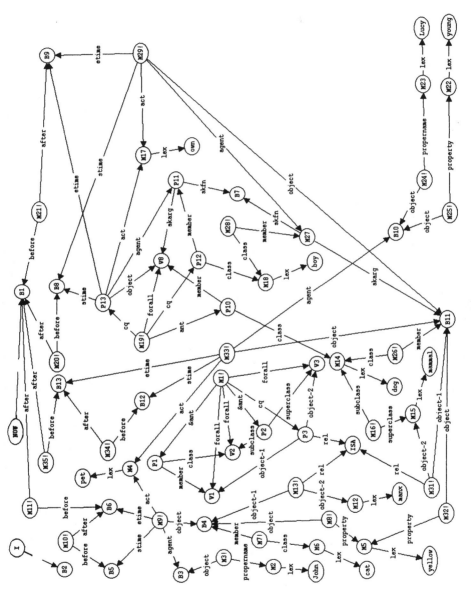

FIG. 4.23. ⟦M33!⟧ = Young Lucy petted a yellow dog.

103

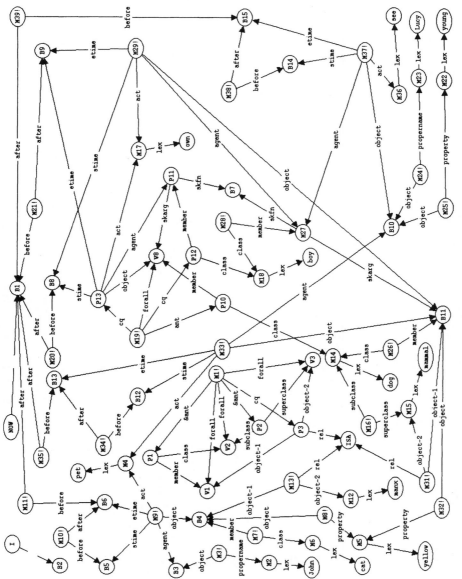

FIG. 4.24. [[M37!]] = The boy saw her.

SNePS networks. Cassie (and SNePS, itself) is still under development, and so can presently read texts only in certain fragments of English. Other uses of Cassie to model readers of narrative texts are discussed in chapters 7 and 8 of this volume.

ACKNOWLEDGMENTS

The work presented here was done in collaboration with the members of the SNePS Research Group and the Narrative Research Group of the Center for Cognitive Science at the State University of New York at Buffalo, to whom we are grateful for their contributions and comments, especially Jürgen Haas, Susan Haller, Johan Lammens, Sandra L. Peters, and Janyce M. Wiebe. This research was supported in part by the National Science Foundation under Grant IRI–8610517. Versions of this chapter were presented (by Rapaport) at the 1989 Conference on Problems and Changes in the Concept of Predication (University of California Humanities Research Institute, University of California at Irvine) and the First Annual SNePS Workshop (Kumar, 1990). The present chapter is a revised version of the first half of Rapaport (1991).

5

COGNITION AND FICTION

William J. Rapaport
Stuart C. Shapiro
State University of New York at Buffalo

This chapter is on *computational philosophy*: the investigation of philosophical issues using computational methods as well as the application of philosophy to problems in computer science. The philosophical issues we explore include predication and fiction. The computational issues are primarily in artificial intelligence (AI). This chapter assumes knowledge of SNePS, an intensional, propositional, semantic-network "knowledge"-representation and reasoning system that is used for research in AI and in cognitive science. The uninitiated reader will benefit from reading Shapiro and Rapaport (this volume).

"Knowledge" representation is the study of the representation of information in an AI system (because the information need not be true, a more accurate name would be "belief" representation; cf. Rapaport, 1992). Shapiro and Rapaport (this volume) look at how predication is represented in such a system when it is used for cognitive modeling and natural-language competence (by which we mean both natural-language understanding and generation; cf. Shapiro & Rapaport, 1991). This chapter discusses appropriate means of representing fictional items and fictional predication in such a system.

FICTIONAL PREDICATION

In Shapiro and Rapaport (this volume), we saw how Cassie (the computational cognitive agent implemented in SNePS) can construct a mental model of a narrative. More specifically, we and our colleagues have been investigating how a

cognitive agent is able to read a narrative and comprehend the indexical information in it: *where* the events described in the narrative are taking place (i.e.,
where in the "story world"—a semantic domain corresponding to the syntactic
narrative text), *when* they take place (in the time-line of the story world), *who*
the participants are in these events (the characters in the story world), and *from
whose point of view* the events and characters are described.

In order to do this, Cassie has to be able to read a narrative (in particular, a
fictional narrative), construct a mental representation or model of the story and
the story world, and use that mental model to understand and to answer questions
about the story. To construct the mental model, she needs to contribute something
to her understanding of the narrative. One contribution is in the form of the
deictic center—a data structure that contains the indexical information needed
to track the who, when, and where.

Another contribution is background knowledge about the *real* world. For
instance, if Cassie is reading a novel about the Civil War, she would presumably
bring to her understanding of it some knowledge of the Civil War, such as that
Abraham Lincoln was the 16th president and was assassinated in 1865, even if
that information is not explicitly stated in the novel. The novel might go on to
make other claims about Lincoln, such as that he was tall or that he had a
particular conversation with General Grant on a particular day in 1860 (even if,
in fact, they never talked on that day—this is a novel, after all). Such a claim
would probably not be inconsistent with anything Cassie antecedently believed
about Lincoln. But some claims in the novel might be inconsistent in this way,
for example, if she read that Lincoln was re-elected to a third term in 1868. So
Cassie has to be able to represent the information presented in the narrative, keep
it suitably segregated from her background knowledge, yet be able to have information from her antecedent real-world beliefs "migrate" into her model of the
story world, as well as to have information from the story world "migrate" back
into her store of beliefs about the real world: There must be a semi-"permeable
membrane" separating these two subspaces of her mental model (Yordy, 1990–
1991).

There are a number of theories in philosophy about the nature of fictional
objects. All of these are *ontological* theories concerned with such questions as:
What are fictional objects? How are properties predicated of them? How are
fictional objects related to nonfictional ones? However, for the purposes of our
project, we need to be more concerned with epistemological or processing/com-
putational/interpretive issues: How does a reader understand a (fictional) narrative? How does a reader decide whether and to what extent it is fictional? How
does a reader construct a mental model of the story world? How does a reader
represent fictional entities and the properties predicated of them? How do readers
integrate their knowledge of the real world with what they read in the narrative?
And so on. Some of these are, indeed, ontological issues, but they are what we
have elsewhere termed issues in *epistemological ontology* (Rapaport, 1985/1986).

Corresponding to the purely or metaphysically ontological question, "What are fictional objects?," we ask the epistemologically ontological question, "How does a cognitive agent represent fictional objects?". And corresponding to the purely ontological question, "How are properties predicated of fictional objects?," we ask the epistemologically ontological question, "How does a cognitive agent represent the predication of properties of fictional objects?"

In this chapter, we examine several philosophical theories of fiction to see what aspects are useful for our cognitive/computational project, and we propose a SNePS representation scheme that answers most of the kinds of questions raised above (and that incorporates an exciting, albeit counterintuitive, proposal for the remaining questions). The proposed representational scheme is to embed the propositions of the fictional narrative in a "story operator" that is formally akin to the belief representations we already have in SNePS (Rapaport, 1986a; Rapaport, Shapiro, & Wiebe, 1986; Wiebe & Rapaport, 1986). We show how SNePS's propositional and fully intensional nature, plus the story operator, allow the best aspects of the philosophical theories to be implemented.

Four Ontological Theories of Fiction

Let us begin by briefly surveying four (out of many more) philosophical theories of the ontological status of fictional objects. We are not concerned as much with criticizing them as with finding what aspects might be useful for our, rather different, purposes.

Castañeda's Theory. Hector-Neri Castañeda's theory of guises and consubstantiation is an all-encompassing theory of the objects of thought and of objects in the world (Castañeda, 1972, 1975a, 1975b, 1977b, 1980, 1989); it includes a theory of fictional objects (Castañeda, 1979, 1989). We discussed the full theory in detail elsewhere (Rapaport, 1978, 1985a), so here, we will content ourselves with a presentation of his theory of fiction.

Castañeda took a uniform viewpoint, with which we agree: All objects in fiction are to be treated alike, whether they are real or fictional (cf. Rapaport, 1985a; Scholes, 1968). They are, in his terminology, *guises*, that is, intensional objects of thought. But there are different modes of predication of properties to guises. If one reads in a narrative about the Civil War that Lincoln died in 1865, this would be analyzed in Castañeda's theory as a *consubstantiation* (C*) of two guises, the guise c{being Lincoln} (i.e., the intensional object of thought whose sole internal property is *being Lincoln*) and the guise c{being Lincoln, having died in 1865} (i.e., the intensional object of thought whose sole internal properties are *being Lincoln* and *having died in 1865*):

C*(c{being Lincoln}, c{being Lincoln, having died in 1865}).

Consubstantiation is an existence-entailing equivalence relation. On the other hand, if one reads another narrative, in which the author has stated that Lincoln was re-elected in 1868, this would be analyzed as a *consociation* (C**) of two guises:

C**(c{being Lincoln}, c{being Lincoln, having been re-elected in 1868}).

Consociation is an equivalence relation that does not entail existence, among guises that are joined together in a mind. But it is the same Lincoln (i.e., c{being Lincoln}) in both cases.

That is an oversimplification, but it raises the following concern: How is the reader to decide whether a sentence read in the course of a narrative is to be analyzed by consubstantiation or by consociation? In fact, we claim, the uniformity with respect to the objects should be extended to the mode of predication: All predications in narrative are consociational, even the true ones.

Castañeda also admitted the existence of story operators into his theory, but found them otiose. A *story operator* is a (usually modal) operator that prefixes all sentences in a narrative: "In story S, it is the case that φ." Not all theorists of fiction find them attractive (cf. Rapaport, 1976, 1985b), but, as Castañeda pointed out, one can hardly deny that they exist. One can take the operator to be the title page of the narrative! His claim was that story operators fail to account for the interesting or problematic aspects of fiction.

An example in the context of SNePS might clarify this. Consider the situation illustrated in Fig. 5.1. Suppose that Cassie has a background belief ("world knowledge," we might say) that: (1) George Washington was the first president. This would be analyzed as a consubstantiation. Suppose that Cassie next reads in a narrative that: (2) George Washington chopped down a cherry tree. This would be analyzed as a consociation. The processing problem is this: If both sentences were to have occurred in the narrative, they would have to be treated alike, using the same mode of predication, namely, consociation. But this is a reasonable modification of Castañeda's theory, and there are no other problems so far, so all is well.

Lewis's Theory. David Lewis's theory of fiction (1978) made essential use of the story operator, and, despite earlier misgivings about them (see previous references), we find they have a useful role to play. But Lewis's version has some problems. He allowed his story operator to be dropped by way of abbreviation. Thus, we might say, "Sherlock Holmes lived at 221B Baker Street," but what we really mean is, for example, "In *The Hound of the Baskervilles*, Sherlock Holmes lived at 221B Baker Street," because, after all, the former is false and the latter is true.

There is an evident advantage to this, for it enables us to distinguish between facts about fictional and nonfictional entities—a worthy endeavor, and one that

Background belief:
(1) GW was the first president **(C*)**
Narrative claim:
(2) GW chopped down a cherry tree **(C**)**

Processing problem:
In narrative, both have to be treated alike;
      same mode of predication (C**)

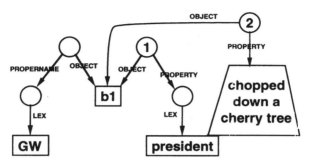

FIG. 5.1.   A narrative for Castañeda's theory.

Cassie must be able to do. In fact, she will do it much the way that Lewis recommended. Consider the following argument:

    Lived-at(221B Baker St., Sherlock Holmes)
    221B Baker St. = a bank
    ∴ Lived-at(a bank, Sherlock Holmes)

Although the first premise is true in the story world (but false or truth-valueless in the real world), and the second is factually true (cf. Rule, 1989), the conclusion is false in both the real world and the story world. But merely replacing the story operator will not help:

    In *The Hound of the Baskervilles*, Lived-at(221B Baker St., Sherlock Holmes)
    221B Baker St. = a bank
    ∴ In *The Hound of the Baskervilles*, Lived-at(a bank, Sherlock Holmes)

fares no better, since 221B Baker St. is not a bank in *The Hound of the Baskervilles*. Nor does:

    In *The Hound of the Baskervilles*, Lived-at(221B Baker St., Sherlock Holmes)
    221B Baker St. = a bank
    ∴ Lived-at(a bank, Sherlock Holmes)

fare any better, since the conclusion is false with or without the story operator. But a uniform application of the story operator works fine:

In *The Hound of the Baskervilles*, Lived-at(221B Baker St., Sherlock Holmes)
In *The Hound of the Baskervilles*, 221B Baker St. = a bank
∴ In *The Hound of the Baskervilles*, Lived-at(a bank, Sherlock Holmes)

and:

Lived-at(221B Baker St., Sherlock Holmes)
221B Baker St. = a bank
∴ Lived-at(a bank, Sherlock Holmes)

are both valid, albeit unsound. The former is unsound, because the second premise is false; the latter is unsound, because the first premise is false.

The difficulty with Lewis's proposal is that "Sherlock Holmes is fictional" is false either way. It is false *with* the story operator restored, because, within the story, Holmes is as real as is anyone. And it is false (or at least truth-valueless) *without* it, because "Sherlock Holmes" is a nondenoting expression. This difficulty is unacceptable.

Parsons's Theory. Terence Parsons's theory of fiction (1975, 1980) was based on his theory of nonexistent objects. In contrast to Castañeda, whose theory had one kind of property but two modes of predication, Parsons's had two kinds of properties (nuclear and extranuclear), but only one mode of predication. Rather than rehearse his full theory of fiction here (see Rapaport, 1985b for a summary and critique), we focus on a distinction he makes between *native, immigrant,* and *surrogate* fictional objects.

Native fictional objects are those who originate in the story in which they are found, such as Sherlock Holmes in *The Hound of the Baskervilles*. Immigrant fictional objects are those who have migrated into a story from elsewhere, such as London in *The Hound of the Baskervilles*, or Sherlock Holmes in *The Seven Per Cent Solution* (Meyer, 1974). But, of course, the London of *The Hound of the Baskervilles* has properties that the real London lacks (and vice versa), which raises obvious difficulties. So the London-of-*The-Hound-of-the-Baskervilles* is a surrogate fictional object, distinct from the real London.

Such distinctions can be made and are useful. But there are a number of questions to be answered before one can accept them: Which London did Conan Doyle discuss? Which London did Sherlock Holmes and Dr. Watson discuss? When is one discussing London and when the London-of-*The-Hound-of-the-Baskervilles*? In general, how does the reader distinguish properties of the "real" London from properties of the London-of-*The-Hound-of-the-Baskervilles*? These are questions that can be dealt with, we believe, in the SNePS proposal to be introduced later.

Van Inwagen's Theory. The final theory of fictional objects in our brief survey is one that we find quite congenial in many respects, though it, too, falls short. Peter van Inwagen's theory (1977), like Castañeda's, distinguished between two modes of predication, and, like Lewis's, it used something like a story operator.

Van Inwagen's two modes of predication were *predication* and *ascription*. "Sherlock Holmes is fictional" expresses a property "predicated of" an existing theoretical entity of literary criticism, namely, Sherlock Holmes. (Other kinds of theoretical entities of literary criticism include novels, short stories, etc.) In contrast, "Sherlock Holmes is a detective" expresses (perhaps elliptically) a property "ascribed to" the same theoretical entity of literary criticism "in" a work of fiction:

A(detective, Sherlock Holmes, *The Hound of the Baskervilles*).

Note that the story is not a logical operator, but an essential argument place in a 3-place predication relation.

There are two problems with this theory. They are, we believe, not serious problems and could be easily resolved. First, in "Sherlock Holmes Confronts Modern Logic" (Hintikka & Hintikka, 1983), the authors called Holmes a "great detective" (p. 155). According to van Inwagen's theory, contrary to what one might expect, it is not the case that:

A(great detective, Sherlock Holmes, "Sherlock Holmes Confronts Modern Logic").

Why? Because "Sherlock Holmes Confronts Modern Logic" is not literature and, hence, not a theoretical entity of literary criticism. This strikes us as an unnecessary aspect of van Inwagen's theory.

Second, assume that in Tolstoy's *War and Peace* it is stated that Napoleon is vain.[1] According to van Inwagen's theory and contrary to what one might expect, it is not the case that:

A(vain, Napoleon, *War and Peace*),

because Napoleon is not a theoretical entity of literary criticism! Again, this strikes us as unnecessary.

A SNePS Approach to Fiction

In order for Cassie to read a narrative, the representations she should construct include a story operator (as in Lewis's or van Inwagen's theory), only one mode of predication (as in Parsons's theory), and only one kind of property (as in Castañeda's theory). Because, at the time of writing, this theory is only beginning to be implemented, there is a strong possibility that this will prove insufficient. The one addition we foresee (urged in earlier writings, e.g., Rapaport, 1976, 1985b, and suggested in conversation by Johan Lammens) is the need to distinguish between real-world entities and their surrogates; but it must be kept in mind that all entities represented in Cassie's mind are just that—entities in her mind—not entities, some of which are real and some of which are fictional.

---

[1] It may in fact be so stated; one of the co-authors confesses to not (yet) having read it; the other has read it but does not recall whether it is so stated. It might suffice for van Inwagen's example that it follow (logically) from what is stated in *War and Peace* that Napoleon is vain; no matter.

The story operator sets up a "story space" that is formally equivalent to a belief space (cf. Rapaport, 1986a; Shapiro & Rapaport, 1991; Shapiro & Rapaport, this volume; Wiebe & Rapaport, 1986). It allows Cassie to distinguish her own beliefs about London from claims (or her beliefs about claims) made about London in a story in precisely the same way that belief spaces allow Cassie to distinguish her own beliefs about John from her beliefs about Mary's beliefs about John (cf. Rapaport, 1986a; Shapiro & Rapaport, 1987; Shapiro & Rapaport, this volume).

But how should this be handled? Consider Fig. 5.2. Suppose that one of Cassie's background beliefs is that Lincoln died in 1865, and suppose that she reads in a narrative that Lincoln was re-elected in 1868. There is a processing problem: Cassie is faced with an inconsistency. There are two solutions. First, the SNePS Belief Revision system (SNeBR; Martins & Shapiro, 1988)—a facility for detecting and removing inconsistent beliefs—can be invoked. The detection of the inconsistency will cause a split to be made into two consistent contexts. But note that the net effect of this is to embed the second statement (the re-election in 1868) in a story operator. So we could start with a story operator in the first place. This is the second solution, as shown in Fig. 5.3. (An implementation of the first solution is given in the next section.)

But now let us complicate the data. Consider Fig. 5.4. Suppose that Cassie's background beliefs include that Lincoln was the 16th president and that Lincoln died in 1865, and suppose that Cassie reads in a narrative that Lincoln was re-elected in 1868. The processing problem here is that we want the first of Cassie's two background beliefs to migrate into the story world. But this is not

Background belief:
(1) Lincoln died in 1865.
Narrative claim:
(2) Lincoln was re-elected in 1868.

Processing problem: inconsistency

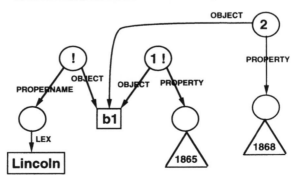

FIG. 5.2. A processing problem for Cassie.

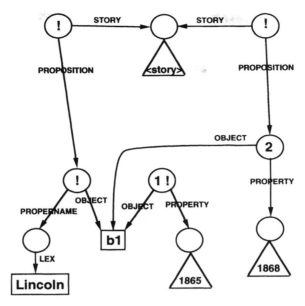

FIG. 5.3.   A solution using a story operator.

Background beliefs:
(1) Lincoln was the 16th president.
(2) Lincoln died in 1865.
Narrative claim:
(3) Lincoln was re-elected in 1868.

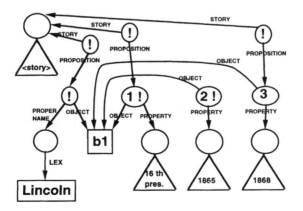

FIG. 5.4.   A more complex narrative.

really a problem because those first two background beliefs are Cassie's beliefs and the third is not. The first one (that Lincoln was 16th president) is both believed by Cassie and is in the story world.

Consider Fig. 5.1 again. If Cassie knows that she is reading a narrative, we want it to be the case that she believes (1) (that Washington was the first president), and we want both (1) and (2) (that he chopped down the cherry tree) to be in the story world. How do we accomplish this? Under the first solution, all propositions from the narrative will be placed in a story context. Under the second solution, we start with a story operator on (2). In general, we put a story operator on *all* narrative predications.

But then we face two problems: Background beliefs of the reader are normally brought to bear on understanding the story, as we saw in Fig. 5.2. And we often come to learn (or, at least, come to have beliefs) about the real world from reading fictional narratives. Thus, we need to have two rules, which we put roughly, but boldly, as follows:

(R1) Propositions outside the story space established by the story context or the story operator (i.e., antecedently believed by the reader) are assumed, when necessary, to hold within that story space by default but defeasibly.

(R2) Propositions inside the story space are assumed, when necessary, to hold outside that story space by default but defeasibly.

The "when necessary" clause is there to prevent an explosion in the size of belief and story spaces. The migrations permitted by these two rules would only take place on an as-needed basis for understanding the story or for understanding the world around us. The "by default" clause is there for obvious reasons. We wouldn't want to have Lincoln's dying in 1865 migrate into a narrative in which he is re-elected in 1868. The "defeasibly" clause is there to undo any damage that might be done at a later point in the narrative if such a migration had taken place, innocently, at an earlier point. Rule (R1) (or such refinements of it as will, no doubt, be necessary as implementation of the theory proceeds) aids in our understanding of the story. Rule (R2) (or such refinements of it as will also, no doubt, be necessary as implementation of the theory proceeds) allows us to enlarge our views of the world from reading literature, yet to segregate our real-world beliefs from our story world beliefs. In this manner, we facilitate the membrane whose semipermeability allows us to understand narratives using our world knowledge, and to learn from narratives—indeed, to understand the real world in terms of narratives (cf. Bruner, 1990).

We close with three final remarks. First, to see how the story operator solves the problem with Lewis's theory, look at Fig. 5.5. (How it solves the problems with van Inwagen's are left as exercises for the reader.) Second, in Figs. 5.1–5.5, we used the linguist's triangle to hide irrelevant details; however, Fig. 5.6 shows how the story operator looks in detail. Finally, a preliminary implementation using SNeBR is presented in the next section.

1. Sherlock Holmes is fictional.
2. Sherlock Holmes is a detective.

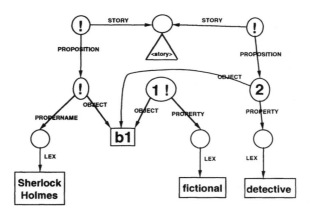

FIG. 5.5.   Handling the problem with Lewis's theory.

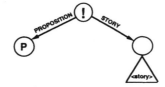

In <story>, P

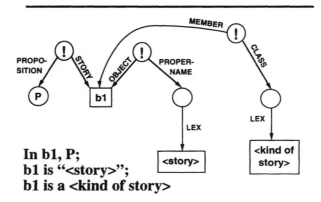

In b1, P;
b1 is "<story>";
b1 is a <kind of story>

FIG. 5.6.   Details of the story operator.

117

A SNePS IMPLEMENTATION OF FICTIONAL REPRESENTATION
AND REASONING

In this section, we present an interaction in SNePSLOG (Shapiro & the SNePS
Implementation Group, 1989; Shapiro, McKay, Martins, & Morgado, 1981), a
Prolog lookalike interface to SNePS–2.1 (which incorporates the SNeBR belief-
revision system), demonstrating the current implementation of parts of the theory
of fiction outlined in a previous section. Explanatory comments are added (signalled by "★★★ COMMENT ★★★"). After SNePS is invoked, user input follows
the ":" prompt, and subsequent lines show Cassie's output. (Some irrelevant
information was deleted or edited for ease of readability.)

```
Welcome to SNePSLOG (A logic interface to SNePS)
Copyright © 1984, 88, 89, 93 by Research Foundation of State
University of New York.
```

```
★★★ COMMENT ★★★: Let the current belief space be the real world.
```

```
: set-context real-world ()
((ASSERTIONS NIL) (RESTRICTION NIL) (NAMED (REAL-WORLD DEFAULT-
DEFAULTCT)))
: set-default-context real-world
((ASSERTIONS NIL) (RESTRICTION NIL) (NAMED (REAL-WORLD DEFAULT-
DEFAULTCT)))
```

```
★★★ COMMENT ★★★: We begin by giving Cassie some background
                 knowledge about the real world. First, she is
                 told (using SNePSLog) that all persons who are
                 assassinated in some year are dead in that year.
                 As a result, Cassie believes that proposition.
```

```
: all(p,y)(Assassinated(p,y) => Dead(p,y))
  all(P,Y)(ASSASSINATED(P,Y) => DEAD(P,Y))
```

```
★★★ COMMENT ★★★: Cassie is told that if a person, p, is dead in
                 some year y1, and y1 is before year y2, then p
                 is dead in y2 (a "no-resurrection" hypothesis;
                 see Acknowledgments section):
```

```
: all(p,y1,y2)([Dead(p,y1), Before(y1,y2)] &=> [Dead(p, y2)])
  all(P,Y1,Y2)([DEAD(P,Y1),BEFORE(Y1,Y2)] &=> [DEAD(P,Y2)])
```

```
★★★ COMMENT ★★★: Cassie is told that if a person is elected in
                 some year, then it is not the case that that
                 person is dead in that year (a "neither Chicago
                 nor Philadelphia" hypothesis):
```

```
: all(p,y)(Elected(p,y) => ~Dead(p,y))
  all(P,Y)(ELECTED(P,Y) => (~DEAD(P,Y)))
```

*** COMMENT ***: Cassie is told that 1865 is before 1868:

```
: Before(1865, 1868)
  BEFORE(1865,1868)
```

*** COMMENT ***: Next, we tell Cassie some specific facts about Lincoln. After each one, Cassie performs forward inference, signalled by the "!", in order to draw conclusions. If she has to reason, she "thinks out loud". First, she is told that Lincoln was elected in 1860, from which she infers that Lincoln was not dead in 1860:

```
: Elected(Lincoln, 1860)!
Since all(P,Y)(ELECTED(P,Y) => (~DEAD(P,Y)))
and ELECTED(LINCOLN,1860)
I infer ~DEAD(LINCOLN,1860)
  ELECTED(LINCOLN,1860)
  ~DEAD(LINCOLN,1860)
```

*** COMMENT ***: Cassie is told that Lincoln was assassinated in 1865, from which she infers that Lincoln was dead in 1865, hence also in 1868. ("BS" is a "belief space"; for its definition in SNeBR, see Martins & Shapiro, 1988.)

```
: Assassinated(Lincoln, 1865)!
Since all(P,Y)(ASSASSINATED(P,Y) => DEAD(P,Y))
and ASSASSINATED(LINCOLN,1865)
I infer DEAD(LINCOLN,1865)
I wonder if DEAD(LINCOLN,Y1)
holds within the BS defined by context REAL-WORLD
I wonder if BEFORE(Y1,Y2)
holds within the BS defined by context REAL-WORLD
I know DEAD(LINCOLN,1865)
I know BEFORE(1865,1868)
I know it is not the case that DEAD(LINCOLN,1860)
I wonder if ASSASSINATED(LINCOLN,Y)
holds within the BS defined by context REAL-WORLD
Since all(P,Y)(ASSASSINATED(P,Y) => DEAD(P,Y))
and ASSASSINATED(LINCOLN,1865)
I infer DEAD(LINCOLN,1865)
I wonder if ELECTED(LINCOLN,Y)
holds within the BS defined by context REAL-WORLD
Since all(P,Y)(ELECTED(P,Y) => (~DEAD(P,Y)))
and ELECTED(LINCOLN,1860)
I infer ~DEAD(LINCOLN,1860)
I know ASSASSINATED(LINCOLN,1865)
I know ELECTED(LINCOLN,1860)
```

```
DEAD(LINCOLN,1868)
BEFORE(1865,1868)
~DEAD(LINCOLN,1860)
ASSASSINATED(LINCOLN,1865)
DEAD(LINCOLN,1865)
```

*** COMMENT ***: So, Cassie's background, or real-world, beliefs consist of six hypotheses—that assassination implies death (WFF1), that death in year y1 implies death in all later years (WFF2), that elected people aren't dead (WFF3), that 1865 is before 1868 (WFF4), that Lincoln was elected in 1860 (WFF5), and that Lincoln was assassinated in 1865 (WFF8)—together with all propositions inferred from these:

```
: describe-context
((ASSERTIONS (WFF1 WFF2 WFF3 WFF4 WFF5 WFF8)) (RESTRICTION NIL)
  (NAMED (REAL-WORLD)))
```

*** COMMENT ***: Next, the story world context is defined, following Rule (R1), to consist, by default, of all of Cassie's current hypotheses. (This implementation of the story world operator does not use an explicit story node; rather, it uses SNeBR's mechanism of contexts; cf. Martins & Shapiro, 1988.):

```
: set-context story (wff1 wff2 wff3 wff4 wff5 wff8)
((ASSERTIONS (WFF1 WFF2 WFF3 WFF4 WFF5 WFF8)) (RESTRICTION NIL)
  (NAMED (STORY REAL-WORLD)))
```

*** COMMENT ***: The story world context is entered; from here until that context is left, Cassie should be thought of as reading a narrative about Lincoln, the Lincoln about whom she believes WFFs 1–5, 8, and all beliefs that she has inferred from them:

```
: set-default-context story
((ASSERTIONS (WFF1 WFF2 WFF3 WFF4 WFF5 WFF8)) (RESTRICTION NIL)
  (NAMED (STORY REAL-WORLD)))
```

*** COMMENT ***: Cassie reads that Lincoln was tall in 1860, from which, being an intelligent reader who thinks about what she reads, she infers nothing:

```
: Tall(Lincoln, 1860)!
```

TALL(LINCOLN,1860)

*** COMMENT ***: Cassie reads that Lincoln was elected in 1868
(thus, Cassie is clearly reading a work of his-
torical fiction) ...:

: Elected(Lincoln, 1868)!

*** COMMENT ***: ...from which she infers that, in the story
world, Lincoln is not dead in 1868. Since this
is inconsistent with her beliefs that Lincoln
is dead in 1865 and that anyone who is dead in
1865 is dead in the later year 1868, SNeBR, the
interactive belief-revision system, is invoked:

Since all(P,Y)(ELECTED(P,Y) => (~DEAD(P,Y)))
and ELECTED(LINCOLN,1868)
I infer ~DEAD(LINCOLN,1868)
  A contradiction was detected within context STORY.
  The contradiction involves the newly derived node:
  ~DEAD(LINCOLN,1868)

*** COMMENT ***: That is, the contradiction involves the propo-
sition that it is not the case that Lincoln is
dead in 1868, which Cassie has just inferred in
her real-world-augmented story world, ...

---

  and the previously existing node:
  DEAD(LINCOLN,1868)

*** COMMENT ***: ... and the proposition that Lincoln is dead in
1868, which Cassie had inferred to hold in the
real world.

  You have the following options:
  1. [C]ontinue anyway, knowing that a contradiction is de-
     rivable;
  2. [R]e-start the exact same run in a different context
     which is not inconsistent;
  3. [D]rop the run altogether.
  (please type c, r or d)
=><= r

*** COMMENT ***: That is, we choose to eliminate the inconsis-
tencies.

In order to make the context consistent you must delete at
least one hypothesis from each of the following sets of
hypotheses:

(WFF1 WFF12 WFF2 WFF3 WFF4 WFF8)

*** COMMENT ***: WFF12 = Lincoln was elected in 1868.

In order to make the context consistent you must delete
some hypotheses from the set (WFF1 WFF12 WFF2 WFF3 WFF4
WFF8)
You are now entering a package that will enable you to
delete some hypotheses from this set.
Do you need guidance about how to use the package?
=><= n
Do you want to take a look at hypothesis WFF1?
=><= y
  all(P,Y)(ASSASSINATED(P,Y) => DEAD(P,Y))
  There are 3 nodes depending on hypothesis WFF1:
   (WFF1 WFF10 WFF9).

*** COMMENT ***: WFF9 = Lincoln is dead in 1865.
                 WFF10 = Lincoln is dead in 1868.

Do you want to look at [a]ll of them, [s]ome of them, or
[n]one?
(please type a, s or n)
=><= n
What do you want to do with hypothesis WFF1?
[d]iscard from the context, [k]eep in the context,
[u]ndecided, [q]uit this package
(please type d, k, u or q)
=><= k

*** COMMENT ***: We choose to keep within the story world the be-
                 lief that assassinated people are dead.

Do you want to take a look at hypothesis WFF12?
=><= y
  ELECTED(LINCOLN,1868)
  There are 2 nodes depending on hypothesis WFF12:
   (WFF12 WFF13).

*** COMMENT ***: WFF13 = Lincoln is not dead in 1868.

Do you want to look at [a]ll of them, [s]ome of them, or
[n]one?
(please type a, s or n)
=><= n
What do you want to do with hypothesis WFF12?
[d]iscard from the context, [k]eep in the context,
[u]ndecided, [q]uit this package
(please type d, k, u or q)
=><= k

*** COMMENT ***: We keep in the story world that Lincoln was
                 elected in 1868. (After all, this is a fact in
                 the story world and must be accepted.)

Do you want to take a look at hypothesis WFF2?
=><= y
  all(P,Y1,Y2)([DEAD(P,Y1),BEFORE(Y1,Y2)] &=> [DEAD(P,Y2)])
  There are 2 nodes depending on hypothesis WFF2:
   (WFF10 WFF2).
  Do you want to look at [a]ll of them, [s]ome of them, or
  [n]one?
  (please type a, s or n)
=><= n
  What do you want to do with hypothesis WFF2?
  [d]iscard from the context, [k]eep in the context,
  [u]ndecided, [q]uit this package
  (please type d, k, u or q)
=><= k

*** COMMENT ***: We keep in the story world that once dead, al-
                 ways dead.

Do you want to take a look at hypothesis WFF3?
=><= y
  all(P,Y)(ELECTED(P,Y) => (~DEAD(P,Y)))
  There are 3 nodes depending on hypothesis WFF3:
   (WFF13 WFF3 WFF7).

*** COMMENT ***: WFF7 = Lincoln is not dead in 1860.

  Do you want to look at [a]ll of them, [s]ome of them, or
  [n]one?
  (please type a, s or n)
=><= n
  What do you want to do with hypothesis WFF3?
  [d]iscard from the context, [k]eep in the context,
  [u]ndecided, [q]uit this package
  (please type d, k, u or q)
=><= k

*** COMMENT ***: We keep in the story world that elected people
                 are not dead.

Do you want to take a look at hypothesis WFF4?
=><= y
  BEFORE(1865,1868)
  There are 2 nodes depending on hypothesis WFF4:
   (WFF10 WFF4).
  Do you want to look at [a]ll of them, [s]ome of them, or
  [n]one?

```
    (please type a, s or n)
=><= n
    What do you want to do with hypothesis WFF4?
    [d]iscard from the context, [k]eep in the context,
    [u]ndecided, [q]uit this package
    (please type d, k, u or q)
=><= k
```

*** COMMENT ***: We keep in the story world that 1865 is before
                 1868.

```
Do you want to take a look at hypothesis WFF8?
=><= y
    ASSASSINATED(LINCOLN,1865)
    There are 3 nodes depending on hypothesis WFF8:
    (WFF10 WFF8 WFF9).
    Do you want to look at [a]ll of them, [s]ome of them, or
    [n]one?
    (please type a, s or n)
=><= n
    What do you want to do with hypothesis WFF8?
    [d]iscard from the context, [k]eep in the context,
    [u]ndecided, [q]uit this package
    (please type d, k, u or q)
=><= d
```

*** COMMENT ***: That Lincoln was assassinated in 1865 is *de-
                 feated*; that is, we remove it from the story
                 world as being the cause of the inconsistency;
                 that is, everything that Cassie antecedently
                 believed about Lincoln is assumed to hold in the
                 story world, except for this belief.

```
    The following (not known to be inconsistent) set of
    hypotheses was also part of the context where the
    contradiction was derived:
    (M11! M5!)
    Do you want to inspect or discard some of them?
=><= n
```

*** COMMENT ***: The propositions that Lincoln was elected in
                 1860 (WFF5, represented by node M5!) and that
                 Lincoln was tall in 1860 (WFF11, represented by
                 node M11!) were not listed as among the hypothe-
                 ses responsible for the inconsistency, so they
                 remain in the story world by default.

```
    Do you want to add a new hypothesis?
=><= n
```

```
*** COMMENT ***: Cassie's reasoning about Lincoln's properties
                 in the story world continues:
```

```
Since all(P,Y)(ELECTED(P,Y) => (~DEAD(P,Y)))
and ELECTED(LINCOLN,1868)
I infer ~DEAD(LINCOLN,1868)
  ELECTED(LINCOLN,1868)
  ~DEAD(LINCOLN,1868)
```

```
*** COMMENT ***: Cassie has just inferred, again, that, in the
                 story world, Lincoln was not dead in 1868. This
                 is no longer inconsistent with her other be-
                 liefs about the story world. We now interac-
                 tively ask Cassie questions about what she
                 believes, including what she has read.
```

```
: ?P(Lincoln,?y)?
```

```
*** COMMENT ***: Cassie begins to reason within the story world,
                 but also using her real-world beliefs. By Rule
                 (1), they were assumed to hold in the story
                 world by default, but defeasibly—as we just
                 saw.
```

```
I wonder if ?P(LINCOLN,?Y)
holds within the BS defined by context STORY
I know ELECTED(LINCOLN,1860)
I know ELECTED(LINCOLN,1868)
I know TALL(LINCOLN,1860)
I know it is not the case that ASSASSINATED(LINCOLN,1865)
I know it is not the case that DEAD(LINCOLN,1860)
I know it is not the case that DEAD(LINCOLN,1868)
I wonder if DEAD(LINCOLN,Y1)
holds within the BS defined by context STORY
I wonder if BEFORE(Y1,Y2)
holds within the BS defined by context STORY
I wonder if ASSASSINATED(LINCOLN,Y)
holds within the BS defined by context STORY
I wonder if ELECTED(LINCOLN,Y)
holds within the BS defined by context STORY
Since all(P,Y)(ELECTED(P,Y) => (~DEAD(P,Y)))
and ELECTED(LINCOLN,1868)
I infer ~DEAD(LINCOLN,1868)
I know BEFORE(1865,1868)
I know ELECTED(LINCOLN,1860)
Since all(P,Y)(ELECTED(P,Y) => (~DEAD(P,Y)))
and ELECTED(LINCOLN,1860)
I infer ~DEAD(LINCOLN,1860)
I know ELECTED(LINCOLN,1868)
```

*** COMMENT ***: Following is Cassie's reply to our question. She believes that, in the story world, Lincoln was tall in 1860, he was elected in 1868, he is not dead in 1868, he was not assassinated in 1865, he was elected in 1860, and he was not dead in 1860:

TALL(LINCOLN,1860)
ELECTED(LINCOLN,1868)
~DEAD(LINCOLN,1868)
~ASSASSINATED(LINCOLN,1865)
ELECTED(LINCOLN,1860)
~DEAD(LINCOLN,1860)

*** COMMENT ***: Now we tell Cassie to think about the real world, in which she believes the propositions represented by WFFs 1, 2, 3, 4, 5, and 8:

: set-default-context real-world
((ASSERTIONS (WFF1 WFF2 WFF3 WFF4 WFF5 WFF8)) (RESTRICTION
((WFF12)))
  (NAMED (REAL-WORLD)))
: %(clear-infer)
(Node activation cleared. Some register information retained.)

*** COMMENT ***: If we just add WFF11 to the real world, following Rule (2), Cassie tries to believe, by default, but defeasibly, that what she read in the story is true in the real world. No inconsistency is detected, so, because Lincoln's being tall in 1860 is consistent with her real-world beliefs, she believes it:

: Tall(Lincoln, 1860)!
TALL(LINCOLN,1860)

*** COMMENT ***: But if we then add WFF12 an inconsistency is created. What she has learned in the story world is inconsistent with what she antecedently believed in the real world, so SNeBR is invoked:

: Elected(Lincoln, 1868)!
Since all(P,Y)(ELECTED(P,Y) => (~DEAD(P,Y)))
and ELECTED(LINCOLN,1868)
I infer ~DEAD(LINCOLN,1868)
  A contradiction was detected within context REAL-WORLD.
  The contradiction involves the newly derived node:
  ~DEAD(LINCOLN,1868)

and the previously existing node:
DEAD(LINCOLN,1868)
You have the following options:
1. [C]ontinue anyway, knowing that a contradiction is de-
   rivable;
2. [R]e-start the exact same run in a different context
   which is not inconsistent;
3. [D]rop the run altogether.
(please type c, r or d)
=><= d

*** COMMENT ***: So WFF12 is not added. The following message,
however, is printed, because we attempted to
add WFF12. That fact that it was not successfully added to the real-world context will be
apparent below.

ELECTED(LINCOLN,1868)

*** COMMENT ***: We ask Cassie again what she believes about Lincoln in the real world (this time, her reasoning
has been edited out, for readability):

: ?P(Lincoln,?y)?

*** COMMENT ***: Note that Cassie now believes, on the basis of
the story, that, in the real world, Lincoln was
tall in 1860. Note, too, that she does not believe that Lincoln was elected in 1868. She infers the following:

DEAD(LINCOLN,1868)
TALL(LINCOLN,1860)
ELECTED(LINCOLN,1860)
~DEAD(LINCOLN,1860)
ASSASSINATED(LINCOLN,1865)
DEAD(LINCOLN,1865)

CONCLUSION

This brings to an end our essay in computational philosophy. We explored
knowledge-representation and reasoning issues surrounding fictional entities and
their fictional (and nonfictional) properties, as well as their interaction with
nonfictional entities. We showed how Cassie could read a narrative and construct
and reason about her mental model of the story expressed by the narrative, and how
information can selectively flow between general real-world knowledge and story
world knowledge.

ACKNOWLEDGMENTS

The work presented here was done in collaboration with the members of the SNePS Research Group and the Center for Cognitive Science at State University of New York at Buffalo, to whom we are grateful for their contributions and comments, especially Jürgen Haas, Susan Haller, Johan Lammens, Sandra L. Peters, and Janyce M. Wiebe. For the descriptors for some of the hypotheses in the Lincoln narrative, we thank Bonnie Webber. This research was supported in part by the National Science Foundation under Grant IRI–8610517. Versions of this paper were presented by Rapaport at the 1989 Conference on Problems and Changes in the Concept of Predication (University of California Humanities Research Institute, University of California at Irvine) and the First Annual SNePS Workshop (Kumar, 1990). Previous versions of this chapter appeared in Rapaport (1989) and as part of Rapaport (1991).

6

THE DEICTIC CENTER: A THEORY OF DEIXIS IN NARRATIVE

David A. Zubin
State University of New York at Buffalo

Lynne E. Hewitt
The Pennsylvania State University

In this chapter, we offer a theory of the deictic nature of fictional narrative. The first part of the chapter presents a theory of the essential components of deictic centering in fiction; the second part details operations that affect the construction and alteration of the deictic center as stories unfold.

DEIXIS IN LANGUAGE

Deixis in its traditional linguistic sense (see Jarvella & Klein, 1982, and Lyons, 1968, for overviews) refers to the fact that certain linguistic forms have direct pragmatic interpretation dependent on parameters of the speech situation, rather than a stable semantic value. In particular, their interpretation is contextually anchored to the identity of the speaker and addressee, their locations, and the time of utterance. When A asks B on the phone, "Will you come here?" the linguistic expressions *you, here,* and *will* are interpreted as "addressee," "location of the speaker," and "after time of utterance," respectively.

Bühler, Fillmore, Clark, and others stressed that there is a unified conceptual centering of events underlying the linguistic fact, an egocentric modelling of reality in which the here, now and I of the speaker (and secondarily, of the addressee) have priority over other elements of the speech situation.

Fillmore (1975) noted that deictic centering is more general and more abstract than the traditional shifters (Jakobson, 1971) of the *here, now* and *I/you* of the speech situation. The deictic verbs *come* and *go*, traditionally considered to convey motion toward and away from the speaker, are a good illustration of the abstractness of deictic centering. Consider the utterance, "Who is coming to the party?" In the most mundane interpretation, *come* conveys motion toward the location of the speaker, that is, he or she is already at the party. But it could be the addressee who is there, or neither may be there, but only intend to be there later, or have participated in the planning, or belong to the group throwing the party, or in some other way have a reason for identifying with the party.

Thus, in its more general/abstract deployment, the spatial center of deixis is a location (either physical or psychological) with which the speaker identifies in the content of the utterance. The linguistic marking of deixis tends to gravitate towards centers of interest or empathy (Kuno, 1987). It is this plasticity of deictic centering that forms the basis for the deictic structure of narrative. Deictic center (DC) theory attempts to model the consequences of shifting deixis out of the *here/now, I/you* of face-to-face interaction, where it is anchored in real-world situations, into the purely textual realm of fiction, where deixis is cut adrift from its physical moorings in the speech situation. In this chapter, we outline the deictic mechanics of this shifted center.

A number of theoretical proposals were made for the structure of narrative discourse, including Labov & Waletsky (1967), Rumelhart (1975), Mandler & Johnson (1977), Kintsch & van Dijk (1978). Our approach finds its antecedents less in these previous linguistic and psycholinguistic approaches to narrative than in Buhler's account of deixis, referred to previously (1982), as well as that of Fillmore (1975) and Jarvella and Klein (1982). We take as our premise that deixis is not just a special subcomponent of narrative language, but rather a central structuring framework from which the narrative emerges (see also Segal, this volume, who uses the term *Deictic Shift Theory* to describe this approach).

Deictic Centering in Fictional Narrative

Deictic center theory presupposes a story world underlying the events of the particular story being narrated. The story world provides the general spacetime coordinates within which the story unfolds. Here we use the term *story* in a sense close to that of ordinary usage, as the totality of events and experiences played out via plotting and characterization in a fictional narrative. The story world is inhabited by the participants and objects that play a role in the story, or are presupposed by the story. The relation between the story and the story world in which it takes place, is fluid. The story is, like all linguistically derived mental representations, partially a construction of the reader or listener, although it is certainly based on text of the author/speaker. In contrast, the story world is mostly a mental construct of the reader/listener; and thus simplifies the task of world construction for an author. Stories are made possible because readers can import knowledge of the everyday world and of other possible worlds into the current story world; this provides the listener/reader with the illusion of mentally inhabiting a fully specified and coherent world (see Rapaport and Shapiro, this volume).

Just as constructing a mental model of the story world involves importing world knowledge into the interpretation of fictional text, so the deictic construction of narrative is derivative of the reader's experience of deictic centering in the *here/now/I/you* of the everyday world. Our folk belief in the unitary nature of experience causes us to construct a deictic center from which to view the unfolding story events, and we use this deictic center as we would use the "I" of face-to-face interaction to anchor our comprehension of the text. The reader tracks the shifted deixis in the text as if placed in that center. The decoupling of deixis in narrative from the speech situation allows the linguistic realization of the deictic center to be altered from that of face-to-face interaction in a variety of ways, from a fictional "I" to impersonal third-person narration.

One way to approach an understanding of the deictic shift in narrative language is to observe typical oral storytelling styles. The storyteller begins by placing his or her initial remarks about the story—who the characters are, where the story takes place, and so on—in the deictic frame of the speech situation. The teller is *I*; the audience is *you*; *here* is where the teller (or the teller and audience) is; and *now* is the current time of interaction between teller and audience. But after an interactional prolog in which the teller establishes rapport with his or her audience and the story begins, the central illusion of narrative takes over: The teller seems to fade into the background and the story world, containing its own deictic center, comes to the fore. This is accomplished by decoupling the linguistic marking of deixis from the speech situation, and reorienting it to the major characters, the locations, and a fictive present time of the story world itself. The story is not addressed to the audience in the way conversation or a lecture is; rather, it opens a conceptual window through which the story world can be glimpsed. The story is self-enclosed. Its deictic structure presupposes its own story world, and not the current interactional context of the teller and audience. In fact, the listener's deictic perspective becomes the one chosen for him or her by the teller. In a successful story, we have the illusion of experiencing the fictional world directly, because we unconsciously adopt the deixis of the DC as our own (Banfield, 1982; Wiebe, this volume).

Just as a given person is limited in his or her experience of the real world, so the DC provides only a limited current view of the story world, like a moving window establishing a perspective from and through which events in the story world are viewed. The window is deicticly centered in the sense that the current contents of the window presuppose a center in space, time, and character from which events are depicted. We call the components of this center the WHERE, the WHEN, the WHO, and the WHAT (see Fig. 6.1).

Figure 6.1 is a first-order approximation of DC structure, in which there is an illusion of direct, unrestricted access to the story world. However, much of the time deictic framing is more complex. The narrator controls not only what is looked at, but from what perspective these things are viewed. In its full form, the deictic center window is constituted by the intersection of temporal, spatial, and personal coordinates forming a *focalizing perspective*, or origin of view,

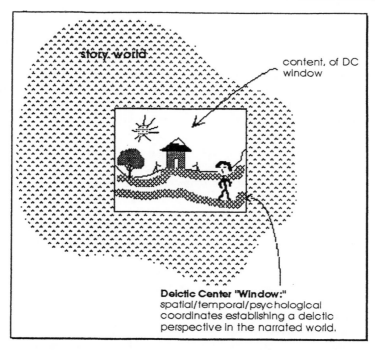

FIG. 6.1. Objective windowing of the Deictic Center.

from which the events of the narrative are made accessible to the listener/reader (c.f. Kuno, 1987, who uses the term *camera angle* to describe perspectival effects in language), and a *focalized perspective*, consisting of the object of view, that is, the content of the deictic window. As noted previously, contents are not always expressed overtly; they may be presupposed or inferred. The window of the deictic center thus provides the listener/reader with two shifting foci, an *origin* and a *content* of perspective, depicted in Fig. 6.2:

> *Focalizing perspective (origin):* Shifting localization in time, space, and person from which the story world is exposed to the reader/listener, establishing a point of view on the events of the story.

> *Focalized perspective (content):* The objective of the focalizing perspective, that is, the content of the deictic window as it moves along its spatial, temporal, and personal coordinates through the story world. This represents the spatial, temporal, personal, and object contents of the story as viewed by the listener/reader through the deictic window.

The windowing of narrative can be manipulated for special effects. If an author wishes to present events as simply and straightforwardly as possible, he or she

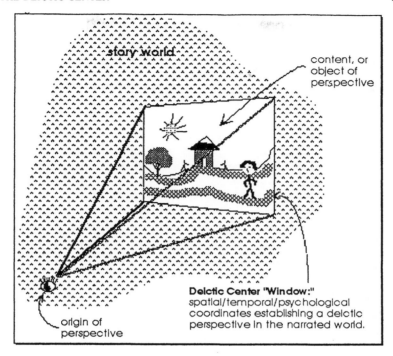

FIG. 6.2.   Perspective windowing of the Deictic Center.

will strive to make the perspectivalization as unobtrusive and objective as possible, as if looking through a clear pane of glass. Traditional third-person, omniscient narration has this character. Figure 6.1 represents such a situation. A different effect is achieved in narratives that are told by a fictional first-person narrator. These offer an illusion more like viewing the story world through a movie camera controlled by the narrator; we only see what this person sees. Similar "camera" effects can be generated more subtly, via use of subjectivity devices in nonfirst-person narration. The "lens" of subjectivity may be metaphorically seen as having special optical distortions or even areas of blindness. The author uses specific linguistic devices to offer us the perspective of a particular character for all or part of a narrative (see Banfield, 1984, 1987; Kuno, 1987; Kuroda, 1973, 1976; and Section VI, this volume).

Organization of the Deictic Center

The four basic components of the deictic center construct we use to account for deictic tracking in narrative, labeled the WHO, the WHERE, the WHEN, and the WHAT are each discussed. Each component may have different status at different times in the narrative; all components have current content and a history.

The components of the deictic center are subject to various operations, by which values can be introduced, maintained, shifted, or suspended as part of the ongoing construction process. These will be described further in the next section.

The WHO: Participant Structure of the Narrative. *Content* is the participant on whom the narrative is focused—at the center of the DC window. The DC representation may include the identity and behavior of this participant, and the (objectively presented) content of perceptual and cognitive states (psychonarration). Scope of the WHO may be expanded to include two or several participants treated as a group, or even to the amorphous mass of a community or society in which the story takes place.

In perspectival context, the WHO divides into the:

Focalizing WHO: the participant whose thoughts/perceptions are represented in the story text, or whose point of view is implicit in the description of the scene—who is at the origin of the deictic focalization (hence, a personal coordinate to the origin of the DC).

Focalized WHO: the participant on whom the Focalizing WHO is focused, isomorphic to the WHO described later. Structurally, the focalized WHO behaves similarly to the WHAT, because the Focalizing WHO tracks both people and things in the story world. Of course, this category may be null, as a focalizing WHO does not always necessarily reflect on other characters.

Ordinarily, the Focalizing and the Focalized WHO are separate characters—one is presented, observed, listened to, evaluated, from the perspective of the other. An especially interesting case is when the same character plays both roles, that is, when the focalizing WHO's intentional state is self-reflective. In such cases, the focalized WHO is a *projected ego,* a projected image of the focalizing WHO, and conceptually distinct from the former, yet objectively the same character in the story. It is in this context type that logophoric and free reflexive pronouns occur (see Chun & Zubin and Li & Zubin, this volume).

History: The deictic window presents the current WHO, but in addition, the listener gradually accumulates a global represention of all the WHOs in the story world—a history. This represention includes properties of participants as accumulated throughout the story (including intentional structures) and association of each participant with particular values of other components, that is, with particular scenes and times. Maintaining such a trace enables readers to more efficiently perform pragmatic matching in managing references to characters, especially in the case of anaphoric references (see Hewitt, this volume). In addition, a previously tracked WHO may be more easily reinvoked if readers have access to memories of previous DCs.

The current WHO is often a subject of intention, and may have thought, feeling or perception relevant to the story. Such intentional properties seem to be an important criterial distinction between WHO and WHAT. This is based on the fact that when the role played by an object in the scene becomes independent and of some duration, the listener/reader tends to attribute pseudointentional states to it, even when none are explicitly described in the text. Fillmore (1968) grappled with the same problem when he distinguished natural forces as a distinct category from agents on the one hand, and from instruments and objects on the other.

The WHAT: Object Structure of the Narrative. *Content.* A part of the current spatial scene may become reified as an object segregated from the scene (see next section) by being foregrounded or individuated. This is accomplished by using a basic level noun in a definite description, using grammatical macroroles rather than oblique slots (e.g., coded as a direct object rather than a locative prepositional phrase). The WHAT-like quality of an entity is accentuated when the entity is independently active or manipulated by a participant. In Example 29 to follow, where the current WHO is eating breakfast, the corncake becomes a WHAT rather than just a scene component by virtue of its linguistic emphasis in a direct object slot, and pronominalization over two clauses: "Kino squatted by the fire pit and rolled *a hot corncake* and dipped *it* in sauce and ate *it*. . . ."

A WHAT may even become an object of intention by a WHO, thus helping to carry the story forward. But it has no intentional structure with which it is associated. That is, a part of the current scene may be focalized as a WHAT, but cannot become an origin of perspective. This component of the DC thus does not exhibit the duality depicted in Fig. 6.2.

In some narratives, a particular object may become very important for the plot. For example, the magic ring referred to in the title of *The Lord of the Rings* (Tolkien, 1965), or the pearl in the novel of that name by Steinbeck (1945/1975), are objects that take on special significance, pivotal in plot generation and recurring in many scenes. These were more than just scene components, yet were not treated as story characters. A WHAT may have a history, in that readers build up an accumulation of information about it, including, among other things, previous locations and associated WHOs. However, a WHAT's ability to be deictically tracked decays more rapidly than a WHO's. The corncake in the previous example is not referred to again, unlike the person eating the corncake. In fact, the WHAT is more volatile than the other components of the deictic center, and may vary from clause to clause. One example of such rapid flux can be seen in cases where a WHO is using a number of different objects (see Example 45 to follow, in which the current WHO is engaged in making a fire, using cornhusks, then lights a candle at this fire).

The WHERE: Spatial Structure of the Narrative. The *content* of the WHERE is the current spatial scene, including the "filling in" of detail not explicitly evoked in the text. The WHERE is deictically centered in an *origin* from which spatial references in the text are interpreted.

The origin is the perspective from which a scene is viewed. This may be precisely localizable, for example, "at the doorway of the hut looking in," or it may be only vaguely localizable, for example, "inside the hut." The default value for WHERE is the position of the current WHO. In subjective contexts, the origin of spatial deixis becomes the current WHO, and the content becomes the actual content of the focalizing WHO's visual field.

(1) Against the sky in the cave entrance Juana could see that Kino was taking off his white clothes. . . . And then she saw how he hooked his amulet neck-string about the horn handle of his great knife. . . . For a moment his body was black in the cave entrance, crouched and silent, and then he was gone. (Steinbeck, 1945/1975, pp. 109–110)

The scene is the interior of a cave. The WHERE-origin is fixed by Juana, the focalizing WHO (positioned at the back of the cave and oriented toward the front). The WHERE content is the front of the cave, where Kino (the focalized WHO) is. The description, "his body was black in the cave entrance," follows from these two specifications; Kino is described as Juana would see him from her vantage point.

The history of the WHERE is its trace within and across scenes, consisting of different scenes in the story world at which spatial centering has occurred; *nesting* relationships for each of these centers on which expansion/contraction effects are based; and *path-traces* that link the current scene to previous scenes in the story. The nesting of WHEREs yields an expansion–contraction effect. This effect causes a current WHERE on one type of scale to either expand to encompass a larger WHERE or contract to focus on a smaller subcomponent of that larger WHERE (c.f. Talmy's granularity; Talmy, this volume), as in the following:

(2) When Mr. Bilbo Baggins of Bag End announced that he would shortly be celebrating his eleventy-first birthday with a party of special magnificence, there was much talk and excitement in Hobbiton. . . .
WHERE = Hobbiton, that is, whole village
Tongues began to wag in Hobbiton and Bywater; and rumour of the coming event travelled all over the Shire.
WHERE = the Shire, that is, entire region
(Expansion from previous WHERE)
No one had a more attentive audience than old Ham Gamgee, commonly known as the Gaffer. He held forth at *The Ivy Bush*, a small inn on the Bywater Road.
. . .
WHERE = The Ivy Bush, an inn, in Bywater, in the Shire
(Contraction from previous WHERE)
(Tolkien, 1965, pp. 29–30)

The WHERE is also typically *path-connected*: The default level of story understanding seems to be to construct path-connections among scenes. This is necessary in order to create the illusion of a spatial universe in which the fictional participants can travel, just as we navigate in the real world. But some readers may be left with isolated scenes, or may go beyond tracing of paths, instead constructing a topographic representation of the story world (c.f. Garling & Golledge, 1993).

The WHEN: Temporal Structure of the Narrative. Events in narrative are not simply chained end-on-end, as suggested in early models of narrative. They have complex relations in which some have beginnings, some have ends, and some are simply ongoing in the deictic window. In Example 3 to follow, multiple past times are evoked, but not in the order in which they occurred in the story world.

One peculiarity of narrative is particularly significant for a deictic center or deictic shift account: Narrative is written in past tense, but its events do not take place in any real past time. That is, the reader takes the past tense of narrative as one of the signals to shift into narrative mode, rather than as a signal of past temporality. As Segal (1990) pointed out, even science-fiction novels that purport to take place in the future, are written in past tense. The reader uses the past tense as a marker telling him or her to create a narrative Now point (or interval; see Almeida, this volume) for the current events of the narrative, during which they begin, end, or are ongoing. This Now point is not referenced against the reader's own realtime experience, but has its own independent status in the story world.

In the case of a focalizing WHO reflecting on past events, an embedded Now point may be constructed, from which the past events' occurrence is projected. This constitutes a *focalizing* WHEN, in which a current time frame in the story is set up, from which other events are presented as past or future. The focalized WHEN may be either a past (flashback) or a future (flash-forward) time. For example:

(3) Bilbo was very rich and very peculiar, and had been the wonder of the Shire for sixty years.... Time wore on, but ... at ninety he was much the same as at fifty.... When Bilbo was ninety-nine, he adopted Frodo as his heir.... "You had better come and live here, Frodo my lad," said Bilbo one day....
Twelve more years passed. Each year the Bagginses had very lively combined birthday-parties at Bag End; *but now* it was understood that something quite exceptional was being planned for *that* autumn. (Tolkien, 1965, p. 29; here, and in all subsequent examples, emphasis added)

In this passage, the WHEN of the starting point is the time of the announcement of Bilbo's 111th birthday party; it then divides into a focalizing WHEN of the current Now, and a series of focalized WHENs relating to past events. The first focalized WHEN is 60 years prior to Now; then the focalized WHEN slowly moves forward to Bilbo at age 99, inviting Frodo to live with him; then jumps forward 12 years to the original WHEN of the passage (marked here, appropriately enough, by "now").

The history of the WHEN adds up to an accumulation of Now-points. This accumulation yields a trace of the temporal relations of the events of the story. In the Tolkien example, at the point at which the WHEN of the time of the announcement of the birthday party is re-evoked after its suspension, it gains the traces of those previously evoked Nows. The linguistic evidence for the importance of these traces lies in the use of the discourse marker "but" and the use of the distal deictic "that": "*but* now it was understood that something quite exceptional was being planned for *that* autumn." The other autumns are evoked and backgrounded by the use of these terms.

The WHO-WHAT-WHERE Continuum.   Story worlds are populated with cognitive and noncognitive entities. Regardless of the particular story world, a listener will begin to construct an intentional representation for a human participant quite easily, but will need more evidence to do so for an animal, and a great deal more to do so for an inanimate object. Thus, humans are quickly and easily promoted to the status of WHO by the listener, animals less easily, and inanimate entities only with difficulty. In addition to promotion of nonhumans, it is also possible to demote humans on the animacy scale. The following examples illustrate a range of treatments of humans, in ascending order of animacy from mere background, to the status of props in the scene, all the way to full intentionality:

(4) *People* passed on the street. (WHERE)
His elbow was bumped by *a passerby* as he walked down the street. (WHAT)
A *woman* stopped him on the street to ask directions. She was lost, and wanted to find her way back to her hotel. (WHO)

Just as readers may be led to "demote" a human referent to the status of a WHAT, they may also promote WHERE-like and WHAT-like entities to WHAT and WHO status, respectively. One example is the reader may construct a fate for an inanimate object, for example, by realizing that as the story progresses, the object will "act" to intervene in the events of the story. In *The Lord of the Rings* (Tolkien, 1965), for example, natural forces were frequently treated as having quasi-intentional states, and animals as acting with deliberate intentionality. Note that this is distinct from actual anthropomorphization of inanimates, in which the entities take on actual cognitive characteristics of human beings (emotion, reasoning, perception) and become a legitimate WHO of the story.

Figure 6.3 illustrates the distinction between WHO, WHAT and WHERE as contents of the deictic window. A percept can freely take on values lower on the continuum shown in Fig. 6.3 without special treatment. In Example 4, a person (obviously an inherently intentional entity) was treated as an inanimate scene component in the second sentence, and as mere background scenery in the

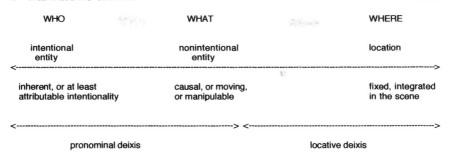

FIG. 6.3.   Deictic continuum of WHO, WHAT, and WHERE.

first. But percepts lower on the continuum need special treatment to be promoted. In Example 5 to follow, an object (a willow tree) originally treated as a scene component, part of the WHERE, is promoted gradually to a WHAT, and then to a fully intentional entity, a WHO. This is accomplished by means of a gradual accumulation of linguistic signs, including syntactic promotion, use of lexical items with inherent animacy and intentionality in their semantics, and change in pronominalization from impersonal to personal:

(5) *[Willows as scene component; syntactically backgrounded in oblique position; no single willow picked out—generic plural used instead]:*
[At the foot of the bank] there wound lazily a dark river ... bordered with ancient *willows*, arched over with *willows*, blocked with fallen *willows*, and flecked with thousands of faded *willow* leaves. ...
[One willow picked out in presentative passage; presentative structure and detailed, lingering description promotes one willow to a WHAT]:
Frodo ... saw leaning over him *a huge willow-tree*, old and hoary. Enormous it looked, its sprawling branches going up like reaching arms with many long-fingered hands, its knotted and twisted trunk gaping in wide fissures that creaked faintly as the boughs moved. ...
[Growing attributed intentionality of willow, use of lexical items suggesting agency]:
Sam ... was worried. "I don't like this great big tree. I don't trust it. ..."
[Sam hears a noise and rushes around the tree to find that ...] Frodo was in the water close to the edge, and a great tree-root seemed to be over him and *holding* him down. ... Sam gripped him by the jacket, and dragged him from under the root. ... Almost at once he woke. ... "Do you know, Sam," [Frodo] said ... "the beastly tree *threw* me in! I felt it. The big root just *twisted round* and *tipped* me in!" "You were dreaming I expect, Mr. Frodo," said Sam. "You shouldn't sit in such a place, if you feel sleepy." ... They went round to the other side of the tree. Pippin had vanished. The crack by which he had laid himself *had closed together* so that not a chink could be seen. Merry was [also] trapped; another crack *had closed* about his waist; his legs lay outside, but the rest of him was inside a dark opening, the edges of which *gripped like a pair of pincers.*

[Willow is promoted further to animate status by exhibiting actions which suggest an intentional response to the hobbits' actions and by having quasi-emotional states attributed to it, such as laughter and anger]:
Frodo ... kicked the tree with all his strength. ... A hardly perceptible *shiver* ran through the stem and up into the branches; the leaves *rustled* and *whispered*, but with a sound now of faint and far-off *laughter*. ... [They light a fire to scare the tree.] Little fingers of fire licked against the dry scored rind of the ancient tree and scorched it. A *tremor* ran through the whole willow. The leaves seemed to *hiss* above their heads with a sound of *pain* and *anger*.
[Willow is fully intentional, speaking and acting as a sentient entity]:
A loud scream came from Merry, and from far inside the tree they heard Pippin give a muffled yell. "Put it out! Put it out!" cried Merry. *"He'll squeeze me in two,* if you don't. *He says so!"*
      "Who? What?" shouted Frodo, rushing round to the other side of the tree.
. . .
[Willow is fully treated as a character, to the extent of getting a name, and being addressed in second person]:
[A man named Tom Bombadil appears and is told about the tree.] "What?" shouted Tom Bombadil, leaping up in the air. *"Old Man Willow*? ... I know the tune for *him*." ... Breaking off a hanging branch [he] smote the side of the willow with it. *"You* let them out again, *Old Man Willow!"* he said. (Tolkien, 1965, pp. 126–132)

Of particular interest in Example 5 is the shift from locative prepositional phrases to subject position as the locus for references to the willow as it is gradually promoted from part of the WHERE, to a WHAT, to a WHO.

Summary

Articulation of the DC has an effect analogous to the deliberate visualization carried out by a writer as the basic components of a plot are elaborated into a story, or to the cinematographer's mise-en-scene as the screenplay skeleton is elaborated into actual camera fields and angles on the set. But whereas these have been analyzed as stylistic elaborations of a basic underlying structure, articulation of the DC is part-and-parcel of the most elementary linguistic coding.

A syntactic representation of a simple sentence cannot be built without making decisions about transitivity, voice, mood, tense, aspect, case frame, NP type, and so on, all choices profoundly affected by the current contents and the history of the DC. So the DC, and the decision matrices it represents, are at the very heart of linguistic coding in narrative discourse context.

DEICTIC DEVICES AFFECTING DEICTIC CENTER OPERATION

Grammatical devices that contribute to the stability and movement of the DC are studied under various rubrics, such as topicalization, focus, extraposition, foregrounding and backgrounding, presentatives, anaphora, tense, aspect, and spatial deixis. The study of each of these phenomena deals with specific, isolated aspects of the structuring of narrative discourse (Givon, 1983; Hopper, 1979). But there is no unified account of how cohesive devices are used to introduce, maintain, shift, and void the WHO, WHAT, WHEN, and WHERE of the DC. Significant steps in this direction were taken by text linguists such as Grimes (1975) and Longacre (1983), but these proposals lacked the hypothesis-generative precision of our DC model.

DC-devices are textual cohesive devices that are used to signal stability and change in the DC of narrative texts. A DC-device is a morphemic or syntactic structure of the text that affects the listener's construction of the DC by setting up candidate actors, places, and times for the DC; by signaling stability or shift in the DC; or by temporarily voiding some component of the DC. In this section, we discuss the general operation of the DC in the comprehension process.

Deictic Operations

Deictic operations are mental operations that the reader/listener performs on the DC during the process of constructing an interpretation for a stretch of narrative text. Much of the coherence of narrative text arises from the performance of these operations. In later sections, we give examples of each operation applied to the WHO, WHEN, and WHERE. (We do not have as many examples of operations relating to the WHAT, however many of the operations listed for the WHO could apply to the WHAT, as well.) The deictic operations are:

1. *Introducing* actors, objects, places, or time intervals into the narrative as potential or actual WHOs, WHATs, WHENs, or WHEREs of the DC.

2. *Maintaining* stability in the DC: Components remain stable either when the listener expects this or when the listener might expect a shift, except for the presence of an antishifting device.

3. *Shifting* the WHO, WHAT, WHEN, or WHERE of the DC from one character, object, place, or time to another. A new WHO is usually introduced before the DC shifts to it. A special instance of shifting is initializing the DC, that is, specifying the initial WHO, WHEN, and WHERE at the beginning of a narrative. Introducing and shifting may be accomplished as a single operation.

4. A special case of shifting is *voiding*. One or more DC components may become indeterminate if the presence and identity of a WHO, WHAT, WHEN, or WHERE is not relevant at that point in the narrative; for example, the WHO and WHEN of the DC may temporarily shift to null during a scene description, or a WHAT that was momentarily important may cease to be tracked if the WHO is no longer attending to it. The voiding operation may be regarded as shifting to a null component.

Principles of the Deictic Center

Textual Economy. As discussed previously, the listener/reader constructs the DC in the process of comprehension, based not only on DC-devices in the text itself, but also on shared knowledge (Smith, 1982) and on what Clark and Clark (1977), following Grice (1975), called the reality and cooperative principles. In consequence of this construction process, much of what happens in the DC can be anticipated by the comprehender and need not be overtly encoded in a DC-device. Put briefly, the text evokes ideas for the comprehender and may remain silent when the comprehender can anticipate them (Slobin, 1979), resulting in considerable economy in the text. Specific aspects of this economy include ellipsis (see Hewitt, this volume, for a discussion of reduced anaphor) and in media res devices. An example of the latter is frequently found in science-fiction and fantasy narratives, where textual economy must be at a premium, given that an entire world differing from our own must be evoked in the reader's mind by means of purely textual devices. One way to avoid sounding too much like an encyclopedia description is to start in media res, plunging the reader into a world of unfamiliar objects, place names, and beings:

> (6) He sat in a room, the sand of which was synthetic and shining with opal tints.
> . . . The windows held no cityview, but a continuously rotating panorama of
> the Khogghut plain: a lie. Traffic noise came through. (Cherryh, 1987, p. 5)

Here, a novel begins with a number of implications: that it is normal for a room to have sand; that there is such a thing as synthetic sand; that windows can typically show something other than the actual outside view; and that the Khogghut plain is a well-known place name. Moreover, the "he" sitting in the room is not named until the second paragraph (this is a marker that he is the current focalizing WHO; see Hewitt, this volume). All of these implications cause the reader to construct a fictional knowledge representation, a sort of possible world in which these "facts" are true. It is this sudden plunge into unfamiliar territory, linguistically treated as familiar, that we term *in media res*.

Inertia. The DC remains stable unless a change is explicitly signaled. The WHO and WHEN stay the same unless they are signaled to change. The WHAT, as discussed previously, tends to decay rapidly unless explicitly evoked. In contrast, since time is sequential, the WHEN has dynamic inertia; that is, a stable WHEN moves forward with each successive event in the narrative, unless a jump or stop is signaled (see Almeida, this volume). Events are inferred to occur in the sequence in which they are mentioned unless signaled to be out of sequence (Clark & Clark, 1977).

Deictic Synchronism. A norm of narrative discourse seems to be that the WHO, WHEN, and WHERE of the DC are maintained and shifted together. A complementary norm seems to be that this synchronism is periodically broken, either by voiding a component of the DC or by shifting them apart. The WHAT routinely violates this principle, as noted previously. In a text segment of character description, the WHEN and WHERE of the DC are voided while the WHO is maintained throughout; in scene descriptions, the WHERE is maintained, voiding the WHO and WHEN.

The principle of *deictic synchronism* leads to specific implicational relationships among DC components. These relationships can be used by the comprehender as inferences in constructing the DC; that is, they are functionally equivalent to DC-devices:

1. Time sequencing entails a WHO and a WHERE; that is, progression in time may be stopped by voiding either the WHO or the WHERE. In the following example, the WHO, WHERE, and WHEN are not yet instantiated; the opening of the novel starts with commentary rather than storyworld building:

(7) It is a truth universally acknowledged, that a single man in possession of a good fortune, must be in want of a wife. However little known the feelings or views of such a man may be on his first entering a neighbourhood, this truth is so well fixed in the minds of the surrounding families, that he is considered as the rightful property of some one or other of their daughters. (Austen, 1966, p. 1)

2. A shift in the WHERE may entail a shift in the WHO, WHAT, or the WHEN; that is, if the WHERE shifts to a new place, time is updated, and/or the WHO shifts to another character. Shift of the WHO may trigger automatic updating of the WHERE, because the reader is aware that the new WHO is in a different location from the previous WHO:

(8) As he fell slowly into sleep, Pippin had a strange feeling: he and Gandalf were still as stone, seated upon the statue of a running horse, while the world rolled away beneath his feet with a great noise of wind.
   WHERE: Somewhere on road between Gondor and Rohan
   WHEN: Few days before major battle
   Chapter ends, blank pages intervene, new chapter begins—no intervening text between above and what follows:
   "Well, master, we're in a fix and no mistake," said Sam Gamgee. . . .
   WHERE: mention of Sam Gamgee resets WHO, which instantly resets WHERE to the last known WHERE for this new WHO, which is far south and east of WHERE of Pippin. WHEN is unknown.
   It was the third evening since they had fled from the Company . . .
   WHEN: Reset backwards from WHEN of Pippin, to some days prior.
   (Tolkien, 1965, p. 206)

Transparency. A further crucial aspect of deictic center structuring is that the amount of linguistic material assigned to subcomponents is often unequal. That is, it is the focalized perspective, or content of the deictic window that is described in the text. The focalizing perspective, or origin, is outside the deictic window, and thus not in view. It is transparent in the sense that the reader does not look at it, but rather through it at the content of the window. This transparency translates into being presupposed by, but not mentioned (or only mentioned in some reduced form) in the text.

Scope.   Scoping principles are closely related to deictic synchronism, as follows.

Individual DC-devices have a specific scope or *mental space* (Fauconnier, 1985), corresponding to a chunk of text, within which the parameters they set are valid. Some scopes, such as the scope of initial adverbials, are broad, that is, valid until they are cancelled by another DC-device signaling a shift. Other scopes, for example, the scope of antishifting devices (discussed later), are narrow, that is, limited to one clause or phrase.

When scopes conflict, narrow scope supersedes broad scope.

(9) Kino stood perfectly still. He could hear Juana whispering the old magic again, and he could hear the evil music of the enemy. (Steinbeck, 1945/1975, p. 7)

In Example 9, the definite subject NP "Juana" should shift the DC, but there is no shift, since this device occurs within the narrow scope of a complement clause (an antishifting device).

Extraposition.   DC-devices will be located at the beginning or end of clause or sentence units to the extent that these dislocations are permitted by the grammar of the particular language.

Initial DC-devices will establish the DC for the next sentences; final DC-devices will signal a pending shift in the DC (e.g., relative clauses).

Cumulative Cohesion.   Cohesive devices in text tend to be redundant (de Beaugrande & Dressler, 1981; Halliday & Hasan, 1976; Zubin, 1977, 1980). In a narrative, there will be intervals of certainty about the DC and intervals of uncertainty during which it is unclear whether or not the WHO, WHEN, or WHERE have shifted. Agreement of several DC-devices will more clearly shift or maintain the DC than will a single DC-device, that is, they have a cumulative effect. On the other hand, absence of DC-devices or conflict among them will correspond to intervals of high uncertainty in the text.

Morphological, Lexical, and Syntactic DC-Devices

In the following sections, we summarize some ways in which individual cohesive devices introduce, maintain, and shift the WHO, WHEN, and WHERE of the DC, providing illustrative examples from a variety of works, but primarily from Steinbeck's *The Pearl* (1945/1975).

TABLE 6.1
Devices in English Contributing to Transitivity

High Transitivity	Low Transitivity
Main clause	Dependent clause
Definite, anaphoric object	Indefinite object
Simple past tense	Progressive or perfect tense
Direct object	No direct object
Affirmative	Negative
Telic predicate	Atelic predicate

Hopper and Thompson (1980) described a number of morphological and syntactic features that alert what they called the "transitivity" of the clause, and showed how these features affect the discourse foregrounding and backgrounding of the information conveyed by the clause. Many of the devices shown in Table 6.1, individually and conjointly, serve either to maintain or to void the DC.

There are three forms of simple *maintenance*, in which the reader expects maintenance of the current character as the WHO:

1. *Conjoined clauses* signal that the DC remains stable within the conjunction (Fillmore, 1975). This reflects the frequent observation (e.g., Brown & Yule, 1983) that the members of a conjunction are conceptually bound close together. Clause conjoining is often combined with other maintenance devices, such as zero-anaphora.

2. *Complement and relative clauses* are antishifting devices. They permit reference to another character, time, or place within their scope, and prevent the DC from shifting there. At the end of the clause, the scope of the device is cancelled, and the narrative automatically continues at the unshifted DC. Complement-taking predicates that seem to fulfill this function include perception predicates, cognition predicates, speech predicates, and causatives.

3. *Initial adverbial clauses* shift the WHEN and WHERE. Brown and Yule (1983) suggested that initial adverbials may in general be a marker of topic shift. In Fauconnier's (1985) terms, initial adverbials would mark a shift to a new mental space that the listener is constructing in the comprehension process, an idea implicit in Geis's (1985) study of initial and noninitial spatial and temporal adverbials. Geis found that initial placement of a spatial adverbial sets up a spatial frame within which the event occurs, whereas noninitial placement does not. Example 10a places John in Chicago in the narrative context, whereas 10b does not:

(10) a. In Chicago, John knew about some good Chinese restaurants.
b. John knew about some good Chinese restaurants in Chicago.

The DC is a type of mental space in Fauconnier's sense, which is crucial to the construction of narrative discourse. Specifically, we claim that initial spatial and temporal adverbials will shift these aspects of the DC.

Devices That Affect the WHO. There are several devices that introduce or maintain an actor as the WHO, as the quotations from Steinbeck's *The Pearl* (1945/1975) in Examples 11–25 illustrate.

1. *Presentative structure:* One type of presentative structure consists of a preposed adverbial phrase/clause + subject NP (usually indefinite):

> (11) Down the rope that hung the baby's box from the rope support a scorpion moved slowly. His stinging tail was straight out behind him, but he could whip it up in a flash of time. (p. 6)

Another type of presentative structure exhibits a "there"/"it" + "be" + NP construction:

> (12) His eyes flicked to a rustle beside him. It was Juana arising, almost soundlessly. On her hard bare feet she went to the hanging box where Coyotito slept . . . (p. 34)

2. *Noun phrases with extended modifiers (e.g., adjectival phrases or relative clauses):*

> (13) And the newcomers, particularly the beggars from the front of the church who were great experts in financial analysis looked quickly at Juana's old blue skirt . . . (p. 11)

> (14) Kino's eyes opened, and he looked first at the lightening square which was the door and then he looked at the hanging box where Coyotito slept. At last he turned his head to Juana . . . (p. 1)

3. *Overall frequency of mention:* Kino and Juana are the most frequently mentioned characters in the story. The DC shifts to them with fewer supporting features than an infrequently mentioned character such as the beggars. For example, after an extensive passage of scene description in which the WHO and WHEN are voided, a simple subject NP shifts the WHO from null to Kino, and thereby sets the dynamic WHEN back in motion. (In this and subsequent quotations, paragraph breaks are marked by: [P].)

> (15) But the Pearls were accidents, and the finding of one was luck, a little pat on the back by God or the gods or both. [P] Kino had two ropes, one tied to a heavy stone and one to a basket. He slipped off his shirt and trousers and laid his hat in the bottom of the canoe. (p. 22)

In addition to the simple maintenance devices listed above, there are also antishifting devices which block a shift to a new WHO. These take several forms:

1. *Definite NPs in direct/indirect-object position:*

(16) And last he turned his head to *Juana* his wife, who lay beside him on the mat ... (p. 1; emphasis added)

2. *Coordinate-clause conjoining:*

(17) And as always when he came near to one of this race, Kino felt weak and afraid and angry at the same time.... He could kill the doctor more easily than *he* could talk to him ... (p. 12; emphasis added)

Note that the italicized subject pronoun refers to Kino, the WHO of the DC, even though the doctor is most recently mentioned.

3. *Subject chaining:* This includes pronominalization and zero-anaphor successive mention of a character as the subject of adjacent clauses (c.f. Hewitt, this volume; Zubin, 1979).

4. *Relative clauses:*

(18) And every year Kino refinished his canoe with the hard shell-like plaster by the secret method *that had also come to him from his father.* (p. 15; emphasis added)

Here, the WHO does not shift to Kino's father because his father occurs in a relative clause.

5. *Indefinite subjects:*

(19) ... he [Kino] squatted down and gathered the blanket ends about his knees. He saw the specks of Gulf clouds flame high in the air. And a goat came near and sniffed at him and stared with its cold yellow eyes. Behind him Juana's fire leaped into flame ... A late moth blustered in to find the fire. [P] The dawn came quickly now.... Kino looked down to cover his eyes from the glare. (p. 4; emphasis added)

6. *Complementation:*

(20) Kino stood perfectly still. He could hear Juana whispering the old magic again, and he could hear the evil music of the enemy. (p. 7)

In this example, the definite subject NP "Juana" is introduced as a potential WHO (c.f. Example 15), but the clause is a complement to the verb "hear," so the DC does not shift.

7. Finally, *switch-reference markers* in other languages often have an antishifting function in narrative (Haiman & Munro, 1983).

There are three devices that shift to another actor as the WHO:

1. *Perception and mental predicates:* In the next example, the verb "feel" shifts the DC briefly to the scorpion, as shown by the deictic verb "come" in its scope:

(21) He [Kino] could not move until the scorpion moved, and it *felt* for the source of the death that was coming to it. Kino's hand went forward very slowly, very smoothly. (p. 7)

2. *Definite noun phrases* (including names) in subject position; the italicized pronoun shifts the WHO to the servant from Kino:

(22) He [Kino] brought out a paper folded many times. Crease by crease he unfolded it, until at last there came to view eight small misshapen seed pearls, as ugly and gray as little ulcers, flattened and almost valueless. The servant took the paper and closed the gate again, but this time he was not gone long. *He* opened the gate just wide enough to pass the paper back. (p. 15)

3. *A shift in the WHERE:*

(23) The gate closed a little, and the servant refused to speak in the old language. "A little moment," he said. "I go to inform myself," and he closed the gate and slid the bolt home. The glaring sun threw the bunched shadows of the people blackly on the white wall. [P] *In his chamber* the doctor sat up in his high bed. He had on his dressing gown of red watered silk that had come from Paris, a little tight over the chest now if it was buttoned. (p. 13; emphasis added)

In Example 23, the shift to the doctor's chamber prepares us to shift to the doctor as the new WHO.

Finally, a device that temporarily voids the WHO (i.e., shifts it to null) is *chained indefinite reference*:

(24) The beach was yellow sand, but at the water's edge a rubble of shell and algae took its place. Fiddler crabs bubbled and sputtered in their holes in the sand, and in the shallows little lobsters popped in and out of their tiny homes in the rubble and sand. (p. 14)

(25) A town is a thing like a colonial animal. A town has a nervous system and a head and shoulders and feet. A town is a thing separate from all other towns, so that there are no two towns alike. And a town has a whole emotion. How news travels through a town is a mystery not easily to be solved. (p. 27)

In the examples just given, the indefinite references ("a town"; "fiddler crabs"; "lobsters") are used to evoke typicality; in story world terms, they set the scene or the mood, but no characters are brought into play as potential WHOs.

Devices That Affect the WHERE. Two devices introduce a location as a potential WHERE. These are (a) *'go'/'take' + noninitial goal adverbial*:

(26) And rage surged in Kino. He rolled up to his feet and followed her as silently as she had gone, and he could hear her quick footsteps *going toward the shore.* (pp. 75–76)

and (b) *preposed adverbials*, that simultaneously introduce and shift:

(27) Thus, *in La Paz*, it was known in the early morning through the whole town that Kino was going to sell his pearl that day. (pp. 53–54)

The devices that maintain a location as the WHERE again consist of simple maintenance and antishifting devices. *Simple maintenance* can take at least three forms:

1. *Clause conjoining* (as in Example 17)
2. *Spatial deictic adverbs "here" and "there"*:

(28) And in the pearl he saw Juana with her beaten face crawling home through the night. "Our son must learn to read," he said frantically. And *there* in the pearl Coyotito's face, thick and feverish from the medicine. (pp. 93–94)

3. *Deictic verbs "come," "go," "bring," "take":* In this example, maintenance of the WHERE is signaled by "come":

(29) Kino squatted by the fire pit and rolled a hot corncake and dipped it in sauce and ate it . . . When Kino had finished, Juana *came* back to the fire and ate her breakfast. (p. 2)

Often, the goal of "come" and "bring" is left unspecified, since these convey movement toward the DC, already known to the comprehender:

(30) Juana *brought* a little piece of consecrated candle and lighted it at the flame and set it upright on a fireplace stone. (p. 49)

The antishifting devices are *complement clauses* (c.f. Example 20), *relative clauses*, and *perception verbs*.

Devices Which Shift the WHERE. There are four devices that shift to another location as the WHERE:

1. *Spatial deictic adverbs:* "here" and "there" (note that these are also
   maintenance devices if they agree with a previous DC-device):

(31) Even in the distance he could see the two on foot moving slowly along, bent
     low to the ground. *Here,* one would pause and look at the earth, while the
     other joined him. They were the trackers, they could follow the trail of a
     bighorn sheep in the stone mountains. They were as sensitive as hounds. *Here,*
     he and Juana might have stepped out of the wheel rut, and . . . these hunters,
     could follow, could read a broken straw or a little tumbled pile of dust. (pp.
     95–96)

2. *Preposed locative adverbials:*

(32) He [Kino] slipped his feet into his sandals and went outside to watch the
     dawn. [P] *Outside the door* he squatted down and gathered the blanket ends
     about his knees. He saw the specks of Gulf clouds flame high in the air. (p. 3)

3. *Verbs with directional valence* (e.g., "come," "go," "enter," "leave,"
   "bring," and "take"): In the following example, "come" successively shifts
   the narrative not only to a new WHERE but to a new WHO:

(33) The news *came* to the doctor where he sat with a woman whose illness was
     age. . . . the doctor grew stern and judicious at the same time. . . . [P] The
     news *came* early to the beggars in front of the church, and it made them
     giggle a little with pleasure. . . . (pp. 28–29)

   In the following example, "go" and "come" in combination signal a shift
   in the WHERE, which begins outside the hut:

(34) The world was awake now, and Kino arose and *went* into his brush house.
     [P] As he *came* through the door Juana stood up from the glowing fire pit.
     (p. 2)

4. *Shift in the WHO:* A shift in the WHO can shift the WHERE. In the
   example below, the place where Juana is becomes the WHERE:

(35) The scorpion moved delicately down the rope toward the box. Under her
     breath Juana repeated an ancient magic to guard against such evil, and on top
     of that she muttered a Hail Mary between clenched teeth. (p. 6)

Devices That Affect the WHEN. An introducing device introduces a time
interval as a potential WHEN and shifts to it; in the following example, this is
accomplished by use of an initial adverbial:

(36) *In the afternoon,* when the sun had gone over the mountains of the Peninsula to sink in the outward sea, Kino squatted in his house with Juana beside him. (p. 30)

The two classes of devices that maintain the WHEN actually maintain its dynamic inertia (i.e., they keep updating the WHEN). Simple maintenance can take three forms:

1. *Tense chaining* (simple past, simple present):

(37) And the newcomers, particularly the beggars from the front of the church who were great experts in financial analysis, *looked* ... *saw* the tears in her shawl, *appraised* the green ribbon ... *read* the age of Kino's blanket ... and *set* them down as poverty people ... (p. 11)

2. *Accomplishment and achievement predicates* (Vendler, 1957):

(38) Then from his bag he *took* a little bottle of white powder and a capsule of gelatin. He *filled* the capsule with the powder and *closed* it, and then around the first capsule he *fitted* a second capsule and *closed* it. (p. 4041)

3. *Clause conjoining* (again, see Example 17).

Antishifting devices signal that an event is out of sequence, but that otherwise events are still sequential. That is, beyond the scope of the antishifting device, sequencing returns to normal. There are two such devices: (a) *Conjunction adverbs:* "while," "after," "before," "when."

(39) And as always *when* he came near to one of this race, Kino felt weak ... (p. 12)

and (b) *Past perfect:*

(40) In the pearl he saw Coyotito sitting at a little desk in a school, just as Kino *had once seen* him through an open door. (p. 33)

One type of device that can shift the WHEN is a *preposed temporal adverbial*:

(41) *And then,* in the first light, he heard the creak of a wagon, and he crouched beside the road and watched a heavy two-wheeled cart go by, drawn by slouching oxen. (p. 92)

There are four devices that can void the time sequence of the WHEN (i.e., shift it to null):

1. *Stative and activity verbs* (Vendler, 1957):

(42) She, who *was* obedient and respectful and cheerful and patient, she *could arch* her back in child pain with hardly a cry. She *could stand* fatigue and hunger almost better than Kino himself. In the canoe she *was* like a strong man. (p. 9)

2. *Habitual and iterative adverbs:*

(43) *For centuries* men had dived down and torn the oysters from the beds and ripped them open, looking for the coated grains of sand. (p. 21)

3. *Imperfective aspect* (Hopper, 1982; Reid, 1977):

(44) Kino *was not breathing*, but his back arched a little and the muscles of his arms and legs stood out with tension and a line of sweat formed on his upper lip. (p. 97)

4. *Absence of a WHO:* In Example 24, the chained indefinite subjects are not embedded within a focalizing WHO, so they void the WHO, that in this case, voids the WHEN.

The Effect of Agreement and Conflict Among DC-Devices

When devices agree with each other, the certainty of a maintenance or shift in the DC is increased. When devices of like scope disagree, the certainty of a maintenance or shift is decreased; that is, the comprehender will be uncertain about the WHO, WHEN, or WHERE of the DC. Note that this is distinct from a voided DC, in which case the comprehender is certain that there is temporarily no WHO, WHEN, and/or WHERE.

Certainty about the identity of the WHO, WHEN, or WHERE of the DC during an interval in the narrative is proportional to the number of DC-devices that agree about the identity of this component of the DC. The following passage illustrates the strong and certain DC resulting from multiple devices that maintain it:

(45) *She* [Juana] uncovered an ember from the ashes and Ø shredded little pieces of cornhusk over it and Ø blew a little flame into the cornhusks . . . *And then* . . . Juana *brought* a little piece of consecrated candle and Ø lighted it at the flame and Ø set it upright on a fireplace stone. (p. 49)

Here we have a pronominal reference to the WHO, followed by three zeroes, conjoined to the next sentence by the high continuity connective "and then," with two further zeroes after one full nominal reference, that is followed by "brought," indicating movement toward the DC.

The following passage illustrates how antishifting devices cooperate to prevent a DC shift:

(46) The four beggars in front of the church knew everything in the town. *They₁* were students *of* the expressions *of young women* as *they₂* went in to confession, and *they₃ saw them₄* as *they₅ came* out and [$\emptyset_6$] read the nature of the sin. *They₇* knew every little scandal and some very big crimes. *They₈* slept at *their₉* posts in the shadow of the church . . . (p. 11; subscripts added)

In this example, the WHO = the beggars, and the WHERE = in front of the church. Four antishifting devices cooperate to prevent shift of the WHO to the women and of the WHERE to the inside of the church: the obviating preposition "of," the indefinite NP "young women," the subordinating conjunction "as," and the perception verb "see," with the beggars as subject. This maintenance of the WHO is supported by the deictic verbs "go" (signalling movement away from the WHERE) and "come" (signaling return). Note that the concerted maintenance of the beggars as the WHO throughout the passage allows the anaphoric pronoun "they" and zero-anaphora (marked with numerals in the passage) to switch back and forth in reference between the beggars and the women. Occurrences 2 and 5 referring to the women are in the scope of the antishifting devices "as" and "of" (cf. the Principles of Scope). Occurrences 1, 3, 6, 7, and 8—referring to the beggars—are not in the scope of such devices. (Occurrence 4 is assigned to the women by a co-reference principle.) Thus, because of the stable DC, the reader is able to keep track of switching reference, despite the use of potentially ambiguous pronouns and zero-anaphora.

Uncertainty about the identity of the WHO, WHEN, or WHERE of the DC during an interval in the narrative is proportional to the number of DC-devices of like scope that conflict concerning the identity of this component of the DC:

(47) . . . he crept into the cover of a thorny tree [P] . . . and peeked out from under a fallen branch. . . . Even *in the distance he* could see the two on foot moving slowly along, bent low to the ground. *Here, one* would pause and look at the earth, while the other joined him. (pp. 95–96)

In this example, the WHO and WHERE start off together in the first sentence. In the second sentence, the initial adverbial signals a shift in the WHERE, but the anaphoric subject pronoun "he" signals maintenance of the WHO. This conflict leads to uncertainty about whether the WHERE has really shifted, or whether or not the WHO is going to shift. This uncertainty is resolved in the last sentence by the initial "here" and the change in subject pronoun: The WHO and WHERE have shifted to the location of "the two on foot."

The following passage reveals a similar conflict, resulting in momentary uncertainty about the DC:

(48) Juana went to the fire pit and uncovered a coal and fanned it alive. . . . [P]
Now Kino got up and wrapped his blanket about his head and nose and
shoulders. He slipped his feet into his sandals and went outside to watch the
dawn. (pp. 2–3)

At this point, the WHERE is inside the hut and Kino is the WHO. But since the
WHO is leaving the WHERE, it is highly probable that one will shift, and we
are left in uncertainty; that is, we do not know if we, the reader, are staying
inside with Juana (shift of the WHO) or going outside with Kino (shift of the
WHERE). This is resolved by the next sentence:

(49) *Outside the door* he squatted down and gathered the blanket ends about his
knees. (p. 3)

The anaphoric pronoun "he" (referring to Kino) signals maintenance of the WHO,
whereas the initial spatial adverbial "outside the door" signals a shift of the
WHERE; that is, the reader is now certain that the WHO is maintained but the
WHERE has shifted.

Stable Dissynchronism of the DC

We identified one nexus of DC-devices resulting in a separation of the WHO
and WHERE that is stable, that is, it does not show the evidence of conflict of
the examples above. This nexus seems to evoke a journey schema (Lakoff &
Johnson, 1980) in the comprehender's mental model of the narrative. The WHO
is composed of the individual or group making the journey, and the WHERE is
their final goal as well as places they pass along the way. What creates the
dynamic quality of the journey in the narrative is the fact that the WHERE keeps
shifting out ahead of the WHO.

The following passage illustrates this effect. Kino and Juana are going to the
town doctor with their baby, accompanied by their neighbors and others in the
town:

(50) a. The people in the door pushed against those behind to see her [Juana]
through.
b. Kino *followed* her. They *went* out of the gate to the rutted path and the
c. neighbors *followed* them. [P] . . . They *came* to the place where the brush
houses
d. stopped and the city of stone and plaster began . . . The procession *crossed*
e. the blinding plaza and *passed* in front of the church. [P] . . . the beggars
from

    f. the front of the church . . . *went* along to see what kind of drama might
    g. develop . . . they *followed* the procession, these endless searchers after
    h. perfect knowledge of their fellow men, to see what the fat lazy doctor
    i. would do about an indigent baby with a scorpion bite. [P] The scurrying
    j. procession *came* at last to the big gate in the wall of the doctor's house.
       (pp. 10–12; emphasis added)

One of the many devices of the text that set up the movement of the procession are the motion verbs "follow," "pass," and "cross" on lines (b), (c), (d), (e), and (g) of the text passage. The verbs "come" (c, j) and "go" (b, f), in addition to expressing motion, express movement toward and away from the DC, respectively. If the WHO (the procession) and the WHERE are synchronized, then "come" and "go" should express movement toward and away from the procession, respectively. But the opposite is the case. To show this, we define a locus as a location that is non-coterminous with the WHO and with respect to which the WHO is moving. Both instances of "come" in the passage express movement toward a locus, not toward the WHO. The word "went" in line (b) expresses movement away from a locus and, in (f), away from a locus and toward the WHO. In other words, the deictic verbs in this passage orient toward loci away from the WHO, as if these were the WHERE of the DC. Thus, either our claim about "come" and "go" is wrong, or the WHO and WHERE are indeed dissynchronous in this passage. We believe that such dissynchronism of DC-devices maintaining the WHO and WHERE will be systematically exploited in narrative to evoke a journey schema.

CONCLUSION

In this chapter, we outlined the linguistic foundations of deictic centering in narrative fiction in English. The work presented is intended as a framework for analysis, with coverage broader than it is deep. The material in this chapter may be used in two ways. The theory and its devices is intended to have direct application to text linguistic studies of narrative fiction. Similarly, psycholinguistic studies of text processing may find our categories helpful.

    On a more abstract level, our results can be taken as arguments for a functionalist approach to the analysis of linguistic structures. The close examination of language of a particular type (here, narrative fiction) inevitably yields insights into the plasticity of application of linguistic material to meet specific communicative goals.

DEICTIC TRACKING IN NARRATIVE

7

TIME IN NARRATIVES

Michael J. Almeida
University of Northern Iowa

INTRODUCTION

Narratives are a type of discourse used to describe sequences of events. Standard examples of narratives are novels, short stories, biographies, and histories. Narratives can be contrasted with other discourse types, such as lyric poetry and expository prose, in which the temporal element is not so central. Because of the nature of narratives, one of the most important tasks for understanding them is determining the temporal relations that exist among the events described in the narrative. These events and their temporal relations constitute what is called the *story* of the narrative.

In this chapter, we concentrate on the study of issues involved in understanding the temporal structure of narratives. These issues are of two major types. The first type has to do with representational questions; here we address the problem of how to represent a story. The second type has to do with processing questions; here we address the problem of how a reader extracts the story from a narrative. Central to our approach is a representation of the present moment within the story, called the *narrative now-point*. Much of the analysis of how different event-types, tenses, aspects, and time adverbials function within a narrative concerns their interaction with, and effect on, this now-point.

THE ONTOLOGY AND BASIC REPRESENTATIONS

In this and the next few sections, we describe our basic representational approach and its underlying ontology. The representations described are implemented as semantic networks in the SNePS Semantic Network Processing System (Shapiro,

1979). A more complete account of our implementation of the representations and processes described in this article can be found in Almeida (1987).

Following Davidson (1967), we make a distinction in our representations between *propositions* and *events*. Propositions are the bearers of truth values; that is, a proposition is the sort of thing that may be true or false. Propositions can be the objects of verbs such as *know* and *believe*. Events, on the other hand, are spatio-temporal entities much like ordinary physical objects. They can be the objects of perceptual verbs such as *see* and *hear*, and they can be the subjects of verbs like *last* and *occur*. Events are often referred to with what Chomsky calls *derived nominals* (Chomsky, 1970), e.g., *explosion, eruption.*

The relationship between the proposition and the event it describes is essentially that of Davidson (1967). For example, Davidson gave as the representation for the sentence *Shem kicked Shaun*: (∃x)(Kicked (Shem,Shaun,x)), where, x is an event "such that x is a kicking of Shaun by Shem" (p. 118). As Davidson puts it, "The basic idea is that verbs of action—verbs that say 'what someone did'—should be construed as containing a place, for singular terms or variables, that they do not appear to. For example, we would normally suppose that 'Shem kicked Shaun' consists in two names and a two-place predicate. I suggest, though, that we think of 'kicked' as a *three-place* predicate" (p. 118). This third argument is the event.

Finally, we view predicates as corresponding to core verb phrases rather than simply to verbs. Thus, in the (tenseless) proposition *Mary play the piano*, the predicate is *play the piano* with argument *Mary*. This analysis is opposed to one in which *play* is considered the predicate with arguments *Mary* and *the piano*. According to Schachter (1976), gerundive nominals without an initial possessive are class names, naming types of activities, types of conditions, and so on. Thus, *going to the beach* is a type of activity, and *being sick* is a type of condition or state. It is these types of activities, and types of conditions, that are taken as predicates in our system. The class of predicates can be divided into two major subclasses: stative predicates, called *properties*, and nonstative predicates, called *acts*. These predicate classes are discussed in more detail in a later section.

The basic case frame for the representation of a nonstative proposition and the event it describes is shown in Fig. 7.1. In this figure, node 1 represents the proposition, node 2 represents the argument of the predicate, which is called the

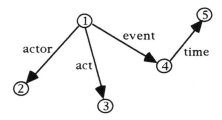

FIG. 7.1.   Basic case frame for nonstative propositions.

actor, node 3 represents the predicate (in this case, an act), node 4 represents the event described by the proposition, and node 5 represents the interval of time occupied by the event. This case frame is intended to be neutral between agentive and nonagentive events. In the current representation, an event is a structured individual that (so far) consists only of a time property. This is not to suggest that this representation of events is complete. There are other components to this concept, such as a location.

The case frame for stative propositions is similar to that for nonstative propositions, except that the argument of the predicate is called an *object* and the predicate itself is called a *property*. We differ from Davidson in associating events with stative propositions as well as with nonstative propositions. As partial justification for this move, we suggest that in sentences such as *John saw a cat on the porch*, what John sees is not simply some object, but a configuration of objects—that is, a state. If such states can be seen, then they are events in our sense of the term. In addition, this move makes the overall representation and interpretation of time more uniform.

THE TEMPORAL LOGIC

The ontology of time used in this project is that developed by Allen (1981, 1984); that is, a purely interval-based approach to the representation of time. Largely because of technical differences between the way that arc labels in Allen's network system work and the way that arcs in SNePS work, we take a different approach to the representation of temporal relations. Instead of defining the basic relations as mutually exclusive, as Allen did, and then disjoining them to produce ambiguous relations, we define the basic temporal relations as ambiguous in the first place, and then, when necessary, use negation for disambiguation. We use the following temporal relations: (a) The *before/after* case frame means that the interval pointed at by the *before* arc is temporally before the interval pointed at by the *after* arc. This relation is ambiguous between Allen's *before* and *meets* relations; that is, we allow the possibility that the distance between the two intervals is zero. Notice that this case frame also represents the related inverse relation. This is true of our other relations as well. (b) The *before/after/duration* case frame means that the interval pointed at by *before* is temporally before the interval pointed at by *after* by the amount of time pointed at by *duration*. When the duration is zero, this relation is equivalent to Allen's *meets* relation. (c) The *subinterval/supinterval* case frame means that the first interval is a subinterval of the second interval. This relation is ambiguous between Allen's *during, starts, finishes*, and *equal* relations; that is, the first interval need not be a proper subinterval of the second. (d) The *initial-subinterval/supinterval* case frame is ambiguous between Allen's *starts* and *equal* relations. Again, the first interval need not be a proper subinterval of the second. (e) The *final-subinterval/supinterval* case frame is ambiguous between Allen's *finishes* and *equal* relations. (f) The *equiv/equiv* case frame is the same as Allen's *equal* relation.

PREDICATE TYPES AND EVENT TYPES

In *Verbs and Time* (Vendler, 1957), Vendler developed a classification scheme for verbs based on what he called their *time schemata*. The notions that make up these time schemata are such things as whether or not a verb can occur in the progressive, whether or not the truth of a sentence using the progressive of some verb implies the truth of the same sentence using the simple form of that verb, co-occurrence restrictions of verbs with various time adverbials, and so on. Actually, although Vendler used the word *verb* exclusively, it seems clear that he really meant verb phrases or predicates in our sense, because many of his examples were not single verbs at all, but entire verb phrases.

The four classes of predicates that Vendler posited are called *activities, accomplishments, achievements*, and *states*. This classification scheme and related schemes were discussed and elaborated upon by many other researchers in various fields, among them Bennett and Partee (1972), Comrie (1976), Dowty (1977, 1979), Mourelatos (1981), Verkuyl (1972), and Vlach (1981). Within AI, these concepts or related ones have been used by Allen (1984), Almeida and Shapiro (1983), McDermott (1982), Steedman (1977), and Webber (1978).

Among the people who discussed these classes, there is wide disagreement about exactly what sorts of things are being classified: verbs, predicates (verb phrases), propositions, or events. As stated earlier, it is clear from his examples that Vendler thought of these classes as a classification of verb phrases or predicates, and we believe that at the most basic level this is correct. However, it is also true that propositions are constructed from these predicates, and the classification, or a related scheme, can be usefully applied to these, as well. In the same way, if we posit events as objects in our representations, it is useful to extend the classes to cover these also. In this section, we give our current formulation of Vendler's original four classes. We also show how we represent these predicates, along with the events and propositions based on them.

Typical examples of activities are: *running, playing the piano, looking for an umbrella, pushing a cart, humming, sleeping*, and *remaining*. The essential properties of activities are: (a) when they involve change (which most do), it is of an indefinite extent; (b) they can occur in both the progressive and the nonprogressive (simple) forms; and (c) in the cases where some definite goal or definite change is implied by these predicates, the actual achievement of that goal or change is not expressible by either form of these predicates. As an example of the third property, the sentence *John was looking for his umbrella* implies the goal of finding the umbrella, but the actual finding of the umbrella is not expressible by either the progressive form or the simple (nonprogressive) form of the predicate *looking for the umbrella*.

Instances of activities are represented as in Fig. 7.2. In this figure, node 1 represents the tenseless proposition *John play the piano*. Node 2 represents the

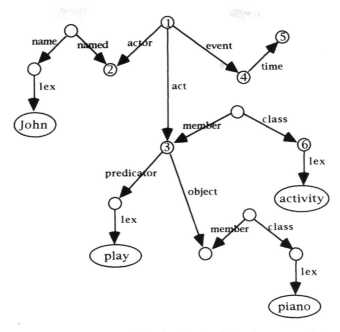

FIG. 7.2.   Representation of "John play the piano" (simple or progressive).

person whose name is *John*. (The assertion that this person's name is John is represented by the *name/named* case frame.) Node 3 represents the concept of *playing the piano*, which is the act of proposition 1 and a member of the class of activities, represented by node 6. Notice that the act is a structured individual consisting of a predicator, *play*, and an object, *the piano*. Node 4 represents the event of John playing the piano, and node 5 represents the interval of time occupied by this event. In SNePS, a node with a *lex* arc coming from it represents a concept that can be expressed by the word pointed at by the arc.

Activity events have the *subinterval property* (Bennett & Partee, 1972). This means that any segment (or interval) of an activity event is an event of the same type (at least down to a certain grain size). So, for instance, any segment of a running-event is also a running-event. A consequence of the subinterval property is that, for activity V, if *John V-ed*, then at some time *John was V-ing*, and if *John was V-ing*, then at some time *John V-ed*. Of course the discourse functions of the simple and the progressive forms are quite different. At any rate, the representation in Fig. 7.2 is neutral between the simple and the progressive form.

Typical examples of accomplishments are *walking to the store, running a mile, playing a sonata, building a house,* and *writing a letter*. The essential properties of accomplishments are: (a) they involve a definite change of some sort; (b) in most contexts, the simple form of the predicate expresses the complete process, from beginning to end, that leads to that definite change; and (c) the progressive form (and the simple form in some contexts) refers to a portion of the complete process, in other words, a subact of the complete act.

Because accomplishments involve definite change, and because the progressive only refers to some portion of the complete process leading to that definite change, an accomplishment sentence *A was V-ing* does not necessarily imply that at some time *A V-ed*. In other words, accomplishments do not have the subinterval property. For example, *John was walking to the store* merely says that John was engaged in some process and says nothing about whether he completed it or not. Therefore, it does not imply that *John walked to the store*. Dowty referred to this property of progressive accomplishments as the *imperfective paradox* (Dowty, 1977). On the other hand, *John was walking to the store* does imply that *John walked to the store for some period of time*. In this context, with an adverbial of duration, the simple form also refers to only a portion of the complete accomplishment.

The imperfective paradox introduces a complication into the representation of accomplishments: How do we represent an occurrence of an incomplete accomplishment without implying the occurrence of the complete accomplishment? Within AI, McDermott (1982) and Allen (1984) both presented ways of handling this property of progressive accomplishments. We also offered a solution to the imperfective paradox (Almeida & Shapiro, 1983), but it was based on an overall representational approach that we no longer use. Our current approach to the representation of incomplete accomplishments is shown in Fig. 7.3. The proposition represented by node 1 could be expressed (assuming the event took place in the past) as *John was walking to the store* or as *John walked to the store (for some period of time)*. Node 2 represents the complete process of walking to the store. Node 4 represents the assertion that the act represented by node 3 is a subact of the act represented by node 2. That is, node 3 represents some portion of the complete accomplishment represented by node 2. The complete act of *walking to the store* is represented as a structured individual consisting of a predicator, *walk*, and a goal (indicated by the *to* arc), *the store*.

The representation of an accomplishment that is understood as being complete is similar to the incomplete case, except in this case the act is the complete process. It is important to emphasize that *acts*, in our sense of the term, are neither propositions nor events, but something akin to procedures. The performance of an act, like the execution of a procedure, generates an event. An incomplete accomplishment event is thus represented by us as a partial performance of some act, the complete performance of which would lead to some definite change as described above.

Typical examples of states are *being sick, being on the table, knowing the answer, believing that Mary walked to the store*, and *resembling Bill*. The standard

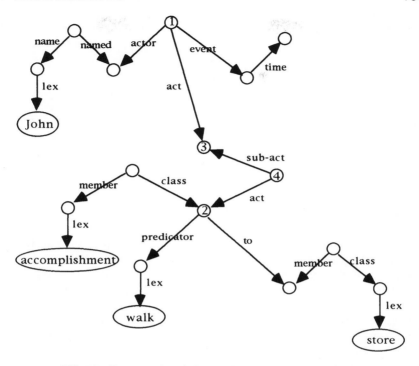

FIG. 7.3. Representation of "John walk to the store" (incomplete).

features of states are that they are not dynamic (they do not involve change), and they cannot occur in the progressive. Intuitively, any part of a state-event is an event of the same type; therefore, like activity-events, state-events have the subinterval property.

Typical examples of achievements are *losing an umbrella, dying, noticing the picture, falling asleep, arriving at the station, realizing something, returning to the house*, and *winning the race*. The principal properties of achievements are: (a) like accomplishments, achievements involve a definite change of some sort; (b) also like accomplishments, the progressive form of these predicates refers to some arbitrary portion of the complete process; and (c) unlike accomplishments, the simple form of these predicates refers not to the complete process but only to the final portion of it.

Examples of achievements that consist of clear and potentially lengthy processes are *dying* and *returning to the house*. Such predicates easily take the progressive form, and in such cases the progressive refers to a portion of the complete process. Again, because of the definiteness of the change involved, and because the progressive form refers to only a portion of the complete process, an achievement *A was V-ing* does not imply that at some time *A V-ed*, the same as with accomplishments. Some achievements are relatively point-like in nature and consequently do not tend to occur in the progressive. Examples of such predicates are *losing an umbrella, finding the treasure*, and *spotting a plane*.

We distinguish between complete and incomplete achievements in the same way we do for accomplishments. Complete achievements have as their act the entire process, whereas incomplete achievements have as their act only a portion of the complete process. So far, the representations for both achievements and accomplishments are basically the same. The way in which they differ—property (c), is discussed later.

TENSE AND ASPECT

The linguistic notions of *tense* and *aspect* play a central role in the analysis of narratives. Tense is used to relate the time of the event referred to in a sentence to the time of the utterance of that sentence. In his well-known analysis of tense, Reichenbach (1947) introduced the important concept of temporal reference points. He distinguished three such points: *Speech Time* (ST), the time at which the utterance is made; *Event Time* (ET), the interval of time occupied by the event; and *Reference Time* (RT), a time point which is determined by the tense of the sentence. A past tense sentence has a Reference Time in the past, *before* the Speech Time.

Reichenbach's analyses of the six basic and perfect tenses in terms of his reference points is shown in the following diagram, in which the arrow shows the direction of time from the past to the future. Times separated by commas are understood as being simultaneous.

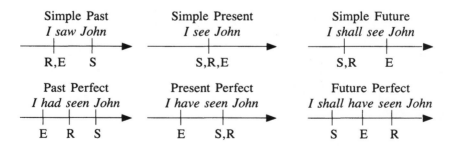

According to Comrie (1976), aspects are "different ways of viewing the internal temporal constituency of a situation" (p. 3). Comrie distinguished two principal aspects. The *perfective aspect* occurs when a situation is referred to without reference to its internal temporal constituency; that is, the situation is seen as a whole. The *imperfective aspect* occurs when explicit reference is made to the internal temporal constituency of a situation; that is, the situation is viewed from within. Thus, the perfective/imperfective distinction has to do with the way events are described. For example, in the sentence *John was reading when I entered,* the second clause, *I entered,* has perfective aspect, whereas the first clause, *John was reading,* has imperfective aspect, because it makes explicit reference to an internal portion of John's reading.

In English, the relation between the progressive and the nonprogressive (simple) form of verbs, providing we restrict ourselves to nonstative verbs and exclude habitual meaning, is one of imperfectivity versus perfectivity. That is, events described using the progessive are viewed imperfectively, whereas in most cases, events described using the simple form of the verb are being viewed perfectively. Statives are already typically viewed imperfectively, so most stative verbs do not take the progressive without a change of sense.

In our survey of the different types of events and their representations, we showed that each event instance has an associated interval of time, indicated by the *time* arc. This interval, the *Event Time,* is to be understood as the complete period of time occupied by the entire event from beginning to end. However, this interval does not function well in the role of Reichenbach's Event Time. Instead, we introduce a new interval of time, called the *Attachment Time* (AT), that is related to an event's Event Time as described below, and that functions as the interval directly related to the Reference Time and to the intervals referred to by time adverbials.

The ways in which Attachment Times are related to Event Times of various types of events is shown in Figs. 7.4–7.7. In these figures, and in most of the subsequent figures, event representations are compressed into the event node, represented by a triangle labelled by its associated tenseless proposition. This is just a convention to prevent the figures from being cluttered by irrelevant material.

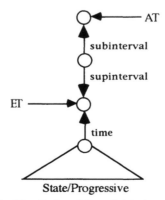

FIG. 7.4. The attachment time of states/progressives.

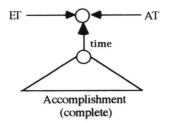

FIG. 7.5.   The attachment time of simple (complete) accomplishments.

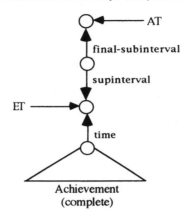

FIG. 7.6.   The attachment time of simple (complete) achievements.

The AT of a state or a progressive is related to its ET as shown in Fig. 7.4. In these cases, the AT is a subinterval of the ET. For example, with *John was sick yesterday*, all we know is that John was sick during some part of yesterday. In itself, this sentence does not tell us when John started to be sick, and it does not tell us if and when John has ceased to be sick. Therefore, we can only place a subinterval of John's illness as definitely during yesterday, and this subinterval is the Attachment Time. By having the AT be only a subinterval of the ET, this representation does not bound the extent of the event. The same is true of a progressive sentence such as *John was running yesterday*.

The AT of a simple (complete) accomplishment is related to its ET as shown in Fig. 7.5. For example, we understand *John painted a picture yesterday* as saying that John both started and completed the painting of the picture sometime during yesterday. Therefore, the event is completely contained within yesterday. We capture this property of complete accomplishments by making their ET and AT identical.

The AT of a simple (complete) achievement is related to its ET as shown in Fig. 7.6. For example, with *John died yesterday*, we understand that John reached the end of the process of dying sometime during yesterday, but we do not know when this process began. In other words, John may have been dying for several

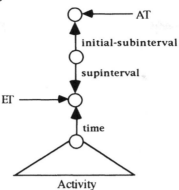

FIG. 7.7. The attachment time of simple activities and simple (incomplete) accomplishments.

days previous to yesterday. Therefore, it is, in general, only some final-subinterval of an achievement event that is bounded by such adverbials. In this way, we capture the third of the properties of achievements. Thus, we represent the difference between accomplishments and achievements as a difference in the ways that their ATs are related to their ETs.

The AT of a simple activity or of a simple (but incomplete) accomplishment is related to its ET as shown in Fig. 7.7. We usually understand a simple activity sentence as referring to the initial segment of the event. For example, *John ran at three o'clock* means that John started running at three o'clock, but says nothing about when he stopped running. Actually, in the most general case, the AT of such events is just an arbitrary, though nonzero, subinterval of the ET. In the next section, we provide additional motivation for the ways in which the ATs and the ETs of the different event types are related.

Now that we have indicated the various possible relationships between Attachment Times and the Event Times, we can show how we represent some of the tenses. Rather than trying to represent all tenses, however, we discuss only the past tenses, because these are the ones we need in our discussion of narrative. For a more complete discussion of tense, see Hornstein (1977) and Harper and Charniak (1986). As was mentioned earlier, tense is used to indicate the relation between the Speech Time and the Reference Time. Therefore, the past tense (both the simple and the progressive forms) is understood as placing the RT in the past with respect to the ST and the AT equal to the RT. Our representation

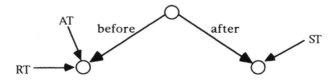

FIG. 7.8. Representation of the past tense.

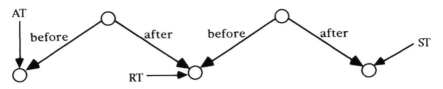

FIG. 7.9. Representation of the past perfect tense.

for the past tense is shown in Fig. 7.8. The other tense we are interested in is the past perfect. Our representation for the past perfect is shown in Fig. 7.9.

NARRATIVES AND NARRATIVE-LINES

The type of approach we use to understand the temporal structure of narratives was introduced by Hinrichs (1986). This approach makes use of a special Reference Time that interacts with the events of the story to produce the temporal structure of the story. Partee (1984) also used this approach. In the Introduction, we defined a narrative as a type of discourse used to describe sequences of events. In general, an extended narrative can be seen as consisting of one or more simpler units—narrative-lines. In the remainder of this chapter, we describe our approach to understanding the temporal structure of individual narrative-lines. Ways in which several narrative-lines can be put together to produce a large-scale narrative were discussed in Almeida (1987).

We define a *narrative-line* to be a stretch of narrative that is "controlled by," or is within the scope of, a single Reference Time. This Reference Time can be understood as representing the present moment of the story, and so we refer to this Reference Time as the *narrative now-point* (Almeida & Shapiro, 1983). It is this sense of a present moment within a narrative-line that allows the combination of the adverb *now* with a past tense sentence to be grammatical in a narrative context. Outside of a narrative context, this combination is not considered grammatical.

The narrative now-point functions within a narrative more or less the way that the actual present (the "real" now) functions in the real world. That is, everything that comes before the now-point is in the past in the world of the story, and everything that comes after the now-point is in the future from the perspective of that moment in the story. Thus, as the story progresses in time, the now-point is moved forward in time, and events that were at one point in the story future become part of the story past.

THE BASIC RULES OF NARRATION

In this section, we present the rules for extracting the story from a basic narrative-line. A *basic narrative-line* is a narrative-line with no temporal adverbials and which follows certain other simplifying restrictions. These basic narrative-lines will constitute a base case for narratives, and other types of narratives will be viewed as extensions to, or elaborations of, this base case.

The basic rules of narration are the rules which hold by default (under ordinary circumstances) in the absence of time adverbials. The only factors taken into consideration by these rules are tense, event type, aspect, and what we call the *Narrative Convention*. The Narrative Convention is that unless we (the readers) are given some sign or information to the contrary, we assume that the events of the story occurred in the order in which they are presented in the text. This is, of course, the same as the "narrative time progression" of Hirschman and Story (1981).

In English, narratives are typically written in the past tense. The past tense is used because in most narratives the events of the story are in the past with respect to the time of narration. The relationship between the events of the story and the real present plays no role in tense selection. Thus, even science-fiction stories about the (to us) distant future are written in the past tense. Because the events of the story are in the past with respect to the (usually fictional) narrator, the simple past and past progressive tenses are used to refer to events in the story present. References to the story past are made using the past perfect tenses, and references to the story future are made using the future-in-the-past tenses.

Perfective Events in the Simple Nonperfect Past

What we call *perfective events*, that is, nonprogressive accomplishments, achievements, and activities, have the temporal effect of moving the now-point forward when they are expressed in the simple past tense. Thus, in the base case, it is the occurrence of such perfective events in the story present that causes the story to develop in time. Perfective events work in the following fashion: their Reference Time, and therefore their Attachment Time, is placed after the current now-point, and then the now-point is updated to just after the Reference Time. The idea that in such cases the special Reference Time (our now-point) is moved to just after the event was introduced by Hinrichs (1986). In our system, this just after relationship is represented by having *epsilon* (ε) as the duration of the interval between the end of the Reference Time and the updated now-point. Each of the different perfective event types is understood in a slightly different way, however, because of the differing relationships between their Attachment Times and their Event Times.

The general pattern for perfective events in the past tense is shown in Fig. 7.10. We use a variable called *now*, whose value is the node which represents the current position of the story present. In many of the figures, numerical subscripts are used to indicate successive positions of the now-point; so "$_1$" indicates the first (or original) value of *now*, "$_2$" indicates the second value of *now*, and so on. It is important to emphasize that at any time during the reading of a narrative-line, there is only one value of the *now* variable. In addition, in this figure and in all subsequent figures showing the temporal structure of fragments

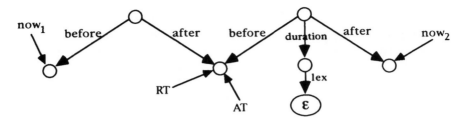

FIG. 7.10.   The temporal effect of perfective events.

of narrative, we do not include the time of narration, the Speech Time. This is simply because, in a purely past tense narrative, the relations between the ST and the events of the story are always the same—the events are before the ST.

With accomplishment events, the entire event is understood as occurring after the current now-point, with the result that the event moves the now-point to just after the end of the time interval that it occupies. This follows from the equivalence of the AT and the ET in the case of complete accomplishments. Sequences of completed accomplishments are very common in narratives. Some typical examples are:

(1) I went to the door, unlocked it, and pulled it open. (Hammett, 1929/1980a, p. 206)

(2) The doctor wrote down an address on a page in his notebook, tore it out, and handed it to Poirot. (Christie, 1937/1984b, p. 73)

The representation for Example 1, a sequence of three accomplishments, is shown in Fig. 7.11. The subscripted *nows* show the successive positions of the now-point, and the subscripted RTs show the successive RTs. (We often abbreviate some of the more commonly used arc labels as follows: *before, after,* and *duration* are abbreviated as *b, a,* and *dur,* respectively; *supinterval, subinterval, final-subinterval,* and *initial-subinterval* are abbreviated as *sup, sub, f-s-i,* and *i-s-i,* respectively.) As Fig. 7.11 indicates, the three successive events are understood as occurring in their entirety in the order in which they are described. When all three of these events have occurred and are therefore part of the story past, the position of the story present is indicated by the fourth *now*. Also, with quoted speech, which occurs frequently in many types of narrative, the events consisting of the making of such statements (as opposed to the content of the statements) are accomplishment events, and they have the same temporal effects as do other accomplishment events.

With achievement events, sometimes only a final-subinterval of the event is understood as occurring after the current now-point. As we have seen, this is modeled by having the AT be a final-subinterval of the ET. Some typical examples of achievements (in italics, emphasis added) in narrative are:

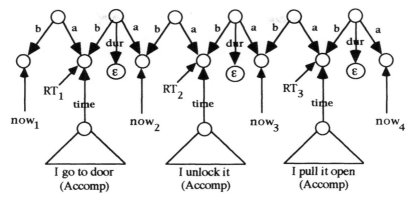

FIG. 7.11.   Representation of "I went to the door, unlocked it, and pulled it open."

(3) ". . . The envelopes are missing too." (said Mr. Leggett)
Mrs. Leggett returned with her daughter, . . . (Hammett, 1929/1980a, p. 147)

(4) *We found an automatic elevator*, rode to the fifth floor, and went down a purple-carpeted corridor to the door just beyond the stairs on the left-hand side. (Hammett, 1929/1980a, p. 170)

The representation for Example 3 is shown in Fig. 7.12. Notice that the position of the start of the returning-event is left ambiguous; we can only be sure of the position of the end of the event.

The situation with simple past tense activity events is more complex than with the preceding two event types, because the relationship between the AT and the ET of simple activities is more complicated. As we mentioned, the most commonly occurring case in narratives is where the AT is an initial-subinterval of the ET. In this case, some piece of the event, including its beginning, occurs after the current now-point, and the now-point is moved to just after that initial-subinterval. The time of the end of the complete event cannot always be determined and so is left ambiguous in the representation. Following are some examples of this case; the activity sentences are in italics (emphasis added):

(5) "Don?" I said. *I walked towards him.* "Donald!" (Francis, 1976/1978, p. 12)

(6) ". . . it would have been difficult to put it in exactly the right position." (said Poirot) *Inspector Raglan stared at the little man.* Poirot, with an air of great unconcern, flecked a speck of dust from his coat sleeve. "Well," said the inspector, . . . (Christie, 1926/1939, p. 131)

(7) "How is your father?"
She laughed. "I was going to ask you." (Hammett, 1934/1980b, p. 591)

In Example 5, a character says something (an accomplishment) and then starts to walk towards another character. The question is, has the speaker stopped

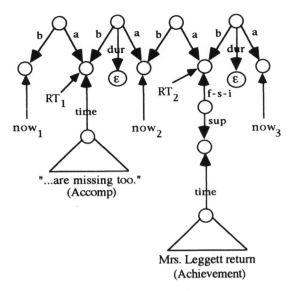

FIG. 7.12.   Representation of complete achievements, Example 3.

walking when he makes the second statement? Because it seems unclear, this is modeled by leaving the end-time of the walking ambiguous with respect to the following event. The representation for this example is shown in Fig. 7.13.

In Example 6, the *staring* is definitely still going on when Poirot flecks a speck of dust from his sleeve. In Example 7, however, we know that the *laughing* is definitely over when the laugher starts talking. This follows from the world-knowledge that laughing and talking are incompatible. The complete boundedness of the laughing can be easily modeled by adding an *equiv/equiv* relation between the AT and the ET.

The representation of simple activities is complicated, however, by the fact that there are instances in which the AT is some arbitrary subinterval of the ET rather than the initial-subinterval. In this case, the times of the beginning and the ending of the complete event are not directly related to either of the now-points. An example of this case is:

(8) A small boy of twelve or thirteen stood there staring at us with . . .
    I said: "Hello, son."
    Collinson jumped around at the sound of my voice.
    The boy said nothing. *He stared at me for at least another minute* . . . , then
    turned his back on me and walked away, . . . (Hammett, 1929/1980a, p. 169;
    emphasis added)

The staring-event described by the italicized sentence obviously did not start at this point in the story, but is instead only a part of the larger staring-event

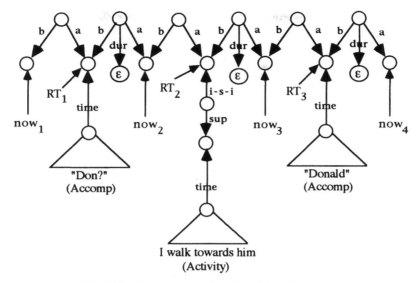

FIG. 7.13. Representation of simple activities, Example 5.

mentioned in the first sentence of this example. Fortunately, such cases are often signaled by the presence of a for-adverbial, such as the one in this example, where the duration is modified by a word such as *another* or *additional*.

The really central property of perfective events is that they imply the passage of time. This passage of time is captured, at least partly, in our representation by the movement of the now-point.

Hinrichs' (1986) approach to the treatment of perfective events differs from ours in that Hinrichs placed each new accomplishment or achievement within or during the then-current Reference Time, rather than after it, as we do. To Hinrichs' overall approach, Partee (1984) added the assumption that in a "linear narrative," the Reference Times strictly follow one another. Neither Hinrichs nor Partee used a representation of the present moment of the story, such as our now-point. Also, unlike us, Hinrichs and Partee treated simple activities in the same way as states and progressives, the handling of which we discuss in the next section.

Imperfective Events in the Nonperfect Past

The *imperfective events* are states and progressive accomplishments, achievements, and activities. When expressed in the simple past (for states) or the past progressive (for the other classes), imperfective events are understood as temporally containing the current now-point, so that the event is viewed from within from the current now-point. Because the now-point is ordinarily just after some perfective event, the imperfective event is tied to that event; that is, the imperfective event is typically seen as also containing the immediately preceding event. If the imperfective event does not contain that event, then these two events are almost always seen as being causally related, with the perfective event causing the coming-into-being of the imperfective event. At any rate, our basic representation is ambiguous between these two cases, so we are not ordinarily concerned with this issue.

These properties of imperfective events are modeled by making the AT of the event (which, remember, is a sub-interval of the ET for states and progressives) equal to the current now-point. In addition, with imperfective events, there is no sense of temporal motion such as there is with perfective events. Therefore, the now-point stays where it is. In this way, successive states and/or progressives can be used to build up complex descriptions. Some typical examples with imperfective events are:

(9) ". . . I haven't seen Macauley since the murder and I haven't even been following it in the newspapers."
　　The telephone was ringing again. Nora gave us our drinks and went to answer it. (Hammett, 1934/1980b, p. 623)

(10) I went up there. Gabrielle, in a low-cut dark silk gown, was sitting stiff and straight on the edge of a leather rocker. Her face was white and sullen. She was looking at a handkerchief stretched between her hands. (Hammett, 1929/1980a, p. 267)

The representation for Example 9 is shown in Fig. 7.14, and that for Example 10 is shown in Fig. 7.15. Notice that in Example 9, we understand that the telephone starts to ring sometime before the speaker finishes his statement. In addition, the

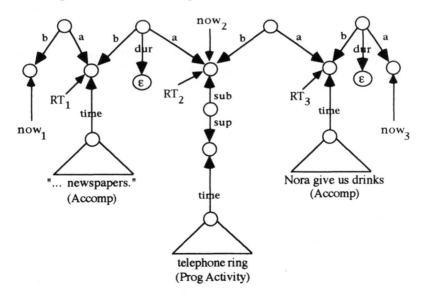

FIG. 7.14.　Representation of imperfective events, Example 9.

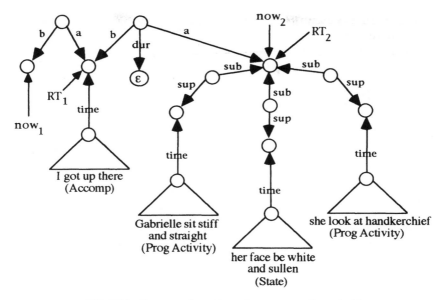

FIG. 7.15. Representation of imperfective events, Example 10.

telephone continues to ring until Nora answers it sometime after she gives out the drinks. If, in this example, the progressive *The telephone was ringing* is changed to the corresponding simple form *The telephone rang*, then we would understand that the telephone started to ring after the speaker completed his statement. Example 10 is a typical illustration of how a complex description of a situation at a single point of time can be built up by a series of progressive and/or stative sentences. We understand all of the events described by these progressive and stative sentences as temporally overlapping at least at the now-point.

Our treatment of states and progressives is essentially the same as that of Hinrichs and Partee. Hinrichs gave the following example (discussed in Partee, 1984) of a state that does not overlap the immediately preceding event:

> Jameson entered the room, shut the door carefully, and switched off the light. It was pitch dark around him because the Venetian blinds were closed. (p. 254)

Clearly the state of its being pitch dark does not start until Jameson switches off the light, and therefore this state cannot overlap or contain the event. Notice, though, that there is a causal connection between this event and the given state.

Events in the Past Perfect Tense

As we stated, the past perfect tenses (both simple and progressive) are used to refer to the story past. An event is placed in the story past by making its RT equivalent to the current now-point, thus making its AT before the current now-point. Because the event is understood as being in the story past, it does not, regardless of its type, cause the now-point to move. Some examples of past perfect sentences in narratives are:

(11) "Are you sure?"
"No, but that's the best we've been able to do so far. There's Fitzstephan now." Looking through the cafe door, I had seen the novelist's lanky back at the hotel desk. "Excuse me a moment." (Hammett, 1929/1980a, p. 244)

(12) There was a sudden brusque movement from Theresa. She had risen and was standing by the mantelpiece. She quickly lit another cigarette. (Christie, 1937/1984b, p. 111)

The representation for Example 11 is shown in Fig. 7.16. In this example, it is clear that at least the beginning of the seeing of the novelist's (Fitzstephan's) back must have preceeded the stating of *There's Fitzstephan now*. Therefore, we could infer that the interval indicated as AT, node 2, is before the interval of the statement, node 1. Example 12 is interesting and unusual in that the sudden brusque movement described in the first sentence is the same event as the rising described in the following past perfect sentence. The use of the past perfect indicates that the rising is being described from a point of time that is after the brusque movement event. Such examples offer some support for the idea that past perfect events are before the now-point rather than before the event just before the now-point.

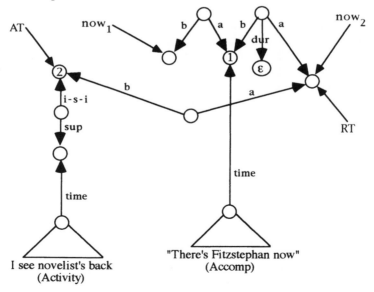

FIG. 7.16. Representation of events in the story past, Example 11.

NARRATIVE LINES WITH FRAME ADVERBIALS

Most extended narratives contain time adverbials. Time adverbials are used to specify temporal relations between events, to place events within calendrical intervals, and to give the durations of events. Time adverbials can be divided into two large classes according to how comfortably they fit into narrative contexts. What we call *nonnarrative adverbials* seem to be by their nature directly related to the Speech Time. Examples of such adverbials are *today, yesterday, tomorrow, this Tuesday,* and *three days ago.* Such adverbials are common in conversation but are somewhat awkward in narratives. When they do occasionally appear in narratives, there is usually a sense that the narrator is identifying very closely with the story present, and so the now-point is identified with the Speech Time. *Narrative adverbials,* on the other hand, are not directly tied to the Speech Time and so are much more free to function in narratives.

In this section, we expand our analysis of narratives to include narrative-lines containing members of the narrative subclass of *frame adverbials. Frame adverbials* refer to intervals of time which are used to bound or frame the temporal locations of events and of Reference Times (Bennett & Partee, 1972). There are two types of such adverbials: *interval*—large intervals of time, and *point*—small intervals of time. We call the interval referred to by such adverbials the *frame-interval.* (Additional classes of narrative adverbials were treated in Almeida, 1987.)

In the case in which the frame-interval gives the temporal location of an event, it is the Attachment Time of the event, and not its Event Time, that is directly related to the frame-interval. Therefore, in all such cases, the AT of the event is asserted to be a subinterval of, that is, during, the frame-interval. Given our earlier analysis of the ATs for different types of events, this means that it is incorrect to say that the frame-interval bounds the event, because it may only bound part of the event.

Since interval frame adverbials refer to large intervals of time, these intervals typically temporally contain not only the event(s) of the sentence containing the adverbial, but also, by default, the events of the succeeding sentences, until some new frame-interval is established. The frame-intervals referred to by point frame adverbials do not generally have this property because of their small size. The remainder of this section surveys several different types of frame adverbials.

The two prepositions *on* and *in* seem to have complementary distributions in the usage considered here, and so they are treated as having the same meaning. *On* occurs with NPs which refer to calendrical days, weekends, and subintervals of a day where the day is also mentioned or is strongly implied. *In* occurs with NPs that refer to calendrical intervals both larger and smaller than a day. In both cases, the preposition can often be deleted with no apparent change in meaning.

Adverbials of the form *on N(day-of-week)* generally refer to the day of that type within an already picked out week. On the other hand, adverbials of the form *on a N(day-of-week)* are used when no such week has been established. For example, compare:

> (13) We went to Boston last week. We arrived there on Monday. (vs. We arrived there on a Monday.)
>
> (14) We went to Boston last month. We arrived there on a Monday. (vs. We arrived there on Monday.)

In Example 13, the first sentence picks out a week as a context and so the continuation sounds best with *on Monday*, which of course refers to the Monday of that week. In Example 14, however, no such week is picked out and so the continuation sounds best with *on a Monday*, because there is more than one Monday in a month.

By default, in a narrative, the "picked out" week is the current week of the story, that is, the week that contains the current now-point. Figure 7.17 shows the representation for the following case: It is a Monday in the story; we then read *On Thursday John walked to the store.* In this figure, node 1 represents the current week, and node 2 represents Monday, which contains the initial now-point. The presentential adverbial *on Thursday* picks out the Thursday (node 3) of the current week, and since Thursday is later in the week than Monday, the now-point is updated to during that Thursday. The RT of the event (an accomplishment) is then related to the now-point in the standard way for perfective events in the simple past tense and this RT is further made a subinterval of Thursday. Finally, the now-point is updated to just beyond this RT and is also made a subinterval of Thursday. In this way, Johns walk to the store is asserted to have been on Thursday, and the story present is updated to that Thursday, as well.

In the stories we examined, one of the most common types of on/in-adverbial has the form *on the following N(day-subinterval)*. Some examples are:

> (15) "The next thing to do is to catch the twelve o'clock train to Torquay tomorrow and verify our brilliant conclusions." [said Tommy]
> Armed with a portfolio of photographs, Tommy and Tuppence duly established themselves in a first class carriage the following morning, and booked seats for the second lunch. (Christie, 1929/1984a, p. 172)
>
> (16) When he returned to the flat on the following evening, Tuppence came flying out of her bedroom to meet him. (Christie, 1929/1984a, p. 57)
>
> (17) On the following night he himself was given a proof. (Christie, 1929/1984a, p. 123)
>
> (18) Franklin Clarke arrived at 3 o'clock on the following afternoon and came straight to the point without beating about the bush. (Christie, 1936/1941, p. 88)

All of the adverbials in these examples have parallel interpretations. The morning referred to in Example 15 is the morning of the day after the day on

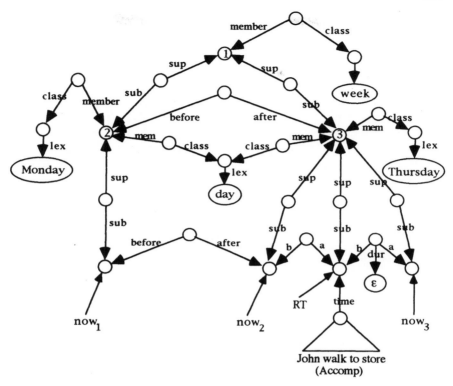

FIG. 7.17.   Representation of "On Thursday John walked to the store."

which the preceding statement was made. In Example 16, the evening referred to is the evening of the day after the day of the immediately preceding occurrences. Similarly, in Example 17, it is the night of the next day that is being referred to, and in Example 18, the adverbial refers to three o'clock in the afternoon of the next day. The basic representation for *on the following N(day-subinterval)* is given in Fig. 7.18. Starting with the now-point during some day, the adverbial updates the now-point to sometime during the relevant subinterval of the next day. The event is then attached to this now-point in the usual way, and is asserted to be during that interval.

On/in the following N may also be used to refer to intervals other than day-subintervals. In order to describe the behavior of this adverbial in general, it is necessary to distinguish between *covering* and *noncovering* interval types. Examples of covering interval types are *days, weeks, months,* and *years.* They have the property that the complete set of instances of any of these types covers or partitions the timeline completely; that is, there are no gaps between successive instances of each of these types. With the noncovering interval types, however, there are gaps between successive instances of each of those types. Examples of

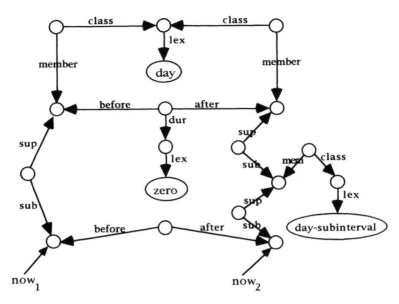

FIG. 7.18.   Representation of "on the following N(day-subinterval)."

such interval types are *Mondays, Aprils*, and *mornings*. Typically, such intervals have *standard covering intervals* which contain them. So, for instance, Mondays are subintervals of weeks, Aprils are subintervals of years, and mornings are subintervals of days.

The general rule for interpreting *on/in the following N* has two cases. If *N* is a covering type, then the interval picked out by the adverbial is the instance of that covering type that immediately follows (or is met by) the current instance of that type. Thus, *on the following day* refers to the day immediately after the current day. If *N* is a noncovering type, then the interval picked out by the adverbial is the instance of that type that is a subinterval of the instance of its standard covering type that immediately follows the current instance of that covering type. Thus, as we have seen, *on the following afternoon* refers to the afternoon which is a subinterval of the day that immediately follows the current day. Adverbials of the form *on/in the previous N(interval)* are analogous to adverbials of the form *on/in the following N(interval)*, with the difference being that these adverbials refer in the opposite direction, that is, to the story past.

Examples of adverbials of the form *on/in that N(interval)* are:

(19) Somehow or other, a spade was duly produced, and that night, late, two figures might have been seen stealing into the grounds of the Red House. (Christie, 1929/1984a, p. 45)

(20) Spade returned to his office at ten minutes past five that evening. (Hammett, 1930/1984, p. 45)

(21) Later that day he drove down to Burminster Street, which runs between Chain Walk and Stafford Quay, . . . (Gilbert, 1982/1983, p. 130)

In a narrative, when a that-adverbial is used to refer to a covering interval, it is always the current instance of that covering type that is picked out. For instance, *that day* refers to the current day. With noncovering intervals, however, the interval picked out may be in the past, present, or future. Example 21 illustrates the use of the that-adverbial where the now-point is already during an instance of the type of interval being referred to. Of course, with a covering interval, such as *day*, this is necessarily the case. In such cases, the movement of the now-point is directed by the use of a modifier such as *later*, so that whereas the now-point to which the event will be related is moved ahead, it is still kept within the interval. When reference is made to a past segment of the interval, the adverb *earlier* is used, along of course with the past perfect tense. When the now-point is not during an instance of the type of interval being referred to, the interval picked out may be in the past or the future. This can only happen, of course, when the interval is of a noncovering type. In this case, the interval picked out is the instance of that type which is a subinterval of the current instance of that type's standard covering type.

Examples of adverbials of the form *on/in the next N(interval)* are:

(22) . . . , and the next day Ilaria drove her in the Fiat to the hairdresser, . . . (Francis, 1984/1985, p. 102)

(23) The next morning, during the drive to the office, Cenci said, ". . ." (Francis, 1984/1985, p. 62)

This adverbial seems to have the same meaning as *on/in the following N*. Interestingly, there seems to be a distinction in usage between *the next N* and *next N*—the adverbial with and without the determiner. The version with the determiner is used in narratives, whereas the version without the determiner is directly related to the Speech Time and is, therefore, a non-narrative adverbial.

Examples of adverbials of the form *at NP(point of time)* are:

(24) Spade returned to his office at ten minutes past five that evening. (Hammett, 1934/1984, p. 45)

(25) At half past five he went into the kitchen and made more coffee. (Hammett, 1934/1984, p. 235)

Although at-adverbials are classified as point-adverbials, it is useful to treat them as being interval adverbials where the interval involved is relatively small. Their representation is similar to the interval adverbial representations given previously.

The interval of an at-adverbial provides, first of all, a measure of vagueness; that is, the size of this interval defines how precisely we are referring to the point-of-time in question. For example, we can modify the adverbial, as in *at precisely eight o'clock, at about eight o'clock, at around eight o'clock*, etc. The other purpose of this interval is to account for the strangeness of sentences such as *At 3 o'clock John painted a picture* and, much worse, *At 3 o'clock John built a house*. The problem with these examples is that the events described are typically lengthy, and yet when combined with the point-adverbial, they are understood as being short; hence, we have a conflict. We account for this conflict by treating this situation in exactly the same way that we treat similar cases with the interval-adverbials; that is, we constrain the ATs of the associated events to be during the interval introduced by the adverbial. Of course, one way in which we can avoid the conflict is to understand the at-adverbial as to give the start-time of the extended event.

One important difference between the at-adverbial and the larger interval adverbials, is that the at-adverbial's interval is so small that succeeding events are unlikely to also be during that time. Instead, we place these events in the smallest interval containing that point of time.

AN IMPLEMENTATION

We implemented a system that can read a simple narrative and produce as output a model of the events of the story along with the temporal relations that hold among those events. The natural language parser is implemented as an Augmented Transition Network, and the story model is represented in SNePS. As the system processes each new sentence, it builds representations for the described event(s) and any new time intervals introduced in the sentence, integrating these representations into the developing story model. In this section, we show a run of our system using as input the following example narrative:

> John was walking to the office. John entered the office at three o'clock in the afternoon. The secretary was busy. The secretary was typing a letter. John waited for ten minutes. John left the office. On Thursday John returned in the morning. The secretary gave John a check. On the following Tuesday John returned to the office. John had lost the check on the previous afternoon.

At the beginning of each run, the system assigns a new value to the variable *now* (the now-point of the story), and it builds representations for the current (within the story) day and week. Reading the progressive accomplishment, *John was walking to the office*, adds the following assertions to the network:[1]

---

[1]Each expression enclosed in parentheses and beginning with "m<n>", where "n" is an integer represents a node labeled "m<n>". The rest of the expression lists the labeled arcs emanating from node "m<n>", the nodes these arcs point to, and any labeled arcs emanating from them, and so on. For example, (m18 . . .) and (m17 . . .) represent the following network:

```
(m18 (sup-interval (b7)) (sub-interval (b1)))
(m17 (event (m16 (time (b7)))) (act (b6)) (actor (b4)))
(m15 (sub-act (b6)) (act (m12 (to (b5)) (predicator (m9 (lex (walk)))))))
(m14 (class (m13 (lex (accomplishment)))))
    (member (m12 (to (b5)) (predicator (m9 (lex (walk)))))))
(m11 (member (b5)) (class (m10 (lex (office)))))
(m8 (named (b4)) (name (m7 (lex (John))))))
(m6 (sup-interval (b3)) (sub-interval (b2)))
(m5 (member (b3)) (class (m4 (lex (week))))))
(m3 (sup-interval (b2)) (sub-interval (b1)))
(m2 (member (b2)) (class (m1 (lex (day))))))
```

The initial value of *now* is node b1, the current day is represented by node b2, and the current week is represented by node b3.

Reading the accomplishment sentence, *John entered the office at three o'clock in the afternoon*, adds the following assertions to the network:

```
(m35 (sup-interval (b8)) (sub-interval (b12)))
(m34 (duration (m33 (lex (epsilon)))) (after (b12)) (before (b9)))
(m32 (sup-interval (b8)) (sub-interval (b9)))
(m31 (duration (b11)) (after (b9)) (before (b1)))
(m30 (sup-interval (b2)) (sub-interval (b10)))
(m29 (sup-interval (b10)) (sub-interval (b8)))
(m28 (member (b10)) (class (m27 (lex (afternoon))))))
(m26 (event (m25 (time (b9))))
    (act (m23 (object (b5)) (predicator (m19 (lex (enter))))))
    (actor (b4)))
(m24 (class (m13 (lex (accomplishment)))))
    (member (m23 (object (b5)) (predicator (m19 (lex (enter)))))))
(m22 (class (m21 (hour (m20 (lex (three)))))) (member (b8)))
```

Notice that the system assumes that the afternoon referred to in this sentence is the afternoon (node b10) of the current day (node b2). Three o'clock is represented by node b8. This sentence causes the now-point to be updated to a time (node b12) during three o'clock.

Reading the stative sentence, *The secretary was busy*, adds the following assertions to the network:

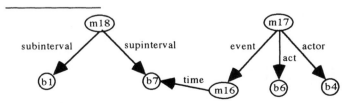

Node labels that appear in more than one expression represent the same node in each expression.

(m43 (sup-interval (b14)) (sub-interval (b12)))
(m42 (event (m41 (time (b14)))) (property (m38 (lex (busy)))) (object (b13)))
(m40 (class (m39 (lex (state)))) (member (m38 (lex (busy)))))
(m37 (member (b13)) (class (m36 (lex (secretary)))))

Since the now-point is not changed, the system understands the secretary to be busy at three o'clock.

Reading the progressive accomplishment sentence, *The secretary was typing a letter*, adds the following assertions to the network:

(m52 (sup-interval (b17)) (sub-interval (b12)))
(m51 (event (m50 (time (b17)))) (act (b16)) (actor (b13)))
(m49 (sub-act (b16))
     (act (m47 (perf-object (b15)) (predicator (m44 (lex (type)))))))
(m48 (class (m13 (lex (accomplishment))))
     (member (m47 (perf-object (b15)) (predicator (m44 (lex (type)))))))
(m46 (member (b15)) (class (m45 (lex (letter)))))

Again, the now-point is not changed and so the secretary is understood to be in the process of typing the letter at three o'clock.

Reading the activity sentence with a duration, *John waited for ten minutes*, adds the following assertions to the network:

(m66 (sup-interval (b10)) (sub-interval (b21)))
(m65 (duration (m33 (lex (epsilon)))) (after (b21)) (before (b19)))
(m64 (sup-interval (b10)) (sub-interval (b19)))
(m63 (duration (b20)) (after (b19)) (before (b12)))
(m62 (has-duration (b19))
     (duration (m56 (quantity (m55 (lex (ten)))) (unit (m54 (lex (minute)))))))
(m61 (initial-sub-interval (b19)) (sup-interval (b18)))
(m60 (event (m59 (time (b18)))) (act (m53 (lex (wait)))) (actor (b4)))
(m58 (class (m57 (lex (activity)))) (member (m53 (lex (wait)))))

This time, the now-point is moved to node b21. Notice that the event is assumed to have taken place during the current afternoon but not during three o'clock.

Reading the accomplishment sentence, *John left the office*, adds the following assertions to the network:

(m75 (sup-interval (b10)) (sub-interval (b24)))
(m74 (duration (m33 (lex (epsilon)))) (after (b24)) (before (b22)))
(m73 (sup-interval (b10)) (sub-interval (b22)))
(m72 (duration (b23)) (after (b22)) (before (b21)))
(m71 (event (m70 (time (b22))))
     (act (m68 (object (b5)) (predicator (m67 (lex (leave))))))
     (actor (b4)))

```
(m69 (class (m13 (lex (accomplishment))))
    (member (m68 (object (b5)) (predicator (m67 (lex (leave))))))))
```

The now-point is moved to node b24. The leaving also takes place during the current afternoon.

Reading the achievement sentence, *On Thursday John returned in the morning*, adds the following assertions to the network:

```
(m96 (sup-interval (b29)) (sub-interval (b33)))
(m95 (duration (m33 (lex (epsilon)))) (after (b33)) (before (b31)))
(m94 (sup-interval (b29)) (sub-interval (b31)))
(m93 (duration (b32)) (after (b31)) (before (b27)))
(m92 (final-sub-interval (b31)) (sup-interval (b30)))
(m91 (sup-interval (b29)) (sub-interval (b27)))
(m90 (sup-interval (b25)) (sub-interval (b29)))
(m89 (event (m88 (time (b30)))) (act (m83 (lex (return)))) (actor (b4)))
(m87 (class (m86 (lex (achievement)))) (member (m83 (lex (return)))))
(m85 (member (b29)) (class (m84 (lex (morning)))))
(m82 (sup-interval (b25)) (sub-interval (b27)))
(m81 (duration (b28)) (after (b27)) (before (b24)))
(m80 (sup-interval (b3)) (sub-interval (b25)))
(m79 (duration (b26)) (after (b25)) (before (b2)))
(m78 (member (b25)) (class (m77 (lex (Thursday)))))
(m76 (member (b25)) (class (m1 (lex (day)))))
```

The system assumes that the Thursday referred to in this sentence is the Thursday of the current week. Also, because the sentence is in a nonperfect past tense, the system assumes that this Thursday is later in the week than the unnamed day during which the previously described events occurred. Therefore, the now-point (node b33) is updated to the morning (node b29) of this Thursday (node b25).

Reading the accomplishment sentence, *The secretary gave John a check*, adds the following assertions to the network:

```
(m107 (sup-interval (b29)) (sub-interval (b37)))
(m106 (duration (m33 (lex (epsilon)))) (after (b37)) (before (b35)))
(m105 (sup-interval (b29)) (sub-interval (b35)))
(m104 (duration (b36)) (after (b35)) (before (b33)))
(m103 (event (m102 (time (b35))))
    (act (m100 (recipient (b4)) (object (b34)) (predicator (m97 (lex (give))))))
    (actor (b13)))
(m101 (class (m13 (lex (accomplishment))))
    (member (m100 (recipient (b4)) (object (b34)) (predicator (m97 (lex (give)))))))
(m99 (member (b34)) (class (m98 (lex (check)))))
```

This event is assumed to have occurred on Thursday morning.

Reading the achievement sentence, *On the following Tuesday John returned to the office*, adds the following assertions to the network:

```
(m125 (sup-interval (b39)) (sub-interval (b45)))
(m124 (duration (m33 (lex (epsilon)))) (after (b45)) (before (b43)))
(m123 (sup-interval (b39)) (sub-interval (b43)))
(m122 (duration (b44)) (after (b43)) (before (b40)))
(m121 (final-sub-interval (b43)) (sup-interval (b42)))
(m120 (event (m119 (time (b42))))
    (act (m117 (to (b5)) (predicator (m83 (lex (return))))))
    (actor (b4)))
(m118 (class (m86 (lex (achievement))))
    (member (m117 (to (b5)) (predicator (m83 (lex (return)))))))
(m116 (sup-interval (b39)) (sub-interval (b40)))
(m115 (duration (b41)) (after (b40)) (before (b37)))
(m114 (class (m1 (lex (day)))) (member (b39)))
(m113 (sup-interval (b38)) (sub-interval (b39)))
(m112 (member (b39)) (class (m111 (lex (Tuesday)))))
(m110 (after (b38)) (duration (m108 (lex (zero)))) (before (b3)))
(m109 (member (b38)) (class (m4 (lex (week)))))
```

The now-point (node b45) is updated to during the Tuesday (node b39) of the following week (node b38).

Reading the achievement sentence, *John had lost the check on the previous afternoon*, adds the following assertions to the network:

```
(m138 (sub-interval (b49)) (sup-interval (b47)))
(m137 (duration (b50)) (after (b45)) (before (b49)))
(m136 (final-sub-interval (b49)) (sup-interval (b48)))
(m135 (event (m134 (time (b48))))
    (act (m132 (object (b34)) (predicator (m126 (lex (lose))))))
    (actor (b4)))
(m133 (class (m86 (lex (achievement))))
    (member (m132 (object (b34)) (predicator (m126 (lex (lose)))))))
(m131 (sup-interval (b46)) (sub-interval (b47)))
(m130 (member (b47)) (class (m27 (lex (afternoon)))))
(m129 (sup-interval (b38)) (sub-interval (b46)))
(m128 (before (b46)) (duration (m108 (lex (zero)))) (after (b39)))
(m127 (member (b46)) (class (m1 (lex (day)))))
```

The afternoon referred to is the afternoon (node b47) of the day (node b46) immediately before the current day (node b39). Both the use of the past perfect tense and this type of adverbial indicate that this event occurred in the story-past. Consequently, the now-point is not changed.

SUMMARY

In this chapter, we examined some of the major issues involved in understanding the temporal structure of narratives. Central to our discussion were the concepts of the *narrative now-point* and a *narrative-line*. The *narrative now-point* is a special Reference Time, used to represent the present moment within the story. Much of the analysis of how different event-types, tenses, aspects, and time adverbials function within a narrative concerns their interaction with, and effect on, this now-point. We define a *narrative-line* as a stretch of narrative controlled by, or within the scope of, a single now-point. By restricting ourselves to basic "well-behaved" narratives, we are able to define and implement a simple set of general rules for extracting the temporal structure of a story from a narrative.[2]

---

[2]My representations for different event types have changed since the work reported in this chapter was done. These more recent representations are described in Almeida (1989, 1992).

8

COMPUTATIONAL REPRESENTATION OF SPACE

Albert Hanyong Yuhan
AT&T Bell Laboratories

Stuart C. Shapiro
State University of New York at Buffalo

The purpose of this chapter is to provide an analysis of the domain of spatial information and the spatial reference frame problem in the context of understanding natural language narratives, and to present a model for solving the reference frame problem.

In the following sections, we provide the analysis of spatial information and the reference frame problem, describe three strategies and six heuristic rules[1] for resolving reference frame problems, and describe the computational system that demonstrates the model for resolving reference frame problems. We then provide examples of an AI system, called Cassie, processing a short narrative requiring various types of spatial information.

Spatial Information and the Reference Frame Problem

Spatial information may include information about the position, motion, orientation, shape, extent, topology, and so on, of objects or events. If direction of any kind is involved, the meaning of a spatial expression depends on what direction was indicated, the ground relative to which the direction was given, the context in which the direction was mentioned, and so on. As Clifford described (1955), spatial information is essentially relational:

> Just as the "George" has only position relative to the other buildings in the town, or the town itself relative to other towns, so a body in space has only position

---

[1]Nine additional rules are proposed in Yuhan (1991).

relative to other bodies in space. To speak of the position of the earth in space is meaningless unless we are thinking at the same time of the Sun or of Jupiter, or of a star—that is, of some one or other of the celestial bodies. (p. 135)

Spatial information about some event or object is given as a relation with respect to some reference, whether that reference is a point, a line, a plane, or anything else, abstract or concrete, explicitly or implicitly expressed. Whereas in linguistic expressions, reference is ordinarily made to some presupposed object, in spatial references about a directional relation, the reference object alone cannot fully clarify the spatial information involved. A grid-like system is needed around the reference object to determine the meaning of directionality. For this reason, understanding of a spatial expression is not complete unless the object serving as the hinge of the reference is properly identified, and the orientation of an imaginary grid-like system serving as the frame of the reference is properly recognized. As Talmy (1978; 1983) noted, the fundamental mechanism of linguistic description of spatial information is the projection of a schema in which a figure object's spatial situation is depicted against a ground object within a stationary reference frame. Henceforth, we define the *reference frame* to be an appropriately established orientational system centered at a certain reference origin. This definition is largely consistent with notions of reference frames discussed in the literature. Our definition of spatial reference frame is an attempt to formalize a recognized problem rather than an attempt to identify a new problem.

In ordinary uses, the ground, which functions as the reference point of the spatial information expression, is given explicitly, whereas the reference frame is mostly implicit. But without determination of the correct reference frame, understanding of spatial information is uncertain and incomplete. Clark's example clearly showed this point:

> [. . .] to the girl lying on the beach, one could say, "There is a fly three inches above your knee," and this could be taken to mean either "There is a fly flying three inches vertically from your knee," or "There is a fly on your leg three inches headward from your knee." (Clark, 1973, p. 44)

This ambiguity arises from the fact that the fly scene can be pictured within either of two competing reference frames: one characterized by the up–down direction determined by the gravitation-based geographical reference frame, and another characterized by the up–down direction determined by the human body's canonical posture based on the ground object's intrinsic reference frame.

We adopt Sondheimer's (1976) terminology, reference frame problem, to refer to the problem of establishing the most appropriate reference frame to interpret a given spatial expression. The decision-making involved in resolving the problem goes beyond recognizing the surface form of the expression. Often, the reference frame problem is not completely resolved by the information in, or inferred from

the utterance. Hearers frequently rely on their visual sense to establish an un-
equivocal reference frame. For instance, in the example of a girl at the beach,
the girl may visually check the competing alternatives. Although reference frame
problems may be resolved in different ways by different people, we consider
only the problems found in narrative texts in which people generally agree on
the reference frames.

AN ANALYSIS OF NARRATIVE SPACE

Semantic Structure of Spatial Events

An event can be represented as a proposition that something occurred at a certain
time and at a certain place. We refer to the time as the *event time*, the place as
the *event place*, and the something that occurred as the *event affair*. The event
affair can be represented as a proposition. For example, in Sentence 1:

(1) In his office yesterday, Jim called Tom.

the event time is "yesterday" (relative to whenever today is understood to be),
the event place is Jim's office, and the event affair is the proposition *Jim call
Tom*. A *spatial event affair* is an event affair involving a motion or station of
any participant. The event affairs expressed by the Sentences 2a and 2b:

(2) a. Mary stayed in the room.
b. Tom pitched a ball to the catcher.

are spatial because the sentences are about Mary's station in the room and the
ball's move to the catcher.

Surface Conflation of Spatial Verbs

A spatial event may consist of two underlying propositional components. One
is the proposition representing the move or station of the figure object, and the
other is the one representing the activity (initiated by the agent) that causes,
accompanies, or contains in it a move of the figure constituent. For instance,
Sentence 2b can be analyzed into two separate deep level propositions—one that
describes Tom's activity of throwing a ball in the direction aligned to the catcher,
and another that describes the ball's move from Tom to the catcher. Thus, the
surface expression, *Tom pitched a ball to the catcher* is thought of as a *conflation*
at the surface level of the two underlying propositions. For convenience, we call
the component that represents the move or station of a figure the *spatial component*, and the component that represents the other activity, the *nonspatial component*. The spatial component is realized as a deep level proposition consisting

of a figure, a deep statio-motional verb (either *BE-LOC* for the figure's station, or *MOVE* for the figure's move), and appropriate spatial case constituents satisfying the statio-motional verb's valence structure. The nonspatial component is realized as a deep level proposition consisting of an agent, a deep verb for the agent's nonspatial activity, and possibly, some other case constituents in the valence structure. Hereafter, we will call this nonspatial activity component associated with the spatial component the *spatially associated activity*, and the act (such as the act of pitching) that constitutes the centroid of the valence structure of the spatially associated activity the *spatially associated act*.

Spatial Deep Cases and Proximity Relations

Spatial relations are usually expressed in English by means of prepositional phrases. At the surface level, a prepositional phrase is begun by a preposition, a compound preposition cluster, or an implicit preposition. Not all spatial prepositions have the same semantic complexity, despite their ostensibly similar syntactic behavior. For example, Sentence 3:

(3) John ran into the room.

can be analyzed as meaning that John was at first at some place outside the room, and John ran to a place X where X is in the room. This analysis indicates that *into* is a surface composition of *to* and *in*. We view *to* as a predicate that states that an abstract place X is the goal of John's move, and *in* as a predicate that states that the abstract place X has the particular spatial relation *in* to the *room.*

Natural language is equipped with a spectrum of spatial relations (such as *in, on, above, under, in front of,* etc.) that relate abstract places to reference objects. Because these spatial relations constitute propositions that assert an abstract place as a satellite place within the semantic vicinity of the ground object, we call them *spatial proximity functions*. These are typically expressed by *directional relations* (such as *in front of, behind, to the left of*), *inclusion relations* (such as *in, out of, on, between, beside*), or *distance relations* (such as *near to, away from*).

Spatial case relations and various spatial proximity functions are both coded in English by spatial prepositions (as well as by some preposition clusters). Clark (1973) analyzed the propositions *into* and *onto* as compositions of *in* with *to* and *on* with *to*, respectively. Our analysis is an extension of Clark's analysis. English spatial prepositions (and preposition clusters) are a surface amalgamation of a spatial deep case marker with a spatial proximity function. For example, the prepositional phrase, "in the room," in the sentence, *John stayed in the room*, is analyzed as a surface realization of something equivalent to "AT some place P where P is-IN the room." In other words, this analysis decomposes the surface prepositional phrase *in the room* into a case component containing a deep spatial case marker AT and an abstract place argument, and a spatial proximity function component that asserts the spatial proximity relation is–IN held by the abstract place to the ground object, *the room.* In Sentences 4a and 4b,

(4) a. The mouse lives under the tree where Tom found the eagle's nest.
    b. The mouse lives under the tree where Tom found many strange rocks.

the places qualified by the two where-clauses are two different places despite their analogous surface syntactic configuration. The analysis that we argue for accounts for this structural ambiguity. That is, Sentence 4a is analyzed as:

- the mouse lives AT a place X,
- X is under the tree Y,
- Tom found the eagle's nest AT Y;

and Sentence 4b is analyzed as:

- the mouse lives AT a place X,
- X is under the tree Y,
- Tom found many strange rocks AT X.

In these two different analyses, X and Y are both nominal concepts antecedent to the relative clause in the sentence. Grammar allows the antecedent of the where-clause in both sentences to be either X or Y, and we adopt whichever interpretation sounds more likely in the real world.

Directional Relations and Their Reference Frames

Object-Inherent Directionality

Some objects (such as *people, houses,* and *cars*) are perceived as having inherent directionality, and others (such as *balls* and *rocks*) are not.

Inherent directionalities vary widely from object to object in their dimensionality and saliency. First, the inherent directionality of an object may be *incomplete*—it may not determine directions in all three basic dimensions. For instance, a *tree* has a very strong inherent up/down but no front/back or left/right directionality. Second, the degree of saliency of the inherent directionality can be quite different from one object to another. A *telescope* seems to have an inherent front/back directionality of mild strength compared to a person. We now examine various ways in which objects come to have inherent directionalities, as a result of semantic extention from the ontological foundations of the three basic directionalities.

Inherent Up/Down.   Objects have come to have an inherent up/down directionality through semantic irradiation, or faded metaphor.

"Semantic irradiation" (Bréal, 1924) is a process of semantic change or semantic extention by which a certain form, which was initially meaningless, comes to be associated with a certain meaning after the form has been repeatedly used in contexts containing the particular semantic material. The *canonical posture* of an object is the normal, usual, and default stance of the object. Due to this posture's being cognitively the most typical, statistically the most frequent, and functionally the most natural, the up/down directionality ontologically originating from the earth's gravity is irradiated into the object giving it an inherent up/down even when not in its canonical posture.

If an expression, originally used metaphorically, becomes widely accepted and becomes an ordinary usage, it is then a *faded metaphor* (Sturtevant, 1917/1961). When the idea of the pressing force of gravity is metaphorically transferred to nongravitational situations such as, "under the thumbtack on the bulletin board," we have cases in which the up/down directional terms appear to be used with their reference frame shifted from the direction of the gravitational force to the direction of the exertion of the force involved.

Inherent Front/Back.   The prototype front/back directionality around the egocentered perceiver is abstracted and extended to other animate (or inanimate) objects, letting them take the role of the perceiver. In this way, the inherent front/back directionality is recognized around other people, other animals, or even inanimate objects that become an extension of the perceiver.

Because mobility is such an important property of animate objects, if an object is designed to move in a particular direction with respect to its body, we attribute to the object an inherent front/back directionality aligned along the path of motion.

The front/back directionalities based on objects' autonomous cognitive or kinetic properties are *autonomously inherent* to the objects. But there is a directionality derived more passively. When people encounter other people, they typically do so front side to front side in order to keep their communication channel open. Clark (1973) called it *canonical encounter*. People encounter objects such as houses, computer terminals, or desks, that have a preferred side to be accessed. This canonical access gives the accessed object an inherent front/back in the direction of the accessing— along the direction of the canonical encounter. This kind of front/back directionality is assigned to objects through their encounter with sentient beings, and so is *passively inherent* to the objects.

The inherent front/back direectionality found in objects' static canonical position is *canonically inherent* to the objects. However, when an object is in motion along a particular path, there may arise a sense of front/back directionality whose reference frame is aligned with the path regardless of the object's own orientation or shape. This directionality is based on dynamically understood contingent characteristics of the object and is *contingently inherent* to the object.

Inherent Left/Right. Left/right directionality does not have an ontological base of its own. If an object has both inherent up/down and front/back directionality, then its inherent left/right directionality depends on whether or not it is viewed as three-dimensional. Every three-dimensional object which has an inherent left/right directionality also has both inherent up/down and inherent front/back directionalities.

Perspectively Imposed Directionality

In natural language, we find that the meaning of some directional terms cannot be attributed to any object explicitly cited or presupposed in the context. Here, we examine the notion of the perspective ego as an imaginary human being implicitly understood in narrative contexts, and claim that such senses of directionalities that cannot be attributed to any object's inherent properties are the ones perspectively imposed by the perspective ego.

The Perspective Ego. Consider Sentences 5a and 5b:

(5) a. There is a tree *in front of* the house.
   b. There is a rock *in front of* the tree.

In (5a), the front/back directionality is part of the house's inherent properties. However, the front/back directionality explicitly mentioned by the same directional term, "in front of," in (5b) cannot be regarded as inherent in either of the two objects explicitly mentioned. The front/back directionality referred to in (5b) is understood from the viewpoint of the language users (the speaker and the hearer) who are imagined to be viewing and talking about the depicted scene. In order to account for some uses of directional relations in natural language, we have to introduce an imagined meta-object[2] from whose point of view the scene is supposed to be viewed, described, and understood. In many studies, the notion of this imaginary entity or something very close to it was captured with a variety of terms, such as *speaker* (Fillmore, 1972), *narrator* (Prince, 1982), *perspective* or *point of view* (Cresswell, 1985; Dijk & Kintsch, 1983; Prince, 1982), *hypothetical observer of the scene* (Cresswell, 1985), the *WHERE* of the deictic center at which the *narrating WHO* is supposed to be located (Rapaport et al., 1989). (For a fuller description of deixis and perspective in narrative, see Galbraith, this volume.)

---

[2]This object is a meta-object in that it cannot be regarded as one of the objects the sentence or the discourse is immediately about. Thereby, it is differentiated from ordinary object-level objects such as people, animals, rocks, trees, houses, and so on. For instance, if a subject is asked to count the number of entities referenced in Sentence 5b the answer will be two, to mean the rock and the tree.

This imaginary entity (see also Prince, 1982) clearly has a human nature made abstract. The speaker or writer speaks or writes the narratives, putting himself or herself in the position of this imaginary entity. The hearer or reader listens or reads the narratives, putting himself or herself in the position of this imaginary entity. The reason a text can be understood by readers the way the writer sees it is that they construct and reconstruct the same imaginary entity with the same characteristics at each passage of the text. The entity is perceived as a separate cognitive character with its own identity. We call this imaginary entity the *perspective ego* and will use the term *perspect* to mean the act of the perspective ego's viewing.

Consider Sentence 6:

(6) One day as the boy was cleaning, hidden from his master's view *behind* a door, he heard the magician say some magic words to a broom. (Lewis & O'Kun, 1982, p. 24)

In this sentence, the door serves as an object that divides the surrounding space into two disjoint subspaces; we cannot tell which direction relative to the door was meant by "behind the door" if it is detached from the context. It is very difficult for us to attribute the front/back directionality of "behind the door" to the inherent front/back of the magician. The magician was not looking at the boy. He was busy performing his magic, changing his posture in various directions. Thus, the most satisfying interpretation of the expression is that the front/back directionality is established by the perspective direction of the perspective ego who is viewing the room from where the magician was working.

Since the perspective ego would not normally be expected to be in any noncanonical stance in order to view the scene, the up/down directionality is not an issue for the perspective ego. (It is aligned with the gravitational up/down.) Left/right is, as we have already seen, dependent on the front/back directionality. Therefore, the question of how the front/back directionality is created is the most important issue for perspectivally imposed directionality.

Encountering and Projecting Perspectives. There are two contradicting front/back directionalities imposed by the perspective ego. One is the front/back directionality coming from the perspective ego's own autonomous inherent front/back[3] projected into the perceived space; the other is the front/back directionality coming from the passive front/back directionality vested around an encountered object due to its contingent encounter with the perspective ego. This difference is similar to the one we noted between autonomously inherent and passively inherent front/back directionalities of objects. Depending on which front/back directionality prevails, a perspective is said to be either *projecting* or *encountering*. Consider the following two text fragments (7a) and (7b):

---

[3]The perspective ego is believed to be a separate cognitive character with its own identity. Thus, it is natural for there to be an autonomously inherent front/back directionality associated with the perspective ego.

(7) a. You must be properly seated to operate vehicle controls correctly. Sit in a comfortable, erect position squarely *behind* the steering wheel so that your feet can easily operate the floor controls (Canadian Automobile Association, 1977).

　　b. The convicted will remain *behind* bars for the rest of his life.

The front/back directionality for "behind" in Sentence 7b is, as in Sentence 6, the one perspectively understood from the view point of the perspective ego who stands and encounters the bars and the prisoners from the outside. In this encountering perspective, the front direction is toward the perspective ego from the bars and *the convicted is behind the bars*. The sentences in (7a) were taken from a booklet with instructions addressed to the second person. In this context, the perspective ego views things from the second person's (that is, *your*) viewpoint. The perspective ego is aligned with *you* seated at the driver's seat "in a comfortable, erect position" prepared to drive the car. The inherent front/back of the perspective ego is projected into the space from him or her in this posture in the car. In this projecting perspective, the front direction is toward the steering wheel from the perspective ego and *you are behind the steering wheel*.[4]

Perspective Up/Down. Another kind of perspectively imposed up/down directionality is psychological, without a matching object in the concrete world. In a perspective situation, the location imagined to be occupied by the perspective ego is given a special perceptual property so that it can serve as the viewpoint for the perspective. Hence, we call the point used by the perspective ego in viewing the scene the *perspective viewpoint*.

Generally, the perspective viewpoint is perceived as somewhat elevated over other places so that the perspective ego can maintain a good, natural perspective. The perspective ego perceives a perspectively created imaginary up/down directionality that is real only in his or her psychological space, and the perspective ego feels that he or she is at a higher height than other places in this imagined up/down directionality. If a character approaches nearer the perspective viewpoint, the perspective ego perceives that the character is making an upward move, and vice versa. When the focal character is moving away from the current WHERE-point, the perspective ego perceives that the focal character is making a downward move because of the focal character's movement(s) away from the current perspective viewpoint. For example:

(8) And I heard my dad stomping *down* the hall. . . . Then I heard the front door open. (Mann, 1973, p. 6)

---

[4]Rather than understanding it perspectively, one may attempt to account for the behindness used in (7a) by appealing to the car's inherent front/back directionality. The inherent front/back directionality of a car and the front/back directionality projected by the perspective ego sitting inside the car in the prototypical way are not, perhaps, different in their origin.

The text (8) describes the scene from a young boy's perspective in which his father walked out on his family. We know that halls are usually level. Nonetheless, the boy perceived that his father stomped *down* the hall. There is no other way of understanding this up/down reference other than appealing to the perspectivally imposed up/down directionality discussed previously.

STRATEGIES FOR RESOLVING THE REFERENCE FRAME PROBLEM

Now, we present a number of strategies, together with some heuristic rules related to those strategies, that help a cognitive agent resolve reference frames following the principles stated in Yuhan (1991). These rules are only heuristic, as they do not guarantee an optimal solution to the reference frame problem. Moreover, some strategies and rules may partially overlap with others in terms of their applicability. Nonetheless, each different strategy has its own merits and justifications. These rules are grouped into three classes: (a) *grammatical rules* are those stated in terms of grammatical factors—the applicability of these rules are tested by examining the expression's grammatical structures, (b) *inferential rules* are those stated as general reasoning rules—the applicability of these rules are tested by invoking inference processes, (c) *default rules* are used when no others lead to a solution.

In this chapter, we present only those rules Cassie currently uses. For a more complete list see Yuhan (1991).

Resort to Overt Messages

The *principle of explicit expression* states that in resolving the reference frame, the cognitive agent first looks for overt messages and clues in the linguistic expression. The strength of such signals can vary widely. Some messages are definite instructions that the cognitive agent is expected to accept unconditionally; others are subtle insinuations merely promoting or demoting one resolution alternative over others. Regardless of its strength, if there is an overt signal that suggests that the reference frame be resolved in a certain way, the processor is obliged to consider it to be most significant. This is encapsulated as:

> *Strategy 1:* Look in the expression for overt linguistic signals that contain a message for reference frame resolution.

This strategy is implemented by the grammatical rules.

Directional Terms of Definite Noun Form.   Consider Example 9:[5]

(9) a. ?Your golf ball is *to the tree's left.*
    b. Your golf ball is *to the left of the tree.*

---

[5]We follow here formal linguists' convention of putting an asterisk or a question mark in front of an unacceptable or an awkward expression.

Our intuition accepts (9b) and rejects, or only reluctantly accepts, (9a). If the ground object does not have an effective inherent left/right directionality, a left/right directional reference using a possessive-phrase construct is inappropriate.

A closer examination of of-phrase and possessive-phrase constructs sheds some light on the basis for this distinction. We seldom say "the eyes of John,"[6] whereas we easily say "John's eyes." We do not say "the desk's owner" but can say "the owner of the desk." However, we comfortably say either "John's image" or "the image of John," and also either "the desk's top" or "the top of the desk."

The degree of semantic dependency each possessed constituent has with respect to its possessor constituent in the listed expressions is not the same. We can hardly think of John's eyes without thinking of John himself, whereas we normally do not link a person to the desk he or she owns. Legs of a desk are quite tightly associated to the desk, but not as strongly as John's eyes are to John.

Another grammatical distinction is seen in the use of the definite article *the* in English front/back directional references. Consider Sentence 10:

(10) [When the professor entered the room, he found that his assistant was] *standing in front of the class* [asking some question of a girl] *sitting in the front of the class.* (Hornby, 1974, p. 352)

Hornby remarked that the phrase "sitting in the front of the class" means [being] "in one of the foremost rows facing the teacher" whereas "standing in front of the class" means "facing the pupils" (p. 352). First of all, the syntactic structures of the two phrases (i) *in front of the class* and (ii) *in the front of the class* are equally

<prep> <NP1> of <NP2>

in their lower level analysis. However, depending on whether or not <NP1> is delimited by a definite article, their phrasing is syntactically different. In (i), the cluster of words *in front of* syntactically functions as a preposition phrase and constructs a prepositional phrase (PP) by taking the noun phrase (NP2) as its prepositional object, whereas in (ii), *in* is the preposition that constructs a prepositional phrase (PP) by taking the noun phrase (NP1 of NP2) as its prepositional object. Therefore, (i) makes a front/back directional reference, and (ii) makes a reference of a containment relation in which a reference of a *whole–part* relation is embedded in the ground object constituent. We perceive the girl sitting in the front of the class as a part of the whole-class while perceiving the assistant standing in front of the class as an individual detached from the class in an encounter with it.

---

[6]Though there is a movie titled *The Eyes of Laura Mars*.

These differences in the two constructs of "in front of" trace back to the difference of the presence or absence of a definite article. The spatial noun *front* is used in (ii) as a definite noun phrase because of the *the* in front of it, whereas it is used in (i) as a nondefinite noun phrase with no determiner. The definiteness property of the phrase "the front" of (ii) indicates that the noun *front* is used *referentially*.[7] On the other hand, being nondefinite, the noun *front* of (i) is used solely to exhibit its *predicative function* (Lyons, 1977). A referentially used noun presupposes or implies the existence of the referent (Russell, 1905; Strawson, 1950).[8] The semantics of the expression are hinged on the referent designated by the inherent properties of the noun concept. For this reason, the expression, "in the front of the class," presupposes or implies for the expression's own sake an inherent front of the class to be referenced. On the other hand, a noun used more to function as a predicate than as a referent indicator does not presuppose or imply the existence of the referent. Its use is proper if the noun concept can be interpreted as an intensionally defined relation in the given context. Therefore, the use of the expression, "in front of the class," is proper merely if a location that has the directional relation *front of* with respect to the class can be intensionally understood. The presence of a definite article before a directional term promotes the intrinsic resolution alternative, in which the ground object's inherent is taken as the reference frame (see Yuhan, 1991).

Hence, the grammatical rule in English regarding reference frame resolution:

G-rule 1: Use of a possessive-phrase construct (instead of an of-phrase construct) or a *definite article* (instead of no article) in a directional reference promotes an intrinsic resolution.

Dummy Agents. In discourses or texts of a certain style,[9] in which the writer/speaker may use an unstressed *we* or *you* to indicate a nonspecific nonfocused agent (Longacre, 1983), a dummy agent "you" or "we" may be introduced. In such a case, if the location of the dummy agent is known to the reader/hearer, the dummy agent exhibits a strong tendency of inviting the perspective ego. In Sentence 11:

(11) With the printer facing you, as shown in Figure 1-3, grasp the left top side of the lid and lift off the entire lid. (Epson, 1982, p. 1-4)

the dummy agent "you" is introduced into the context and its position is determined propositionally by the phrase "With the printer facing you," as well as analogically by the figure. At this point, the perspective ego is invited to the

---

[7]It is untrue, though, that all uses of definite noun phrases are referential. For details about such notions as *nondefinite* or *referential use*, see Lyons (1977, chap. 7).

[8]We have no intention of reopening the controversy of Russel and Strawson's arguments about whether it is necessarily an implication or only a presupposition.

[9]Longacre (1983) terms discourses of this style, *procedural discourses*.

place where the dummy agent "you" is located, and provides a perspectivally imposed directionality that anchors the reference frame of the left/right directional reference in the context. Hence, the grammatical rule:

> *G-rule 2:* A definitely located dummy agent *you* or *we* promotes a perspective resolution in which the perspective viewpoint is *invited* to the place of the dummy agent.

Resort to Discourse Coherence

According to the discourse coherence principle, a cognitive agent expects a newly read expression to have a semantic interpretation relevant to the current discourse context, and therefore tends to look for a reasonable way to have the new information be interconnected to some components in the context. In reference frame resolution, the readers/listeners have a strategy:

> *Strategy 2:* Examine the discourse context for a coherence connection. This strategy is implemented by the inferential rules.

> ***Typical Acts at the Deictic WHERE-Point.***   Important aspects of a coherent discourse are cohesiveness of the text and the deictic center. The notion of a deictic center in narratives is discussed extensively in other chapters of this volume. Tracking the deictic center in a narrative is not a trivial problem. Nevertheless, when the WHERE-point is identifiable, it tends to play a significant role in resolving the reference frame problem.
>
> One such situation is where an event is placed at a location and the event is one expected at the location as part of a series of events normally developing at that location. In such a case, the inherent properties of the location are more accessible, and resolution-demanding expressions are more likely to cohere to the location. Hence, we have an inferential rule:

> *I–rule 1:* If both the figure and the ground objects are located at a place L and the figure's *spatially associated act*[10] is typically expected at L, then an inherited resolution is promoted in which L serves as the host object.

Consider this situation (12):

> (12) Mary and Tom were in the theater watching a show. Tom was sitting in front of Mary.

In (12), the reader/listener notes that Mary and Tom were in the theater as audience. Because the audience is normally seated in a theater hall while watching

---

[10]The *spatially associated act* denotes the nonspatial act component of a surface conflated spatial verb. A surface conflated spatial verb is an association of a deep spatial verb with a spatially associated act.

a show, *typicality reasoning* on generic concepts of a theater and the audience make the cognitive agent realize that the spatially associated act, *Tom's sitting at a place P*, is one of the typical acts that Tom was expected to do, due to his being in the theater hall. The rule captures that, in a circumstance like this, the directional reference, *the place P is in front of Mary*, is likely to be interpreted with its reference frame anchored in the inherent front/back directionality of the theater hall. The point of this argument is clearer considering a similar situation (13):

(13) Mary and Tom were in the theater fixing the electric wirings. For a short break, Tom sat in front of Mary, lighting his cigarette.

In (13), too, Mary and Tom were in the theater hall and Tom sat in front of Mary. However, here, *Tom's sitting* is not an event in which Tom was typically expected to be involved as an electrician working in the theater hall. This difference blocks the rule for the inherited resolution from being applied to (13).

Figure Object Attached to the Environment.   The reader/listener tends to favor interpretations that have a strong connection to the context. One such situation is when the figure object is *directionally attached* to the environment. Consider Sentence (14):

(14) Tom was sitting *in front of* Mary.

First of all, let us suppose this sitting event is placed in a hall and that the hall is perceived as an environment of the directional reference. Let us further suppose we know Mary's location in the hall, but not her orientation there. If the reference frame of the directional reference *in front of* is believed to be anchored in the inherent front/back directionality of Mary, we realize that the directional reference in (14) does not yet help us to learn about the directional relation of Tom's location with respect to the hall. On the other hand, if Mary's orientation in the room is known to us or if the reference frame is believed to be anchored in the inherited front/back directionality of the hall, then Tom is directionally attached to the environment.

Whether or not a directional reference causes the figure object to be directionally attached to the environment depends on whether the directionality in which the reference frame is anchored is bound to the environment. That is to say, the orientation of the directionality in question is fixed with respect to the environment.

From this, we claim that a directionality not bound to the environment is less likely to be considered as the anchor of a reference frame when having the figure object attached to the environment is important. Thus, in situations in which environmental interconnection is expected, the amount of attention that an object receives in terms of serving as the anchor of a reference frame varies, depending on whether or not its inherent directionality is bound to the environment. In general, when a strong contextual interconnection of a directional reference with its surrounding environment is expected, directionalities that are bound to the environment are more likely to be significant in the context. From this, the following rule is derived:

I–rule 2: When a contextual connection of the directional reference to the environment is perceived to be important, and the ground object's inherent directionality is bound to the environment, then an intrinsic resolution based on that particular directionality is promoted.

Default Resolutions

When no remarkable clue leading to a particular solution is found, the cognitive agent settles on an interpretation that requires minimal context (the principle of computational economy). This is the strategy:

Strategy 3: Rely on default solutions when no particular solution is found enhanced.

The following describes a few rules that define default solutions.

Default Inherited Solution of Up/Down.   Because up/down directionalities have their ontological foundation in the terrestrio-gravitational environment where most events of concern to people happen, it is natural that, in the absence of other information, people understand an up/down directional relation in this way.

Hence, we have a default rule:

D–rule 1: When the directional reference is in an up/down directionality, if no other alternative is enhanced, then the language user accepts by default an inherited resolution in which the terrestrio-gravitational environment serves as the host object.

Default Intrinsic and Perspective Solutions of Front/Back.   Front/back directionalities have their ontological foundation in the way in which a sentient being encounters objects in the environment. This object-centered nature of front/back directionalities leads the language user to prefer an intrinsic resolution in the absence of a reason for something else. However, if the language user does not see an inherent directionality associated with the ground object, an intrinsic resolution is not appropriate. In this case, the language user has to settle on the next simplest resolution. When the ground object cannot be regarded as an encountering sentient being and if there is no conspicuous object to serve as a host, the next closest alternative to the ontological foundation comes from the language user's regarding the ground object as an encountered object rather than as an encountering one. This is realized as a perspective resolution.

Hence, we have a default rule:

D–rule 2: When the directional reference is in a front/back directionality, if no other alternative is particularly enhanced and if the ground has an inherent directionality, then the language user supports by default an intrinsic resolution.

A COMPUTATIONAL MODEL OF LANGUAGE PROCESSING

Cassie (Cognitive Agent of the SNePS System—an Intelligent Entity) is an AI system built to demonstrate the robustness of our model of natural language narrative understanding. Cassie reads a simple narrative, understands the story, paying particular attention to spatial information, resolves the spatial reference frame problems based on a coherent model of the story kept in her "mind," and maintains and tracks the deictic center. (See Shapiro & Rapaport, this volume, for a general introduction to SNePS/Cassie.[11])

Cassie's main component is ENGRAMMAR, a GATN (Shapiro, 1982) grammar that determines all aspects of Cassie's sentence processing. ENGRAMMAR uses the English morphological analyzer provided with SNePS (Shapiro & the SNePS Implementation Group, 1991) and SNIP, the SNePS Inference Package. ENGRAMMAR's sentence processing is divided into four phases:

1. In the *Initial Interpretation* phase, Cassie recognizes the surface form of the sentence, identifies previously known entities referred to by definite descriptions and pronouns, resolves the spatial reference frame, and constructs a SNePS network for the direct interpretation of the sentence. Spatial information is handled by a special spatial module, called in two kinds of situations: to analyze the spatial case of a verb of location or of motion, or to analyze the spatial expression describing the location of an event. In either case, the spatial module separately identifies any given quantity of distance, the spatial localization function, and the ground object against which the localization function localizes the figure object. If the localization function is a directional relation, spatial processing of this information will conclude at the end of the sentence when the spatial reference frame is resolved. Otherwise, the spatial module builds a SNePS representation of the spatial information before returning to the main sentence processor.

---

[11]Although this version of Cassie was implemented separately from the other versions of Cassie described in this book, the same design principles were used. In this chapter, we refer to this version of Cassie as simply "Cassie."

2. The *Extended Interpretation* phase is, in this project, devoted to filling in spatial information from spatially conflated surface verbs, such as *sit, stay, lie, go, run, throw, fly*. The conflated information is unbundled into spatial primitive verbs, such as *BE-LOCated, MOVE,* or *BE-ORIENTed*. This phase also attempts to determine where the figure and the deictic HERE will be located at the end of the activity.

3. The *Immediate Inference* phase in this project is devoted to tracking any MOVing entities, the deictic center, and the contextual goal.

4. The *Extended Inference* phase is provided for simulation of conscious reflection upon what has just been read, for example, when a person reads a detective novel. This phase is not used in the current project.

The two interpretation phases are driven by the grammar, assisted by inference only for finding previously known entities and for resolving the spatial reference frame. The two inference phases are driven by language-independent domain rules represented in the SNePS network.

EXAMPLES OF THE SYSTEM IN ACTION

To demonstrate Cassie's ability to read a narrative and understand the spatial information in it, we present excerpts from a run[12] in which Cassie read the following story[13]:

S1: Mary, Tom, and Bob went to a theater together in order to see Bob's uncle's show.

S2: They walked to the front of the hall.

S3: Bob sat two rows in front of Mary.

S4: And, Tom sat just behind her.

S5: They had a few minutes before the show would start.

S6: Mary was turned around in her seat talking with Tom.

S7: Then, she saw a person who looked like Bob walking down the aisle toward her with a tall girl on his left.

S8: Recognizing Mary, he stopped in front of her to say hello.

S9: Mary glanced back and saw that Bob was still there in his seat.

S10: The person standing in front of Mary was Jim who was Bob's twin brother.

S11: She had met him once before.

---

[12]The version of SNePS/Cassie used for the work reported here was implemented in Franz Lisp and ran on a VAX 780 machine using the UNIX operating system.

[13]This narrative was written by a graduate student who was a native speaker of English. The story was first explained verbally to the writer with an aid of a diagram of the situation. Then, the writer was asked to write a short paragraph to describe the situation. The writer was not aware of the theoretical claims to be made by this research, although he was told that the text would be used for a study of spatial references. The code number assigned to each sentence is only to refer to it in this book.

S12: Jim and the tall girl found seats a little distance away to Mary's left.
S13: Then the lights in the hall dimmed.
S14: They saw Bob's uncle standing behind a lectern to the left of a microphone.

In the following excerpts, Cassie's output is in typewriter font. Normally, after each phase of sentence processing, Cassie prints a terse English version of what she has understood, and also displays the SNePS structures she has built. Because of limited space, we will only show the terse English edited only by adjusting the spaces and line arrangements.

```
S1: Mary, Tom, and Bob went to a theater together in
    order to see Bob's uncle's show.

Initial Interpretation
======================
#> I understand that
      a group of individuals namely, Bob, Tom and Mary
      went to a theater;
   and I understand also that
      it was in order to enable another affair, which is
      that a group of individuals namely, Bob, Tom and
      Mary might see a show.
```

The terse English sentence indicates that Cassie understood the sentential relation between Bob, Tom, and Mary's going to a theater and their seeing a show. We notice that Cassie understood their seeing a show merely as a possible event while taking their going to a theater as a solid fact.

```
Extended Interpretation
=======================
#> Particularly, I note that,
      due to m35 the <going> act of a group of individuals
      namely,  Bob, Tom and Mary,the Figure Objects, a
      group of individuals b4, b3 and b2
       where b4 is related to an individual b7 in such a
          way that b7 has a kinship relation of being uncle
          to individual b4
       where b7 possesses an individual b8 where b8 is a
       member of class show
          and b7 is a member of class uncle
       and b4 is named Bob
       and b4 has the property of being human
       and b4 has the property of being male
      and b3 has the property of being human
       and b3 has the property of being male
       and b3 is named Tom
      and b2 has the property of being human
```

```
        and b2 has the property of being female
        and b2 is named Mary
    MOVEed
    to a place b6 where b6 has a Spatial Relation of
        "ideal-point"
        to the Ground Object, individual b5 where b5 is a
        member of class theater,
    and that, PRESUMABLY at the end,
    the Figure Objects became BE-LOCated
    at place b6, the destination of the MOVE.
```

Here, Cassie extends the interpretation of the motional act m35, the act of "going to a theater," extracting first the figure objects' motion in terms of the deep verb MOVE, and second the result that the figure objects are presumably BE-LOCated at the goal location at the immediately next time interval after the event time of the MOVE act. Cassie understood that these two underlying deep events are very closely sequenced together in time and were both conflated and expressed by one surface phrase. Therefore, in Cassie's cognitive space, these deep level events are understood as happening in some subintervals of the event time of the going-to-a-theater event while the event time of the MOVE is before the event time of the BE-LOCated.

In the interests of space and readability, in future displays of Cassie's terse English, we will replace occurrences of b2 by Mary, b3 by Tom, b4 by Bob, and b5 by the theater, edit out repetitions of the properties of these entities, and, in general, replace low-level descriptions of entities by higher level English descriptions after their first introduction.

```
Immediate Inference
===================
Going into an INFERENCE.
#> Furthermore, I infer that, PRESUMABLY,
    Bob, Tom and Mary were BE-LOCated at a place in the
     theater;
    In other words,
    the Figure Objects, Bob, Tom and Mary
    were BE-LOCated at a place b10
     where b10 has a Spatial Relation of "in"
      to the Ground Object, the theater
    at a time interval b20
     b20 is after a time interval b1
      where b1, which is the EPISODE starting time,
       is the Event-Time of m35 an asserted event,
       the <going> act of Bob, Tom and Mary
     and b20 is before a time interval b9
      where b9 is the Event-Time of m30 an unasserted
        event,
        the <seeing> act of Bob, Tom and Mary.
```

In the immediate inference phase, Cassie goes through a series of inferences to try to figure out the locations where the individuals that Cassie has learned have moved will eventually be BE-LOCated. Cassie knows that a theater has a hall and an aisle as its parts, and that, if someone goes to a theater and the purpose of going there is to see a show there, then the person is presumably IN the theater at some time point, that is after the person goes there but before the person sees the show. First Cassie believes that Bob, Tom and Mary are AT the theater, then infers that they are presumably IN the theater shortly thereafter. Without any reason to reject the presumption, Cassie finally thinks that Bob, Tom and Mary are IN the theater at the time b20, that is after the event time b1 of their going to the theater, and before the event time b9 of the conjectured event of their seeing the show.

```
Deictic-NOW is maintained as b20
Deictic-HERE is maintained as b10
Deictic-WHO is maintained as m16
m30 is maintained as a contextual goal
```

Cassie updates the contextual parameters, including the deictic center, before she reads the next sentence in the story. The deictic-NOW is the time that Bob, Tom and Mary were in the theater. The deictic-HERE is the place in the theater where Bob, Tom and Mary are; the deictic-WHO is the group consisting of Bob, Tom and Mary. Cassie also understands that the conjectured event that Bob, Tom and Mary may see a show in the near future, is the goal of their being at the deictic-HERE, and maintains m30 as the contextual goal event at this point.

```
S2: They walked to the front of the hall.
```

The second sentence contains a few interesting problems that have to be addressed. First, Cassie has to resolve the pronoun *they* appropriately. Second, the noun *hall* is introduced in the text with a definite article although it had never been mentioned before.

```
Initial Interpretation
======================
#> I understand that
 Bob, Tom and Mary
 walked to the front part of the hall part of the
   theater.
```

The terse English report indicates that Cassie has solved the both problems successfully. First, Cassie understands that the pronoun "they" in the input sentence refers to the group of the three people, Bob, Tom and Mary. Second, Cassie succeeds in understanding that the *hall* is related in a whole/part relation to the *theater* that was introduced in the previous sentence. When a noun (object) which has not been mentioned before is first introduced with a definite article, Cassie thinks that an expectation of the object's existence should be foreshadowed in the context. To find out the expectation that will account for the *hall*, Cassie initiated a SNePS inference. Due to Cassie's rule that states that *the theater has a hall as a part of its whole*, Cassie knows there must be a hall which is a part of the theater that they went to. Thus, Cassie succeeds in integrating the newly given object *hall* into the running narrative context.

```
Extended Interpretation
=======================
#> Particularly, I note that,
   due to m106 the <walking> act of Bob, Tom and Mary,
   the Figure Objects, Bob, Tom and Mary
   MOVEed
   to a place b24 where b24 has a Spatial Relation of
     "ideal-point"
    to the Ground Object, individual b23
     where b23 is a part of an individual b22
      where b22 is a part of the theater
       and b22 is a member of class hall
      and b23 is a member of class front,
   and that, PRESUMABLY at the end,
   the Figure Objects became BE-LOCated
   at place b24, the destination of the MOVE.
```

In the extended interpretation phase, Cassie again extracts a MOVE and a resulting BE-LOCated from a conflated surface verb, in this case, "walked."

Note that Cassie does not take the English expression "the front of the hall" as a directional reference. It rather analyzes the phrase as referring to the front part of the theater hall. Although such part references as this evidently originate from directional references, they have rather specific idiosyncratic meanings.

```
Immediate Inference
===================
Going into an INFERENCE.
NOTHING reportable deduced through the immediate
  inference
```

Cassie finds no particularly interesting inferences through the inference phase.

```
Deictic-NOW is maintained as b21
Deictic-HERE is maintained as b10
Deictic-WHO is maintained as m16
m30 is maintained as a contextual goal
```

The deictic-NOW point has been updated, whereas the deictic-HERE, deictic-WHO and the goal–event stay the same.

```
S3: Bob sat two rows in front of Mary.
```

The expression "two rows in front" is a directional reference that raises a spatial reference frame problem. For the expression to be properly understood, the associated front/back directionality has to be resolved and determined.

```
Starting the process of the reference frame resolution.
Contextual expectation is examined by an inference
```

In this particular case, Cassie could not resolve the reference frame problem using grammatical clues alone. So, the system initiated inferences to solve the problem based on the contextual connection. One important tactic is examining whether there is a contextual expectation that may provide a candidate host object for an inherited resolution. Therefore, the system tries to examine in what contextual connection Bob (the figure) is expected to be located at the place b32 at the most updated time b31. I–Rule 1 is invoked and resolves the reference frame since Bob and Mary are both in the theater hall and Bob is indeed expected to take a seat in this context.

```
Initial Interpretation
=======================
#> I understand that
     Bob sat at a place in-front-of Mary.

Extended Interpretation
=======================
#> Particularly, I note that,
     due to m123 the <sitting> act of Bob,
     the Figure Object, Bob
     was BE-LOCated
     at a place b32
      where b32 has a Spatial Relation of "in-front-of"
       to the Ground Object, Mary
       with the inheritedly resolved reference frame of SR
       anchored to the canonical front/back directionality
       of the Host Object, the theater hall.
```

The detailed English report made during the extended interpretation indicates that the spatial reference frame problem has been resolved by inheriting the canonical front/back directionality of the theater hall.

```
Immediate Inference
===================
Going into an INFERENCE.
```

```
#> Furthermore, I infer that, PRESUMABLY,
   Bob was BE-LOCated at a place in a seat;
   In other words,
   the Figure Object, Bob
   was BE-LOCated
   at a place b37
    where b37 has a Spatial Relation of `in"
     to the Ground Object, individual b36
      where b36 is a member of class seat
   at a time interval b38
    b38 is after a time interval b31
     where b31 is the Event-Time of m129 an asserted
       event,
        the <BEing-LOCated> act of Bob
      and b31 is the Event-Time of m123 an asserted
      event,
        the <sitting> act of Bob
    and b38 is before a time interval b9
     where b9 is the Event-Time of m30 an unasserted
       event,
       remembered as a contextual goal event,
       the <seeing> act of Bob, Tom and Mary.
```

As indicated in the detailed English report of the immediate inference results,
Cassie now understands that Bob is in a seat at the most updated time interval
b38, and updates the deictic-NOW to that time interval.

```
Deictic-NOW is maintained as b38
Deictic-HERE is maintained as b10
Deictic-WHO is maintained as m16
m30 is maintained as a contextual goal

S4: And, Tom sat just behind her.
```

The syntactic structure of this sentence is very close to that of the previous
one. It contains a pronoun "her" which should be resolved for its actual reference.
It also has a directional reference whose spatial reference frame is resolved by
I–Rule 1.

```
Starting the process of the reference frame resolution.
Contextual expectation is examined by an inference
Directional attachment is examined by an inference
```

Since this sentence shows no special features not previously encountered, in
the interest of saving space, we will omit the output of Cassie's interpretations
and inferences.

Cassie now understands that Tom is also BE-LOCated in a seat in the theater hall.

```
Deictic-NOW is maintained as b44
Deictic-HERE is maintained as b10
Deictic-WHO is maintained as m16
m30 is maintained as a contextual goal
```

S5: They had a few minutes <before the show would start>.

This sentence has a complex sentential structure, containing an embedded adverbial clause led by an adverbial conjunction.[14]

```
Initial Interpretation
======================
#> I understand that
   Bob, Tom and Mary
   had an interval.
```

This sentence conveys no notable spatial information. For our purpose, therefore, there is nothing that requires an extended interpretation or any further inference.

```
Deictic-NOW is maintained as b45
Deictic-HERE is maintained as b10
Deictic-WHO is maintained as m16
m30 is maintained as a contextual goal
```

S6: Mary was turned around in her seat talking with Tom.

The interesting points of this sentence include: the pronoun; the prepositional phrase, "in her seat," that specifies the place of the narrated event; the present participle phrase, "talking with Tom," that describes another action of Mary's that takes place simultaneously with the action expressed by the main clause;[15] the spatial expression, "was turned around," that describes an orientation that is neither a motion nor a location.

---

[14]In fact, this sentence is a good example of a garden-path sentence. The adverbial conjunction "before" can be easily thought of as a preposition. Therefore, Cassie can well be misled at first to think that the sentence is simply *They had a few minutes before the show* until she finds that the sentence does not end at the word "show" but continues with more words, namely, "would start." Furthermore, a prepositional phrase after a noun phrase can be construed as a reduced relative phrase attached to the noun phrase, as in *the soldier with a rifle on his shoulder guarded the gate*, rather than as a detached adverbial phrase, as in *the poacher shot an elephant with an automatic rifle*. A garden path sentence can seriously drain a system's resource if the system takes a wrong path. Depending on which alternative the parsing grammar of Cassie is arranged to pursue first, this input sentence can cause Cassie to go through many expensive backtrackings before it gets to the right analysis of the sentence. In order to save time, we use the angle bracket diacritics to indicate that the utterance delimited by the paired angle bracket is one constituent.

[15]Cassie understands this correctly, but this understanding is not reflected in the terse English reports.

```
Initial Interpretation
=======================
#> I understand that
   at a place in a seat,
   Mary was turned around.
```

The prepositional phrase "in a seat" was recognized by Cassie as a description of the place of Mary's being turned around.

```
Immediate Inference
===================
Going into an INFERENCE.
Debris of some failed inference are erased[16]
#> Furthermore, I infer that,
   Mary was BE-ORIENTed to the rear part of the
    theater;
   In other words,
   the Figure Object, Mary
   was BE-ORIENTed
   toward a place b69
    where b69 has a Spatial Relation of "ideal-point"
     to the Ground Object, individual b68
      where b68 is a member of class rear
       and b68 is a part of the theater
   at a time interval b51
    where b51 is the Event-Time of m218 an asserted
       event,
       the <being-turned-around> act of Mary.
```

After the immediate inference, Cassie understands that Mary is oriented toward the rear of the theater.

```
Deictic-NOW is maintained as b51
Deictic-HERE is maintained as b10
Deictic-WHO is maintained as m16
m30 is maintained as a contextual goal
```

---

[16]In the immediate inference phase, Cassie tries to reason out certain expectations that will help her to understand how the story coheres. In the process of the inference, many fragmentary propositions often become asserted even though the inference fails to lead the system to confirm the main issue for which the inference was performed. Although they are truthful pieces of information, we view such fragmentary assertions in the process of inferences as transient assertions existing only on the subconscious level. Therefore, Cassie purges and does not keep such fragmentary pieces of information.

The deictic-NOW is updated to be the time of Mary's turning around. The rest of the Deictic Center and the contextual goal are unchanged.

```
S7: Then, she saw <a person (who looked like Bob) walk-
    ing down the aisle  toward her with a tall girl (on
    his left)>.
```

This sentence starts with a time adverbial word, "then," that signals a special time relative to the deictic-NOW. Because the sentence is syntactically quite complicated, containing three personal pronouns to be resolved, one definite core noun phrase to be fused with the context, one relative clause, one present participle phrase, and a number of prepositional phrases, we used diacritics to facilitate the processing.

```
Starting the process of the reference frame resolution.
Starting the process of the reference frame resolution.
Contextual expectation is examined by an inference
```

The two directional references in the input sentence each require a separate reference frame resolution. The order of resolutions depends on the embedding level of the expressions in the recognized sentence structure. Because the expression "on his left" is syntactically more deeply embedded than "down the aisle," it is resolved first. Due to the overt clue indicated by the possessive delimiter for the directional term, it is quickly resolved by relying on grammatical rule G–Rule 1. As the other expression, "down the aisle," is not resolved by any grammatical rules, Cassie tries to resolve it by inference rules. Failing to do so, Cassie finally resolves it inheritedly, using the default resolution rule D–Rule 1.

```
Initial Interpretation
======================
#> I understand that
   Mary saw
   a walking act of a person.
```

The initial interpretation shows that Cassie resolved the pronoun "she" as meaning Mary, and also that Cassie indeed parsed the input sentence suitable to the story context. Essentially, the syntactic structure of the sentence recognized by Cassie is, to describe it informally:

then, Mary saw the event that <a person (who looked like Bob) was walking down the aisle toward Mary herself with a tall girl (who existed on the person's left)>.

Cassie also inferred that the definite noun clause "the aisle," refers to the aisle which is a part of the theater, as the report made after the extended interpretation will show us.

Extended Interpretation
========================
#> Particularly, I note that,
   due to m298 the <walking> act of a person,
   the Figure Object, individual b76
    where b76 is the Ground object of a Spatial
      Relation of "left-side"
     for location, individual b83
      where b83 is the locative of m288 an asserted
        event,
       the <existing> act of a girl
     with the intrinsically resolved reference frame of SR
     anchored to the canonical left/right directionality
     of the Ground Object itself
    and b76 has the property of being human
    and b76 has the property of being male
    and b76 is the object of m270 an asserted event,
     the <looking-like> act of a person
    and b76 is a member of class person
   MOVEed
   via a place b80
    where b80 has a Spatial Relation of "downward"
     to the Ground Object, individual b70
      where b70 is a part of the theater
       and b70 is a member of class aisle
     with the inheritedly resolved reference frame of SR
     anchored to the canonical up/down directionality
     of the universal terrestrio-gravitational world
    and b80 has a Spatial Relation of "toward"
     to the Ground Object, Mary
    and that, PRESUMABLY at the end,
    the Figure Object became BE-LOCated
    at some place b94 on the path;
   and also that
    due to m288 the <existing> act of a girl,
    the Figure Object, individual b81
     where b81 has the property of being human
      and b81 has the property of being female
      and b81 has the property of being m278
      and b81 is a member of class girl
    was BE-LOCated
    at a place b83
     where b83 has a Spatial Relation of "left-side"
      to the Ground Object, b76
      with the intrinsically resolved reference frame of
      SR

```
anchored to the canonical left/right
 directionality
of the Ground Object itself.
```

Cassie extends the initial interpretation of the progressive walking act of the person who looks like Bob into the person's MOVE to a presumed BE-LOCation somewhere on the path.

```
Immediate Inference
====================
Going into an INFERENCE.
Debris of some failed inference are erased
NOTHING reportable deduced through the immediate
 inference
```

In this experimental system, Cassie deduces no interesting information in the immediate inference even though it would be reasonable to have inferred from the fact that the person b76 was walking down the aisle toward Mary with a tall girl b81 on his left, that the girl also was moving down the aisle toward Mary.

```
Deictic-NOW is maintained as b75
Deictic-HERE is maintained as b10
Deictic-WHO is maintained as m16
m30 is maintained as a contextual goal

S8: Recognizing Mary, he stopped in front of her to say
    hello.
```

Syntactically, this sentence consists of three embedded propositional structures. Under the main sentence, it has one presentential present participle adverbial phrase and one postsentential to–infinitive adverbial phrase. It contains two personal pronouns and one directional reference to be resolved.

```
Starting the process of the reference frame resolution.
Contextual expectation is examined by an inference
Directional attachment is examined by an inference
```

Here, Cassie tries to resolve the reference frame of the directional reference "in front of her." Cassie finds no grammatical clue for the resolution and tries in vain to resolve it through SNePS inferences by relating it to the context. Eventually, Cassie resolves it relying on the default rule D–Rule 2.

```
Initial Interpretation
======================
#> I understand that
   a person stopped at a place in-front-of Mary;
```

```
and I understand also that
   it was in order to enable another affair, which is
      that
   a person might say hello.
```

Cassie has correctly parsed the main clause and the postsentential to–infinitive adverbial phrase, properly understanding their propositional relations.

```
Extended Interpretation
=======================
#> Particularly, I note that,
   due to m329 the <stopping> act of a person,
   the Figure Object, individual b76
    where b76 is the agent of m336 an asserted event,
      the <recognizing> act of a person
     and b76 has the property of being male
   was BE-LOCated
   at a place b98
    where b98 has a Spatial Relation of "in-front-of"
    to the Ground Object, Mary
    with the intrinsically resolved reference frame of SR
    anchored to the canonical front/back directionality
    of the Ground Object itself.
```

By extending the interpretation of the surface expression of a person's stopping in front of Mary, Cassie further understands that the person, b76 is BE-LOCated in front of Mary based on the canonical front/back directionality of Mary. Note that Cassie understands this is the same b76 who was walking down the aisle.

```
Going into the Immediate Inference
==================================
Going into an INFERENCE.
Debris of some failed inference are erased
NOTHING reportable deduced through the immediate
 inference
Deictic-NOW is maintained as b95
Deictic-HERE is maintained as b10
Deictic-WHO is maintained as m16
m30 is maintained as a contextual goal

S9: Mary glanced back and saw that Bob was still there
    in his seat.
```

This sentence exhibits a coordination of two clauses conjoined by a coordinative conjunction "and," where the two clauses share a same subject. Cassie can handle certain usages of syntactic constituent coordination. As we saw with the example of "Mary, Tom, and Bob" in the first sentence, Cassie understands coordination of arbitrarily many core noun phrases that all together constitute a group of individuals. Cassie also understands coordination of clauses either sharing the same subject or having different subjects.

In the input sentence, there is one genuine spatial expression that states that "Bob was still there in his seat." However, we find in the input sentence one interesting kind of expression, "Mary glanced back." This pseudospatial expression borrows spatial EXTENTION notion to visual perception in order to express "glancing" as if the perception of glancing moves from the perceiving agent to the perceived object via the path of sight. The pseudospatial expression in the input sentence exhibits a use of an adverbial particle, "back," borrowed from a spatial preposition; we view the use as a self-grounded directional reference. In a self-grounded directional reference, the figure object itself serves as the ground of the spatial reference. Thus, an expression such as "Mary glanced back" is understood as "Mary glanced back of herself."

```
Starting the process of the reference frame resolution.
Contextual expectation is examined by an inference
Directional attachment is examined by an inference
```

Given the self-grounded directional reference, Cassie, finding no obvious grammatical clues, tries—but fails—to resolve the reference frame using inferential rules. Finally, the reference frame is resolved by default rule D–Rule 2.

```
Initial Interpretation
======================
#> I understand that
    Mary saw an existing act of Bob;
     and I understand also that
    Mary glanced via a place backward from Mary.
```

Cassie correctly parsed the sentence made of two coordinated clauses sharing one subject, "Mary," and correctly resolved the reference frame of the directional reference by the pseudospatial expression.

```
Extended Interpretation
=======================
#> Particularly, I note that,
    due to m368 the <existing> act of Bob,
    the Figure Object, Bob
    was BE-LOCated
    at a place b108
     where b108 has a Spatial Relation of "in"
      to the Ground Object, individual b107
        where b107 is a member of class seat
          and b107 is possessed by an individual Bob;
  and also that
    due to m359 the <glancing> act of Mary,
```

```
      a pseudo-motion, the perception of
       the Figure Object, Mary
      EXTENDed
      via a place b104
       where b104 has a Spatial Relation of "backward"
        to the Ground Object, Mary
        with the intrinsically resolved reference frame of SR
        anchored to the canonical front/back directionality
        of the Ground Object itself.
      NOTHING reportable deduced through the immediate
        inference
      Deictic-NOW is maintained as b103
      Deictic-HERE is maintained as b10
      Deictic-WHO is maintained as m16
      m30 is maintained as a contextual goal

      S10: The person standing in front of Mary was Jim
           who was Bob's twin brother.
```

There are a number of challenging problems in this particular sentence. It contains one spatial proposition consisting of a front/back directional reference whose reference frame has to be resolved, one reduced relative clause made of a present participle phrase, and one relative clause led by a relative pronoun, "who."

```
      Starting the process of the reference frame resolution.
      Contextual expectation is examined by an inference
      Directional attachment is examined by an inference
```

Cassie first tests the contextual expectation in an attempt to resolve the reference frame of the directional reference "in front of Mary" in a duplicated context after erasing the target expectation from the context. The test turns out to be futile. Then, Cassie tests the possibility of directional attachment. Cassie finds that I–Rule 2 is applicable and so does resolve the reference frame.

```
      Initial Interpretation
      ======================
      #> I understand that
         a person had the identity status of being Jim.
```

Cassie's terse report shows how she understood the top level skeleton of the input sentence. Grasping the top level propositional structure of a sentence with a complicated syntactic structure is unlikely without properly parsing the whole sentence correctly.

```
      Extended Interpretation
      =======================
      #> Particularly, I note that,
```

```
due to m430 the <standing> act of a person,
the Figure Object, b76
was BE-LOCated
at a place b112
  where b112 is a base equivalent to b98
    and b112 has a Spatial Relation of "in-front-of"
      to the Ground Object, Mary
      with the intrinsically resolved reference frame of
      SR
      anchored to the canonical front/back direction-
      ality
      of the Ground Object itself.
```

Cassie derived that the person is located at the place where the person is standing. The reference frame of the "in front of" directional reference was intrinsically resolved. Cassie made the correct inference and identified the person standing at location b112, namely, a place in front of Mary, as b76, the person who stopped to say hello at location b98, the place in front of her. Cassie also understood that the two locations b112 and b98 are indeed equivalent.

```
Immediate Inference
===================
Going into an INFERENCE.
Debris of some failed inference are erased
NOTHING reportable deduced through the immediate
 inference
Deictic-NOW is maintained as b111
Deictic-HERE is maintained as b10
Deictic-WHO is maintained as m16
m30 is maintained as a contextual goal

S11: She had met him once before.

Initial Interpretation
======================
#> I understand that
   Mary had met a person.

Deictic-NOW is maintained as b122
Deictic-HERE is maintained as b10
Deictic-WHO is maintained as m16
m30 is maintained as a contextual goal
```

This sentence exhibits a perfective aspect and contains two personal pronouns both of which are resolved correctly.

```
S12: Jim and the tall girl found seats a little
     distance away to Mary's left.
```

The sentence contains one directional reference whose reference frame has to be resolved, one definite article phrase whose reference should be resolved by SNePS inference, a plural of a countable noun, and a distance specification coupled with a direction.

```
Starting the process of the reference frame resolution.
Contextual expectation is examined by an inference
Contextual expectation is examined by an inference
```

Attempting to resolve the reference frame of the directional reference "a little distance away to Mary's left" by inference, Cassie performs a few tests to examine the contextual expectations regarding the locative case of the event. The situation appears to warrant the applicability of G–Rule 1 which is activated by the possessive construction used in the directional expression. However, the effect of the rule is weakened because the figures are not close to the ground. When the first test does not work out, Cassie goes into another test in which the focus is on the expectation regarding the event place. This test eventually reveals that I–Rule 1 is applicable to the situation and so resolves the reference frame.

```
Initial Interpretation
======================
#> I understand that
   at a place left-away Mary,
   a group of individuals
    namely, a person and Jim
   found some counts of seats.
Deictic-NOW is maintained as b124
Deictic-HERE is maintained as b10
Deictic-WHO is maintained as m16
m30 is maintained as a contextual goal
```

After the input sentence is all processed, Cassie updated the deictic-NOW to *b124*. Information not shown here indicates that this time is somewhere between b122, the last deictic-NOW and *b9*, the event time of the yet-unrealized goal event.

```
S13: Then the lights in the hall dimmed.
```

This sentence contains one definite noun phrase in which another definite noun phrase is embedded. It is not much of a problem for Cassie to recall "the hall" from the story context. However, "the lights" are some individuals which have never explicitly been introduced in the story context. Inference will find *the lights* with the help of a reasoning rule that intuitively states that *for any hall, there exist some lights that are parts of the whole hall.*

```
Initial Interpretation
======================
#> I understand that
   the light part of the hall part of a theater dimmed.
```

Cassie's terse report after the initial interpretation indicates that Cassie correctly related the light to the context.

Because there are no new or unusual spatial issues involved, we omitted the extended interpretation and immediate inference reports. Only the Deictic-NOW is updated to a new time.

```
Deictic-NOW is maintained as b126
Deictic-HERE is maintained as b10
Deictic-WHO is maintained as m16
m30 is maintained as a contextual goal

S14: They saw <Bob's uncle standing behind a lectern
to the left of a microphone>.
```

This sentence contains a pronoun and a previously mentioned kinship noun phrase that each has to be resolved and two directional references whose reference frames have to be resolved.

```
Starting the process of the reference frame resolution.
Starting the process of the reference frame resolution.
```

Both directional references are found within the scope of the dummy agent, "they," that introduces a perspective viewpoint in the input sentence. This sentential structure activates the grammatical rule, G–Rule 2, and resolves the reference frames of both directional references.

```
Initial Interpretation
======================
#> I understand that
   Bob, Tom and Mary
   saw
   a standing act of an uncle of Bob.

Extended Interpretation
=======================
#> Particularly, I note that,
   due to m515 the <standing> act of an uncle of Bob,
   the Figure Object, Bob's uncle
   was BE-LOCated
   at a place b135
    where
```

```
    b135 has a Spatial Relation of "left-away"
     to the Ground Object, individual b136
      where b136 is a member of class microphone
     with the perspectivally resolved reference frame
       of SR
     anchored to the encounter left/right direction-
       ality
     of the Perspective Ego
     invited to the inviting object Bob, Tom and Mary
    and
     b135 has a Spatial Relation of "behind"
     to the Ground Object, individual b134
      where b134 is a member of class lectern
     with the perspectivally resolved reference frame
       of SR
     anchored to the encounter front/back direction-
       ality
     of the Perspective Ego
     invited to the inviting object Bob, Tom and Mary
Deictic-NOW is maintained as b133
Deictic-HERE is maintained as b10
Deictic-WHO is maintained as m16
m30 is maintained as a contextual goal
```

The terse report shows that the pronoun "They" was resolved as referring to the group Bob, Tom, and Mary. The expression "Bob's uncle" was also understood as referring to the same Bob's uncle that Cassie first read about at the beginning of the story.

The extended interpretation report indicates that the reference frames of the directional references "behind a lectern" and "to the left of a microphone," were both perspectivally resolved by a perspective ego invited to the group Bob, Tom and Mary who are viewing the scene.

SUMMARY

We sketched an analysis of spatial information in narratives. We pointed out that understanding directional information requires having a reference frame, and we discussed the reference frame problem—the problem of deciding what the reference frame is for any given description of directional information. We presented six heuristic rules for solving the reference frame problem, and showed the output of a computer program that reads narratives containing directional information, uses the heuristic rules to resolve the reference frame problems, and demonstrates a fair amount of understanding of the narrative text.

9

Preschool Children's Introduction of Characters Into Their Oral Stories: Evidence for Deictic Organization of First Narratives

Judith F. Duchan

State University of New York at Buffalo

Children's spontaneous narratives have been studied in a variety of ways (Peterson & McCabe, 1983, 1991). Some researchers looked at the overall structuring, aiming to determine possible conceptual schemas that govern children's story production. Candidates for this global approach are (a) the high point analysis developed by Labov and Waletsky for stories told by adolescents and adapted for analyzing stories told by younger children (Peterson & McCabe, 1983), (b) story grammar analysis developed by Rumelhart (1975) for cultural myths and adapted for those told by children (Mandler & Johnson, 1977; Stein & Glenn, 1979), and (c) contrastive analysis of story forms used by members of different cultures (Heath, 1983).

Other approaches analyzed children's narratives for the existence of particular language forms. For example, Peterson and McCabe (1983, 1991) studied connectives, Miller and Sperry (1988) studied children's first use of past tense, Gee (1991) examined poetic and expressive forms, and Hewitt and Duchan (in press) studied a child's use of discourse indicators of characters' subjective states.

An additional rendition of story structuring is developed in this book and elsewhere by our cognitive science group in Buffalo (Rapaport et al., 1989; Segal, Duchan, & Scott, 1991; Wiebe, 1990a). The approach conceptualizes the overall story as being structured around one or more deictic centers, and looks for language forms that could provide evidence that such structuring exists. For example, we found evidence that story settings function to shift one's mental orientation to a deictic center for a story world that exists in a time, place, and perspective different from that in which the story is told (Rapaport et al., 1989; Segal, Duchan, & Scott, 1991), and that once the new center is established, it can be presupposed.

Deictic shifts and presupposed centering can be found in stories told by young children. (Excerpts from children's stories used in this chapter are taken from Sutton-Smith, 1981. The story numbers refer to Sutton-Smith's numbering system, and are included for story identification). In the following setting, the child indicates both the place and characters and in so doing establishes a center for subsequent events to occur.

(4) Once upon a time there was a little house,
     and people lived inside it. (Alan, age 5, story 7, p. 127)

As shown elsewhere in this book, once the deictic center has been established, one can interpret deictic verbs such as COME and GO from that reference point. So, characters introduced in the middle of stories can be described as approaching or leaving a presupposed place, without mentioning which place. In the following story, 4-year-old Ephra establishes a spatial center as the home of an elephant, from which characters introduced in the setting leave and into which later characters arrive:

(5) Once upon a time there was a elephant
     and he lived happily
     and the monkey lived right next door
     and then a mountain lion scared them
     and frighten them away
     and so somebody else came
     and that's it. (Ephra, age 4, story 14, p. 85)

A common way stories have of shifting to a new center is to move into the subjective perspective of a character in the story. Five-year-old Ann shifts from an objective perspective in the story world to the subjective perspective of Red Riding Hood. In line i of the excerpt to follow, she objectively describes what the fox (sic) did, a description that could not be from the perspective of Red Riding Hood, because she was not there when the event took place. In line iii, the center has shifted to the perspective of Red Riding Hood, as can be seen from the fact that the fox is now named "grandma," and the deictic term THERE is used when Red Riding Hood is first discovering the character whom she takes to be her grandmother. The THERE refers to a location away from the HERE of Red Riding Hood. Finally, Ann ends the story with a sentence that can be interpreted as Red Riding Hood's subjective reminder to herself not to "do that again."

(6) i   The fox ran in and put the grandmother in a closet.
    ii When Red Riding Hood opened the door

iii there was grandma.
iv "Why do you have such big ears?"
v "They're good to hear with."
vi "Why do you have such big eyes?"
vii "They're good to see with."
viii "Why do you have such big teeth?"
ix "They're good to eat with."
x She ran away from her grandmother.
xi She wouldn't do that again. (Ann, age 5, story 3, p. 129)

In order to determine whether or not children conceptualize a story deictically, one can examine the deictic terms they use to introduce new elements into the story. For example, if they introduce a character into a story in the setting when the first deictic center is being established, they should use terms which serve to establish a place, such as terms identifying a character's or place's existence. If they understand deictic structuring, one would not expect them to include terms in their setting descriptions, that presuppose the audience's knowledge of a center. Specifically, one should find terms such as THERE in settings contexts and terms such as COME or GO in contexts of established centers. And for contexts of deictic shifts, one might predict a high incidence of discourse markers indicating that a shift is about to take place, such as the marker THEN (Duchan, Meth, & Waltzman, 1993; Schiffrin, 1987; Segal, Duchan, & Scott, 1991) along with verbs of departure, such as "went" (Rapaport et al. 1989).

Although it has not been studied directly, there is evidence that children structure their stories deictically, and that deictic terms and the types and locations of these terms in the narrative reflect the deictic structuring of the narrative. Villaume (1988), in her study of literate first and second graders, found that the children favored different introductory devices, two of which she called *existential patient* and *self-propelled patient*. The existential patient most often contained THERE constructions, such as the following: "There once was a dog." These tended to occur in setting contexts. Self-propelled patients occurred later in the text, where a character enters an already formed story scene via verbs of motion, such as BRING and CAME. Thus, as in conversations, children may use deictic terms in narratives differently, depending on whether a deictic center is being established, is being maintained, or is shifting.

The aim of this study was to examine children's use of deictic terms in stories in order to determine whether children's stories have deictic structuring. Because we and others (Segal, Duchan, & Scott, 1991; Villaume, 1988) noted a prevalence of deictic terms in clauses that introduce characters, we chose them for study. They are: CAME, WENT, THERE, and THEN. We added to these terms, HERE and NOW, which have a semantic affiliation with THERE and THEN, to balance the group semantically. The specific approach was to determine how often these six terms occur in contexts of character introduction, how the clauses introducing characters were shaped, and where such introductions occurred in the story. Our hope was that children's use of these terms would give insight into the ways they are conceiving of the deictic organization of their oral stories.

METHOD

Subjects and Data Collection

The narratives analyzed in this study were taken from a set of children's oral stories collected and published by Sutton-Smith (1981). The stories were volunteered by 22 verbally precocious middle- to upper-class 2- to 5-year-olds who were enrolled in a preschool or public school in New York City. The stories were told to *storytakers* who were graduate students in psychology. The storytakers were frequent visitors in the children's classroom over a 2-year period. At the beginning of Sutton-Smith's study, the storytakers were introduced to the children as: "people who like to collect stories from children, and someone to whom you may tell a story at any time you wish." The storytakers wrote down the story verbatim at the time it was told to them. The takers expressed preference for third-person fictional stories by asking children who began a personal experience story to "make up" a story rather than to tell something that really happened.

Sutton-Smith's book grouped together the stories told by each child. A child's early stories may have been told when the child was age 2 and later stories when the child was age 4. The result is that a particular child may have contributed stories to more than one age group. There were 292 stories produced by the preschoolers. No single child told more than 10% of the stories. Four children told 20 or more stories, 9 told between 10 and 19 stories, and 8 children told between 1 and 9 stories. Preliminary analyses of the data by age groups revealed that individual children within the same age group and from different age groups did not differ significantly from one another in the way they used deictic terms. Because of the relative homogeneity of the data, and because the question being asked was not a developmental one, the stories were grouped and analyzed together.

Data Selection

Because the study involved an examination of the language of character introduction, the analysis required that the *characters* of the children's stories be identified. Many characters in the children's stories were inanimate objects, so the definition of character was kept broad, and included any object, animate or inanimate, that was a participant in the story. The referring expressions introducing a participant occurred in verbless phrases (e.g., a horse) and in clauses (e.g., the horse came). On occasion, there were several introductions in a single clause or phrase, as in 4-year-old David's introduction of "a cow and a horse" in the following:

(7) and in the farm there was *a cow* and *a horse* (David, age 4, story 16, p. 78)

The only exclusions from the category of first mentioned participant were direct and oblique objects (object of prepositions) that were not later rementioned as subjects. The oblique object, "doggie," in the following clause was not counted as a participant because it did not occur later in the story in subject position:

(8) The cookie went on the doggie (Alice, age 2, story 1, p. 48)

(See Appendix for a more detailed description of the coding system and examples.)

Once the first mentions of participants were identified, the clauses or phrases surrounding them were examined to determine the presence of the following six selected lexical items: COME, GO, HERE, THERE, NOW, THEN. These items were selected because they were found to vary with the deictic structure (Rapaport et al. 1989), because some of them (THERE, COME) occur often in stories and in contexts of character introduction (Villaume, 1988), and because they form a coherent semantic domain allowing for analysis of spatial and temporal facets surrounding character introductions.

The frequencies of occurrence of the six lexical items in introductory clauses were compared. In addition, analyses were done to determine the syntactic frames for frequently occurring items, those items' location in the story, and the ways the items occurred together in the same story.

RESULTS AND DISCUSSION

There were a total of 1,186 clauses and phrases of introduction in these stories. Some of the introductory clauses and phrases (hereafter referred to as *introductory clauses*) contained more than one participant. There were 1,302 participants introduced by the 1,186 introductory clauses. The number of introductory clauses varied considerably for different stories, even for the same child. For instance, 2-year-old Bill told 18 stories in all, 6 with 1 introductory clause, 8 with 2, 2 with 3, 1 with 5, and 1 with 6. The 6 deictic terms under study occurred 735 times in introductory clauses. Of these 735, 31% (229/735) were CAMEs, 12% (86/735) were WENTs, 1% (8/735) were HEREs, 27% (197/735) were THEREs, 1% (5/735) were NOWs, and 29% (210/735) were THENs.

The 6 deictic devices also occurred in clauses that did not introduce characters, with differing frequencies. CAME and THERE were the most dedicated to introductory clauses, with 74% of all occurrences of CAME and 88% of all occurrences of THERE falling into first mention, introductory contexts. In contrast, only 27% of the occurrences of WENT and 39% of the occurrences of THEN appeared in clauses of introduction. HERE and NOW, which occurred only occasionally, differed in their degree of dedication to introductory contexts, with 25% of the occurrences of HERE in contexts of first mention, and 50% of the occurrences of NOW occurring in such contexts.

The low incidence of HERE and NOW in the children's stories is in keeping with what is expected from the deictic theory framework, that argues that stories are deictically located in a center away from the current here-and-now. While such terms are interpretable in the shifted here-and-now of a story context (for examples see 1, 2, and 3), the use (unlike the direct point of the conversational context) is esoteric and not as easily interpreted as those used in the conversational present.

Clauses Containing Verbs CAME and WENT

Introductory clauses frequently contained either COME or GO as a main verb (most often expressed in a narrative past tense as CAME and WENT). As noted previously, CAME was the more frequent of the two introducers, occurring nearly three times more often than WENT, although the two verbs are logically symmetrical. The clausal shape also differed for CAME and WENT introductory clauses. CAME most often introduced participants with an unelaborated verb phrase as exemplified below:

(9) Alligator came. (Ezra, age 3, story 9, p. 89)

Of the 229 introductory clauses containing CAME, 139 (61%) were bare, in that they had no indicator of locale from or to which the introduced character came. Indeed, for only 19 (8%) of all CAMEs in first mention contexts was a locale specified for the verb, as depicted in the following two examples:

(10) and a big apple came down from a tree (Ezra, age 3, story 9, p. 89)

(11) a kitty came in the house (Alice, age 3, story 7, p. 49)

WENT, by way of contrast, occurred infrequently as a bare verb and frequently with an object or prepositional phrase specifying locale. Of the 86 WENT clauses, only 12 (14%) were bare; all the others specified a locale.

This difference in locale of CAME and WENT is support for a deictic structuring of the discourse, with CAME serving to introduce characters into already established deictic centers and WENT to introduce characters into newly created centers. Indeed, it is the WENT clause that specifies the shift to the new place, with the new locale being indicated in the phrase following the verb (e.g., "went to the woods" shifts the deictic center to the woods).

Relative Prevalence and Within-Clause Co-Occurrence of the Six Deictic Terms

The six terms—CAME, WENT, HERE, THERE, NOW, and THEN—were used singly in a clause for 37% (438/1186) of the introductory clauses, and in combination with one another in 13% (150/1186) of the introductory clauses. Together, these accounted for 50% (588/1186) of the total number of introductory clauses. The remaining clauses of introduction did not contain any of the deictic terms.

Of the stories with more than one term in the same clause, nearly all (96%, 144/150) contained THEN, and of these THEN + X clauses, 75% (108/144) were of the type THEN + CAME. The within-clause co-occurrence of THEN and CAME supports earlier findings that THEN serves as a marker of discourse discontinuity (Duchan, Meth, & Waltzman, 1992; Schiffrin, 1987; Segal, Duchan, & Scott, 1991), in this case, marking the arrival of a new character into an already established deictic center.

A second context of discourse discontinuity that would lend itself to the occurrence of THEN involves the departure verb WENT, because verbs of departure function to locate the deictic center in a new place, resulting in discontinuity. Of the total THEN + X clauses, only 12.5% (18/144) were THEN + WENT combinations. One reason for the low percentage of THEN occurrences in WENT contexts was that many of the WENT clauses (49% or 42/86) occurred in setting contexts where the deictic center was first being established. For those contexts of WENT in which the center had already been established, 40% (18/44) contained THEN. In these discontinuity contexts in which WENT created a deictic shift, THEN was used. This co-occurrence suggests that the verb WENT combined with the adverb THEN were indicating a discontinuity in the story, in this case a place shift.

The Story Location of Introductory Clauses Containing the Six Deictic Terms

Although all stories contained participants and clauses of introduction, not all stories contained the six deictic terms. Of the 292 stories, 212 (or 73%) contained one or more of the terms in contexts of character introduction. Stories that had introductory clauses with deictic terms either contained one or more examples of the same term, showing device invariance (35%, or 103/292); or contained two or more different devices (37%, or 109/292). For example, 3-year-old Ephra told 3 stories and introduced 18 characters in them. Of the 18 introductions, 9 were introduced with deictic terms, and in all cases the term was the same (CAME) (e.g., "and then came a giraffe"—story 3). On the other hand, Danielle, another 3-year-old, introduced 63 characters, 39 of which were introduced by one or more of the select devices. She used all of the following singly or in combination: THEN, CAME, WENT, and THERE.

An analysis of those stories containing more than one of the introductory clauses with deictic terms was carried out to determine where in the story these clauses occurred. Each of the introducing clauses containing a deictic term was indexed according to its location in the sequence of the story. The stories were divided into linguistic lines by numbering each phrase (for those phrases which contained no verb) or each independent clause. Figure 9.1 displays the absolute distribution of the most frequently occurring terms in introducing contexts, namely: CAME, WENT, THERE, and THEN.

There were two types of distribution contours. The first contained a first line peak followed by a rapid fall. This narrow-peak pattern occurred for both WENT and THERE. A first line preference was especially pronounced for THERE, comprising 52% (103/197) of the first-mention THEREs. Twenty-seven percent (23/86) of the introducing WENTs occurred in the first line of the story, and another 22% (19/86) occurred in the second line, together comprising nearly half (49%) of all introducing WENTs.

The second contour shape presented a rise from first to second lines, a peak in lines 3 or 4, and a gradual fall. The frequency distribution of THEN and CAME both fit this broad-peak pattern. THEN differed from CAME in that it never occurred in the first line of the stories, whereas CAME occurred in the first lines of 13 of the 292 stories.

A sequential analysis of the co-occurrences of different devices revealed that for those 41 stories containing both THERE and COME introductory clauses, 36 (88%) had the THERE clause located earlier in the story than the COME clause. Even more strongly, in all the 14 cases in which THERE + WENT occurred in separate clauses of the same story, THERE preceded WENT. The co-occurrence of CAME + WENT in introductory clauses was not as regularly ordered. In three of the stories, the WENT clauses preceded all clauses with CAME. However for the remaining five stories, the occurrences of WENT and CAME were interspersed in unpredictable order throughout the text. (As is shown in Fig. 9.1, in most instances WENT occurred early in the story and instances of CAME occurred later, but the figure includes all stories and not just those that contained more than one device.)

The first line occurrence of THERE might be expected by those, such as Villaume (1988), who saw children's first lines (Once there was an X) as formulaic. What is not formulaic is the children's understanding that the introduction of a character in a THERE clause at the story's beginning establishes a center into which later characters come (as evidenced by their use of CAME and WENT to introduce characters later in the story). Thus, whereas the existential–deictic function of the term THERE may not be interpreted deictically by children who produce THERE as a formulaic beginning of their story, those same children are understanding that character introductions at story beginnings structure the story deictically. This is exemplified by the following story beginning produced by 4-year-old Ephra:

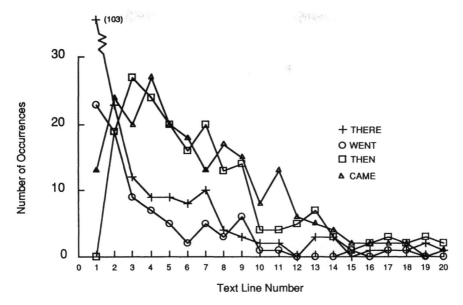

FIG. 9.1.   Most frequently occurring terms in introducing contexts.

(12) Once there was a squirrel.
and one day his mother squirrel came along. (Ephra, age 4, story 4, p. 82)

The squirrel, once introduced, provides a place of origin for the term CAME, allowing for the interpretation that the mother was accompanying the squirrel, with the squirrel's place of presence providing the center into which the mother squirrel enters.

What was not predicted by the deictic center theory is the first line occurrences of the departure verb WENT. Indeed, this occurrence of WENT in a context in which the deictic center is being established runs counter to what would be predicted. WENT, according to deictic theory requires that the departure is from a known locale, and thus should occur once the originating locale is established.

Examination of the WENT clauses reveals that young children might be presupposing that the place in which their story is situated is at home. This is suggested by the following examples from the first lines of children's stories:

(13) My cat went to the doctor (David, age 3, story 7, p. 76)

(14) Once a man went to the post office
and mailed a letter (Ephra, age 4, story 7, p. 83)

In addition, there were a number of uses of WENT occurring in the first line of stories which did not indicate a departure from the overall scene (i.e., were not a deictic shift to a new location), but rather described a movement of an object within the scene, as indicated by the following story by 3-year-old Danielle:

(15) Batman went over Superman
and Wonder Woman came
and then Robin came
Mommys and daddys came
Superman went over Robin (Danielle, age 3, story 4, p. 70)

Danielle seems to use WENT in the above story to describe a motion within the scene, rather than as a deictic shift away from the scene. Her within-scene conceptualization is indicated by her description of characters going over one another, followed by a description of new characters entering what seems to be the original scene. For example, Superman was part of the first scene, as indicated in the first line, and also part of the scene to which Robin came.

For those children who are using WENT in their first lines as a departure verb (as in example 14), they may be assuming the locale and existence of home as a center for their stories. If this is the case, the stories beginning with WENT are still deictically centered, and indeed, involve a shift at the beginning into the story frame, because the children were telling their stories at school and not at home. This home-as-presupposed-center based account would explain how WENT, which occurs prior to establishing a center, could be consistent with a deictic center interpretation of children's stories. Bolstering this home-as-center theory, the verb WENT is followed by a place indicator in story beginnings, offering the story a location. This consistency is not true for THERE, a term usually followed by the specification of a character rather than a place, nor is it true for CAME, which occurs as a bare verb. Thus, WENT at story beginnings indicate that the story is not taking place at home, but in the place indicated.

Deictic Center Theory Versus Other Renditions of Children's Story Structuring

This study was of the deictic organization of narratives told by normal language learners, between the ages of 2 and 5. The children used THERE, CAME, WENT, and THEN to introduce characters into their stories. They used the terms THERE and WENT to introduce characters at the beginning of their stories, and they used CAME and THEN to introduce characters after the story had begun.

The children's use of deictic terms in their stories is compatible with a theory that holds that narratives are organized around deictic centers, centers that are different from those used in conversational interactions (e.g., Banfield, 1982; Clarke, 1986; Hamburger, 1973; Segal, Duchan, & Scott, 1991). In narratives, the elements of the situation must be introduced and the deictic center must be established. In conversations, deictic terms originate from the perspective of the speaker in the site and time in which the conversation takes place. The deictic center is consistent and predictable; it is a speaker's perspective taken with regard to elements in the situation. The time and location of the events do not have to be introduced, nor do decisions have to be made for where to establish such a center.

The deictic center theory is compatible with certain aspects of other findings on the structuring of children's stories. For example, the deictic center view recasts the story grammar view of stories beginning with a grammatical node of "setting" into a functional view of story setting. Within the story grammar, categories are learned through memorization, statives and habitual statements locating the story in time and place. Introductions of characters are placed at the beginning of stories because that is where the grammar dictates they should be. Within the deictic center view, the structure derives from functional needs. Characters are introduced at the beginning of the story as part of the need to establish the story's deictic center. They occur at the story's beginning because narratives do not begin on the here-and-now deictic plane that originates in the speaker, and therefore, they require that a center be established.

Some analyses have divided stories into separable episodes within which the plot is organized. Analysts using the deictic center theory examine stories for deictic continuities and discontinuities. Discontinuities occur often in places in which new characters are introduced, in which old characters move from one place to another, or in which time shifts occur. These are the places where THEN and CAME occurred in the children's stories in this study. It is at these places of indicated discontinuity that story grammarians are likely to designate a beginning of a new episode (Segal, Duchan, & Scott, 1991).

The results of this study show that young children are aware of deixis in their story construction, and that they structure their stories in keeping with a coherent deictic center that includes personal, spatial, and temporal elements.

ACKNOWLEDGMENTS

This research was supported by NSF Grant No. IRI8610517 to G. Bruder, J. Duchan, E. Segal, W. Rapaport, S. Shapiro, and D. Zubin and is based on data published in Sutton-Smith (1981).

This paper grew out of theoretical formulations developed by colleagues in the Cognitive Science Graduate Group at SUNY at Buffalo. Of particular importance were ideas and editing from Alan Duchan, Mary Galbraith, Lynne Hewitt, Jeff Higginbotham, Erwin Segal, and Rae Sonnenmeier.

APPENDIX

Rules used to determine the first mention of participants in children's stories (underlined elements indicate the portion of the phrase counted as a participant):

1. A simple noun phrase that served as the subject of a main or embedded clause, and that also introduced a person, event, or place into the story, was counted as a single participant. Numbers = total number of participants for that segment.)

    a. Peter went over the castle.   = 1
       (Alice, age 3 story 4, p. 49)

    b. and a fly got on the worm.   = 1
       (Alice, age 3, story 6, p. 49)

2. A compound noun phrase that served as subject of a main or embedded clause, and also one that introduced more than one entity into the story was counted as a multiple participant introduction. Each entity introduced was counted once.

    a. Mommys and daddys came.   = 2

    b. The sisters. brothers, mothers,
       and fathers were all sleeping   = 4
       (Farrah, age 4, story 9, p. 102)

3. A noun phrase that was not understandable, yet served as subject of a clause of introduction, was counted as a participant.

    a. The dillow went over the dillow.   = 1
       (Danielle, age 3, story 7, p. 71)

4. If the first mention of an entity was with a pronoun whose referent was not known, the entity was still counted as a single first mention.

    a. She made pee on the floor.   = 1
       (Beatrice, age 2, story 1, p. 52)

5. If an entity was introduced once under one description, and mentioned a second time under a second description or paraphrase, it was only counted once.

    a. Someone said something. . .
       Then he opened his lunchbox. . .
       It said "ouch."   = 1
       (Abe, age 5, story 4, p. 120)

6. If several entities were introduced at first as a group and then reintroduced as individual members of the group, the group mention was counted as one, and the individualized mentions were each counted as introductory mentions of participants.

    a. The monkey had <u>hats</u>.
       <u>Blue hats</u> and <u>white hats</u>.   = 3
       (Bill, age 3, story 19, p. 56)

    b. He had <u>two helpers</u>
       The helpers were named <u>Frankenstein</u>
       and <u>Godzilla</u>   = 3
       (Ingbert, age 4, story 4, p. 111)

7. If the first mention of an entity was a specific form and subsequent mentions were general forms or groups, both specific and general mentions were counted as participant introductions.

    a. One day <u>a robber</u> came and took some
       things off the roof
       and took some plants outside
       and the next morning <u>daddy</u> looked for the plants
       and there wasn't any
       and <u>everybody</u> said "where's the plants?"   = 3
       (Ephra, age 3, story 2, p. 81)

8. A noun phrase containing a possessive pronoun or noun that was later rementioned as clausal subject was counted as a participant introduction.

    a. The little fiddle went over <u>Cathy</u>'s head   = 1
       and then Cathy kissed everybody.
       (Danielle, age 3, story 5, p. 70)

    b. There was <u>a big big monster</u>
       bite <u>my finger</u> off
       then I saw a long long book.   = 2
       (Ezra, age 3, story 7, p. 88)

9. If the first mention of an entity was in a title or a description of what the story is about, and then rementioned in a nominalized form at the beginning of the story, both title mentions and story mentions are counted as introductions.

    a. <u>Little Red Riding Hood</u>
       <u>Little Red Riding Hood</u> went into the
       forest.   = 2
       (Danielle, age 4, story 16, p. 73)

10. Descriptions of more than one entity in a single simple noun phrase were counted as a single participant.

    a. and there were <u>two cats</u>   = 1
       (Garrett, age 4, story 6, p. 104)

    b. Once upon a time there were
       two gorillas and <u>three cats</u>   = 2
       (Ingbert, age 5, story 7, p. 112)

11. General expressions such as "anyone, someone, no one, all, another one, none" were each counted as a single participant.

    a. <u>Someone</u> bit him in the water.   = 1
       (Cathy, age 3 story 9, p. 59)

    b. and <u>everyone</u> was named
       once upon a time   = 1
       (Ingbert, age 5, story 14, p. 114)

12. Formulaic compound noun phrases that are usually taken to mean a single entity, were counted as one participant.

    a. <u>Cat in the Hat</u>   = 1
       (Cathy, age 2, story 1, p. 57)

13. A noun phrase that was introduced in object position of a main or embedded clause was counted as a participant only if it also occurred later in the story in subject position. (The later occurrence can be either nominalized or pronominalized.)

    a. They pushed on <u>the people</u>
       The people got hurt.   = 1
       (Clarence, age 2, story 2, p. 62)

14. A noun phrase serving as clausal complement was counted as a participant.

    a. Now there was <u>a pa ka</u>.   = 1
       (Cathy, age 3, story 12, p. 61)

15. Noun phrases which were first mentioned in verbless phrases were counted as participants.

a. <u>A monkey</u>
   <u>a dog</u>
   <u>a book</u>
   <u>a fish</u> = 4
   (Adam, age 2, story 1, p. 47)

16. If a noun phrase occurred outside a clause and was not a recognizable word, it was not counted as a participant.

a. cha cha doo choo = 0
   (Cathy, age 3, story 12, p. 61)

10

PSYCHOLOGICAL EVIDENCE THAT LINGUISTIC DEVICES ARE USED BY READERS TO UNDERSTAND SPATIAL DEIXIS IN NARRATIVE TEXT

Gail A. Bruder
State University of New York at Buffalo

INTRODUCTION

This chapter briefly reviews the psychological literature relevant to spatial tracking in narratives; describes some linguistic devices that Zubin (Zubin & Hewitt, this volume) has suggested serve to introduce, maintain or shift the Deictic Center in narrative; and describes psychological studies conducted to test the validity of these devices. The main focus of the studies was to assess readers' abilities to track the spatial component of the Deictic Center, or the WHERE. (See Bruder & Wiebe, this volume, for a description of research related to tracking psychological point of view—the WHO—in narrative.)

Background

The psychological literature pertaining to narrative tends to fall into one of several categories: structural descriptions of narrative (Segal, this volume, provides a brief discussion of structural description approaches, such as frames, story grammars, and scripts), causal relations in narrative (cf. Trabasso & Sperry, 1985; Trabasso & van den Broek, 1985), inference in narrative (cf. papers in the issue of *Discourse Processes* edited by Graesser, 1993; for an alternative viewpoint on inference, see McKoon & Ratcliff, 1992), and deixis.[1] This chapter focuses on deixis in narrative, and we briefly review the literature relevant to that topic.

---

[1]The literature on general text comprehension is voluminous and is not covered here. For a description of an early influential model of text comprehension see Kintsch and van Dijk (1978). For a more recent treatment of this topic see Just and Carpenter (1987).

Black, Turner, and Bower (1979) explored the role of deixis in narrative comprehension. They argued that coherence in narrative is dependent on maintaining a consistent point of view. Deictic verbs such as "come" and "bring" indicate movement toward the established point of view, and "go" and "take" indicate movement away from the established point of view. They tested the hypothesis that understanding narrative would suffer if the point of view indicated by deictic verbs differed from that previously established. In one series of studies, they used complex sentences wherein the first clause established an initial point of view by describing the identity and location of the focal character. The second clause contained a deictic verb that was either consistent or inconsistent with the point of view established in the first clause. For example, the alternative completions for the phrase "Bill was sitting in the living room reading the paper" might be: "when John came [consistent] into the living room," or, "when John went [inconsistent] into the living room." As predicted, they found inconsistent point of view sentences took longer to read, were rated as less comprehensible, had poorer recall of the deictic verb, and were edited more (in the direction of deictic consistency). A similar pattern of the effects of inconsistent deictic terms on reading time, recall, and editing was found when the point of view was established by character alone without mention of a particular location. Black, Turner, and Bower explained their approach and predictions using a metaphor—a cameraman filming a movie and being instructed as to where to set up the camera by the text. Their metaphor was a precursor to later models of tracking point of view and deixis, including our own Deictic Center model.

Our model, like other models of narrative comprehension, takes as its starting point the assumption that the reader builds a mental model of narrative (cf. Johnson-Laird, 1983). This model of narrative includes a representation of the important characters and events, as well as a representation of their current location in time and space. The contents of this mental representation guide the interpretation of subsequent text.[2]

In the following sections, I describe a number of factors found in the literature to influence the identification and location of characters. Of particular interest are those related to deixis.

Factors Implicated in Locating Characters

Morrow (1985a) tested the role of spatial prepositions in locating characters on a path between a source and goal room. Subjects memorized a layout of rooms before reading short narratives describing a character moving through those rooms. Sentences were of the form: "He walked from/though/past the study [source or path

---

[2]This type of model has been contrasted (cf. Morrow, 1985b) with one in which the surface characteristics of the text itself, such as recency of mention, controls the interpretation of subsequent text including ambiguous referents. A number of studies (cf. Morrow, 1985b; Stark, 1987) found that factors other than recency play a role in the tracking of characters.

room] to the bedroom [goal room]. Readers indicated where the character was by identifying the room of the layout referred to by the next sentence. For example, a subsequent sentence might be: "He did not find his glasses in the room." Subjects were more likely to select the goal room than the source/path room when the prepositions used were from/to or from/into. Subjects were more likely to select the path room when the prepositions were through/to or past/to. When "into" was used as the second preposition ("into the bedroom") the goal room was selected most frequently, regardless of whether the other preposition is "through" or "past." Morrow used simple past tenses in the above studies.

In that same series of studies, Morrow also tested the combined effects of verb aspect and prepositions on determining character location. He found that verb aspect added to the role of prepositions in locating a moving character. When past progressive aspect was used ("walking" rather than "walked"), readers with "walking through/past" overwhelmingly chose the path room as the referent, and did so more often than readers with past tense verb aspect. Although less overwhelming, readers also selected the path room more often with walking from/to or walking from/into. Morrow concluded that both prepositions and verb aspect combine to determine the spatial location of characters. (Zubin has argued that the WHERE, WHEN, and WHO aspects of the Deictic Center tend to be maintained or shifted together in what he calls Deictic Synchronism (see Zubin & Hewitt, this volume).

In a related series of studies of spatial tracking, Morrow, Greenspan, and Bower (1987) found accessibility of objects (in the memorized layout of rooms) was influenced by the location of the protagonist. They tested accessibility by having readers respond as quickly as possible as to whether or not two objects were in the same room. Readers were faster when the objects were in the same room as the protagonist.[3]

Factors Implicated in Identifying Characters

Morrow (1985b) studied the role of character status and foregrounding on the selection of the character referent for an ambiguous pronoun. He contrasted protagonist and nonprotagonist characters and manipulated whether events involving the character were forgrounded or backgrounded. He constructed congruent narratives, in which the protagonist was foregrounded; and incongruent ones, in which the nonprotagonist was foregrounded. Of particular interest is the fact that temporal connectives had an influence on the results. With incongruent narratives, Morrow found that the effect of foregrounding on selecting the non-

---

[3]Bower and Morrow (1990) summarized their research and characterized it as providing evidence that readers use a spatial layout to track the events in narrative. More recent research, however, indicates that their results depend on the reader's attention to the protagonist's location (see Wilson, Rinck, McNamara, Bower, & Morrow, 1993). That is, results replicated only when protagonist probes were used in the task.

protagonist as the referent depended on the temporal sequence of story events, for example, "Harry [nonprotagonist] walked toward the ferris wheel after Tom [protagonist] went into the hall." The nonprotagonist was more likely to be selected as the referent when the foregrounded event was the most recent in story time.

Stark (1987) also found an effect of temporal connectives on the accessibility of characters. Using computerized presentation, Stark had readers read narratives phrase by phrase and interrupted this reading by presenting a name probe. Readers were to respond as quickly as they could as to whether or not that name referred to a character in the current story. Access, as measured by reaction time, was faster to the more distant (in recency of mention) character when the temporal connective "meanwhile" (as opposed to "then") was used just prior to the probe.

Stark found three additional factors that were related to character identification. When the sentence prior to the name probe referred to a goal relevant to one character, access to that character's name was facilitated. The other two factors were related to spatial location. Access to a character's name was facilitated when a prior sentence referred to that character's location, or described a scene from that character's perspective.

OUR APPROACH AND OUR PSYCHOLOGICAL RESEARCH

As is evident from other chapters in this volume, our approach assumes that the readers construct a mental model of the narrative—including a deictic center—in order to infer temporal, spatial, and perspectival relations among characters, objects, and events in the narrative. What follows is a description of a series of studies that use a variety of approaches to measure spatial tracking, with special emphasis on linguistic devices used to indicate spatial deixis. Taken as a whole, the convergence of evidence from these varied approaches provides convincing evidence for the psychological reality of the linguistic devices for readers of narrative.

Based on the work of Zubin (1989; Zubin & Hewitt, this volume), we tested two linguistic devices. These devices are: *preposed adverbials* and *deictic verbs of motion.* Zubin suggested that preposed adverbials, such as "in La Paz" or "outside the door," serve to introduce and/or to shift the WHERE of the DC. If there are no preposed locatives, the current WHERE is maintained. Locative adverbials in a noninitial position may indicate a potential shift. Similarly, deictic verbs may serve to maintain or to shift the WHERE depending on the context. Maintenance of the WHERE occurs with deictic verbs "come" and "bring" when the goal (location) is the current WHERE (explicitly by mention or implicitly by no mention of different goal location)—for example, "When Kino had finished, Juana came back to the fire. . ." (Steinbeck, 1945/1975, p. 5). When mention is made of a specified goal location which differs from the current WHERE, "come" can serve to shift the WHERE to that new location—for example, "They came to the place where the brush houses stopped. . ." (Steinbeck, 1945/1975, p. 10).

"Went" indicates movement away from the current WHERE. Because of this movement, it has the potential for shifting the WHERE. This shift is actualized if the sentence following includes a preposed adverbial or a reference to something in the new location—for example, "He slipped his feet into his sandals and went outside to watch the dawn. "Outside the door. . ." (Steinbeck, 1945/1975, p. 3). However, "went" used merely to describe a departure would not shift the current WHERE—for example, "[Four beggars] were students of the expressions of young women as they went into confession and they saw them as they came out. . ." (Steinbeck, 1945/1975, p. 11). A shift in the WHO can also indicate a shift in the WHERE—for example, "[Juana] combed her black hair. . . Kino squatted by the fire pit" (Steinbeck, 1945/1975, p. 5). The WHERE shifts from where Juana is to the fire pit as is evident in a later sentence where Juana "came back" to the fire pit.

In this section, I describe five studies testing the role of preposed adverbials and/or deictic verbs in shifting or maintaining the WHERE of the DC. The sections are organized according to the approach taken and the specific question asked. For example, in some studies we were interested in the overall interpretation of the narrative and did not monitor the online processing used to arrive at this interpretation. In other studies, we did attempt to assess the online processing of the narrative in relation to these linguistic devices. An overview of the studies, their approaches, the devices tested, and the texts employed are shown in Table 10.1.

Assessing the Interpretation of Narratives

Study 1: Preposed Adverbials, Deictic Verbs, and the WHERE. In our first attempt to evaluate the role of various linguistic devices, we (Segal, Bruder, & Daniels, 1984) conducted a study to evaluate readers' interpretation of narrative as a function of manipulations of spatially relevant devices. To do this, we looked at readers' interpretation of the WHERE following manipulations of preposed adverbials and deictic verbs.

TABLE 10.1
Overview of the Five Studies Reported:
The Approach, Devices Tested, and Text Used

Study	Approach	Devices	Text Used
1	Interpretation of narrative	Preposed adverbials Deictic verbs	*The Pearl*
2	Interpretation of narrative	Deictic verbs	*The Pearl*
3	Online interpretation of narrative	Deictic verbs	*Lake Wobegon Days* *Leaving Home*
4	Online comprehension difficulty	Preposed adverbials	*The Pearl*
5	Online accessibility of DC information	Preposed adverbials Deictic verbs	Constructed

Because Zubin's (1989) analysis of linguistic devices was based primarily on Steinbeck's (1945/1975) *The Pearl*, we used that as our narrative. We divided the first chapter into 30 segments from 2 to 17 sentences in length. We modified some segments (e.g., adding references to an animal) in order to test the location of the WHERE. Each segment appeared on a separate page and was followed by a series of from 2 to 6 statements about that segment.

There were three versions of the narrative. Twenty-five sentences differed across these versions, whereas the remaining sentences remained the same. The versions were created by varying the 25 sentences in the original version by changing "come" to "go," "go" to "come," and moving or removing preposed locative adverbials.

Sixty subjects were randomly assigned to one of the three versions. Subjects were students at The State University of New York at Buffalo, or were friends or acquaintances of the researchers. The subjects were instructed to proceed through the test booklet at their own pace and to read the segments and test statements in order without returning to a prior page. Readers were instructed to read the segment and to use a 6-point scale, ranging from *definitely false* (1) to *definitely true* (6) to indicate whether or not they agreed with each of the test statments.

Of the total of 115 questions, we predicted from Zubin (1989) that 16 would be biased in one direction or the other. The results of the study showed that responses to 15 of these 16 questions differed in the predicted direction (based on the manipulation of the lingusitic device). However, only two of the questions yielded statistical significance. In one of these two, the manipulation involved a preposed adverbial; for the other, the manipulation involved a switch of the deictic verb. The significance of the two test sentences, and the trend in the direction predicted for all but one of the remaining test sentences provided some initial support for the role of preposed adverbials and deictic verbs in tracking the deictic WHERE.

Study 2: Deictic Verbs and the WHERE.   In a subsequent study, we (Bruder, 1988) looked more closely at the role of deictic verbs "come" and "go" in the interpretation of narrative. For this study, the passages tested the role of deictic verbs in shifting the WHERE, in disambiguating the WHERE, and in influencing the selection of what character's perspective was being reflected in the narrative.

The beginning of *The Pearl* (Steinbeck, 1945/1975) was divided into 31 short passages. The paragraph structure in the original narrative provided a natural basis for segmenting most of the passages. Eleven of the passages[4] were used to test the deictic verbs. Of these, 10 passages had either "came" or "went" in the original version. For the 11th passage, "come" was substituted for the verb

---

[4]As can be seen in Table 10.2, modifications were made in the passages in order that we might test the current location of the WHERE.

of motion in the original, preserving direction of motion conveyed in the original passage. (See Table 10.2 for examples of different types of passages.)

Two versions of the narrative were prepared. For each passage with "came" in the original version, a new version was created by substituting "went." Likewise, for each passage with "went" in the original, a new version using "came" was constructed. Both versions were given to an equal number of readers; each reader had about 5 of 11 passages with "came" and the rest with "went." Each passage was followed by two to four statements about the passage. Some of these were foil statements to disguise the interest in location and character identity.

The subjects were 75 male and 95 female introductory psychology students who participated as part of a laboratory requirement. Each subject read one passage at a time and after each, indicated whether statements about the passage were true or false. Subjects also indicated how certain they were about their answer, using a scale from *very uncertain* (1) to *very certain* (4).

I converted the evaluations of true and those of false, which totalled 8 possible values, to scores ranging from 0 (*very certain the statement was false*) to 7 (*very certain the statement was true*). Separate analyses were done for each of the test statements. In interpreting the means, it should be kept in mind that means of 3 or 4 resulted from averaging high and low scores. Very few subjects actually selected either of the very uncertain ratings (in the converted scores, 3 was used to indicate *very uncertain the statement was false*; 4 to indicate *very uncertain the statement was true*). Although not all of the test statements yielded statistical significance, none of the foil statements (statements about sentences that did not differ across versions) showed significant differences.

In 7 of the 11 passages, the location of characters or objects was tested in order to determine the role of deictic verbs in establishing characters' or objects' location. We assumed that mention of entities without a specified location would lead the reader to place them in the current WHERE. We defined the current WHERE as the location of the main characters and events prior to the target sentence with the deictic verb. The following describes the tests of location of these characters or objects as a function of the context.

In the first five passages, the target sentence specified movement to a destination other than the current location (WHERE). In these cases the new location was specified and we predicted that "come" would shift the WHERE. In the first two of these five passages, "came" was more likely than "went" to shift the WHERE to the new location. These statements about these passages inquired as to the whereabouts of a character other than the one who moved (in the deictic sentence). In the third and fourth passages, the statements measured the subjects' sense of location of objects perceived by the moving character after the deictic sentence. The trend was in the predicted direction for the third passage but not so for the fourth. Both deictic verbs in the fourth passage seemed to shift the WHERE to the new location. Finally, in the fifth passage, prior background knowledge seemed to locate the character tested.

I. Tests of Location

Example 1: [The servant gives the pearls back to Kino who is at the gate][a]. "The doctor has gone out, " he said. "He was called to a serious case." And he shut the gate quickly out of shame.

And now a wave of shame went over the whole procession. They melted away. The beggars came/*went*[b] back to the church steps. [Some curious little children stopped playing in the dirt and looked up at them.][c] (Steinbeck, 1945/1975, p. 15).

	CAME	WENT
The Children were near the church.	3.23	1.69

$F(1, 154) = 18.76, p < .001$

| The Children were near the gate to the doctor's house. | 4.13 | 5.54 |

$F(1, 154) = 18.64, p < .001$ (In the other passage of this type, $F(1, 158) = 40.52, p < .001$.)

Example 2: [Now the servant has left the doctor's chamber and is at the gate asking Kino if he has any money][a] And this time he spoke in the old language. "Have you any money to pay for the treatment?"

Now Kino reached into a secret place somewhere under his blanket. He brought out a paper folded many times. Crease by crease he unfolded it . . .[d] The servant took the paper and closed the gate again [and left. He came/went[b,e] back with the packet of ugly little pearls][c]. (Steinbeck, 1945/1975, p. 15).

	CAME	WENT
The servant is approaching the Doctor's chamber with the pearls.	3.94	5.79

$F(1, 155) = 22.34, p < .001$

| The servant is approaching the gate with the pearls. | 3.51 | 1.29 |

$F(1, 155) = 33.29, p < .001$ (In the other passage of this type, differences were not significant.)

Example 3. [It is now later that morning][a] [Juana was preparing a fire][c]. She broke little pieces of brush.

Now Kino got up and wrapped his blanket about his head and nose and shoulders. He slipped his feet into his sandals and came/*went*[b] outside to watch the dawn. Kino squatted down and gathered the blanket ends about his knees. (Steinbeck, 1945/1975, p. 3).

	CAME	WENT
Juana is inside the brush house.	3.36	4.20

$F(1, 158) = 4.31, p < .05$

II. Tests of Character and Perspective

Example 4. [The servant approaches the doctor's chamber][a] [The doctor] poured his second cup of chocolate and crumbled a sweet biscuit in his fingers. The servant *came*/went[b] to the open door and stood waiting to be noticed. [He looked at the silent figure.]c (Steinbeck, 1945/1975, p. 14).

	CAME	WENT
The doctor looked at the silent figure.	4.54	3.17

$F(1, 89) = 6.04, p < .05$ (females only; for males $F < 1$)

| The servant looked at the silent figure. | 2.76 | 4.15 |

$F(1, 88) = 5.91, p < .05$ (females only, for males $F < 1$). (In the other passage, of this type, in one of the two test statements, the effect was significant for only the female subjects, $F(1, 88) = 4.96, p < .05$.)

Note. Minor deviations from the original, such as substitutes of a name for a pronoun, are not noted here.

[a]A brief summary subjects read to put the passage in context.

[b]Indicates the alternatives; the italicized word was in the original.

[c]Sentence or phrase not in the original.

[d]Some segments which were read by subjects are deleted here and indicated by ". . .".

[e]Sentence was not the original version. The sense of the original sentence is closest to "come."

Thus, we find some evidence that "came" shifts the WHERE to the new location mentioned; "went" may also shift the WHERE, thus leading to a lack of significant differences.

The sixth and seventh passages had an undefined destination. These could be used to assess "came" as an indicator of movement toward the current WHERE. In passage 6, readers with the "came" verb were more likely to place the character at the current WHERE than were those who read a version containing "went" (see example 2 in Table 10.2). In passage 7, readers showed no differences.

In the eighth passage, I tested the role of deictic verbs in disambiguating the WHERE. In this passage, the WHERE was not identified prior to the deictic sentence (see example 3 in Table 10.2). That is to say, the current WHERE could be outside or inside, or with one of the other characters. This leads to a conflict about how to interpret the deictic verbs. If the characters start out in the same location, whether it be inside or outside, the character who moves cannot "come" into the location of the other character. One resolution of ambiguity would be to assume the characters started out in different locations. Another would be to assume they started out in the same location and to interpret "came" as signalling a shift in the WHERE to a new location for the moving character. The results indicated that more readers followed the first alternative and had the characters originate in different locations when "came" was used.

In passages 9 and 10, I tested the role of deictic verbs in establishing the perspective being taken. I did this by looking at the interpretation of an ambiguous character reference. If other factors do not disambiguate the reference, this pronoun should be interpreted as referring to the character from whose physical point of view the event was unfolding—the character at the WHERE (typically the WHO). We predicted that "come" would establish the destination as the WHERE and lead the reader to adopt the point of view of the stationary character already there. "Go" would indicate the moving character was at the WHERE and was leaving it. This interpretation led the reader to adopt the point of view of the moving character (see example 4). Only female subjects showed statistically significant differences. (See Bruder & Wiebe, this volume, for a further description of gender differences relative to interpreting point of view.)

The last (eleventh) passage tested perspective taking in a different situation. This passage used a deictic verb to describe a general behavior pattern of a single character. We expected "come" would lead the reader to adopt the point of view of the individuals at the WHERE and take their view of the character's general behavior. Our prediction was not supported.

To summarize, our predictions were supported in half the passages, whereas none of the foil statements showed any significant differences. We take these results as evidence that "come" can shift the WHERE to a new location, that deictic verbs can disambiguate the location of the moving character, and that deictic verbs can help identify the character whose point of view is being taken (the WHO).

Study 3: Deictic Verbs and the WHERE.   In this study, we (Bruder & Scott, 1989) again used a series of passages to test the effects of deictic verbs on shifting the WHERE, disambiguating locations, and influencing the perspective taken. For this study, we used different sources for our narratives and presented the passages and test statements by computer. By using the computer to prevent our subjects rereading passages after receiving the test statements, we were able to assess the initial interpretation readers obtained from passages.

There were 21 passages derived from the short tales in *Lake Wobegon Days* (Keillor, 1985) and *Leaving Home* (Keillor, 1987). We used the basic themes and much of the language from the original stories. In addition to using "come" and "go" as deictic verbs, we used "bring" and "take" as alternatives in three of the passages. There were three different versions of each passage, one with a nondeictic verb (often the one used in the original tale) and one with each of the deictic verbs. Examples of the passages are shown in Table 10.3. Each subject received approximately an equal number of passages of each type (nondeictic verb, deictic verb "come" or "bring," deictic verb "go" or "take").

The subjects were 48 female and 51 male introductory psychology students who participated for laboratory credit. Subjects were told that we were interested in their impressions of stories and that some of the statements they would see were factual and others were a matter of opinion. The passages were presented sentence by sentence on a microcomputer. Each sentence was replaced by the next when the subject pressed a key. Following an entire passage, subjects received three test statements, one at a time. Subjects indicated whether they agreed with the statement by selecting a number on a 6-point scale, ranging from *strongly disagree* (1) to *strongly agree* (6). The agreement scores for each statement were subjected to analysis of variance. We report the results for shifts in the WHERE, disambiguation of the WHERE, and for perspective.

All six passages testing shifts in the WHERE used the deictic verbs "come" and "go" (none used "bring" and "take"). The shift was tested in one of two ways: by asking questions about the location of events or characters mentioned prior and subsequent to the sentence with the deictic verb (three passages), or by probing the subjects' selection of referents for pronouns (three passages).

The first of the three passages testing character/event location yielded a significant difference between "coming" and "going" in the predicted direction. This occured with only the second of the two test statements, $F(1, 93) = 6.52$, $p < .03$ (see example 1 in Table 10.3). In the second passage, the nondeictic verb was less likely to lead to a shift than were either of the deictic verbs. The contrast of the nondeictic verb with "came" was significant: $F(1, 93) = 5.66$, $p < .03$. The contrast with "went" was not. In the third passage, the tendency to shift with the verb occurred with all three types of verbs, and therefore, there were no significant differences.

Of the three passages involving identification of a character referent, passages four and five showed a bias toward the last-mentioned subject, regardless of the

I. Shift

Example 1. Jack and Jeanette Bakke went to Florida. They stayed with Jack's sister and her husband and their four kids in their mobile home near Winter Green. It was cold and miserable there. Jack's brother-in-law smoked so much that Jack and Jeanette felt like they were smoking themselves. It made her nervous and she ate more greasy food. . . .[b] They flew back to Minneapolis the very next day. Coming/Going/Walking[c] out of the Minneapolis airport terminal, they began the bitterest fight of their marriage over whether it had been a good vacation. (Based on passage from Keillor, 1987, pp. 33–34)

	COMING	GOING	WALKING
Jack and Jeanette began their fight before they walked out of the airport terminal.	3.47	3.41	3.19
They began their fight after they walked out of the terminal.	4.11	2.94	3.61

II. Disambiguation

Example 2. It was Wednesday night. Roger was worrying about his unplanted corn and thinking about his daughter Martha's new black kitten. Earlier, Roger had laid down the law that a cat stays outdoors, even when it's cold. "That's what it has fur for, put it outside, it'll take care of itself." She pleaded with him to let it stay inside in the warm house. He said, "Now, just do it." As she came/went/stomped[c] upstairs to bed, she whispered "murderer." He heard her. (Based on passage from Keillor, 1987, p. 1)

	CAME	WENT	STOMPED
Roger was upstairs when he heard Martha whisper "murderer."	4.06	1.94	2.15

Example 3. Last Sunday at Lake Wobegon Lutheran Church, Pastor Ingqvist looked out over the faces and asked "any additional announcements this morning." Of course there wouldn't be any because you're supposed to tell him if you are going to stand up and make one. Darlene's mother stood up . . .[b] To stand up and announce a collection for your own daughter. . . . She said good morning to everyone as they came/went/walked[c] out, . . .[b] (Based on passage in Keillor, 1987, p. 170)

		CAME	WENT	WALKED
Darlene's mother stood just outside the church door to collect money.	Female:	4.87	4.18	4.19
	Male:	2.94	3.79	4.19
Darlene's mother stood just inside the church door to collect money.	Female:	3.33	4.35	3.75
	Male:	5.31	4.32	4.75

III. Perspective

Example 4. It was a cold morning and Lyle's car was dead—again. . . .[b] Just then Carl came over, let himself into the kitchen, poured a cup of coffee and called out to Lyle. "Where are you?" "I'm in the garage,," Lyle shouted. Carl poked his head in the garage as Lyle sat in the dead car. Carl came/went/sauntered[c] over to the car as Lyle gave it one last try. He opened the door. (Based on passage in Keillor, 1985, p. 241)

		CAME	WENT	SAUNTERED
Lyle opened the car door to let Carl get in.	Female:	2.50	1.47	1.35
	Male:	1.38	2.25	1.95
Carl opened the car door to let Lyle get out.	Female:	2.88	3.20	3.47
	Male:	3.18	2.94	2.84

[a]We modified the stories cited to make them more concise and appropriate for the study.
[b]Segments presented but not shown here are indicated by ". . .".
[c]Alternative verbs used in the three versions.

verb. In the sixth passage, the difference between deictic verbs was not significant. Subjects receiving either "came" or "went" showed more of a tendency to attribute the referent to the character who moved in the deictic sentence than did subjects who received the nondeictic verb. The difference was significant with "came" (vs. the nondeictic verb), $F(1, 91) = 4.46, p < .05$. The difference between "went" and the nondeictic verb was not significant.

There were seven passages to test disambiguation (passages 7–13) and all but one used the deictic verbs "come" and "go." Four of these seven passages yielded significant differences, as predicted, on at least one of the two test statements. In one of these passages, the deictic verb disambiguated the location of a character in the sentence with the verb, $F(1, 93) = 26.99, p < .001$. In another passage, the verb disambiguated the location of a character at the WHERE, $F(1, 93) = 31.82, p < .002$ (see example 2 in Table 10.3). In the third significant passage, the difference was between the verbs "bring" and "take," $F(1, 93) = 5.03, p < .05$. The contrast by gender interaction failed to reach significance. In the fourth significant passage, the contrast by gender interaction was significant for the second statement, $F(1, 93) = 4.43, p < .05$; but not for the first. Females showed disambiguation in the direction predicted, whereas males displayed the opposite effect (see example 3 in Table 10.3).

There were eight passages of perspective taking (passages 14–21), and all used test statements about who thought or did something. Only two yielded significant effects in the predicted direction. In both cases, there was a significant gender by type of verb interaction. In one case, this interaction was significant for the first statement, $F(1, 93) = 9.56, p < .003$, but not the second (see example 4 in Table 10.3). In the other passage, the interaction with gender was significant for the second statement, $F(1, 93) = 6.45, p < .02$, but not the first.

Generally, deictic verbs did not differ in shifting the WHERE. Regardless of which deictic verb was used, there was a tendency to stay with the last mentioned subject (the one moving in the deictic sentence) and shift the WHERE accordingly. The only passage to show significance used the imperfective past tense. Morrow (1985a) suggested that imperfective aspect makes the path more prominent than the goal. In this study, perfective aspect may move the reader to the goal, therefore shifting the WHERE, regardless of the deictic verb. It is interesting that, in two of the passages, the nondeictic verb appeared less likely to shift the WHERE than did the deictic verbs. The two verbs, "shuffled" and "scampered," are more descriptive of the act of moving, and may lead the reader to focus on the activity (and, thus, the path) rather than on the new location (the goal).

The passages testing perspective also showed a tendency for readers to stick with the subject of the last sentence as the referent. When we did find a difference, females assigned perpective to the stationary character with "came," and the moving character with "went." Males either showed no effect or one opposite that of the females. One possible explanation is that females interpret "came" with reference to the current WHERE and assign the WHO on that basis; males may interpret "came" as indicating a shift of the WHO to a new WHERE. However, this could occur either because males assign the WHO to the moving character and shift the WHERE, or because they shift the WHERE with "came" and then assign the WHO to the moving character.

Finally, we found that when two test statements were presented, it was more often the second that was sensitive to the influence of the deictic verb. Subjects may respond to the plausibility of the first statement or be insensitive to the distinction being tested until a contrasting statement is provided.

This study provides some support for the role of deictic verbs in the interpretation of the WHERE (the strongest support was with disambiguation). We are not entirely surprised that the predictions were not supported in each passage; there were probably a number of other lingistic and contextual factors that influenced the readers' interpretation of passages. This study also provides data showing differences between male and female subjects in the interpretation of deictic verbs. In some of the situations where two interpretations of "come" are possible (one to maintain, one to shift the WHERE), males and females seem to make different choices. Females seemed to take the perspective of the stationary character toward whom the other character is "coming." Males, on the other hand, seemed to take the perspective of the active character, the one who was "coming."

To combine the results of studies 2 and 3, both were designed to investigate the role of diectic verbs:

1. Results show that deictic verbs serve to disambiguate and shift the WHERE, with the influence greater for disambiguation than for deictic shift. In the latter case, both approach and departure verbs may shift the WHERE, although "come" seems to do so more consistently.

2. In terms of perspective, both studies show similar gender differences. Females tend to take the perspective of the stationary character with "came" and the moving character with "went." That is, the deictic verb defines the WHERE, and the WHO is imagined to be in that location. Males tend to show either no effect or one in the opposite direction.

Monitoring the Difficulty of Comprehension

As was seen in the previous studies, linguistic devices can influence the interpretation of narrative. However, these studies provide evidence that natural narrative is redundant and, even with manipulations of devices, readers might be able to reach a given alternative interpretation of narrative based on the preponderance of nondeictic information. In these instances, the linguistic devices related to deixis may or may not be the major factors in the readers' interpretation. It is possible, nonetheless, that when differences in deictic devices do not result in different interpretations, the deictic devices might influence how easily or quickly the reader arrives at the interpretation.

Study 4: Preposed Adverbials and the WHERE. In order to look at this aspect of the readers' tracking of spatial deixis in narrative, we conducted a reading time study (Bruder, Engl, & Schultz, 1985) using reading time as an indicator of comprehension difficulty.

We predicted that comprehension would be more difficult, as indicated by slower reading times, when the explicit signal of a deictic shift (a preposed locative adverbial) was removed or moved from the initial position in the sentence. We also reasoned that the difficulties imposed by failing to mark a deictic shift might not show up in the sentence with the misleading deictic device. Readers might not become aware of a conflict between the WHERE in their DC and the location of events in the narrative until a subsequent sentence makes this obvious. Until some conflict in location occurred in the narrative, the readers might maintain an erroneous WHERE. To test this possibility, we looked at reading times for the target sentence and for the subsequent sentence. We expected deletion of adverbials to be more detrimental to comprehending subsequent sentences than shifting the location of the adverbial, because in the latter case, the information about the new location was available.

The narrative in this study consisted of most the first chapter of *The Pearl* (Steinbeck, 1945/1975) (approximately 200 sentences). For our target sentences, we selected eight that had preposed locative adverbials in the original text and eight that had none. Three versions of the narrative were prepared, so that each target sentence appeared in a different form in each of the versions. Versions of the target sentences included: one with a preposed locative adverbial; one with a locative adverbial in a noninitial positon; and one in with no locative adverbial. These three versions were used both for the target sentence that had a preposed adverbial in the original version and for the target sentence with no such adverbial. Therefore, combining the three versions with the two types of target sentences yielded six different test types. At least one of the target sentences occur in each of the six test type conditions. The particular target sentence in each condition differed for different groups of subjects.

Subjects were 39 volunteers including high school, undergraduate and graduate students. They received a fee of $4.00 for participating in the one hour experiment. Subjects viewed one sentence at a time on a computer monitor and signalled for the next sentence by pressing the space bar. Sentence reading times were measured by the time between space-bar presses. Subjects received a short practice passage from a mystery novel in order to get used to the task. Subjects were tested on reading comprehension in order to make sure they were reading and understanding the story. (We stopped the computer after every 30 or so sentences and asked subjects to answer questions about the most recently read segment.)

Because sentence length variability caused by using natural text affected reading times, we needed to correct reading time scores for sentence length. We did so by obtaining correlations between sentence length (in words) and reading time for each subject (using only nontarget sentences). These correlations were high ($M = .82$), indicating most of the variation in reading time could be attributed to sentence length. We obtained a predicted reading time for target and subsequent sentences using the regression line (based on the correlation between reading time and sentence length) for each subject. Using these predicted times, we obtained adjusted reading time scores for target and subsequent sentences. These reading times were expressed as difference scores (actual minus predicted reading times). Negative values indicate that reading time was faster than predicted. Figure 10.1 shows these scores for each of the types of sentences and conditions tested.

The main result of interest was the significant three-way interaction of target/subsequent sentence by original version by presentation version, $F(2, 72) = 3.97$, $p < .03$. The manipulation seemed to have more of an effect on reading times for subsequent sentences than on the target sentence (within which the deictic device manipulation was made). We used two contrasts to evaluate the effect of preposed adverbials. One contrast showed that subsequent sentences

Target Sentences

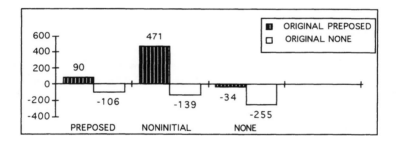

Subsequent Sentences

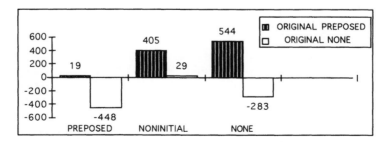

FIG. 10.1. Mean difference scores (predicted–actual) in milliseconds for target and subsequent sentences as a function of orginal and experimental versions of target sentences for study 4.

were significantly slower in the no adverbial test condition than in the other test conditions when the original narrative had a preposed adverbial, $F(1, 72) = 5.10$, $p < .01$. That is, if there was an adverbial signalling a deictic shift, and it was deleted in the presentation, readers had difficulty in comprehension. In the second contrast for subsequent sentences, the difference between reading times for the preposed and noninitial test condition (when a preposed adverbial occurred in the original version) approached significance, $F(1, 72) = 2.82$, p. $< .10$.

These results provide some support for the role of preposed adverbials in signalling a shift in the WHERE of the DC. Although the second contrast did not reach statistical significance, it did repeat the trend noted in the initial study, as described in the previous section.

Assessing the Currently Active DC in the Reader's Mental Model

Another measure of how readers keep track of location is suggested by the research of Morrow, Greenspan, and Bower (1987). They found that probing for information about location of objects was faster if the readers' situation model was currently at that location. Reaction time was used as an indicator of accessibility. Daniels (1986) used this approach to explore "where" the reader is (in his or her deictic model) at the end of a short narrative.

Study 5: Preposed Adverbials, Deictic Verbs, and the WHERE.   In line with our prior tests of the DC theory, Daniels (1986) examined the influence of preposed adverbials and deictic verbs ("come," "go") on readers' tracking of location in short narratives. Two main differences between this and our other research were the use of constructed narratives to closely control the movement of the DC and the use of reaction time to measure the WHERE currently active in the readers' mental model of the depicted situation.

The hypotheses tested by Daniels (1986) were: (a) the use of "come" with no new goal location maintains the current DC (WHERE), whereas "go," with a goal location, shifts it to a new location (if the WHO is the one who goes); and (b) preposed adverbials shift the DC to a new location, whereas their absence maintains the DC.

Daniels assumed that subjects would take longer to respond to statements that referred to locations other than the current WHERE at the end of the narrative. If the lexical items—preposed adverbials or "go"—do shift the WHERE, then subjects should take longer to respond to a statement about the prior WHERE. In order to assess this, Daniels measured her subjects' reaction time in responding to evaluating the truth of a statement referring to the original WHERE of a narrative. When the DC was maintained (no shift), the WHERE referred to in the statement was still the WHERE. When the DC was shifted, the WHERE referred to in the statement was no longer the current WHERE.

Daniels constructed and presented 50 short (four-sentence) narratives describing everyday events or situations. At the end of each narrative, a target statement was presented and subjects had to respond whether that statement was true or false. Although only true statements were of interest, Daniels used approximately half of the narratives as foils in which false test statements were given. False test statements were included in the study in order to make sure subjects actually read the narratives and made a true/false judgment on the content of the test statements. See Table 10.4 for an example of these narratives and the test statement that followed.

The results indicated that response time was slower ($M = 2.77$ sec.) when a preposed adverbial signalled a shift in the WHERE, than when no movement occurred in the narrative ($M = 2.49$ sec.). This difference was significant, $t(11) = 3.11$, $p < .05$. Similarly, when 'go' was used to create movement to a new WHERE, the average response time was slower (3.77 sec.) than when no such movement was indicated (2.64 sec.). This difference was also significant, $t(8) = 4.74$, $p < .01$.

Daniels concluded that these results generally support the notion of the DC (WHERE) as a model of readers and validate the lexical items tested.

CONCLUSION

The studies described here indicate a more context-sensitive and complex role of deictic verbs than was evident in earlier research (Black, Turner, & Bower, 1979), and add preposed adverbials to the list of factors influencing readers' construction of space from narrative. These studies also provide a method for testing the psychological reality of the Deictic Center. Our findings were consistent with the predicted role of preposed adverbials and deictic verbs in signalling the reader about the current location of events described in the narrative—the WHERE. We found evidence that readers track the current

TABLE 10.4
Example of a Passage Used to Test Accessibility of Information in Study 5

Sentences Presented	Role of the Sentence
John and Mary were eating dinner when there was a knock at the door.	[sentence establishes the WHERE]
*John got up and went to answer the door.	[sentence shifts the WHERE]
*John looked up to see his partner come in.	[sentence maintains the WHERE]
Kevin greeted John with a bottle of champagne and a big hug.	[sentence continues the passage]
They had just won a large advertising account.	[sentence continues the passage]
Test Statement:	
Mary is in the dining room.	[sentence to test accessibility]

Note. Only one or the other of the starred sentences was presented to a particular subject.

WHERE and shift that WHERE when signalled to do so by preposed adverbials or decitic verbs. Failure to provide appropriate signals of shifts in the WHERE may make it more difficult for the reader to track it. In addition, our findings confirm (Zubin, 1989) that the WHERE and the WHO are closely related.

The fact that these positive findings were replicated across studies with similar and different methodologies is important in confirming the role of these linguistic devices. Another contribution of most of this research is finding evidence for the role of these linguistic devices on narrative interpretation when natural narratives are used. The role of these linguistic devices in maintaining or shifting the WHERE was evident in spite of the great degree of variability among these narrative passages.

ACKNOWLEDGMENTS

Much of the research reported in this chapter was supported in part by The National Science Foundation, Grant No. IRI–8610517.

SUBJECTIVITY IN NARRATIVE

11

REFERENCES IN NARRATIVE TEXT

Janyce M. Wiebe
New Mexico State University

Specific references are references to particular entities, for example, "a car" in (S1) and "the car" in (S2), as opposed to "a car" in (NS1) or "the car" in (NS2):

S1. John bought a car yesterday.
S2. John couldn't get to work today because the car wouldn't start.
NS1. John wants to buy a car, but he hasn't chosen one yet.
NS2. The car is a four-wheeled vehicle.

A specific reference has a *propositional content*—the proposition attributing to the referent properties that correspond to the nouns and modifiers in the reference. For example, the propositional content of "Mary" is that the referent is named Mary; the propositional content of "the car" is that the referent is a car, and the propositional content of "he" is that the referent is male. During language comprehension, the recipient (the hearer or reader) must determine the set of beliefs with respect to which the propositional content of a reference is to be understood. In the prototypical case, this set consists of the propositions that he or she believes that the producer (the speaker or writer) believes that he or she and the producer mutually believe. This chapter identifies two contexts in which the propositional content of a specific reference is not understood with respect to this set of beliefs—*subjective* and *objective* sentences in third-person fictional narrative text—and identifies some implications for understanding specific references.

This work has grown from work in philosophy (e.g., Castaneda, 1970/1977), linguistics (e.g., Fodor, 1979), and artificial intelligence (e.g., Rapaport, 1986a) on the interpretation of references in *opaque contexts*. Opaque contexts are the objects of sentences with third-person subjects and with main verbs that are either propositional-attitude verbs, such as "believe," "know," and "hope," or other psychological and perceptual verbs, such as "want," "hate," and "see." Under one interpretation of such a sentence (the de dicto as opposed to the de re), the propositional content of references in the object are understood with respect to the beliefs of the subject of the sentence. References in subjective sentences have a similar property, even in those that do not have the syntactic form described previously.

In the next section, I provide background information about subjective sentences in third-person narrative text. The next three sections identify the set of beliefs with respect to which the propositional content of a specific reference is understood in conversation, objective sentences, and subjective sentences. In other work, I developed an algorithm for distinguishing between subjective and objective sentences in third-person narrative text (Wiebe, 1990b); this algorithm can be used to choose the proper set of beliefs with respect to which references should be understood in this genre. In the section entitled, "Understanding References," I show some implications of this choice for computational approaches to the resolution of specific references. The next section considers the *de re/de dicto* distinction in light of the issues raised in earlier sections, the next draws some parallels between the interpretation of references and the interpretation of subjective elements, and the last section discusses some issues for future research.

Throughout this chapter, only specific references are considered.

SUBJECTIVE SENTENCES

Sentences of fictional narrative can be characterized as either *subjective* or *objective* (Banfield, 1982). In contrast to sentences that objectively narrate events or describe the fictional world, subjective sentences present the consciousness of a character within the story. They express characters' evaluations, emotions, judgments, uncertainties, beliefs, and other attitudes and affects. Some present a character's thought or perception (*represented thought* or *represented perception*; Banfield, 1982); others report a character's *private state*—a perceptual state such as seeing, a psychological state such as wanting, or an experiential state such as feeling ill—that is, a state that is not open to objective observation or verification (Quirk, Greenbaum, Leech, & Svartik, 1985).[1] We call the character whose consciousness is presented by a subjective sentence the *subjective character* of that sentence.[2] Further, an *objective context* is a maximal block of objective

---

[1]See Wiebe (1990b) and the references therein for alternative categorizations of subjective sentences.

[2]A text may take the point of view of an overt narrator, to whom beliefs, emotions, and so on, are attributed (Chatman, 1978). In this chapter, texts with overt narrators are not considered. Note that a sentence with an overt narrator is not an objective sentence.

sentences, and a *subjective context* is a maximal block of subjective sentences with the same subjective character.

The following passages illustrate different kinds of subjective sentences (throughout this chapter, sentences in cited passages are indented to reflect paragraphing in the original texts).

(1) (a) "What are you doing in here?" (b) Suddenly she (Zoe) was furious with him (Joe).
    (c) "Spying, of course."
    (d) "Well of all dumb things! (e) I thought you ran away." (f) Joe Bunch was awful. (Oneal, 1971, p. 130)

Sentence (1b) is a private-state report: It reports Zoe's private state of being furious with Joe. Sentence (1f) is a represented thought: It presents Zoe's thought, and it expresses her evaluation of Joe (that he is awful).

(2) (a) Certainly, Dennys thought, anything would be better than this horrible-smelling place full of horrible little people.
    (b) There was a brief whiff of fresh air. (c) A glimpse of a night sky crusted with stars. (L'Engle, 1986, p. 25)

Sentence (2a) is Dennys' represented thought, and (2b) and (2c) are Dennys' represented perceptions.

The feature of subjective sentences important to the current work is that they reflect the subjective character's beliefs, which may be false in the fictional world (noted by many literary theorists, such as Banfield, 1982; Cohn, 1978; Dolezel, 1973; Kuroda, 1973, 1976; Uspensky, 1973). For example:

(3) This was David's boy. (Bridgers, 1979, p. 91)

The sentence is the represented thought of a character named Dwayne; it is about a female character whom Dwayne incorrectly believes to be a boy. Another example is the following:

(4) She (Morgaine) was indeed a witch, he (Chei) thought. (Cherryh, 1988, p. 64)

Sentence 4 is the represented thought of Chei. Morgaine is not actually a witch, but Chei believes she is one. (The word "witch" is not used as a figurative term in (4) or in (8), to follow; Chei believes there are such things as witches.)

Before leaving this section, it should be noted that a sentence of quoted speech such as (1a) is really a mixture of genres. First, it is a narrative sentence whose main verb phrase contains a communicative verb, and whose object is a quoted string (though the discourse parenthetical, such as "Zoe said," may be only implicit, as in (1a)). Second, the contents of quoted strings are conversational utterances. My discussion of references in third-person narrative text applies to references in the discourse parenthetical (if there is one), not to any in the quoted string.

References in Conversation

In conversation, references are directed by the speaker toward the hearer. To understand a reference, the hearer cannot consider only his or her own beliefs, or only what he or she believes the speaker believes; he or she may also have to consider what he or she believes the speaker believes that he or she believes, and so on. Clark and Marshall (1981) and Perrault and Cohn (1981) described some of the complexities of this process.

Clark and Marshall showed the potential relevance of a conjunction of beliefs that comprise the speaker and hearer's mutual beliefs:

(MB) S believes that P, and S believes that H believes that P, and S believes that H believes that S believes that P . . .

where "S" stands for the speaker, and "H" stands for the hearer, and "P" is the proposition mutually believed. Clark and Marshall pointed out that speakers and hearers cannot consider an infinite series of conjuncts during processing, and they suggested heuristics that speakers and hearers might use to assess their mutual beliefs in a finite amount of time.

Perrault and Cohen showed that beliefs acquired privately about objects, people, places, and so on, can override some of the conjuncts of mutual belief. They gave the following example, adapted from Donnellan (1966):

(5) S and H are at a party. They watch together as water and gin are being poured in two identical glasses and given to women W1 and W2, respectively. Unbeknownst to H, S sees W1 and W2 exchange glasses. Later S tells H: "The woman with the martini is the mayor's daughter." (Perrault & Cohen, 1981, p. 222)

The speaker is referring to W2, even though she herself does not believe that W2 is the woman with the martini. However, she believes that the *hearer* believes that W2 is the woman with the martini, and, because the hearer does not know that the speaker has changed her belief, the speaker also believes the hearer still believes that the speaker and hearer mutually believe that W2 is the woman with the martini.

Of course, from the hearer's perspective, the reference does reflect the series of conjuncts in (MB). However, the hearer can also acquire a private belief that affects her understanding of the speaker's reference. Cohen, Perrault, and Allen (1982, p. 257) give the following example (I replaced "system" by "hearer" and "user" by "speaker"):

(6) Suppose that at first the hearer and speaker agreed that Kirk was the captain (of the Enterprise). Then suppose that the hearer found out through direct,

> private access to the Enterprise that Kirk had been replaced by Spock. The
> hearer would therefore believe that Spock was the captain, while believing that
> the speaker believed that Kirk was. The speaker's utterance of "the captain of
> the Enterprise" still clearly identifies Kirk, and should be understood as such
> by the hearer.

The hearer understands that the speaker is referring to Kirk because, although
the hearer believes that Spock is the captain, he or she believes that the speaker
believes that Kirk is the captain and also that the speaker still believes that the
hearer and speaker mutually believe that Kirk is the captain.

Perrault and Cohen showed through example that any finite number of conjuncts of (MB) might not be true for a successful reference; what is required
(taking the hearer's perspective) is some nested belief of the form, "H believes
that S believes . . . (MB)." If a more nested environment than H believes (MB)
is required, then the hearer understands the reference in spite of some private
belief that he or she holds or some private belief that he or she believes the
speaker holds. (Note that Cohen, 1978, specifies a finite representation of mutual
belief.)

The importance of this discussion for our purposes is that the hearer cannot
consider only what he or she believes or only what the speaker believes in order
to understand references in conversation. He or she has to consider what he or
she believes the speaker believes that he or she believes, and he or she has to
distinguish what he or she privately believes (and what he or she believes the
speaker privately believes) from what he or she believes they mutually believe.

Before leaving this discussion of conversation to consider narrative text, there
is something obvious about conversation that needs to be noted, so that objective
sentences can be contrasted with it. In conversation, a hearer always has the
option of questioning the veracity (or sincerity) of the speaker's utterances. Even
the most gullible listener with the greatest belief in the speaker's authority might
question the truth of the speaker's utterances, if things begin to sound too pre-
posterous. In particular, the hearer can question the propositional content of
references. That is, the hearer may believe that a reference reflects a false belief
of the speaker (as discussed previously in this section)—he or she may believe
that the speaker holds the false belief, he or she may believe that the speaker
holds a false belief about what the hearer believes, and so on.

REFERENCES IN OBJECTIVE SENTENCES

Objective sentences narrate events independently of any character's consciousness. The major difference between objective sentences and conversation is that
the reader does not question the truth of an objective sentence. This is because
objective narration actually creates the fictional world, to which the reader has
no other resource but through the text itself:

> A fictional narrative statement is immune to judgments of truth or falsity; in fiction, (these judgments) are suspended. It is inappropriate to say that a fictional statement is false. Rather, it creates by fiat a fictional reality which can only be taken as fictionally true. (Banfield, 1982, p. 258)

In conversation, people talk about a reality to which they have independent access, but, in objective narration, what is narrated is created in the fictional world (Banfield, 1982; Hamburger, 1973; Kuroda, 1976).

For example, consider a reader's response to the following narrative statement, assuming that he or she interprets it to be objective:

(7) Shea Stadium was a large stadium in Chicago.

Even if he or she knows where Shea Stadium and Chicago are, he or she will not question the truth of (7), but instead will simply update his or her model of the fictional world. That is, even if he or she knows that, in the real world, Shea Stadium is in New York City, from (7) he or she understands that, in the fictional world being created, Shea Stadium is in Chicago. (Chicago and Shea Stadium may themselves turn out to be completely different in the fictional and the real worlds.)

A reader understands that the propositional content of references in objective contexts is (fictionally) true. This means that the reader does not have to question whether a reference reflects a false belief of a producer (either a producer's own false belief, or a producer's false belief about the reader's beliefs, or about the reader's beliefs about a producer's beliefs about the reader's beliefs, etc.). The reader cannot have private beliefs about what is true in the fictional world that would allow him or her to disagree with the propositional content of a reference, although he or she may have beliefs about the fictional world—for example, that it does not correspond to the real world. In contrast to conversation, in which the hearer has independent access to the world under discussion (the real world), the reader of a narrative text does not have any other access to the fictional world than that provided by the text.[3] Consider a use of the reference "the king." In conversation, the hearer may believe both that the referent is actually a usurper and that the speaker is expressing a false belief about the referent. It is also possible that the hearer believes the speaker is expressing the false belief that the hearer believes that the referent is the king. The reader of a narrative text, however, cannot have the private belief that the referent of the king is a usurper, or that a producer has the mistaken belief that the reader believes that the referent is the king. If the propositional content of a reference in an objective context is that a character is the king, then it is simply so.

---

[3]Actually, the author relies on the hearer bringing to the fictional world the knowledge he or she has about the real world. However, the reader accepts any discrepancies, and updates his or her model of the fictional world accordingly.

REFERENCES IN SUBJECTIVE SENTENCES

As noted previously, subjective sentences reflect the beliefs of the subjective character, that may be false in the fictional world. This is true not only for the main proposition of the sentence, but also for the propositional content of references. In the following passage, Morgaine is referred to as "the witch" in Chei's subjective sentence, reflecting his false belief about her.

> (8) He (Chei) reckoned even that it was a spell *the witch* had cast over him, that from the time she surprised him with that look into his eyes, from that moment his soul had been snared. (Cherryh, 1988, p. 86; italics mine)

As in conversation, the reader does not automatically assume that the propositional content of references in subjective contexts is true; this is in contrast to objective contexts, in which he or she does automatically assume this. As in objective contexts, however, subjective sentences are not understood with respect to the relationship between a speaker and a hearer; subjective and objective contexts differ from conversation in this respect. A subjective sentence is not directed by the subjective character toward an addressee (Banfield, 1982; Kuroda, 1973, 1976). Rather, the pragmatic situation might be thought of as the reader "overhearing" the character's thoughts, or the reader "perceiving" the fictional world through the character's senses (or a combination of the two; cf. Brinton, 1980). The subjective character is clearly not addressing the reader—the reader does not exist in the fictional world. The reader may believe that a reference reflects a false belief of the subjective character, and yet he or she will not try to understand the disparity between his or her own beliefs and the subjective character's in terms of beliefs about their mutual beliefs (in fact, he or she does not have any such beliefs). Subjective sentences are propositionally transparent (Castañeda, 1970, 1977); they reveal, unobscured by any communicative relationship between the subjective character and the reader, the subjective character's model of the fictional world.

UNDERSTANDING REFERENCES

Representation

A single text can contain subjective contexts attributed to different characters, as well as objective contexts. So, simply to understand references in a narrative text, the reader must maintain (a) a model of objects, places, characters, and so on, and their properties that are actually in the fictional world (cf. Webber's 1983 discourse models, Kamp's 1984 discourse representation structures, and Rapaport's 1988a notion of the mind of an AI/natural-language-understanding system), and (b) for each subjective character, another model of the objects, characters, and so on, and their properties the character believes are in the fictional world (cf. Fauconnier's 1985 mental spaces). Where one character's beliefs differ from another character's beliefs or from what is true in the fictional world, the models are distinct, and where they correspond to one another, the models overlap.

The last section noted the most obvious situation for which these models must be maintained to understand references in subjective contexts, namely, when a character has a false belief about an individual. Another situation in which the reader's and character's beliefs about the fictional world must be distinguished is when the reader (and perhaps another character) knows more than the subjective character knows. For example:

(9) Perhaps the man understood. Perhaps he did not. (Cherryh, 1988, p. 24)

These sentences are the represented thoughts of the character Vanye about Chei. Although the reference "the man" does not reflect a false belief of Vanye's about Chei (Chei really is a man), it does reflect Vanye's limited knowledge about Chei: At this point in the novel, the reader, but not Vanye, knows Chei's name.

Representation of Proper Names. This and related work (Rapaport, 1986a; Rapaport, Shapiro, & Wiebe, 1986; Wiebe & Rapaport, 1986) shows that when representing an individual in a natural-language-understanding system, it is important to represent the individual in a way that is neutral with respect to any properties ascribed to it. In particular, the individual must be represented independently of attributes used to refer to it, even a proper name. For example, the reader may know that a character has two names and that some of the other characters know only one of the names. In Ludlum's *The Parsifal Mosaic* (1982), for example, the characters at the State Department know an individual by the name Arthur Pierce, but the reader knows he is a Russian spy whose real name is Nikolai Petrovich Malyekov. The individual cannot be represented as Arthur Pierce, or as Nikolai Petrovich Malyekov, but has to be represented as an individual whom the reader believes has both names, but whom the reader believes some of the other characters believe has only the name Arthur Pierce. References to this individual can reflect different beliefs the reader holds, and that he or she believes the other characters hold (in objective and subjective contexts, respectively).

Belief Spaces. The reader's and characters' models of the fictional world can be represented by *belief spaces* (as in Rapaport's 1986a computational model of de re and de dicto belief reports). A belief space is labeled by a stack, and represents those things that the bottom member of the stack believes that . . . the top member of the stack believes. The reader is always the bottom member of the stack, reflecting the fact that other agents' beliefs are not directly represented, but rather, what the reader believes those other agents believe.

The belief space $BS[the\ reader, a_1, a_2, \ldots, a_{n-1}, a_n]$ consists of the propositions P such that the reader believes that a_1 believes that a_2 believes that $\ldots a_{n-1}$ believes that a_n believes that P, together with the propositions that follow from the propositions P. As we shall later see, the important belief spaces in this chapter are $BS[the\ reader]$ and $BS[the\ reader,\ c]$, where c is a character. The former will be referred to as the reader's belief space, and the latter will be referred to as c's belief space.

Shapiro and colleagues (Maida & Shapiro, 1982; Rapaport, 1985a; Shapiro & Rapaport, 1987) argued that the terms of an AI representation language, if it is to be used to represent the mind of a cognitive agent, should be interpreted as intensional entities (in particular, as Meinongian objects of thought; Meinong, 1904). Under this interpretation, there is not necessarily a one-to-one correspondence between entities actually in the world and concepts of those entities. For example, the cognitive agent might believe two concepts are actually concepts of the same individual, that is, that they are *coextensional*. Once the cognitive agents holds such a belief, then anything he or she believes about one of the concepts he or she simultaneously believes about the other. Because we are concerned with nested beliefs, we need the following generalization: If the belief that two concepts are coextensional appears within a belief space, then anything believed about one of them in that belief space is also believed about the other in that belief space.[4]

Note that a single proposition may appear in more than one belief space. An example is the situation from *The Parsifal Mosaic* described previously: Although the proposition that the individual in question is named Nikolai Petrovich Malyekov appears in the reader's belief space and not in the belief spaces of the characters at the State Department, the proposition that he is named Arthur Pierce does appear in all of these belief spaces.

The Current Belief Space and References

In this section, we consider reference resolution in light of the observations made in previous sections about references in subjective and objective contexts. The main idea of this section is that references should be understood with respect to the *current belief space* (*CBS*), the belief space of the reader while an objective context is processed, and the belief space of the subjective character while a subjective context is processed. This explains some interesting referential phenomena in third-person narrative text.

As an overview, we begin with sr, a specific reference, and p, a predicate corresponding to the propositional content of sr. For example, if sr is "the car," then p is the predicate *car*. The referent of sr will be a concept c such that the proposition $p(c)$ is in *CBS*. For example, if "the car" appears in a subjective

---

[4]Beliefs that two concepts are coextensional, especially nested beliefs of that sort, clearly pose hard problems for knowledge representation (cf. Asher, 1986; Konolige, 1986; Maida, in press; McCarthy, 1979; Moore, 1980; Rapaport, 1986a; Shapiro & Rapaport, 1987, for relevant work in knowledge representation). Because this chapter is not about belief representation, per se, the issues involved will not be discussed here.

context of John, the referent will be a concept c such that $car(c)$ is in John's belief space.[5] Depending on the sort of reference sr is and on what is currently believed, $p(c)$ may or may not already be in *CBS* before sr is resolved. We first consider specific definite references and then specific indefinite references. In order to focus on the specific phenomena I wish to illustrate, I idealize reference resolution in these sections, ignoring many complexities.

Nonanaphoric Specific Definite References. In general terms, a specific definite reference refers to an individual who is already known. Examples of definite references are "Ellen," "the mirror," and "she." Context may be required to identify the referent, so the referent should first be sought among the concepts recently evoked in the narrative (if it is found among them, the reference is *anaphoric*); this is the topic of the next section. In the present section, we consider specific definite references that are *nonanaphoric*, that is, whose referents are not recently evoked concepts.

Let sdr be a specific definite reference and p a predicate corresponding to the propositional content of sdr. Further, assume that the referent of sdr could not be found among the concepts recently evoked in the text. Then sdr should be resolved as follows:

i. If there is a concept c such that the proposition $p(c)$ is in *CBS*, then the referent should be chosen from among the set of such c.

ii. Otherwise, if there is a concept c such that $p(c)$ is in a belief space other than *CBS* and $p(c)$ is consistent with *CBS*, then the referent should be chosen from among the set of such c. Let $c1$ be the concept chosen. Then $p(c1)$ should be added to *CBS*.

iii. Otherwise, a new concept c should be created to serve as the referent of sdr, and the proposition $p(c)$ should be added to *CBS*.

If there are possible referents given only the propositions in *CBS*, one of them should be chosen as the referent (branch i). In *The Parsifal Mosaic*, for example, a set of characters believe that there is someone named Parsifal, but each believes it is a different person. When Parsifal appears in the subjective context of one of these characters, the referent is the person who the subjective character believes is named Parsifal. (There would be a set of possible referents from which to choose if more than one person were believed by the subjective character to have the name Parsifal.)

---

[5]There may be more than one predicate, $p_1 \ldots, p_n$ that together correspond to the propositional content of the reference. For example, if sr is "the little red car," then there are three predicates, *little, red,* and *car*. In this case, the referent of sr will be a concept c such that $p_1(c)$ A $\ldots$ A $p_n(c)$ is in *CBS*. One sort of complexity we ignore is the interaction among components of a noun phase. For example, the referent of "a fire alarm" is not something believed to be a fire and believed to be an alarm (cf. Hobbs, Stickel, Martin, & Edwards, 1988 for a computational treatment of compound nominals).

If the test in (i) fails, then other belief spaces should be considered (branch ii). To see why, suppose that *sdr* is "Ellen" and that it occurs in a subjective context of John. Because branch (i) was not taken, the belief that someone is named Ellen is not yet in John's belief space. But someone may have been referred to earlier as Ellen, and, unless there is some reason to believe that John believes that this person is not named Ellen (in which case, the proposition that she is named Ellen would not be consistent with *CBS*), then that person should be taken to be the referent. (There are many cases where there is a set of possible referents from which to choose. The simplest one is if, for all *c*, any proposition *p[c]* that appears in a character's belief space also appears in the reader's belief space, where *p* is as above. Then the choice is among concepts *c*, such that the reader believes that *p[c]*.)

Once we have the referent, *c1*, the proposition *p(c1)* should be added to *CBS*. In the above example, the fact that Ellen occurs in John's subjective context indicates to the reader that John believes that the referent is named Ellen.

If the tests of both (i) and (ii) fail, then *sdr* is a definite reference to a new concept (branch iii). This kind of reference is acceptable in both objective and subjective contexts. In conversation, however, a specific definite reference would not be completely acceptable to the hearer if he or she were not already familiar with the referent.

In objective contexts, a definite reference can be used to introduce something new into the fictional world. An example is "the jockey" in the following—the first mention of the jockey in the story:

(10) The jockey came to the doorway of the dining room, then after a moment stepped to one side and stood motionless, with his back to the door. [McCullers, 1931/1952, p. 58]

In a subjective context, a specific definite reference is understood to refer to an individual with whom the subjective character is familiar (Fillmore, 1974). This is so, regardless of whether or not the reader is already familiar with the referent. For example:

(11) (a) She [Hannah] winced as she heard them crash to the platform. (b) The lovely little mirror that she had brought for Ellen and the gifts for the baby! [Franchere, 1964, p. 3]

Neither the mirror, the gifts, the baby, nor Ellen have been mentioned before in the novel (the pronoun "them" in (11a) is an anaphoric reference to some luggage mentioned in the previous sentence). For each, a new concept is created to serve as the referent, and an appropriate proposition is added to Hannah's belief space.[6]

---

[6]We consider only a small subset of the reader's beliefs. Some we are not considering are beliefs about the sense in which the referent is familiar to the subjective character and beliefs about the temporal extent of this familiarity.

That is, by virtue of understanding the references in (11b), the reader comes to believe that Hannah (the subjective character) believes that there is a mirror, some gifts, a baby, and a person named Ellen.

Anaphoric References. An anaphoric reference accesses a concept recently evoked in the narrative (typically, pronouns and definite descriptions such as "the jockey" are anaphoric). We first consider anaphor resolution in computational linguistics (ignoring many details),[7] and then consider the role of *CBS* in this process.

The clearest case of anaphoric reference, the only one we will consider here, is when an anaphor corefers with a noun phrase that explicitly appeared earlier in the text (called its *antecedent*).[8]

So that the referent of an anaphor can be recovered from the previous context, an ordered list of previously mentioned concepts is maintained (the *history list*). To find the referent of an anaphor, this list is searched for possible referents, starting with the first element. (Although recency of mention should partly determine how the elements of the list are ordered, other factors should also be taken into account, cf. Sidner, 1983.)

When any sort of reference is encountered, once the referent has been found, it is added to the history list in anticipation of later anaphoric references to it. If it already appears on the list, then the old entry is deleted and a new one is added.

There are syntactic constraints governing the relationship between an anaphor and its antecedent. For example, they must agree in number and gender. Thus, when a concept is added to the history list, any syntactic properties of the reference that may be relevant for resolving later anaphoric references should be included in the list entry.

Now, consider finding the referent of an anaphoric reference. Let c be a concept on the history list, ar an anaphoric reference, and p a predicate corresponding to the propositional content of ar. Then c should be ruled out as a possible referent for ar if the syntactic properties stored with c on the history list and the syntactic properties of ar do not agree. (There may also be syntactic constraints from the sentence in which ar appears, such as those on the use of reflexive pronouns. In addition, c is acceptable only if the sentence would make

---

A new concept that is the referent of a definite reference in a subjective context is new in the sense that it is created to serve as the referent when the reference is processed by the reader. However, the reader believes that, with respect to the current moment within the fictional world, the concept is not new to the subjective character.

[7]Hirst (1981) provided an extensive survey of computational linguistics work on anaphor resolution, and Allen (1987) gave an excellent synthesis of the computational results.

[8]An anaphoric reference may refer to an entity that is merely related to a previously mentioned entity. For example: "John tried the lamp, but the lightbulb was burned out." One understands that "the lightbulb" refers to the lightbulb of the previously mentioned lamp. There are many similar sorts of complications; compare, for example, Webber (1983) and Sidner (1983).

sense if c were the referent.) In addition, c might be rejected on the basis of the content of ar. It is here that *CBS* should be consulted—c should be ruled out if $p(c)$ is inconsistent with the propositions in *CBS*. However, if $p(c)$ is consistent with *CBS* (and no other constraints are violated), then we can accept c as the referent, even if $\neg p(c)$ is in another belief space. Consider the following example:

(12) (a) His [Dwayne's] brain worked slowly through what he knew about this person [Casey] (b) David's kid. (c) The name stumbled into place. (d) This was David's boy. (e) David was in the war, and here was his kid in the arcade scared of something. (f) He wasn't sure of what. (g) What in the arcade could scare a boy like that? (h) He rubbed his head under his baseball cap. (i) He could see tears in Casey's eyes. (j) He could tell they were tears because *his* eyes were too shiny. (k) Too round. (l) Well, it was all right to cry. (m) He'd cried when they took him to that place a few years back. (n) Now Casey was in a new place, too, feeling maybe the same as him. (o) If he just knew what to do about it.

(p) "Let's don't play that game anymore," he said. (q) "I don't like that one."

(r) Casey wiped *her* face on her sleeve . . . (Bridgers, 1979, pp. 91–92; emphasis added)

The interesting references in this passage are "his" in (12j) and "her" in (12r)—both refer to Casey, even though one is masculine and one is feminine. Because Casey can be either masculine or feminine, it is syntactically permitted to be the antecedent of both masculine and feminine references (but not of those such as "it").

Examples (12a)–(12o) are Dwayne's subjective sentences, and examples (12p)–(12r) are objective. Although Dwayne correctly believes that Casey's name is Casey, he incorrectly believes that Casey is a boy. Suppose $c1$ is the concept of Casey. When Casey in (12i) is understood to refer to $c1$, an entry for $c1$ is made in the history list. When "his" in (12j) is encountered, *CBS* is Dwayne's belief space. Because *male(c1)* is consistent with *CBS*, $c1$ is not ruled out as a possible referent of "his," even though *male(c1)* is in the reader's belief space. Similarly, an entry for $c1$ is made when Casey is resolved in (12r). Since (12r) is objective, *CBS* is the reader's belief space. Thus, $c1$ is not ruled out as a possible referent of "her" in (12r) because *female(c1)* is consistent with *CBS*.

Suppose that a concept c is taken to be the referent of an anaphoric reference ar (that is, c is the first, or only, concept on the history list that is not ruled out as a possible referent). Because $p(c)$, the propositional content of ar, need only be consistent with *CBS*, it may not already be in *CBS*. If $p(c)$ is not already in *CBS*, it should be added to it. The reason is the same as the one given for (iii).

The question arises as to how long entities should remain in focus. In computational linguistics, this question has been related to discourse structure.[9] (The

---

term "discourse" in this context is neutral with respect to genre. It is a text or conversation considered as a structured whole.) It was suggested that a discourse is composed of hierarchically related discourse segments, such that within a segment, sentences are locally coherent. One aspect of this coherence is that within a discourse segment, anaphoric references can be resolved to concepts evoked in that segment, but once a segment has ended, those concepts are no longer available for anaphoric reference (but note that there can be discourse returns to segments, and semantic returns to concepts evoked in previous segments; Allen, 1987). As a consequence, each segment should have its own local history list.

Some phenomena I observed in narrative suggest that each subjective and objective context is a discourse segment composed of subsegments. Thus, following the approach outlined in the previous paragraph, each subjective or objective context has its own local history list (as does each subsegment within a context) (Nakhimovsky, 1988; Nakhimovsky & Rapaport, 1988). Further, there may be a level of discourse structure at which a discourse segment can include more than one context; because such a segment would have its own history list, an entity could remain in focus across context boundaries. This would explain cases I observed in which a subjective context is followed by an objective one, the subject character of the subjective context is referred to by a pronoun at the beginning of the objective context, and there is a reference to someone else in the subjective context that is possible antecedent of the pronoun, and this reference is more recent than the last reference to the subjective character (see "he" in (12p)). The following modified version of (12) is a more convincing illustration:

(13) Dwayne wasn't sure what John was scared of. What in the arcade could scare a boy like that? He rubbed his head under his baseball cap. He could see tears in John's eyes. He could tell they were tears because his eyes were too shiny. Too round. Well, it was all right to cry. He'd cried when they took him to that place a few years back. Now John was in a new place too. Maybe that was why he was crying.
"I want to leave," he said.

Even though John is the last-mentioned male entity, the referent of "he" in the last sentence is taken to be Dwayne, the subjective character of the first paragraph.

I am investigating this view of the discourse structure of narrative text and also the related processing issues, such as how it can be determined whether or not a new context is part of a larger discourse segment.

Specific Indefinite References. A specific indefinite reference, in general terms, refers to an individual who is not already known. In a subjective context, such a reference is understood to refer to an individual with whom the subjective character is not familiar (Fillmore, 1974). Interestingly, even if the referent is actually an individual with whom the reader is familiar, the author must still use an indefinite reference—a definite reference would imply that the subjective character, too, is familiar with the referent. In a subjective context, in general, whether a specific reference is definite or indefinite is determined by the familiarity of the subjective character with the referent, regardless of whether or not the reader is familiar with it.

The following is a strategy for understanding specific indefinite references in third-person narrative text (a situation in which another strategy might be better will be identified later):

> Let *sir* be a specific, indefinite reference and p a predicate corresponding to the propositional content of *sir*. Then a new concept c should be created to serve as the referent of *sir* and the proposition $p(c)$ should be added to *CBS*.[10]

The reader's believing that the referent of *sir* is actually an individual with whom he or she is already familiar can be represented by including, in the belief space of the reader, the proposition that c and $c1$ are coextensional, where $c1$ is the concept of that individual that already existed.

Suppose that *sir* appears in a subjective sentence. The reader may decide that the referent is actually an individual he or she is already familiar with after reading later sentences. For example, suppose that the following passage appears in the middle of a novel:

> (14) Zoe looked up. A man was coming toward her. My, he had shocking red hair.

Suppose that in earlier objective sentences, a man was referred to as "John" and was described as having very red hair. Thus, there are already propositions in the reader's belief space that someone is named John and has very red hair; let $c1$ be the concept of that person. Under the above strategy, a new concept, c, is created to serve as the referent of "a man," and the proposition $man(c)$ is added to Zoe's belief space. After reading the third sentence, the reader may come to believe that c and $c1$ are coextensional, given the clue that the man has shocking red hair.

However, suppose that it is at the time "a man" is processed that the reader decides the referent is actually John. This is a situation in which the above strategy may not be the best one. That is, rather than creating a new concept c

---

[10]Suppose that a specific, indefinite reference appears in a subjective context of Mary, and a concept c is created to serve as the referent. An interesting question is what should the reader believe about the temporal extent, within the fictional world, of Mary's unfamiliarity with c? In the following passage, the subjective character is familiar with the referent before the current moment in the fictional world: "Mary was curious. A man had been sitting in a car across the street, watching her house, for two hours." The current moment is the time at which Mary is curious. However, Mary has been aware of the referent of "a man" for at least two hours. (I owe this point to an anonymous referee.)

to serve as the referent and then having to add to the reader's belief space the proposition that $c1$ and c are coextensional, we may simply want to add *man(c1)* directly to Zoe's belief space.

Another interesting feature of specific, indefinite references in subjective contexts is that they may imply that the subjective character is not sure what sort of thing the referent is. This may occur when the head noun is a superordinate term, such as "plant" or "vehicle," rather than either a basic-level term, such as "flower" or "car," or a subordinate term, such as "violet" or "station wagon" (Rosch & Lloyd, 1978). Often, it should be understood from the use of the superordinate term that the subjective character cannot classify the referent at the basic level. For example:

> (15) Slowly Hannah raised her head and blinked her eyes. Small dots of purple covered the ground around her and she reached out to explore. Violets! (Franchere, 1964, p. 25)

When she first sees the violets, Hannah can identify them only as small dots of purple.

There are other reasons to use a superordinate term in a specific indefinite reference. For example, a superordinate term is used when the reference is plural and refers to a group composed of individuals in different basic-level categories (Murphy & Wisniewski, 1989). In any event, the fact that a superordinate term was used is a source of information about the subjective character's beliefs about the referent or referents. (Peters & Shapiro, 1987a, 1987b, and Peters, Shapiro, & Rapaport, 1988, described a representation for natural category systems in which the fact that something was classified only at a superordinate level can be expressed.)

The following passage illustrates the observations made in this section:

> (16) There they [the King and his men] saw close beside them a great rubbleheap; and suddenly they were aware of two small figures lying on it at their ease, grey-clad, hardly to be seen among the stones. (Tolkien, 1965, p. 206)

The King and his men have come upon two hobbits, Merry and Pippin. The King and his men do not know the hobbits, but other characters also present in the scene do know them. In a subjective sentence attributed to the King and his men, the hobbits are referred to with an indefinite reference, "two small figures," reflecting the fact that the King and his men do not know them. In addition, the superordinate term "figures" reflects the fact that the King and his men do not know what the referents are ("hobbit" is a basic-level term in this novel; the kinds of sentient beings are hobbits, dwarves, elves, men, etc.).

Suppose the reader does not decide until after processing "two small figures" that it is Merry and Pippin whom the King and his men have come upon. Once "two small figures" is processed using the strategy given earlier, the following are some of the propositions about Merry and Pippin that appear in various belief spaces. The belief spaces of the reader, and of the characters in the scene other than the King and his men, include the following propositions about two concepts c_1 and c_2: c_1 is named "Merry," c_2 is named "Pippin," c_1 is a hobbit, and c_2 is a hobbit. The belief space of the King and his men include the following propositions about two other concepts c_3 and c_4: c_3 is a small figure, and c_4 is a small figure. When the reader decides that the referents of "two small figures" are, in fact, Merry and Pippin, two more propositions appear in the reader's belief space: that c_1 and c_3, and c_2 and c_4, are concepts of the same individual.

Conclusion

This section identified some consequences for reference resolution of the fact that although references in objective sentences reflect true information about the fictional world, those in subjective contexts reflect the beliefs of the subjective character.

DE RE AND DE DICTO REPORTS

Introduction

This work has grown out of the work on de re and de dicto belief reports in philosophy, linguistics, and AI. This section considers the de re/de dicto ambiguity with respect to some issues raised in earlier sections.

The terms *de re* and *de dicto* have been used in different ways; here, I use them to describe an ambiguity to which particular types of sentences, those with opaque contexts, are subject. Another term for this is *ambiguity with respect to description* (Fodor, 1979). Recall from the first section that opaque contexts are the objects of sentences with third-person subjects and main verbs that are either propositional–attitude verbs, such as 'believe', 'know', and 'hope', or other psychological and perceptual verbs, such as 'want', 'hate', and 'see' (we use the term "private-state" for such verbs). We only consider such sentences that have "believe" as the main verb (although similar comments apply to those with other private-state verbs), and, following usual practice, we call them "third-person belief reports."[11]

The ambiguity is generally viewed as follows. In a de re belief report, the speaker believes the propositional content of references in the subordinated clause; in a de dicto report, the speaker believes the subject of the sentence believes the propositional content of those references. Consider the following:

---

[11]In this section, "report" refers to a syntactic form of sentences. However, I should point out that report is also used in this work to refer to a type of subjective sentence, and not all subjective sentences that are syntactically reports are interpreted to be the type of subjective sentence called a report (cf. Wiebe, 1990a).

(17) John believes that the morning star is beautiful.

If (17) is de re, then "the morning star" reflects the speaker's belief that the referent is the morning star; if it is de dicto, then "the morning star" reflects the speaker's belief that John believes the referent is the morning star. In the first case, the speaker may not believe John believes that the referent is the morning star; in the second case, the speaker may not himself or herself believe the referent is the morning star.[12]

Analyses of belief reports do not generally consider whether genre affects how reports are interpreted. In the next section, I suggest that analyses of de re reports in conversation should take into account the mutual beliefs of the speaker and hearer, and I contrast this with reports in objective contexts. Next, following Fodor (1979), I suggest that "pure" de dicto interpretations are unlikely in conversation; given this and the observations made in previous sections, I then draw parallels between the interpretation of references and the interpretation of *subjective elements* (linguistic elements that express attitudes and affects).

The De Re Interpretation and Mutual Belief

As discussed previously, references in conversation are understood to reflect the speaker's beliefs about the hearer's and speaker's mutual beliefs; they are not always understood to simply reflect the speaker's beliefs about the entities referred to. I suggest in this section that this extends as well to references in the subordinated clauses of de re belief reports.

We first reconsider references in conversation from the speaker's perspective. Even in nonopaque contexts, the speaker's beliefs may not in fact be reflected by his or her references. For example, because of the communicative situation, a speaker may use a reference whose propositional content the speaker does not believe, but the speaker believes the hearer believes. One example, (5), was given previously. Donnellan (1966) provided another example:

(18) Suppose the throne is occupied by a man I firmly believe not to be the king but a usurper. Imagine also that his followers as firmly believe that he is the king. Suppose I wish to see this man. I might say to his minions "Is the king in his countinghouse?" I succeed in referring to the man I wish to refer to without myself believing that he fits the description. (pp. 290–291)

---

[12]According to Quine (1976), de dicto reports are referentially opaque and de re reports are referentially transparent—substitution of coreferential expressions into the opaque context of the former does not necessarily preserve truth value, whereas substitution into the latter does. According to Castañeda (1970/1977), de dicto reports are propositionally transparent and de re reports are propositionally opaque—in the former, the speaker believes that references in the opaque context convey the content of the believer's belief, but, in the latter, the speaker may not believe this.

The same can be true of a reference in the object of a de re belief report. That is, given the above scenario, I might utter the following, even if I do not myself believe the propositional content of "the king"; I might do so if I believe my hearers believe the propositional content of this reference:

(19) The queen believes that the king is in his countinghouse.

Now let us take the hearer's perspective. Even in the objects of de re belief reports, the hearer does not always understand references as simply reflecting the speaker's beliefs about the referent. Consider understanding (19). If the hearers do not know I believe the man on the throne is a usurper, then they will not detect my "dishonesty," and they will understand the reference as reflecting my belief that the man is the king. However, suppose they do know I believe he is a usurper. Then they understand "the king" as reflecting my belief that they believe the man is the king, my belief that they believe I believe he is the king, and so on, even though they do not believe I believe he is the king. In this case, the hearers do not understand the reference as reflecting my belief in the propositional content of the reference. Thus, in conversation, even references in the objects of de re belief reports are subject to the sorts of complexities that were identified by Clark and Marshall (1981) and by Perrault and Cohen (1981).

Now consider (syntactic) private-state reports in objective contexts. One sort that can be objective is a report with a negated factive verb (such as "know" or "realize") and a propositional object. For example:

(20) John did not know that Mary was in the cell next to his.

Either this sentence is another character's reflection about John's lack of knowledge, or it is an objective sentence. Let us assume the latter. As with other references in objective contexts, the reader understands that the propositional content of the reference in the object of the report is true; the fact that the sentence is syntactically a knowledge report is irrelevant. The de re/de dicto ambiguity lies in whether or not this reference also reflects the beliefs of the subject of the report. If it is understood that it does, then the report is interpreted to be de dicto. Otherwise, it is interpreted to be de re. In either case, the propositional content of the reference is understood to be true.

De Dicto Reports and the Speaker's Beliefs

It is difficult to find clear cases of "pure" de dicto reports in natural conversation. (A "pure" de dicto report is one in which a reference does not reflect the speaker's beliefs about the referent, but only the speaker's beliefs about the subject of the report's beliefs about the referent.) Fodor (1979) argued that the speaker is always responsible for references, even in the objects of belief reports interpreted de dicto—that is, the speaker cannot use a description in the subordinated clause of a belief report that the speaker does not believe correctly describes the referent, even if the speaker believes the subject believes it does. The difference between a de dicto and a de re belief report, she claimed, is that in the former, but not the latter, the speaker believes that the subject of the report believes the propositional content of references, too. (Note that Fodor, whose work predates Clark & Marshall, 1981, and Perrault & Cohen, 1981, did not consider the communicative relationship between the speaker and the hearer, so she did not consider, for example, the possibility that a reference reflects the speaker's beliefs about the hearer's beliefs.)

Fodor made her argument by considering examples in which the speaker and subject disagree about what would be a correct description of the referent. Examples in which they agree would not reveal anything, she argued, because there would then be no way of determining who is responsible for the reference. I will not present her entire argument here, but just show her analysis of an example from Postal (1967/1974).

(21) Charley believes that the book which *was* burned was *not* burned.

Both de re and de dicto interpretations of (21) ascribe a false belief to Charley.

By the definition of a de re report, the speaker believes the propositional content of "the book which *was* burned"; thus, what the speaker disagrees with must be Charley's belief that the book was not burned.

A de dicto interpretation of (21) ascribes a contradictory belief to Charley—by the definition of a de dicto report, Charley believes the propositional content of the reference "the book which *was* burned," and the main assertion of the sentence is that Charley believes that the book was not burned. Fodor contended that a speaker cannot reasonably utter (21) unless the speaker herself believes the propositional content of "the book which *was* burned," and, therefore, as in the de re case, what the speaker disagrees with must be Charley's belief that the book was not burned, and not Charley's belief that the book was burned. Fodor's evidence is that a speaker could reasonably utter (22) but not (23):

(22) Charley believes that the book which was burned was not burned. Silly old Charley. Of course it was burned. (p. 255)
     (The speaker disagrees with the propositional object of "believe.")

(23) Charley believes that the book which was burned was not burned. Silly old Charley. Of course it wasn't burned. (p. 255)
     (The speaker disagrees with the propositional content of the reference.)

"Whichever opinion as to the state of the book is expressed by the content of the noun phrase (in the object of the report) is the one to which the speaker is committed. He may be ascribing it to Charley, but he is also, in using it in his report, endorsing it himself" (p. 256). If the speaker has no opinion either way about the book, then neither the reference "the book which was burned" nor "the book which was not burned" can be used. Thus, (24) and (25) are both inconsistent:

(24) Charley assumed that the book which was burned was not burned, but I don't know whether it was burned or not. (p. 256)
(Speaker has no opinion about the propositional content of the reference.)

(25) Charley assumed that the book which was not burned was burned, but I don't know whether it was burned or not. (p. 256)
(Speaker has no opinion about the propositional content of the reference.)

We now consider examples similar to the ones above, except that in these, a de dicto reading does not ascribe a contradictory belief to the subject. Even without the contradiction, we find the same phenomena. Thus, the speaker could reasonably utter (22'), but not (23') or (24'):

(22') Charley believes that the book which was burned was written by Shakespeare. Silly old Charley. It was obviously written by Burns. (p. 255)
(The speaker disagrees with the propositional object of "believe.")

(23') Charley believes that the book which was burned was written by Shakespeare. Silly old Charley. Of course it wasn't burned. (p. 255)
(The Speaker disagrees with the propositional content of the reference.)

(24') Charley believes that the book which was burned was written by Shakespeare, but I don't know whether it was burned or not. (p. 256)
(The speaker has no opinion about the propositional content of the reference.)

In contrast to (24'), (26) is fine, since it is the truth of the propositional object of "believe" that the speaker has no opinion about:

(26) Charley believes that the book which was burned was written by Shakespeare, but I don't know whether he wrote it or not. (p. 256)
(No opinion as to the propositional object of "believe.")

Returning to third-person narrative text, there is no question that pure de dicto reports appear in subjective contexts (see example [8]).

PARALLELS WITH THE INTERPRETATION
OF SUBJECTIVE ELEMENTS

The language-use context of a reference (i.e., whether it occurs in a subjective context, an objective context, or in conversation) affects how the reference is understood. This is not an isolated issue. There are lexical and grammatical elements whose interpretations are similarly affected by language-use context—those that express subjectivity, as analyzed by Banfield (1982).

Banfield equated subjectivity with that expressed by *subjective elements*. Examples of subjective elements are exclamations, as in (15), which express emotion, and epithets, such as "the idiot," which express evaluation of the referent. In any context, Banfield argued, the subjectivity expressed by such an element is attributed to the subject of consciousness, or the SELF. In conversation (or any context in which "I" could appear), the SELF is the speaker, so the subjectivity expressed by subjective elements is attributed to the speaker.[13] Banfield showed, however, that subjectivity is not tied by definition to the speaker. In a narrative subjective sentence, the subjective character is the SELF, even when he or she is referred to in the third person. Consider the following sentence:

(26) The idiot was standing next to her.

If uttered in conversation, "the idiot" expresses the speaker's subjectivity. But if (26) is a narrative subjective sentence, then "the idiot" expresses the subjectivity of the subjective character (who is potentially the referent of "her").

Given Fodor's contention that the speaker is always responsible for references, and the fact that references in subjective sentences reflect the beliefs of the subjective character, we relate the issue addressed in this chapter to Banfield's theory as follows: Belief in the propositional content of a reference is attributed at least to the SELF (in the case of a belief report, the SELF may believe that the subject of the sentence believes it as well).[14] As mentioned previously, Fodor did not consider the communicative relationship between the speaker and hearer, so she did not consider the possibility that, for example, a reference reflects the speaker's beliefs about the hearer's beliefs. Thus, the above statement needs to be revised to account for this relationship. However, one might consider the following to be an example of an analogous phenomenon (note that a kinship

---

[13]This is a simplification of Banfield's theory. For example, see her *revised principle of the priority of the speaker*, developed to account for complexities that arise in the interpretation of echo questions and a type of subjective sentence not considered in this chapter, represented speech (Banfield, 1982).

[14]Even when the SELF is a subjective character, a reference in a (syntactic) belief report might reflect the SELF's belief that the subject of the sentence believes the propositional content of a reference, as well. Suppose the following sentence is interpreted to be the thought of a character Rick: John believed that Mary was rich.

In this case, Rick, not John, is the subjective character, so all references reflect Rick's beliefs. However, the sentence may be interpreted to be either de dicto or de re from the perspective of Rick. Under the former interpretation, but not the latter, Rick believes that John, too, believes the propositional content of "Mary." On the other hand, if the sentence is interpreted to be the type of subjective sentence called a "private-state report" (see note 11 and Wiebe, 1990a), the sentence is a report of John's belief, John is the subjective character, and because the subject of the report believes the propositional content of "Mary", the sentence is simply de dicto.

term such as "Daddy" is another type of subjective element): my uttering (27) with the intention of referring to the child's father rather than to my own.

(27) Daddy will be here to pick you up soon.

Thus, it may be that the communicative relationship between the speaker and hearer also potentially affects the interpretation of subjective elements.

Subjective elements cannot appear in objective sentences. The reason, Banfield argued, is that there is neither a speaker nor any other subject of consciousness in an objective sentence to whom subjectivity can be attributed. The absence of a SELF can also explain the fact that references in objective sentences are simply understood to reflect true information—since there is no SELF to whom to attribute belief, the question of belief in the propositional content does not arise.

CONCLUSION

I conclude by mentioning some open questions related to those addressed in this chapter. First, it is assumed we are given fully fleshed-out belief spaces; given these, and the sort of reference to be understood, we identify some specific situations in which propositions are added to belief spaces as a result of understanding references. An important question is: what strategies should be employed in general to add propositions to belief spaces? (Wilks and colleagues dealt extensively with this question, cf., Ballim, Wilks, & Barnden, 1991; Wilks & Ballim, 1987; Wilks & Bien, 1983.)

Second, the content of a reference may be important in determining which belief space is the current one. For example, where p is a predicate corresponding to the propositional content of a reference r, and c is a concept, suppose that $p(c)$ is inconsistent with the propositions in *CBS*, but is a proposition in another belief space. This may suggest that we are wrong as to which belief space is the current one, not that c should be rejected as the referent of r.

Third, it is in the absence of a speaker that subjectivity and belief in the propositional content of references can be attributed to an agent referred to in the third person. However, I do not define the term "speaker," as used in that context. I do not attempt to define it here, but merely point out that containing a first-person pronoun is a sufficient but not a necessary condition for a sentence to have a speaker. Thus, a sentence in an expository text in which the author is referred to as "I" has a speaker, even though the sentence is not verbally uttered. But in the absence of a first-person pronoun, what is important is whether or not a first-person pronoun could potentially appear without changing to whom subjectivity is attributed. (Banfield showed that deictic elements, tense, and aspects can place constraints on whether or not both a first-person and a second-person pronoun could appear in a sentence.)

Finally, in objective and subjective narrative sentences, the author is not a speaker or even a SELF, in Banfield's terms (note that by "the author," I mean the actual writer of the text, not an overt narrator; see note 2). Experimental fiction aside, the author cannot be referred to in the first person, and subjectivity cannot be attributed to him or her. However, the author is clearly communicating with the reader, in some sense of that word. For example, part of understanding a narrative text is recognizing the author's intentions with respect to whether sentences should be interpreted as subjective or objective. Pollack (1986) noted that in narrative, one must infer both the author's and the characters' plans. This aspect of fictional narrative has important implications for computational models of pragmatic processing.

ACKNOWLEDGMENTS

I am indebted to Mary Galbraith, Sandra L. Peters, William J. Rapaport, Stuart C. Shapiro, David Zubin, and the other members of the Narrative Research Group of the SUNY Buffalo Center for Cognitive Science and the SNePS Research Group for many discussions and ideas, and to William Rapaport, Sandra Peters, Toby Walker, Diane Horton, Peter Heeman, and anonymous referees for valuable comments on earlier drafts of this chapter. This research was supported in part by National Science Foundation grants IST–8504713 and IRI–8610517, and the preparation of this chapter was supported in part by the Natural Sciences and Engineering Research Council of Canada.

12

DISCOURSE CONTINUITY AND PERSPECTIVE TAKING

Naicong Li
Language Systems, Inc., Woodland Hills, CA

David A. Zubin
State University of New York at Buffalo

In Brown's (1958) classic paper on categorization, *How Shall a Thing Be Called*, he observed that the choice among full NP referring expressions for a specific referent is determined by a variety of context-dependent cognitive factors. For example, the thing in which I drive to work might be called a "vehicle," "car," "Toyota," "Tercel," or even an "artifact," depending on the social or discourse context. An extension of Brown's thinking suggests that the choice of an anaphoric referring expression—full NP, pronoun, or zero (in languages such as Mandarin with zero anaphor)—might likewise be a function of context-dependent cognitive factors. In this chapter, we briefly review proposals based on the *linear* and *rhetorical* structure of discourse, and then turn to the effect of perspective taking on the selection of an anaphoric referring expression.

LINEAR AND RHETORICAL CONTINUITY

Givon's (1983) work on topic continuity set the stage by laying out the basic relationship between the form of an anaphoric referring expression and what he called the "accessibility" of its referent to the listener (Fig. 12.1). Basically, the less accessible the referent, the more robust the anaphoric referring expression (both its phonological form and semantic content). Conversely, the more accessible the referent, the more reduced the anaphoric referring expression. What Givon had in mind was a cognitive model of the speaker and/or listener's discourse representation that draws on the psychological and natural language proc-

accessibility of referent	high<-->low
robustness of form/meaning	reduced<-->robust zero < pronoun < simple NP^a < complex NP^b

Note. From Givon (1983). Adapted by permission.
[a]For example, (DET+) noun.
[b]For example, [PP or adjP+] noun.

FIG. 12.1.   Continuity Scale. Adapted by permission.

essing literatures. In accordance with the former (cf. Cowan's 1988 review) the model is divided into (a) a global representation of the discourse as well as background knowledge (reminiscent of long-term memory), and (b) a processing window (reminiscent of focal attention and/or short-term memory) in which a representation for the current clause(s) is constructed.[1] Furthermore, (c) the processing window contains a *focus stack*,[2] reminiscent of the NLP literature (Grosz, 1981; Reichman, 1978; Sidner, 1983) in which previously mentioned participants in the discourse world are ranked according to their relative (and absolute) accessibility to the listener in his or her search for the target of an anaphoric referring expression. Position in the focus stack is determined by an open-ended set of factors, such as recency of mention, mention within the same rhetorical/episodic unit, status in the story world (central vs. peripheral character), presence of another (higher ranking) participant in the stack, or grammatically focal versus oblique coding of the previous mention (e.g., subject vs. object of preposition). As depicted in Fig. 12.1, the robustness of an anaphoric referring expression iconically reflects the accessibility of the intended referent, that is, its position in the focus stack. The listener can thus use the robustness of the anaphoric referring expression to pick out a referent from the focus stack, at least as an initial hypothesis about the intended referent.[3]

Givon chose to operationalize and measure accessibility by looking at how recently the participant was evoked (referential distance), and whether or not another eligible participant was co-present in the preceding context (referential competition). In applying *linear continuity*, as we call it, to Mandarin data, Chen (1986) found the following figures: average referential distance for zero: 1.25; for

---

[1]Evidence for this distinction in the psychological literature (cf. Clark & Clark, 1977) showed that a listener's memory for clause(s) under current processing is highly literal, whereas memory for previous clauses shows extensive effects of thematic integration into a global discourse structure.

[2]Givon (1983) calls it "discourse file" or "register."

[3]Li and Zubin (1986), following Marslen-Wilson, Levy and Tyler (1982), contended that *pragmatic matching*, as a parallel process, is the ultimate arbiter in anaphoric resolution.

pronouns: 2.03; for full NPs: 6.29. He found average referential competition for zero to be .08; pronouns: .23; and full NPs: .88. Thus, for zero anaphora, the average distance one has to look back in the text to find the preceding reference to the participant is 1.25 clauses. This distance increases for the pronoun *ta*, and jumps substantially for full NP references. If one looks for a competing participant in the immediately preceding context, one finds one for zero anaphor only 8% of the time. This index of referential competition likewise increases for pronouns and full NPs. Chen's data provide clear confirmation of Givon's linear continuity principle.

Fox (1987) argued that linear continuity is only part of the story. Equally important is the hierarchical structuring of the discourse into rhetorical units (Mann & Thompson, 1985), for example, into clause groups characterized by a common goal or action schema and composed of super- and subordinate layers of structure. Chen showed that, for Mandarin discourse, the choice of anaphoric referring expressions along the scale in Fig. 12.1 is systematically related to rhetorical structure. Example 1 shows that a shift from one goal/action schema to another motivates the use of a pronoun (instead of a zero anaphor) even when linear continuity is high. The pronoun at the beginning of line (1b) has a referential distance of one clause and no referential competition, characteristic of zero anaphora. But at this point there is a break in the action type as well as in the goal structure. (See Table 12.1 for explanations of the abbreviations used in the close translations in the examples that follow.)

(1) a. You ge xiaohai, Ø qi zhe yi liang jiaodache, Ø jingguo zhexie shuiguo.
      exist CL kid   ride DUR one CL bike   pass   these fruit
   b. Ranhou, *ta* ting xialai, Ø ba yi luo shuiguo tongtong ban dao che shang.
      then   *he* stop down   BA one CL fruit   all   move to bike up

   (a) There was a kid, [who] was riding a bike, and passed the fruit. (b) Then he stopped, and moved the whole basket of fruit up to the bike (Chen, 1986, p. 204)

Example (2) shows the inverse effect: Continuity of goal structure and action schema motivate the use of zero anaphora across a hiatus of linear discontinuity. In (2b), the text shifts to Lao Li for two clauses and then back to Zhang Dasao with a zero anaphor (indicated by Ø in this and subsequent examples) at the beginning of (2c). But in Fox's and Chen's view, this linear interruption of reference to Zhang Dasao was not an interruption in rhetorical structure because the clauses of line (2b) are rhetorically subordinate: They provide an explanation for Zhang Dasao's action of replacing the chopsticks. Line (2c) is thus a direct continuation of the rhetorical structure of (2a).[4]

---

[4]Fox (1987) asserted that in this case, the popped over material has to be short and to have simple internal structure for reduced anaphoric referring expressions to be used in resuming the same rhetorical line.

TABLE 12.1
Abbreviations Used in the Examples

BA	preverbal objective marker	CL	classifier	CRS	current relevant state
CSC	complex stative construction	DUR	durative aspect	NOM	nominalizer
PAR	particles	PFV	perfective aspect	¶	paragraph break

(2) a. *Zhang Dasao* zuocai, Ø duan cha, Ø rang keren, tian tang,
     ZD   cook   serve tea   entertain guest add soup
     Ø huan kuaizi—
        change chopsticks
   b. *Lao Li* chi gaolexing, Ø ba kuaizi   diao zai dishang liang hui—
     LL   eat pleased   BA chopsticks drop on ground two time
   c. Ø ziji tiao fei de chi, Ø kuajiang ziji de   shouyi,
     self pick fat NOM eat   praise self NOM skills
     Ø tongshi   bingju.
     same-time together-do

(a) Zhang Dasao prepared dishes, served tea, entertained [her] guest, added soup, replaced the chopsticks—(b) Lao Li was so pleased with the food that [he] had dropped the chopsticks twice—(c) [and she] picked the fat for herself, praised her own cooking, and did all these at the same time. (Chen, 1986, p. 181)

Fox's taxonomy of rhetorical structure allows any discourse to be hierarchically segmented into rhetorical units, with at least minor discontinuity across the boundaries. Chen (1986) was able to show that in a sample of oral discourse, pronouns with a referential distance of only one clause (a referential distance which would usually trigger zero anaphora) follow a rhetorical boundary 88% of the time.[5]

PERSPECTIVE: EXPRESSIVE VS. REPORTIVE FRAMING

We argue that rhetorical structure is only part of the story, as illustrated in (3), taken from a written narrative. The character, Li Xiangnan, is mentioned in (3a) and (3b). Lines 3a–3j represent the content of his perception, but do not refer to him. In (3j), reference to this character is accomplished with a zero despite the fact that there are 21 intervening clauses containing reference to several potentially competing participants,[6] as well as numerous breaks in the goal and schema

---

[5]Why rhetorical structure should have this effect on the choice of referring expression was suggested by Tomlin and Pu's (1989) experimental research. They showed that the visual segmentation of a cartoon-style stimulus presentation results in zero anaphora within image frames, and pronominal or full NP anaphora across frames.

[6]Note that person/gender/number properties are irrelevant for the match between zero and its referent.

structure of the story. Such data clearly fall outside the domain of both the linear and the rhetorical continuity hypotheses. The choice of anaphoric referring expressions in such passages involves *perspective taking* (or "*subjectivity*") in discourse. We propose a cognitive model in the context of frame semantics (Fillmore, 1978) for this phenomenon, and investigate its effect on the choice of anaphoric referring expressions in Mandarin.

(3) a. ¶ *Li Xiangnan* zaozao qilai, yigeren zou dao waimian.
       LX   early get-up alone   walk to outside
   b. *Ta* xiwang ganshou yixia Beijing zaochen
      he hope   feel   a-little Beijing morning
      de shengqibobo de qifen [3 clauses omitted]
      NOM dynamic NOM atmosphere
   c. ¶ Dandan de [. . .] chenwu longzhao zhe Hufanqiao
        thin   NOM   morning-fog envelop DUR H
      yidai de jiedao. [7 clauses omitted]
      area NOM street
   d. ¶ Malu duimian, [. . .] ji ge zaoqi   de jinhuang toufa de waiguoren
        street across   a-few CL early-rise NOM blond hair NOM foreigner
   e. —yi ge piaoliang nulang, ji   ge nanxing—
      one CL pretty   woman a-few CL males
      liuliudada, [. . . 2 clauses omitted]
      stroll
   f. ¶ Wu liu ge laotou   zai lubian jingshendousou,
        five-six CL old-man DUR road-side energetic
      yitaianxiangde da zhe taijiquan:
      calmly   practice DUR Taichi
   g. [4 clauses] ¶ Ji liang saiche wushengde cong malu shang
                    a-few CL racing-bicycle silently from street on
      jisu liangguo, [1 clause omitted]
      fast sweep-past
   h. ¶ Yi qun shiliuqisui   de guniang—shi tixiao
        one group 16–17 NOM girl   are PhysEd-Institute
        de ba—[1 clause omitted]
      NOM PAR
   i. cong shenpang tengtengde paoguo.
      from body-side   run-past
   j. Ø Neng gandao tamen na qingchun huore de
        can feel   they that youthful hot   NOM
      huxi, zhengteng de hanqi.
      breath steaming NOM perspiration

(a) Li Xiangnan got up very early, went out alone. (b) He wanted to feel the dynamic atmosphere of Beijing's morning [. . .]. ¶(c) Thin [. . .] morning mist envelops the streets of the Hufangqiao area. [. . .] ¶(d) Across the street, [. . .] a few early rising foreigners with blond hair—(e) a pretty woman, a few males—are strolling, [. . .] ¶(f) Five or six old men are practicing Taichi beside the road, energetic and calm, [. . .]. .¶(g) A few racing bicycles sweep past in the street silently and swiftly, [. . .] ¶(h) A group of girls—sixteen or seventeen years old—probably from the Institute of Physical Education—[. . .] (i) run past by [his] side. (j) [He] can feel their youthful and vigorous breathing, their steaming perspiration. (Ke, 1986, pp. 357–358)

Frames are stereotypic representations of scenes or event types drawn from the speaker's background knowledge, composed of cultural and naive physical beliefs. They are thus part of the speaker's cognitive representation of the world, and not exclusively a component of individual lexical items, or even of the lexicon as a whole, to which frame semantics has most extensively been applied. Frame semantics (Lakoff, 1987; Zubin & Choi, 1984; and cf. Talmy, 1983) reduces the problem of uncontrolled polysemy to an analysis of the interaction between lexical meanings and the contexts in which we use them. To cite one classic example, Fillmore (1978) noted that the lexical item "morning" is exasperatingly variable when you try to map it onto clock time, but that this variability is under the control of social and discourse context. If I say, "we'll discuss it in the morning" to a colleague at work, I mean between 9:00 a.m. and noon; if I say it to my housemate, I mean between 7:00 and 9:00 a.m., before I leave for work. To my fishing buddy, I could mean 4:00 a.m., and to a friend on the graveyard shift, I could mean after midnight.

We propose an abstract application of frame analysis to discourse organization in which two distinct types of perspective framing, depicted in Fig. 12.2a & b, are responsible for a host of textual coding properties, one of which is the choice of anaphoric referring expressions. In building our models of perspective framing we draw on the linguistic, literary critical, and NLP literature on subjectivity in language: Banfield (1982), Cohn (1978), Fillmore (1974), Galbraith (1990), Kuroda (1973), Langacker (1985), Wiebe (1990b), and others.

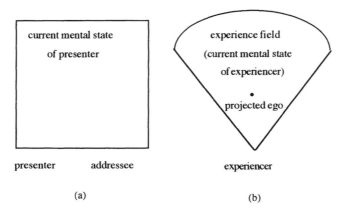

FIG. 12.2.   (a) Reportive frame. (b) Expressive frame.

The reportive frame (Fig. 12.2a) consists of a presenter (i.e. a speaker or writer), an addressee, and the presenter's dynamic mental model of the ongoing discourse that takes the addressee into consideration. This mental model contains the entities pertaining to the story world, and the relations among them. Note that the frame represents the consciousness of the presenter during his or her actual process of narrating or speaking. The expressive frame (Fig. 12.2b) consists of an experiencer, an experience field containing objects of experience and their relations (mental model of here-and-now experience). Among these objects of experience, there can be one representing the experiencer when he or she is an object of his or her own mental process. Here the model represents the consciousness of a person who is experiencing, rather than presenting, something to an addressee. The text codes only the enclosed area of the frames: the dynamic mental model of the presenter as he or she is speaking/writing (Fig. 12.2a) and the dynamic mental model of the experiencer as he or she is experiencing (Fig. 12.2b).

In interactional discourse, speakers use both types of framing in constructing their utterances. Thus, a speaker can choose to express his or her experience in an immediate/unmediated way (expressive framing), or report it in a less direct way (reportive framing). The sensation of stomach pain can be directly expressed with an interjection-like utterance in Mandarin, as in (4a):

(4) a. Teng   si (wo) la!   b. Wo duzi   teng   de shoubuliao le.
    pain/ache dead I PAR   I stomach ache/pain CSC can't-stand CRS
    "Oh my stomach!"   "My stomach aches (so bad)
    I'm gonna die!"   I can't stand it."

A characteristic of such interjections is that they are not addressed to a listener so much as they are uttered in his or her presence. On the other hand, the speaker can transform the experience into a report about his or her internal state, for example to a doctor, as in (4b). Note that because we do not have direct access to another person's mental state, in interactional discourse we can only report about it (as in b'), but not express it in an unmediated way (as in a') (Banfield, 1982; Chun & Zubin, 1990):

(4) a.' ??Teng   si (ta) la!   b. Ta duzi   teng   de shoubuliao le.
    pain/ache dead he PAR   she stomach ache/pain CSC can't-stand CRS
    "Oh her stomach!"   "Her stomach aches (so bad)
    She's gonna die!"   She can't stand it."

Unlike in interactional discourse, in narrative texts expressive framing (illustrated in Examples 5–7) can be used to capture the here-and-now of a third-person experiencer's mental world.

(5) *Represented Thought:*
    Li Ming hanliumanmian. Tamen zhende faxian le zhe shi ziji gan de ma?
    LM   sweat-all-over-face they really discover PFV this is self do NOM PAR
    "Li Ming was sweating. Did they really discover that self (= LM) did this?"

(6) *Represented Perception:*
Zhuangkuo de Beijing cheng zai yanqian zhankai.
grand   NOM Beijing city at eye-front spread-open
"The city of Beijing spread out before [his] eyes."

(7) *Represented Feeling/Emotion:*
Yi zhen beishang yong le   shanglai.
one CL sadness well PFV up-come
"A wave of sadness welled up [in him]."

In contrast, a text may use reportive framing, as in Examples 8–10, to talk about the internal states of the experiencer. Here, the text presents the content of the experiencer's mental state from an external vantage, that of the writer, or of an omniscient observer. The distinction between expressive and reportive framing does not entirely coincide with the distinction between subjective and objective sentences/context/text. In particular, certain types of reportive framing may be called subjective because they present private mental states, although in a reportive style. Note that Banfield (1982) used "subjective" or "objective" to talk about specific sentence types, whereas we use "expressive" and "reportive" to denote cognitive structures underlying the interpretation of specific morpho-syntactic and lexical structures in the text.

(8) *Reported Thought:*
Li Ming haipa tamen yijing   faxian   zhe shi ta gan de.
LM   afraid they already discover this is he do NOM
"Li Ming was afraid that they had discovered that he did it."

(9) *Reported Perception:*
Li Ming fukan   zhe Beijing cheng.
LM   look-over DUR Beijing city
"Li Ming looked over the city of Beijing."

(10) *Reported Feeling/Emotion:*
Li Ming hen nanguo
LM   very sad
"Li Ming felt very sad."

Table 12.2 summarizes the distinction between expressive and reportive framing with a set of contrastive properties.

FRAMING EFFECTS ON REFERENTIAL CONTINUITY

Expressive framing affects the coding of the experiencer and objects of experience in ways that violate the linear or rhetorical continuity hypotheses in a number of ways.

TABLE 12.2
Properties of Reportive and Expressive Framing

Reportive	Expressive
1. Communicative—directed at an addressee, coding takes addressee into account.	1. Noncommunicative—coding does not take addressee into account, may not even be directed at an addressee.
2. Reports "objectively" about the story world (may include information about the internal state of an experiencer).	2. Directly and vividly portrays the mental process of an experiencer (may include aspects of the story world.)
3. May give an abbreviated summary presentation of the story world.	3. Full, expansive, detailed presentation.
4. Events may (or may not) be temporally deflected (distant in space and time) from the story world's deictic center.	4. Here-and-now, blow-by-blow portrayal of events as they happen.
5. Indirect, transformed coding of experiencer's cognitive process.	5. Direct coding of experiencer's cognitive process.
6. Experiencer is equivalent to other focal characters in the story world.	6. Experiencer is qualitatively different from other characters in the story world.
7. Experiencer may (or may not) be at the deictic center of the story world.	7. Experiencer is by definition at the deictic center of the story world: He or she is the *Origo* of Buhler's (1982) deictic theory.
8. Experiencer is an entity in the presenter's discourse model, and hence must be coded in the text.	8. The text does not code the experiencer (because he or she is the origin of the discourse model), but rather the content of his or her experience field.*

*Pointed out by Langacker (1985).

Suppressed Coding of Experiencer

Example 3 is a clear case. The use of zero to refer to a character after 21 intervening clauses is allowed because the passage expressively codes the content of this character's perceptual experience, and because this character is not an object of his own perception, textual reference to him is suppressed, leaving a syntactic slot unfilled. This is a device used in Mandarin discourse to code the here-and-now experience of a character in an unmediated way. Example 11 shows that body parts make effective metonymic substitutes for the suppressed experiencer in expressive framing. This phenomenon suggests a naive cognitive model in which body parts are the locus of experience, that is, there is a ground–figure relation between the body part and the experience itself.[7]

---

[7]Further examples can be found in (3i), (6), (16d), (17a,c). A similar phenomenon was observed in Korean (Chun & Zubin, 1990).

(11) a. Secai pu   yan, shenglang pu   er reqi   pu   mian.
color pounce-on eye sound-wave pounce-on ear warm-air pounce-on face
b. ¶ Yanqian de zhe huo ren zhengzai tiao disike, [. . .]
eye-front NOM this CL people DUR dance disco

[Xiaoli has entered a noisy dance hall.] (a) Colors assailed [her] eyes, Waves of sound assailed [her] ears, warm air assailed [her] face. (b) ¶ The people in front of [her] eyes were dancing disco. (Ke, 1986, p. 116)

Both the linear and rhetorical continuity hypotheses predict that the first mention of a character should be a full NP. This is true of reportive framing. But Example 12, taken from the beginning of a novel, shows that expressive framing may begin with zero coding for the experiencer. The passage presents the subjective experience of a woman as she follows a man out of the train station. The zeros in (2d) and (12e) are the first references to her. The suppression of overt coding of an experiencer is indeed unconditional, and thus is not anaphoric. For a more detailed discussion of different ways of coding the experiencer, see Li (1990).

(12) a. . . . Yu, hai zai xia, dan mingxiande bian xiao le.
rain still DUR fall but obviously become lighter DUR
b. Ø Biancheng niumao ban de yusi,   feifeiyangyang
become   ox-hair like NOM rain-tread, softly-spreading
c. liao   de ren   lian shang liangsousoude.
brush CSC person face on   cool
d. Ø Gen zhe *ta*   chu zhan, Ø zouchu na menre,
follow DUR *him* exit station walk-out that stuffy
wuzhuo de qifen.
dirty   NOM atmosphere
e. Ø Likai mojianjiezhong de   renliu.   Ø Yi ke
leave crowded   NOM people-stream one moment
ye meiyou ting . . .
even not   stay

(a) ". . . The rain, still falling, had become obviously lighter. (b) [It] changed to ox-hair-like thin thread, softly spreading, (c) and was cool on one's face. (d) Following him, [she] exited the station, [she] walked out of the stuffy and dirty atmosphere. (e) [She] left the crowded stream of people. [She] didn't stay for one moment. . . ." (Lu, 1986, p. 139)

Objects of Experience

In contrast to the experiencer, the coding of the objects of experience in expressive framing obeys the linear continuity hypothesis, although with certain restrictions. In considering the objects in the experience field, we need to distinguish two types of entities: the projected ego—the conceptual image of the experiencer in his or her reflective thought process, and other objects of experience.

Experiencer as an Object of His or Her Own Experience. Example 13 shows that when the experiencer becomes an object of his or her own scrutiny, this reflective image of self in his or her experience field is overtly coded in the text. Lines 13a and 13b give a summary report of Li Xiangnan's thought process. Lines 13c–13e switch to expressive framing. In (13e), he becomes an object of his own thought. This projection of ego is coded by a distinctive marker, the reflexive pronoun *ziji*. In narrative, such unbound (and noncontrastive) *ziji* is used only to code the projected ego. They occur only in, and are therefore reliable markers of expressive framing (Li, 1991; Zubin, Chun, & Li, 1990). Further examples can be found in (5), (14d,e), (15d), (16g,h), (17d,f,h,j), (19b). Because in this case, the referent of *ziji* is unique (i.e., there is no referential ambiguity), the coding of the projected ego does not violate the linear continuity hypothesis. Note that although the projected ego is overtly coded, the experiencer is still suppressed in the text.

(13) a. Li Xiangnan yibian xunsu tiaozheng zhe ziji de   xinli,
      LX   while quickly adjust   DUR self NOM psychological-balance
    b. yibian jinliang xiande hen suibiande tan zhe Guling
       while try-hard appear very casually talk DUR Guling
       de   qingkuang. [22 clauses omitted]
       NOM situation
    c. Huang Pingping shuo de   yanzhong qingkuang shi shenme?
       HP   say NOM serious   situation   is what
    d. Zai yanzhong neng yanzhong dao nar   qu?
       more serious can serious   to where go
    e. *Ziji* you zugou de   zhengzhi caineng,
       self have enough NOM political ability
       ye   you zugou de   naishouli.
       also have enough NOM endurance

[Li Xiangnan, a political reformer, is walking in the streets of Beijing with Huang Pingping (a girl) who informs him that his situation is quite serious now.] (a) Li Xiangnan was quickly adjusting his psychological balance, (b) while trying hard to appear casual in talking about the situation in Guling. [. . .] (c) [. . .]What is the serious situation that Huang Pingping was talking about? (d) How serious can it be? (e)Self (= LX) has enough political capability, also enough endurance. (Ke, 1986, pp. 22–23)

Note that in expressive framing, "ziji" tends to be used when the experiencer is self-reflective (vs. emotional). For more discussion see Li (1991).

Other Objects of Experience. The coding of other objects of experience in an expressive frame obeys the linear continuity hypothesis as well, but with one restriction. Reduced anaphora corresponds to accessibility in the experiencer's

mental model, and not in the speaker or listener's, because these are irrelevant
to expressive framing. Compare Examples 14 and 12. In (14), Yu Gentu, the
experiencer, has discovered an ancient tomb, and the unscrupulous Yu Wanggou
is trying to get information from him. Line 14a is in reportive framing, which
introduces the experiencer, and lines 14b–14e expressively frame his thought
process. Initial mention of Yu Wanggou as an object of Yu Gentu's thought in
Line 14c is a full NP. Subsequent continuous references to Yu Wanggou in Lines
14c–14e are zero anaphors, in accordance with the linear continuity hypothesis.

(14) a. Yu Gentu chui zhe yanpi bu kengsheng,
         YG   hang DUR eyelid not make-sound
         xin li que   zai dazhuanzhuan:
         heart in whereas DUR whirl
     b. na yitian, Ø faxian   gumu   de shihou,
         that one-day,   discover old-tomb NOM time
         sizhou mingming meiyou ren   na!
         around clearly   no   person PAR
     c. Yaoshi *Yu Wanggou* kanjian le, Ø dangchang
         if   *YW*   see   PFV   there-and-then
         hai hui   bu guolai?
         still would not come-over
     d. Ø zhunshi yuanyuande   kanjian ziji zai dixia   kouba,
         must-be from-far-away see   self at   ground-down dig
         Ø qi le   yixin,
         raise PFV suspicion
     e. Ø lai   zha ziji li! Zhe ge huatou   shouduan shi man duo de.
         come bluff self PAR this CL slippery-fellow trick   is quite many
     f. Zheme yi xiang, xin li shaowei tashi le   xie, ta tai qi yan shuo, . .
         thus once think heart in slightly steady CRS some he lift up eye say

[Yu Gentu, the experiencer, has discovered an ancient tomb, and the unscrupulous Yu Wanggu is trying to trick him into revealing its location.] (a) Eyes
cast down, Yu Gentu did not answer, but his mind was awhirl: (b) that day,
when [he] discovered the old tomb, there had been nobody around! (c) If Yu
Wanggou had seen what was happening, wouldn't [he] have come over right
there and then? (d) Must be that from far away [he] saw self(= YG) digging
on the ground, got suspicious, (e) and now is bluffing self(= YG)! This slippery
fellow is indeed full of tricks. (f) Thinking like this, [his] mind calmed down
somewhat, he lifted up [his] eyes and said, ... (Xu Xiaoyu, 1982, p. 14)

This contrasts with Example 12. In Line 12d, initial mention of the character
whom our experiencer is following is the pronoun *ta*, in violation of linear
continuity, but this instance of reduced anaphor is in accordance with the fact
that this character is already in the focused consciousness of our experiencer.

FRAME SHIFTING

We suggested that, whereas the linear and rhetorical continuity hypotheses are valid within a reportive frame, in an expressive frame they may be violated, although the general principle of accessibility holds with respect to the experiencer's mental model. From these observations it follows that accessibility is not preserved across framing boundaries. In a shift from reportive to expressive framing, for example, a participant may have already been accessible to the speaker and listener, but not to the experiencing character.[8]

Expressive → Reportive (E → R)

Likewise, a shift from expressive to reportive framing creates a barrier to accessibility, at least for objects of experience. In Example 15, the experiencer Lei Tonglin is listening to his now-retired superior Huang Gongyu. Lines 15b–15f expressively frame Lei Tonglin's thought process. Huang Gongyu is initially introduced in (15b) with a full NP "this old man"—and then shifts to pronouns and zero anaphors in accordance with the linear continuity hypothesis. At Line 15g however, the point at which the text shifts back to reportive framing, the coding of Huang Gongyu goes back to full NP in spite of the fact that he has just been evoked in the previous clause and has no referential competitor.

> *{Reportive framing}*
> (15) a. ¶ Lei Tonglin de   yishiliu
>   R   LT   NOM stream-of-consciousness
>   geng   shi shengdongbuxi.
>   even-more is alive
>
> *{Shift to expressive framing}*
> E b. *Zhe laotour,* zhengou luosuo   de,
>   this old-man really long-winded NOM
>   [6 clauses omitted] Zhe dou kuai shiyidian   le,
>   this already almost eleven-o'clock CRS
>   c. Ø hai mei   baxiu de yisi,   rangburang ren zou?
>   still has-no stop NOM intention let-or-not one leave
>   d. Ø Rang ziji chu   jizi?   Ziji de   wenzhang
>   ask self publish collection self NOM articles
>   shuliang hai tai shao, [4 clauses omitted]
>   number still too few

---

[8]The shift from reportive to expressive framing initiates the use of indefinite referring expressions in Mandarin (Chen, 1986) and in English (Fillmore, 1974; Wiebe 1990b), and ga marking in Japanese (Watanabe, 1989), for a participant that was accessible in the preceding reportive frame. Also see Wiebe (this volume) and Hewitt (this volume) for more discussions about anaphoric expressions in subjective context in English.

e. Jiujikuan de   shir   ta hai ji   zhe na! [4 clauses omitted]
   relief-fund NOM matter he still remember DUR PAR
f. Ta shibushi meitian   dou yao ba ta gei ren xingguo
   he whether every-day all   must BA he for one do
   de   haoshir   guo yi bian naozi, Ø fuxifuxi a!
   NOM good-deed pass one CL mind   review-review PAR
   {Shift to reportive framing}

R g. ¶ *Huang Gongyu* de   jianghua dao le   zui
      HG   NOM talk   come-to PFV most
   shizhi   de   bufen le.
   important NOM part CRS

[Lei Tonglin has been listening to his retired former superior Huang Gongyu at Huang's house.] (a) Lei Tonglin's stream of consciousness was even more alive. (b) This old man, [he] is so long-winded, [. . .] It's already close to eleven o'clock, (c) [he] still doesn't seem to have the intention to stop, will [he] let one (= LT) leave or not? (d) [He] is asking self (= LT) to publish a collection? The number of self's (= LT) articles is still too few, [. . .] (e) He still remembers the matter of the relief fund! [. . .] (f) Does he go over in [his] mind and review the good deeds he has done for other people every day? ¶(g) Huang Gongyu's talk came to the most important part. (Ke, 1986, p. 267)

A modified version of (15g), (g1), shows that attempting to follow the linear continuity hypothesis by using a zero or a pronoun to refer to Huang Gongyu produces an incoherent text continuation.

g1. *Ø (/ta) Shuo dao zher, Ø bujin   yanfande deng le
            speak to here   can't-refrain-from fed-up   cast PFV
    Lei Tonglin yi yan.
    LT   one look
    "Speaking up to this point, [_/he] (= HG) couldn't help but cast a fed-up look at Lei Tonglin."

On the other hand, if the reportive frame of (15g) had instead referred to the experiencer, as in (g2) and (g3), then continuation with zero or pronoun would be perfectly coherent, even though the linear continuity for LT is low at this point of the text.

g2. Ø Xiang dao zher, Ø bujin   yanfande deng le
       think to   here can't-refrain-from fed-up   cast PFV
    Huang Gongyu yi yan.
    HG   one look
    "Thinking up to this point, [he] (= LT) couldn't help but cast a fed-up look at Huang Gongyu."

g3. Ta yanfande deng le Huang Gongyu yi yan.
he fed-up   cast PFV HG   one look
"He (= LT) cast a fed-up look at Huang Gongyu."

$E_1 \rightarrow R \rightarrow E_2$

A reportive frame often functions as a transition between two expressively framed passages with different experiencers and serves to introduce the new experiencer. This is illustrated in (16). In R_1, the character Liu Yao is topicalized, and then suppressed in E_1. In R_2, the second experiencer is topicalized, and then suppressed in E_2.[9] Note that each experiencer is an object of experience in the other's expressive frame, and correspondingly evoked with overt referring expressions: "this old Cao" in (16c), and "this Liu Yao" in (16e).

{*Reportive framing*}

(16) R_1 a. Liu Yao yibian bei   zhe shou manbu,
　　　　　 LY   while clasp-behind-back DUR hand stroll

　　　 b. Ø yibian yong yanjiao   de   yuguang kan zhe shenbian
　　　　　 while use eye-corner NOM side-view look DUR aside
　　　　　 Cao Lifu aizhuang de   shenti
　　　　　 CLF   short-sturdy NOM body

E_1 　 {*Expressive framing*}

　　　 c. [. . .] Zhe wei Lao Cao [. . .11 clauses] He zheyang
　　　　　　　 this CL *LC*   with this-kind
　　　　　 de   ren   gongchu,
　　　　　 NOM person coexist

　　　 d. Ø xinli   zong   yao   shishi tifang zhe diar. . .
　　　　　 heart-in always should always careful DUR a-little

　　　 {*Reportive framing*}

R_2 e. ¶ Cao Lifu yibian shenqingxianyide liuda zhe, Ø simian
　　　　　 CLF   while leasurely   stroll DUR around
　　　　 guanshang zhe xiaoqiaoliushui, cangsongcuibo, yibian zai xiang:
　　　　 admire   DUR bridge-water   evergreen-trees while DUR think

　　　 {*Expressive framing*}

　　　 f. *zhe wei Liu Yao*, shi renmen gongren
　　　　　 this CL *LY*   is people commonly-consider
　　　　 de [. . .] you poli   de   ren.
　　　　 NOM   has daring-spirit NOM person

　　　 g. Ke ziji que   changchang gandao: yue   shi zheyang
　　　　　 but self however often   feel   the-more is this-kind
　　　　 de   ren, yue   you zhe bi   yibanren geng
　　　　 NOM person the-more have DUR compare ordinary-people

---

[9]Although the projected ego is explicitly coded with *ziji*.

E₂   nan   zhuomotou   de   difang. [4 clauses omitted]
      more hard figure-out NOM poin
   h. Ziji yinggai jinyibu miqie he   ta de   guanxi ...
      self should further close with he NOM relation

(a) Liu Yao was strolling with [his] hands behind [his] back, (b) while observing from the corner of [his] eye the sturdy body of Cao Lifu who was
walking beside [him,. . .]. (c) This Old Cao, [. . .] Coexisting with such a
person, (d) [he] has to always be careful. . .¶(e) Cao Lifu was strolling leisurely, admiring the small bridge and stream, and the evergreen trees, while
thinking: (f) this Liu Yao, is a person commonly considered as having a
daring spirit. (g) But self (= CL) often felt: this kind of persons are more
difficult to figure out. [. . .] (h) Self (= CL) should get closer to him. . .(Ke,
1986, p. 655)

E₁ → E₂

On the other hand, the text may directly shift from one expressive frame into
another, as illustrated in (17). This text, in which a good deal of material has
been elipted in order to highlight the frame boundaries, shifts from an expressive
representation of Fan Danni's thought process to Lin Hong's, and from hers to
Fan Danlin's with no intervening reportive framing, and correspondingly no
proper introduction of the experiencers. The reader has to infer who the origin
of experience is from the content of the thought process.

              {Expressive framing—Fan Danni}
(17) E₁ a. ¶ Huangdong de   jiu, [. . .] zai dengguang xia   shanliang,
            sloshing   NOM wine   at lamp-light below glitter
            zai Ø yanqian   shanliang.
            at   eye-front glitter
       b. Touguo jiubei   Ø kan shijie, [. . .] dou shi guangliang
          through wine-glass   look world   all is bright
          er mohu   de.
          and obscure NOM
    E₁ c. Gezhonggeyang de   dianying jingtou zai Ø yanqian shanguo. [. . .]
          various-kind   NOM movie   frame   at   eye-front pass
       d. Yi ge lianer tiantian de   nushouhuoyuan
          one CL face sweet   NOM sales-girr
          zai chong ziji weixiao, [. . .]
          DUR to   self smile
              {Expressive framing—Lin Hong}
    E₂ e. ¶ Deng Qiubai he Fan Shuhong liang wei laoren,
            DQ   and FS   two CL elder
       f. haiyou ziji de   shishi   de   fuqin,
          also   self NOM deceased NOM father

E₂ g. tamen jingli   de   rensheng qidian   xiangtong,
   they experience NOM life   starting-point same
   jieju   hedeng xuanshu a. [. . .]
   ending how   different PAR

   h. Fan Danlin gangcai yue   ziji yiqi   qu canjia
   FD   just-now invite self together go join
   yi   ge taolunhui, qubuqu ne? . . .
   one CL meeting   go-or-not PAR
   {*Expressive framing—Fan Danni*}

E₃ i. ¶ Ta wei fuqin gandao chouchang, raner, [. . .]
   he for father feel   melancholy but

   j. ziji zenme hui you zheyang yi ge huanjue?
   self how   can have such   one CL illusion
   Lin Hong hen you dian weidao. . .
   LH   quite have some flavor

(a) [Fan Danni's mental state] The sloshing wine, [. . .] glittering in the lamp light, in front of [her] eyes. (b) Seeing the world through the wine glass, [. . .] all is bright and obscure. (c) Various kinds of movie frames passed in front of [her] eyes. [. . .] (d) a salesgirl with a sweet face is smiling to self [= FDN], [. . .]¶ (e) [Lin Hong's mental state] The two elders Deng Qiubai and Fan Shuhong, (f) and self's [= LH] deceased father, (g) their life's starting points are the same, yet the endings are so different. [. . .] (h) Just now Fan Danlin invited self [= LH] to go and participate in a discussion meeting, should [she] go or not?. . . ¶ (i) [Fan Danlin's mental state] He feels melancholy for his father, yet [. . .] (j) Why is self [= FDL] having such an illusion? Lin Hong is quite attractive. . .(Ke, 1986, pp. 804–805)

FRAME EMBEDDING

Rather than switching back and forth between reportive and expressive frames, the text may start with a reportive frame, shift to expressive framing, and then briefly pop back out to the reportive frame, so that the pieces of expressive framing are conceptually embedded in the reportive frame. Example 18 illustrates this effect. The experiencer, Gu Xiaoying, wanders into a family gathering and looks over the members of the family. Lines 18a–18c topicalize GX in a reportive frame. Starting with (18d), we get into the content of his thought process in an expressive frame, except for short reportive clauses (italicized) in (18d), (18g), (18i), and (18l). Each of the two levels of the framing has its own continuity, as if two threads of the plot were running in parallel. The coding of the experiencer GX is consistently suppressed with the use of zero in the expressive frame, and is consistently evoked with the overt pronoun *ta* in the pops to the reportive frame. Also note that in the expressive frame, the women are identified in succession as "this one," because GX does not know who they are. In the reportive pops, however, they are identified by name, because they have already been introduced to the reader in the narrative.

{*Reportive framing*}

(18) R a. ¶ Gu Xiaoying de   yanjing youxiande
        GX   NOM eye   leisurely
        sichu   zhangwang zhe, Ø chou le huir yan,
        around look   DUR   smoke PFV a-while cigarette

     b. Ø cai bu yinrenzhuyide   cong yipang guancha qi
           then not attention-drawing from aside   observe up
        zhe yijia   ren   lai. [5 clauses omitted]
        this family people come

     c. Ta zixi   pinwei, pingjia de shi liu ge nuxing.
        he carefully savour evaluate NOM is six CL female

{*Expressive framing*}

E R d. ¶ Zhe ge—*ta kan zhe Chunping*—Ø yikan
          this CL *he look DUR Chunping*   one-look
        jiu   zhidao shi dajie,
        then know is eldest-sister

     e. Ø sishilaisui de   yangzi. [16 clauses omitted]
        forty-some NOM look

     f. Ø Shaidiao fang zai yibian.
        screen-out put at aside

  R g. ¶ Zhe ge—*ta kan zhe Xiaping*—Ø kan   nianji dagai
          this CL *he look DUR Xiaping*   look age   probably
        shi er   de   le, [27 clauses omitted]
        is second NOM CRS

     h. Ø Mei   kantou,   Ø ye shaixuan xiaqu, Ø jianjue
        nothing worth-seeing also screen   down   firmly
        bu zai   kan ta.
        not again look her

  R i. ¶ Zhe ge—*ta muguang kan zhe Dongping*—zhen piaoliang,
          this CL *he gaze   look DUR Dongping* so   pretty

     j. Ø xiang ge Indu   meiren. Ø Dagai shi zhe yijia nuxing
        like   CL Indian beauty   maybe is this family female
        zhong zui   piaoliang de ba.
        among most pretty   NOM PAR

     k. Ø Xian fang xia zan   bu xikan,   Ø hao de   fang dao
        first put down for-now not scrutinize   good NOM put to
        zuihou manman pinchang.
        last   slowly savour

  R l. ¶ Ø Xian kan zhe yi ge—*ta kan zhe Qiuping*—[...]
          first look this one CL *he look DUR Qiuping*

(a) Gu Xiaoying's eyes looked around leisurely, [he] smoked for a little while,
(b) then began to observe this family from the corner of his eye. ¶¶4 clauses
] (c) What he was savoring and evaluating were the six females. ¶(d) This
one—he looked at Chunping—just one look [he] can tell that [she] is the

eldest sister, (e) forty something. [17 clauses of unfavorable evaluation] (f) Screen [her] out and put [her] aside. ¶(g) This one—he looked at Xiaping— judging from [her] age [she] probably is the second, [. . .] (h) Nothing worth observing, also screen [her] out, absolutely not look at her again. ¶(i) This one—his eyes looked at Dongping—is so pretty, (j) like an Indian beauty. [She] is probably the prettiest among the females of this family. (k) Put [her] aside and not study [her] for now, keep the good ones for the end to savor slowly. ¶(l) This one—he looked at Qiuping—[. . .] (Ke, 1986, pp. 539–541)

FRAME BLENDING

Previous sections presented instances of expressive and reportive framing that are cleanly segregated from each other in the text in the sense that the structure of any clause in the text is based on one or the other. Equally prominent in narrative is a specialized form of frame embedding that we call "frame blending." Rather than the segmental embedding illustrated in (18), there is an undertone of reportive features within the clauses of an expressive frame, or alternatively, the traces of expressive language within a reportive frame. A relatively continuous transition from one type to the other can be illustrated by the constructed example:

(19) a. Tamen ganma zheme ding zhe wo? Shi zai huaiyi wo ma?
    they   why   thus   stare DUR me is DUR suspect me PAR
    "Why are they staring at me like that? Are they suspecting me?"

   b. Tamen yong yi zhong qiguai de   yanguang kan zhe ziji.
    they   use one CL   strange NOM gaze   look DUR self
    Taman zai   huaiyi ziji ma?
    they DUR suspect self PAR
    "They were staring at self strangely. Were they suspecting self?"

   c. Tamen yong yi zhong qiguai de   yanguang kan zhe ta.
    they   use one CL   strange NOM gaze   look DUR him he
    Ta xiang tamen keneng huaiyi ta le.
    think they maybe suspect him PFV
    "They were staring at him strangely. He thought maybe they suspected him."

   d. Tamen kan zhe ta de   na zhong yanguang shide ta yishidao
    they   look DUR he NOM that CL   gaze   make he realize
    tamen yijing kaishi huaiyi ta   le.
    they already begin suspect him PFV
    "The way they looked at him made him realize that they had begun to suspect him."

Version 19a is pure expressive framing, called "internal monologue" in the subjectivity literature. The text gives an exact rendition of the actual thoughts of the experiencer, making it structurally equivalent to quoted speech. Version 19b shifts *wo* to *ziji*, as discussed previously. This produces the slight reportive undertone characteristic of what Banfield called represented thought. In version 19c, the shift to the pronoun *ta* and the final perfective aspect marker are characteristic of reportive framing, but otherwise the lexical choices (e.g., *qiguai*) are expressive. Version 19d is a description of the experiencer's thought with little commitment to the actual process. This is the characteristic reportive framing of psychonarration. A similar series moving from expressive to more strongly reportive framing can easily be constructed for English (cf. Fillmore, 1974).

(20) a. Why are they looking at me that way? Do they think I'm responsible?
b. Why were they looking at him that way? Did they think he was responsible?
c. Why were they looking at him that way, he thought. Did they think he was responsible?
d. He suspected they thought he was responsible from the way they were looking at him.
e. His paranoia prevented him from realizing that they were looking at him with admiration, and not with suspicion.

Blending helps to solve the problem of expressing emotion. Emotions do not have words like thoughts do, and so the narrative expression of emotion is necessarily reportive to some extent. In other words, the expressive framing of emotion must take on the traces of reportive framing in the conversion from the felt emotion to language. This shows up, for example, in the pronominal emergence of the experiencer in Example 20, that in Mandarin is highly expressive of the experiencer's emotions. Note that if we replace the third-person pronoun *ta* with *ziji* (the reflexive which codes the projected ego), the sentence immediately sounds self-reflective and thus, less emotional.

(21) a. Zheme chang shijian yilai, *ta*   xiang shi aiqing shang de   zei,
        such   long time since *she* as-if is love on   NOM thief
b. zhuilaizhuiqu, qiulaiqiuqu, duolaiduoqu, *ta* shou gou   le!
   pursue   beg   hide   *she* suffer enough CRS!

For such a long time she'd been like a thief in the matter of love, like a beggar; pursue, beg, hide—enough suffering! (Ke, 1986, p. 717)

CONCLUSION

We tried to show that the theory of referential continuity, as reflected in Fig. 12.1, and the concept of accessibility on which it rests, can provide a basis for an interesting set of hypotheses concerning the choice of anaphoric referring expressions in narrative data. In particular, we defined two types of perspectival framing (expressive and reportive) and examined the continuity theory within and across perspectival frames.

ACKNOWLEDGMENTS

This research was supported in part by National Science Foundation Grant No. IRI–8610517. We would like to express our gratitude to members of the Deictic Center Research Project of the Center for Cognitive Science at SUNY, Buffalo for their comments and discussions. Special thanks go to Soon Ae Chun, Erwin Segal, Mary Galbraith, Janice Wiebe, Lynne Hewitt, Sandy Peters, William Hanks, and Randy LaPolla for their comments on an earlier version of this chapter.

13

EXPERIENTIAL VERSUS AGENTIVE CONSTRUCTIONS IN KOREAN NARRATIVE

Soon Ae Chun
David A. Zubin
State University of New York at Buffalo

INTRODUCTION

This chapter presents an analysis of agentive and experiential constructions based on differences that can be explained by the notion of subjectivity, a property of cognition that underlies all language use. We describe these constructions; introduce the concept of subjectivity; present the morpho-syntactic relations between these two constructions (demonstrating a productive structural opposition akin to voice in the grammar of Korean); present the distributional effects that are brought about by the expression of different degrees of subjectivity in interactional discourse and in narrative; and describe the cognitive folk models that underly the two constructions.

Experiential and Agentive Constructions

There are parallel syntactic constructions in Korean, depicted in (la) and (lb), into which a variety of perception and psychological verbs can be inserted.[1]

(1) a. *Suni-ka/nun*   *Toli-lul*   *coahanta.*
     Suni-NOM/TOP Toli-ACC like   'Suni likes Toli.'

---

[1]Psychological verbs include verbs of perception (see, look, hear), verbs of cognition (think, know, seem), and feeling state verbs (feel, like). The syntactic constructions in question are not limited to psychological verbs. In particular, the structure in (1b) with overt action predicates is described as "passive." See also the discussion of Table 13.2.

b. *Suni-eykey/ka/nun*   *Toli-ka*   *coh-ta.*
Suni-DAT/NOM/TOP Toli-NOM likable   'Toli is likable to Suni.'[2]

Both versions contain an experiencer and an object of experience, but the case marking differs. In (1a), the experiencer is nominative and the object of experience, or stimulus, is accusative. In (1b), the experiencer is dative or nominative and the stimulus is nominative. We call sentences like (1a) the agentive construction and those like (1b) the experiential construction. Although various syntactic characterizations were proposed for the experiential construction,[3] its inherent semantics and how they differ from those of the agentive construction were neglected. Either it is derived from the agentive construction, suggesting that the two are synonymous, or a more or less fortuitous semantic feature is attached to the experiential construction.

THE SUBJECTIVITY CONTINUUM

At the base of the analysis presented in this chapter is the view that language is a subjective enterprise.[4] All utterances are subjective in the sense that they presuppose a cognizer. But the degree of subjectivity is greater when the cognizer is encoded in the utterance, as in (2a).

(2) a. It *seems to me* that the weather is cold today.
    b. It's cold today.

Even in those cases where there is no overt cognizer as in (2b), a cognizing agent is implied. The difference is in the degree of subjectivity: (2a) is more subjective than (2b). In any use of language, there must be a speaker/cognizer, whose role is to provide the consciousness through which a pure "objective" event is perceived and understood. The degree to which an utterance affords direct access to this consciousness—that is, the degree to which it creates the impression that the contents of that consciousness are directly exposed—is what

---

[2]Where possible, we translate the experiential construction in Korean with a superficially parallel inversion construction in English. This does not, however, capture either the distributional possibilities or the semantic effects of the Korean, which are central topics of this paper.

[3]Experiential constructions have been noted in Russian, Japanese, Georgian and German, in addition to Korean. They have variously been called psych constructions, inversion constructions, double-subject constructions, dative subject constructions, impersonal constructions or unaccusative constructions. See Postal, 1970; McCawley, 1975; for examples of previous treatments of this phenomenon.

[4]The term "subjective" is naturally understood in relation to its opposite notion, "objective," and although these contrasting notions may be useful in understanding the cognitive models behind the experiential and agentive constructions, this should not be taken to imply that language itself can be objective.

is meant by the phrase *degree of subjectivity*. Thus, the objective phenomena that occur in the world are liable to be expressed in a number of ways, each different expression coloring the event for a different degree of subjectivity.

One might view events in the real world in terms of a typology of event phenomena. "Action" is one type of real-world event; "perceptual state," "speech event" and "emotional/psychological state" are others. These objective events may be expressed in different forms, varying in the degree to which a subjective viewpoint is encoded. The description of an event may be relatively external, or objectified, as in *John kicked the dog*, or it may be relatively more internal, as in *It looked to me as though John kicked the dog*. In the first sentence, the cognizer is placed outside of the event as an observer; on the other hand, the second type of sentence directly encodes the cognizer as a part of the utterance— the expression names the interpreter of the event. Schematically, this difference can be represented as in Fig. 13.1:

FIG. 13.1.   Point of view and the cognizer.

The difference between the agentive and experiential constructions lies in the degree of subjectivity. The agentive construction has an external observer/cognizer objectively describing the psychological state of some experiencer (Suni in [1a]), whereas the experiential construction identifies the cognizer with the experiencer (Suni in [1b]), and is thus more subjective.

Although the encoding of subjectivity may vary from language to language, all languages seem to have the capacity to express differences in subjectivity. From the examples given in the preceding paragraphs, it can be seen that English does not grammatically encode such differences. In contrast, Korean does morphosyntactically encode such differences in subjectivity.

MORPHO-SYNTAX

Table 13.1 gives a morpho-syntactic breakdown of typical predicates in the two constructions. For each predicate in the experiential column there is a lexically related predicate on the agentive side and that the morpho-syntactic relation is complex but systematic. In other words, Korean presents a speaker with a systematic set of coding options based on the same lexical material. In (A), -*ha*- is added to derive the agentive version from the experiential one; in (B), the expe-

TABLE 13.1
Morpho-Syntactic Relations Between Experiential and Agentive Predicates

Experiential	Agentive	Translation
Adjective-ta	**Adjective-ha-ta**	
A. kulip-ta	kulipwe-ha-ta	"miss, long for"
musep-ta	musewe-ha-ta	"be afraid of"
pulep-ta	pulewe-ha-ta	"be envious of"
kwiyep-ta	kwiyewe-ha-ta	"love"
silh-ta	silhe-ha-ta	"dislike"
mukep-ta	mukewe ha-ta	"feel heavy"
tulyep-ta	tulyewe-ha-ta	"dread"
elyep-ta	elywe-ha-ta	"be difficult for"
mip-ta	miwe-ha-ta	"hate"
yeppu-ta	yeppe-ha-ta	"be pretty, good"
Noun + ha-ta	**Noun + ha-ha-ta**	
pulanha-ta	pulanhae-ha-ta	"feel insecure"
yukwaeha-ta	yukwaehae-ha-ta	"feel pleasant"
ciluha-ta	ciluhae-ha-ta	"feel bored"
pulkwaeha-ta	pulkwaehae-ha-ta	"feel upset"
sinkiha-ta	sinkihae-ha-ta	"be amazed"
pilyoha-ta	pilyolo-ha-ta	"need"
Noun + iss-ta	**Noun + iss-ha-ta**	
masiss-ta	masisse-ha-ta	"feel tasty"
mesiss-ta	mesisse-ha-ta	"feel dandy"
caemiiss-ta	caemiisse-ha-ta	"be interested in"
Verb-i-ta	**Verb-ta**	
B. po-i-ta	po-ta	"see"
tul-i-ta	tut-ta	"hear"
ttel-i-ta	ttel -ta	"tremble"
Verb-ci-ta	**Verb-ta**	
nwiuchie-ci-ta	nwiuchi-ta	"repent"
nukkie-ci-ta	nukki-ta	"feel"
mite-ci-ta	mit-ta	"believe"
heyalie-ci-ta	heyali-ta	"figure out"
pese-ci-ta	pes-ta	"take off"
mancie-ci-ta	manci-ta	"touch"
Noun-toi-ta	**Noun-ha-ta**	
C. huhwe-toi-ta	huhwe-ha-ta	"regret"
kekceng-toi-ta	kekceng-ha-ta	"be concerned"
ihae-toi-ta	ihae-ha-ta	"understand"
hontong-toi-ta	hontong-ha-ta	"be confused about"
uysim-toi-ta	uysim-ha-ta	"be doubtful of"
sangsang-toi-ta	sangsang-ha-ta	"imagine"
Noun-sulup-ta	**Noun-ha-ta**	
salang-sulup-ta	salang-ha-ta	"love"
calang-sulup-ta	calang-ha-ta	"be proud of"
conkyeng-sulup-ta	conkyeng-ha-ta	"be respectful"

TABLE 13.2
Semantic Range of the Parallel Constructions

Cognitive activity:	memory: *kieknata vs. kiekhata*
thought, feeling, memory, etc.	thought: *saengkanata vs. saengkakhata*
Cognitive disposition:	heavy: *mukepta vs. mukewehata*
easy, difficult, heavy, possible, etc.	difficult: *elyepta vs. elyewehata*
Perception:	see: *poita vs. pota*
see, hear, feel, touch, taste, etc.	hear: *tulita vs. tutta*
Affective states:	fear: *musepta vs. musewehata*
fear, pleasure, shame, boredom, etc.	boredom: *ciluhata vs. ciluhaehata*
Bodily sensation:	cold: *chupta vs. chuwehata*
cold, hot, hungry, sick, etc.	sick: *aputa vs. apahaehata*

riential predicates are derived from the agentive ones with *-i-* or *-ci-*; and in (C) both experiential and agentive predicates are derived from nouns.

Table 13.2 gives the range of psychological predicates that enter into these parallel constructions. There does not seem to be any limitation, so that the constructions must be considered highly productive. Semantically, the experiential construction extends into spatial metaphor. Morpho-syntactically, the two constructions are exploited far beyond the domain of psychological verbs.

INTERACTIONAL DISCOURSE

Example 3 is a series of potential tums in a conversation between a speaker (A) and a listener (B) about a third person (Changho).

(3) A: *Na-nun ne-wa Cbangho-ka   kathi issnun kes-ul poass-nuntey . . .*
    l-TOP you-and Changho-NOM together being-ACC saw-and . . .
    "I saw you with Changho and . . ."

    a. *Na-nun Chango-lul cohahae.*   "I like him."(AGT)
    b. *Na-nun Changho-ka coha*   "I like him."(EXP)
    c. *??Ne-nun Changho-ka coha*   "You like him."(EXP)
    d. *Ne-nun Changho-ka coha?*   "Do you like him?"(EXP)
    e. *?? Changho-nun ne-ka coha*   "Does he like you?"(EXP)
    f. *Changho-nun ne-lul coahani?*   "Does he like you?"(AGT)
    g. *Ne-nun Changho-ka cohun ka poa*   "You like him, it seems."(EXP)
    h. *Changho-nun ne-ka coh tey.*   "He said that he likes you."(EXP)
    i. *Changho-wa na-nun ne-lul cohahae.*   "He and I like you."(AGT)
    j. *Changho-wa na-nun ne-ka coha.*   "He and I like you."(EXP)
    k. *?? Changho-wa na-nun kakca ne-ka*   "He and I each like you."(EXP)
    coha

It is well known that the experiential construction is limited to use with first person subjects (cf. Kuroda, 1973).[5] Turns a and b show that the speaker, A, can use either construction to describe his/her own feelings for Changho; (3c) shows that the speaker A cannot use the experiential construction to describe B's feelings about Changho, except if A is making an inquiry about B's feelings, as in (3d), in which case the experiential construction is fine. But if the inquiry is about Changho's feelings for B, as in (3e), the experiential construction is odd. Only the agentive construction can be used, as in (3f).

What unifies these facts is accessibility to the mental world of the experiencer by a cognizer, namely, the speaker. A, the speaker, can make direct access assertions about his/her own feelings, or can make an inquiry into the feelings of the interlocutor B, in effect making a request for a direct access conduit to B's mental state. Example 3e is odd in the experiential construction because neither A nor B have direct access to Changho's feelings. Examples 3g and 3h show that the experiential construction can be licensed by the presence of an evidential which specifies the conduit through which the speaker has access to the experiencer's state. In (3g), this conduit is B's appearance and behavior; in (3h), it is Changho's own words. What is asserted in (3g) and (3h) is the evidential link, not the experiential state itself. Thus, (3g) and (3h) help to confirm that the basic issue underlying the choice between the two constructions is the accessibilty of the experiencer's mental world to a cognizer, in this case the speaker.

Examples (3i) and (3j) further clarify this point. In (3i), A and Changho can be coded as a conjoined subject in the agentive construction with no implication about their personal relationship. But in (3j), the experiential construction pre-supposes that A and Changho have intimate shared knowledge about B—for example, if A and Changho are siblings and B is the sister-in-law. This is con-firmed by (3k), where a distributive quantifier blocks the shared knowledge interpretation, making the experiential construction unacceptable.

NARRATIVE DISCOURSE

The facts of interactional discourse suggest a single unifying pragmatic factor controlling the occurrence of the experiential construction: accessibility of the experiencer's mental world to a cognizer. This factor is equally manifested in the use of the agentive and experiential constructions in narrative discourse. The accessibility explanation offered for the limited distribution of the experiential construction in interactional discourse suggests that this construction ought to be

---

[5]German shows a similar restriction, but only with a few archaic predicates. For example, in interactional discourse, *mich dünkt* is acceptable, but **dich dünkt* or **ihn dünkt* are not possible, although in narrative *ihn dünkte* suggests direct access to the mental state of the character. In contrast, the verb *denken*, with an "agentive" case-marking pattern, has no such restriction.

used in narrative for a direct representation of the thoughts and perceptions of a character; in fact, it ought to be limited to such contexts. In contrast, the agentive construction ought to give an objective, external perspective on the character, even when presenting his or her mental state.[6]

It is a widely held view that a narrative text invites the reader to identify with a perspective from which the story is presented.[7] Narrative is made up of contexts that may be viewed as more or less subjective. Objective context may be understood to be portrayed or reported by a narrator as an observer. Hence, the reader, adopting the narrator's point of view, also views the events of the story world as an observer. In subjective contexts, the reader can directly participate in the story via the character's thoughts and perceptions. The character whose consciousness is adopted is called the *subjective character*, and the phenomena that the reader experiences through that character are labeled *represented thought* and *represented perception* (Banfield, 1982). Typically, the text will present perceptions, thoughts and feelings without referring to the experiencer at all. The reader's focus is not on the experiencer as an actor in the story world, but rather, on the direct experience of thoughts, feelings and perceptions through that character.

We predict that the experiential construction will be used in subjective contexts for the straightforward expression of a subjective character's mental state, because in subjective context, the reader has direct access to the subjective character's psychological state. We also predict that the agentive construction can occur in either objective contexts, or in subjective contexts to express a nonsubjective character's mental state.[8] The agentive construction is licensed in objective contexts because the reader, taking the narrator's perspective, views events as an external observer. In the agentive construction in subjective context, it is possible to describe a nonsubjective character's mental state because the subjective character cannot have direct access to any character's mental world except his or her own.

Examples 4 and 5 are parallel episodes of narrative discourse.[9] In (4), several linguistic features suggest represented thought of the subjective character *Suni*: the deictic *come . . . stand*, the reflexive *caki*, the nonembeddable fragment and

---

[6]This point is essentially parallel to Kuroda's claim about adjectival versus verbal predicates in Japanese narrative.

[7]This view was implicit in Fillmore's (1975) work on deixis; it was also articulated by Banfield (1982) and Cohn (1978), among others in literary criticism, and by Kuno (1987), Kuroda (1973), and others in linguistics.

[8]The agentive construction appears to occur in subjective context to describe the subjective character's mental state. But rather than directly representing the thought or perception of the character, it gives a psychological report (Wiebe, 1990b) of his or her general psychological disposition from an external "objective" point of view (cf. Examples 7a & 8a). The agentive construction also occurs in passages of reflective thought, in which the subjective character is the observer of his own objectivized mental state, as in example (9a).

[9]These and subsequent examples are based on sentence-types found in Han (1980) (except as otherwise indicated), but details have been altered for purposes of linguistic argumentation.

exclamation, and the causal conjunction. In this context, the experiential construction (a) is more coherent than the agentive (b), because it supports a constant psychological viewpoint from within Suni. In Example 5, linguistic features such as the deictic *go . . . stand*, the adverbial *obviously*, the plain pronominal possessor and the progressive aspect all suggest an external, objectified view of Suni, and in this case the agentive construction (b) is coherent. This illustrates the basic effect of represented perception and thought versus objectified expression. The experiential contruction supports the subjective context because it conveys more direct access to the character's mental world, precisely the point of represented thought. On the other hand, the agentive construction supports the objective context, because it suggests an external view of the character.

(4) *Suni-nun   kewul   ap-ey   wase sessta*
    Suni-TOP mirror   front-to   come-stand
    papo kathi ulkin! ulkoissnun (caki) elkul-ul   po-ni,
    fool like   crying   crying   (self) face-ACC see-cause,
    a. *(Suni-nun)Toli-ka   teuk miwessta.* (EXP)
       Suni-TOP Toli-NOM more hateful
    b. *?Suni-nun Toli-lul   teuk miwehaessta.* (AGT)
       Suni-TOP Toli-ACC more hate
    "Suni came and stood in front of the mirror. Crying like a fool!
    (Suni) seeing herself crying like that, Toli was even more hateful (to her) than before."

(5) *Suni-nun   kewul   ap-ey kase sessta   kunye-nun punmyengh ulko issessta.*
    Suni-TOP mirror front-to go stand   she-TOP obviously   crying was
    ulkoissnun (kunye-uy) elkul-ul   po-nmye,
    crying   (her)   face-ACC see-and,
    a. *?Suni-nun Toli-ka   miwessta.* (EXP)
       Suni-TOP Toli-NOM more hateful
    b. *Suni-nun Toli-lul   miwehaessta.* (AGT)
       Suni-TOP Toli-ACC more hate
    "Suni went and stood in front of the mirror. It was clear that she was crying.
    As she looked at her face crying, Suni hated Toli even more."

Examples 6 a, b, and c provide further evidence of the direct access function of the experiential construction. The introductory sentence of (6a) sets up a represented thought context for Insu in the following sentence. Here, the experiential construction is fully acceptable, just as it was in the represented thought context of Example 4. Example 6b is projected thought; more specifically, it is Suni's report of Insu's mental state, as Insu views it. Here, the experiential construction is strange, but still marginally acceptable. Finally, (6c) presents Suni's psychological report about Insu's mental state, that is, from Suni's point of view. There is no sense of direct access to Insu's mental world and the experiential construction is impossible. Thus in moving from (6a) to (6c), the context portrays decreasing access to Insu's mental world, and the experiential construction becomes less and less acceptable.

(6) a. *Insu-nun   ancase cangmi kkoch-ul pomye saengkakhaessta.*
Insu-TOP   sitting   roses-ACC   seeing thought
cacki-nun i cangmi kkoch-ul coahanta. (AGT)
caki-nun   i cangmi kkoch-i cohta. (EXP)
self-TOP this rose-ACC/NOM like
"Insu was thinking as he sat looking at the roses. (To him) These roses were nice."

b. *Suni-nun Insu-lopute manun iyaki-lul   tuless-nuntey,*
Suni-TOP Insu-from   many story-ACC heard-and
    ku-nun cangmi kkoch-ul coahanta. (AGT)
    ? ku-nun cangmi kkoch-i cohta. (EXP)
    he-TOP   rose-ACC/?NOM like
"Suni heard many stories from Insu, you know, he liked roses."

c. *Suni-nun Insu-eytaehae manun iyaki-lul tuless-nuntey*
Suni-TOP Insu-about   many story-ACC heard-and.
    ku-nun cangmi kkoch-ul coahanta. (AGT)
    * ku-nun cangmi kkocb-i cohta (EXP)
    he-TOP   rose-ACC/*NOM like
"Suni heard a lot of stories about Insu, and he liked roses."

The next piece of evidence has to do with aspectual inferences derived from the two constructions. In (7), the initial sentence sets up a character description. In the sequel, only the agentive construction in (7a) is coherent. In contrast, the initial sentence in (8) sets up a narrative episode with a here and now deicticly anchored to the story world. In the sequel, both constructions are coherent, but each has a different interpretation. (8a) is a psychological report giving a general disposition of Insu, explaining why he stopped, perhaps from another character's or the narrator's perspective. (8b), on the other hand, transparently presents what Insu is thinking at that moment of the story.

(7) *Insu-nun uskinun namca-ta.*
Insu*TOP* funny   guy
a. *Ku-nun cangmi kkoch-ul cohahanta.* (AGT)
b. *?? Ku-nun cangmi kkoch-i cohta* (EXP)
    he-TOP roses-ACC/?NOM like
"Insu is a funny guy. He likes roses."

(8) *Insu-nun kkoch cip   ap-ey sessta.*
Insu-Top flowershop front-LOC stood.
a. *Ku-nun cangmi kkoch-ul cohahaessta.* (AGT)
b. *Ku-nun cangmi kkoch-i cohassta.* (EXP)
    he-TOP roses-ACC/NOM like
"Insu stopped in front of the florist to look. He liked the roses."

The Agentive construction can describe a general psychological disposition, or it can summarize. As used in (8a), it gives a report about the mental state of the character, rather than tying us to the character's here-and-now. The lack of connection to a deictic center results in interpretations that are habitual, durative, timeless, or generic. On the other hand, the experiential construction, in directly representing a character's consciousness, is tied to that character's here-and-now in the story world. This leads to a punctual, perfective interpretation, as in (8b).

Further support for the cognitive analysis of these constructions is provided by the use of the so-called long-distance reflexive *caki* in the complement of psychological verbs, as in (9a & b). The reflexive *caki* expresses reflective consciousness in a context where the experiencer is an objectified element of his or her own consciousness (cf., reflective *Adam considered himself to be inadequate* vs. nonreflective *Adam felt inadequate*).[10]

(9) a. *Insu-nun {caki-ka/?Ø}   Suni-lul silhehanta ko nnukkiessta.* (AGT)
Insu-TOP {self-NOM / ?Ø} Suni-ACC dislike   that felt
"Insu felt that he disliked Suni."
b. *Insu-nun {?caki-ka/Ø}   Suni-ka silhta   ko nnukkiessta.* (EXP)
Insu-TOP {? self-NOM/ Ø} Suni-NOM dislikable] that felt
"Insu felt Suni to be dislikable."

In (9a), the agentive construction presents an objectified view of Insu's dislike for *Suni*, but since the whole is located within *Insu*'s mental world, as indicated by the matrix psychological verb, it is *Insu*'s objectification of his own feeling; he as observer is regarding a separate intensional entity (experiencer), who happens to be himself. This reflective consciousness promotes the use of *caki* versus *zero* in the complement. On the other hand, in (9b), the experiential construction invites the reader to directly access Insu's mental state. *Insu* himself is transparent, and *zero* is consequently more acceptable in the complement than is *caki*.

It is the usual case that each experiencer has complete access to his or her own mental world; hence, the preference for the experiential construction with first-person subjects. An experiencer is less likely to have access to other human minds, but the potential for access does exist, especially in narrative. However, as Wierzbicka (1980) pointed out, we have little access to the minds of animals. The inaccessibility of animal minds is reflected in a comparison of (10) and (11):

(10) *Suni-nun twis kelum-ul chessta.*
Suni-TOP back step-ACC took
Suni stepped back.
a. *Kunye-nun Insu-lul musewehassta.*(AGT)
she - TOP Insu-ACC afraid-of
She was afraid of Insu.

---

[10]See Zubin, Chun and Li (1990) for a fuller discussion of this point.

b. *Kunye-eykey/nun Insu-ka musewessta* (EXP)
she - DAT/TOP Insu-NOM frightening
Insu was frightening to her.

(11) *Ku kae-nun twis kelum-ul chessta.*
The dog-TOP back step-ACC took
The dog stepped back.

a. *Ku kae-nun Insu-lul musewehassta.*(AGT)
the dog-TOP Insu-ACC afraid-of
It was afraid of Insu.

b. *?Ku kae-eykey/nun Insu-ka   musewessta.*(EXP)
the dog-DAT/TOP Insu-NOM frightening
Insu was frightening to it.

Example 10 shows both constructions are acceptable with a human experiencer if a context for represented thought is set up. Example 11 shows that in the same context, the experiential construction (11b) is odd with an animal experiencer, unless, of course, the whole is embedded in a story such as London's *Call of the Wild* (1915), that personifies the animal character.

The following data, taken from Korean narrative stories, instantiate the claims that are made in this chapter. These examples illustrate the narrative effects available through the use of experiential and agentive constructions. Example 12 is taken from an episode in which the reader participates in Yuceng's fear of Molan.

(12) a. *Yuceng-un   enusai   mom-ul tosalinta.*
Yuceng-TOP abruptly body-ACC withdrew.
sulmyesi kongpo-ka moliewassta.
slowly   fear-NOM crowd came

b. [*nunap-ey   anca   cangnankkuleki-chelem cocaltaenun*]
eye-front-LOC sitting prankster-like   chatting

c. *Molan-i   kapcaki museweciessta.* (EXP)
Molan-NOM suddenly fearsome

"a. Yuceng abruptly withdrew. Slowly fear came crowding in. b. There sat (Molan), chattering like a mischievous kid. c. Suddenly Molan was frightening (to her)." (No Won, 1986, p. 175)

The context is represented thought, with Yuceng as the source. In line (1), the spatial metaphor *fear came crowding in* helps the reader to identify with her emotional state. In line (3), the experiential construction with deleted experiencer continues the identification with Yuceng as a subjective character by directly representing her thought process.

Example 13 is necessarily a bit more complex due to the contrast between the two construction types. The entire passage is represented thought, with "he"

(Youngha) as the subjective character. Youngha is thinking about Yuwha and Yuwha's hatred toward Hyenwu. Line a (No Won, 1986) contains the experiential construction that directly represents Youngha's mental state: Youngha's concern for Yuwha. In Line c (No Won, 1986), the agentive construction gives Youngha's projection of Yuwha's mental state: Yuwha hates Hyenwu. The reader has direct access to Youngha's mind, hence the experiential construction, but not to Yuwha's mind, hence the agentive construction.

(13) a. ***ku-nun Yuwha-ka   kekcengsulewessta.*** (EXP)
        he-TOP Yuwha-NOM   concerned. (He = Youngha)
    b. [*Kewuy kwangki-ey   kakkawul*] *cengto-lo salanamun*
        almost madness-to   near   degree-with survived
    c. ***Hyenwu-lul   cungohakoiss-nuntey,*** (AGT)
        Hyenwu-ACC hating-but
    d. [[*salanghanun salam-ul ilun*] *sulpum ttaemun-ila*] *ko haki eynun*
        loving   person-ACC lost   sadness because-is   to-say
    e. *com   cinachita siphessta.*
        somewhat above seemed.

    (a) Yuwha was a concern to him [Youngha] (c) Although (Yuwha) was hating Hyenwu, (b) the survivor, with near madness, (e) it [her hatred] seemed (to him) to be more (d) than the sadness of losing her lover. (No Won, 1980, p. 46)

COGNITIVE MODELS

The analysis in this chapter follows Gerdts and Youn (1988) in positing distinct underlying structures for the two constructions. In relational grammar, they argued that the experiential construction contains a locative case-marked experiencer in the initial stratum, while the corresponding agentive construction has the experiencer as a marked agent. This initial level case marking suggests distinct cognitive models for the two constructions. Table 13.3 provides a simple schematic of what we think the folk cognitive models underlying the two constructions might look like.[11] Specifically, the experiential construction has a locative basis, whereas the agentive construction has a force-dynamic one. In the experiential construction, the experiencer is categorized as a location that is approached by a stimulus, the object of experience. In some cases, this stimulus emanates from a source.

---

[11]We are indebted to pioneers in Cognitive Semantics such as Ronald Langacker and Leonard Talmy for their insights into the underlying cognitive structure of these constructions, and in particular, for insisting that such constructions are not maps of reality, but rather conventionalized construals of it.

TABLE 13.3
Folk Models of Mental Events

Construction Type	Experiencer		Object of Experience
Experiential construction		*motion*	
	LOC	←	Stimulus (Source)
Agentive construction		*energy*	
	AGENT	→	Object

We argue that Korean experiencers metaphorically conceive of themselves as locations approached by stimuli. This is shown by the extensive use of *ota* (to come) and *tulta* (to enter) in predications of mental events, as in (14).

(14) a. *sulmyesi kongpho-ka (Suni-eykey) molie-wassta.*
  slowly   fear-NOM   (Suni-DAT) gather-come
  "Slowly fear gathered in to Suni."

  b. *nolae soli-ka   (Suni-eykey) tulie-wassta.*
  song sound-NOM (Suni-DAT) heard-come
  "Suni heard the sound of music coming to her."

  c. *kulen nukkim-i   (Suni-eykey) tulessta.*
  that feeling-NOM (Suni-DAT) enter
  "That kind of feeling came to Suni."

  d. *mom-i   (Suni-eykey) ttelie-wassta.*
  body-NOM (Suni-DAT) shiver-come
  "shiver overcame Suni."

  e. *(Suyen-eykey) Min paksa-uy mosup-i   tteola-wassta*
  (Suyen-DAT) Min Dr.GEN   figure-NOM surface-come
  "The figure of Dr. Min came to Suyen('s mind)."

  f. *kapet-uy   kamkak-i   (Kanguk-eykey) cenhae-wassta.*
  carpet-GEN touching-NOM (Kanguk-DAT) transmit-come
  "Kanguk became aware of how the carpet felt."

  g. *papokathun saengkak-i   (Suni-eykey) tulessta.*
  foolish   thought-NOM (Suni-DAT) enter
  "A foolish thought came to Suni."

Furthermore, the case-marking pattern of the experiential construction as in (15) is exactly parallel to that of a locative expression, even when it is not intuitively obvious that a stimulus is approaching a location. Compare the literal locative in (15a), and the experiential construction in (15b).

(15) a. *Toli-eykey sopho-ka   wassta* b. *Toli-eykey Suni-ka   musepta.* (EXP)
  Toli-DAT package-NOM come   Toli-DAT Suni-NOM fearful
  "A package arrived to Toli."   "Suni is fearsome to Toli."

An interesting phenomenon to consider in this respect is the fact that body part metonymy (Lakoff, 1987) is not only possible, but frequent in the experiential construction. The body part used in the expression is the relevant organ to which the stimulus must come, in order for it to be experienced. This model for perception is depicted in Table 13.4.

Instead of having the experiencer specified in the dative/locative, a visual experience can come to the eyes, an auditory experience to the ears, a tactile experience to the skin, affect to the heart or body, and thought to the head or brain. This systematic metonymy emphasizes the experiencer as a location because the actual site of experience, in the folk model, is substituted for the whole person, who is usually not mentioned. (Note the lack of overt possesor in Table 13.4). In contrast, this body part metonymy is not possible in the Agentive construction. This reflects the folk assumption that people, and not any specific part of them, are the default source of agency. Note the strangeness in English of *his mind wanted to leave*, or *his foot kicked open the door*.

Finally, the case marking of the experiential construction places focus on the object of experience, and not only backgrounds the experiencer in an oblique expression, but also promotes its deletion in both interactional and narrative discourse. This is consonant with the claim that the experiential construction allows the reader to view the story world through the thoughts and perceptions of the experiencer, who remains more or less transparent. In constrast, the agentive construction portrays the experiencer as an agent, that is, as a salient actor in an objective presentation of the story world.

CONCLUSION

In this chapter, we attempted to account for two types of constructions in Korean. The difference between experiential and agentive constructions is signalled at the surface level by systematic differences in derivational morphology and case marking. The semantic distinction is accounted for in terms of the notion of subjectivity: the agentive construction has an external cognizing observer who has no access to the mental world of the experiencer, whereas the experiential construction incorporates the cognizer as the experiencer in the utterance who has direct access to his or her own mental state. We also discussed the effect of these semantic and pragmatic differences in interactional and narrative discourse. The experiential construction is exploited in subjective contexts in narrative to give the reader the feeling of direct participation in the story world, whereas the agentive construction is used in objective contexts where the reader is acting as a mere observer of the scene, just like a narrator. A locative/directional model for the experiential construction is proposed, and a force dynamic model for the agentive construction. One avenue for future research is an investigation into the similarity of the case pattern [DAT–NOM–PREDICATE] used both in the ex-

TABLE 13.4
Body Part Metonymy for Experiencer

Type of Experience	Body Part Metonymy	Example for Experiencer
sight	eyes	*pulpich-i nun-ey pointa* light-NOM eye-DAT visible "The light was visible to (his) eyes."
sound	ears	*phili soli-ka kwi-ey ulinta* recorder sound-NOM ear-DAT heard "The sound of a recorder was audible to (his) ear."
touch	skin	*chukchukhan kamkak-i phipu-ey nukkiecinta.* wet feeling-NOM skin-DAT felt "Wet feeling was sensible to (his) skin."
affect	heart/mind	*Suni-ka kasumsok-ey kulipta.* Suni-NOM heart-DAT longed-for "In (his) heart was longing for Suni. "
thought	head/brain	*Suni-uy saengkak-i meli-ey nassta* Suni-GEN thought-NOM head-DAT strike "The thought about Suni struck him. "

periential construction discussed here and in passive constructions, and on the stativity versus activity of these constructions.

ACKNOWLEDGMENTS

This research was supported in part by National Science Grant No. IRI–8610517. We would like to express our gratitude to members of the Deictic Center Research Project of the Center for Cognitive Science at SUNY, Buffalo for their comrnents and discussion. Special thanks go to Naicong Li, Dan Devitt, Donna Gerdts and Karin Michelson for sharing their ideas and support. Thanks also to Eve Sweetser, Lloyd Anderson and Susan Fleischman for their comments on the earlier version of the chapter. All errors and mistakes are our responsiblity.

14

ANAPHOR IN SUBJECTIVE CONTEXTS IN NARRATIVE FICTION

Lynne E. Hewitt
The Pennsylvania State University

The study of narrative fiction in psycholinguistics, text linguistics, and discourse analysis focused on plot elements (Mandler & Johnson, 1977; Rumelhart, 1975; Stein & Glenn, 1979) or on narrative framing devices (Bamberg & Damrad-Frye, 1991; Gee, 1986; Hopper, 1979; Labov & Waletsky, 1967). These are vitally important aspects of narrative discourse. To examine the unfolding of plot is to explore which aspects of experience are tellable or newsworthy—what it is that makes us wish to tell stories, to give a recognizable pattern to events. To study the unique aspects of narrative language structure is to understand how we set narrative apart from other forms of speech. But as McCabe (1991) pointed out, the study of narrative is an unfolding process, and new ways of looking at it teach us to understand it in new ways.

A large and critically important area of narrative structure is either left out or given only incidental treatment when plot and frame are given overriding importance. The area these approaches fail to address is subjectivity—the aspect of fiction that offers us the illusion of direct experience of another's private mental states. Several chapters in this volume address subjectivity in fiction from various points of view (cf. especially Chun & Zubin, Galbraith, Hewitt, Li & Zubin, and Wiebe, this volume). The work presented in this chapter offers evidence for the psychological reality of subjectivity based on findings from linguistic analyses of text.

Banfield (1982), one of the pioneers in the study of subjectivity, argued that the depiction of individual experience is the reason-for-being of modern written narrative fiction. In fact, those who study subjective contexts are finding that much of the text of modern fiction, especially popular fiction, is constructed as a means of portraying the subjective experience of the characters (Banfield, 1982; Wiebe, 1990a, 1990b, and this volume). Some authors achieve specialized effects, the result of which is to heighten suspense or to deepen the reader's appreciation for conflicting motivations, by writing entire novels from various characters' subjective perspectives (hereafter, *subjectivity*)—see, for example, *Cyteen*, by Cherryh (1988a). A casual survey of a rack of popular fiction in such genres as romance, mystery, and spy novels will quickly reveal that, except for dialogue, the majority of the language used is presented from the subjectivity of a character.[1]

Psycholinguistic Approaches to Anaphor and Narrative

There is agreement among psycholinguistic researchers that nonsyntactically-bound anaphoric evocation of a referent indicates a high degree of psychological accessibility. Prior to the advent of psycholinguistic studies of anaphor, the traditional approach was text-based, approaching comprehension of anaphoric reference as a process in which recently mentioned noun phrases are searched until a match is found. The referential hierarchy derived by Givon (1983) via text linguistic methods assumes this traditional model, focusing on the notions of recency of mention and referential competition. Psycholinguistic studies of the last decade examined readers' processing of anaphor using constructed texts and tasks tapping priming effects, reading times, and response times to probes to try to map the memory structure of readers during anaphoric processing (e.g., Anderson, Garrod, & Sanford, 1983; Dell, McKoon, & Ratcliff, 1983; Garnham, 1984; McKoon & Ratcliff, 1980; Murphy, 1985; O'Brien, Duffy, & Myers, 1986). Some researchers in this tradition (e.g., Garnham, 1984) advocated a conservative approach to theories of anaphoric reference, using syntactic and semantic constraints to account for the majority of cases. An alternative approach involves pragmatic inference and mental models. Examples of researchers who found support for this latter approach are Marslen-Wilson, Levy, and Tyler (1982) and Anderson, Garrod, and Sanford (1983). In these models, the listener tracks the intentions of the speaker, and resolves conflicts by drawing on an array of inferencing strategies. Fox (1987) arrived at a similar theory of anaphoric devices in conversation using conversational analysis. She claimed that speakers and hearers cooperate in using and interpreting anaphor within a structural subset of

---

[1]Gee (1991), a student of modern children's oral narratives, contrasted modern with premodern forms of narrative. He argued for the relevance in the modern world of narrative as practiced in premodern societies, where personal narratives are always embedded in a social context of symbols and structures integral to a coherent group tradition. He did not consider what may be going on in modern, written narratives that is distinct from this. One way of looking at modern fiction is as extended and elaborate linguistic invocations of individual subjectivity embedded in age-old plot and symbolic structures. In this sense, a novel mirrors our modern Western experience of the world, in which our needs and duties as individuals are in constant tension with our roles as members of social groups.

conversation that she called a "sequence." In expository prose, Fox claimed that anaphoric reference is possible if the previous mention of that person is "in a proposition that is active or controlling" (p. 139). She related these two models of anaphor using the notion of discourse *focus* or *topicality*. Sidner's (1983) approach to the resolution of definite anaphor also relied on the notion of discourse focus. These models imply the existence of a mental model comprised of structural subunits used by both writers/speakers and readers/listeners to produce and resolve anaphoric referencing.

Just as some psycholinguists and linguists offered models of anaphor resolution based on inferencing and mental models, so also in the field of psycholinguistic studies of narrative comprehension, researchers agreed that readers/listeners use mental models to interpret narratives. Bower and Morrow (1990) described a mental model approach to the study of narrative composed of two major parts: "descriptions of the cast of characters. . . . important because they usually explain characters' goals, plans, and actions as the plot develops" (p. 44); and "a mental map of the physical settings in which actions occur" (p. 44). To explain referencing in narrative, they used the constructs "foreground" and "background" (Hopper, 1979). (The "on/off narrative line" account of Labov & Waletsky, 1967, is a similar approach also cited by Bower & Morrow.) Characters and objects in the foreground can be readily referenced by pronouns and definite noun phrases, those in the background less easily. Bower and Morrow saw the foreground as the locus of story activity. It was held to be in the "attentional focus" (p. 45) of the reader.

One problem with using a foreground/background distinction alone to account for narrative effects is that it is purely structural, offering no explanation for the differing story world status of foreground versus background effects. In fact, analysis of subjective language in a story shows that any single binary distinction fails to capture the complexity of the story's operation. Analysts rely on linguistic and topic analyses to determine the foreground or background status of a given piece of text: Certain phrases indicate backgrounded events; or events occurring around the protagonist are considered foregrounded, whereas those relating to minor characters backgrounded; or foregrounded events occur in main rather than subordinate clauses. But in resolving any particular anaphoric evocation, the reader uses a multitude of textual cues, and will easily disregard simple reading heuristics in which main characters get pronouns and minor characters do not, if given sufficient linguistic reason to do so. And what of the case of two equally important characters: How would one resolve anaphoric referencing conflicts then?

Anderson, Garrod, and Sanford (1983), using simple constructed narratives, found that the main character was most likely to be pronominalized when subjects were given the task of continuing an incomplete narrative. In these narratives, there was a main character important throughout the passage, and a scenario-dependent character. They theorized that pronominalization of the main character reflected its status as the "thematic subject," citing work by Karmiloff-Smith (1980). However, they acknowledged that "some scenario-dependent characters might also serve as potential thematic subjects" (p. 438). A more complete theory of narrative may help shed light on which characters are most highly activated, and/or accessible for pronominalization.

Role of Subjectivity in Narrative

The research presented in this chapter argues for a model of narrative that includes a theory of why stories are the way they are. One component of such a theory is the importance of subjectivity in narrative. That is, one vital component of the reader's experience of a story is the way in which it offers vicarious experience of other's lives. Because this is part of the pleasure, and indeed purpose, of reading fiction, it is a large part of the endeavor of the reader. In this view, readers do not pay attention to a main character's motivations just because they explain a given event in the text, or because they assume the main character is always most important for reference tracking. Rather, in much of the language of fiction, readers are experiencing those events as if filtered through the consciousness of those characters. And it is the language of the text, including anaphoric referencing strategies, that creates this illusion.

In this chapter, I present the results of an examination of use of pronominalization and zero anaphor to evoke participants in subjective contexts in narrative fiction. I test the hypothesis that the participant whose subjectivity is being represented will be invoked with a reduced anaphoric form (i.e., in English, via pronominalization or zero) significantly more often than other participants. That is, the subjective experiencer is always the most highly psychologically activated nominal, and is therefore the best candidate for anaphor resolution (in nonsyntactically-bound contexts). As Zubin (1989; and Li & Zubin, this volume) argued, the character from whose point of view events are being viewed is, in a sense, transparent—the most activated character becomes the most linguistically invisible, because less referential material is needed to evoke him or her. Confirmation of the previous hypothesis would provide evidence for the validity of the experiential theory of narrative, because it would offer confirmation for the importance of subjectivity in linguistic processing of text.

Procedure

In order to develop a means to test the hypothesis, I needed a means of quantifying the degree of "anaphoricity" of participants in a text. Givon's work on referential hierarchies (1983) offered a means of tracking participants through a text by examining their evocation from clause to clause. Givon's theory of anaphor resolution is more closely linked to text-based approaches, where a given reference is held to be more available if it is closer to its first evocation, has few competitors, and persists in being mentioned for several clauses. This approach does not address pragmatic inferencing and mental model approaches, although it is not necessarily opposed to them. Givon (1983) described three quantitative measures of participant continuity: *referential distance*, or the number of clauses between one evocation of a referent and the next; *referential competition*, or the number of competing referents in a span of three clauses; and *persistence*, or the number of contiguous clauses in which a given referent continues to be evoked. Because these measures focus on counting clauses rather than classes of nominals used to evoke referents, none is precisely suited to the task of tracking the degree to which a given participant is evoked via anaphor. Of the three, persistence is most closely linked to the continuing importance of a given referent. It focuses on the number of sequential clauses in which a participant appears. However by focusing on clauses alone, it does not allow the examination of the type of reference used, whether it is a full nominal or some type of anaphoric device.

In developing a measure suited to my needs, I modified the measure of persistence by counting the number of reduced anaphoric evocations (pronouns and zeroes) of a participant after a fully specified evocation (either by name or a noun phrase) until the next fully specified evocation, irrespective of clause boundaries. I then calculated the percentage of total evocations that were reduced anaphoric evocations. For example, in *Exile's Gate* (Cherryh, 1988b), the character, Vanye, in his own subjective context, was evoked by a full nominal 9 times, and by a reduced anaphoric expression 99 times, to yield a number indicative of 91.7% (99/108) "anaphoricity."

In deciding which nominals deserved to be tracked as participants, humans alone were included, because other noun phrases in the texts used were not represented as possible subjective characters. That is, it is possible that the psychological states of an animal, or even a rock or a tree, might be represented in a story, but in these narratives only one example of the representation of a psychological state in an animal occurred. I discuss this example separately. Otherwise, only human characters were represented as having private psychological states in the narratives examined, and therefore, only references to human actors were tracked.

Identification of Subjective Contexts

Subjective contexts in narrative are defined as passages in which the private mental state of a character is being represented. Identification of such contexts is based on analysis of the language used. Banfield (1982) enumerated a variety of specialized contexts in which private states are portrayed. In *internal monologue*, the thoughts of the character are depicted in the character's own language. This can be identified by the presence of first-person, present tense, online narration. In *psychonarration*, the character's mental states are described by use of mental verbs and psychological descriptions. In addition to these two relatively straightforward and well-understood types of psychological contexts, there is a third, less well recognized, but common type in which a character's thoughts and perceptions are represented linguistically but not in the character's own thoughts or by means of psychological verbs. This third type of context was termed *represented thought and perception* by Banfield. She inventoried a large number of syntactic structures that only occur in these specialized subjective contexts. Wiebe (1990a & b; this volume) expanded on Banfield's work, developing a much more extensive list of indicators of subjectivity. Using these indicators, it is possible to provide linguistic evidence to show that certain contexts are intended to be taken as the representation of a character's private states.

In order to be able to compare anaphoric referencing in subjective contexts, it is necessary to draw boundaries between objective and subjective contexts and between one character's subjectivity and another's. In some texts, the indications of such boundaries are clear. For example, typographic indicators such as paragraph and chapter boundaries may be used to demarcate contexts (Wiebe, 1990b; see also Bruder & Wiebe, this volume). Another clear boundary would be a transfer from representing one character's thoughts to those of a different character. In some texts, however, the boundaries are not obvious, at times designedly so. This is the case with one of the texts used for the research reported here—*The Pearl* (1945/1975) by Steinbeck.

In *The Pearl*, long segments devoted to the exclusive portrayal of one character's subjectivity are absent. Evocations of the main character's internal states are not infrequent (usually via psychonarration and represented perception), but they tend to blend seamlessly with objective sentences, as in the following passage:

(1) Kino was young and strong and his black hair hung over brown forehead...
He lowered his blanket from his nose now, for the dark poisonous air was
gone and yellow sunlight fell on the house... (Steinbeck, 1945/1975, p. 5)

Clearly, the first sentence and the one that follows it, (here omitted) is purely an objective description of Kino. He is not thinking about, nor is he able to observe, his appearance. But the next sentence contains several indicators of subjectivity: narrative past tense in a sentence containing "now" (Banfield, 1982), a definite article for a referent not recoverable from the context (the dark poisonous air), and the imputation of factuality to a description the reader is likely to interpret as being in Kino's belief space (that night air is poisonous)—see Wiebe, this volume.

Much of *The Pearl* wavers from clause to clause between objective, subjective, and middle-ground contexts. Therefore, measuring the number of reduced anaphoric evocations is misleading. Local factors, such as referential competition, may frequently outweigh the subjective context as factors in determining the level of anaphora that can be tolerated without leading to confusion. In fact, Kino, being the protagonist and present in most scenes, would be likely to be pronomi-nalized more often as the chief actor and most available participant, even if he were never to be depicted as a thinker or perceiver (see Anderson, Garrod, & Sanford, 1983). In this light, subjectivity may be irrelevant to anaphor resolution at the local level.

Although subjectivity may not influence local anaphor resolution phenomena, it might still serve as a factor in extended pronominalization. A true test of this conjecture is not possible with a text such as *The Pearl.* I, therefore, sought out texts in which clearly demarcated alternations of subjective perspective could be found. I located a novel, *Exile's Gate* by Cherryh (1988b), a science fantasy. The passage chosen has useful properties for the purposes of analyzing anaphoric referencing. It contains only three characters. Two of the characters are compan-ions, and the third a stranger to them. Two are human males, the third an alien humanoid female. The subjectivity of the two males is represented, but never that of the female character. Because of the differences in knowledge state of the characters, the subjective contexts are clearly delineated by the characters' respective styles of referencing. Each man, in his own subjective context, thinks of the other as "the man" and of himself by name. The lone male thinks of the female alien as "the woman" or "the qhal," because he does not know her name. The other, companion to the woman, thinks of her as "Morgaine." For example:

(2) "Vanye" is subjective character.
... when Vanye pressed his hand over the man's heart he felt it beating steadily.... (Cherryh, 1988b, pp. 24–25)

(3) "Chei" is subjective character.
... Chei was far gone in the pain that began about his ankle ... he tried not to react when the man probed the joint... (Cherryh, 1988b, p. 27)

In Example 2, "the man" refers to Chei; in Example 3, "the man" refers to Vanye. (I use the term "subjective character" in the same sense that Wiebe (Bruder & Wiebe, this volume) and Zubin (Zubin & Hewitt, this volume) use the term "focalizing WHO.")

Another aspect of *Exile's Gate* that makes it useful for the purposes of this investigation is that one of the main characters never has her subjectivity repre-sented. This character, Morgaine, the only female, is the decision-maker in her association with Vanye. She is clearly a co-protagonist with Vanye. Any differ-ences in pronominalization between Vanye and Morgaine cannot be attributed to Morgaine's being a secondary character. Moreover, one of the subjective characters, Chei, is in fact not a protagonist of the novel; he is a main character for this stretch of text, and diminishes in importance later on. (As this novel is one in a series featuring Vanye and Morgaine, a reader of the series would be able to predict that Chei will not have the same continuing importance.) If, despite his equivocal status as temporary main character, Chei's degree of pronominalization is equal to that of Vanye, it bolsters the argument that subjectivity may be a more important factor in pronominalization than status as main character.

I examined 134 lines of text (6.5 pages) for each of the two subjective characters, Vanye and Chei, in *Exile's Gate*. In *The Pearl*, I examined 126 lines (4 pages) of text in Kino's subjective context, selecting a passage where Kino is most clearly marked as the subjective character, with some unambiguous represented thoughts, and some represented perception. As noted previously, there is a disparity between the two texts, in that many more sentences in *Exile's Gate* are unambiguously represented thought than in *The Pearl*. Because of the high subjectivity of *Exile's Gate*, the likelihood of a reader continuing to interpret sentences as subjective (even those lacking overt indicators of subjectivity) is very high (see Bruder & Wiebe, this volume; Wiebe, 1990a, 1990b). This might not be the case in the passages from *The Pearl*.

A comparison of the persistence of reduced anaphoric invocations for subjective versus nonsubjective characters in subjective contexts reveals the strongest trends in the most clear-cut contexts, as predicted. Thus, whereas examination of *The Pearl* yielded trends in the predicted direction, the findings for *Exile's Gate* showed much larger disparities (see Table 14.1).

In order to further explore disparities in anaphoric usage for subjective versus nonsubjective characters, I identified which chains of anaphoric references were the longest for each character in each story. As can be seen from Table 14.2, there is a large disparity between the two groups.

TABLE 14.1
Percentage of All Evocations That Are Reduced:

The Pearl (Subjective Character = Kino)	
Kino:	72.5%
Juana:	62.9%
Coyotito:	57.9%

Exile's Gate (Two Subjective Characters)	
1. Subjective character = Vanye	
Vanye:	91.7%
Chei ("the man"):	60.0%
Morgaine:	42.9%
2. Subjective Character = Chei	
Chei:	94.4%
Vanye ("the man"):	36.8%
Morgaine ("the woman" or "the qhal"):	33.3%
Morgaine & Vanye ("these strangers"):	87.5%

Note. Phrases in parentheses indicate actual fully specified forms evoked by character when character does not know the name of the person.

TABLE 14.2
Longest Chains of Reduced Anaphor Following Full Form

Subjective Characters:	
Kino	12
Chei	52
Vanye	78
Nonsubjective Characters:	
Morgaine & Vanye (as a unit)	7
Chei	5
Vanye	3
Juana	4
Coyotito	5

In examining the data in Table 14.2, the contrast between the two novels is almost more striking than the differences among the participants. Not all of the clauses in the data from *The Pearl* are subjective, and many are indeterminate. This lack of pure subjectivity without interruption dilutes the data, which shows Kino to persist with a reduced anaphoric evocation an average of two times longer than Juana or Coyotito. In contrast, in the clearly subjective contexts of *Exile's Gate*, with two participants alternating as subjective characters in clearly demarcated passages, the subjective character persists in reduced form more than 10 times as often as the nonsubjective. The longest chain of reduced references to Kino is 12. The longest chain for Chei as the subjective character is 52 anaphoric evocations, and in the contexts where Vanye is the subjective character, it is 78. The longest chain for a nonsubjective character is seven (referring to Morgaine and Vanye as a unit by means of the pronoun "they"). The contrast between Kino, on the one hand, and Vanye and Chei, on the other, is all the more striking as Kino is clearly the main character in the passage chosen, even when his subjectivity is not being represented.

I also examined the instances in which a full nominal evocation of a character was followed by another full reference to that character. For example, in *Exile's Gate*:

(4) Morgaine understood it. Morgaine did all that she did for that thing she served. ... (p. 31)

In this example, the first nominal evocation of "Morgaine" is not followed by reduced anaphor, but by another full nominal. The percent of fully specified forms not followed by any reduced form is reported in Table 14.3. This measure offers perspective on nonavailability of a character for easy pronominalization.

Examination of Table 14.3 shows that, again, the trends are less clear in the case of *The Pearl*. Contrary to expectations, the nonsubjective character Juana is slightly less likely than the focalizer Kino to be fully specified in the next clause: 38%

TABLE 14.3
Percent of Full Nominals Followed by Another Full Nominal
in the Next Evocation

The Pearl (Steinbeck, 1945/1975)	
Kino:	44%
Juana:	38%
Coyotito:	50%

Exile's Gate (Cherryh 1988b)	
1. Vanye = subjective character:	
Vanye:	11%
Chei:	50%
Morgaine:	58%
2. Chei = subjective character:	
Chei:	14%
Vanye ("the man"):	66%
Morgaine ("the woman"):	66%
Morgaine & Vanye ("these strangers"):	0%

versus 44%. On the other hand, the subjective characters in *Exile's Gate* are significantly less likely than the nonsubjective to be fully specified in the next evocation. In this text, only 11% and 14% of the subjective character's fully specified evocations are followed by another full nominal; the nonsubjective characters are almost five times more likely to be evoked by name rather than by reduced anaphor.

Exceptions

There were two interesting exceptions, in addition to the case of Juana mentioned in the above paragraph, to the patterns of pronouns for subjective characters and nouns for nonsubjective ones. Although this study focused on the human actors in these stories, one pattern observed in a nonhuman actor in *The Pearl* is worth recounting. At a critical juncture in the plot of this novel, a scorpion becomes the focus of narration for several sentences. The scorpion is evoked three times and followed by "it" or zero anaphor for 3, 7, and 2 consecutive instances. Its high availability reflects the narrative importance of its presence in the scene. Clearly, the scorpion is not being portrayed as a fully subjective character, although its vague sensory experience is conveyed in one clause, where it feels for "the source of the death that was coming to it" (p. 6). In this instance, its importance and, hence, psychological activation are boosted by plot factors. Two additional factors make the pronominalization of this participant easier: the referential options of the English pronoun system, and pragmatic checking relating to our knowledge of what humans typically do versus what scorpions are capable of. "It" cannot refer to human actors, humans do not have stinging tails, and so on. These considerations may also help account for Juana's relatively high availability for pronominalization even in Kino's contexts; the marking of gender on English pronouns allows her to be referred to unambiguously.

A similar example occurs in *Exile's Gate*, in Chei's subjective context. Chei reflects on the other two characters whose names he does not know. He has been captured and is therefore thinking a great deal about his captors and their motives. The disambiguating force of number combines with the plot structure (in which Chei perceives his captors as a nameless unit) to produce chains of "they" far longer than the evocations of either of the two characters alone (see Table 14.3). However, the extremely long sequences of pronominalization and zero that mark evocations of the subjective character are much longer than the longest sequence of "they": 78 compared to 7. In comparison to the multiparagraph use of reduced anaphora for the subjective character, the use of "they" is merely a local phenomenon.

In order to verify that the patterns displayed in the descriptive statistics hold up to further examination, chi-square analyses of the patterns of reference found in the texts studied were also performed.[2] Tables 14.4A, 14.5A, and 14.6 present this data; all of these were significant at the $p < .001$ level, indicating that the distribution of the data is highly unlikely to occur by chance. The numbers in Table 14.4A reflect the total number of times Vanye and Chei were referred to in the contexts studied, collapsing the data for these two characters in order to contrast the number of reduced versus full evocations occurring in subjective versus nonsubjective contexts. Table 14.4B presents a nonsignificant chi-square supporting the combination of numbers for Chei and Vanye, showing that the number of references to each are equivalent.

Table 14.5A compares the total evocations of Vanye and Chei with the total evocations of Morgaine and "these strangers"—the nonsubjective characters. Again, data for Chei and Vanye was combined. It should be noted that references to Vanye and Chei in their nonsubjective contexts are included on the right hand

---

[2]Woods, Fletcher, and Hughes (1986) warned against the illegitimate uses of chi-square analyses in language research, when the assumption of independence may be violated. They argued that words used sequentially in a text cannot be treated as data points occurring independently of each other. Although it is true that one occurrence of a grammatical form may influence another, in the study here reported, each occurrence of the dependent variable of interest (reduced vs. full evocations), is logically independent of any other occurrences. That is, on no occasion would it be grammatically necessary to have a full form rather than an anaphor.

Another aspect of the design of this study that might be questioned is the assumption of random sampling from the total population. The texts selected were not chosen randomly; nor were the contexts in those texts chosen randomly. Rather, they were chosen specifically so that the operation of the independent variables of interest could be examined. Given the difficulties of ever obtaining a true random sample, owing to resources and other limitations, I offer Woods, Fletcher, and Hughes' (1986) defense of sampling procedures in linguistic studies. They advocate a pragmatic approach, in which consumers of research first judge the results as though they were based on a random sample, and then weigh the magnitude of the possible effects of nonrandomness for evaluating the conclusions drawn.

TABLE 14.4A

Number of References: Subjective Versus Nonsubjective Contexts
in Vanye and Chei's *Exile's Gate* (Cherryh, 1988b)

	Subjective Character	Nonsubjective Character
Reduced anaphor	217	22
Fully specified form	16	22

Note. χ^2 (1 N = 257) = 54.53, $p < .001$. References to Vanye and Chei have been summed.
See Table 14.4B.

TABLE 14.4B

Total References to Vanye and Chei in Subjective
Versus Nonsubjective Contexts

	Subjective Contexts	Nonsubjective Contexts
Chei	125	21
Vanye	108	19

Note. χ^2 (1, N = 273) = .001, $p > .95$, N.S.

side of the table under nonsubjective characters. To justify this inclusion, references to Vanye and Chei in their nonsubjective contexts are compared with references to other nonsubjective characters in Table 14.5B. Table 14.5B shows that a chi-square comparison of Vanye and Chei and the other nonsubjective characters yields nonsignificant results, indicating that in their nonsubjective contexts they behave similarly to other nonsubjective characters. The data re-

TABLE 14.5A

Number of References: Subjective Versus Nonsubjective Character
in *Exile's Gate* (Cherryh, 1988b)

	Subjective Characters	Nonsubjective Characters
Reduced anaphor	217	53
Fully specified form	16	45

Note. χ^2 (1, N = 331) = 67.41, $p < .001$.

TABLE 14.5B

Number of References: Nonsubjective Character in *Exile's Gate*
(Cherryh, 1988b)

	Vanye & Chei	All Others
Reduced anaphor	22	53
Full nominal	22	45

Note. χ^2 (1, N = 142) = .07, $p > .80$, N.S.

TABLE 14.6

Number of References: Subjective Versus Nonsubjective Characters
in *The Pearl* (Steinbeck, 1945/1975)

	Subjective Character (Kino)	Nonsubjective Characters (Juana & Coyotito)
Reduced anaphor	66	33
Fully specified form	25	21

Note. χ^2 (1, N = 145) = 37.26, $p < .001$.

ported in Table 14.5 gives a sense for the inequality of references to subjective versus nonsubjective characters. Not only are there more than twice as many total references to the subjective characters, but the vast preponderance of subjective character references are reduced (217 reduced vs. 16 full), and the references to nonsubjective characters are much more evenly distributed (53 reduced vs. 45 full).

Table 14.6 presents the chi-square analysis of the data for *The Pearl*, also yielding a significant finding regarding the distribution of the data. This offers evidence that Kino is indeed more available for reduced anaphoric referencing than the nonsubjective characters, Juana and Coyotito. However, as noted previously, the effect of Kino's being the main character cannot be discounted as the primary explanation for this data, because there are no competing minor characters' subjective contexts to compare with Kino's.

Discussion

These data uphold the general hypothesis that clear subjective contexts allow for greater pronominalization and zero anaphor for the subject thereof. It is important to recall, however, that the ultimate decision on any given instance of reduced anaphor must rely on many other factors. For example, in the following example, pragmatic checking disambiguates "he" and "him" (grammatical position may also play a role):

> (5) Vanye set his own foot in the stirrup, stepped up, and rested his leg across the low cantle and blanket roll till he could get hold of the man and haul him upright enough. Then he slid down behind him. . . (Cherryh, 1988b, p. 24).

The reader knows that one man is disabled, and the other helping him; certain types of actions, such as grabbing hold of a man and hauling him up into a saddle, are not plausibly attributable to a seriously injured person. In addition, since the reader is aware that the current actor is Vanye, it makes sense to attribute the subject pronouns to him, and the object pronouns to Chei, the disabled man who is not moving under his own ability.

In contrast to the local resolution principles that apply to examples such as this, different forces come into play in subjective contexts. For example:

(6) The words made no sense at all to him. He thought of the wolves, the ones he had named—he had known their faces, he had known their ways. They were terrible, but he knew them, what they would do, when they would do it: he had learned his enemy and he had known the limits of his misery. (Cherryh, 1988b, p. 28)

The paragraph following this one is nearly as long, and similar in tone and content; it also contains no full noun phrase referring to the subjective character (here, Chei). In fact, it is followed by a paragraph break after which we are in the subjectivity of Vanye; we leave Chei's subjectivity not having had a reference to Chei by name for over six paragraphs. In contexts such as that in example 6, extended sequences without a fully specified form for the subjective character offer evidence that the subjective character is the most psychologically activated candidate for anaphor resolution. This finding supports not only the model of fiction argued for here, in which subjectivity is a crucial factor, but also all types of mental model approaches to language comprehension. Readers must be able to build a very clear picture of the mental spaces inhabited by characters if they can process chains of 78 reduced referring expressions without excessive numbers of breakdowns.

One alternative explanation for the findings of this study deserves consideration.[3] In this view, the high degree of pronominalization of the subjective character reflects the shifted deixis of represented thought. That is, where a first-person narrator version would have used first person, represented thought contexts use third-person pronouns. Thus, example 6 could just as easily read: "The words made no sense at all to me. I thought of the wolves . . ." This explanation fails to take into account at least two factors. First, it does not address use of full nominals in subjective contexts; people seldom think of themselves by name, yet full nominals evoking the subjective character do occur in represented thought. Second, the deictic shift of represented thought offers more scope to the writer than merely shifting the deixis from first to third person. It also allows inclusion of aspects of events and scenes that are not being actively tracked or considered by the subjective character. The subjective context filters the story world through the character's consciousness; it does not merely recount the thoughts of the character.

In example 7, although the events could theoretically be narrated in first person, the use of represented thought allows for effects that the intrusiveness of an active narrator would obscure:

(7) But—a brief darkness then; and a snap like a burning log, that brought him out of his sleep reaching for his sword, aware first that Morgaine was at his left and that their guest was to his right and moving staggering to his feet and

---

[3]My thanks to William Rapaport for offering this alternative explanation.

reeling away among the trees at no slight speed. Fire burned in the leaf mold. That was the result of Morgaine's weapon; he knew it well enough—knew that was the sound that had waked him and he scrambled up sleep-dazed as he was and overtook the man before he had gotten as far as the horses he strove to reach—overtook him and seized him at the shoulders, bearing him down in a crash to the leaves at the very hooves of the gray warhorse. (Cherryh, 1988b, p. 28)

Example 7 shows that events and actions not consciously being thought about by the character can be represented subjectively in a represented thought context. In the first line, the phrase "a brief darkness then" represents Vanye's perception of having dozed off only briefly before he is awakened by the snapping twig. The advantage of the third-person mode of presentation is that it makes no claims for Vanye's narrative ability; if it was shifted into first-person, part of the reader's perception of Vanye would be that he is a skilled, and garrulous, storyteller. In fact, the author is at pains to portray him as taciturn.

Aspects of the pronominalization pattern of example 7 are worth calling attention to. Like example 6, it also follows several paragraphs that do not mention the subjective character by name. There are several clauses at the end of the paragraph when both Vanye and his opponent are evoked via pronominalization. These sentences are relating an action sequence, and local factors involving pragmatic checking are probably involved here. But note that it is Vanye, the subjective character, who gets the most reduced: He is evoked via zero ("overtook him"). In fact, the appearance of this zero is indicative of a continuing subjective context for Vanye; the pure action sequence does not make us pop to an objective interpretation. The operation of such devices allow us to experience the illusion of sharing the experience of a person who could not in fact tell his own story with such immediacy. Reference via reduced anaphoric expressions is one way of conveying that immediacy to the reader.

ACKNOWLEDGMENTS

I am grateful to David Zubin for first proposing that I investigate the behavior of anaphora in subjective contexts, and for first recognizing that these contexts are likely to show interesting differences in the behavior of pronouns and zeros. My discussions of subjectivity owe greatly to ideas discussed at length with Mary Galbraith and Janyce Wiebe. I am also grateful to the other members of the erstwhile Graduate Group in Cognitive Science, almost all of whom are represented in this book, for many fruitful discussions of subjectivity in narrative fiction. In addition, I would like to thank Erwin Segal and Gail Bruder for advice on statistical design and interpretation.

Preparation of this chapter was supported in part by a graduate assistantship awarded by the Center for Cognitive Science at the University of New York at Buffalo.

15

RECOGNIZING SUBJECTIVITY AND IDENTIFYING SUBJECTIVE CHARACTERS IN THIRD-PERSON FICTIONAL NARRATIVE

Gail A. Bruder
State University of New York at Buffalo

Janyce M. Wiebe
New Mexico State University

INTRODUCTION

In this chapter, we discuss the importance of the distinction between subjective and objective sentences, give an overview of an algorithm for recognizing subjective sentences (in continuous narrative) and identifying their subjective character, present a general description of our approach to psychological testing of discourse features used by the algorithm, and describe the results of a series of six studies testing these features.

Comprehension of text, including narrative text, depends on the interpretation of individual sentences, as well as the integration of that local information with global contextual information. Theories of text comprehension must explain understanding on both these levels. In addition, there are some important differences between fictional narrative and other types of text. Readers of fiction must track the spatio-temporal location of events, the focal characters currently in the scene, and the psychological point of view (POV) from which the events are portrayed. The narrative research group at SUNY at Buffalo is operating on the assumption that people use mental models of the story world to interpret local information and integrate it with global information in narrative fiction. The Deictic Center (DC) is part of this mental model and includes current temporal (WHEN), spatial (WHERE), and character (WHO) information. Character information is most central to this chapter and the WHO is perhaps the most complex of the components of the DC. In our earlier formulations (Bruder et al., 1986), the WHO was a single construct representing the character whose actions, thoughts, and beliefs the narrative is currently following. However, a narrative can follow the actions of a character as perceived by another, that is, it can take a character's *psychological point of view* (Uspensky, 1973). We include two constructs in the WHO. The current character in focus in the narrative is the focal WHO; the character from whose perspective the events are presented is the focalizing WHO.

As Galbraith so convincingly argues in chapter 2 (drawing on the work of Banfield, 1982), readers must distinguish between *subjective* and *objective* sentences. Objective sentences are those whose narrative content is taken simply as true (in the fictional world). Subjective sentences are those whose content is mediated by the epistemology of a character, and is structured by the character's perceptions, thoughts, knowledge, intentions, goals, and other psychological attributes. The propositional content of subjective sentences must be understood with respect to a character's judgment and experience, and is thus open to question. The character whose epistemology governs subjective sentences is our focalizing WHO, or, the *subjective character*.

There are several areas of narrative understanding that are crucially determined by the reader's ability to track the psychological POV (that is, to recognize subjective sentences and identify their subjective characters). First, readers cannot simply integrate the content of a subjective sentence into their representations of the story, but instead have to integrate that content into their representations of a character's attitudes or beliefs. A subjective sentence reflects a character's beliefs, even if those beliefs are false (Banfield, 1982; Cohn, 1978). Second, subjective sentences can contain linguistic elements that express a character's emotion, evaluation, and so on. Readers have to understand that these elements express the character's attitudes, rather than the author's or narrator's. Third, subjective sentences can reveal information about a character's intentions. Understanding a character's thoughts may be needed in order to understand why the character performs a particular action. Finally, readers must determine the current psychological POV in order to understand the discourse structure of the text: A change in POV affects how the reader understands the relation of a sentence to preceding ones (Black, Turner, & Bower, 1979; Nakhimovsky & Rapaport, 1988).

Tracking the psychological point of view was first investigated in Artificial Intelligence by Wiebe and Rapaport (1988) and Wiebe (1990b, 1994). To determine the current POV, readers cannot consider sentences in isolation, because most subjective sentences are not explicitly marked for point of view. Wiebe's approach was to examine naturally occurring narratives for regularities in the ways that authors continue, resume, and initiate characters' points of view, and to develop an algorithm that tracks point of view on the basis of the regularities found. Certain combinations of sentence features and aspects of the current context provide the reader with evidence for particular points of view. Sentence features included tense, aspect, lexical items that potentially express subjectivity, the types of states of affairs denoted, and the identities of the actors or experiencers of those states of affairs. Relevant aspects of the discourse context are things such as whether the previous sentence was subjective or objective, whether a paragraph break separates the current and previous sentences, and the identity of the subjective character of the previous subjective sentence.

Next, we give an overview of Wiebe's algorithm, then we report on our empirical investigations of two of the textual regularities (used by the algorithm) in human readers' interpretation of POV in fictional narrative. These regularities were the presence or absence of paragraph breaks and the presence of potential subjective elements (e.g., lexical items that potentially express subjectivity). We wish to point out that our psychological research evaluated the influence of these regularities on human readers. At this preliminary stage, our research did not test whether the algorithm's behavior simulates that of human readers. As is evident below and in Wiebe (1990b, 1994) there is more to the algorithm than the two regularities we tested.

OVERVIEW OF WIEBE'S ALGORITHM

The main components of the algorithm are a function, *POV*, that maps features of the current sentence, and the current *context*, into an *interpretation* of the sentence, and function *newContext*, that maps the current context and the interpretation of the current sentence into an updated context:

POV: featureSet × context → interpretation.
newContext: interpretation × context → context.

There is also a function, *newContext'*, which maps a paragraph or scene break and a context into an updated context.

The following illustrates the functioning of the algorithm, starting from the very beginning of the text (assuming no breaks, for simplicity):

POV(features of sent. 1, initial context) = interpretation of sent. 1
NewContext(interpretation of sent. 1, initial context) = context of sent. 2

POV(features of sent. 2, context of sent. 2) = interpretation of sent. 2
NewContext(interpretation of sent. 2, context of sent. 2) = context of sent. 3

An interpretation is either that the sentence is the subjective sentence of a particular character or that the sentence is objective (and optionally has an *active character*). (An active character is a character who just performed an action.) A context consists of (a) the identify of the subjective character of the last subjective sentence that appeared in the text, if there was one, (b) the identity of the last active character, if there was one, (c) the identities of any characters whose points of view were taken earlier in the text, and (d) the current *text situation*.

context = < LastSubjectiveCharacter, LastActiveCharacter, PreviousSubjectiveCharacters, TextSituation >

The current text situation encodes such things as whether a subjective sentence has appeared in the current scene and, if so, whether or not objective sentences and/or paragraphs breaks have appeared since the last subjective sentence. It also encodes which *expected subjective characters* there are—characters whose points of view are likely to be taken in the current context.

The text situations are divided into groups, numbered 1–4. Each type of potential subjective element is associated with the situations in one of these groups and also with those in all lower numbered groups. For the current sentence, the potential subjective elements it contains are among the features input to function *POV*. If one of these elements is associated with the current text situation, and some other conditions are met, then the interpretation of the current sentence (the output of *POV*) will be a subjective one. Below is a brief description of the text situations in the four groups:

1. *continuing–subjective*: The current sentence follows a subjective sentence without a paragraph break;

2. a. *broken–subjective*: The current sentence follows a subjective sentence but after a paragraph break;
   b. *interrupted–subjective*: The current sentence follows an objective sentence but an earlier sentence in the current paragraph was subjective;

3. a. *postsubjective–active* and
   b. *postsubjective–nonactive*: A subjective sentence has appeared in the current scene and a paragraph break and an objective sentence have appeared since. These text situations differ only in whether an active character has appeared in the current paragraph (active) or not (nonactive);
   c. *presubjective–active*: A subjective sentence has not appeared so far in the current scene, but an active character has appeared in the current paragraph;

4. *presubjective–nonactive*: A subjective sentence has not appeared so far in the current scene and a sentence with an active character has not appeared so far in the current paragraph.

There is an expected subjective character in the situations in groups 1–3, but not in the situation in group 4. The situations in groups 1–3 have increasing numbers of types of discontinuities relevant to POV, that is, objective sentences and breaks.

In the current version of the algorithm, the association of elements with situations is based on examinations of texts. That is, textual analysis was performed to determine in which text situations a potential subjective element usually indicates subjectivity. The general hypothesis behind this aspect of the algorithm is that the fewer the number of discontinuities since the last subjective sentence, the more readers expect a subjective sentence to appear, and thus the more they are inclined to interpret things that are potentially subjective to indeed be subjective.

The algorithm performs functions *POV, newContext,* and *newContext'*. Recall that one of the inputs to *POV* is a *featureSet*. Computationally deriving the *featureSet* of a sentence involves the resolution of ambiguities that are outside the scope of the algorithm presented in Wiebe (1990b). Therefore, we assume the existence of a component that produces the necessary information, that is, it performs the following function:

features: sentence → featureSet

A featureSet includes the potential subjective elements in the sentence, the types of states of affairs denoted (e.g., action, private-state), and other information. What composes a featureSet, and the possible feature values were specified in detail in Wiebe (1990b).

COMPARISON OF OUR APPROACH WITH THAT OF RELATED PSYCHOLOGICAL RESEARCH

Although the experimental investigation of point of view dates back at least to Black, Turner, and Bower (1979), research with extensive narrative is more recent. Bower and Morrow (1990) conducted a number of studies supporting their claim that readers construct situation models during comprehension. As Morrow, Greenspan, and Bower (1987) indicated ". . . evidence suggests that readers build situation models organized around protagonists and guided by the spatial and temporal information conveyed by prepositions . . ." (p. 167). Research supporting the notion that readers build mental models in accordance with spatial, temporal, and character information in the text is consistent with and contributed to our conceptualization of the DC. But there are a number of differences between that line of research and the psychological research reported here. We briefly describe these differences and how they impact our research.

Psychological research typically identifies factors of interest and then systematically varies these while holding others constant. To date, most research on time and space in narrative used constructed narrative to ensure that factors of interest are varied appropriately and other factors are held constant. In our research, we did the same thing, but used natural narratives. For example, we identified a variable—such as the absence of a paragraph break before a subjective sentence in a continuing subjective context—and then selected passages from natural narrative that displayed this feature. We experimentally varied this feature by creating a version with a paragraph break inserted before the crucial sentence.

We then contrasted readers' responses to the two versions of these natural narrative passages, where the versions differed only in their display of that paragraph break. Differences between the responses to the versions were therefore attributed to the presence or absence of a paragraph break.

A disadvantage of natural narrative is that difference passages (in which the manipulation is embedded) are more likely to vary on a large number of other dimensions than is the case with constructed narrative. This may make it more difficult to obtain consistent and clear effects of a single manipulation, but we found effects by averaging over passages. The gain in using natural narrative is that results are closer to the way in which factors operate in the real world. In addition, natural narrative is more likely to include factors that researchers have not yet identified as relevant—providing opportunity for serendipitous discoveries.

Another difference between our approach and that of much other relevant research involves the nature of the response measures used. For example, Bower and Morrow (1990) used reaction time to measure access to information. They interpreted their measures to be an indication of what information is currently in the mental model. Although we, like Bower and Morrow (1990), used reaction time to infer the current contents of the DC and used reading time as a measure of comprehension difficulty (see Bruder, this volume), we did not limit ourselves to these measures. In our studies of POV, we are most interested in readers' interpretations of passages, so we directly probe these interpretations. Direct measures of the contents of a reader's mental model are appropriate when subjects have conscious access to that content. Indirect measures are required when subjects do not have such access or when there is a need to disguise the hypotheses or manipulations of interest. We feel it unlikely that subjects could determine what we are manipulating: Our natural materials are rich and varied and our manipulation is typically applied to one target sentence per passage.

The major difference between our approach to POV and that of Bower and Morrow, 1990, is our model of the WHO and POV. In addition to the focal WHO (i.e., the *protagonist* of Morrow, Greenspan, & Bower, 1987), our DC theory includes a focalizing WHO—the subjective character whose POV is being presented. Our model of narrative includes the readers' representation of both the objective story world and their representation of the belief spaces of characters. Our research, unlike that of Bower and his colleagues, focuses on the factors that indicate whether the sentences are objective or subjective.

THE PSYCHOLOGICAL EXPERIMENTS

General Description of Our Method

Two of the regularities that Wiebe (1990b) detected in narrative fiction that indicate POV are the presence of paragraph breaks and the presence of linguistic indicators of subjectivity. As indicated earlier, our research goal was to establish the psychological effects of these two discourse devices on a reader's rendering of POV for sentences in fictional narrative. In order to do this, we required sentence types that had the potential for alternative POV interpretations. Take, for example, the sentence "John was furious." This is a private-state sentence. A *private-state* is a psychological, perceptual, or experiential state and a *private-state sentence* is any sentence about a private-state. One interpretation of a private-state sentence is as a *private-state report*. A private-state report simply reports a character's private-state and is taken to be true in the fictional world. In that respect, it is similar to an objective sentence. (Wiebe's algorithm considers a private-state report to be a subjective sentence because such a sentence represents the consciousness of a character). What is relevant here is that the propositional content is taken to be true—John really was furious.

An alternative interpretation of such a private-state sentence is that of a *represented thought* or *represented perception* (Banfield's, 1982 terms). If it is Mary's belief that John was furious, the sentence represents Mary's belief about the private-state of John. That Mary holds the belief about John is taken to be true in the fictional world, but whether or not John is furious is uncertain.

We investigated the interpretations of such subjective sentences in fictional narrative as a function of the presence or absence of the discourse devices of interest.

All of our studies used between 6 and 10 passages from published novels that met the following criteria: (a) the passage had a sentence (the target sentence) of a type that allowed for alternative interpretations (such as a private-state sentence), (b) we could perform the manipulation of interest on that sentence (e.g., remove a paragraph break if that was the factor of interest), and (c) one of the potential alternative interpretations of the target sentence was as a represented thought of a character in the passage.

We drew conclusions about readers' interpretations of the POV of the sentences of interest by evaluating their acceptance of the truth of the propositional content of the sentence. That is, we asked the readers to indicate their agreement with test statements referring to that sentence. For our example above, "John was furious," our test statements would be: "John was furious" or "Mary believed that John was furious." The first type of test is simply a restatement of the propositional content. The second type of test taps into the represented thought interpretation of the passage sentence; we call this our represented thought test statement.

If readers interpret the target sentence as a represented thought, then they should agree more with the represented thought test statement than with the restatement. If readers interpret a sentence as a private-state report or an objective sentence, then they should be more in agreement with the restatement than with the represented thought test statement. For each passage sentence of interest we obtained a difference score reflecting the difference in the degree to which readers accepted each of the test sentences. We used these difference scores as our basic data in evaluating the POV interpretation for the target sentence as it appeared in the original version and after the manipulation was applied (the experimental version).

Of course, we did not have the same reader read both versions. Half the readers received the original version of a passage; the other half received the experimental version with the changed target sentence. Because we always used an equal number of passages to test each hypothesis, we also had each reader receive an equal number of original and experimental passages. This permitted us to compare a reader's average difference score for the original passages with an average difference score for the experimental passages. All our predictions refer to the outcome of this comparison. Specifically, we predict a shift away from the original version interpretation of POV (according to the algorithm) when we change the discourse device that supports this interpretation over an alternative one.

The Paragraph Break Studies

Three of the six studies reported here were directed toward paragraph breaks as discourse devices related to POV. A summary of the results of the studies is presented in Table 15.1. As indicated earlier, paragraph breaks are important devices in determining POV. According to Wiebe (1990b), shifts in POV from one character to another usually require a paragraph break. Of course, the presence of a paragraph break does not always indicate a shift in POV; this depends on the

TABLE 15.1
Summary of Studies

Study	Passages	Results for Predictions Tested
1	6	Presence of paragraph break related to shift in POV.
2	4	Insertion of paragraph break decreased represented thought interpretation for target, but not for subsequent subjective sentence.
	6	Removal of paragraph break increased represented thought interpretation for target sentence and decreased interpretation of subsequent subjective sentence as represented thought of experiencer.
3	4	Insertion decreased represented thought interpretation for target and subsequent subjective sentences.
	4	Removal of paragraph break did not significantly increase represented thought interpretation for target sentence, but did decrease interpretation of subsequent subjective sentence as a represented thought of experiencer.
4	8	Removal of subjective elements decreased represented thought interpretation of the target sentence.
5	8	Removal of subjective elements decreased represented thought interpretation of the target sentence.
6	8	Addition of subjective elements failed to increase represented thought interpretation.

TABLE 15.2

Sample Passages and Test Statements Testing Paragraph Break Manipulations

"Drown me?" Augustus said. "Why if anybody had tried it those girls would have clawed them to shreds." He knew Call was mad, but wasn't much inclined to humor him. It was his dinner table as much as Call's, and if Call didn't like the conversation he could go to bed.

Call knew there was no point in arguing.[a] That was what Augustus wanted: argument. He didn't really care what the question was, and it made no great difference to him which side he was on. He just plain loved to argue. (McMurtry, 1985, p. 161)

Test Statements:

Call felt that Augustus wanted an argument.

Augustus did want an argument.

In a panic, he shook her. "Lynette, it's me, Jeremy. Wake up now!"

At first she was rigid. Then she turned around and dug her sharp-boned little face into his shoulder. She shook with sobs. Jeremy didn't know how to stop them or even if he should try to. He just sat getting wet from her hot tears. Anxiously he waited. She felt fragile in his arms as if anything at all might break her.

The flames sank away. Only the flowing red treasure heap of embers was left and the cold mist at his back and the sense of being in a land with no familiar landmarks in the dark.[b] How could she not know her mother was dead? She had to know it. (Adler, 1987, p. 45)

Test Statements:

Jeremy wondered how Lynette could not have known her mother was dead.

Lynette wondered how she could not know her mother was dead.

Jeremy felt Lynette had known about her mother's death subconsciously.

Lynette felt she had known about her mother's death subconsciously.

[a]The experimental version moved the first paragraph break from in front of "Call" to insert it before "That was . . .".

[b]The experimental version added a paragraph break before "How could she . . .".

context and other sentence features. Here, we briefly describe the materials, subjects, and results for these three studies.

Study 1. Our initial study (Bruder & Wiebe, 1990b), used six passages from various novels cited by Wiebe (1990b). These included *Lonesome Dove* (McMurtry, 1985), *No One Hears But Him* (Caldwell, 1966), and *The Magic of the Glits* (Adler, 1987). Sample passages with their corresponding test statements are shown in Table 15.2. For four of the six passages, the manipulation involved paragraph breaks. We focus our discussion on this discourse device. In these four passages, we introduced a paragraph break before a private-state sentence that was a represented thought in the original version, according to the algorithm. We predicted that introducing a paragraph break would decrease the readers' tendencies to render a represented thought interpretation. In two of the passages, however, the break inserted was actually moved from in front of a prior sentence in order to avoid having single sentence paragraphs. (See the first sample passage in Table 15.2). Because this resulted in the removal of a paragraph break before another private-state sentence, we included the effects of removal in our data.

The prediction for this situation was an increase in the readers' tendencies to render a represented thought interpretation.

Because of the small number of tests of each prediction, we combined the data in a manner that permitted a single test of paragraph break effects.

The subjects (readers) were 44 introductory psychology students who participated in the study for laboratory credit. Subjects were run in groups of about 10 and were allowed to take as much time as they wished. The instructions emphasized there were no right or wrong answers, and that we were interested in their impression or understanding of the passages. On each page of the test booklet was one passage followed by the test statements. Subjects were told to circle a number from *strongly disagree* 1 to *strongly agree* 6 to indicate whether or not they agreed with each test statement.

We found a statistically significant effect of paragraph break manipulations in the directions predicted. This provides support for the validity of the paragraph break discourse device as an influence on POV.

Study 2. In our next study (Bruder & Wiebe, 1990a), we included enough passages to separately evaluate the effects of paragraph break insertion and removal on private-state sentences. We also expanded our examination of subjective sentences beyond the target sentence we focused on in study 1.

This study used 10 passages, all from McMurtry (1985), none of which had been used in study 1. Because of the need to have even numbers of passages for each hypothesis tested, we used four passages to test paragraph break insertion and six to test paragraph break removal. We also included in this study a test of the POV taken in a subjective sentence immediately following the target private-state sentence. According to the algorithm, the subjective character of a private-state sentence is the subjective character of a subsequent subjective sentence if no paragraph break or objective sentence has intervened. Testing the subjective character of such a subsequent subjective sentence provided additional evidence about the interpretation of the manipulated private-state sentence. Finally, we included a few tests to check whether or not the POV of a character was established prior to the private-state sentence. All passages had to conform to the following requirements: (a) a subjective sentence (S1) with a subjective character occurred early in the passage; (b) later, the passage had a private-state sentence (S2) with an experiencer of the private state who was not the subjective character of the S1 sentence; and (c) still later, the passage had at least one subjective sentence (S3).

Following each passage, we had paired test statements for all of the subjective sentences of interest in that passage.

The subjects were 101 male introductory psychology students who participated for laboratory credit. The procedures followed were similar to those in study 1.

As in all our studies, the results are based on the basic data of differences in agreement scores for the paired test statements. We discuss the results for each type of subjective sentence and each type of manipulation.

The subjective sentences (S1) prior to the private-state sentence (S2) did not differ across the versions of passages, and we looked at these only to confirm that subjects were establishing the POV of a character before the target private-state sentence. However, we were unable to do so because the difference scores actually indicated a slight tendency for subjects to agree more with the restatement than the represented thought statement. Because subjects were consistent in this tendency across passages, we suspected it reflected a response bias. The response biases were not equally distributed across subjects. The main use we made of these S1 difference scores was as covariates to neutralize individual differences in response bias for the examination of S2 and S3 scores.

The introduction of a paragraph break significantly decreased the represented thought interpretation of the S2 sentence, as predicted. In the subsequent subjective sentences the tendency to continue a subjective character's POV seemed weak and no significant effect of the break was obtained.

The deletion of paragraph breaks had a significant effect on both the private-state sentence (S2) and the subsequent subjective sentence (S3) in the directions predicted. Experimental removal of a paragraph break decreased the readers' tendency to interpret the private-state sentence (S2) as a private-state report and made it less likely that subsequent subjective sentences would be interpreted as reflecting the POV of the experiencer of the S2 sentence.

The evidence from these studies generally supported the importance of paragraph breaks in interpreting POV. But there were two issues we felt we needed to address in our final paragraph break study of this series. We briefly describe study 3 with our main focus on these two issues—one concerning the type of subjects, and the other, the wording of our test statements.

Study 3.   We were concerned that the wording of one of our test statements in previous studies may have influenced the subjects' responses to the other. That is, the use of words such as "believed" in our represented thought test statement may have implied that the propositional content of the target sentence was in doubt. We decided to test this by adding an additional manipulation to our materials. For half of the passages, we used the nonfactive verbs (e.g., "believed," "felt") we used in the previous studies. For the other half of the passages, we used factive verbs (e.g., "was aware," "knew"). In our analyses, we could therefore compare the effects of our paragraph break manipulations when we used factive verbs, to the effects when nonfactive verbs were used.

The second concern was that the mean difference scores in study 2 did not clearly indicate a represented thought interpretation when they were predicted to do so. We suspected a response bias to agree with restatements. We did not have this response bias problem in study 1 (and both studies showed the predicted paragraph break effects). We therefore looked for a difference between these two studies that was not related to our manipulations. One obvious difference between the studies was the fact that study 2 had only male subjects. Male readers might show more of a response bias than female subjects. Therefore, in the third study, we used approximately the same number of male and female subjects so that we could evaluate the bias and determine whether or not it was related to our manipulation.

This study used eight passages from *Lonesome Dove* (McMurtry, 1985) that were used in either study 1 or study 2. Four of the passages were used to test paragraph break insertion and four were used to test paragraph break removal. As in study 2, we tested S1, S2, and S3 sentences. The subjects were 62 male and 64 female introductory psychology students who participated for laboratory credit. The procedure was the same as in studies 1 and 2.

When we looked at the S1 sentences, we did find that males showed a bias toward accepting restatements, whereas females showed no consistent preference for either test statement. In this study, subjects were less consistent in their S1 scores and we did not feel the need to use them as covariates for our tests of S2 and S3 sentences.

Males had significantly more response bias than females in the tests of paragraph break insertion. However, there were no significant differences between males and females in the effects of that manipulation. Paragraph break insertion significantly decreased the represented thought interpretation of the private-state sentence (S2) immediately following the break. However, a similar effect on the subsequent subjective sentence, S3, only approached significance.

When paragraph breaks were removed, we predicted a shift away from the private-state report interpretation (which was assigned by the algorithm to the original version of S2). Because the interpretation would favor the restatement, we were not certain whether or not a gender-related response bias would be evident, and it was not. The effect of removing paragraph breaks was in the predicted direction, but it was not significant for the private-state sentence. The prediction for the S3 sentence was somewhat more complex. If the S2 sentence was a private-state report, then the experiencer of S2 was the subjective character and a subsequent subjective sentence should have that experiencer as the subjective character. However, if removing the paragraph break shifts the reader toward a represented thought interpretation, then the subjective character of S2 and of S3 should not be the experiencer of S2. The subjective character of S2 and S3 should be whoever was the subjective character of the sentence prior to S2. The test of this prediction was the only case in which we contrasted two represented thought statements, one for the experiencer of S2, and the other for the previous subjective character. We expected no bias toward a restatement when none was involved in the comparison, and we found none when we looked for differences between males and females. We did find, as predicted, that the removal of paragraph breaks significantly decreased the likelihood that the reader would select the experiencer of S2 over the previous subjective character as the subjective character of S3.

There were no significant differences due to the use of factive versus nonfactive verbs for either paragraph break insertion or paragraph break removal passages.

Subjective Element Experiments

Along with the studies on paragraph breaks, we also conducted three studies in which we manipulated the discourse device of potential subjective elements and examined the effects on the interpretation of the target sentence containing that manipulation. We briefly describe these studies, but first need to point out some minor differences in these studies compared with the paragraph break studies. First, the sentences undergoing manipulation of subjective elements were not all private-state sentences. Second, we only tested the subjective sentence that contained our manipulation—we did not test subsequent subjective sentences.

Study 4. In our first study in the series, we required passages that contained subjective sentences with potential subjective elements that were subjective in that context. We selected eight such passages from *Lonesome Dove* (McMurtry, 1985). We removed one or two subjective elements from a single such target sentence in each of the passages and tested whether or not this would decrease the tendency to interpret the sentences as represented thoughts of a subjective character. The elements removed from the various passages included: attitude adverbials ("surely," "much less"), shifted past tense, habituals ("often," "always"), as modifier ("as willful as a child"), perceptual term ("nowhere in sight"), or a quantifier ("much"). Following each passage there were paired test statements referring to the target sentence. As in previous studies, these pairs included one restatement and one represented thought test statement.

The subjects were 22 male and 19 female introductory psychology students who participated for laboratory credit. The procedure followed was similar to that in the previous three studies.

In this study, there were no significant differences between male and female subjects. In spite of the small number of subjects used in this study, removing subjective elements significantly decreased the tendency for readers to render a represented thought interpretation.

Study 5. This study served as a replication of study 4 with different passages, subjects, and subjective elements removed.

We selected a set of eight passages from McMurtry (1985) that met the criteria stipulated for study 4, but had not been used in that study. Although the specific subjective elements removed differed considerably from those in study 4, there was partial overlap in the type of element removed. We removed the following elements: attitude adverbials, attitude adjectives, shifted past tense, intensifier subjunct, and content subjunct. (There were some additional conditions in this second study that are not described here.) As in study 4, the test statements following each passage included a restatement and a represented thought statement referring to the target sentence that contained the manipulation. A sample passage is shown in Table 15.3.

TABLE 15.3

Sample Passage and Test Statements Testing the Removal of Subjective
Elements (subjective element underlined, experimental version in brackets)

"I wish they'd talk, so we'd know what they were thinking," Sean said. The silent Spettles made him nervous.

Call was annoyed with Gus, who had still not returned. Pea had reported seeing him just after dawn, riding east in evident health. Call noticed the Texas bull, standing about fifty yards away. He was watching the two pigs [He watched the two pigs], who were rooting around a chaparral bush. Probably they were trying to root out a ground squirrel, or perhaps a rattlesnake. The bull took a few steps toward them, but the pigs ignored him.

Needle Nelson was scared of the bull. The minute he noticed him he went to get his rifle out of his saddle scabbard. (McMurtry, 1985, p. 291)

Test Statements:
The bull watched the two pigs.
Call noticed that the bull watched the two pigs.

The subjects were 49 male and 48 female introductory psychology students who participated for laboratory credit. The procedures were the same as in study 4.

As in study 4, there were no significant differences between male and female subjects in the effects of the manipulation. Removing the subjective elements significantly decreased the tendency to render the represented thought interpretation of the target sentence.

Study 6. As with our paragraph break research, we felt it important to test the role of subjective elements by adding them to sentences, as well as by removing them. We therefore needed to find passages with target sentences without such subjective elements, and add them to these sentences. Our prediction was that adding subjective elements would decrease the tendency to interpret such sentences as objective sentences or private-state reports.

Using passages that had been submitted to the algorithm for other purposes, we were able to find six with a target statement that was "not subjective" according to the algorithm, and a seventh that was a private-state report. For methodological reasons, we required an even number of passages and, in order to accomplish this, we selected an eighth passage in which the target statement was a represented thought due to the context. Even though the sentence was already a represented thought according to the algorithm, the addition of a subjective element might increase readers' tendencies to interpret this sentence as a represented thought.

The subjective elements added to the target sentence were varied, including content disjuncts ("evidently," "apparently," "fortunately"), attitude and evaluate adjective ("poor," "curious"), tense shifts and focusing subjuncts ("just"). Some passages had a single element added, some had two. An example passage is shown in Table 15.4.

The subjects were 48 male and 48 female introductory psychology students who participated for laboratory credit. The procedure was the same as in the prior studies.

TABLE 15.4
Sample Passage and Test Statements Testing the Addition
of Subjective Elements

Jake was tolerant of the cowboys but careful to keep himself a bit apart from them. He never chimed in when they talked about the life they would have on the trail, and he never spoke to Lorena about the fact that the herd would be leaving in ten days. He didn't work much on the branding, either, though once in a while he spent a night helping them gather more stock. Mostly he let it appear that the drive had nothing to do with him.

Fortunately Lorena wasn't pressing [didn't press] him, but she kept an eye on him. If he wanted to stay, that was one thing, but if he planned on going he was going to have to figure out a way to take her. (McMurtry, 1985, p. 187)

Test Statements:
Lorena kept an eye on Jake.
Jake felt that Lorena kept an eye on him.

Note.   Subjective elements underlined; original version in brackets.

As in the previous studies examining subjective elements, there was no significant difference between male and female subjects. Although the trend was in the predicted direction, it was not statistically significant. We have not tried to repeat study 6 with new passages. At this point, we cannot claim support for the prediction that the introduction of subjective elements will influence subjects toward a represented thought interpretation of sentences that would otherwise be interpreted as factual (objective or private-state reports).

CONCLUSION

We believe our research provides considerable support for the importance of two regularities, paragraph breaks and subjective elements, in determining POV in narrative. This validates Wiebe's selection of such regularities and her incorporation of these into her algorithm for recognizing subjective sentences and identifying the subjective character. Of course, we have only tested the psychological validity of these regularities; we have not yet evaluated the algorithm's behavior as a simulation of human behavior.

At this point, we should also point out a major difference between the paragraph break and subjective element studies that has implications for the generality of the conclusions drawn. The paragraph break studies have one regularity manipulated; the subjective element studies involve a number of different types and tokens of manipulated subjective elements. Our results reflect an averaging across passages (as well as subjects) and do not provide support for individual subjective elements. Nor can they be used to evaluate different classes of subjective elements. Finally, there are also a number of subjective element types and tokens selected by Wiebe that we have not yet tested.

A final word on the variability across passages and subjects is appropriate. In all of our studies, we gave different versions (original or experimental) of the same passages to different subjects. The effects of our manipulations are not quantitatively equivalent across the passages. This probably reflects differences in subjects and in passages. We assume that, in natural narrative, numerous cues converge to signal POV. When we manipulate just one, albeit a major one, it may not always lead to a clear shift in POV. We leave it to future research to investigate the variations among passages and subjects, as well as the types of subjective elements, and to incorporate the findings into the algorithm and into our theory of narrative understanding. In order to generalize our findings, it is also crucial that we replicate our findings with other passages from different books and genres.

In spite of these qualifications, we see our results as providing significant support for the algorithm with regard to the two discourse devices—paragraph breaks and subjective elements—that it uses (along with other information) to recognize subjective sentences and to identify their subjective characters in fictional narrative.

ACKNOWLEDGMENTS

Much of the research described in this chapter was supported in part by The National Science Foundation under Grant No. IRI–8610517.

EXTENSIONS OF DEICTIC THEORY

16

Expanding the Traditional Category of Deictic Elements: Interjections as Deictics

David P. Wilkins
Max Planck Institute for Psycholinguistics, Nijmegen

PROLOGUE

The bulk of this chapter is an abridged and re-edited version of an earlier paper (Wilkins, 1992).[1] The primary purpose of that paper and, hence, this chapter is to argue that the traditional American linguistic view of deictic elements must be expanded to embrace interjections alongside the more standard members such as pronouns and demonstratives. To rescue interjections from the periphery of linguistic concerns requires a demonstration of two points: (a) that interjections share specific linguistic and communicative properties with more standard deictic elements, and (b) that it is possible to render a convincing account of the semantic structure and pragmatic usage of interjections. Through this prologue and the epilogue, I attempt to expand this argument, and extend the demonstration of the two forementioned points by tying interjections in with the narrative and deictic center concerns that form the focus of this book, but that were not explicitly covered in the original paper.

It is, in fact, a narrative concern that first drew my attention to interjections as an interesting lexical class. In dealing with oral narratives in Mparntwe Ar-

---

[1]The original was abridged in the following way. The introductory abstract was removed. A section entitled *Interjections and speech acts* was cut altogether, with only the most basic argument concerning the illocutionary purpose of interjections being preserved and placed here in a newly created section. A discussion of the phonology of interjections was cut, a discussion of forms that function both as interjections and as particles of other types was taken out, and the vast majority of the original 25 footnotes were excised.

rernte, a Pama-Nyungan Australian language spoken in Central Australia, I found that it was frequently the case that the transition between the narrative and a direct quotation went unmarked. No verb of saying or thinking occurred, and the narrator did not overtly identify the reported speaker. This lack of overt transition can be related, in part, to the fact that Australian languages do not make a strong distinction between direct and indirect discourse (cf. Rumsey, 1990). However, what interested me was that the first word in such a direct quotation was frequently an interjection. Indeed, except for meta-comments by a narrator, interjections only occur in direct discourse, and often at the initial boundary of the reported utterance. As a very simple example, consider the following excerpt from a short hunting narrative:

> **Ikwerenge arrerne-lhe-ty.alpe-rlenge,**   **lyeke-le**
> after.that   put-REFL-go.back.and.do.-dif.subj(when), thorn-ERG
> **atnilhe tanthe-ke. "Yekaye!" Kemirre-mele**
> bottom spear-past   ouch!   get.up-same.subj(when)
> **anteme re   tne-ke.**
> now   s/he stand-past
> *After that, when he got back and sat down, a thorn stuck into (his) bum. "Ouch!"*
> *(he cried). Then he got up and stood (there).*

Here, the only word in the direct quotation is the interjection "Yekaye!" that can be glossed variously as "ouch, wow, gee." There is nothing in the Arrernte like a "he cried" or "he screamed," that seems to be required in a natural English translation. As it comes from an oral narrative, the narrator's intonation tells us unambiguously that it is the character's wording that is expressed, not the narrator's. Thus, we momentarily shift from the perspective and deictic center of the narrator into the immediate, unpleasant, subjective experience of one of the characters of the narrative. That entails an understanding of the unique properties of that speaker's deictic center perspective.

It is not my intention to suggest that this property of Arrernte narrative is exotic—quite the contrary. For instance, Haberland (1986) noted that cases of direct speech occur in Danish that also lack any introductory verb. He noted that "[t]he lack of need of a speech act describing verb is obviously connected with the fact that, in spoken language, direct speech is always displayed," and so, "[i]t is only in 'texts' that a verb of saying achieves its real importance in structuring the dialogue reported" (p. 247). More important for this chapter, however, is the fact that it is widely known in the literature on direct and indirect discourse that "interjections are most suitable for evoking direct speech acts" (Fónagy, 1986, p. 287) and, "interjections and expressions with purely conversational functions have to be omitted in any indirect quotation" (Kiefer, 1986, p. 211).

This correspondence between interjections and direct quotation is easily demonstrated for English. A search through Carroll's (1971) *Alice's Adventures in Wonderland* for that ubiquitous interjection "Oh!" (including interjectional phrases containing "Oh," such as "Oh dear!") reveal 45 instances, all of which occur in direct quotations of speech or thought. Indeed, on the very first page of the text the first spoken words are those of the White Rabbit saying to himself, "Oh dear! Oh dear! I shall be too late!" Of these 45 instances, 23 have "Oh" as the first element in the direct quote, and of these 23 quotes, 10 follow immediately from narrative text and 13 mark shifts in conversational turntaking. So, although Carroll was careful to include all his "saying" and "thinking" verbs to tie the direct quotation to the reported speaker, "Oh!" is quite an effective marker of direct quotation, and a way of indicating a shift from narrator's perspective to character's perspective, or from one character's perspective to another's.

Thus, in the context of this volume, it is possible to see this chapter as contributing to a better understanding of one set of linguistic elements (i.e., interjections) that signal a shift in cognitive stance to that of the more subjective and immediate experience of one of the characters. Critical to the analysis is a recognition of the particular deictic properties of interjections. In the epilogue, we return to a more direct demonstration of how interjections function in narrative.

INTRODUCTION

It is common to treat interjections as peripheral to the real concerns of linguistics. Indeed, it is even common to treat interjections as though they were outside of the concerns of linguistics altogether—placed, so to speak, into that wastebasket labelled *paralinguistic phenomena*. Given the dubious reputation interjections have acquired, it may be useful to begin by briefly pointing out how research into this "decorative edging to the ample, complex fabric" (Sapir, 1921, p. 6) is relevant to theoretical research in semantics, pragmatics, morphosyntax, and historical linguistics.

What Does Studying Interjections Have to Do With Issues Central to Linguistics?

As far as semantics is concerned, it has frequently been claimed that interjections are devoid of any real semantic content and have no inherent conceptual structure (see, e.g., Leech, 1981). In this view, interjections merely invoke associative interpretations through pragmatic rules (Erman, 1987; Levinson, 1983). Such claims were typically made in the absence of any attempt to fully characterize the interpretation and functions of particular interjections. It is, therefore, important to examine this claim closely and explicate precisely any semantic content that interjections may possess. I contend that interjections are semantically rich and have a definite conceptual structure that can be explicated (cf. Ameka, 1992a). In identifying the semantic structure of interjections, a contribution is made to theories of lexical semantics in general, and theories of meaning in particular. Of course, to support the claim that interjections have a rich semantic structure, the class of items to be investigated must be clearly defined. As such, the reader must be forewarned that this chapter proposes a definition of interjection that, to some, may seem unorthodox, because it does not adhere to the widely held notion that "[i]nterjections are purely emotive words which have no referential content" (Quirk, Greenbaum, Leech, & Svartik, 1972, p. 413).

One of the current, key problems in pragmatics is defining exactly where the boundary between pragmatics and semantics falls (see for instance Verschueren, 1987). The two most extreme positions are that (a) there is no (linguistic) semantics, there is only (linguistic) pragmatics (the "radical pragmatics" approach, cf. Cole, 1981; Levinson, 1983), and (b) there is no (linguistic) pragmatics, only (linguistic) semantics (the "radical semantics" approach, cf. Wierzbicka, 1987a).[2] The truth almost certainly lies somewhere between these extremes; however, it is only through detailed studies of linguistic phenomena that require both a semantic and pragmatic account, such as interjections, that the exact interaction between linguistic semantics and linguistic pragmatics will be understood.

If it is accepted that interjections are simultaneously lexemes and utterances, then many interesting questions are raised for theories of grammar, more particularly theories of morphology and syntax. For instance, how does an element of the lexicon become instantiated as a complete utterance? Further, how does the grammar treat utterances that are both verbless and nounless (given that interjections are neither nouns nor verbs)? Indeed, one may argue that most syntactic theories are not concerned with *utterances* (i.e., real-world "etic" productions), but are concerned, instead, with *sentences* (i.e., abstract "emic" structures produced by the grammar). For such theories, there still remains the question of the nature of the relationship between sentences and utterances, and this leaves the need to account for the relationship between interjections as utterances, and the morphosyntactic component of a grammar that is concerned with producing sentences. More specifically, can a grammar have as part of its lexicon elements that are never instantiated as part of sentences (i.e., abstract units), but are only instantiated as, or as part of, utterances (i.e., real-world, contextualized units)?

As noted later, interjections often develop out of more standard parts of speech, such as verbs (*fuck*; *welcome*; *damn*) and nouns (*rats*; *Christ*; *shit*), that are clearly part of the lexicon. If one were to argue that such interjections are outside of the lexicon, or even outside of language, then one would need to account for the historical shift from sign within the central lexicon to sign beyond the lexicon. In fact, a detailed study of the origins of interjections would give indications of (a) the nature of relations between elements within the lexicon, (b) types of

---

[2]I placed square brackets around the word *linguistic* because theories and approaches to semantics and pragmatics may differ on the question of whether they are concerned with explaining linguistic phenomena only, or whether they are also concerned with explaining nonlinguistic semiotic behavior.

morphology associated with certain pragmatic functions, and (c) the nature of constraints on semantic and pragmatic change.

In the previous discussion, I tried to indicate some of the crucial questions that interjections pose for linguistic theory at all levels. It would appear that it is precisely because interjections are a peripheral phenomenon that they throw up issues that strike at the heart of widely held assumptions current within linguistics. Linguistics must not only define its core, it must also define its periphery in an unambiguous and motivated way, and only after that is done may it proceed to provide an account that works not only for the core phenomena, but also for the peripheral phenomena. At the very least, I hoped to demonstrate why studies of interjections should be taken seriously. This done, I am in a position to address the specific concerns central to this chapter.

Overview of the Chapter

There are many issues a chapter on interjections could profitably address; however, I restrict myself to an investigation of some of the semantic and pragmatic features of interjections. I start by providing and justifying the definition of *interjection* used throughout this chapter. An uncontroversial observation is that interjections are both lexemes and utterances. I continue by examining the semantic and pragmatic consequences of being simultaneously an utterance and a lexeme. I observe that we can account for the context bound nature of interjections by observing that their semantic structure must include basic deictic elements. As a consequence of this observation, I conclude that (a) interjections are a subtype of deixis and (b) the semantic structure of certain linguistic items must provide a means by which pragmatic rules can map the item into context in order to gain a complete interpretation.

THE DEFINITION OF INTERJECTION

There are a number of approaches that one could take in identifying a class of elements that may be labelled *interjections*, and each distinct approach is likely to yield a slightly different set of forms. Interjections may, for instance, be defined using formal (i.e., structural) criteria, or semantic or pragmatic criteria, or some combination of these three. The advantage of using only one type of criteria to identify interjections, rather than using a combination, is that such a procedure allows the investigator to examine whether or not the set of elements thus defined also manifests other regular features describable in terms of the other two domains (i.e., the domains that did not supply the criteria for the identification of the forms). For instance, if interjection is defined using semantic criteria, it is then possible to investigate whether or not the forms identified on semantic grounds also share structural and/or pragmatic features. Because I am particularly interested in the question of whether or not elements identified on the basis of formal criteria tend to share semantic and pragmatic traits, I have chosen to define interjection in formal (i.e., structural) terms. The following, therefore, represents a preliminary attempt at a formal definition of interjection, and it is this sense of interjection that is to be understood throughout this chapter.

(1) *Interjection:* A conventional lexical form that (commonly and) conventionally constitutes an utterance on its own, (typically) does not enter into construction with other word classes, is (usually) monomorphemic, and (generally) does not host inflectional or derivational morphemes.

A few comments concerning this definition of *interjection* are in order. First, I use *conventional lexical form* to indicate that interjections have a fixed and largely arbitrary phonological/phonetic/visual shape known to the majority of members of the speech community within which the interjection is found. On perceiving this form, that group is able to interpret its sense. Second, although all words are conventional in the sense just indicated, they do not conventionally constitute an utterance on their own. That is to say, whereas, for instance, the word *black* may constitute an utterance on its own in answer to the question, "What color was her car?", *black* is not commonly used as an utterance on its own and it is not a word that English speakers think of as one they could use as an utterance without any preceding linguistic context (cf. Ameka, 1992b). In other words, to be an interjection is to be a sign that speakers conventionalize as an utterance. Third, note that, without the hedges, the definition in (1) identifies the clearest members of the interjection class. Roughly, this corresponds to Ameka's (1992b) and Wierzbicka's (1992) notion of "primary interjection," at least as far as the formal criteria they accept are concerned. With the hedges, this definition casts a wider net and catches elements that were called "secondary interjections" by Bloomfield (1933), and "interjectional phrases" and "complex interjections" by Ameka (1992b). The crucial claim I make is that all elements identified by the broader definition, regardless of apparent surface complexity, head an entry in the lexicon. The hedges are added in recognition of the fact that (a) a conventional lexical form may have other uses besides its use as an interjection (e.g., God); (b) phrases may become conventionally fixed and used as interjections (e.g., "Bloody hell!", "Thank you."); and (c) it is not always clear whether, for instance, interjections in certain languages host imperative and/or vocative inflections or whether these inflections are fixed as part of the interjectional form.

Given that the proposed definition of interjection is meant to be based on formal criteria, I clearly avoid any mention of the semantic or pragmatic functions of interjections. Thus, I avoid the common claim that interjections are purely emotive. Similarly, I avoid Wierzbicka's (1992, p. 165) claim that interjections refer "to the speaker's current mental state or mental act," and Ameka's (1992b, p. 106) similar claim that interjections "express a speaker's mental state, action or attitude or reaction to a situation." Although the semantic and pragmatic functions shared by interjections are open to empirical investigation, the notion that interjections make reference to the speaker's (current) mental state is a natural consequence of the formal requirement that an interjection constitutes an utterance on its own. In most theories of speech acts, all utterances convey something about the speaker's mental state, inasmuch as they convey the assumption(s) the speaker makes, and the intention(s) the speaker encodes through an utterance composed of conventional signs. This point is elaborated later.

In the definition of interjections given above, the observation is made that they (generally) do not host inflectional or derivational morphemes. This criterion is often used to identify the class of particles in a language, and would suggest that, on formal grounds, interjections are typically a subclass of particles (cf. Laughren, 1982). This has led, in some areas, to confusion between what counts as a particle and what counts as an interjection. James (1972, 1973a, 1973b)—who championed the cause of interjections, arguing that "they are semantically quite complex" (1973b, p. iii), and remarking on the absurdity of the claim that interjections are simply expressions of emotion (1973b, p. 5)—dealt with a number of forms that are not interjections in terms of the definition given here, but are, instead, part of the broader class of particles. Thus, forms like *well* (as in *Well, what do we have here?*) and *say* (as in *Say, Mona lives on Forrest Street!* or *Suppose Mona lived, say, on Forrest street* [James, 1973b, p. 9]), treated by James as interjections, are not classed here as such precisely because they do not conventionally occur as utterances on their own. Indeed, James' (1973b) distinction between "sentence-initial interjections" and "sentence-internal interjections" makes no sense within the present characterization of interjections.

INTERJECTIONS AS LEXEMES AND UTTERANCES

As indicated previously, the unique formal feature of interjections is that they are simultaneously lexemes and utterances. Although this has long been recognized, the semantic and pragmatic consequences of this observation have remained largely unexplored. Among other things, interjections should both be described and subclassified in the same manner as other lexemes, as well as being described and subclassified in the same manner as other utterances. Because one of the central aims of this paper is to explore some of the conditions under which a lexeme may constitute a whole utterance, I begin this discussion by examining interjections as utterances.

Interjections as Utterances

Sapir (1921, pp. 6–7) said interjections were "the nearest of all language sounds to instinctive utterance," and Bloomfield (1933, p. 176) classified interjections among the "minor sentences." In recognizing interjections as utterances (or sentences) there must be an attendant claim that, like all utterances, they convey a complete proposition about the world within the given context of the utterance. Given the view that a complete proposition requires both a predication and one or more referential arguments for which the predication holds true, then interjections must, in some way, both predicate and refer. As utterances/sentences, interjections are regarded as "primitive," "instinctive," or "minor" primarily because they "do not consist of a favorite sentence-form" (Bloomfield, 1933, p. 176). That is to say, the fact that they are highly reduced in form, being limited to a single lexeme, and the fact that they contain neither a verb (the canonical predicating element) nor a noun (the canonical referring element) means they are definitely odd utterances/sentences, at least from the point of view of theories that take as their starting point the idea that there is such a thing as a normal sentence that consists minimally of an NP (which minimally contains a noun) functioning as subject, and a VP (which minimally contains a verb), functioning as predicate.

The implication of the observations in the preceding paragraph is that, if interjections are utterances, we must state how interjections both predicate and refer. In a brief, but informative, discussion of minor sentence types and the semiotic structure of discourse, Weinreich (1980, p. 68) noted that the solution to the "old and treacherous problem of minor sentence types and impersonal verbs" rests on "a conscientious separation of semantic and grammatical criteria." More particularly, he pointed out that we should revise the general logical view that requires the semantic structure of a proposition to be of the form "$f(x,y)$," allowing propositions to be of the form "$f(,)$," "$f(x,\_)$," or "$(x,\ )$," and that we should also revise the notions that each element of semantic structure should correspond to an element of syntactic structure, and that each element of syntactic structure should correspond to an element of semantic structure. Thus, although in English *It rained.* has an element in subject position, Weinreich argued that it does not correspond to anything in semantic structure and, semantically, the predication is of the type "$f(,)$." In this way he made sense of the notion "dummy subject" and allowed for the cross-linguistic comparison of argumentless predications. This is relevant to our discussion, because it does not rule out the possibility that, semantically, interjections are complete predications of the form "$f(x,y)$," even if there is not a distinct element in syntax that corresponds to each of the elements of semantic structure. Weinreich (1980) also compared the descriptions of elliptical sentences, interjections, and stunted propositions. Importantly, he recognized that arguments of semantic structure that do not appear in surface syntax can be identified and filled by discourse-deixis (p. 69).

At this point it is useful to make the common observation that the size of an utterance (i.e., the number of morphemes an utterance contains) is inversely proportional to the amount of information that is recoverable from context. This observation governs ellipsis, the form of imperatives, the reduction of full NPs to pronouns and of pronouns to zero anaphors as referents are tracked through discourse, and so on. Thus, for example, where the question *What color is her car?* could simply be answered by the sentence *Black.*, we find an instance of an elliptical utterance. Here, the answer to the question is dependent on the fact that the question is a full source sentence and contextually provides the elements that are ellipsed from the answer (i.e., "her car," "is," and "color"). Ellipsis, then, is characterized by the fact that there are elements understood within the semantic structure of the elliptical utterance that are not present in the surface structure, but are recoverable from some other linguistic structure in the discourse context. There are also cases where it is the extralinguistic context that provides the semantically/pragmatically understood element missing from the utterance. For instance, it is cross-linguistically common for imperative sentences to have a conventionally more reduced structure in comparison to declarative sentences and interrogative sentences in the same language (cf. Givon, 1979). With respect to imperatives, Sadock and Zwicky (1985, p. 173) observed that:

> Languages regularly suppress subject pronouns and/or affixes that agree with the subject, at least in some parts of the imperative paradigm. Especially interesting is the fact that personal suffixes are frequently absent, even in languages that quite strictly mark features of the subject on the main verb.

The lack of morphemes referring to the subject in imperatives may be explained by noting that imperatives have a predictable subject, the addressee, that is supplied by extralinguistic context. That is to say, the semantic structure of imperatives conventionally codes that an addressee is the performer of the verb action and, pragmatically, the actual filler of this role (i.e, the referent) is to be provided by the extralinguistic context. That this is conventionally coded in the semantic structure of, and pragmatic constraints on, imperatives is iconically reflected in the lack of surface syntactic elements to code a fully predictable subject. Interjections are the most reduced form an utterance can possibly take, unless one allows silence to constitute an utterance, and my claim is that interjections, like imperatives, have arguments provided by extralinguistic context. The motivation for such reduction can be found in Grice's (1975) "maxim of quantity," and Haiman's (1985) concept of "economic motivation," which suggest that what is familiar, predictable, and common will be given a reduced expression.

The step from imperatives to interjections may be taken by noting that certain types of interjection often find their source in imperative verbs. In Mparntwe Arrernte, the interjections "Me!" (take this!) and "Ngke!" (give that here!) have no cognate forms in the language, but are cognate with the Warlpiri imperative form of the verbs for "take" "*Ma*-nta!" (take it, and give) "Yu-*ngka*!" (give it here), respectively. These Mparntwe Arrernte interjections only occur with the intonation pattern given to imperative sentences in the language. Thus, like utterances, and unlike lexemes, interjections may be associated with a characteristic intonation pattern. As the source of both of these interjections is a transitive verb, it is reasonable to ask whether, and how, the underlying object argument is to be identified from the interjection. Once again the entity to be taken or given is understood from the extralinguistic context. Both "Me!" (take this!) and "Ngke!" (give that here!) always occur with accompanying deictic gestures that indicate the object in question. A person will hold an object out toward a person and say "Me!" (take this!), and a person will point to an object (with finger, lips, nod of head, or eyes) and say "Ngke!" (give that here!). There are also three interjections in Mparntwe Arrernte that are overtly related to verbs in the imperative. The emphatic imperative forms of "impe-" (to leave X behind), "lhe-" (to move/go away), and "are-" (to see, to look) are equivalent in form to "Impaye!" (leave it alone), "Alhaye!" (go away), "Araye!" (have a look!). The reasons for claiming these forms are interjections rather than regularly inflected forms of the corresponding verbs are three-fold: (a) they are used with such high frequency as utterances on their own that they have become conventionalized as such; (b) children tend to learn these interjectional forms before learning the verbs on which they would be based, a fact that is not true of the emphatic imperative forms of other verbs, and probably correlates with their high frequency of use (especially to children); and (c) these forms, like the two interjections mentioned previously, are conventionally associated with nonvocal gestures, that is not the case as far as the emphatic imperative forms of other verbs are concerned. Examples from English of interjections and interjectional phrases that arise from the imperative form of verbs are "Damn!," "Dammit!," "Fuck!," "Fuck off!," "Look out!," and "Hold on!." Similarly, in Spanish, the imperative form of *andar* (to go, to walk; to move) is the source for the interjections "¡Anda!" and "¡Ándale!," both of which mean (hurry up! move on!, you don't say!), and in French, an imperative form of *tenir* (to hold) yields the interjections "Tiens!" ("Tenez!"), (look!, hey!, here!, well!, indeed?!, hullo!).

Forms that are originally interjections may even become verbs. Thus, "Shoo!" (Middle English "Schowe!"), originally an interjection to frighten animals away, gained a transitive verbal counterpart "to *shoo* (away)" meaning "to frighten someone or something away by saying 'shoo!,' or through some similar means." The interjection "Wow!" has also given rise to a transitive verbal counterpart "to wow" meaning "to do something very good which causes other people to say 'Wow!' " (e.g., "She *wowed* them with her new designs"). Similarly, in Pitjantjantjara (Goddard, 1983, 1987 [Central Australia: Pama-Nyungan]), the interjection "Pai!," which is usually directed at dogs and means (clear off!, be off!), is the source of the transitive verb *paini*, meaning "to drive someone/something away; to shoo off, to hunt away."

The purpose of showing that interjections may have their origin in imperative verbs, and that interjections with an imperative intonation pattern commonly correspond to transitive verbs, was to (a) demonstrate that it is just a short step from having one argument position filled (referentially) by extralinguistic context (the case of imperatives) to having all arguments filled by extralinguistic context (the case of interjections); (b) show that at least some interjections must be semantically close to other elements in the lexicon, in that we have seen verbs giving rise to interjections, as well as interjections giving rise to verbs; and (c) exemplify the close relationship that interjections may have with specific speech act types; vis-à-vis the relationship of certain interjections to imperatives.

The discussion returns to the relationship between interjections and speech acts shortly; however, we are still concerned with the issue of how interjections both predicate and refer.

Interjections as Deictics

The solution to the problem of reference comes from recognizing that all interjections are indexical. Forms ranging from "Ouch!" to "Yes!," and from "Huh?" to "Thank you.," which all meet the formal definition of an interjection, are all context-bound and directly index entities in the extralinguistic context as fillers of the argument positions in the proposition underlying the interjections. Although it is a common observation that interjections (typically in the sense of emotive interjections) are context bound, Peirce is among the few to have observed that interjections are primarily indexes, rather than symbols or icons. He noted (1955, p. 119):

> Thus any given street cry, since its tone and theme identifies the individual, is not a symbol but an Indexical Legisign [i.e., a conventional indexical—DPW]; . . . it may be well to consider the varieties of one class more. We may take the Rhematic Indexial Legisign. *The* shout of "Hullo!" is an example of the ordinary variety— meaning, not an individual shout, but this shout "Hullo!" in general—this type of shout. A second variety is a constituent of the Dicent Indexical Legisign, as the word "that" in the reply, "That is Farragut."

This is a guiding insight for the treatment of interjections; they share with words like *I, you, this, that, here,* and *now* the fact that they must be tied to the actual speech moment (i.e., the situation of utterance) before their complete interpretation (i.e., full referencing) can be made. When I say "Yippee!" I am indexing *myself* and something (i.e, "*this* thing") *here* that just *now* made me aware of some proposition that has made me feel excited and more than happy (here and now), and so I say "[jɪpiː!]" in order to show how I am feeling *right now*.

Of course, interjections differ from what are normally taken to be deictics (shifters, indexicals) by virtue of the fact that they are not merely referring expressions (or are not merely used for referencing), but also function to predicate something with respect to the argument or arguments that they index. In this sense, interjections are similar to deictic verbs like "come," or members of the grammatical category tense, because these elements also semantically predicate and refer indexically at the same time. That is to say, a past tense can be analyzed semantically as a two-argument predicate that takes an unspecified event as one argument and predicates that this event happened before the present speech moment, the indexed second argument of the predication.

I claim that included in the semantic decomposition of all interjections are one or more of the following basic deictic referencing elements: *I, you, this, that, now*, and perhaps *here* and *there*. These elements in the decomposition provide the function of referencing in interjections and account for the classification of interjections as (complex predicational) deictics.

Evidence of the Deictic Nature of Interjections. Evidence that deictic elements are part of the decomposition of interjections comes from a number of sources. One source of evidence is the fact that deictic elements are frequently incorporated into interjections. In English, for example, the forms "Thankyou.," "Gimme!," "Welcome!," and "Dammit!"—whose orthographic representations demonstrate that they are each single lexemes rather than phrases—clearly incorporate the deictic forms *you, me, come*, and *it*, respectively. The deictic *here* is an element of the fixed *interjectional phrases* "*Here* goes!," "*Here* goes nothing!," and "*Here* we go again." Furthermore, spatial prepositional elements frequently take on deictic directional senses in interjections and interjectional phrases. Thus, "off" is used to indicate movement away from the speaker in such interjectional phrases as "Fuck off!," "Buzz off!," "Piss off!," "Kiss off!," "Rack off!" (Australian), "Back off!," "Nick off!" (Australian), "Take off!" (Canadian), and the more outmoded phrases, "Be off!" and "Off with you!" Similarly, the preposition/particle "out" can be used as an interjection on its own (i.e., "Out!") indicating that the addressee should move out of the place where the speaker is.

Another source of evidence is the fact that simple deictic forms themselves may be the source of interjections, or may be used on their own as interjections. In Warlpiri, the interjection "Mpa!" (take it!), which is basically equivalent to Mparntwe Arrernte "Me!" (take this!) discussed previously, is apparently based on the truncation of *nyampu* (this; here) (David Nash, personal communication, 1989). Literate Warlpiri people often write this interjection as "Yimpa." that is the same form as the Warlmanpa demonstrative meaning "this; here."[3] This, then, is akin to an English speaker's use of "Here." when handing something to someone else. Similarly, in English, "There!" may be used to mean something like "See, I told you so" or "Just as I expected." Moreover, a number of deictic forms in English are repeated to give interjectional forms. Thus we have *There, there*, used to calm someone down and/or give them consolation, *Now, now!*, used to placate or reprove someone, and *Come, come!*, used to hurry someone up or to get someone to behave in a sensible fashion. It may also be desirable to add to this list *That's that!*, used to terminate any further discussion of a particular matter, or used to indicate that some particular matter or event is settled and has come to its natural conclusion.

---

[3]Note that Warlpiri and Warlmanpa are neighbouring, and closely related languages in Central Australia.

The final source used here as evidence for the fact that interjections are complex predicational deictics that contain basic deictic elements in their semantic decomposition, is the use of deictic gestures as part of, or as an accompaniment to, interjections. In American Sign Language (ASL), for instance, where the majority of signs are restricted to a certain orientation within a fairly fixed signing space, many of the interjections are signed with a deictic movement in the direction of the particular entity (or entities) to which the interjection refers. So, for example, the sign that can be glossed as SMART ASS!; TOUCHÉ!; SICK-OF(-index) may be signed towards the addressee or towards someone outside of the conversation, depending to whom the speaker is referring. Similarly the sign that may be glossed as POOR BABY!; POOR THING (; PITY) may also be signed towards the addressee or towards someone else, and when it is used in a sarcastic or ironic sense it may also be signed directly towards the speaker. Thus, a deictic gesture is built into these signs just as they are built into the basic ASL pronominal and demonstrative forms.

Except for the important fact that ASL interjections are clearly part of the general spatial-gestural linguistic mode of ASL as a language, the deictic orientation of these ASL forms is very similar to certain interjectional gestures used by English speakers. For example, when Americans "give someone the finger," they not only raise their middle finger upwards, they also direct it towards the individual who is the target of their contempt. A reasonable gloss for this gesture would be the interjection(al phrase) "Fuck you!" that commonly accompanies it. It has already been noted, with respect to the Mparntwe Arrernte interjections, that deictic gestures may obligatorily accompany verbal interjections.

In sum, then, the facts that conventional deictic elements are commonly incorporated as part of interjections, deictic elements may give rise to interjections, and deictic gestures may be built into (or may accompany) interjections, are taken as strong evidence in support of the conjecture that all interjections contain basic deictic elements in their semantic decomposition. At the very least, these facts argue that interjections must be included in any serious investigation of deixis.

Once the claim that interjections are deictic elements is accepted, it is then possible to put forward some observations that are true of deictic elements generally. Previously we observed that languages may have conventionalised non-linguistic gestures that correspond to verbal interjections. The other areas of the lexicon that, cross-linguistically, commonly have gestural equivalents are the deictics par excellence, pronouns and demonstratives. Pronouns and demonstratives have their equivalents in conventionalised pointing gestures. For example, Arrernte speakers employ a small set of conventional signs during everyday interactions: singular pronouns are commonly signalled by pointing the index finger towards the relevant person. For first-person singular, the gesture involves pointing toward one's own upper chest or neck with the palm at a 45° angle from the body, whereas for the second-personal singular, the palm is facing upwards and the index finger points to the middle of the addressee's chest. For third-person singular, the palm is face down and pointed towards the direction of a person outside the signed conversation. The demonstratives "this" and "that" may be signalled by a pointing gesture of the lips (by women), or by pointing with the index finger (palm downwards). Although less structured than the Arrernte system, English speakers also regularly use conventional pointing gestures to signal "I," "you," "this," "that," "here," and "there."

Furthermore, although interjections frequently violate the phonological patterns of a language (e.g., English "pssst!"), interjections are not the only linguistic elements that, cross-linguistically, tend to be phonologically aberrant, and, once again, it is pronouns and demonstratives that share this same trait with interjections. For instance, in English, the phoneme /ð/ in initial position in a word occurs only in a small set of semantically similar words: *this, these, that, those, there, they, them, their, thou, thy, thine, then, the, thus, than*, and *though*. This set consists predominantly of demonstratives and pronouns, and is completed by discourse markers and determiners that have deictic semantics. In Mparntwe Arrernte, the only free-form monosyllabic words of #CV# structure are pronouns (e.g., /ŋə/ '2nd sg. nom.,' /ɹə/ '3rd. sg. nom.') and interjections (e.g., /mə/ 'take this,' /yə/ 'I'm attending').

In short, we claim that, cross-linguistically, deictic linguistic elements (inclusive of interjections) are more prone to be phonologically aberrant, and are the elements most likely to have corresponding nonlinguistic gestures. To my knowledge, no one has claimed that pronouns and demonstratives are not part of the core of the language system. However, they commonly manifest two of the properties that are typically used to demonstrate why interjections should be considered peripheral linguistic phenomena. To be consistent, at least with respect to these criteria, we must treat interjections and pronouns and demonstratives alike; they must all be considered as linguistic elements whose shared semantic/pragmatic features predict aspects of their form, their use, and their association with nonlinguistic signs.

Defining Interjections: Interjections as Lexemes.   Having demonstrated the deictic nature of interjections, it is time to show what is meant by the claim that one or more of the basic deictic elements are to be included in the semantic decomposition of interjections. I use the Natural Semantic Metalanguage (NSM) approach to semantic decomposition advocated by Wierzbicka (1980, 1988, 1989, 1991, 1992) and her followers (e.g., Ameka, 1987, 1992b, 1992c; Evans, 1992; Goddard, 1989; Wilkins, 1986, 1989). This is a method of reductive paraphrasing in which linguistic elements are defined by a proposition, or series of propositions, presented as active, declarative natural language sentences, composed from a metalexicon of natural language words that are semantically simpler than the terms being defined. The metalanguage will consist of simple English lexical items and syntax, and is used because it has the advantage of being relatively easy to understand for the layperson with no prior knowledge of NSM. Although Wierzbicka advocated a metalanguage containing approximately 30 lexical semantic primitives,[4] including "I," "you," and "this," in practice she uses many more items for the purposes of clear and comprehensible definitions. These other lexemes are semantic molecules (or semantic elements) that have been previously defined, and this chapter uses the richer defining vocabulary, rather than primitives. All the basic deictic elements I suggest are part of the semantic decomposition of interjections may be found on the list of approximately 170 words Wierzbicka (1987b) gave as the practical defining vocabulary for the definition of English speech act verbs.

Using the above method, a suggested definition for Mparntwe Arrernte "Me!" 'take this!' would be:

(2) **"Me!"** (Mparntwe Arrernte: Central Australia)
 I_U want you$_A$ to take this$_I$ thing I_U am holding out to you$_A$.
 I_U say '[mɐ!]' because I_U want to cause you$_A$ to do it right now$_T$.
 I_U assume you$_A$ will do it.

In the above definition, I improved on Wierzbicka's approach by adding subscript letters to those deictic elements in the decomposition that are to be understood referentially through matching to extralinguistic context. These definitions are meant to capture what Grice called the *timeless* (1989), or decontextualised, meanings of the items. So, although "I" and "you" are primitives in the decomposition of "Me!" 'take this!,' they have no interpretation, by virtue of having no reference, until they are contextualised and the utterance takes on what Grice (1989) called its *occasion-meaning*. Thus, the subscripted deictics are meant to demonstrate that each deictic element must be filled referentially before the interjection can be fully meaningful.[5]

"Me!" ('take this!') derived originally from a verb meaning "to take," and this fact can be related to the elements in the first line of the decomposition I_U *want* *you$_A$ to take this$_I$ thing.* Further, a necessary accompaniment to the utterance of this interjection is a conventional deictic gesture involving the speaker holding the entity in question out towards the addressee; this is captured in the definition by

---

[4]The current set of primitives according to Wierzbicka (1989, 1991) is *I, you, someone, something, this, place (where), time (when), after, (world), the same (other), two, all, no (do not want), if (imagine), be like, because, can, do, happen, part (of), kind of, think (of), want, say, know, very, good,* and *bad.*

[5]The subscripts could, of course, be anything, but for mnemonic convenience I have employed the following conventions: 'you' takes 'A' for 'addressee' [i.e., you$_A$]; 'I' takes 'U' for 'utterer' [i.e., I_U]; 'this' and 'that' take 'I' for 'index(ed entity)' [i.e., this$_I$; that$_I$]; 'now' takes 'T' for 'time (of speaking)' [i.e., now$_T$]; 'here' takes 'P' for 'place (of speaking)' [i.e., here$_P$]; and 'there takes '-P' for 'not at place (of speaking)' [i.e., there$_{-P}$]. Note that 'O' may be subscripted to variables (X, Y, Z) to indicate 'other' (i.e., someone outside the current discourse). Where more than one contextually given entity fulfills the same role, numbers are added to subscripts to distinguish individuals.

the phrase *this_I thing I_U am holding out to you_A*. Finally, "Me!" 'take this!' is always said with the intonation pattern of a mild imperative. This corresponds to the final two lines of the decomposition—"I_U say '[mɐ!]' because I_U want to cause you_A to do it right now_T. I_U assume you_A will do it."—that give the illocutionary purpose and the illocutionary force of the interjection. The definition conveys that Mparntwe Arrernte speakers, by knowledge of convention, recognize that they can usually get other speakers to perform a specific act by the utterance of the arbitrary vocal form [mɐ!].[6] The use of "right now_T" in the decomposition corresponds to the immediacy understood to be conveyed by the shortness and sharpness of such interjections. The four things that must be provided by immediate context for this interjection to have a full interpretation are the particular speaker, the exact addressee, the thing that is being transferred, and the precise time of utterance.

The interjection to which "Me!" 'take this!' often forms a response, "Ngke!" 'give that here!,' may be defined as follows:

"Ngke!" (Mparntwe Arrernte: Central Australia)
I_U want you_A to give me that_I thing I_U am pointing to.
I_U say '[ŋgɐ!]' because I_U want to cause you_A to do it right now_T.
I_U assume you_A will do it.

The parallels in semantic structure between "Ngke!" 'give that here!' and "Me!" 'take this!' are immediately apparent when one compares the two definitions. In fact, given that "Ngke!," like "Me!," is always said with a mild imperative intonation pattern, it is not surprising to find that the final two lines of the semantic decomposition of both forms are essentially identical. A comparison of the first line of the definitions of each of these two interjections reveals why the two forms tend to constitute a common *adjacency pair* (cf. Levinson, 1983) in which "Ngke!" 'give that here!' is the first utterance and "Me!" 'take this!' is the rejoinder. As mentioned previously, "Ngke!" derives historically from a verb meaning "to give" and the first line of the decomposition makes this association explicit (i.e., *I_U want you_A to give me that_I thing*). The fact that there is a necessary pointing gesture that accompanies the utterance of the interjection is captured by the phrase *that_I thing I_U am pointing to*. "Ngke!" 'give that here!' tends to be used when an item that the speaker wants is closer to the addressee, or is easier for the addressee to get, and the speaker wants the addressee to pass that item to him/her. Thus, the deictic element "that_I" occurs in the decomposition to indicate this fact that the particular object to be transferred is out of the easy reach of the speaker. Clearly, then, the components "give" and "that_I" appearing in the decomposition of "Ngke!," are matched by the components "take" and

---

[6]In these definitions, 'I say "[X]" . . .' is meant to convey that the speaker utters a particular phonetic form (knowing that it conveys something to other speakers of the same language). Thus, this phrasing does not convey that the speaker is uttering the word(s), but that he or she is uttering the form of the word(s).

"this₁" in the decomposition of the response form "Me!." Interestingly, the interjection "Ngke!" 'give that here!' may also be directed to a baby when the speaker is about to pick that baby up and s/he is holding his/her arms out towards the baby. In this usage it may be understood to mean something like, "come on little one, give yourself to me."

One convincing way to demonstrate both the value of natural language definitions, and the need to recognize that interjections have a complex semantic structure that can be explicated, is to compare semantically similar interjections from two different languages. To this end, the Italian interjection "To'!" 'take this, here you are' (*prendi!*) will be discussed against the background of the previous discussion of Mparntwe Arrernte "Me!" 'take this!.'

Like Mparntwe Arrernte "Me!" 'take this!,' Italian "To'!" 'here you are!' is always said with an imperative intonation pattern, and is only felicitous if it is said while the speaker is holding the object to be taken out towards the addressee. As a reflection of these similarities, I claim that the first part of the definition of "To'!" 'here you are' is exactly the same as the whole definition of Mparntwe Arrernte "Me!" 'take this!.' However, "To'!" differs from "Me!" in two significant respects.

Firstly, for some Italian speakers, "To'!" 'here you are' is only felicitous if at some prior stage, the current addressee had asked the speaker to give her/him the particular object that the speaker is currently holding out. In this sense "here you are" is a better English gloss than "take this." Other Italian speakers do not feel that "To'!" 'here you are' entails a prior request for the object, and according to my limited sample of Italian informants, the difference is between what the informants themselves identify as Northern Italian and Southern Italian. Apparently, for Northern Italian speakers "To'!" is only felicitous if there is a prior request for the object by the addressee, while Southern Italians consider it felicitous to use "To'!" even if the addressee never indicated that he or she wanted the object being transferred. In this sense the Mparntwe Arrernte use of "Me!" 'take this!' is exactly parallel to the Southern Italian use of "To'!" 'take this!.'

The second difference that Italian "To'!" 'take this!, here you are' manifests, in comparison to the Mparntwe Arrernte form, appears to hold true for all Italian speakers. While "Me!" 'take this!' can be said by any Mparntwe Arrernte speaker to any other Mparntwe Arrernte speaker (to whom he or she is permitted to speak), in Italian, "To'!" 'here you are' may only be said to a person that the speaker can address using the informal second-person singular form *tu*. It is considered rude and insulting to use "To'!" to someone whom you are expected to address using formal, polite forms. If it is accepted that interjections are a normal part of the linguistic system, then it should not be surprising to find that culturally important distinctions, such as formality and politeness, which are coded in other areas of the lexicon of a language, are encoded in the meanings of interjections.

It seems reasonable to presume that the differences between Italian "To'!" 'here you are' and Mparntwe Arrernte "Me!" 'take this!,' reflect differences in the meanings of the two forms. If interjections are denied any conceptual structure, then it would be difficult to demonstrate this difference explicitly. However, in taking the position that interjections have an explicable conceptual structure, one is able to construct the following NSM definition for "To'!" 'here you are' which allows one to see immediately the similarities and differences between the meaning of "To'!" and the meaning of Mparntwe Arrernte "Me!."

(4) "To'!" (Italian)
I_U want you$_A$ to take this$_I$ thing I_U am holding out to you$_A$.
I_U say '[to?]' because I_U want to cause you$_A$ to do it right now$_T$.
I_U assume you$_A$ will do it,
(because you$_A$ have said that you$_A$ want me$_U$ to give this$_I$ thing to you$_A$.)
I_U know I_U could not say this to everyone,
but I_U assume I_U can say it to you$_A$ because you$_A$ are someone I_U say '[tu]' to.

Thus far, definitions have only been given for very similar interjections that fall into what Ameka (1992b, 1992c) called the class of *conative interjections*; that is, interjections directed at an auditor and demanding an action or response from the addressee in accordance with the speaker's wants. To demonstrate that the definitional approach advocated here is not restricted to this group of interjections, and to provide a clearer view of the nature of the semantic information that may be encoded in interjections, this section concludes with a discussion of two very different interjections.

The first interjection to be examined is the ASL sign I gloss POOR BABY < sarc >. The manual part of this sign is essentially the same as the sign often glossed as PITY (n,v); SYMPATHY; MERCY. I have only observed what might be regarded as the sarcastic use of the PITY sign, as a sign used on its own as an utterance, and, through discussions with native and nonnative ASL signers, I am confident that the sign I describe should be considered a distinct item, with a distinct meaning, related to the PITY sign. The sign involves the middle finger projecting outward from a spread hand held upward and parallel to the signer's body, and the signer moves this hand shape up and down with slight circular motion towards the direction of the target of pity. This part of the sign looks as though the signer were gently stroking or petting something, the object of pity, with the projected middle finger. A further aspect of the sign is a sad facial expression involving an exaggerated pout (with bottom lip protruded). As noted previously, this sign can be directed towards the addressee, the speaker, or some person outside the conversation.

The interjection POOR BABY < sarc > is used at a time when the speaker finds out that something has happened, is happening, or will happen to someone else who thinks that this event is a bad or worrisome thing for them, and who might expect to be pitied because of their involvement in this 'unfortunate' event. In using this interjection, the speaker indicates that he or she does not really feel sorry for this other person, and does not really think that the event in question is something important enough for that person, or anyone else, to be worried about. For instance, if someone saw on the television that the President was disappointed at not getting a pay raise, then he or she could show an addressee that he or she was basically unimpressed by this news by signing POOR BABY at the television. This would indicate to the addressee, through a mock show of sympathy, that this is a trivial problem for the President, other people are in a worse situation, and the President should be worrying about more important things. The use of this sign is generally lighthearted and the speaker assumes that the addressee will be amused by his or her use of this interjection. These observations may be captured in the following definition.

(5) [POOR BABY] < sarc > (American Sign Language)
Something/Someone here$_P$ has caused me$_U$ to know something about person X$_{[U/A/O]}$ just now$_T$.

I$_U$ now know: that something has happened (is happening/ will happen) to person X$_{[U/A/O]}$, and person X$_{[U/A/O]}$ would think this is something bad and would not want this thing to have happened (to be happening/ to happen) to them,
and person X$_{[U/A/O]}$ might think that people would feel sympathy for them because of this.

I$_U$ say (sign) '['POOR BABY']' in the direction of person X$_{[U/A/O]}$, while pretending to show sympathy (on my face), because I$_U$ want to show you$_A$ that I$_U$ do not really think that the bad thing that has happened (is happening/ will happen) to X is very bad at all, and so I$_U$ do not feel any real sympathy for X$_{[U/A/O]}$.

I$_U$ assume you$_A$ will be amused by my$_U$ saying/doing this.

Note that in this definition the deictic element "here$_P$" indicates that something or someone in the immediate environment is the source of the information concerning the target of mock pity. Furthermore, the variable argument X is subscripted to show that the target of mock pity could be either the speaker (U), the addressee (A), or someone else (O)—the particular choice being indicated in context by the direction in which the sign is aimed. Finally, this interjection is an informative one, rather than one that attempts to get the addressee to do something.

The final interjection to be discussed in this section is Italian "Cincin!" 'cheers!' In the classification schema proposed by Ameka (1992b), this form would not be considered an interjection, but, instead, would be classed as a one-word formula (or a one-word routine). However, forms like "Cincin!" 'cheers,' "Thankyou.," and "(Good)Bye.," which are all considered one-word formulae by Ameka, meet the definition of an interjection proposed previously. They are conventional lexical items that constitute an utterance by themselves, they are contextually bound, and, as will be demonstrated with respect to "Cincin!" 'cheers,' their features of use and their semantic structure are similar to other interjections which have been discussed previously. It is true, however, that they form a distinct pragmatic and semantic subtype of interjections because they are tied to specific, and very common, situations, and their function is mainly to acknowledge, promote, and/or maintain social relations in accordance with cultural conventions.

Like the English use of "Cheers!" the Italian use of "Cincin!" is typically tied to a situation in which there is a social gathering of two or more people, and the majority of people are drinking something. Unlike English "Cheers!," Italian "Cincin!" does not appear to necessarily imply the drinking of alcoholic beverages. Thus if the group is drinking Italian sodas, it would be perfectly reasonable and felicitous to say "Cincin!" without it sounding amusing. In the same situation, an English speaker could say "Cheers!," but it is taken to be amusing in the sense that the addressees are asked to imagine that what they are drinking is like an alcoholic beverage. These facts also seem to be associated with the fact that Italian speakers do not find it odd or amusing if children say "Cincin!," whereas English speakers find it amusing and/or precocious if children say "Cheers!."

The person who says "Cincin!," like the person who says "Cheers!," must accompany the utterance with a conventional deictic gesture that involves raising their drinking vessel and holding it out towards their addressee(s). The purpose of the utterance and the accompanying gesture is to get all the people involved in the gathering to demonstrate that they all have good feelings about being together. Once again, "Cincin!" appears to be different from its rough English gloss "Cheers!" in that "Cheers!" indicates not only the sense that the people have good feelings about being together, but also that everyone should be feeling happy. "Cincin!," unlike "Cheers!," can be used, without sounding odd, in situations where everyone is very sad, as after a funeral. In such a situation, this interjection is used to express solidarity in the face of adversity, as well as to acknowledge that everyone is feeling the same way for the same reason. Thus, "Cincin!" is typically used where a group has gathered socially for a particular purpose, and it is used to get people to show that they are feeling the same way with respect to the particular focus of the occasion. When speakers utter "Cincin!," they expect their addressee(s) to respond by raising their glass(es) as a demonstration that they feel the same way as the speaker. All of these facts may be brought together and structured into the following definition.

(6) "Cincin!" (Italian) 'Cheers'

We$_{U\&A1(\&A2\ldots)}$ are going to drink now$_T$

I$_U$ raise my glass towards you$_{A1(\&A2\ldots)}$ and say '[tʃintʃin]' because:

I$_U$ want us$_{U\&A1(\&A2\ldots)}$ to show that we$_{U\&A1(\&A2\ldots)}$ feel the same way about X right now$_T$,

and I$_U$ want to show that we$_{U\&A1(\&A2\ldots)}$ have good feelings about being together here$_P$.

I$_U$ assume you$_{U\&A1(\&A2\ldots)}$ will raise your$_{U\&A1(\&A2\ldots)}$ glass to show that you$_{U\&A1(\&A2\ldots)}$ feel the same as I$_U$ do right now$_T$.

Thus far, five distinct interjections from three different languages were defined using the same methods, principles, and metalanguage. As lexemes, it is reasonable to expect that interjections should be amenable to lexical decomposition along the same lines as other lexical items, and this was shown to be the case. The relatively unique feature of interjections as lexemes is that they have deictic arguments as part of their semantic decomposition, and these arguments must be matched, by pragmatic principles, to entities within the extra linguistic context before the interjections can be understood to be fully meaningful.

Interjections and Illocutionary Purpose

But what about 'real' interjections? What about Goffman's (1981) *response cries* and Wierzbicka's (1992) *emotive interjections*? This section briefly examines one standard example of what many consider to be prototypical interjections (i.e., interjections that express the speaker's current emotional state and do not encode an addressee). As such, we also arrive at the question of whether forms like "Ow!" and "Wow!" have an illocutionary purpose; the whole question of illocutionary purpose appears to be bound up with conventionality.

In discussions of convention (e.g., Grice, 1989; Lewis, 1975), it has been typical to assume that linguistic conventions, from word to utterance, are only learned from communicative interactions involving speakers and addressees. However, it is clear that we learn certain conventional symbolic behaviours that do not involve intended interpreters (i.e., addressees). Conventional signs and behaviours minimally require only social, not communicative, interaction that allows an individual to observe and learn those signs and behaviours. As Goffman (1981) noted, interjections (his response cries) tend to be socially situated acts, even if they are not conversationally situated, and they are "available to someone who is present to others but not 'with' any of them" (p. 104).

No one will deny that the interjection "Ow!" is a conventional form that does not require an addressee, but the question is why does a person choose to use a conventional form like "Ow!" rather than some nonconventional form? It has been common to claim, as Ameka (1992b) did, that real interjections are spontaneous, immediate responses to situations. However, it is necessary to assess what is meant by spontaneous and immediate. When one experiences real, sharp, excruciating pain, there tends to be a host of immediate nonlinguistic, nonconventional vocal and nonvocal gestures that can be, and are, made spontaneously instead of conventional forms. The use of a conventional form seems to indicate at least some time taken for an assessment of the situation and the choice of the appropriate form. In the same way that Goffman (1981, pp. 97–98) noted that "a man who utters *fuck* when he stumbles in a foundry is quite likely to avoid that particular expletive should he trip in a day-nursery," persons who hurt themselves amongst adult companions may say "Fuck!" or "Shit!," but will say "Ow!" or "Ouch!" under similar circumstances if a child or their boss is around. These conventional responses to a situation are not so immediate and spontaneous that they do not allow for assessment, selection, and, if necessary, censorship of one's own utterance. I claim that the use of a conventional linguistic gesture, even if there is no addressee, necessarily signals that the speaker has a communicative purpose. In the case of the person who says "Ow!," his or her purpose is to show that he or she is feeling some pain right at the moment and is showing it in the manner that other English speakers use to demonstrate the same thing in similar situations. In line with the preceding discussion, I define "Ow!" as follows:

(7) "Ow!"
    I_U suddenly feel a pain (in this$_I$ part of my$_U$ body) right now$_T$ that I_U would not have expected to feel.
    I_U say "[aʊ!]" because I_U want to show that I_U am feeling pain right now$_T$ [and because I_U know that this is how speakers of English can show (other speakers of English) that they are in pain (in a situation like the situation here$_P$)]

English informants with children have observed that when their children say "Ow!," it is not usually the case that the children are experiencing any real or significant pain. Instead, children tend to use this interjection knowing that it will get their parents' attention, and knowing that it can be used to start a chain of events that may lead to their sibling getting into trouble. The real signals of pain to which these parents are attuned are nonconventional screams, crying, and, in some instances, silence. At an early age, then, children appear to recognize the conventional nature of this interjection, its illocutionary purpose, and that, although it has no real addressee, it can be used communicatively precisely because it is conventional.

To reiterate, even if emotive interjections like "Ow!" and "Wow!" encode no addressee (i.e., they have no "you" in their decomposition), they can still be said to have an illocutionary purpose (i.e., they have "I_U say [X] because . . ." in their decomposition). The illocutionary purpose of emotive interjections is to show how the speaker feels at the exact moment of speaking in a fashion that is conventional and appropriate to the situation at hand. On these grounds it is possible to say that emotive interjections are exclamative speech acts and are to be treated like exclamatory sentences (see, e.g., Elliot, 1974). [For a description of "Wow!" see the epilogue.]

CONCLUSION

Givon's complete entry for interjections reads as follows (1984, p. 84):

Most languages display this mixed-bag category with expressions such as "yes," "no," "hey," "oh," "hi," "wow," "ouch," etc. or their functional equivalents. It is not a unified category functionally, morphologically or syntactically and it is highly language specific.

Much of this chapter is an attempt to show that views such as those expressed in the previous quote are essentially wrong. Such views are no more true of interjections as a word class than they are of nouns and verbs. Using a formal definition of interjection it is possible to identify, cross-linguistically, a form class of items that are simple lexemes conventionally used as utterances. For English, this definition identifies all the forms that Givon listed and more. Contrary to Givon's assertion, it is clear that this is a unified category both morphologically and syntactically, given that interjections host no inflectional or derivational morphemes, and given that they do not enter into construction with any other lexemes. Furthermore, the class of items thus identified share important semantic and pragmatic features. They are all context-bound items which require referential arguments to be provided by the immediate discourse context. These arguments are coded in the semantic decomposition of interjections by the use of basic deictic elements. Interjections are also speech acts that, at minimum, encode an illocutionary purpose. Thus, all interjections contain an *I say "[X]" because* ... in their semantic decompositions. These facts were demonstrated for a varied range of interjections from a diverse selection of languages, and argue that there is clearly a reasonable degree of functional, semantic, and pragmatic unity to this word class.

Contrary to the view that interjections have no conceptual semantic structure, it was demonstrated that interjections tend to have a complex semantic structure that is amenable to semantic decomposition. This chapter used the Natural Semantic Metalanguage approach to semantic decomposition in order to render the definition of the various interjections discussed, and it is hoped that the value of such definitions for the cross-linguistic comparison of interjections is readily apparent.

I argued that interjections are the most reduced form an utterance can take, and that the motivation for such reduction is to be found in the functional principle that determines that the more information that is recoverable directly from context the more reduced an utterance will be. Once again, this relates to the context-bound nature of interjections; all of their referential arguments are provided by extralinguistic context. One should not underestimate the importance of this observation. Linguistics recently went through a period in which the main object of study was complete, decontextualised sentences. This allowed the illusion of isomorphism between semantic structure and syntactic structure. The more recent concern for studying real, contextualised utterances caused certain problems for formal analysis, precisely because not all the elements one would want to propose as belonging to semantic structure have overt manifestations in syntactic structure. If we realize that the degree of isomorphism between semantic and syntactic structure is mediated by pragmatic and functional concerns, then it is not a problem to explain how and why the rich semantic (utterance) structure of interjections may be conveyed by a single lexeme.

The claim that interjections are complex deictics that contain one or more basic deictic elements in their decomposition provides the basic framework that allows one to explain how interjections may be regarded as complete utterances conveying complete propositions appropriate to the discourse situation, and why they are necessarily context-bound. There are three pieces of evidence that were adduced in support of the deictic nature of interjections: (a) interjections commonly have basic deictic forms incorporated as part of their lexical form; (b) basic deictic elements often give rise to interjections or form the root from which interjections are derived; and (c) interjections frequently require an accompanying deictic gesture, or have a roughly equivalent physical gesture that includes a deictic component. Furthermore, two features of interjections commonly considered a sign of their peripherality—they tend to be phonologically aberrant and they tend to have corresponding physical gestures—also characterize pronouns and demonstratives. The conclusion is that these two features tend to associate generally with deictic elements. Thus, although research into deixis has basically ignored interjections, they should constitute an interesting and important part of deixis studies.

On the issue of the relation between semantics and pragmatics, there are some observations that can be made on the basis of the present research. At the 1987 Concluding Round Table of the International Pragmatics Conference (Verschueren, 1987), Fillmore recounted how he had come under fire for suggesting that one "could talk about pragmatic information being encoded in linguistic form" (p. 43; see also Fillmore, 1975). Indeed, according to Fillmore, another participant (Fraser) claimed that if Fillmore insisted on this point of view, then the International Pragmatics Association was not big enough for the two of them and there should be a vote to say which member stayed and which one left. Such tension arises from the common view that if something is conventionally encoded in linguistic form, then it is to be presumed to be within the domain of semantics. Fillmore's statement (Verschueren, 1987, p. 18) that "there are many linguistic structures that appear to be dedicated to specific pragmatic purposes," and that certain things are simultaneously semantic and pragmatic and "that there are lots of lexical items . . . that require for their interpretation an anchoring in some kind of real situation" (p. 43), seems essentially correct, given the present discussion of interjections. Still, the view that information that is conventionally encoded in linguistic structures is semantic, not pragmatic, is also persuasive. I believe the approach taken here would make sense to both sides. Lexemes, such as interjections, may conventionally indicate and encode aspects of the particular contexts for which they are appropriate. This is semantic. Thus, a form may indicate that an addressee must be present in context, or that an object in context must be in a particular spatial relation with respect to the speaker. However, the speaker's recognition that the lexeme is appropriate for use within the context, and the addressee's ability to appropriately match the semantically specified features that need to be found in context to the actual features of the discourse context, are both matters of pragmatics. Interjections are only fully interpretable when they are placed in context, because only then can the deictic elements in the decomposition be understood referentially. The component 'I$_U$' in the definition of an interjection must be matched by pragmatic rules to the actual discourse context for it (and thus the interjection) to have any interpretation. Note that if one allows some of one's semantic primitives to be pragmatic units, such as basic deictic elements, it becomes obvious how a lexeme could be simultaneously semantic and pragmatic.

Interjections are hard to handle in linguistic terms, not because they are peripheral to the concerns of linguistics, but because they embody all the concerns of linguistics. They are lexemes and utterances; they have to be described semantically and pragmatically; they require "the examination of our relation to social situations at large, not merely our relation to conversation" (Goffman, 1981, p. 90). As utterances they are verbless and nounless, so we must be concerned about their relation to sentences and what their position is with respect to the grammatical component. Their relation to other areas of the lexicon must be investigated not only synchronically, but also through a study of their diachronic development. They need not only be declarative forms, but they may be interrogative, imperative, or exclamative—both in their intonation pattern and in the speech acts they convey. They are not only associated with the strictly linguistic component, but also with nonlinguistic, gestural means of communication. Formal syntactic approaches are not in a position to handle them, nor are formal semantic approaches. Similarly, radical semantic and radical pragmatic approaches fall short. Interjections point to the inadequacies of received wisdom, and so it has been easier to dismiss them than it has been to accommodate them. However, as Goffman (1981, p. 12) noted with respect to response cries, imprecations, and self talk, "these utterances are too commonly met with in daily life, surely, to justify scholarly neglect." This chapter attempted to grapple with some of the difficult linguistic issues which interjections raise, and to demonstrate why interjections merit serious linguistic investigation. Müller's enlightened quote from 1862 provides an appropriate conclusion:

> One short interjection may be more powerful, more to the point, more eloquent than a long speech. (Müller, 1862, p. 368)

EPILOGUE

It is now possible to discuss some aspects of how the previous account of interjections relates to narrative concerns. Returning first to the issue of direct and indirect discourse raised in the prologue, it is possible to note that another linguistic property shared by interjections and the utterance-bound deictic elements on which their meaning is based (i.e., "I," "you," "here," "now") is the fact that, whereas such elements can occur in direct quotation, they must be deictically shifted in indirect quotation. A direct quote like " '*Shit! I'm bored,*'

Sally said," would need to be rendered in an indirect quote in something like the following manner: 'Sally said that she had just come to the unpleasant realization that she was bored.' In the indirect quote, 'I' becomes 'she,' present tense is rendered in the past, and the immediate subjective expressiveness of the interjection is rendered more objectively through the descriptive proposition 'she had just come to the unpleasant realisation that.' Accounts which treat interjections as *nonreferential* (Fónagy, 1986) or *noncontentful* (Coulmas, 1986b) fail to notice this parallelism, even though they faithfully report the facts concerning interjections and then separately report the same phenomenon for the traditional class of deictics (i.e., pronouns, demonstratives, tense, etc.).

Focusing on the analysis of interjections in fictional narrative, we examine the issue of interjections in relation to Deictic Shift Theory. In Deictic Shift Theory, as outlined by Segal (chap. 1), the crucial cognitive act in narrative interpretation is the reader's shift from the real world situation in which the text is encountered, to a locus within a mentally constructed story world. Segal notes that the events in the narrative "tend to occur within the mental model at the 'active' space-time location to which the reader has been directed by the syntax and semantics of the text," and it is this location, the deictic center, that "serves as the 'center' from which the sentences are interpreted." Crucially, however, this deictic center location in the story world can shift as the narrative unfolds, and especially crucial for the current chapter is the observation that deictic terms refer to the entities and events in the constructed mental model of the story world. Is the account of interjections as deictics that has been given previously, especially the proposed style of semantic decomposition, compatible with Deictic Shift Theory? I believe so.

Consider the following excerpt from Tony Hillerman's *Coyote Waits* (1990, p. 243).

> Largo cleared his throat, producing a rumble.
> "We had a man killed here in Ship Rock today," Largo said. "Shot."
> This was not anything like what Chee had expected.
> "Shot? Who?"
> "Fellow named Huan Ji," Largo said "You know him?"
> "Wow," Chee said. He sat stock still digesting this.

As the reader will have guessed, I am concerned with the interpretation of the one word interjectional utterance "Wow." In my original paper, I proposed and justified the following definition for "Wow" (compare with definitions of the same interjection offered by Ameka, 1992b, p. 109 and Wierzbicka, 1992, p. 164). Note that 'X[pr-of-this$_1$]' in the definition refers to the particular property of the thing indicated (i.e., 'this$_1$ something') that is the source of surprise. Although the property is itself a variable argument (X), it is tied specifically to a deictic argument ('this$_1$ something').

"Wow"
I_U have just now$_T$ and here$_P$ become aware of this$_I$ something that I_U
wouldn't have expected.
This$_I$ something is much more X[pr-of-this$_I$] than I_U would have expected
and this causes me$_U$ to feel surprised,
and to feel that I_U could not imagine this$_I$ something being more
X[pr-of-this$_I$] than it already is now$_T$.
I_U say "[waʊ!]" because I_U want to show how surprised I_U am feeling
right now$_T$.

As speakers of English, the author (Hillerman), the reader, and the fictional
character Jim Chee would all possess something like the general, conventionalized, context-independent lexical semantic knowledge that is represented in this
definition for the lexeme "Wow." However, to be fully interpretable, "Wow"
must be contextualized. Indeed, this utterance of "Wow" requires us to identify
the active spacetime location that has been modelled for this fictional story world
at this point in the novel, and all the deictic elements that occur in the propositional
structure of the definition must be tied to entities and events in the current mental
model of the story world that the reader has constructed through engaging with
the narrative. Without the active deictic center information, a reader would be
at a loss to fully understand the source of surprise for Chee. At this point, more
than two thirds of the way through the novel, the reader is able to say that: (a)
'I_U' indexes the speaker Jim Chee, an officer of the Navajo Tribal Police who
is on injury leave, but who is unofficially investigating the murder of Delbert
Nez, a fellow policeman and friend; (b) 'now$_T$' indexes the time of the speaker's
new awareness and experiential state of surprise, which is late afternoon, in late
Autumn, some months after the original murder under investigation, during a
conversation with Chee's superior Captain Largo; (c) 'here$_P$' indexes the location
of the conversation that is inside the aluminum trailer where Jim Chee lives and
that is parked on the low north bluff of the San Juan River, in the Navajo
Reservation in New Mexico; (d) 'this$_I$ something' indexes the news conveyed
by Largo that a man named Huan Ji, one of the people under investigation in
connection with the original murder, had been shot dead; and (e) 'X[pr-of-this$_I$]'
refers to the extreme property of the news that causes Chee to feel so surprised,
and can be interpreted as the property of relevance (or newsworthiness) to Chee,
because he had seen Huan Ji's vehicle leaving the scene of the original murder
and, as a result, had gone out to talk to him, and found Huan Ji had been lying
about something. Of course, a reader need not associate the definitional deictic
elements to deictic center information that has this much detail (it might suffice,
for instance, to record that the deictic center here$_P$ was simply 'Chee's trailer'
or 'Chee's home'). Some readers and even the author might disagree with aspects
of this account, but that is all part of individuals coming to their own understanding of a text. Such variation in details does not mean that either the definition
or Deictic Shift Theory is wrong; on the contrary, both are meant to allow for
individual variation in particularized interpretation.

Chee's utterance of "Wow" leads the reader to a cognitive stance viewed from the perspective of Chee himself, and through this utterance, this fictional character externalizes his internal subjective emotional state. Readers can only achieve that cognitive stance if they know what the interjection means, and they have deictically shifted from the real world into the fictional story world and constructed a mental model with an active deictic center that allows the interjection to gain a contextual interpretation. In this sense, then, Deictic Shift Theory and the account given for interjections are fully compatible, and, indeed, they are mutually dependent on one another. It remains only to observe that such a structured representation of lexical semantic knowledge as I argue for here is a crucial prerequisite for any serious theory of narrative understanding, not just Deictic Shift Theory.

ACKNOWLEDGMENTS

For advice and help in producing this chapter, I wish to thank Gail Bruder, Lynne Hewitt, Harald Baayen, Sotaro Kita, and Paulette Levy. Elsevier Science Publishers gave permission to reprint some of the material. I would also like to thank the following people for their comments on one or more of the prior manifestions of this chapter: Avery Andrews, Felix Ameka, Matthew Dryer, Nick Evans, Donna Gerdts, Jeri Jaeger, Kean Kaufmann, Madeleine Mathiot, Jacob Mey, Karin Michelson, David Nash, Janet Smith, Robert D. Van Valin, Jr., Anna Wierzbicka, Wolfgang Wolck, David Zubin, Jan-Ola Ostman, and an anonymous referee for the *Journal of Pragmatics*. As always, I owe a great debt to the Yipirinya School Council and the Yipirinya School Community for their help in the original collection and analysis of Mparntwe Arrernte data. Barbara Villanova-Wilkins was particularly helpful with respect to the collection and interpretation of Italian data, and Robin Shay and Lisa Marchand kindly helped with the interpretation of the data from American Sign Language. The original research was supported in part by a Faculty Research Grant from the University of California, Davis. The Cognitive Anthropology Research Group of the Max Planck Institute for Psycholinguistics, Nijmegen, provided me with the atmosphere, time, and resources that enabled me to work on abridging the text and to do the research for, and writing of, the prologue and epilogue.

17

Wayfinding Directions as Discourse: Verbal Directions in English and Spanish

David M. Mark
State University of New York at Buffalo

Michael D. Gould
Universidad Complutense de Madrid

Verbal directions for wayfinding represent an interesting, important, and neglected topic for research involving many facets of communication. The topic is important for several reasons, ranging from theoretical to empirical, from basic to applied:

- Telling someone how to get from one place to another is a common and important activity in most societies. In fact, many people rely on obtaining such information when needed, and would have difficulty finding their way around without the availability of verbal information from strangers while en route.

- Work by Lakoff (1987), Johnson (1987) and others, on the role of metaphor and image schemata in the forming of cognitive models and in reasoning about abstract domains, claimed that the Path image schema, with a source, a path, and a goal, is one of the most central conceptual schemata. The path or journey through physical (geographic) space represents the basis for our understanding of, and language for, projects, relationships, and so on (Johnson 1987). Thus, the study of wayfinding itself may be a window on the core principles of cognition.

- Spontaneous provision of verbal directions for wayfinding requires the direction-giver to perform both spatial and verbal cognitive tasks (perhaps simultaneously), and thus provides an interesting area for studying possible interference between verbal and spatial tasks.

- Current technology, especially the development of microcomputers, created considerable recent interest in on-board provision of navigation assistance to vehicle drivers, and includes studies of the relative value and effectiveness of graphic (map or map-like) versus verbal presentation of navigational information (see Gould, 1989; Mark, 1985, 1989a; Mark, Gould, & McGranaghan, 1987; Mark and McGranaghan, 1986; Streeter, Vitello, & Wonciewicz, 1985).
- Many of the properties and principles related to the understanding of fictional narrative apply to verbal wayfinding directions, as well. In particular, the use of spatial deictics in narrative offers interesting parallels for how spatial terms are used in wayfinding directions.

DEIXIS

When reading a story, a reader keeps track of the location (WHERE), time (WHEN), focal character (WHO), and point of view (WHOSE) for each part of the story. This deictic (or indexical) information contributes a mental data-structure—the Deictic Center (DC)—used by the reader to help in understanding the story (Bruder, Duchan, Rapaport, Segal, Shapiro, & Zubin, 1986; Rapaport, Segal, Shapiro, Zubin, Bruder, Duchan, & Mark, 1989). The story contains various cues to indicate when the reader should change elements in the DC, and whether to retain or discard the previous DC.

This chapter reports some aspects of our studies of verbal directions for wayfinding. Included is a consideration of deictic terms and their relationship to the use of such terms in fictional narrative. We begin by describing these studies.

METHODS

Experiment 1A

Adult subjects were approached in public places in the Buffalo, New York area, and asked for driving directions to particular other public places. (For all of the North American data, the directions were requested by one of the authors, DMM.) The experimenter approached adult lone subjects and asked: "Excuse me, can you tell me how to get to PLACE?"—where PLACE represents the name of the chosen destination. Subjects who appeared to be with other people were not approached in order to avoid the complications that might arise if directions were given by two or more people in combination. Initially, potential subjects of apparent Asian ethnic origin were avoided, because most Asians in the Buffalo area are not native speakers of English, and we wanted to avoid cross-linguistic complications. Later, all nonwhite potential subjects were avoided, because we became aware that Sissons (1981) found statistically significant correlations between helpfulness and both race and sex in an experiment in which strangers were asked for change for a coin. Again, we wanted to avoid such complicating factors if, indeed, they would exist in Buffalo. Whenever a dialogue with a subject developed, the experimenter pretended to be planning to drive to the destination from the current location and to have only a general familiarity with the area. Responses were recorded using a concealed tape recorder, and later transcribed and verified.

When the directions were complete, the experimenter walked away toward the assumed location of his car, and when out of hearing distance from the subject, recorded the following information onto the tape: (a) whether or not any visual aids were used by the subject, and if so, what they were, what directions of pointing corresponded to which direction word spoken, and, if cardinal direction words were used, whether the directions were correct; and (b) background information on subject, as judged by the experimenter (general age group, ethnicity, sex, etc.). No personal information was solicited from the subjects, and we did not solicit or otherwise record their names or other material that would allow individuals to be readily identified. Later, tapes were transcribed using a portable tape recorder, checked by the same researcher using a high fidelity audio system, checked again by another researcher, and finally analyzed with respect to the research objectives. When quotations from the transcripts are given in this chapter, the experimenter's utterances are enclosed in brackets ('{}'). The experimental design was approved by the Human Subjects Review Committee of the Faculty of Social Science, State University of New York at Buffalo.

The first experiment was carried out at two shopping malls in the Buffalo area: Boulevard Mall and Eastern Hills Mall. Shopping malls were used because a fairly large number of individuals were able to be asked for directions between the same pairs of localities. In each case, the destination was the other mall. The study area has a gridded road network, and one can get from one mall to the other by following a path including a north–south leg of about 1 mile, and an east–west leg of about 6.6 miles (see Fig. 17.1). As is generally true of gridded transportation networks, there are many shortest paths of approximately equal length. A total of 14 subjects were approached at Boulevard Mall, and 18 at Eastern Hills Mall, in order to obtain 10 sets of directions at each site.

Experiment 1B

Because our work is exploratory, we also obtained small numbers of interviews in Santa Barbara, CA, and in Vancouver, BC. In Santa Barbara, 5 people were approached in front of Lucky's Supermarket on Calle Real, Goleta, and asked for directions to the campus of the University of California, Santa Barbara; there are several reasonable possible routes, the shortest of which is rather complicated. In the Vancouver area, 6 subjects were interviewed at shopping malls in the eastern suburbs of that city; three people at Coquitlam Centre Mall (Coquitlam) were asked for directions to Lougheed Mall (Burnaby), and three at Lougheed Mall were asked for directions to Coquitlam Centre Mall; the complexity of the route between these malls is similar to the situation in Buffalo.

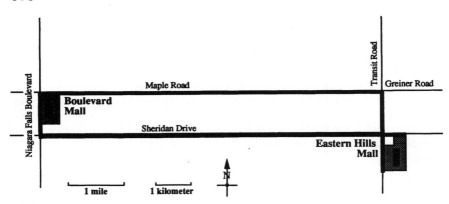

FIG. 17.1. The most frequently chosen routes between two shopping malls near Buffalo, NY.

North American Subject Characteristics

The 31 North American subjects who responded with usable transcripts included 16 males and 15 females. As noted above, ages were estimated in the field; the average estimated ages both for the male and for the female subjects was 38, with ages ranging from about 20 to about 60 years old. For most excerpts from English-language transcripts to follow, subject identifiers are given. The first letter is a "B," "S," or "V," to indicate Buffalo, Santa Barbara, or Vancouver, respectively. The second letter, if present, is the first letter of the name of the mall at which the data were collected. The number is the subject number for that mall; the numbering included subjects who stated that they were not able to give directions; thus, numbers as high as 17 are given.

Experiment 2

During the summer of 1989, we obtained 22 sets of spoken directions in Valencia, Spain. The methodology was the same as in the North American experiment, with the exception that two interviewers were used (separately) in order to add a sex-related and a native/non-native speaker factor into the experiment. One interviewer was a male non-native speaker of Spanish (one of the authors, MDG), whereas the other was a female native speaker and a former resident of the origin (testing) location.

Subjects were approached in a parking lot within an urban neighborhood and asked:

Perdon. ¿Sabes como ir a Nuevo Centro desde aqui por coche?
Excuse me. Do you know how to go to Nuevo Centro from here by car?

where Nuevo Centro is the only major shopping mall in the city. The optimal route (chosen by all 22 subjects) is about 2.5 miles in length. It consists of two rather straight segments, and includes only two or three major choice points (see Fig. 17.2). The complexity of this route is similar to the route chosen by most subjects in Buffalo (Experiment 1A). The testing environment in Valencia differed slightly, however, in that all subjects were tested outdoors, where a wider variety of reference objects were available than in the shopping malls of North America.

In the Spanish experiment, subjects were selected only if they were drivers, judged by their arrival to or imminent departure from the parking area by car or motorcycle. Persons who appeared to be under driving age, extremely elderly, or merely passengers were not questioned (though some saw fit to answer anyway!). Other selection criteria were that the potential subjects appeared friendly and were alone, though some individuals within small groups were also approached. Given their automobile license plate designations, all subjects were presumed to be natives of Valencia, but not necessarily residents of the neighborhood where testing occurred. The interviewers attempted to minimize bias by speaking only when necessary to prompt the subject to continue. Subjects' questions (such as "Have you got that?" or "Do you know were I mean?") were answered affirmatively by nodding or responding *sí*.

Spanish Subject Characteristics

The 22 subjects included 13 males and 9 females. The average estimated age of both males and females was 35 years, with ages ranging from about 17 to 70 years. As in the North American research, ages were estimated in the field upon completion of each direction-giving session.

RESULTS

In this section, we summarize the results of Experiments 1A/B and 2, and compare the Spanish and English directions. For clarity, we always begin by presenting English-language results, and follow this with Spanish results. First, we give

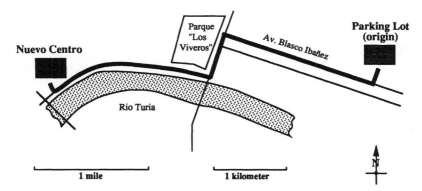

FIG. 17.2. The route chosen by all 22 subjects in Valencia, Spain.

results for our study of deictic references. This is done under three subheadings: "Go" and "Come," "This" and "That," and "Here" and "There." Next, we discuss reference frames for directions. We then analyze the occurrences of words indicating distances and cardinal directions, and the evidence for the use of repetition to indicate relative distance. This is followed by a discussion of turns, with emphasis on the verbs used to denote those turns. Style of presentations compares the use of the imperative, or future-tense description, or other grammatical forms in directions. Lastly, we discuss the use of metaphor in the transcripts.

DEICTIC REFERENCES

Go and Come

It is reasonable to assume that, at the start of a direction-giving act, the DC is set so that the WHERE point is the current physical location (e.g., the mall or other public place at which the question is being asked; this is essentially a "You are here" point), and the WHEN point is the time of asking. The DC may remain that way, in which case the entire trip would occur in the future, and the locations would all be away. In that case, the deictic word *go* would be used rather than *come*, and the directions would be given either as commands or in the future tense. Alternatively, the direction giver might reset either the WHERE point to be some other point along the route (perhaps the destination, or some complicated place or decision point) or perhaps the WHEN point to some time in the future.

English-Language Data. The 31 transcripts in the English-language study support the deitic center notions. A total of 128 occurrences of "go" (including "going") were observed, with 30 of the 31 subjects containing at least 1 occurrence. In contrast, the transcripts contained only 13 occurrences of "come" (including "coming"), and these were found in 10 of the transcripts. (Some of the occurrences of "come" were in the form "come to.") Thus, although about one third of the subjects used "come" at least once, "go" exceeds "come" by about a 10:1 margin.

The use of the deictic "come," indicating a WHERE point away from the current location, may be even less frequent than the above counts imply. Later, we discuss the issue of whether "come to" should be treated as a figure of speech. Eliminating the uses of "come to" for the moment, there were only six cases in which "come" was used. For example:

> Well, if you go out the mall here, and then you would take a left, at the big intersection, um, {OK} you just go straight Sheridan. {OK} Its about . . . its around, its like 20 minutes from here. {OK. Is it on Sheridan?} Yeah, it'll take you right on. . . Yeah {OK} *You're **coming** in from the back entrance* when you go that way, so you're avoiding some traffic. [Subject B-B-9]

Apparently, the speaker concentrated on the destination, and the entrance to it. Here is another example:

> You go down to Maple. {OK} There'll be a K . . . *if you're comin' up Transit* . . . you go past Glen Campbell Chevrolet, {OK} a Tops, and this'll be Maple, and you'll see a K-Mart off to the left. [Subject B-E-5]

"There'll be a K," followed by a pause, strongly suggests concentration on the landmarks in the region of the left turn onto Maple Road, that could reset the speaker's WHERE point to that intersection. Yet another example involved a bridge:

> From here? No, I can't. . . . {OK} First of all, yes, OK. There's a bridge. {OK} *You come out of the parking lot here*, there'll be a bridge. [Subject: B-E-12]

From a viewpoint at the bridge, the traveller would be coming toward that point as he or she leaves the parking lot.

Three transcripts from Vancouver used "come":

> Uh . . . OK, uh . . . go back out to Barnett Highway {OK, Yeah}. Just follow that *and it'll come* . . . just keep going all the way, it'll go up a hill [Subject: V-C-2]

> [5 second pause]. . . Where are you parked, out here? {Yeah} There's an entrance . . . go up here and around {OK} the road here, turn right, go up to the lights. {OK} Turn left, follow that all the way out *and you come all the way* . . . then you go all the way up the hill, eh, *then you come down the other side* {OK} *and come into Port Moody*, and just, just, it'll turn. Stay on that, its Barnett Highway {Yeah}, just follow that all the way out {Oh, OK} and its right on your left hand side, just keep going. [Subject: V-L-1]

> Oh, yeah, OK, uh, you go, . . . *come on here*. Um, you keep yourself on that . . . , you know, where the cars go {Yes}, . . . [Subject: V-C-3]

The occurrence of "come" in the transcript of subject V-C-3 occurred when the subject led the interviewer some 20 feet or so to the glass doors of the mall entrance, in order to show the recommended route out of the mall parking lot. Thus, it was not really part of the wayfinding directions. Even V-C-2 might be a "come to" that was truncated, rather than some other occurrence of "come."

It seems that in the cases of "come" and "coming," the direction-tellers had set their WHERE points to places at or beyond the landmarks being described. In most of the previous cases, there is evidence that the teller had jumped ahead, and was then backtracking to bring the direction-receiver along. Subject B-B-9 had reached the destination in her mental trip. B-E-5 makes a truncated reference to the K-Mart landmark, then returns to a previous point on the route; B-E-12 had mentioned the bridge, and then returns to describe the receiver "coming" out of the parking lot toward that bridge.

Now we return to the issue of the use of "come to." The three samples differed in the frequency of occurrence of "come to." Many of the eight uses of "come" found in the six Vancouver transcripts were in the form "and then you'll **come to** [landmark]." The phrase "come to" occurred in 1 of 20 Buffalo, 1 of 5 Santa Barbara, but 3 of 6 Vancouver transcripts. Perhaps "come to" should be treated as a figure of speech in Vancouver, being used where other dialects of English might use "reach" or "pass" or "see." It is not clear whether use of "come to" indicates that the subject has set his or her WHERE point to the location of the landmark before describing it.[1]

On the other hand, "come to" may sometimes operate in this fashion as a true deictic, as appears to be the case in this Santa Barbara example:

> ... the easiest way is to go down Hollister to, um, go past two, wait, no three signals, and turn left on, uh, Storke Road {OK} and then you go into... you go through Isla Vista, and then head back this way on, uh, I can't remember what the name of that street is ... *but when you come to the end of Storke Road*, you'll only be able to go left or right, go left and go, you'll be going back toward the campus {OK} and then there's a kiosk where you go in. [Subject: S-4]

As in the cases described, the speaker has focused her attention on the corner, as she tried to recall the name of the cross street, and so a deictic "come" would be consistent with the teller''s WHERE point being set to the corner of Storke Road and the unnamed street.

Spanish-Language Data.   The Spanish directions contained far fewer occurrences of the "come" and "go" deictic terms. Although there were about two thirds as many subjects in Spain as in North America, *vas* (you go) was used 22 times [compared to 128 in Experiment 1A/B], and *vienes* (you come) was used 3 times [compared to 13 in Experiment 1A/B]. However, the ratio is similar to the 10:1 ratio observed for the North American data.

An interesting observation is that Spanish allows the use of an egocentric spatial reference frame in which the observer is motionless and landmarks along the road approach and pass him or her, creating what Talmy (1990) called *fictive motion*. Following is an example of fictive motion:

> ... *veras como* ***viene*** *la estacíon de autobuses y enseguida* ***viene*** *Nuevo Centro.*
> ... you will see it when the bus station comes and following [that] comes Nuevo Centro.

---

[1]"Going" is also used nonspatially in English, in situations such as "and you are going to pass a hospital"; such occurrences were not counted as valid instantiations of "go."

A similar reference frame, but tied to a moving observer, is sometimes used in English when the observer is seated within a large moving vehicle, such as a moving bus or train. It did not occur in the 31 North American transcripts. Otherwise, deictic "come" and "go" in Spanish seem to behave similarly to what we observed for driving directions given in English, typified by the following segment:

> ... *por esta avenida **vas** hasta el final y giras hacia* ...
> ... by this avenue go until the end and turn toward ...

This and That

English-Language Data. "This" and "that" are deictic, demonstrative pronouns. The 31 transcripts included in this study include 40 occurrences of "that" and 13 of "this," further indicating that the story is taking place at a location somewhat removed from the current WHERE. Most of the "that's" are direct references to a noun phrase in the preceding sentence.

Spanish-Language Data. The Spanish deictic pronouns *esta, este* (this) occurred 17 times and *esa, ese* (that) occurred 5 times. Typical examples are seen below:

> *Tienes que coger **esta** avenida [Blasco Ibañez] y seguirla hasta* ...
> *Osea siempre a **esta** parte del río, siempre a **esta** parte.*
> You have to take this avenue [Blasco Ibañez] and follow it until ...
> As I said always on this part of the river, always on this part.

A third form of deictic pronoun, *aquel*, did not appear in any of the directions. This pronoun is described in the linguistics literature to be negatively defined with respect to the speaker and the listener; it means "near neither person" (Hottenroth 1982, p. 134). The aquel form is rare in everyday conversation. As discussed elsewhere in this chapter, the language used by the 22 Spanish subjects for direction-giving was noticeably simplified, compared to that found in literature, when talking to both the non-native Spanish-speaker and to the native.

Here and There

English-Language Data. In the data from the two North American experiments, there were 39 occurrences of "here" and 19 of "there." Most of the difference was due to subjects at Boulevard Mall in Buffalo, where the occurrences of "here" exceeded "there" by 17 to 3. Most of the time, the word "here" was used to refer to nearby landmarks or streets along the route that could either be seen from the point of the dialog or immediately upon exiting from the mall. Note that the emphasis on nearby locations ("here" outnumbering "there") contrasts with the pattern for "this" and "that."

Spanish-Language Data. Hottenroth (1982) described the tripartite system of deixis and compared it to the binary system used by English and other languages. In our Valencia transcripts, the forms of "there" outnumber "here," but only by a slight margin (20:14). The specific data are: *aquí* (here), 14; *ahí* (there, where the listener is) 13; *allí, allí* (there, at some other place), 7.

REFERENCE FRAMES

Reference frames are an important part of spatial language. In verbal directions for wayfinding, the up–down contrast of the VERTICALITY image-schema is frequently observed. The orientation of "up" and "down" can be based on topography (up = uphill), on river flow (down is downstream, in the direction of flow), or on the compass combined with a north = up conventional binding (Mark, Svorou, & Zubin, 1987). The direct use of compass directions was seldom observed in either the English or Spanish transcripts, with only 5 of 31 English-speaking and 0 of 22 Spanish-speaking subjects including them. Another reference system, based on the CONTAINER image-schema, uses an in–out contrast in a radial reference scheme, with "out" often, but not always, being directed away from the central business district.

English-Language Data. We found that "out" was the most commonly used reference-frame word, being used 46 times by a total of 31 subjects. However, in 31 of these cases, the word "out" was referring not to a geographic reference frame, but to a reference frame based on the current location, telling the recipient to go out of the parking lot, the mall, and so on. Thus, only 15 occurrences of "out" were used in the "out-of-the-city" sense. "Down" was mentioned 33 times, by 20 of the 31 subjects, and was almost always in a geographical context. It seemed to be used for every cardinal direction. "Go down the street" seemed to simply reflect an ego = up personal reference frame, the one that gives rise to "a stranger came up to me on the street" rather than "a stranger came down to me on the street." "Up" was less common again (15 occurrences), and usually referred to an uphill or a northward direction. Finally, "in" was used least often. "In" was used geographically only three times, by 2 subjects; other times, "in" was used for a mall-based or parking lot–based reference frame.

Spanish-Language Data. The reference frames for "up" and "down" were present in the Spanish directions, but with much less frequency than in the English directions. The verb "bajar" (to go down) took the command form *bajas* (go down) 4 times, compared to 33 in Experiment 1A/B. The verb "subir" (to go up) occurred as *subes* (go up) only once, compared to 15 times in Experiment 1A/B.

DISTANCE AND DIRECTION

One might expect that wayfinding directions would contain distances that the traveller should drive, and might use cardinal directions to indicate orientations. Alternatively, people sometimes use estimated travel times instead of ground distances.

English-Language Data

Among the 31 transcripts, distances in miles were mentioned 9 times, by 8 subjects. For the Buffalo subjects, 7 of the 11 male subjects included at least one distance estimate (in miles), whereas only 1 of the 9 female subjects there did. Distances in miles were found in 2 of 5 Santa Barbara transcripts (1 male, 1 female), and in none of the 6 Vancouver transcripts. Only 3 of the 31 transcripts contained travel time estimates, 2 by female subjects in Buffalo, the other by 1 male in Vancouver. Sex-related differences in the indication of distances seem clear in Buffalo.[2]

Cardinal directions (north, south, east, west) were even less common. Only 5 of the 31 subjects mentioned them; far more often, directions were given using egocentric directions (left/right) or by using reference frames. As in the case of distances, males used them four times more often than did females. Interestingly, the same woman gave the only distance and the only direction mentioned by any of the 9 female subjects in Buffalo, and she had a European accent! Furthermore, her statement suggested that she would probably have chosen a left/right frame or indicated direction by pointing, but could not, because she could not orient herself inside the mall:

> I usually take the, uh, uh, I don't know which way we're facing, now. {OK} But if you go south, there's the Thruway. [subject B-E-6]

Only 5 of 31 English-speaking and none of the 22 Spanish-speaking subjects included them. Anecdotal reports suggest that cardinal directions may be more commonly used in the American Midwest, but this awaits further study.

Spanish-Language Data

If distances and cardinal directions were uncommon in the North American data, they were much less common in Valencia. Only 1 occurrence of distance was found throughout all 22 transcripts:

---

[2]Because all North American driving directions were given to a male interviewer, we realize that we must be cautious in interpreting sex-related differences in the transcripts as sex-related differences in the abilities or mental models of the subjects. It is conceivable that the observed sex-related differences would be exactly reversed in directions given to a female interviewer; we intend to conduct such an experiment in the future.

Estará de aquí a unos 5 kilometros lo menos . . .
(It will be here [will come] in some 5 kilometers . . .)

Furthermore, no occurrences of time estimates, such as "about 5 minutes," were found, nor were any mentions of cardinal directions. Of course, since there was only one distance and no directions, there could not be significant sex-related differences; we note, however, that the lone Valencian subject giving a distance was male.

REPETITION AS AN INDICATION OF DISTANCE

Repetition in directions can be used as an indication of distance. They also are an indication that the person is mentally traversing an image of the route, in some egocentric reference frame.

English-Language Data

We observed 3 cases in which repetition apparently was used by direction-givers to indicate distance in English in our sample of 31 transcripts; the first from Buffalo (Boulevard Mall to Eastern Hills Mall), and the others from Vancouver. All 3 of these subjects were female.

> Then when you get on Maple you wanna go right, you wanna go past, uh, there's Chi-Chi's {OK. Yeah, I know that. . .} there's, uh, lots of theaters. **Keep going straight down, going straight down,** until you hit—I'm trying to think how many major lights, but you wanna hit Transit.

> . . . turn left on the big road, and then turn right and then **keep going and going and going** 'til you get up the hill {OK}, I mean, that's all straight through Port Moody {Yeah}, up hill and still **keep going and going and going** until you hit Lougheed Mall!

> Turn left, going onto Lougheed Highway {Yeah} that way, and keep going straight. I mean, just totally **straight straight straight straight straight straight.** {OK} And you'll go through all these lights and these bypasses and {OK} keep going straight, and you'll, you'll reach, um, Port Coquitlam, and from there, there'll be signs everywhere, so, you got that?

Spanish-Language Data

One of the 22 Spanish transcripts contained a large amount of repetition; 3 others contained two or more occurrences of repetition. Following is an excerpt from a sample transcript:

*Pues mira, sales por aquí **todo recto, Blasco Ibañez todo recto***
y cuando llegas al parque del Real, de los Viveros... Tu por la orilla de los
*Viveros, **todo recto, todo recto, todo recto**, y ya llegara a Nuevo Centro.*
(Well look, you leave for here totally straight Blasco Ibañez totally straight
and when you arrive at the royal park, of los Viveros . . .
You [go] for the bank of the Viveros park, totally straight, totally straight,
and there you will arrive at Nuevo Centro.)

DESCRIPTION OF TURNS

Another interesting property of the transcripts was the description of turns that
the traveller would make during the trip. It was first noted in the Spanish transcripts that a large number of verbs and other terms was used to describe turns.
Subsequently, we analyzed the English-language transcripts in the same way; we
present those data first for comparability with other sections of this chapter.

English-Language Data

The 31 English-language transcripts contained a total of 49 linguistic representations of turns. This low number is in part because the routes in Buffalo and
Vancouver could be negotiated making only one turn (excluding moves out of
the current mall and into the destination mall). The 26 transcripts from these
areas contained 41 turn descriptions (1.6 per person); the excess turns were either
in repetitions or reviews, or involved the source or destination mall. There is a
relatively low diversity of turn descriptions in our English-language data, and
also some apparent regional differences.

The most common way to describe a turn was the simple verb "to turn." This
verb was used for 21 of the 49 turns. It was used for all 10 turns mentioned in
the Vancouver transcripts (100%), for 4 of 8 in Santa Barbara (50%), but for
only 7 of 31 in Buffalo (23%). Buffalo subjects tended most frequently to use
the verb "make" (14/31, 45%). It appeared in a number of uses, with a simple
"make a left[right]" 13 times, "make a left[right] hand turn" in 2 cases, and
"make a left[right] turn" once. The simple form "make a left" was used twice
(25%) in Santa Barbara, and "make" was not used at all in Vancouver. Only
three other verbs were used to indicate turns: "take a left[right]" in 5 Buffalo
cases and one other; "go left[right]" in 4 Buffalo transcripts and 1 other; and
"hang a left[right]" just once, in Buffalo.

The Spanish transcripts contained many occurrences of *mano* (hand) in turn
descriptions. For comparative purposes, we tabulated the uses and contexts of
"hand" in the English-language data. The word appeared only 11 times among
the 31 transcripts (0.35 occurrences per subject), and was most often used (8 of
11) in the phrase "left[right]-hand side" to describe the side of the street on
which a landmark or the goal could be expected. It was used only twice among

the 49 turn descriptions; the other use was to indicate which lane of a multilane highway should be used.

Spanish-Language Data

It is interesting to note the variety of expressing the act of turning in this small sample. Nine different verbs or verb phrases were used to indicate turns or the need to turn. The verb "coger" (literally: to take) was used most frequently, and is illustrated in the following passage.

> *Cogeis **a mano izquierda** para salvar los jardines, luego **a mano***
> ***derecha** a este lado del río . . .*
> (Take a left hand [turn] to avoid the gardens, later a right hand [turn]
> on this side of the river . . .)

A more unusual form of indicating a turn is the use of the verb "girar" (literally: to gyrate).

> *Vas hasta el final y **giras hacia allá** . . .*
> (Go until the end and turn toward there . . .)

The following driving directions (male interviewer; male subject, approximately 40 years old) contain no reference to turning, although the directions given are accurate and complete:

> *¿Pero cómo vas, en coche? {Sí, en coche.} Pues mira, sales por aquí*
> *todo recto, Blasco Ibañez todo recto y cuando llegas al parque del*
> *Real, de los Viveros . . . {Sí} Tu por la orilla de los Viveros, todo recto,*
> *todo recto, todo recto, y ya llegara a Nuevo Centro. {Muy bien}*
> *Osea siempre a esta parte del río, siempre a esta parte. Ya veras*
> *como viene la estacíon de autobuses y enseguida viene Nuevo Centro.*
> *{Muy bien, gracias} Sales por aquí, así y vas siempre a orilla del río,*
> *a orilla del río y ya llegaras. {Vale gracias} Adios.*
> (But how are you going, by car? {Yes, by car.} Well look, you leave for here
> totally straight Blasco Ibañez, totally straight and when you arrive at the royal
> park, of los Viveros {Yes} You [go] for the bank of the Viveros park, totally
> straight, totally straight, totally straight, and you will arrive at Nuevo Centro. {Very
> good} As I said always on this part of the river, always on this part. You will see
> it when the bus station comes and following comes Nuevo Centro. {Thanks} Leave
> for here, like this and go always on the bank of the river, on the river bank and
> you will arrive at it. {Okay thanks} Goodbye.)

The 22 Spanish transcripts contained 34 mentions of turning; with an average of 1.5 turn descriptions per transcript, the total turn frequency is very similar to the English-language data. Thus the variety of turning verbs is all the more notable: the 49 English-language turns were described using only 5 verbs, whereas the 34 Spanish turns used 9 different verbs or verb phrases (see Table 17.1).

STYLE OF PRESENTATION

We examined the transcripts to determine the grammatical style (tense, voice, etc.) used, and review the results in the following section.

English-Language Data

Of the 31 transcripts in English, 22 of them began with commands ("do this," "go there"). Six subjects used commands throughout; only one of these was in Buffalo. The most common pattern, seen in 11 cases, was to begin by giving commands, but to later switch into future-tense description, in which the listener''s trip is described to him or her in advance of travel. Six of the 11 were from the west, and together these two categories (command-only; command, future) included all 11 west coast subjects. Other command-first styles included 5 subjects; all of these were in Buffalo. Furthermore, of the 11 Buffalo subjects to begin with commands, 9 were male.

Other styles, used by 7 of the 9 female subjects in Buffalo, included 3 cases of a hypothetical style ("Uh. I would go out and take, uh . . ."; subject B-B-10); 2 cases that expressed the traveller''s wants to him ("Then when you get on Maple you wanna go right, you wanna go past, uh, . . ."; subject B-B-6); one presented multiple possibilities; one was very mixed; and two began with present-tense description, as in the following example:

{Excuse me, can you tell me how to get to Boulevard Mall?} Um, sure. It's . . . you go out here, this is Transit Road {OK} If you take Transit to , um, I guess it would be easiest just to go up to, Maple {OK} and then take Maple all the way

TABLE 17.1
Frequency of Verb Forms Describing Turns in Spanish

Corner-Turning Verbs (22 subjects tested)	
coger (to take[a turn])	11
tirar (to throw [a turn])	8
dar la vuelta (to make a turn)	4
torcer (to turn [oneself])	4
doblar (to turn)	2
echar (to throw [a turn])	2
desviar (to deviate)	1
volver (to revolve, turn around)	1
girar (to girate [turn])	1

until you see it. {OK} It's on, it'll be on your left-hand side, almost at Niagara Falls Boulevard. {OK} OK? {Thank you} Sure. [subject B-E-10].

We note that all 11 Western subjects (5 male, 6 female) started with a command, as did 9 of 11 Eastern male subjects. In contrast, only 2 of 9 Eastern female subjects started with a command; we have no explanation for this effect at this time, although the association between sex and command-first style among Buffalo subjects is strong.

Spanish-Language Data

Thirteen of the twenty-two direction sessions began with the simple form of command. The "You have to . . ." form of advice was used in 6 of 22 of the direction sessions. The descriptive mode, which more or less resembles a tour, was used in 3 of 22 direction sessions.

CONVENTIONAL METAPHORS

English-Language Data

The Road "Takes You."   One interesting spatial metaphor is the idea of a road as a transportation device. In a literal sense, the road is stationary and it is a vehicle travelling along that road that "takes" the person. Here, the source domain of the metaphor is a vehicle travelling along a road, and the target domain is the use of a trajectory along that road by the listener, in what Talmy (1990) called fictive motion. This "road-as-conveyer" metaphor is widespread, occurring in 10 of the 31 English-language transcripts (32%). Here are two examples:

> . . . actually all you have to do is get on Maple Road and Maple'll *take* you to Transit [B-B-7]

> Ward Memorial *takes* you right out to the campus, . . . [S-3]

"Follow" That Road!   According to the basic meaning of the word, one can only follow something that is moving. In 5 transcripts, speakers used what we term a *follow metaphor*, in which a person is told to follow a road. This is similar to a case discussed by Talmy (1990), in which a road "runs through the mountains." The road itself is substituted for the trajectory of a vehicle moving along it. If that metonymic substitution is made, then it is a simple step to tell someone to follow the road, meaning follow a hypothetical vehicle travelling along it. Here are three examples:

> Make a right onto Walden and *follow* Walden straight out. [B-E-15]

. . . over to the freeway, just keep on your right hand lane. {OK} *Follow* that all the way along. [V-E-15]

Turn left, *follow* that all the way out and you come all the way . . . then you go all the way up the hill, eh, then you come down the other side {OK} and come into Port Moody, and just, just, it'll turn. Stay on that, its Barnett Highway {Yeah}, just *follow* that all the way out. [V-L-1]

Mixed Metaphors.   It was not uncommon for speakers to mix two or more of these metaphors together, often within a single sentence:

1. *You take it, it takes you:*
   Take Maple out. Maple'll *take* you right to the Mall. [B-E-3] (This mixes metaphors if one believes that taking a road is in fact metaphorical.)
2. *"Follow" and "take" metaphors:*
   And, uh, you go over the Freeway and *if you just follow that road out,* it, it will *take* you to the campus. [S-2]
   That'll *take* you out to Clark Road. *Just keep following that road all the way,* it'll *take* you right to Lougheed Mall. {Oh, OK} It'll *take* you right there. [V-C-2].

Spanish-Language Data

The same basic metaphors (take, follow) were found in Spanish as in English, although the relative frequencies were different. The take metaphor was found in Spanish only as part of turns (*coges* (take [a turn]), 11 occurrences), and not in the "take this road" construction that was fairly common in the English data. Although we are aware of Sandor's (1986) warning regarding the attribution of metaphor to another culture''s literal discourse, we feel safe in interpreting these rather directly mapped metaphorical statements, and we have found two native speakers, from Spain and Chile, to corroborate this interpretation.

The "follow the road" metaphor was more common in Spanish than in English. *Sigues* (follow [the road, river]) occurred 28 times among the 21 transcripts from Valencia; in contrast, "follow" occurred only 5 times in the 31 English-language transcripts. On the other hand, *te lleve* (it [road, river] takes you) occurred only twice in the Spanish data, but in about one third of the English-language transcripts. Another interesting metaphor, which appears in English as well, is *pegada* (stick to [the right]).

SUMMARY

In the introduction to this chapter, we suggested that verbal directions for wayfinding represent an interesting and important topic for research, and that the topic was important for several reasons. Here, we summarize our findings using the same framework.

Relation to Narrative Understanding

Properties and principles related to the understanding of narrative text, especially stories, seem applicable to verbal wayfinding directions. Many linguistic phenomena, such as deictic terms, summaries, and repetition to indicate distance or temporality are shared by narrative and the natural discourse involved in giving directions. The study of verbal directions for wayfinding provides a good area in which to test robustness of results of models posited for narrative text understanding, given the unprepared, natural quality of the former.

Relation to Models of Spatial Cognition

Spontaneous provision of verbal directions for wayfinding usually requires the direction-giver to perform both spatial and verbal cognitive tasks, perhaps simultaneously. Again, the unassuming (covert) environment within which we have collected these directions assures that our transcripts reflect natural, unprepared, everyday spatial language.

Relation to Vehicle Navigation Aid Systems

Current microcomputer technology has generated considerable recent interest in onboard provision of navigation assistance to vehicle drivers. This interest includes studies of the relative value and effectiveness on graphic (map or map-like) versus verbal methods of assistance. Many drivers perform better using verbal (aural) driving directions than using paper maps or a map/verbal combination when navigating an unfamiliar environment (Streeter, Vitello, & Wonciewicz, 1985). Because many people have difficulty reading maps (Streeter & Vitello 1986), more attention should be paid verbal directions for vehicle navigation aids.

Relation to Cognitive Linguistics

Work on the role of metaphor in the forming of cognitive models and in reasoning about abstract domains by Lakoff, Johnson, and others, claimed that the Path image schema, with a source, a path, and a goal, is one of the most central. The path or journey through physical (geographic) space represents the basis for our understanding of and language for situations as diverse as projects, relationships, and so on (Johnson, 1987), and thus the study of wayfinding may be close to the core of cognitive principles. Indeed, many core image schemata are spatially derived, and some are geographical.

ACKNOWLEDGMENTS

This chapter represents part of Research Initiative #2, *Languages of Spatial Relations*, of the National Center for Geographic Information and Analysis (NCGIA), supported by a grant from the National Science Foundation (SES–88–10917); support by NSF is gratefully acknowledged. The authors also wish to thank the members of the Center for Cognitive Science at the State University of New York at Buffalo, who made valuable suggestions during earlier presentations of these ideas, and William Rapaport for comments on an earlier draft of this chapter.

18

Deixis in Persuasive Texts Written by Bilinguals of Differing Degrees of Expertise

Carol Hosenfeld
Judith F. Duchan
Jeffery Higginbotham
State University of New York at Buffalo

INTRODUCTION[1]

Uncle Sam Wants You! This culturally familiar phrase is usually accompanied by a picture in which a father figure, "Uncle Sam" points out to the audience the "you" in an effort to persuade young men of military age to join the Armed Services. This familiar sample of persuasive writing takes a deictic perspective wherein Uncle Sam, the person who points from his own perspective to the "YOU," the audience member to whom the phrase is directed. Reinforcing of the deixis is the pointing finger of Uncle Sam, making direct deictic contact with his audience.

Our project in this chapter is aimed at determining how deixis in persuasive texts, such as the Uncle Sam text, compares with that of narrative. In addition, we examine the sensitivity of rating instruments used in bilingual education for rating persuasive texts. Our ultimate goal is to develop methods to be used in teaching students persuasive writing.

We take persuasive text to be a type of discourse that functions to convince someone to agree with a position held by the writer and often, as a result, to act

---

[1]This study was part of a larger project conducted by Carol Hosenfeld. The large study also included having the subjects reflect on the process by which they produced the revised handout (see Hosenfeld & Segal, in preparation). Additionally, the revision required changes in spelling, grammar, and rhetorical skill. Because the spelling was of no concern here, we did not duplicate spelling errors in this data.

in a particular way. Persuasion differs from narrative in that its aim is not to entertain but to persuade. Typical treatments of persuasive texts, sometimes called argumentative texts, have not considered the deictic elements as central to the genre (Connor, 1987; Folman & Sarig, 1990; Leggett, Mead, Kramer, & Beal, 1988). They have emphasized, instead, organizational patterns of logical argument such as cause and effect, detail and example, particular to general, general to particular, and argument to counterargument (Connor, 1987; Connor & Lauer, 1988; Leggett et al., 1988; Young, Becker, & Pike, 1970). The function of the persuasive discourse is seen as an inducement of an evaluation in the mind of the reader comparable to that subscribed to by the writer (Young et al., 1970).

The contention here is that competent handling of deictic perspectives in persuasive text is essential to its effectiveness. For example, a persuasive text that fails to make clear its intended audience, or one that shifts from one addressee to another without explanation, can falter in its goal of persuasion. Similarly, a text written by an expert should show sufficient control of deixis to best serve the persuasive goals. Finally, helping learners with deictic problems improve their handling of deixis in persuasive texts should help them arrive at a better product.

In this chapter we investigate three aspects of deixis as it pertains to persuasive text: deixis of time, space, and person. We describe the commonalities and differences across a group of persuasive texts written by bilingual speakers whose first language is not English. Then, we compare the deictic structuring of these texts with the way the texts were rated by experts using a global rating scale. We also compare our subjects' use of deixis with that used in narrative, and show the differences in effectiveness in our subjects' handling of deixis. Finally, we consider the implications of these findings for the teaching of persuasive writing.

METHOD

This project involves an analysis of deixis in 17 persuasive texts written by university faculty (4), university writing teachers (4), graduate students (5) and undergraduate students (4) at the State University of New York at Buffalo. All subjects had first languages other than English, and all texts were written in English.

The subjects were asked to create a persuasive text by revising an already written handout (see appendix). The persuasive text used in this study is of a particular type, one that involves a revision of an already formed text, with the information provided. What our subjects were to do was to recreate a text to improve upon it.[2] Their instructions were as follows: "You are the new director

---

[2]This text did not conform to the type of persuasion that was found in other studies of persuasion, such as those by Connor and Lauer (1988) or Folman and Sarig (1990). In Connor and Lauer, for example, the subjects were to select a problem, identify an audience who could solve the problem, develop a solution and evaluate the solution. The authors then evaluated the produced text based on components that fit the nature of their task, not all of which would be appropriate for evaluating our subjects' performance.

of the International Living Center [ILC] at the State University of New York at Buffalo. One of your first tasks in your new job is to revise a handout designed to recruit (enlist) incoming American freshmen to live in Richmond, a special residence hall where American students have the opportunity to live with international students." The subjects were told to "use as much of the text as you can, while revising to improve it."

The compositions were scored holistically by raters trained in evaluating the compositions of nonnative writers of English. A discourse analysis was performed on the compositions, tracking the use of deictic indicators in the areas of person, place and time across 18 different persuasive texts.

Once we identified the deictic indicators, we analyzed them to determine whether they clustered within paragraphs. We also analyzed the effect of format framing on the use of indicators and the degree of vividness that the indicators portrayed. We then compared the texts and their deictic organization with global ratings from a standardized assessment tool to determine the sensitivity of such a measure to differential use of deixis, as well as differential abilities in persuasive writing.

RESULTS

The Commonalities Across Texts

We found certain types of similarities across texts regardless of the expertise of those writing them. The similarities were in all areas of deictic organization, time, space, and person.

Temporal Deixis. Our writers expressed time relations using present and past-perfect constructions (has been, have been), future constructions (will be, will make, will have opportunities), and constructions expressing habitual action (students learn, they develop skills, they have dances). Sometimes habitual actions were cast in future tense (there will be dances). Hypothetical events were also depicted, requiring a frame shift to a future time in which events hold temporal relations to one another, rather than to events of the present (If you do X, Y will happen).

In our persuasive texts, the time at which the text was created, the writing time, and the time when they were read—the reading time—were cast as the deictic "now." Evidence for this assignment of current time is provided by the interpretation of the phrase "5 years ago" used to described when the ILC was established. A reader, unless provided with other information, is to assume that 5 years ago is 5 years prior to this year in which the reading is taking place. The further assumption called for is that the reader also takes the time of writing to be this year.

This now of writing and reading time was portrayed in two ways. One was as prior to the time of the events being predicted or hypothesized. So the hypothetical events are interpreted as occurring after the time when the text was written or read, and after a future decision is made to live at the ILC.

The aim of the persuasion of these texts was to predict that those who might live at the International Living Center in the near future will benefit in ways that are similar to the benefits gained by those who lived there in the past. A second way the now was portrayed was in relation to past time. Past time for the texts in this study, is a time when previous affiliates (previous students at the ILC) received its benefits. The contrast between past benefits obtained by others and future benefits obtained by the reader is pivotal to the structure of persuasion in these compositions.

The future time for these texts is different from the future typically depicted in stories. Even science fiction texts that are read as being about the future, are written in past tense. Stories are also not to be read as the now of the writing or reading present, but rather as a now experienced within the time frame of the story.

Furthermore, the progression of time within the discourse frame differs for narratives and our persuasive texts. The story time now for narrative moves on as the story progresses (see Almeida, this volume). This was not typically the case for the persuasive texts in this study. New events described were not necessarily temporally related, but more like a list of events insensitive to time (you will have dances, take trips, have potlucks).

Spatial Deixis.   The texts all were aimed at persuading individuals to "come" to a center, to a place that was depicted as the "here" of the text. Thus, the texts we examined all involved the creation of a shifted spatial center—the International Living Center. Once created, the center was sometimes referred to as "a setting" or with the deictic term "here." This easy alternation between deictic expressions (here) and ones referring to a specified place and to a general locale is shown in the following:

(1) The *International Living Center* has been in existence during five years. Its purpose is to create *the setting* where foreign students can interact with Americans. *Here* foreign students receive ongoing orientation into the American way of life and American students learn to live with many cultures (Subject O, para 1).

Once the spatial center was established, it became a focal location for situating other events. Thus, for example, socials take place at "nearby attractions" (Subject 0, para 4). The term "nearby" is to be interpreted as near the ILC, the place which is serving as the spatial center. And events that are not specified as to their location are able to be seen as taking place at the ILC or Richmond Hall, the presupposed center. For example, one can safely assume that potluck suppers described in (2) take place at the ILC.

(2) Most obvious among these is the opportunity to taste a variety of foods at the monthly potluck suppers sponsored by the Center (Subject B, para 2).

The shifting from the place at which the text is being read to the ILC is reminiscent of the spatial shift that takes place in a narrative text. In that case, the shift is from the place of reading to the story world.

Person Deixis. The audience, however identified, functions as the addressee, as the "you" of the deictic frame. That is, readers were indirectly invited to identify with the specified group. So, when writers write about a positive experience, they hope their reader will want to have that experience.

(3) *Many of you* have no experience eating food from other countries; here, there are delicious and wonderful surprises (Subject N, para 3).

Similarly, when writers wrote about misguided views of a group, they were probably hoping their reader would be persuaded to change their position:

(4) It has been assumed by many *uninformed students* that to be majoring in international affairs or foreign languages is necessary to successfully benefit from living in Richmond (Subject D, para 2).

(5) *They* fail to realize that they don't have to travel to each and every country all over the world in order to experience other cultures (Subject D para 3).

Sometimes, just by casting a position on an issue as a misbelief, the audience is invoked indirectly as someone holding that misbelief. It can be read as "you might be thinking X, but Y is true."

This invocation for the reader to identify closely with the positions being attacked or promoted in the text is likely to be inherent to many persuasive texts. They thereby differ from narrative texts, which do not require such identification to be successful. Narratives can still be enjoyed, whether or not the reader is in accord with the beliefs of an author or character.

Vividness. As with other discourse genres, the same place, person, or time may be referred to in a variety of ways, within the same persuasive text. Similar referring expressions are sometimes found in clusters, as when one subject used "here" to refer to the ILC many times in one paragraph, and not in the next; or when another subject identified an addressee in third person (American student), and then shifted to "you."

Sometimes, changes in terms used to indicate deixis occurred together across different deictic domains resulting in an alternation in textual vividness. For example, our writers tended to use more instances of "you" "here" and "come" in sentences that were formatted as headings or listings (see Tables 18.1 and 18.2). The grouping of changes across deictic domains could be identified as an overall change in stance in the text from a distant one to one that was more engaging, or more vivid. The vivid stance is one that made a direct personal appeal to the audience, such as is the case in the poster where the Uncle Sam figure points to indicate the "you."

Individual Differences

Because the task was one in which a given text was revised, the similarities between individuals responding to the task were likely to have been more pronounced than would have been the case had the subjects been instructed to create their persuasions anew. Nonetheless, there were marked differences in the texts written by these subjects, some of which are described later.

Temporal Deixis.   Time was used differently by various authors. Some emphasized the past mistakes and misconceptions held by potential readers, and others emphasized the future benefits offered by the ILC. One author placed the reader in the temporal frame of a hypothetical future that included the following phrases: "you could be overseas on dry land"; "if you accept this offer it could make you part of the most unique and exciting residential experience on campus" (Subject A).

Some texts built a temporal structure in which the past was first emphasized, and then the hypothetical future. The persuasive argument involved contrasting a place having a desirable past history with the future potential for pleasurable affiliation. Other texts focused on the present, with a description of activities that are currently desirable and potentially available sometime in the future.

Spatial Deixis.   Writers also differed in their depiction of spatial entities in the texts. All established the ILC as the center, and occasionally referred to it as "here." But some used the ILC as a spatial contrast with other places, and others did not.

TABLE 18.1
The Six Titles Used by Subjects to Begin Their Persuasive Texts

---

A. YOU COULD BE OVERSEAS ON DRY LAND AT THE INTERNATIONAL LIVING CENTER.
C. WHAT ABOUT AN INTERNATIONAL LIVING EXPERIENCE?
F. COME AND LIVE IN THE I.L.C.!
I. COME TO THE INTERNATIONAL LIVING CENTER
    ENJOY THE INTERNATIONAL EXPERIENCE
J. WELCOME TO INTERNATIONAL LIVING CENTER
K. IT PAYS TO BE "INTERNATIONAL PERSON"!

TABLE 18.2
Subheadings Used by Some Writers to Highlight Information
in Their Persuasive Texts

C: THIS IS AN INVITATION FOR YOU TO APPLY FOR THIS PROGRAM.
C: YOUR LIFE WILL BE MUCH THE RICHER FOR THE EXPERIENCE. ONCE AGAIN,
   WE INVITE YOU TO APPLY.
J. THE INTERNATIONAL LIVING CENTER AT SUNY-BUFFALO CAN PROVIDE ALL
   OF THE ABOVE FOR YOU.
J. IF YOU DESERVE THE BEST, WHY YOU TAKE THE BETTER?
K. *What Are Your Benefits of Living at Richmond?*
   Awareness of International Cultures:
   Enjoyment of a Variety of Cross-cultural Interactions:
   Long-lasting Friendship:
   Capability to become an "International" person:

Note. In these instances, the text was either in capital letters, bold print, indented, or separated
from the rest of the text.

Some writers elaborated place entities, contrasting the ILC with other places, both near and far. This was done, on occasion, by spatially nesting the ILC in relation to other spatial entities. For example, the "here" for one subject was the dormitory in Richmond Hall (which is part of the ILC in Ellicott Complex) at the State University of New York at Buffalo. Multiple references to the "there" also occurred, with places being of contrastive locations away from "here." Those used by different writers included places from which residents of the ILC came that were "far away," "overseas," "other countries," "every country all over the world."

Person Deixis.   The texts also differed in the way in which they deictically referred to people. In particular, they varied in the degree to which the author and audience were specified. The writer of the passage was sometimes identifiable to the reader through the use of a noun phrase:

(6) For further information contact (Michael Zem) the Director of the International Living Center.

For other texts the identity of the author was ambiguous. The "we" in (7) could be a director, staff member, or someone living at the ILC.

(7) We have dancing (Subject D para 3).

The audience was also referred to in varying ways. One way an audience was identifiable in our texts was through an expression indicating a third person (e.g., foreign students, uninformed students, many Americans). Some authors designated their audience as American students, others as foreign students, and still others as both American and foreign students. A frequent indicator of audience, and one more familiar and direct was the use of the pronoun "you." (The directions were for them to write to an audience of American students.)

Formatting Techniques. The authors used a variety of formatting techniques to highlight elements of their text. Six of the texts were titled. All of the titles had deictic elements (see elements in bold in Table 18.1). Some of the titles contain an implied "you" (C, F, I, J, K), one specifies "you" explicitly (A). Several others contained the deictic term "come" (F, I).

A few authors used subheadings to differentiate or highlight sections of their text. Like the headings, the subheadings tended to contain explicit or implicit deictic references, as can be seen from the examples in parentheses listed in Table 18.2.

Finally, last lines or paragraphs of several texts often were directed to an identified audience, as can be seen by the examples in Table 18.3.

One author framed half of her text with question–answer exchanges, as seen in Table 18.4. The questions presupposed an addressee and the author shifted the deictic perspective from that of a reader, asking a question, to someone speaking for ILC, who is answering the question.

Global Ratings and Their Relationship to Subjects' Use of Deixis

The texts were given to a group of expert raters for global rankings. The trainers used the Test of Written English (ETS, 1990) a method in which they were specifically trained. The TWE requires that the raters rank the proficiency of the writers along a 6-point scale. The scoring method presumes that it can be used generally, for different discourse genres. The lowest rating (assigned a value of 1) includes descriptors such as: may be incoherent, undeveloped, and contain severe and persistent writing errors. A middle category (assigned a value of 3) includes: inadequate organization or development, inappropriate or insufficient details. The most positive, highest rating (assigned a value of 6) includes categories such as: well organized and well developed; uses clearly appropriate details to support a thesis. (Although the TWE is based on samples in which the length

TABLE 18.3
Deictic Elements Within Last Lines of Persuasive Texts

A. For further information, contact Michael Zem, the Director of the International Living Center, Richmond Quadrangle, 636–5555.

C. YOUR LIFE WILL BE MUCH THE RICHER FOR THE EXPERIENCE. ONCE AGAIN WE INVITE YOU TO APPLY.

H. Welcome to the International Living Center!

I. More detailed information is provided in the Appendix. We hope you are interested in the program. Please contact ILC at this number as early as possible. Thank you.

J. Remember, if you deserve the best, why you take the better?

K. It pays to be an "international person"! So, come and join us at Richmond.

TABLE 18.4
Question–Answer Sequences Constructed by One Writer to
Involve the Reader as an Active Addressee

J. How much to pay?
1,200 for a semester plus vacation periods.
Where to apply?
Write to ILC or by calling up.
When to open?
September 2nd, Friday.
What to bring?
Nothing but smiling and personal belongings.

of time was controlled, that was not the case in the current study, suggesting that the ratings should be interpreted with caution.)

It was predicted that the highly rated texts would differ from those achieving low ratings, with the higher scored texts using deixis in different ways. Our raters did not rate any of the texts in the categories of 1 and 2, the lowest ratings, so the span of the scale was over those rated from 3 to 6. Within this span, the global ratings were not related to the subjects' use of deixis. A statistical analysis of the realtionship between global ratings and the degree of vividness (as measured by the proportion of vivid terms over the total number of person terms) did not reveal a significant relationship. Similarly, there was no significant relationship between the proportion of vivid terms over the total number of words for each of the essays.

The lack of relationship between global ratings and our subjects' use of deixis can be revealed by examining 2 subjects who received a level 4 rating (just above the mid-level of competency). These individuals differed markedly in their use of the deictic "you" (see Figs. 18.1 and 18.2). The figures represent two ways subjects referred to themselves and their audience. The inner circle contains a vivid representation in which the audience is shown deictically by second-person pronouns "you." The outer portion of the circle contains less vivid representations of the author or possible audience members, or of other persons referred to (third persons, neither audience or author). The outer circles for both subjects contain referring expressions such as pronouns "they" or noun phrases: "others," "new friends," "American students." As can be seen in the diagrams, the 2 subjects differ significantly in their use of "vivid" or "less vivid" terms. The subject in Fig. 18.1 used the vivid deictic term "you" and "your" 28 times, and the less vivid noun phrases 18 times, whereas the subject in Fig. 18.2, receiving the same rating, used the deictic term "you" only once and less vivid terms 25 times.

The single regularity found between global ratings and features in the text did not relate to deixis, but instead to the overall length of the text, with the longer texts typically receiving the higher ratings. Furthermore, because the scale fails to consider the persuasiveness of the text, the method may fail to differentiate more from less persuasive texts. Additionally, one of our texts that was judged to be most

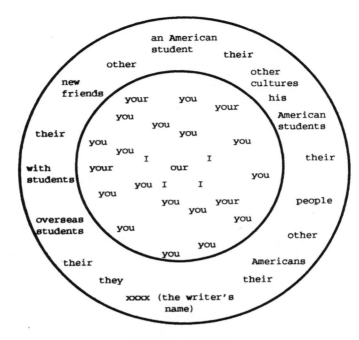

FIG. 18.1.   Subject A.

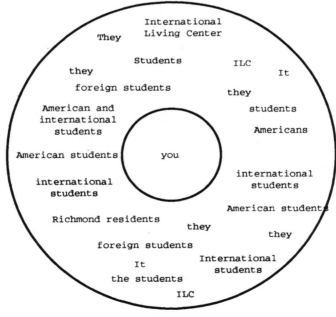

FIG. 18.2.   Subject P.

expert in its persuasiveness (Hosenfeld & Segal, in press), was judged by our raters as ranking only 4 on a 6-point scale. (This is the subject whose essay is depicted in Fig. 18.1 above, with the vivid expressions of audience referencing).

Comparisons of Deictic Structuring for Persuasive and Narrative Texts

The use of deixis in these persuasive texts differed in significant ways from that used in narrative texts. One significant departure was that the writer and the audience were more foregrounded in these texts than for narrated texts studied elsewhere in this volume. Further, the default time in persuasion is the time experienced by the reader (and maybe the writer), whereas in narrative, the time is shifted to the story time, which is not coincidental with the time of reading (or writing). The default now in narrative is what is current in the story world.

Spatial and person deixis contributed mostly to the cohesion in these persuasive texts, deemphasizing temporal relations between events that is so crucial to narrative discourse. Spatial deixis, although prevalent, was not a focal organizing principle, and provided a general frame for making persuasive arguments.

Person deixis offered an interesting addition to our understanding of deixis. Elsewhere in this volume are discussions of how readers determine whether sentences should be read as objective, in the world of the story, or as subjective, in the experience of a story character. In this data, the objectivity or subjectivity of a sentence may vary, depending upon how the reader sees the test. Sentences will be more likely to be read as objective by a reader who is susceptible to the persuasion than one who is suspicious. If the reader does not trust the veracity of the writer, the descriptions may be read as beliefs or lies of the writer and subjective. (The ILC is a great place, or so you, the author, says.)

Stories, unlike these persuasive texts, are event-based, with the the temporal relations between activities serving as a major organizing mechanism. Almeida makes this explicit in his chapter when he says: "The temporal element is more central in narratives than in other discourse types such as lyric poetry or expository prose." Table 18.5 outlines how other aspects of our persuasive texts differed in deictic structuring from narrative texts.

Implications for Teaching Students to Write Persuasive Text

Our writers differed in how they used deixis in their texts, and some of the difference led to reader confusion. For example, for some texts, the identity of the intended reader was not made clear. Other times, it was clear, but shifted between American and foreign students. The lack of specification or shifting of the references to audience occasionally resulted in confusion on the part of the reader.

A third problem occurred when authors identified the wrong audience, violating the instructions. For example, some writers addressed their comments to foreign students rather than American students, even though the instructions

TABLE 18.5
Comparisons of Deictic Structuring of These Samples of Written Persuasion
(Per) and the Deictic Structuring of Narrative Discourse (Nar)

Temporal Deixis

1. Per: The deictic now is the same as the time of writing or reading. (The International Living Center is now 5 years old.)

   Nar: The deictic now is usually shifted from the time of writing or speaking to the story time. (Now it was night.)

2. Per: The temporal focus is on future eventualities (future tense) but a future relative to the time of reading.

   Nar: When the temporal focus of a story is on a future experience, the future is referenced to the time in the story and not to the time of the reading. (She would go tomorrow.)

3. Per: The depiction of future events are often cast as hypothetical, a shifted reference frame, but one centered in the now of the readers consciousness. (If x occurs the circumstances of now will change.)

   Nar: The future of narrative is based in the temporality of the story world. The hypothetical shift is not inherent for narrative, except as one conjured up by the reader in creating a possible-world sense of how the story might evolve.

Spatial Deixis

1. Per: The spatial center is not crucial to the genre, since its structure is more focused on the logical relations among the elements than on where things happen. However, if the logical elements involve a spatial representation, the spatial center can be in the presumed location of the reader (the reader should **go** to the ILC to live), or a shifted center (the reader should **come** to the ILC to live). In the first case the center is with the reader, and moves as the reader moves, in the second the center is at the ILC and the reader approaches it.

   Nar: In narrative the spatial center is usually more prominent, since events take place in a locale, and plot is often structured through movements from one locale to another.

Person Deixis

1. Per: Since the focus is to convince the reader of something, the deictic "who" that takes first-person pronouns, for persuasive texts will often be the writer of the text. (**We** would like for you to come to live in the ILC.)

   Nar: The "who" of narrative is typically an identified character whose perspective is reflected in the text. (Call me Ishmael—"me"—narrator, not author).

2. Per: The audience for whom the text is written is likely to be made explicit in persuasive writing and likely to be the focalized "you" (Uncle Sam wants **you**.) Even if not explicit, the author of a persuasive text is likely to have a foregrounded mental model of a reader so as to be effective in the act of persuasion.

   Nar: The focus for narrative is to get a reader to experience the events, rather than to think in a new way. The reader of the narrative is not as likely to be as highlighted, and is not likely to be located in the fictional world. The "you" of the narrative is not the reader, but a character in the story world (Wiebe, this volume).

3. Per: Subjective elements of persuasion have to do with the beliefs of the audience. If the audience or reader is persuaded, the sentences can be interpreted as objective, as fact. If the reader is not persuaded or suspects the veracity of the writers' statements, then the sentences are taken to be subjective, and part of the belief system of the writer.

   Nar: Subjective elements in narrative are ascribed to the characters, not the writers. Objective sentences in narrative are treated as descriptions of the narrative world and their validity is not questioned.

---

specified that they were to convince American students of the advantages of living at the International Living Center.

Authors who violated the instructions and geared their texts toward the wrong audience (foreign students rather than American students), may have merely forgotten or misinterpreted the instructions. An error such as this would not warrant work on controlling deixis, but rather, would require a lesser effort of reminding the writers to whom they are supposed to be addressing their comments.

Authors who did not identify an intended audience or who shifted their audience in mid-discourse, had the potential for losing discourse effectiveness. This outcome would argue for instruction in persuasive writing in which the student is taught how to be clearer and more consistent in specifying and writing to a particular addressee. That is to say, the student needs instruction in deixis.

CONCLUSION AND IMPLICATIONS

This study shows that deixis can be important to the structuring of persuasive texts. Evidence of its existence is in the use of expressions to identify the intended audience. The authors used expressions such as a "you," "American students," or "foreign students" to refer to their readers. Expressions were also used to identify places and time, and these were used deictically to establish and refer to deictic centers.

There were some texts in this study whose rendering of deixis was confusing. When global ratings were examined, these texts with problem deixis did not get singled out as being different from other texts. Nor did the global ratings relate the quality of the persuasive texts from one another.

It is possible that the global ratings are sensitive to language proficiency and not to genre requirements of persuasion. The way evaluators are to evaluate texts in the global instruments does not include features that would address deixis, nor even features that evaluate the persuasive argumentation of texts such as these. The global ratings, given these results, may be deixis and genre blind, and thus fail to do an adequate job of distinguishing levels of proficiency.

Finally, we found many differences between the deictic structuring of these texts and narratives. The implication, then, is that deixis is an area of language that is particularly sensitive to context, including the contexts provided by the discourse genre in which it appears, so it cannot be taught apart from those genres.

APPENDIX

The International Living Center has been in exsistence during five years. It's purpose is to create the setting where foreign students can interact with Americans. Here foreign students receive ongoing orientation into the American way of life and American students learn to live with many cultures.

It has been assumed by many uniformed students that to be majoring in international affiars or foreign languages is necessary to successfully benefit from living in Richmond. They fail to realize that they don't have to travel to each and every country all over the world in order to experience other cultures. Many Americans have no experience eating food from other countries; here, there are delicious surprises. Monthy pot luck suppers have brought together tasty dishes.

The only chance we get to interface with foreigners is not at the ILC. However, with all our socials it's very easy. We have dancing, trips to nearby attractions, competition to play basketball and volleyball and share holiday customs, going to the movies and to learn each others games.

What is the chief benefit? It's not tasting exotic foods or dancing to different kinds of music. Its the fine intercultural freindships that are forged by students in this environment. Think of the economic and social benefits they will accrue if they are able to bring to there future positions the skills of intercultural communication refined here.

19

NARRATIVE STRUCTURE IN A COGNITIVE FRAMEWORK

Leonard Talmy
State University of New York at Buffalo

INTRODUCTION

This chapter lays out a framework of factors and relationships intended to represent the structure of narrative. Here, narrative is understood to encompass productions of a certain kind, whether these are conversational, written, theatrical, film, or pictorial. The ultimate goal is to develop a comprehensive framework for ascertaining and characterizing the structure of all existent and potential forms of narrative, as well as the larger context within which narrative is situated. Such a comprehensive framework would include the parameters that are necessary in order to characterize the joints of articulation around which narratives and contexts of any kind can vary. The framework set out in this chapter is a step in that direction. This framework was constructed as a working grid for heuristic purposes—much will need to be added, and much will need to be revised. The goal was not to exhaustively and impeccably analyze a smaller circumscribed area. Rather, it was to discern the main structural articulations of a broader and largely unbounded domain.

The Cognitive Approach to the Analysis of Narrative

Our treatment of narrative adopts the presuppositions of cognitive science, cognitive psychology, and cognitive linguistics in assuming the existence of a mind that has produced the narrative work as well as of a mind that is cognizing the narrative work. Unlike some approaches that limit their scope of attention to the confines of the narrative alone, or deny the existence of individual minds, this approach describes a wealth of structural interrelationships that could only be observed by the adoption of a wider scope that includes the existence of both generative and interpretative mental activity. Thus, in our theoretical framework, a particular portion of spacetime can be a "work" only insofar as there is a mind that has assembled it and a mind that perceives and cognizes it as such; otherwise, it is merely some physical pattern.[1]

Further, the mental faculty for the generation and experiencing of narrative in its broader sense may well constitute a specific cognitive system in its own right. This system would generally function to connect and integrate certain components of conscious content over time into a coherent ideational structure. This same cognitive system would operate, for example, not only over the components of a discourse that one had heard recounted, but also over components of one's daily experience to give rise in consciousness to the presence of a unified conceptual entity, whether that of a story or that of one's life. That is, we posit that the same cognitive factors are at work in generating the conscious experience of something as a story that one has heard or the life that one has lived. This putative cognitive system for generalized narrative can be referred to as the "narrative cognitive system." We here only adopt it as a heuristic position that narrative represents the operation of a relatively distinct cognitive system dedicated to it, rather than part of the operation of a more general cognitive system or the interaction of several distinct cognitive systems. But this position is at least provisionally adopted because of the seemingly distinctive qualitative character of generalized narrative in human cognition.

The fact that the human mental faculty for narrative may constitute a particular cognitive system has led to a crucial characteristic of the present analysis. As background to this characteristic, we note that a major direction of the author's work has been to determine the properties of conceptual structuring that apply in common across many or all the different cognitive systems that constitute human mental functioning insofar as these are accessible to consciousness. (In this work, the partitioning of mental functioning into distinct cognitive systems has followed traditional divisions and is regarded as a heuristic issue). This line of research has dealt principally with the properties that govern the conceptual structuring found in one particular cognitive system, that of language (see Talmy 1975, 1976, 1978, 1983, 1985, 1988a, 1988b, 1994). In addition, this research has examined some of the relations between this conceptual structuring of language and that found in other cognitive systems (see Talmy 1988b; in preparation). These other cognitive systems have included visual perception, reasoning,

---

[1]More accurately, only the prototypical work must have an intentional author. In principle, a perceiving mind is capable of experiencing some naturally occurring formation or unintended formation by a sentient entity as being a narrative. Of course, a producer of a narrative can lack any separate entity to perceive the narrative, but that producer will function as a perceiver as well, even if only in the course of production.

memory, expectation (i.e., the simulation of projected future occurrence), kinesthesia (in particular, the system for sensing and experiencing force and pressure), and what may be posited as a "culture system" that structures conceptions pertaining to the ambient culture. And to these cognitive systems can now be added the putative narrative cognitive system.

In a comparison of these cognitive systems, the general finding is provisionally that each system has certain structural properties that are uniquely its own, certain further structural properties that it shares with only one or a few other systems, and certain structural properties that it shares in common with most or all the other systems. These last properties would accordingly constitute the most fundamental properties of conceptual structuring in human cognition. Certain aspects of this fundamental structure were described in Talmy (1988b). But their greatest expansion and detailing to date appears in the present chapter in the "Parameters" section. The parameters that are included and described in that section are those factors that to this point in the present line of research seem the most general and common across the range of cognitive systems. Because they have been included in the present treatment of narrative, most of the examples used to illustrate the parameters pertain to narrative structure. But their cognitive generality is nevertheless intended.

To sum up our cognitive approach, narrative is seen as something that by necessity is cognitively produced or experienced, rather than as anything that could exist autonomously in its own right; that it accordingly represents the operation of a cognitive system; and that its characteristics accordingly share those properties that are common across cognitive systems generally and can, in turn, be used in ongoing research to amplify the nature of those properties. It is this cognitive perspective that distinguishes the present analysis from most other treatments of narrative.[2]

The Cognitive Approach to the Narrative Context

As indicated earlier, narratives per se are understood as necessarily situated within a larger context. Heuristically partitioned, this context encompasses—in addition to the narratives proper—their producers, experiencers, containing societies, and the surrounding world. Because our analytic framework is cognitively based, how will its factors and constructs apply to the divisions of this context?

---

[2]After this chapter was almost complete, I became aware of the work of Genette (1980) and other structural narratologists and of the considerable overlap between their approaches and mine. The negative aspect of this circumstance is the disciplinary compartmentalization that led a linguist to embark on a project without having first consulted the relevant literature in a neighboring field. The positive aspect is that two different paths have led to so many similar conclusions, thus, supporting a sense of the validity of the comparable findings. This partial coincidence may involve more gain than loss, because even the comparable components of the present work are situated within a different overall framework with a cognitive perspective.

First, as already discussed, this cognitively based framework will apply directly to the cognition of the producer of a narrative, both generally and in the course of producing the narrative, as well as to the cognition of the experiencer of a narrative, both generally and in the process of experiencing the narrative.

In addition, the cultures and subcultures in which the producers and experiencers of narratives cognitively participate can constitute a largely coherent cognitive system that informs much of the conceptual structure, affectual structure, presuppositions, values, and, in general, the "world view" of those individuals. This culturally based cognitive system within the psychological organization of these individuals can affect or determine a set of narrative characteristics, and so it is an additionally appropriate target for the kind of analytic framework proposed here.

Finally, the surrounding physical world for humans is seldom—perhaps it intrinsically cannot be—simply a matter of autonomous physics. Rather, the characteristics that are atributed to it, at any level of organization, are (it can be argued) entirely determined by the cognitive processing of the stimuli impinging on the individual and by the cognitively generated schemas that are otherwise imputed to it. To be sure, the ways in which human cognition performs this processing and imputation reflect a biological evolution in which organisms precursor to humans interacted with the exigencies of their environments. But, regardless of its origins, human cognition presently has a particular set of characteristics that shape everything pertaining to mind and behavior. Accordingly, in order to characterize the ways in which the surrounding world is represented in narrative (as well as in much else of human concern), we must look to the ways in which human cognition structures such representations, aside from whatever independent examinations we may make of the surrounding world in accordance with a notion of an autonomous reality. In this regard, the "surrounding world" can now be understood more broadly to comprise not only the physical world, but also the cultural and producer/experiencer portions of the full narrative context. Thus, once again, a cognitively based framework of analysis is called for.

Narrative Structure Across History and Cultures

With respect to narrative structure, it seems that within any one historical tradition, new articulation points develop gradually. That is, some set of elements that previously appeared to constitute a single packet can, in time, be broken into component parts by innovative authors.

It also seems to generally be the case that an articulation of this sort showing up late in one tradition may have been present early in another tradition. Some analysts believe certain phenomena of narrative are only found in recent literature. But that perspective probably arises from insufficient consideration of the varied narrative formats of the world's cultures. For example, in some traditions, children's storytellers play with their stories in ways that Western authors have only recently undertaken. Such a storyteller can ask the children in the audience:

Which way would you like the story to go from here? Would you like me to go back and change the way the story went at that unpleasant point? Or, Here are several endings for the story, which one would you like to hear?

Organization of the Framework

In the present heuristic framework, the structure of narrative is seen as dividing into three main modules. These modules are *domains*, *parameters*, and *strata*. The strata are the basic structuring subsystems of narrative; those recognized and treated here are: Temporal structure, spatial structure, psychological structure, the connectivity system, and import. These subsystems are concurrenly in coordinate effect through the course of a narrative. One image for their operation is the working of a polygraph machine in which separate styluses trace out the concurrent functioning of several different subsystems of a single body's physiology. The term *strata* has been chosen for the components of this module for its suggestion of a parallel relationship between multiple subsystems, but not for any sense of relatively higher or lower placement among the subsystems.

Although each stratum can be individually regarded for its structural properties (as we treat them in the section on strata), a number of these properties are the same or similar across strata. These common properties are abstracted from the individual strata and are gathered together as parameters. These parameters include: the relating of one structure to another, level of partitioning, degree of differentiation, veridicality, and prototypicality.

As already indicated, the strata, with their common principles of organization, apply not only to a narrative work itself, but also to other domains of the entire narrative context. Though only a few of them are treated here, these domains include: the author(s) of the work, the experiencer(s) of the work, the culture (with its shared presuppositions, values, etc.) within which the work and its authors and experiencers are situated, and the spatio-temporal physical world.

This chapter sequences the presentation of the three modules from the more general to the more specific. We use the term *a structure* to refer to any module, member of a module, or definable part of such a member. The sections to follow regularly describe not only individual structures, but also relationships between structures within a member, across the members of a module, and across the modules. Table 19.1, which lists these concepts and the sections in which they are defined, is provided to help the reader move back and forth easily among them for fuller comprehension of the points.

DOMAINS

The context in which a narrative can exist includes not only the narrative work itself, but also the sentience that creates and experiences the work and that manifests the culture and appreciates the world in which the work is situated.

TABLE 19.1
Contents in the Heuristic Framework, Including the Section Headings
in Which They are Described

Domains	Parameters	Strata
Physical World	Relating of One Structure to Another	Temporal Structure
Culture or Society	Embedding	Spatial Structure
	Alternation	
	Concurrence	
Author(s)	Correlation	Psychological Structure
	Abstraction	The Individual
Addressee	Relative Quantity	The Group/Society
The Work	Scope	The Atmosphere
	Granularity	
	Density	
	Degree of Differentiation	Connectivity System
	Continuous–Discrete	Causality
	Uniplex–Multiplex	Viewpoint Connectivity
	Distributed–Concentrated	Psychological Connectivity
	Approximate–Precise	Motivational Connectivity
	Vague–Clear	Epistemic Connectivity
	Sketchy–Elaborated	Sequiturity
	Implicit–Explicit	Continuity of Identity
	Veridicality	Plot Structure
	Prototypicality	Import

This total context can be heuristically divided up into some five portions, here termed domains. These are: the spatio-temporal physical world with all its characteristics and properties; a culture or society with its presuppositions, conceptual and affectual structuring, values, norms, and so on; an author of a work (or a collectivity thereof); the addressee/experiencer of the work (or a collectivity thereof); and a work itself. The work comprises both its physical characteristics, and its contents. The work's physical characteristics involve aspects of its medium—for example, print arrayed over the pages of a book, film projected onto a screen, or the performers and scenery on a stage for a play. The contents of a work are its cognition-related characteristics, encompassing both the affective and intellective, and including the implicit/inferable as well as the explicit/overt. In a narrative, such contents comprise the "story world."[3]

A principal cognitive model on the basis of which the context for narrative and other artistic manifestation can be analyzed is that of communication. Humans

---

[3]To refer to the generic case, rather than just to the case of written prose, the term "book" can be replaced by "work," and the term "reader" can be replaced by "addressee/experiencer." The term "author" is already general enough that it need not be replaced by a term such as "creator." Although the "story world," as just characterized, is only part of the domain of the work, the word "world" will otherwise often be used equivalently to the word "domain."

probably have an innate cognitive system for communicative structure consisting of domains like those just listed. Such communication is usually that of spoken language, but the innate communicational system posited here would function in a more general and meta-modal fashion. Thus, for narrative, the author communicates the contents of the work to the addressee in the context of the culture and the world. However, the conduit metaphor for communication—however adequately it may describe our naive sense of the process—does not adequately characterize either the narrative process or spoken discourse. An author or speaker does not simply aim to transmit his or her ideational content to the addressee—or (to phrase this without a notion of transference), to evoke in the addressee the replication of ideational content equivalent to his or her own. Rather, the author or speaker often wants to engender in the addressee certain conceptual or emotional responses that he or she does not currently experience—for example, surprise, interest, or hurt. To accomplish this, the author or speaker must orchestrate the selection, sequencing, and pacing of material in a way that is likely to cause the desired effects, given his or her understanding of the addressee's psychology.

Although each of the domains listed could be further expanded, only a few are subjected to such elaboration here. In particular, I focus on the various forms or genres a work can take and explore some relations between authors and addressees.

The Work: Properties of the Narrative Prototype

Within the domain of the work, I assess the properties of different genres in order to address one issue: What factors make a work a prototypical narrative? Narrative can be treated as a prototype phenomenon with a core that trails off in various directions. Three dimensions relevant to characterizing narratives are presented. The concurrence of a particular value on each of these dimensions is needed for a prototypical narrative.

Main Cognitive System Engaged. The first dimension consists of the particular type of cognitive system that is primarily engaged by the work. Most prototypical narratives involve the experiencer's *conceptual cognitive system.* This is the cognitive system that establishes *concepts*—ideational, denotative components with referential content—and organizes them in a *conceptual structure.* Less prototypical are works that primarily address or engage other cognitive systems, such as a musical work that induces a sequence of affects or atmospheres in the listener, or a painting that induces in the viewer that class of responses associated with the perception of visual form.

The designation of the conceptual–ideational system as primary for narrative is not intended to deny the incidental or even systematic evocation of emotion or affect by works basically focused on the conceptual–ideational system. Nor, on the other hand, should we underestimate the degree of narrativity in nonprototypical works. For example, a symphony that progresses through a sequence of energetic and calm passages can evoke in the listener a sense of the unfolding of a coherent and meaningful succession of exciting and tranquil events.

Degree of Progression. The second dimension relevant to characterizing narrative is that of the *degree of progression.* We are probably designed to have the experience about the world that it can consist of "events" that "occur" in "succession" through "time." These, taken together, are what I call *progression.* This is not the only experience we can have about the world, but it is a fundamental one, and a work can evoke this particular category of experience. The more a work evokes this experience of progression, the closer it is to the narrative prototype.

The evocation of progression does not require the conveying of an actual succession of distinct events. The depiction of a single event—or even of a static scene—can serve as long as it is designed to be experienced as an excerpt from a progression, where a prior and/or subsequent sequence of events is implied or can be inferred.

One prominent type of nonprogression involves the consideration or evocation of the constant characteristics of some situation. This includes, for example, a physics textbook describing the principles of magnetism, a painting of still life, or a section within a narrative that portrays a static scene.

A seemingly similar type of nonprogressional material might be a rhetorical political work that characterizes some societal situation. However, there can be progressional aspects in such a work. For example, the work can build up its characterization along a particular slant designed to induce emotions and attitudes in a certain sequence, culminating in persuasion of the reader to a cause. Here, what is nonprogressional is the synchronic situation being characterized, whereas the progressional is the marshalling of emotions and the "and therefore" quality of the call to action arising from the description of the disliked state of affairs.

One preponderant—though perhaps not absolute—property of a work that evokes an experience of progression is the following: It is so designed that different parts out of the totality of the work will be cognized by the experiencer at different times. There are two main ways in which this part-at-a-time effect can be achieved, either or both of which may be operative: The work reveals different parts of itself through time, or the experiencer directs his or her attention to different parts of the work through time.

A work that reveals different parts of itself through time can be considered intrinsically *dynamic.* Examples of genres of this type are storytelling, a play, a puppet show, a film, a stand-up comedy routine, an improvisational comedy theater performance, a mime performance, a religious ceremony, a dance performance, music, video art, and kinetic sculpture.[4]

---

[4]Kinetic sculpture is the only item on this list that does not strictly conform to the aegis of successively revealing different parts of itself, because the whole of the sculpture can be seen at all times, but it could be argued that its different states of conformation constitute different parts of the sculpture's totality.

Other works are intrinsically static, but the experiencer can interact with them by successively directing his or her attention to different parts of the whole. Static works may be classed into two groups on the basis of whether or not there is a cultural convention that ordains a particular sequence in which attention is to be directed (even though it would be physically possible to direct one's attention otherwise). Works that involve such a convention include a book, a cartoon strip, a sequential fresco, and an Australian aboriginal sand tracing depicting mythic treks.

Other types of static work are designed for random access by the experiencer's focus of attention. Examples of such works are a painting or tapestry with a number of different depicted components, a sculpture that is designed for viewing from different angles, an architectural structure that one can view from different interior and exterior points, and a geographic-sized art work, as those by Cristo.

One interesting observation that emerges from this analysis is that any tapestry or painting that depicts a story by showing a number of figures and activities that, together, suggest a succession of events (but one the viewer must piece together through his or her own self-determined sequence of visual fixations), is as much an example of interactive fiction as any modern, computer-based form.

The prototype requirement for narrative that it be progressional is abetted to the extent that a genre's succession is determined—whether by physical shifts of exposure or by conventions for directing attention—rather than open to attentional random access.

Degree of Coherence and Significance. The third and final dimension considered here is that of *coherence and significance*. A high degree of coherence and significance are required for the narrative prototype. Coherence is the property that the parts of the work fit together into a sensible whole. That is, relative to the average human conceptual system, the parts of the work can be cognized together in a way that they constitute a higher level entity that can be experienced as a unity. A work loses coherence to the extent that parts of the work are contradictory, nonrelevant, or random with respect to each other. Significance is the property that the parts and the whole of a work can be experienced as fulfilling some purpose or mission on the part of the author. Coherence and significance are, respectively, categories within the strata of connectivity and import, described later, but are brought together in the present dimension because of their related functions with respect to defining narrative.

It can be seen why the dimension of coherence and significance must be added to the previous two dimensions, with the positive poles of these three dimensions in effect, for a work to be a prototypical narrative. A work could be prototypical in being ideational and progressional, but without coherence and significance would little qualify as a narrative. An example of this combination of dimensional values is a diary or a chronicle, which recounts a succession of ideational events but lacks story character to the extent that the entries do not cohere. Even less of a narrative would be a collection of references to a succession of unrelated events, whose juxtaposition would thus not only lack coherence but also significance. On the other hand, to the extent that a diary is seen as someone's personal history or story, or that a chronicle is seen as the history or story of, say, a kingdom, would the recounted succession of events be accorded a sense of coherence and purpose and thus come closer to being experienced as a narrative.

The Addressee's World

An author composes his or her narrative and sets all its structural features on the basis of his or her assumptions about how the addressee processes incoming content. For example, an author can set the rate at which story events take place relative to assumptions about the effects that different rates will have on the average addressee. Authors may slow the rate of events to engender a sense of calm in the addressee, or quicken the pace to engender a sense of excitement. Similarly, authors can set the level of detail based on their assumptions about the effects different levels of detail will have on the average addressee. They can pick a lower level of detail to induce in the addressee a sense that what is currently being described is less important, and increase the level of detail to induce a feeling in the addressee that the present material is important. To have the intended effect, these authorial choices must be based on an assumed (for the addressee) baseline of rate and detail relative to which deviations, such as slow or fast rate or higher or lower level of detail, are defined.

Of course, such baselines differ across cultures and subcultures. If we are to correctly judge the intentions of an author from another culture or period, we must first—or simultaneously—assess the likely baseline of the intended addressees.

Interrelations Between Different Domains

We describe a few out of the numerous possible interrelations between the various domains.

The Work and the Culture/World.   We first consider how the story world, within the domain of the work, relates to the domain of the physical ("real") world and the domain of the cultural world. One relationship here, perhaps the principal one, can be termed the *correspondence of characteristics.* That is, the story world is treated or conceptualized as if it were a real and exhaustive world, in the same way we treat and conceptualize the sociophysical world around us. Further, there are regular relations between the presumed contents of the story world and the world around us, with aspects of the latter systematically projected into the former. Even when some of the content of the worlds differs dramatically, as in science fiction, there is still a great degree of correspondence in the conceptualization of how the worlds work.

The Work and the Addressee.   Another type of interrelationship is that between the domain of the work and the domain of the addressee. One relationship within this type consists of the degree of separation or intermingling of the two domains. In Western works, the norm is a lack of interaction or exchange between individuals in the story world and individual addressees. But some authors play with the usually impermeable boundary between the story world and the addressee's world—for example, by having characters in a play address audience members, or by bringing audience members onto the stage. Some genres intrinsically bridge the two domains, for example, the genre of the interactive street mime, who develops his or her brief narrative episodes in the course of interacting with individuals gathered around or passing by.

A further relationship within the work–addressee type pertains to the balance of the necessities for comprehension along a continuum that runs between the work and the addressee. On one end of this continuum, some narratives are assumed to be self-contained and self-explanatory; that is, all the experiencer need do is to progress through the narrative, and all its relevant contents will be conveyed (that is, if we presuppose the addressee's prior familiarity with the form and medium of the narrative's genre). But other narrative types are assumed not to be sufficient in themselves and, rather, to rely on the addressee's prior familiarity with some portion of the story or story world. For example, the story of a storytelling ballet would be inaccessible to a naive viewer. Such a viewer would no doubt pick up on some aspects of the story, but could not understand the whole plot. For this, the viewer must have knowledge of the story from outside the presentation of the work itself.

The Author and the Work.   A further type of domain interrelationship is that between the author and the work. If the performers of an enacted work can be considered to be part of the domain of the work, then those performers can be thought to bridge the domains by being coauthorial with the work's main author with respect to certain aspects of the work. These aspects are determined by the performers' intonational emphases, timing, accompanying affect of the delivery, and so on—in short, the interpretation. Such aspects can be considered authorial because they affect the meaning and import of the work.

The Author, the Work, and the Addressee.   We finally consider a type of interrelationship involving three domains, those of the author, the work, and the addressee. One relationship of this type pertains to the timing in which these domains come into play. Typically, in the Western tradition, the author composes the work first and then the addressee experiences the work. But other forms are composed "online" as the work is being experienced by the addressee. The term *improvisational* is generally used for this type of work. Examples occur in music (e.g., some recent jazz in the West, or classical Indian music) improvisational dance and improvisational theater performances.

In another relationship of the three-domain type, the addressees are coauthorial with the main author(s) of the work. For example, if the performers of an improvisational comedy act are now considered to be the main authors of the work, then the addressees—that is, the audience members—become coauthorial when the performers ask them for suggestions on aspects of the piece to be improvised. Similarly, in some traditional storytelling or puppet shows for children, the children are asked to choose the way the story will end, or are told that they can demand a return to some point in the story to change certain events. More subtly, one way the audience addressees can become coauthorial is when their online reactions to an ongoing performance influence the performers to alter their delivery, whether these performers are the main authors (as in improvisational comedy) or are coauthorial with the playwright by virtue of their interpretations.

More recent forms of coauthoriality and cocomposition include interactive forms in which the addressee makes choices with respect to the progression of the work. An example is interactive video, in which the work is composed with multiple alternatives at various nexuses; the user can choose the particular alternative that gets realized. Comparably, some modern books are written to allow the reader alternative routes for flipping back and forth within the text.

PARAMETERS

A number of properties run across many and varied structures within the total narrative context. Sets of these properties can be seen to range along particular parameters, and, in turn, sets of these particular parameters can be seen to group together under certain general parameters.

The Relating of One Structure to Another

The wholes or parts of domains or strata can be related in different ways. A number of parameters that involve the relationship of structures are described in this section.

Embedding.   One relationship is that of embedding, both within and across different strata or different domains. To consider strata first, spatial structure can be conceptualized as a larger containing framework with progressively finer levels hierarchically nested therein, as, for example, where a character's location is understood as involving a particular city within the nation, street in the city, house on the street, and room in the house. The same can occur for temporal structure; in fact, the traditional organization of plays is built around such concentric inclusions, where each incident occurs within a particular scene that takes place within a certain act, that occurs within the overall temporal scope of the play.

Such embeddings may also occur across different strata. For example, a reader's attention could be within the physical spatial structure of the story world, and then enter psychological structure by entering the mental world of one of the characters who is located at some point within that space. This mental world has its own structure including aspects of space, but it is still understood as embedded within the spatial structure of the story world as a whole. Such an entrance into a mental world is not understood in the same way as, say, a shift to some new location or scene that is otherwise part of the spatial structure of the story world. The mental world the reader has entered is, rather, more like some subrealm at a particular location within the main fabric of story space. In contrast to the intrastratal example of one physical space embedded within another of the same type structure, this example refers to the interstratal embedding of the psychological structure of a character's mind within the physical spatial structure of the story world.

Embedding is also found with domains. For example, one story can be embedded within another, as when Shakespeare's *Hamlet* embeds a play within itself, each with its own story world. The film *Saragosa Manuscript* has as its main organizing principle the repeated nesting of one story within another.

Alternation. *Alternation* is the relationship among two or more structures in which only one structure is manifest at a time and each one has a turn at appearance, prototypically more than once. As with embedding, alternating structures are cognized one at a time rather than concurrently, but where an embedded structure is taken to be subsumed by the embedding structure or to be localized at some portion of it, alternating structures are treated as wholes relating to wholes with equal priority. Alternation can occur over any scope or scale. Thus, an alternation between the points of view of two different characters in a a narrative can take place every other sentence, as in an exchange of dialog, or every other chapter, as when a narrative presents the progress of a story by turns from the perspectives of the different characters. Other structures frequently alternated in a narrative are different spatial locations, points in time (as with recurrent flashbacks), and subplots or side stories. Virtually any structure can be alternated, including authors, as when a series of different directors each handle a different portion of the single story presented in a film.

Concurrence. *Concurrence* is another relationship that can hold within or across structural units. Concurrence differs from embedding in that in the latter case, a reader can enter the embedded structure and fully disregard the containing structure. But with concurrence, both structures are manifest coextensively. One structure that is concurrent with another can be taken to be equipollent with it, or instead, relate to it in the way that a secondary or more abstract structure relates to a principal or more concrete structure—a type of concurrence termed *overlay.* For example, the work may have an overall atmosphere, one of menace or inexorable doom, for example, whereas subparts of the story will be light. This lightness can be experienced as an overlay upon a subterranean impending menace whose presence does not fully disappear during the light interlude. Other examples of overlay are where a narrative section is intended to tell two or more stories at once on different levels, as, say, a parable with its metaphoric interpretation resting upon its literal interpretation, or where the author has two concurrent purposes, say, to educate while entertaining.

Correlation. Narrative structures that are in *correlation* are also largely concurrent. But where the concurrent structures discussed in the preceding section are generally of contrasting or conflicting character (often included for the effect of incongruity that their clash will produce in the addressee), correlated structures are generally designed to complement or reinforce each other toward the generation of a harmonious effect.

One example of correlation is the existence of corresponding points across a set of different strata in a narrative. Thus, the notion of correlation is the same as the foundational basis of the present analytic system, namely, the polygraph notion in which the different strata of a narrative are linked in their progression. Another example is the correlation of different media or genres, as the synchronization of dialog, image, and music in a film or in a multimedia presentation, or the correlation of the progression in the contents of a story world with the succession of components of the physical medium of the work, as where a story is told by a series of poems with each poem appearing self-contained on each successive page of a book. Finally, a multiplex number of structures can exhibit different types of correlation with respect to each other: They might function jointly, interactively, or independently.

Abstraction. One structure may bear the relation of *abstraction* to another structure within the narrative context. That is, one structure may consist of selected aspects abstracted from another structure. Perhaps the main manifestation of this relation is the way that the contents of a story within the domain of the work can be abstracted from the far richer particulars of the domains of the physical and sociocultural worlds, including the nature of the human psyche and human behavior. Thus, a story typically does not behave like a video camera set up to record all the particulars occurring within its frame and span of operation. Moreover, the abstraction process is not haphazard, but selects aspects understood as structural and of concern.

The abstractions incorporated in a story may correspond to conceptual abstractions already present and regularly generated in our cognition. To explain, note that the texture of everyday life does not much correspond to the cognitive structures in terms of which we experience and categorize. Consider, for example, such conceptual/affectual/actional constructs as jealousy, bravery, and childrearing. In the everyday world, the components out of which such constructs are built are dispersed through time and space, there is much intervening material of no direct relevance, typical components of the construct may be absent and atypical ones present, and so on. Yet, our cognitive processing succeeds in forming the constructs out of the raw experiential material by culling the relevant components, gathering them together, and organizing them into the target patterns. It is cognitive constructs such as these an author may use as structures in the narrative.

In the visual medium, cartoons and caricatures are abstractions from the full detail of the physical objects that they represent. Further, in certain respects, the features that they abstract may well bear some of the same relationships to the original as just discussed. Thus, those features tend to comprise the visual structure of aspects of the original that are of concern to us.

Higher Level Structure.   Virtually any structural factor in narrative can be organized so as to exhibit a second-order structural pattern, and that, in turn, to exhibit a third-order pattern, and so on. An example is shown by Costello, Bruder, Hosenfeld, and Duchan (this volume) in their analysis of temporal structure. The first-order structural phenomenon of relating different out-of-sequence story events to the reader's unidirectional temporal progression is itself shown to be further orchestrated in the story so as to exhibit a progressive asymptotically zeroing-in pattern of flashbacks that alternately overshoot and undershoot a central temporal point.

Relative Quantity

The general parameter that is here called *relative quantity* is basically realized at three levels, with each level serving to embed the next smaller level. From larger to smaller, this parameter includes *scope*—the relative amount of some structure within the narrative context that is presently under consideration; *granularity*—the relative size of the subdivisions into which the amount is internally partitioned in one's attention; and *density*—the relative number of elements within any such subdivisions that enter into consideration.

Scope.   Scope refers to the quantity of some narrative entity that is being considered together at the same time for the structural properties that exist at that choice of quantity. The narrative entity could be a whole domain such as the work with its story world, or one or more strata such as the temporal, spatial, or psychological. For example, one can adopt full scope over a story's temporal and spatial structure so as to track the large-distance geographic movements of a character over the whole period covered in the work. Or, one could pick the relatively small temporal and spatial scope of a character moving about in a room in the course of a half hour.

There are several ways of reckoning different magnitudes of scope. One reckoning involves the proportion out of the total entity at issue that is excerpted for consideration. This type of reckoning has two main levels of magnitude: *global* (i.e., with consideration of the entire entity at issue), and *local* (i.e., with consideration of only a normatively small portion of the whole). But a narrative could make relevant various magnitudes of scope between global and local, or could distinguish magnitudes finer than average local down to microlocal.

Another way of reckoning is based on cognitive capabilities and would yield the following two main levels of scope: (a) what can be experienced within a single scope of perception and span of attention, and (b) what must be assembled in memory because it is larger than a single scope of perception or span of attention. For example, in nonnarrative real life, one can consider an ant crawling across one's palm within a single scope of perception and span of attention. But one can consider a bus trip that one has taken across the country only by assembling aspects of the total experience within one's memory; the whole exceeds one's scope of perception and span of attention. Comparably, within a story of sufficient length, certain structural features of the story will lie within one's span of attention and other features will exceed that span. While scope of perception may apply little to written prose (though it may well do so to poetry that depends in part on the visual arrangement of the words on the page), scope of perception can pertain to the sensory input from dynamic works.

The parameter of scope can pertain to more than space and time. A work can include a greater or lesser scope of import (one of the strata treated later); of the sociocultural domain that is brought into the narrative; of the author's capacities that have gone into the making of the narrative; and of the addressee's capacities that are engaged by the narrative—with the general consequent judgment of the narrative that it is a relatively more major or minor work.

Granularity. The parameter of *granularity* applies relative to a particular level of scope. Within a particular chosen scope, the granularity is the coarseness or fineness of the descriptive grid—that is, the general magnitude of the subdivisions that result from the further partitioning of the chosen scope of material. For example, if we select from a narrative a spatial structure of local scope, perhaps a room the deictic center is in, the narrative might present its material at these two different levels of granularity. One level could constitute a yards-sized metric, a level at which might appear such objects as furniture and people or such features as the room's architectural design. A finer level of granularity could be measured in inches, a level at which might appear such entities as details of wallpaper design, ashtray locations, and facial features. Comparably, at the global level of scope, in a narrative whose story spans geographic distances, a courser granularity might pick up national regions, whereas a finer granularity could present towns.

Density. Relative to a particular granularity, the parameter of density is the relative number of elements extant at that particular granularity that are selected for mention. Thus, to continue the previous example with local scope of spatial structure, a sparse description at the yard-type level of granularity might mention, with respect to furniture, only a sofa and a TV, while a denser description would also mention the armchair, floor lamp, coffee table, and so on. Likewise, at the inch-type level of granularity, a sparser level of density might only mention a few items, like the wallpaper design feature and the ashtray location, but a denser description might also include the crack in the ceiling, the sunbeam hitting the family portrait, and the stain on the butler's tie.

Genres as a whole can differ greatly in the level of their density. Thus, a story presented in a film is more dense in the detailing of material objects and physical features, which occupy and characterize the spatial structure, than the same story written in prose. Across visual genres, a printed or filmic cartoon version of a story will have sparser physical detailing than a standard film version. Further, within a single genre, authors often differ as to the level of density they select; some give innumerable details at a particular level of granularity, and others do not. Finally, the level of detailing can be varied purposively and in correlation with other factors within a single narrative. For example, Hill (1991) noted that, as a narrative approaches a crucial dramatic point, the story time generally slows down relative to reader time and detailedness increases.

Degree of Differentiation

The general parameter *degree of differentiation* encompasses a number of simpler parameters that pertain to various ways in which any entity or structure within the total narrative context can be more or less differentiated or speciated. The parameters presented here may overlap, some of them may pertain to certain types of narrative structures more than to other types, and many of them tend to correlate. Still, they are largely independent and distinct.

The Continuous–Discrete Parameter. This parameter is the axis that runs from the continuous to the discrete, where the latter is the more differentiated. This parameter pertains to any nonhomogeneous structure within the narrative context. At the continuous end of the parameter, that structure is understood as comprising a single unified continuum or gradient that manifests some progressive transition. At the other extreme, the structure comprises two or more entities that are distinct and separate from each other, with clear boundary lines between the entities, and with each entity bearing a particular relation to the others.

This parameter can pertain, for example, to scene shifting: Does a character jump from being in one room to being in another, or do we follow him or her along a single continuous path? In the application of this parameter to psychological structure, the author could have us jump from one character's mind or viewpoint to that of another character, or he or she could have us move imperceptibly from the thoughts of one character to those of another. Also in the stratum of psychological structure, the psyche of a person can be represented as a unitary entity with relatively continuous relations and smooth shifts between otherwise distinguishable moods and attitudes, or it can be represented as composite—in the extreme case, composed of discrete selves in the multiple personality. The short story "The Haunted House" by Woolf (1944) sets it as a deliberate design feature of the narrative to shift gradually in many categories of structure—certainly so in regard to our sense of where we are with respect to the particular location within the house, the identity of the current character, and the time of the events. The present parameter applies as well across domains. For example, where an audience is involved with an author in the cocreation of a work (several forms of which were described earlier), the structure consisting of the author and addressee domains can exhibit various degrees of discrete separation or of a melded gradient across the two contributory domains.

The Uniplex–Multiplex Parameter. For any particular type of structure in a narrative context, the parameter of *plexity* (cf. Talmy, 1988b) pertains to the number of instantiations of that structure. The structure is *uniplex* if there is a single entity manifesting it, and *multiplex* if there are two or more entities manifesting it. This latter case would then represent the more differentiated pole. The multiplex case, further, immediately engages the parameter of correlation: Do the plural entities function jointly, interactively, or independently?

The parameter of plexity can readily be seen to pertain to the author domain—are there one or more authors of the work and, if more than one, are their activities united, cooperative, complementary, at odds? It pertains as readily to the addressee domain; here, one multiplex form is the audience. The correlation parameter could apply here with respect to the ways in which the overt ongoing reactions of various or multiple audience members to a work, via feedback, affect the concurrent and subsequent processing of the work by each addressee within the audience. Comparably, whereas the analysis in this volume generally assumes or concludes that there is only a single viewpoint (i.e., origin of perspective within a deictic center) present at any time, the plexity parameter should alert us to the possibility of a narrative deploying a plural number of viewpoints, whose form of correlation would then further need ascertaining.

The Distributed–Concentrated Parameter. This parameter pertains to whether some single entity is spread out over a larger area or is localized within a small area. More precisely, this parameter constitutes the degree to which some entity within the narrative context, on the one hand, is distributed over the next-larger structure with which it is associated or manifests itself, or, on the other hand, is concentrated or focused relative to that structure. If the single entity is composed of constituents, then this parameter involves the degree to which the constituents are dispersed over a larger area or gathered together within a smaller area in a containing structure. Distinct from this parameter, but readily associable with it, is the degree to which the entity is amorphous as against crystalized, that is, its closeness to the prototype of well-formed entityhood. It is assumed here that greater proximity to the status of being a focused and well-defined entity correlates with greater differentiation. Although this parameter can apply to physical material, as in a description of cosmic dust coalescing over time into a star, in narrative, we find it applies most often to concepts and themes.[5]

To illustrate, the movie *Schindler's List* (Spielberg, 1993) shows the trajectory of Schindler's ever closer involvement with the Jews with whom he deals—from seeing them as useful for his business, to maintaining them against Nazi removals for the sake of his business, to protecting them against Nazi assault out of sympathy for them, to a desperately felt cause to preserve them. The progression along this trajectory is subtle, and, while watching the later stages spanning most of the latter portion of the movie, the viewer might regard them as still involving only pragmatic business concerns plus an increasing sympathy. It is only near the end of the movie, in the scene where Schindler weeps, obsessed over how he might have saved yet one more Jew, that the audience realizes the actual emotional state of desperate empathy that Schindler was feeling in those later stages. Schindler's emotional state is presented in a concentrated, well-defined, acute form. The viewer realizes that this same emotional state must also have been present throughout the later stages, but distributed there in a more diffuse form.

The Approximate–Precise Parameter.   The contrast between *approximation* and *precision* is the difference between a broad-band (or rough-and-ready) and a fine-structural characterization of any structure. An example in narrative could be the depiction of the personality of a character either with broad brush strokes or with a fine-etched articulation. A physical world motor–visual example of this distinction can be made in regard to gestures. In order to show someone the outline of an oval object, one could make a quick ovoid sweep of the whole hand or, one could move one's forefinger slowly and with tightened muscular tension to describe a fine-lined ellipse. (I assume that this type of gestural difference is a crosscultural universal and is innate.)

Suspecting a correlation across the domain of the author and that of the work, one might think to associate certain psychological characteristics in the author with the present two parametric modes in a narrative: indifference and carelessness with the approximation mode, and care and carefulness with the precision mode. Although this association may be common, it is not necessary. Thus, care and carefulness can also accompany the appearance of approximation, as seems, for example, to be the regular association for some schools of Japanese art.

The Vague–Clear Parameter.   This parameter pertains to whether the author's or addressee's understanding of some conceptual entity, or whether the narrative presentation that manifests or mediates such understanding, is vague

---

[5]Note that this parameter is readily distinguished from the earlier parameter of density. That parameter was named density for one sense of this word, the sense of a large number of plural objects per containing structure, the opposite of sparse. The other main sense of the word—a large quantity concentrated in one small volume—was not intended for that earlier parameter.

or clear. On the vague end, this understanding or presentation is murky, where whatever components it may have and their interrelationships are poorly worked out. On the other end, the understanding or presentation is well-developed in its clarity, with its components and their interrelationships well worked out. The pole of clarity is the more differentiated end of the parameter. One may readily associate with conceptual contents at the clarity pole the notion that they are comprehended intellectively, but at the murky pole, the notion is that they are sensed or apprehended viscerally. Contents at the clarity pole are identified; those at the vague pole are more pregnant with the potential of discovery or of being figured out.

The Sketchy–Elaborated Parameter. This parameter pertains to the extent to which some conceptual structure is addressed and dealt with. A conceptual entity can be less extensively addressed, in which case it is sketchy or schematic, or more extensively dealt with, in which case it is more elaborated or specified— the latter being the more differentiated pole. It is necessary to distinguish this parameter from the preceding one because a matter that is clearly understood and worked out need not exist nor be presented with full elaboration, but can be sketched out. However, a matter that is only vaguely understood need not exist nor be presented sketchily, but can get highly elaborated. One can write much and with great elaboration about amorphous murk.

The Implicit–Explicit Parameter. This parameter pertains to the degree to which any factor or system is *implicit* or *explicit*. At the implicit end, the factor or system is effectively present, as judged by an addressee's cognitive response to a work and perhaps by an assessment of the author's intent, but is not in its own right directly apparent. At the explicit end, the factor or system is perceptibly manifest or is expressed overtly and directly in its own right. Implicit content comes to be present in the addressee's cognition through various processes: it can be presupposed, perhaps as part of the cultural or physical world context; inferred from the explicit content via conventional reasoning processes acting in accordance with background knowledge; inferred on the basis of what was not included amidst the explicit material relative to some baseline of expectations; or it can exist in the form of second-order patterns in the explicit material that then have to be discerned. The explicitness pole of the present parameter is assumed to be the more differentiated, because the conceptual content of explicit material is more certain and univocal, whereas implicit conceptual content is generally more ambiguous.

Note that, although the poles of the present parameter tend to align with the respective poles of the preceding two parameters, it is in principle distinct from those parameters. Thus, with respect to the vague–clear parameter, a narrative can be quite explicit about vague material, whereas an implicit suggestion or innuendo can be quite clear and unmistakable. Comparably, with respect to the sketchy–elaborated parameter, explicit material can be quite sketchy, whereas an author can take pains to arrange for the implicit evocation of a particular elaborate pattern of presuppositions and inferences in the addressee.

An author who intends that certain conceptual content be evoked in the addressee may purposely choose to make it implicit so that it will be less accessible for observation, for being set within a comparative framework, or for questioning, and thus to be outside the conscious awareness or control of the addressee. The aims of such a choice could be to abet persuasion, or the subliminal dramatic effect, or the shock and impact of discovery when the addressee pieces together what had been unstated.

Veridicality

The parameter of *veridicality* pertains to the closeness that some structure within the total narrative context has to the concept of correctness or truth in the judgment of a character in the narrative, a performer of the work, the author, the addressee, or some outside analyst. For an example at the high end of the parameter, in works of fiction that have achieved the status of classics, the experience of a critical mass of critics and the lay readership is that the author correctly captured certain truths about the nature of the human psyche or society and incorporated them in the story. Or, for an example at the low end of the parameter, an actor that experiences a play as generally nonveridical may find that he or she just can't believe in his or her role, perhaps that his or her character's lines or personality "ring false," and consequently, may deliver a poorer performance for not being able to throw himself or herself into the part.

Requirements for veridicality can vary in accordance with the type of narrative structure to which it is applied. Thus, the genre of nonfiction has a higher requirement for a veridical correspondence of the textual descriptions to the external world than does fiction. And the concept of an addressee's willing suspension of disbelief refers to a particular differential application of the parameter. The addressee forgoes or even seeks noncorrespondence of a narrative to superficial probabilities of occurrence customarily attributed to the external world in exchange for greater veridicality in the abstracted representation of certain deeper psychological or societal structures. A work does not have to use implausible descriptions of the world in order to get at deeper truths, but it can use the former to highlight the latter.

Prototypicality

Any structure within the total narrative context is generally subject to ascriptions of prototypicality. That is, the author, the audience, or members of the culture at large have certain expectations, norms, and forms of familiarity pertaining to that structure as a result of experiences with the historical tradition or with exposure to narrative contexts. By the nature of this characterization, such prototypes will vary for different structures in different genres, for different individuals or groups within a culture, for different periods within a single cultural tradition, and for different cultures. Authors, or movements of authors, that compose their works to deviate substantially from the current prototypes may be considered by contemporaries to be avant-garde and their works to be experimental. By the same token, the addressees of works with prototype divergence may experience surprise or startlement over the novelty—experiences that can become affectually tinged in a negative direction (e.g., shock), or in a positive direction (e.g., exhilaration). In fact, a principal reason for including the parameter of prototypicality in the framework of the present analysis is the necessity, as we see it, of tracking the cognitive effect of an ongoing narrative on an addressee. After all, that profile of responses is something an author generally takes great pains to engineer, and the breaking of norms is a major vehicle for engendering certain desired responses in the addressee.

Cultural traditions can exhibit a second-order difference in the degree to which they exert pressure on authors to maintain the inherited prototypes or, on the contrary, to challenge them. Thus, certain long periods in Chinese art and literature maintained themselves with great conservatism, whereas, in this century, the West has rewarded authorial experimentation.

Interrelations Between Different Parameters

As with the module of domains, the various general and particular parameters of the present module can interrelate with each other. For example, the parameter of alternation could apply to the parameter of scope: Two structures in a text could alternate either locally or globally. Or, the continuous–discrete parameter could apply to the granularity parameter; for example, a narrative could address an issue or a scene from two distinctly separated levels of granularity, perhaps alternating between them, or could address it along a continuous range of granularities. Or, again, the veridicality parameter could apply to the abstraction parameter: In the judgment of the addressee or of some analyst, has the author correctly captured something about the nature of the human psyche in the abstractions from his or her understanding of it that he or she incorporates into the narrative?

Another way that different parameters may interrelate is as alternatives shifting in their prominence in accordance with the weighting or interpretation they are given. Thus, depending on particulars of their treatment or of their interpretation by an experiencer, two structures may, in the course of a narrative, be able to bear to each other all of the relationship parameters of embedding, alternation, concurrence, and correlation, as discussed previously. For example, a love story that unfolds against the backdrop of a nation at war may at times seem to be a small event embedded within a larger historical epic; or seem to be a drama as intense for its interiority as are the social events for their external power, so that scenes of the one appear to alternate on a par with scenes of the other; or seem like a desperate attempt to wrest a nominal life out of the pervading horrors, hence to appear as a concurrent overlay on the upheaval, one that might even have depended on the turmoil for its occurrence; or seem to consist of stages whose unfolding correlates with the developments in the war.

STRATA

We turn to the last module of the structures of the narrative context, the strata that operate within and across domains. The strata are the basic, or ground-level, structuring systems of a domain, prototypically so of the domain of the narrative work, but perhaps as readily so in the other domains of the total narrative context. The strata are understood as being in effect coextensively. Thus, in the domain of the work, one can track several different strata of a narrative, noting the concurrency and correlations across these several systems. As noted earlier, an apt metaphor is that of the polygraph, where each line represents one mode of activity taking place as the narrative progresses.

Temporal Structure

The temporal stratum, that is, the dimension of time, (a) has internal structure in the form of events and textures, (b) has contents such as processes and activities or situations and circumstances, (c) uniquely has the property of progression, and (d) has systematic correspondences with other narrative structures, as discussed in the following sections.

Events and Textures. Temporal structure consists of the structure of the contents of the temporal stratum. One basic unit of this structure can be termed the *event*. It is assumed that an event does not have intrinsic existence as an objective entity in any domain, but rather is a cognitive construct, resulting from human conceptualization acting on what would otherwise be a continuum of experience of a domain. This conceptualization acts to partition the continuum, to delimit a portion of it as a separate event.

An event can vary with respect to a number of parameters, including many of those described previously. Thus, an event may be discrete, with a clear beginning and ending point, or it can be continuous, experienced as unbounded within the scope of attention that has been partitioned off by the cognitive processes of event formation. The contents of an event may change over the span of the event, in which case the event is dynamic, constituting a process or activity. Or the contents of the event can remain unchanged over its span, in which case the event is static, constituting a situation or circumstance. An event can be global, spanning, for example, the full length of a narrative, or local, or even "microlocal", thought of as covering just a point of time (e.g., a flash of light plus burst of sound that a story could present as a point–durational event). Further, one event could relate to another event along any of the relationship parameters described earlier, for example, could be embedded in it, alternate on a par with it, concurrently overlay it, or exhibit part-wise correlations with it.

A perhaps second-order aspect of temporal structure can be termed its *texture*, that is, the patterns that various events exhibit relative to the overall temporal progression and to each other. In our experience with the world about us, different temporal textures are exhibited, for example, by a waterfall's unbounded continuity that includes a myriad of local nonrepeating variations; by the gradual slow increase and differentiating change that we assemble in our memory from periodic viewings of a flower bud unfolding into full blossom; or by the evenly pulsing rhythm of a throbbing headache. A person can experience his or her whole life to have had one or another temporal texture, for example, a stately cadence of successive discrete phases, or a helter-skelter jumble of overlapping events impinging on him or her. Comparably, a narrative can assert or describe a similar variety of temporal textures for any structure within the story world, or can exhibit them in its own pacing, or can evoke them in the addressee.[6]

The Relations of Narrative Time to Addressee Time.   Temporal structures can also be related across domains, for example, between story time and addressee time. Although *story world time* is the temporal progression attributed to the story world that the narrative sets up and within which it places its particular story,[7] *story time* is the temporal character of what is selected for explicit depiction or implicit allusion to constitute the story. *Addressee time*, quite simply, is the progression of the addressee's life in the course of the everyday world.

In order to observe relevant deviations, we must establish a baseline relationship between story time and addressee time. This baseline will be exact continuously coextensive, forwardly directed, same-rate progression. That is, time and events in the story progress with exactly the same continuity, direction/sequence, and rate as they do in the addressee's world as the addressee attends steadily to the progression of the narrative. This set of correspondences can be termed *coprogression*. Although useful as a baseline, such coprogression is not the norm, and works that aim to achieve it are generally deemed experimental. Examples include quasi-documentary-style films that purport to leave the camera on as events before it unfold in their natural way, like Andy Warhol's film (Warhol,

---

[6]Although a wide variety of temporal textures may structure our experience and narrative works, the grammatical (closed-class) forms of languages are limited to the expression of only a small subset of these textures, with such typical meanings as durative, punctual, iterative, and telic (terminally bounded)—collectively termed *aspect*.

[7]This progression through time is generally taken and supposed to be taken as the same as that of our everyday world, though some works may play with that assumption.

1969) of a couple having sex or, perhaps more challenging to the viewer's attention, his film (Warhol, 1964) showing a stationary building through the course of a full day.

There are two main types of deviation from this baseline. In one type, story time deviates from coprogression with the addressee, who is directing steady attention at a conventional rate to the work. In the second type, the addressee deviates from this steady paced processing.

Under the former type (with the addressee attending in the conventional way), story time can deviate in several ways. First, the story may present only certain discontinuous excerpts selected from the presumed continuous progression of events in the story world. Here, the addressee still progresses forward in story time, but only certain moments and scenes are selected for presentation, with the intervening periods gapped. Another deviation from the baseline is when story time is out of sequence relative to addressee time. This would include backward jumps in the tale, as for flashbacks or returns from flash forwards. As noted earlier, such temporal jumps can themselves form a higher level pattern. An example is the pattern of flashbacks that progressively zero-in, alternatively overshooting or falling short, on a particular temporal point and the event that occupied it.

Still another series of narrative temporal characteristics can be attributed to deviations of the rate of story time from the baseline. First, then, a rate deviation can be steady, so that the rate of the narrative's progression is, by some constant degree, slow or fast relative to the addressee's experience of the rate of events in the everyday world around him or her. Second, the rate of story time can change, either slowing down or speeding up. Hill (1991) observed that story time tends to slow down (and the density of detailing tends to increase) as the story approaches a critical or emotionally charged point. Third, story time can exhibit different rates at which this change in rate takes place—that is, it can be gradual or abrupt (or somewhere in between) in its slowing down or speeding up. A story's abrupt shift from a slow to a fast pace can be used by an author to induce in the addressee an intensification of certain emotional responses, such as fright or excitement. This abrupt change in pace may be a recurrent component of certain other emotions, such as surprise.

Next, we turn to situations where the addressee deviates from the baseline of directing steady attention in a forward progression and at a normative rate to the work. One category of deviation involves discontinuity of attending. For example, a reader can put a book down and pick it up some time later. In this way, forms of discontinuity are introduced into the consciousness of the experiencer that have nothing to do with any discontinuities in the temporal progression of the story. Some works are intentionally constructed to involve addressee discontinuities. An example is the movie adventure serial. The very concept of a "cliffhanger" at the end of one episode depends on the notion of addressee discontinuity. Another category of deviation pertains to forward sequencing. As an example of this, a reader may choose to skip around in a book, rather than read it in the canonical sequence of the printed format. Some recent works directly address the reader's ability to resequentialize the print by explicitly suggesting paths for skipping around. A third category of addressee deviation involves the rate of attending. Thus, a reader can choose to read a written work faster or slower relative to some norm of processing the text, or a viewer could intentionally run a film faster or slower than its canonical speed.

One motivation for an addressee to undertake deviations from the baseline is to introduce certain additional controls over the effects the work will have on his or her cognition. For example, by setting a book down, a reader can think over events in a novel before reading further. By skipping around in a book, a reader could gain a sense of the story's overall design and character. Or, by playing a video in slow motion, a viewer has greater opportunity to process the details of the scenes.

Many of the same relations just described between story time and addressee time can also occur within the story—for example, between the time characteristics of one part of the story and the time characteristics of the consciousness of a character or of the viewpoint of a deictic center. An interesting example is the science-fiction story "Divine Madness" by Zelazny (1971), where the protagonist starts going backwards in time through the last portion of his life, before that process stops and he resumes living forward in time. As this character "rewinds," some aspect of his psyche is aware of this backwards rewind, noting it as it happens. The viewpoint is located at that aspect of his psyche, and we, the readers, are watching through that viewpoint. From this perspective, we are really moving forward in its own time awareness, even though the contents of what appears in that awareness is a rewind of what had once been forward progression. Further, as this viewpoint progresses along its own temporal line, it is in addition able to project its temporal perspective point through all the same types of deviations described above: it can project this perspective point back and forth in time, speed it up or slow it down, and so on.

Relations of the Temporal Stratum to Other Narrative Structures. All structures within the total narrative context, other than that of time itself, can change through the progression of time. Put more analytically, only the stratum of time has the intrinsic property of progression. Particular related instantiations of any other structure can be correlated with different points of the temporal stratum. Where such instantiations are different from each other, that structure has undergone "change," and where they are the same, it has exhibited "stasis."

Changes through time can involve the structure of space (in particular, changes in the location of material objects over time constitutes the concept of motion) or psychological structure (for example, changes in the cognition of a character or the atmosphere of the narrative over time). Some structural units must, by definition, change with time. Plot structure is one example. Change through time is also particularly relevant in the domain of the addressee, in whom the progression of a narrative engenders a continually updated model of the narrative's content and a succession of psychological states consequent on the updates.

Spatial Structure

The stratum of spatial structure exhibits two main subsystems. One consists of all the schematic delineations that can be conceptualized as existing in any volume of space. This subsystem is a matrix or framework that contains and localizes. Static concepts relevant to it include region and location, and dynamic concepts include path and placement. The second subsystem consists of the configurations and interrelationships of material occupying a volume of the first subsystem. The second subsystem is thought of more as the contents of space. Such contents can constitute an *object*—a portion of material that is conceptualized as having a boundary around it as an intrinsic aspect of its makeup and identity—or a *mass*, having no boundaries intrinsic to its makeup. An analogy may exist between material as the contents of spatial structure and events as the contents of temporal structure. Both types of contents exhibit a similar array of structural properties, such as being either bounded or unbounded.

The material aspect of space can bear certain static relations to the matrix aspect of space, for example, material can occupy a region and be situated at a location, and can bear certain dynamic relations to it—material can move along a path. Spatial properties that material entities exhibit in themselves or relative to each other can also be related to schematic delineations of the containing framework. In particular, spatial properties that a single object or mass of material exhibits include the contour of its external boundary, that is, its shape, and interior disposition. The spatial properties that one material entity can have with respect to another include geometric relations, for example, those specified by such English prepositions as the ones in: X is *near/in/on* Y, as well as ones specified more elaborately. And the spatial properties that a set of material entities can exhibit as an ensemble include their *arrangement*, potentially to be conceptualized as a gestalt of geometric patterning.

In addition to these static spatial properties, a single material entity can exhibit such dynamic properties as change of shape—twisting, swelling—and one entity can execute such paths relative to another entity as the ones expressed by English prepositions such as those in: X moved *toward/past/through* Y, whereas a set of entities can alter their arrangement, scatter, converge, or the like.[8]

As we conceptualize it, the second subsystem, the contents of spatial structure, need not be limited to physical matter but can readily generalize to more abstract forms. For example, in a narrative, we can apply all our usual conceptions of

---

[8]The schematic concepts of spatial structure represented by the structuring system of language (i.e., by its grammatical or closed-class forms) was detailed in some depth by Talmy (1975, 1978, 1983) and Herskovits (1986). Typological patterns with respect to which languages differ from each other in their representation of spatial structure was described by Talmy (1985).

spatial relations to understanding the location and motion of a deictic center, the angle and direction of our viewing from that deictic center to an entity to which we are attending, and the size and shape of the zone of this attentional projection.

Spatial structure can also vary along most of the parameters outlined previously. It can exhibit hierarchical embedding, as when we see, or when a narrative describes, a restaurant as a containing structure within which are situated in a particular pattern of arrangement a set of tables, chairs, and people, each of which exhibits its own shape and internal disposition. Spatial structure can pertain to anything from the microlocal to the global—from a ladybug on the palm of a character in a story, to that character's geographic scale travels. Thus, the O'Henry story (1903) about a safecracker at one point has a character look and move locally about his old apartment, but globally depicts this character as first localized in prison, then leaving there and going to a nearby restaurant, then traveling to another town to get to his old apartment, then traveling to some relatively distant town where he settles down and remains for the rest of his life. The geometric pattern of this trek is significant to the import of the story.

Spatial structure can be relevant to all the domains of the total narrative context and to their interrelations. For example, a playwright or director may aim to evoke a particular effect in the addressees by arraying the audience in one configuration or another relative to the performance area, or may interrelate the domains of the performance and of the audience, as with such arrangements as theater in the round or actors passing through the audience. Another cross-domain relationship can be a discorrespondence between the familiar physical world and the story world, as where narrative objects and characters exhibit novel sizes, size changes, or embedding relations, as in *Alice in Wonderland* (Carroll, 1971) or the film *Fantastic Voyage* (Fleischer, 1966), with its miniaturized humans sailing through the bloodstream of a normal-sized person.

Psychological Structure

Although much that is psychological can have particular associations with elements in—or particular distributions over—the spatial and temporal strata, psychology constitutes a distinct stratum by itself, with its own essential quiddity and governing principles.

The psychological stratum encompasses all the possible contents of cognition. A sizable sampling through the stratum conveys the variety of its contents: consciousness/awareness/self-awareness; attention; perception; thought/concepts and conceptualizations/reasoning and inferencing; presuppositions/unnoticed assumptions; attitude/opinion; affect/mood; values, ethics, morals; ascriptions along the dimensions of importance/goodness; world view/philosophy of life; motivation/desires; intending/goal having; planning/expecting/anticipating; agency: actualizing a relation between intentions and realizations; choice/decision; memory: remembering, forgetting; and personality.

Certain portions of this list of psychological phenomena group together as subsystems. Two such may be conceptual structure and affectual structure. Conceptual structure, the subsystem pertaining to the more analytically ideational portion of psychological experience, includes the beliefs, opinions, presuppositions, information, or explanations held or expressed by a psychological entity. The affectual structure includes those things relating to feelings, emotions, mood states, desires, drives, or urges.

Although we may believe that all such psychological phenomena are, in reality, wedded intrinsically to individual sentient biological organisms, our experience of such phenomena can be freer. We can attribute these phenomena—and a work of fiction can take advantage of this freer attributional characteristic by assigning these phenomena—to any one of three main levels: the individual, the group or society, and the atmosphere. We consider each of these in turn.

The Individual. The individual level is perhaps the most prototypical for psychological structure. An *individual* is what can be conceptualized as a sentient, cognitive entity in which all or some of the above set of psychological phenomena are localized together. The crucial notions for the concept of individual are the sentience of the entity and the colocalization of the psychological phenomena in that entity. In addition, it is usually the case that psychological characteristics localized within an individual are also interrelated so as to constitute a form of gestalt unity. But this property is subject to variation, as in the presentation of an entity as having nonintegrated attitudes, or even selves in the case of split or multiple personalities. The prototypical individual is any human and, secondarily, any sentient animal; within the immediate narrative context, the prototype individuals are the author and the addressee outside the story world, and the narrator and characters inside the story world. An individual, of course, need not be a human or animal, or even a biological organism. Any so-posited entity which is treated as if psychological properties are concentrated within it can serve the function, including inanimate objects, ghosts, extraterrestrials, and so on, as well as such abstractions as the viewpoint of the deictic center.

Individual psychological structure can exhibit most of the parameters previously discussed and interact with most of the other strata of this section. For instance, a character's conception or mood can be explicit or implicit, clear or vague; it can embed within, alternate with, overlay, or correlate with another conception or mood; it can extend globally or locally and can change through time. As examples of global change through time, an author can have different periods, an addressee's tastes can change, and a character in a novel can evolve. As an example of local changes of psychological state through time that variously involve alternation, overlap, and so on, we can track a protagonist through her evening at home as her thoughts and feelings include terror, regret, relief, reverie and here-and-now awareness (see Costello, Bruder, Hosenfeld, & Duchan, this volume).

As indicated previously, the viewpoint of a deictic center may be understood as a kind of individual with psychological structure, that is, a sentient cognitive entity with characterological/personality, affectual, and world view characteristics, among other psychological properties. It may be that a viewpoint is typically defective, at least in some works, regarding the psychological properties that appear in it, perhaps evincing primarily the property of perception. But, in some works, or by other analyses, the viewpoint will also include attitude and affect. For example, consider a line like the following as though it were from a story depicting an ocean scene when no story characters are present: "Its body glistening, the porpoise leapt gracefully out of the water, rose majestically into the air, executed a beautiful somersault at the top of its arc, and dove back into the water barely perturbing the surface." Such a scene is presumably being seen from the perspective of a viewpoint located above the ocean surface and near the porpoise. This perspective does include perception, as in the characterization of the events that took place and in the use of the word "glistening." But it also includes evaluation, as in the use of the word "gracefully," it includes attitude and affect in the use of the words "majestically" and "beautiful," and it exhibits expectations in its use of the word "barely," which alludes to a deviation from norms. These additional inclusions are all elements of psychological structure beyond the merely perceptual, and the viewpoint is exhibiting them.

Because the concept of the individual emerges in this section (it is the locus of coalescence of particular psychological properties), we further consider structures resulting from relationships across different types of individuals. As a precursor, we establish that the concept of a *narrator*—that is, an apparent individual who recounts a story—as well as the possibly novel concept of the *narrator's addressee*—that is, the apparent individual to whom the narrator recounts the story—depend on the embedding of one story world within another. The outer story world includes the narrator, the narrator's addressee, and the inner story world, all three the creation of the author. Within this outer story world, the inner story world appears to be the creation of the narrator.

Interrelationships, then, include the following: Where the narrator is identified with one of the characters in the inner story world, then the narrator is a participant in the inner story and nonquoted commentaries include the pronoun "I"; where there is no such identification, the pronoun "I" typically does not appear outside of quotes, and the narrator is understood as a causally noninvolved observer. Where the author is identified with the narrator, the inner story is understood to represent events that the author has witnessed or believes. Where there is a triune identification of the author, the narrator, and a character of the inner story, the work is understood to be autobiographical to the extent to which the author is not thought to be lying. Where a character of the inner story is identified with an individual in the domain of the sociocultural world other than the author, the work is understood to be biographical to the extent to which the author represents actual events. Where the narrator's addressee inside the work is intended to be overtly identified with the addressee outside the work, the nonquoted commentary may include the pronoun "you" or such formulations as, "The reader will now be thinking . . . ," and so on; otherwise, this pronoun and comparable formulations are typically not used, and the outer addressee can have the experience of someone listening in or looking on as the narrator recounts the story to the fictional narrator's addressee.

The Group/Society. Another level of organization to which psychological structure can be attributed is that of the group or of a society composed of first-level individuals. A principal parameter operative at this level ranges from the case where a single set of psychological properties is attributed to the group as a higher level unit, through the case where one such set is attributed equally to all the components of the group that then exhibit them in concert, to the case where different sets of psychological properties are attributed to different components of the group that then interact with respect to these differences.[9] Aside from considerations of narrative, people regularly make the first or second kind of attribution to various sociological categories, such as those of class, race, gender, nation, as well as the bowling league down the street; and some sociological and anthropological theories ascribe such properties as world view and affect style to a culture as a whole or to the conceptually abstracted medium within which individuals interact (examples of the latter are practice theory and conversation analysis).

With respect to the narrative context, group psychology in its various manifestations is understood to be at work where a plural number of authors collaborate on a work, where there is a plurality of addresses such as an audience, in the cast of a play, or in any group identified within the story world. Special forms of groups that have appeared in narrative are the classical Greek chorus, often understood to express the collective moral position of the society, the normative questions of the average member of the society, and the like; or the presentation of a succession of viewpoints expressed by individuals around, say, a neighborhood, as a device to show the variety or the uniformity of the views of the society. Further, the psychological manifestations of the individuals in any portion of a narrative, including the whole story, can be regarded at either the individual level as a distribution and succession of separate individuals, or at the group level as a collective interaction.

The Atmosphere. Finally, we can consider the third level of psychological structure, that of atmosphere. *Atmosphere* is the experience we can have that certain psychological characteristics are pervading some portion of ambient space,

---

[9]This last case includes the recent work on distributed cognition (e.g., Hutchins, 1991), in which various members of a team or of a society have partially complementary forms of expertise, all needed in interaction for overall goals to succeed.

some materially defined region, or some event, rather than being localized within some object or associated with a set of such objects. And, even though we may rationally believe that it is impossible, we generally attribute such psychological characteristics to that region or event as a property of it or as inhering in it, rather than experience them as feelings arising in ourselves in response to perceiving that region or event. The psychological character of an atmosphere generally involves the affectual subsystem of psychological structure more than it involves the conceptual subsystem with such properties as thoughts, opinions, choice, or the like. This affectual subsystem especially involves mood states, for example, menace, light cheeriness, horror, coziness, sturdy security, disgusting squalor, opulence, or spirituality.

Our cognitive capacity to experience atmospheric characteristics in relation to our surroundings or some entities occupying those surroundings is probably innate and largely automatic—that is, the occurrence and product of its functioning within us is barely amenable to internal conscious control. It is a regular concomitant of our environment as we move through it or look about it. Householders, store proprietors, city officials, and so on, often arrange and outfit their domains with care so as to engender particular desired senses of atmosphere in themselves, their customers, or their citizenry.

Authors regularly take pains to orchestrate the operations of our innate capacity so that we will experience particular atmospheres in association with various portions of their story world, as well as with the story world as a whole. In addition to shaping the usual sensory phenomena to this end, films regularly use background music to engender the experience of a certain atmosphere pervading a scene. Thus, the same scene could be apprehended in two different ways with different accompanying music, as eerily threatening or as lightly humorous. A written work can accomplish similar atmospheric effects by the choice of language and the orchestration of ideas. For example, Kahane (1994) shows how a book establishes an atmosphere of sanity-threatening fractionation through the use of periodic, almost subliminal allusions to danger (e.g., one reference to Bluebeard) and of startling, seemingly disjunct jumps in topic and scene.

The Connectivity System

The *connectivity system* pertains to the concurrent association or the temporal succession of phenomena within some particular structure in the total narrative context. Most generally, the connectivity system can be taken to be a so-conceived body of principles that govern, patterns that characterize, factors that determine, or generalizations that constrain this association or succession of phenomena. Further, *connectivity structure* is the overall pattern—simultaneous or cumulative—that appears in the selected narrative structure under the application of a connectivity system. If a particular connectivity structure is in accord with the conditions of a connectivity system under consideration, the phenomena encompassed by that structure are generally said to be consistent insofar as they are considered temporally, and coherent insofar as they are considered in their temporal succession. We discuss connectivity systems of only the temporal type, including the systems of causational, motivational, expectational, and epistemic structure.

Causality. A principal connectivity system is that of physical causality, which consists of the physics of material and energy in space and time. Because it is our conceptualization that determines the nature of a connectivity system, the system of physical causality need not be limited to that of modern physics, but can as readily pertain to early physics (e.g., in classical or medieval science), naive physics, cartoon physics, or science-fiction story physics. Included here could be such conceptions as that matter has physical continuity (it does not disappear and reappear or jump about, but continues in place or along a trajectory); or that two solid objects cannot occupy the same space but at most can only abut at their boundaries; or that time progresses steadily in one direction. Such a connectivity system could be governed by force dynamics (see Talmy, 1976, 1988a), a system of concepts built into the semantic structure of language and seemingly other cognitive systems, in which a body can have an intrinsic tendency toward rest or toward motion, another body can oppose that tendency, the first body can resist that opposition, the other body can overcome that resistance, where a stronger object can block a weaker one or force it to move, and where a weaker object can hinder or act in vain on a stronger one.

Viewpoint Connectivity. The viewpoint of the deictic center has its own connectivity principles. In some ways it does follow the usual physical patterns, but in other important ways, the viewpoint is not constrained by or subject to the same principles of physics as a material entity. For example, viewpoint physics diverges from material physics with respect to certain aspects of spacetime structure. The viewpoint can jump about in story world space not subject to principles of continuity, and if need be, can appear amidst otherwise solid objects; thus it is not subject to the principle against colocation. Comparably, it can first appear at one story world time and then jump to another, shifting either forward or backward, thus it is not subject to temporal continuity or unidirectional progression. The viewpoint has no causal effect on the story world. That is, it can appear anywhere without any consequences to what would otherwise be taking place there. Related to these physical freedoms, the viewpoint can appear in different structures or parts of strata, for example, in both material and psychological structures. The viewpoint can jump across domains, as when a work suddenly redirects the addressee's attention to the author or to the addressee, perhaps with the use of an "I" or "you" pronoun in the text; or when the text calls attention to itself qua text, entailing that the addressee loop his or her attention away from the contents of the text, through the self, and back into the text again. Few other entities have such freedom.

But there are also a number of ways in which viewpoint physics is consonant with material physics. Although the viewpoint does not affect its surroundings, it can be affected by them, at least insofar as the viewpoint's decisions as to how long to stay, what to observe, where to go next are concerned. Further, although the viewpoint ignores some properties of spatial structure (e.g., it can exhibit path discontinuities and can occupy the same location as another object), it does obey other aspects of spatial structure—for example, it remains within the confines of a designated spatial region and observes its abstract schematic structure. Further, with regard to temporal structure, the viewpoint has its own ticking clock that, for its own perspective, does determine a forward progressing timeline. Although the viewpoint may flit backwards and forwards in story world time, the resulting observations are registered on the time line of the viewpoint itself as onto a steadily forward progressing tape.

Psychological Connectivity in General. An analysis of connectivity similar to that for the viewpoint can be undertaken for the system of psychological structure. Such "psyche physics" would need to cover a range of connectional patterns, for example, those in the marshaled progression of rational thought; the gradual coalescence of an amorphous apprehension into a crystalized idea; stream of consciousness-type thought sequences, flitting about in imagined space and time—each related to the last by little more than a shared conceptual component and a similar affectual vector; or, indeed, abrupt shifts of contents.

Although such examples of psychological connectivity may apply most directly to the individual, some distinct forms of psychological connectivity may govern at the other psychological levels, those of the group and the atmosphere. Thus, the group level is subject to principles pertaining to the spread of mass hysteria, to propaganda and the manufacture of public consent, to a society's slide from vigor to malaise, and so on. And some atmospheric transitions may be considered harmonious, whereas others are jarring or unnatural. Much as science fiction as a genre includes much deliberate play with the principles of physical connectivity, it also plays with the principles of psychological connectivity of alien individuals (e.g., with inexplicable motivations), groups (e.g., with telepathic communication that yields novel behavior), and races (e.g., with unfathomable world views and societal goals directing their course).

Psychological connectivity also applies across the various domains. It certainly applies to the story world, with its individuals, groups, and atmospheres. In fact, given the earlier argument that the viewpoint is a kind of individual within the story, viewpoint physics could be merely a particular application of psyche physics to that domain. In addition, it applies to our conceptualizations of the individuals and groups in the world around us, informing our understandings of the way various individuals experience things and behave through time, of group dynamics, and of the history of ideas and the successions of societal zeitgeists. It also applies to the author, whose successive moods or shifts between creative flow and blockage might affect successive sections of the work. Moreover, the principles of psychological connectivity in the domain of the addressee are among the most important in the narrative context. The author aims to structure the work in a way that will engender a particular succession of mental states in the addressee.

Motivation Connectivity. A psychological connectivity system is not likely to consist of a disparate collection of factors, but rather, to exhibit forms of consistency and integration. For example, psychological connectivity can be built around a coherent theoretical construct, for example, that of psychodynamics. It can also contain coherent subsystems. One such subsystem is that of *motivation.* This subsystem consists of the tendencies toward particular types of action that are thought to be associated with or caused by particular psychological states. For example, fear with respect to an object makes one tend to distance oneself from that object; anger, to approach the object so as to harm it; desire, to approach the object so as to acquire it; interest, to attend to the object; and boredom, to attend to something else. Desire for a state of affairs, that is, having a goal, makes one undertake a sequence of actions that one thinks will culminate in that state of affairs. The multiple concatenating, embedding, and overlap of motivations on the part of various individuals or groups over various levels of scope can constitute an important—often the main—connectivity of a narrative.

Epistemic Connectivity. Another organized subsystem of a connectivity system can be *epistemic structure.* This is the structure of "who knows what when." More precisely, for any narrative-related domain, this is the cross-sectional and longitudinal profile of what each individual and group knows and when they know it. In a mystery novel, this subsystem can be the main engine of plot progression for the characters within the story and for the reader.

Thus, within the story, this subsystem affords the rationale for such activities as covering up, throwing off the track, investigating and spying, giving a false sense of security to or decoying a suspect, and tricking the truth out of the real murderer.

For the reader, the subsystem orchestrates the author's setting up a mystery, leaving clues as well as false trails, introducing a succession of seeming explanations that do not prove out, and the delay until the final resolution at the end. Accordingly, the epistemic experiences that can be engendered in the addressee by the present subsystem include puzzlement, hunches as to the truth, increases and decreases in one's sense of certainty, a sense of letdown over one's previous explanatory picture falling apart, and the gratification one can feel over the consistency and coherence of all the pieces finally fitting together.

Epistemic structure can also apply to the author—in ways that may leave traces in the work—for example, in the surety of the author's knowledge about the subject matter. Or the author may be the type that fully plots out the work before composing it, or the type that begins the work and does not know where the story will go, but lets the logic of the story and the psychology of the characters unfold in their own way.

Sequiturity. Yet another connectional subsystem that can be identified may be whimsically termed *sequiturity*. This is the body of principles and normative expectations that pertain to the sequencing of ideas. Included here would be one's sense of the adequacy of the logical flow or the overall logic of a discourse; or of whether or not each idea (over any magnitude of scope) follows reasonably relative to the prior idea, or is instead a non sequitur; or of the pertinence of successive portions in a flow of information. This sequiturity subsystem is presumably most relevant to the domain of the addressee, specifically for his or her psychological processing of conceptual connectivity. But it is also relevant to the author, who must sufficiently think through his or her body of material to understand its logical interconnections so as to be able to shape the work to have the desired effect on the addressee's sequiturity system, whether this is to accord with it or, indeed, to subvert it, as with some propaganda.

The sequiturity system of an individual such as an addressee is readily subject to diminution or disruption in its functioning by the intense activity of other cognitive systems, as when perceiving striking sensory stimuli or experiencing strong emotion. Thus, films that have striking visual effects or that rouse strong emotions can succeed even with less coherent plots.

Continuity of Identity. One further connectivity subsystem—certainly one of the strongest, if not the strongest—is that of the *continuity of identity*. One of our cognitive capacities is the ability to draw a conceptual boundary around some portion of the contents of consciousness (including what is perceived or conceived) and to ascribe unitary "entityhood" to the material within that boundary. Such an entity could be a physically inanimate or animate object, an event, an institution, a personality or soul, and so on. Our cognition can further operate to ascribe to such an entity a distinctive identity, so that it is conceptualized as unique and distinguishable from other entities. Finally, the identity of such an entity is conceptualized as maintaining continuity through time regardless of any other changes that the entity may undergo. Only the genesis or dissolution of the entity may sometimes act as boundaries to this continuity. The concepts of same and different ultimately depend on the concept of identity and its continuity.

To illustrate, in the transformation of Kafka's character, Gregor Samsa (Kafka, 1936), into an insect, the reader readily accepts the idea that the essential identity of Samsa continues on despite the physical change. Likewise, with little question we attribute a single continuous identity spanning decades to, say, "The General Electric Corporation" despite what may have been complete or near complete changes in personnel, physical plant, and product. In a comparable way, once we have formed a concept of the existence of someone, we assume the continuity of their existence despite their absence, short or long. Thus, one can maintain the sense of unbroken friendship with a colleague one sees daily as well as with a colleague one sees only every four years at a conference. In this way, we can conceptually maintain numerous relationships interwoven through our single time line. The operation of the cognitive faculty of ascribing continuity when applied to personal identity is presumably the source of such notions as life after death, transmigration of souls, or the eternity of the soul that are found in many spiritual systems and cultures. Finally, it would seem that the main venue for the ascription of identity continuity is oneself. Each individual has the experience of a continuous identity of self, the "I." I assume that, through evolution, our cognition is so organized as to strongly generate this psychological construct of the experience of one's self and its continuity. This experience may be one model or the main model on which other attributions of the continuity of identity are based.

The attribution of entityhood with a distinctive identity can vary along various parameters to manifest larger forms of connectivity beyond simple continuity. For example, what had been considered one entity with a single identity can then be understood to divide into several entities with separate identities. And we can as readily conceptualize the reverse process of merger. Examples are our understanding of streets or rivers that fork or unite, often with distinct names for each of the three involved segments. Further, several distinct identities may be comprehended under a single larger identity, as with an anthology of short stories. Something understood as a single identity-bearing entity can also be understood as having several distinct and different instantiations, a concept to which the terms *version* and *variant* are applied. Thus, what one is able to consider to be the same story can be told in book and film versions, or in short story and novel versions, or as the related folk tales of two different cultures. Finally, within the same complex of phenomena, one can establish distinct alternatives of entityhood and identity continuity. Thus, if a craftsperson in a story carves a tree into a canoe, we foreground the change in identity from tree to canoe and background the continuity of the physical material, the wood, as an entity with its own identity. On the other hand, if the tree has a spirit and the craftsperson is a magician, then we foreground the continuity of the material with its indwelling spirit and background the change in form.

A so-conceptualized entity with a continuing identity is the main organizing aegis for the operation of a connectivity system. Further, we appear to be innately predisposed to accord primacy to certain types of so-conceived entities as the basic venues for the attribution of connectedness. A principal entity type of this sort is the conceptual construct of one's self. Under the aegis of this single identity, all the experiences one has had are in general conceptually united so as to constitute the ideational entity thought of as one's "life." In accordance with different cognitive styles and sometimes their current mood, individuals vary in the ways that they thread together selected components of their experience into different conceptions of their lives (see Linde, 1993). The same process of choosing a kind of linkage through selected components, when applied to another main type of organizing entity—a nonsentient entity like an institution, a nation, or a planet—yields what is generally termed its *history*. Likewise, this same process when applied to another type of entity—one taken to be a narrative because its values along three particular dimensions place it near the prototype—yields what is generally known as its *story*.

It is by the operation of this aegis function that, for example, we do not cobble together bits and pieces out of various books lying before us from which to fashion a story, but rather limit ourselves to the confines of a single book to integrate its contents into a story. Comparably, we do not mix together excerpts from the experiences of ourselves and other people so as to form the conception of a single life, but rather limit ourselves to the experiences directly associable with our biological self.

The crucial point is that we appear to be innately endowed with a strong cognitive processing mechanism that generates an experience of connectedness through any body of conceptual content that is considered to be an entity—often despite properties of that body of material that, by the operation of other cognitive systems would be assessed as rather disparate in content—and this mechanism is responsible for an often intense fascination with a life or a story. The absorption that children generally exhibit in the telling of a story—a cognitive form manifesting at an early age—must be accounted for within a general understanding of cognition, and is here claimed to result from the operation of the posited connectivity-forming mechanism and to its strong claim on our attention.

Plot Structure.   The final connectivity system to be addressed is that of *plot structure*. The notion of plot structure can be characterized by combining the three dimensions relevant to prototype narrative discussed previously. To repeat them, the narrative prototype has the value of conception/ideation on the dimension of the main cognitive system engaged, a high value on the dimension of degree of progression, and a high value on the dimension of degree of coherence and significance. Then, plot can be regarded as the conjunction of the narrative–prototypical poles of these three dimensions for a particular work. Thus, a plot would be the coherent and significance-bearing progression of referential content in a work. Although the term *plot* is not used for it, the generalization of the concept would apply as well to the life story or life history of an individual or to the history of a nonsentient entity, as such ideas were presented in the discussion just preceding.

The category of plot becomes foregrounded—that is, itself becomes the object of attention—for example, in novels where there is intentional unclarity as to what actually took place, or where some single sequence of events is viewed from different characters' perspectives.

Import

Import is the stratum that pertains to the meaning, significance, or implications of any structure within a larger schema of relevance, as assessed from the perspective of any psychological entity, such as an individual or a society. When applied to an intentional agency that has created or composed a structure, import can also pertain to the purpose of the whole or any part of that structure, the function that the agency intends it to serve. Import varies along all the usual parameters, so that any structure can include different imports that range from the local to the global, that embed, overlap, and correlate, or that exhibit different forms and degrees of connectivity. We generally value the creation of an agency to the extent to which it (a) has an import of relevance to ourselves as judge, (b) has a coherent overall import, and (c) accomplishes that import with the choices that went into it.

For an addressee, the import of the whole or any part of a work is assessed by its significance for various components of his or her psychology, such as interests, values, and aesthetics. For example, a work will be thought to have depth if it accords with a sense for and need of an expanded understanding and emotional enrichment with respect to matters of importance to him or her. And it will be experienced as having beauty if it accords with his or her aesthetics with respect to language, organization, depiction, or the like.

Another main realm in which the category of import holds sway is the author's intentions for his or her narrative with respect to the addressee. All of the choices and selections the author makes in assembling the narrative can be guided by this factor of intended import—for example, at the local level, an author's purpose for a particular paragraph, sentence, or even word could be to induce puzzlement; to keep the addressee's interest and attention active by changing the pace; or to establish particular information or mood needed for subsequent developments. At the global level, an author's preponderant intention for his or her work is to have certain psychological effects on the addressee.

What differs from work to work is what this effect is to be. Generally, this matter is the charge of the field of rhetoric. Examples of intended psychological effects for the work as a whole are: to make the addressee wiser or morally better, to orchestrate certain sequences and waves of emotion in the addressee that should (as the author's conceptualization may have it) cleanse or refresh him or her, or to rouse the addressee to certain actions.

SUMMARY

This chapter presented the beginnings of a framework that lays out the main structural delineations of narrative and of the larger narrative context. The framework can be used to guide the analysis of particular narrative works. But it also links up with endeavors in other fields in cognitive science and the humanities (including linguistics) to help in progress toward an integrated understanding of human conceptual structure.

For a concrete example of the application of parts of this heuristic grid to a complete short story, see Costello, Bruder, Hosenfeld and Duchan's (this volume) analysis. In that chapter, they explore various contrasts and correlations across spatial, temporal, and psychological structures. In particular, note their analysis of various lengths of time spent at various physical and mental locations and the relationships with affect (both in the characters and in the reader).

ACKNOWLEDGMENTS

I am indebted to Gail Bruder, Judy Duchan, and Lynne Hewitt for much beneficial discussion as well as for helping convert the original form of this chapter—an outline with nonconnected sentences and paragraphs inserted at the various headings and subheadings—into a connected prose paper.

20

A STRUCTURAL ANALYSIS OF A FICTIONAL NARRATIVE: "A FREE NIGHT," BY ANNE MAURY COSTELLO

Anne M. Costello
Gail A. Bruder
Carol Hosenfeld
Judith F. Duchan
State University of New York at Buffalo

In the beginning of this volume, we present Joyce Daniel's story, "A Trip to the Dentist's Office" and follow it with a number of questions to the reader involving movement in time, space, and character. We use the story to provide the reader with an introduction to our deictic center theory of narrative understanding.

When that story was written, our treatment of the DC envisioned a "moving window" constructed by the reader, with guidance from the text. This DC was used by the reader to track the movement of events in time and space as the story unfolded, one sentence at a time. Joyce's story permits us to demonstrate in a simple fashion the shifting of time and space in a simple story and to consider the linguistic devices that influence that shifting.

As our work progressed, so did the complexity and sophistication of our DC model. One of the most important advances was our work on subjectivity, that has to do with how readers know when events in the story should be interpreted from a character's point of view. Another expansion of our work, just begun (see Talmy, this volume) is to consider more global structure of the narrative, beyond that indicated by shifts in the DC. The story we use to close this volume allows us to explore more of the global aspects of narrative, such as patterns in temporal shifts from long backward transits to shorter ones, patterns in spatial transitions from static to planned movement to erratic unplanned motion, and patterns in affect expression from positive to negative and from high to low levels of intensity. Before presenting this story and our interpretations of its structure, we describe the circumstances of its creation.

The story was written by Anne Maury Costello, a professional writer. Anne joined our research group in fall 1991, and was working on the story at the time. She felt the research group discussion helped her overcome a block and graciously shared with us both her story and her insights into the writing of the story. Although we are delighted to have Anne's participation in our group, we are reluctant to take any credit for the story she produced. We first present the story and then our analysis of it. We numbered the paragraphs for purposes of analysis, keeping to Anne's original paragraph marking.

THE STORY: "A FREE NIGHT" BY ANNE MAURY COSTELLO

1. She had been in the house by herself only a few minutes when she first heard the rustling noise in the chimney.

2. It was very cold outside, reassuring in this age of global warming. Time was, combating the cold yielded her a righteous joy. Stuffing an old pillow up the chimney early each January was an act in defense of siege. She would mutter to herself a New England saying of her Granny's: "When the days begin to lengthen, that's when the c-c-cold begins to strrrengthen." It had been a book-learned New England, with inaccuracies.

3. She had not bothered with the pillow lately, it hadn't seemed to matter much whether the house was drafty or not. Winters had been mild, she'd sniffed at them, Maryland winters, she thought, not Buffalo, not Great Lakes winters with all the statistical delights of baseball, how many inches of snow, how many degrees below zero, what wind chill, how early the Lake froze. She longed for the days when she'd expected metal to shatter like glass, days when ice creaked underfoot.

4. She remembered clear, post-storm, brilliant days when the air was full of shards of dancing light as the sun drew water vapor from the snow which froze in particles and hovered there, sparkling like mica dust. Canadian high pressure when she stood in the middle of Delaware Park in the middle of the city of Buffalo and saw past the sun to the starry night beyond. Those were her own winter days, after Granny's time, they were her own stories, Buffalo stories, not Granny's stories from Boston, from the Philippines, from Hawaii.

5. Granny's stories about Paul, the oldest. Born at Ft. Slocum, in Boston Harbor. Nineteen eight. That was a cold winter. She was barely twenty, a bride, never been in a kitchen before she was married, no idea of how to take care of a baby. Granddaddy was a Spartan, a West Pointer, she adored him. Give the baby fresh air, make him tough, he'd said. The next morning, she went into the nursery, there was a snow drift over the crib. A white mound. She plunged in, grabbed the baby, sent his father across the ice of Boston Harbor in a sleigh to get the doctor, while she rubbed the baby. No rubbing alcohol, she found a bottle

of fine brandy her husband had been saving, and rubbed and warmed the baby with that. The doctor said, "Nothing's wrong with this baby except that he's drunk!" Uproariously funny. Granddaddy was furious at the wanton waste.

6. Tonight, the wind blew cold, shaking the house. Jack had gone to play poker with the guys. She looked forward to poker night, a free night, she had things she planned to read, TV she planned to watch. As soon as he left, she sat in his chair, by the good reading light, and started to read the paper slowly, savoring solitude. The gusts of wind rattled in the chimney, and icy chips of snow gritted against the window.

7. Thinking she was reading, she stared at the paper. She heard the wind. While her eyes went down the page, her mind walked through the steps to stuffing the pillow up the chimney. First, she would put on an apron, she liked what she was wearing, and she didn't want to get it sooty. The children had obviously had fires in the fireplace while she and Jack were on Kauai, just after New Year's; such a shame to have to go that particular week, when the kids were, migrating birds, hesitating there, with them. But Jack's aunt was alone.

8. Life in a nutshell, she'd said: The children well and happy and home and we have to go spend what we can't afford for a week in Paradise because Jack's aunt, his schedule . . . "Oh, Hawaii!" people said, "Oh, marvelous!" and then, "Oh, the kids! All the kids?" All the living kids, she'd think. "Yes, everybody home. Isn't that always the way? Things come in the wrong order." An inconvenient Paradise. She had laughed a Granny laugh. Life's little ironies, she would have said, quoting again.

9. She put the paper down. The wind was really noisy in the chimney. She thought some more about the apron, then she said what the hell and got up, went halfway down the basement stairs to the ledge where they stored intrinsically dirty things like the chimney pillow, took it out of its paper bags, causing a tiny shower of soot, walked back up the stairs, kicked the basement door shut, walked across the hall and over the living room rug to the fireplace, pushed the standing screen aside, knelt down and stuffed the pillow up the chimney, adjusting it so that it blocked as much as possible of the flue opening, and replaced the screen.

10. She wiped her hands on a piece of Kleenex and sat down again to read the paper. She had read a full column and had started another when she heard the rustling noise the first time.

11. It was more a fluttering than a rustling, a busy, fluttering noise. It would increase in intensity, become very urgent, and then taper off, calm down, or stop suddenly. It was never very loud, but she could hear it clearly.

12. She didn't want to think further, she resumed reading, and the rustling started up again, a fluttering, really. She heard thumping on the porch; Jack had returned.

13. "Forgot the chips," he said, trailing firm white pressings from his sneaker treads across the carpet to the cupboard.

14. "Jack, " she said. "There's a bird in the chimney, and I don't want to get it out. It can die there. I don't care."

15. "A bird? I don't hear anything." He had stopped and turned to look at her, at the chimney. He was on his way back out. He had the green leather box with the chips in it under his arm, his coat was so thick the box was almost hidden in the density. His cheeks were red from the cold, he was breathing quickly, moving decisively.

16. "If there's a bird in there, I'll get it out in the morning. It won't die."

17. He looked at her, gave her the space to insist on emergency action while clearly not wanting to stay.

18. "Bye, dear," he said.

19. "Bye, honey, have a good game," she said. The doors banged behind him. She went upstairs to get her book. Interesting book, required just enough concentration.

20. She came back downstairs and settled in Jack's chair, with the quilt around her, and the big heavy book on her lap. The fluttering began again, became very fast, very intense, and then stopped.

21. The bother of getting the bird out preoccupied her. They had had birds before. Two birds. Dreadful black sooty things when they flopped free, careening around the downstairs, leaving ash splats on the walls and ceiling. Silent as bats. That was four years ago, a bad time for them, the worst, and the birds had seemed a final, extra, gratuitous horror. She had been revolted by them. Opening the windows, getting the birds to fly low enough to go out, how had she and Jack done it? Another time, they would have laughed.

22. Soot all over everything, she thought. What a mess. The fluttering started up again.

23. She moved to her chaise in the bookcase corner. The light wasn't as good, but it was a bit further from the fireplace, and a better place to squirm.

24. She was an environmentalist, but not a fanatic, not a reincarnation believer, she didn't care about some wild animal dumb enough to get stuck in her chimney and die there, slowly, from hunger, thirst and cold, fluttering its stupid, replicable life away. It was probably a starling, or an English sparrow, the two from before were starlings, disgusting birds.

25. Granny'd had a story about starlings, from when she and Granddaddy were in Washington, just before Paul went to West Point. They'd moved into a lovely apartment in Tilden Gardens, new then, on Connecticut Avenue near the brand new Bureau of Standards. And there were starlings everywhere.

26. Granddaddy had offered to shoot them. He was a fine shot, he'd volunteered his services as an officer and a citizen. Granddaddy in his breeches and his Sam Brown belt. The Chief of Police had come to see them, that was the best part of the story. He had more gold braid than a Belgian railway conductor,

Granny'd laughed. He had thanked them, but not even Granddaddy could shoot birds from an apartment window.

27. From the chaise the sound in the chimney was just as loud, erratic and unnerving. She thought she was reading the book, but her hands were feeling what she must do. She must protect herself from the life in the bird, she must put on the apron, this time, and she must put on gloves. She wrapped the quilt around her feet.

28. She assigned herself to read the volume in her lap. A reporter remembering the battle fronts of his long career. A nonparticipant. Granddaddy, US Coast Artillery, had aimed guns at armies, commanded "Fire!" and scores of men had died. Then Granddaddy had been captured, had died. Daddy, much the same.

29. Sometimes, before their own initiation into loss, Jack had called her Big Red One, his redheaded one woman history, affectionately but also out of what seemed to her a boyish admiration for her family of dead soldiers. Paul was a dead soldier. Granny had survived, had carried that. She had talked of Paul with joy. Betsy, Paul's widow, was her favorite daughter-in-law.

30. Still in Los Angeles, the war still on, Daddy, Granddaddy and Uncle Weyman still alive, she remembered Granny telling the last story of Paul, how he was testing bomb sights, in Hawaii, in '37. He had said over the radio: "Tell Betsy to put the chops on, I'll be home in half an hour," and then the bomb had exploded inside the plane.

31. She sat in her chaise and wondered how Granny had walked upright on the earth.

32. A dead bird would be nothing, to Granny. She thought: I have one dead son, she had one dead son, she survived, I'll survive, that's what happens.

33. She went into the kitchen, got her work gloves, a big limp plastic bag that had once held a bunch of broccoli, the flashlight, and a large paper bag. She put on the gloves and drew the plastic bag over her right hand. That way, she hoped to avoid panic at the bird's wild struggle when it felt her hand close around it; that way she needn't feel the beak peck at her hand, the claws scratch. She would pull the plastic bag back off her hand and over the bird clutched therein, put the plastic bag in the big paper bag, and take the whole beating process to the back yard, where she would release the bird. She braced herself for the flailing, the wildness; she returned to the living room.

34. She pushed the screen aside and knelt down on the hearth, flashlight in hand. She shone the beam of light up along the side wall of the fireplace, toward the fluttering noise. The beam made clear the stripes on the sooty chimney pillow, the black bricks of the flue, and in the space between the bricks and the pillow, the label that was attached to the pillow. It fluttered in the draft. She moved the pillow a little, the label made a different noise. She put down the flashlight, and laughed. She had the night ahead of her. She laughed until she cried.

COMPREHENSION QUESTIONS FOR THE READER

1. Whose "book-learned New England" is referred to in paragraph 2 (P2)? Is it that of "she" or of Granny?

2. In P5, does the shift in reference terms from "Granddaddy" to "his father" to "her husband" and back to "Granddaddy" indicate a shift in point of view?

3. Do you feel a shift in the pace and/or abruptness with which the events are described when the story reports what is happening to "she" versus what happened to Granny?

4. Does the scope of WHERE vary throughout the story? Is there a pattern which contributes to the feel of the story?

5. In reading the story, do you feel that the subjectivity or point of view shifts back and forth between "she" and Granny? Or do you perceive Granny only through the protagonist's mind?

6. In P1, there is mention of a first heard rustle. In P10, we again hear about the rustle "heard recently for the first time." Did you read this as both referring to the same event? If so, how did you resolve the temporal sequence of events? That is, did you perceive P2 through P9 as occurring before P1 and P10 in story time?[1]

INTERPRETATIONS AND COMMENTS ON THE STORY

Author's Note

I am a writer, and on the strength of that, Judy Duchan invited me to join the Narrative Group on Wednesday afternoons. When I started coming, I had just begun a story about a woman who has a free evening: Her husband is going out to play poker, and she is going to stay home. The discussions of the Narrative Group were relevant to the writing task I had set myself.

I had never heard the term *deixis*, but, of course, focusing the reader's attention was central to the writing task. In particular, I was interested in the use certain gifted writers make of time and place in short stories. For example, I invite you to read any of Alice Munro's stories in *The Beggar Maid*, or the more recent ones in the *New Yorker*. In these stories, a few crucial events, widely separated in time and revealed to the reader via letters, newspaper articles, or remembered scraps of conversation, illuminate a universe. It is the movement of the narrative through point of view and time that makes these stories so moving.

Fascinated by the possibilities, I was having a go at this, and in the interest of disciplining my craft, had resolved to tell the story in the most straightforward

---

[1]Although initially our research group had differing views on interpreting the "first rustle," we finally agreed the rustle was the same. Anne confirmed the interpretation that the rustle in P1 and P10 is, indeed, the same.

and economical manner possible. This is often a very destructive concept for a writer like me in the early stages of writing a story, because I can easily decide that the whole thing is best, and most economically, presented by silence, and I go for a walk instead of writing anything at all.

I was in one of those stuck places in which I had in my mind a lovely space, not very clear, a sort of white fog, that actually was the story for me. It was the space itself that appealed to me: The character I imagined had a piece of time laid out before her, what would she do with it? I knew something of her, and that her husband was going out to play poker, and that because it was a cold night, she would stuff a pillow up the chimney to keep out the draft, and then various things would occur that would take her, and the reader, into an experiential world she knew about through the reminiscences of people long dead.

I wanted the reader to feel that funny chord change, that harmonic shift, that click, that release, when she came back, really all the way back to the present with the reader, a few minutes into her free night, that now had become free in a different sense.

I knew I wanted to do that, and I hadn't the slightest notion how I was going to go about it. That is fine, the whole thing about writing fiction is the business of going off blindfolded. It takes you where it wants you to go, or, as the famous novelists of my childhood used to say in interviews: "Why, the characters just take on lives of their own."

I had the first sentence, and like the first sentence of a number of things I have written, it has not changed. I thought of the story as something to follow the sentence: "She had been in the house by herself only a few minutes when she first heard the rustling noise in the chimney."

I wanted to convey that she was alone in the house and expected to be that way awhile—that condition is stated first—and that the rustling noise was an intrusion on her solitude. The briefness of the time between when she begins to be in the house alone, and when she hears the rustling noise is important, because it keeps the time frame tight on the events. That seemed important to me, because most of the words in the story are about events well into the past. Memories that take an instant of real time to be recalled, or even to be relived, seem to have taken much longer when one "comes back" from them. I wanted the reader to be safely anchored in the real time of the woman alone in the house—anchored on a long line.

It was very cold outside, reassuring in this age of global warming. Time was, combating the cold yielded her a righteous joy. Stuffing an old pillow up the chimney early each January was an act in defense of siege.

These three sentences presage the directions that will be taken by the shifts throughout the story. The first sentence keeps to the immediate experience of the woman: "It was very cold outside, reassuring in this age of global warming." The night was cold, and the reference to global warming brings in the quotidian, the TV and newspaper language the woman and the reader both routinely encounter. It reaffirms the safe anchor in real time that unites the woman and the reader in the present. It also links the woman to ecological concerns, with their demands of attention to detail and extra effort.

"Time was" signals a shift. Not only does it refer to the past, it is a folksy, old-fashioned way of doing so. Both "combating" and "stuffing" let the reader expect a continuing narrative in the era of "time was." "Combating" and "siege" also serve to introduce the military theme in the story.

> She would mutter to herself a New England saying of her Granny's: "When the days begin to lengthen, that's when the c-c-cold begins to strrrenghten." It had been a book-learned New England, with inaccuracies.

With the introduction of the Granny, this past has been enclosed, defined as that of someone who, the reader is invited to guess, has passed to her reward.

So much for setting the stage. There were overwritten paragraphs about how imprecise the Granny's memory was, and I was really confused about the theme of the story. I had thought that it would be about the moral questions brought on by the woman's belief that she could, if she chose, free a bird stuck in the chimney. I thought she would rummage around in her memory for Granny stories that would let her make a free choice. I had even given the story the word processor file name "morality" the first time I saved it.

After my first encounter with the Narrative Group, I decided to tell the story without naming the central character. I thought if I just concentrated on her focal point—the place and time and person at the center of her awareness, as it shifts and changes—the story could be economically told.

The Granny stories that serve to buttress the woman's willingness to take what is dished out are little illustrations of the woman's stock of memory. The shifts in the story also serve to adumbrate the woman's true wealth: her history and connectedness to her family's history. Although sandbagged by loss, she has, by the end of the story, a kind of amplitude. She can resist several kinds of cold by drawing on the past. The capacity of humans to move back and forth through time, through relationships and places—the agility that undergirds grammar and intelligence—could be called the subject of this story.

Temporal Structure of the Story

The intent of this section is to provide one possible description of the temporal structure of a "A Free Night." The temporal structure of a narrative can be described for a number of domains, including that of the story world, and the narrative that portrays the story within that world. The structure is illuminated by contrasting story world time and the readers' time as they read the story (narrative or story time). We can also describe the temporal structural system in terms of several parameters (see Talmy, this volume). Finally, we can track and describe the shifts in the WHEN of the DC as they occur in the narrative.

Relationship Between Story World Time and Narrative Time

For this description of the temporal structure of the story, we first consider three aspects of the comparison of story world and narrative (reader) time. Narrative time flows continuously forward as the reader reads the story, sentence by sentence. But the narrative does not refer to story world time in the sequence in which that time progresses. We describe the shift in story world time referred to by the narrative (this shift in story world time does not necessarily lead to a shift in the DC) along three dimensions. These are: (a) the direction of the temporal shifts (i.e., does the narrative take us backward or forward in story world time?), (b) the temporal distance covered by the shift in time (i.e., do we move across decades, years, or minutes to reach our destination in the story world?), and, (c) the duration of the temporal interval portrayed before further shifts occur (i.e., how long is the story world time described by the narrative?). (See Table 20.1 for a graphic presentation. Note that this table also includes some of the affect structure information from Table 20.3 in order to allow for a comparison of these structures.)

Direction of Temporal Movement. Talmy (this volume) indicates the importance of the rate of temporal movement, as well as an aspect of which direction time moves. The readers' time (narrative time) typically moves forward in an incremental fashion (unless the reader jumps ahead in the narrative or rereads prior sections). Similarly, time within a story world typically advances in a manner similar to that of the real world (exceptions could occur in science fiction, etc.). But as a narrative progresses, the order in which story world time is portrayed does not have to map the order in which those events occurred. We might move backward in story world time through flashbacks, or jump forward in story world time.

In this particular narrative, backward movement in time seems to occur under two circumstances: (a) unbidden memories, typically unpleasant, occasioned by current objects or events; and (b) voluntarily recalled memories.

The forward movements in time also seem to occur under two different circumstances: (a) time seems to move continuously forward for most of the description of the protagonist's experiences in the house; and (b) there are small but distinct jumps forward in time as the protagonist moves into a plan to solve a problem.

Distance Involved in Temporal Shifts in Story World Time. The temporal shifts in story world time referred to by the narrative appear to be characterized by their relationship to the two key events in the story—the death of Granny's

TABLE 20.1
Temporal and Affective Structure of "A Free Night"

1908	1920s	1937	1940s	1960s	1987	Time In House[a][b] (M/DC)	Time In House DC	Affect[c] (0)	Paragraph/Events
							$DC_{1,2}$	M P	1: hears rustle first time
				M_2			$DC_{1,2,3}$	L N	2: remembers long ago winter
			M_2	M_3		M_1			3: remembers current winters; longs for past winters
				M_2			$DC_{1,2,3}$	M P	4: describes Buffalo winters
E_2/DC_2		M_2					DC_1	HN/HP	5: recalls Granny story;
							DC_2 DC_1	L P	6: wind blows/Jack had left
						M/DC_3	$DC_{1,2}$ P_2	0/L N	7: plan pillow/recall Hawaii
						M/DC_2	$DC_{1,3}$	M N	8: last yr/Hawaii
							$DC_{1,..n}$	0	9: stuff pillow
							DC_1	0	10: hear rustle (see p1)
							DC_1	L N[d]	11,12: fluttering noise continues
							$DC_{1,..n}$	L N 0	13–18: Jack returns/leaves
							DC	L N	19,20: gets book & returns
						DC_2/M_4	$DC_{1,3,4}$	H N	21: recalls birds after loss
						M_1	$DC_{1,2}$	L N	22: hears flutter
							DC_1	L N	23: moves to her chaise
						M_2	$DC_{1,2}$	H N	24: thinks of birds again
	E_1/DC_2		M_1				DC_1	0/L P	25,26: Granny in Washington
			M_1				$DC_{1,2,3}$ P_2	L P	27: plan to get bird
			$E_2 M_2$				$DC_{1,2}$	0	28: Grandaddy, Daddy died
			$E_1 M_1$		M_1		$DC_{1,2}$	L N/LP[e]	29: before her loss/recall Granny
							$DC_{1,2}$	M N	30: remembers hearing about Granny's loss
			E_1				DC_1	H N	31: thinks about Granny's loss
			E_1		M_1		$DC_{1,3}$ P_2	H N	32: she & Granny lost sons
								H N	33: plan to get bird out
							DC	0/H P	34: discovers pillow

Note. Time Line of Events in the Story World is on the horizontal; Time Line of Events in the Narrative Line is on the vertical. Overlap in subscripts reflects embedding of events in stories she remembers. Dashes across the affect column indicate a break in the affect. Shifts in the DC from one time period to another are indicated by boxes around those paragraphs.

[a] DC = Deictic Center; [b] M = Memory; E = topic Event; P = future plan. [c] Degree of Intensity: H = High, M = Medium, L = Low. Valence is indicated by P = Positive, N = Negative, and 0 = Neutral. [d] Alternating affect from low negative to neutral. [e] Alternating affect from low positive to low negative.

son and the death of the protagonist's son. An overall pattern of the shifts in time might be characterized as "landing" on either side (before/after) of the key event with the distance from the key event decreasing until the shift lands at this key event. This provides a sense of the attraction of a powerful negative event (death of a son) on the protagonist's thoughts, as well as the repulsion created by thinking about that event. The pattern is clearer with respect to Granny's son, but can also be discerned with regard to the protagonist's loss. The main difference seems to be that the death of the son of the protagonist is visited several times, but briefly. The following describe that movement with respect to Granny and the protagonist:

1. Granny's experiences (through the memory of protagonist). The key event here is the loss of Granny's son, Paul in 1937. Initially, the shift is back past this event to an early time (1908) when the potential for loss of a son was a false alarm and a humorous event. A bit later, the memory returns to a somewhat less distant event (1920s?) when Granny is in Washington with a grown son and husband. Somewhat later in the narrative, the memory travel falls short of the critical event, landing in the 1940s with the first mention of death in Granny's experience—her husband and "Daddy." Finally, the death of Paul in 1937 is visited.

2. The Protagonist's experience. The shifts in time of the protagonist's thoughts or memories also over- and undershoot the critical event of the loss of her son. She recalls winters before the death and then winters after the death. She also shifts to memories of Granny's stories (involving various locales) she would have heard before the loss, and then to her own travel to Hawaii which occurred after the loss. Finally, in P8 we get the first indication that not all of her children are living.

Duration of the Temporal Interval Between Shifts in Story World Time.
Another aspect of the temporal structure of this particular story is the duration of narrative time spent at a particular point in story world time, as well as the interval of story world time represented between shifts. In particular, the narrative time spent at a particular time in the story provides a feel for the affect association with that (story) time.

There is difference between the experiences of Granny and the protagonist in terms of the duration of narrative time and story time. The description of Granny's experience relating to Paul takes longer in narrative time (as well as being more specific, explicit, direct) and covers more story time than the descriptions of the protagonist's experience relating to her lost son, which are brief, elliptical, and metaphorical (birds). With Granny we get both pleasant and unpleasant events described in some detail and encompassing hours or days. For example, the story of the snow on the baby clearly takes place over days.

There are occasions, however, when the duration of the description of experiences of the protagonist are quite prolonged (in narrative time). These seem to serve the function of postponing or delaying the occurrence of unpleasant events. For example, the paragraphs describing the interaction of the protagonist when her husband Jack returns to get the poker chips are quite detailed and consume a good part of the narrative time. With the dialog, the rates of progression of narrative and story world time appear to be synchronized. This interval seems to postpone the inevitable chore of taking care of the bird. In fact, during this interval, the protagonist indicates to Jack that she will "get it out in the morning."

The descriptions of actions to be carried out in the future also seem to take considerable narrative time, as do the actions leading up to the climax of the event (i.e., stuffing the pillow or getting hold of the bird). The detail of all the steps leading up to the climax both postpones it and allows the reader/protagonist to become girded for that climax. Again, the rate of progression of narrative time seems to correspond with that of the story world.

Factors Involved in Temporal Shifts in Story World Time and in the DC

Another aspect of temporal structure is the way in which shifts in story world time are initiated. Not all shifts involve shifts in the WHERE of the DC. For example, the WHEN of the DC may remain at the time of the protagonist's sitting in her house even when the events she is remembering took place long ago. Here, we briefly describe factors that shift the story world time portrayed, whether or not this leads to a DC shift.

Intrusions from the environment of the protagonist seem to distract her from current activities. These intrusions lead the protagonist to remember past experiences that share some characteristics with the intrusive stimuli. For example, the fact that it is cold outside leads to memories of past winters (P2, P3, P4) as well as Granny's winter experience (P5). More ominously, intrusions of rustling bring back memories of birds in the chimney (P21) and the death of her son.

On other occasions, the shift is to a future time. Intrusions stimulate planning future actions to deal with the related problem. Again, the coldness outside and the rustling in the chimney serve this function—leading the protagonist to plan how to deal with these stimuli.

However, there are a number of shifts in the DC, and these seem to be related to the vividness of the description of events or the intensity of the affect related to the event.

In P5, the DC does seem to shift from the protagonist sitting in the house to Granny in Boston. Although the beginning of that paragraph depicts a memory (leaving the DC in the house), the DC shifts to the time of the event with the detailed description. This shift is most clearly indicated by "The next morning," referring to the morning after the baby was put to bed with the window open. This shift is further supported by the fact that a preposed adverbial in P6, "tonight," is used to shift the reader back to the protagonist in her house.

At times, the DC seems to shift back and forth within the same paragraph, indicating a very brief time spent at a highly emotional moment. In P21, "they had had" indicates the DC is still in the protagonist's current time (in the house). But "careening . . . , leaving ash splats" seems to shift the DC to the time of that event. The next sentence, "That was four years ago," returns the DC to the protagonist in her house. "She had been revolted" maintains that DC, but the next sentence, "Opening the windows, getting the birds to fly . . . ," seems to again shift the DC to the event time. But "how had she and Jack done it" and, "Another time, they would have laughed," returns the DC to the time of the protagonist in her house. The shifts in the DC during this paragraph may provide the reader with the feel of the protagonist's avoidance of certain areas of her past, as the reader shifts back and forth between current and past story world time and the related events.

Parameters and the Temporal Structure of the Story

In this section, we discuss a few of the parameters suggested by Talmy (this volume) as important in the structure of narrative. The temporal structure of this story provides clear examples of *embeddedness*, as we track the timeline of events in Granny's life embedded in the protagonist's memories, that are embedded in present time as the protagonist sits in her house listening to rustling in the chimney. (See P5 in the story for an example.)

Another parameter of particular relevance to time in this story is *scale*, including the *granularity* and the *density* of time intervals. For example, the temporal intervals represented in Granny's experiences are of a coarser grain (P5, P25, P26) than are the intervals when the protagonist is in the house (P9, P13–P20, P33). That is, the temporal intervals in Granny's stories seem to represent hours rather than the minutes represented in the protagonist's experiences. There is also more density in description in the protagonist's experiences. In Granny's stories, many of the hours are skipped as the reader moves from one day to the next (P5), or over even longer time intervals (P25, P26). With the protagonist, we get a more dense description of each minute in P9, P13–P20, and P33.

A third parameter is the *vagueness* about the precise time in the story which is referred to and the time interval covering the events described. We know specifically, almost to the minute, when Granny's son Paul died (P30) and the duration of time during which this death occurred (instantaneous). But the time of the death of the protagonist's son is vague (4 years ago), as is the duration of the event (see P8 and P21, where the death is alluded to).

Spatial Structure

Space plays an essential role in deictic structuring of narratives. This structural system includes geographic space, and animate and inanimate objects and their arrangement in and movement through space. In this section, we examine particular aspects of spatial deixis in narrative, including change through time (motion), scale, embeddedness, explicitness, and density (see Talmy, this volume).

As a story progresses, changes can occur in any of these aspects of space. A narrative can depict a different geographic location in the story world; motion in these locations can be slow, moderate, or rapid, planned or unplanned, erratic or predictable. Focus can be upon a small, medium, or large part of the overall setting (scale); a description of a setting can be sparse or detailed (density). (For more possibilities, see Talmy, this volume.)

What follows is: (a) a description of variations in the four aspects of space listed previously that occur in Anne's story, and (b) a description of how those aspects change as the story unfolds.

Variations in Location, Motion, Scale, and Density

Location.   The central location is the house in Buffalo, New York, where the protagonist is physically located throughout the story. Within the house, she most often sits at the hearth and occasionally takes trips: upstairs, to the basement, to the kitchen, and to another chair. (See Fig. 20.1 for a layout of the house.) When she is sitting at the hearth, she is forced by noises to focus on the chimney. The protagonist's mental space has representations of the house; this includes memories of past configurations, as well as the possibility of projecting future spatial representations for planning purposes.

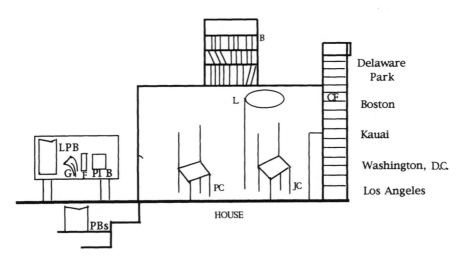

Legend: JC = Jack's chair; PC = Protagonists's chair; L = Lamp; CF = Chimney flue; B = Bookcase;
PB = Paper bags; G = Gloves; F = Flashlight; Pl B = Plastic bag; LPB = Large paper bag;;

FIG. 20.1.   Space represented in the story, "A Free Night."

While in the house, her memory shifts to different geographical spaces. These locations are often connected with either the experiences of Granny or herself. There are "Granny's stories from Boston, from the Philippines, from Hawaii." The protagonist has her own memories of being in Maryland, Kauai, Los Angeles, and Buffalo.

Motion. Several patterns of motion emerge in the story. Motion in the story is moderate or rapid, planned or unplanned, erratic or predictable. One pattern of motion is moderate and planned and occurs when the protagonist moves to different locations in the house to get what she needs to re-establish the warmth and silence in the living room so that she can carry out her plans for the evening. Another pattern of motion is rapid, unplanned, and erratic. This pattern occurs twice—both in memory. One is her memory of the two birds that zigzagged throughout the downstairs 4 years earlier (P21). The other, is where she moves back and forth in space and time in memory (P29–30).

Scale. The scale of the WHERE varies throughout the story. There are three levels of scale: small, medium, and large. Small scale spaces that predominate in the story include the chimney and the chair. Medium scale spaces include the house, or parts of the house, including the kitchen and living room. The only notable large scale space is Delaware Park. Mention of other locations, such as Kauai or Los Angeles, does not indicate the scale; we are told about the events that occur in those locations, but not about the locations, themselves.

One pattern that emerges is change in focus upon a small to a large part and back upon a small part of the overall setting. This shifting of scale from small to large or to medium and then back to small again is manifested in several sections of the story. For example, whenever the protagonist attends to the noise in the chimney, as she does in P10, P11, and P12, the scale becomes small. The scale enlarges as the story portrays a conversation between the protagonist and her husband, or as the protagonist remembers a Granny story, and then it becomes small again as her attention shifts to the noise in the chimney.

Density. The density of the WHERE also varies throughout the story. Reminiscences tend to be spatially sparse as are descriptions of the protagonist sitting in the chair. On the other hand, descriptions of movement within the house are dense. For example, when the protagonist takes action, to close the chimney flue with a pillow (P9) or to free the bird in the chimney (P33–34), the descriptions are detailed with both the objects and series of movements involved in these actions.

Tracking Variations in Spatial Structure

The story begins in a house in Buffalo, New York. The protagonist, looking forward to a evening alone, sits in her husband, Jack's, chair by a good reading light. As the story unfolds, that chair becomes an important deictic center—a place she has chosen to sit during the evening, but one she physically leaves on four occasions.

Her first movement from Jack's chair is to a ledge halfway down the basement stairs. She gets a pillow there to keep out a draft coming down the chimney and settles back into Jack's chair. Her second movement from his chair is to a bookcase upstairs where she gets a volume to read. She comes back downstairs and resettles in his chair with the heavy book on her lap. Her third movement is short: She moves from Jack's chair to her chair, which is less well lit, but where the fluttering noise from the chimney is fainter. Her fourth movement is into the kitchen to get the things she needs to release the bird from the chimney flue; she then goes to the chimney hearth. Except for the short movement, all the movements are described in detail qualifying as dense.

Interspersed with her actual movements are moves into memory (mental spaces). Although the protagonist never physically leaves the house during the entire story, she moves to many different geographic locations in her mind: to Delaware Park, Fort Slocum, Kauai, Washington, Los Angeles.

Even when the protagonist is not moving in the story, changes in space take place. The scale in the story alternates from moderate or large spaces to small ones. As the story opens, there is shifting among medium (her house; Granny's house) and large spaces (Delaware Park). The scope then narrows as the focus of the story is directed toward the protagonist in the chair and the wind in the chimney. A transition occurs with the phrase, "She heard thumping on the porch; Jack had returned." With this phrase, the protagonist shifts her attention to still another small part of the setting—the pounding of Jack's sneakers on the porch; the transition prepares us for an opening up to a larger scale that involves the conversation between the two people as one enters and exits the house in P11–P19. The scale becomes small again in P20, when the protagonist attends to the noise in the chimney once again.

Another illustration of this closing and opening of the scope of the setting occurs around the movements mentioned earlier. While she is moving through the house, space opens up to a more moderate scale; when she returns, it narrows to a focus on the chair or the chimney. (For a paragraph-by-paragraph description of spatial structure, see Table 20.2. This table also includes some of the affect information from Table 20.3, so a comparison of these two structures can be made.)

Affective Structure

Our work on subjectivity and deixis (see the chapters on subjectivity in this volume) has treated affective statements in narrative as subjective ones and as located in the mental space of a focalizing WHO. The emphasis of our previous work was to determine how shifts are indicated between objective events in the story world and subjective ones thought and felt by characters in the story (see

TABLE 20.2

Spatial and Affective Structure of "A Free Night"

P	Text	Location/Scale[a]	Type of Motion	Affect[bc]
1	The protagonist in her house hears the rustling noise in the chimney for the first time.	House	–	0
2, 3	She reminisces about winters	House	–	MF/LN
4	She recalls post-storm, brilliant, winter days in Buffalo, and evenings when she stood in the middle of Delaware Park	Buffalo#, Del. Park#	–	M P
5	She recalls a Granny story about how Granny sent Granddaddy across the ice of Boston Harbor to get a doctor for her new baby, Paul.	Fort Slocum#, Boston Harbor#	Moderate Rapid/Planful	HN/NP
6	Cold wind shakes the house and rattles in the chimney; ice strikes the window. With Jack gone for his poker night, she sits in his chair looking forward to solitude.	House	–	L P
7, 8	As her eyes go down the paper she thinks about stuffing a pillow up the chimney. That the children probably had fires in the chimney reminds her of a trip to Kauai.	Jack's chair, House, Chimney#, Kauai#	–	0/L N
9	She gets up out of Jack's chair, walks down the basement stairs, stops at a shelf and takes the chimney pillow out of the bags, walks back upstairs, kicks the basement door shut, walks across the hall and living room rug to the fireplace, pushes the screen aside, kneels down, stuffs the pillow up the chimney, replaces the screen.	space from Jack's chair to basement to chimney	Moderate and Planful	M N
10	She sits back down in Jack's chair, continues reading and hears the rustling noise.	Jack's chair	–	0
11	She hears a fluttering noise coming from the chimney flue; it is louder, fainter, stops.	Chimney flue	–	L N[d]
12	She resumes reading, hears the noise again, and hears Jack thumping on the porch.	Flue, Porch	–	L N[d]
13	Jack travels across the room to get the poker chips	Across the room	Mod/Planful	L N
14	Remaining seated, she speaks to Jack.	Living room	Mod/Planful	L N
15	Jack is on his way back out.	Across room	–	0
16–18	They converse about the birds in the chimney.	Living room	–	L N[d]/0
19	Jack leaves, she goes upstairs to get a book	chair to upstairs	Mod/Planful	L N
20	She comes back downstairs, settles in Jack's chair with a quilt around her.	upstairs to chair	Mod/Planful	L N
21	Preoccupied with the bird in the chimney, she recalls when two black birds zigzagged through the downstairs leaving black splats on walls and ceiling.	Downstairs#	Fast/Erratic	H N
22	Still remembering the messy, soot-covered downstairs, she is pulled back to the present by the sound in the chimney.	Downstairs#, Chimney flue	–	L N
23	She moves from Jack's chair to her chaise to distance herself from the noise.	Her chaise	Mod/Planful	L N

(Continued)

477

TABLE 20.2
(Continued)

P	Text	Location/Scale*[a]	Type of Motion	Affect[bc]
24	She contemplates on how she is not responsible for a bird dumb enough to get stuck and die in her chimney. She recalls two birds she and Jack released four years ago.	Chimney flue	–	H N
25–26	That thought evokes a Granny story: Granny and Granddaddy lived in an apartment in Washington, DC. Granddaddy's offer to shoot starlings from the window was refused by the Chief of Police.	Washington, DC#	–	0 L P
27	She hears the erratic sound in the chimney. Looking at the book as though reading, she plans how to protect herself from the bird, wraps the quilt around her feet.	Chaise Chimney flue	–	L P
28	Telling herself to read, she reads a reporter's remembrances of many wars. This evokes the memory of Granddaddy and Daddy who died in the war.	Chaise Battlefield#	–	0
29–30	She recalls a time (in Buffalo) when Jack called her "Big Red One"; an earlier time when Granny (in Los Angeles) survived Paul's death; and even earlier time when (Granny still in Los Angeles) Daddy, Granddaddy, and Uncle Weyman were still alive; and at a later time when Paul had died in Hawaii.	Buffalo# Los Angeles# Hawaii#	–	L N[e] L P[e] M N
31–32	Seated in her chaise, she wonders how Granny survived the death of her son and she thinks that she too will survive the death of her son.	Chaise	–	H N H N
33	She goes into the kitchen to get her gloves, a plastic bag, a flashlight, a large paper bag. She puts on gloves, and draws the bag over her right hand; she plans, step-by-step what she will do when she catches the bird. She returns to the living room.	Chaise to kitchen to living room to basement# & back	Moderate Planful	H N
34	She pushes the screen aside, kneels down on the hearth, shines the beam of the flashlight up the chimney toward the noise, and sees the pillow label fluttering. She moves the pillow and hears a different sound. She laughs until she cries.	Hearth Chimney flue	–	0 H P

Note. Dashes across the affect column indicates a break in the affect (see Table 20.2).

[a]# indicates a mental location (memory, plan). The terms used to indicate the location also indicates the scale. For example, the chair is a small scale location, the house is medium scale, Buffalo would be large scale.

[b]H = High, M = Medium, L = Low.

[c]Valence is indicated by P = positive, N = Negative, and 0 = neutral.

[d]Alternating affect from low negative to neutral.

[e]Alternating affect from low positive to low negative.

478

Wiebe, 1990b; Bruder & Wiebe, this volume). What Talmy's (this volume) grid asks for is not only a tracking of the deictic shifts, but also a tracking of the contours of affect as it changes during the telling of a story.

The affective structuring in Costello's story takes place in the mind of the protagonist, and thus, the focalizing WHO remains the DC focus throughout. That is not to say that the emotional content is static, however. Borrowing from Talmy's (this volume) ideas of atmosphere, this analysis aims at tracking atmospheric, emotional themes in the character's subjectivity, and identifying the linguistic devices that convey those emotions.

Themes Relating to Affect

The story is rich in emotional content. Throughout are expressions from the protagonist of deeply felt emotions as well as expressions that create in the reader feelings of suspense, mystery, and release. In this section, we outline ways in which the emotional content of the story is conveyed thematically and linguistically in an effort to arrive at a sense of the story's affective structure. In the next section, we examine parallels between the affective structure of the story and the deictic structure of time and space in the story world.

The story contains emotionally packed contrasts between mundane elements—cold and warmth; birds and pillows. For example, it begins with images of the winter in Buffalo. The winters of the past are compared with the present, the winters of Granny's stories are compared with those experienced directly by the protagonist. In these early paragraphs the winter's cold is associated with withstanding a siege, and with the joy that results from overcoming cold's challenge. The cold is welcomed as an opportunity to withstand difficult circumstances: "the c-c-cold begins to strrrengthen." Past winters, when everyone was alive, are remembered as joyful. The winter of Granny's story when she almost lost her son to the cold is remembered as being "uproariously funny"—a win against the cold.

Whereas intense cold is associated with resolve and sometimes joy upon meeting life's challenges, warmth is used in this story to create feelings of safety, coziness, an evening at the hearth. The cold of outside impinges as a draft coming down the flue of the chimney and enters the warmth and safety of the inside. The protagonist conjures up a plan to meet the challenge of the cold by stuffing a pillow up the chimney. She remembers Granny's baby nearly freezing and Granny meeting that challenge by rubbing and warming him with brandy, saving his life. Cold challenges life; warmth protects and saves it.

Similarly, there are objects in the story that anchor emotional content into polar oppositions. The pillow, used to conquer the cold leak, is cast as a safety measure. The elaborate journey to get the pillow in the basement and the return is associated with emotional resolve to cope with difficulties. The counterpoint to the pillow is the bird, which becomes associated with fear, with repugnance, with entrapment. The feared bird, imagined as causing the fluttering noise in the chimney, becomes associated with birds of the past: the two that were caught in the house at the time of her son's death. Those birds are depicted as "dreadful," as having "gratuitous horror," as "disgusting birds." Birds are also associated with children when the protagonist describes her children back home in Buffalo as "migrating birds."

The protagonist resolves to protect herself "from the life of the bird," or worse, from the death of the bird, by embarking on a second journey through the house. This time she goes to get gloves and a plastic bag to retrieve the bird from the chimney. The final relief and climax of the story comes when she discovers the noise was from the pillow, not a bird. The pillow, a safe, solid, inanimate object wins out over the dreaded bird—it is neither alive nor dead, but inanimate.

The characters of the story also represent affective contrasts. Granny and her losses and coping abilities are repeatedly placed in contrast with those of the protagonist who is trying to cope: "A dead bird would be nothing, to Granny." Granny's stories are distant and funny. Granny doesn't need to plan, she somehow copes with winters, with birds, with near death, and with death itself. Granny's stories allow distance, they are of events that happened somewhere else, at a time long ago. Granny's abilities to cope with cold, birds, death, represent a challenge of survival to the protagonist: "I have one dead son, she had one dead son, she survived, I'll survive, that's what happens."

Emotion is also built up by creating parallels between physical and emotional struggles. Physical struggles are thematized at first as against the cold: People combat the cold (P2) and defend against siege (P2). Later, deaths of family members are described—deaths that result from combat of soldiers at war (P28, P30). These physical combats are associated with combating fear—the fear of the noise in the chimney—and then associated with combating grief, the grief from a son's death. The cold and fear are combated with physical force, placing the pillow in the chimney and then removing it. These physical remedies are associated with a resolve, that is then associated with the resolve to combat the grief and conquer it.

The reader of the story experiences emotion by identifying with what the protagonist is feeling. But the emotion of the reader goes beyond that of empathy. The story also creates for the reader a set of emotions on a different plane, one that exists outside of the protagonist's experience. The reader is made to experience suspense not felt by the protagonist. For example, an event is alluded to, but not described. A noise is heard, but its source and significance is not disclosed. Why is the noise significant? Later a mood of ominousness is added to the mystery. "Such a shame to have to go that particular week" makes one wonder what happened that week? Still later, one reads, "That was four years ago, a bad time for them." What happened? The suspense begins to dissipate when the event is described as a loss (P29) and becomes fully resolved three paragraphs from the story's end: "I have one dead son" (P32).

Tracking Variations in Affective Structure

The affect structure of the story is most directly trackable by examining the feelings of the characters, especially the protagonist as the story unfolds. As can be seen from Table 20.3, one can examine the story, paragraph by paragraph, and assign affect tones to sentences or whole paragraphs, based on its affect terms (joy, savoring, disgusting) or on feelings engendered by the story's content (wondered how Granny had walked upright on the earth). Often the feeling tone of a paragraph is consistent throughout, as if the paragraphs were organized to express single affect tones, and new paragraphs begun when the tone shifts (e.g., P2, P3, P4). Other times, feelings alternate within a paragraph, as if the paragraph was designed to express the experience of conflicting emotion (P5). Some paragraphs do not exude a feeling state, but are neutral, as when the protagonist first hears a noise (P1, P10).

The feeling tones varied in degree of intensity, ranging from low to high. Affect shifts in tone were most dramatic after high intensity paragraphs that were followed by paragraphs low in tone or neutral in valence (no intensity) (P5 vs. P6; P24 vs. P25).

The affect tones also differed in valence. Some were positive, some negative, and some neutral. The first part of the story was mostly positive, interspersed with some negative (section 1 from P1–P5). Section 2 was slightly positive or neutral, and then moved to a consistently negative tone (P11–24). The shift was then to mostly positive, with some neutral and negative (P25–30). The last section was all negative, ending abruptly in a positive sentence (P34).

AN ATTEMPT TO INTEGRATE TEMPORAL, SPATIAL, AND AFFECTIVE STRUCTURE

Temporal and Spatial Structure

Generally in the story, shifts in time are related to shifts in space. When the protagonist and/or reader moves to memories in the past (the protagonist's or Granny's) there is a shift in location (cf. Zubin & Hewitt, this volume). The main exception is when memories involve the central spatial focus of the story—the chimney (the focalized WHERE). Here temporal shifts occur, but the WHERE remains at or near the chimne (see P2, P7, P21, P22, P24).

In the movements of the protagonist within the house (within the present time), the temporal and spatial movement are closely coordinated—with explicit steps seeming to take a realistic amount of time (see P9, P33, P34). Interestingly, when spatial motion is absent (the protagonist is sitting in a chair) the time the reader experiences seems longer than the time that would have passed in the story world.

TABLE 20.3
Tracking the Affect in "A Free Night"

P		Degree[a]	Valence[b]
1	Beginning of problem? First heard noise		0
2	Reassured by cold; reverie of combating cold joy, resolve, act in defense of siege. New England and Granny—cold, strong severe cold = threat and challenge; joy	M	P
3	Discouraged, things don't matter; misses Great Lakes winters. Mild cold = no challenge, boring; something missing	L	N
4	Post storm delight, in Buffalo; her own stories of fond winter personally experienced memories opposed to Granny's told stories resolve against winter; beauty of winter her own stories—strength and joy Granny's stories—strength and joy	M	P
5	Granny's story of near tragedy, winter, baby's near death, snow drift over the crib relief, baby ok, "uproariously funny" Granddaddy was furious . . . conquering against winter, cold and near death	H H	N P
6	Cold outside vs. calm inside, savoring solitude	L	P
7	Recollections—remembering specific but unspecified event (pillow, apron, Hawaii, Kids, migrating birds, hesitating at home, longing, lonely	L	0 N
8	Conflict between wanting to be home with kids and having to be with sick aunt, Irony—wonderful place but can't enjoy it, Granny's laugh associated with life's ironies	M	N
9	Resolve—"what the hell"—journey ending in putting pillow in chimney to solve problem		0
10	Hears rustling noise		0*
11, 12	Noise both urgent and calming; worry	L	N[c]
13–18	Rustling = bird, it can die. Jack returns, presents Jack with problem, he doesn't help, she doesn't force the issue	L	N[c] 0[c]
19	Goes to get book to take her mind off things		0
20	Worry continues as she tries to ignore the fluttering	L	N
21	Recollection of earlier time, dreadful birds; 4 years ago, a bad time for them, birds the final horror, another time they would have laughed at the birds	H	N
22	Soot all over everything, fluttering noise	L	N
23	She tries to resolve the worry by moving	L	N
24	Tries to minimize the problem, stupid life of bird, disgusting bird, reminds her again of the earlier horrible episode, starlings	H	N
25, 26	Granny, and starling episode, Granny stories ended with Granny's laughing	L	0 P
27	Can't ignore it, new resolve, must do something, "Must protect herself from the life of the bird"	L	P
28	Death, Granddaddy, Daddy, distant, as characters in a historical novel		0

(Continued)

TABLE 20.3
(Continued)

P		Degree[a]	Valence[b]
29	Initiation into loss; loss = death, affection from Jack	L	N[d]
	toward her, admiration from Jack toward her family of dead	L	P[d]
	soldiers; Granny had survived death of soldiers, of her son	L	N[d]
	Paul	L	P[d]
30	Granny told story of Paul's death	M	N
31	And she wondered how "granny had walked upright on the earth"—pathos, moves from seeing Granny as having coped to identifying with Granny's grief (Granny as idol—Granny as experiencer)	H	N
32	A dead son, resolve to survive is cast as passive—"that's what happens"—rather than as an active coping with grief	H	N
33	Vivid horrific description of plan to get bird and free it—to avoid panic; braced herself to cope with terror	H	N
34	Finds rustling not bird but label on pillow, she laughed until		0
	she cried—relief	H	P

[a]Degree of intensity: H = High; M = Medium; L = Low
[b]Valence: P = Positive; N = Negative; 0 = Neutral
[c]Alternating affect throughout this dialog from low negative to neutral
[d]Alternating affect in this paragraph, from low positive to low negative

Temporal Shifts and Affect

As indicated previously, shifts in time (either to memories, or more dramatic shifts in the WHEN to past times) are closely associated with affect. As can be seen in Table 20.1, there are close correspondences between deictic shifts and shifts in emotional intensity represented in the narrative. Those shifts appear to be of two different types.

Some shifts in the WHEN are triggered by stimuli, rather than intentional recollecting on the part of the protagonist. These may result in either positive or negative affect, but they do not seem to be triggered by affect (the shifts in P5, P7).

Other shifts in the WHEN appear to be a result of intense negative affect. This may result in a shift from a past event to the present time, when the memory is very negative (P9, P22). Or, it may result in a shift to a past memory when the highly negative affect is in the present (P24–P25, P26).

Other relationships between affect and time include the detailed, explicit memories associated with Granny's experiences and the fleeting, vague memories associated with the protagonist's loss. This not only reflects the feelings of the protagonist—avoidance—but may move the reader to a sense of unease or uncertainty. Granny's tragedies are concrete to the reader and are coped with. The protagonist's tragedy is much more vague and the reader may find that the vagueness provides a sense of being unable to comprehend and thus, cope. (Refer to Table 20.1, at the correspondence between temporal and affective structure.)

Spatial Components and Affect

There are a number of ways the story associates spatial with affectual elements. Two of the seven high-affect paragraphs are spatially associated with Granny, who is somewhere outside of the house and outside of Buffalo (P5 in Boston; P31 at an undefined other place). Granny, in some other place (and time), is realized as a model of how one might experience and cope with the emotional content of life.

Four of the remaining high-affect paragraphs contain a description of birds trapped in the protagonist's house (P21, P24, P33, P34). The fast, erratic movement of the birds in P21 is particularly horrifying and one in which movement is portrayed as being out of a character's control. In the last of the high-affect paragraphs, P32, the protagonist wonders how she can survive the death of her son. It is an internal thought with no particular marking as to space. The coping that needs to be done is not related to a place, but involves a state of mind, an emotional acceptance regardless of where the protagonist is situated.

The image of the bird in the chimney is one of spatial confinement, as contrasted with the image of the previous birds flitting about the house. Both cases are associated with negative affect, but the birds on the loose connote terror, as opposed to more moderate feelings of fear of the bird that remains trapped in the chimney.

The chimney with the cold leaking in and then with the noise that sounds like a trapped bird takes on a negative valence that becomes thematic for the story. To counter these negative feelings, the protagonist plans and carries out activities that remove her from the chimney: first to get a pillow (P9); then, a book (P19, P20); and finally, to sit in her chaise away from the chimney (P23). All three trips to somewhere else in the house are planned and done with commitment and resolve. They are associated with neutral affect, and thus offer successful ways of countering the negative feelings engendered by chimney events. A fourth effort to escape the fears conjured up by the noises in the chimney follows her thoughts about her son's death (P32). She begins this trip into the kitchen to gather materials to capture the bird. These first movements are conveyed with neutral affect (P33). This emotion abruptly turns negative in the middle of the paragraph, as she thinks about what will happen when she returns to the chimney. This passage differs from the other trips in that it includes a plan that carries with it an emotional trauma and it is a direct confrontation of a negative feeling rather than an avoidance of a minor irritation. Before she can complete this journey, she must garner resources to confront the horror of the flailing bird. (Refer to Table 20.2 to compare the spatial and affectual structures.)

Time, Space, and Affect

Although much of the prior section implicitly provides a sense of these components interacting to comprise the structure of the story, here we try to pull out some additional structure that involves all components.

The overall theme of the story emerges from considering all three lines on the structural grid of the story. The theme has to do with coping with loss. And time, motion and affect are closely related to the coping, or lack thereof, portrayed. When the protagonist is actively coping—moving in time and space to solve a problem—space is densely populated with motions; time seems to move quickly and affect is voided. While moving, "she" is not thinking or feeling. When the protagonist is stationary, time seems to also be virtually stationary—or to drag by slowly—and affect is negative: either revulsion or depression.

Time and motion provided an interesting metaphor for coping. The passage of time is often portrayed as the solution to, or palliative for, loss. And this is reflected by the protagonist's statement, "she survived, I'll survive, that's what happens." But this passive passing of time does not seem to be working for our protagonist. Passive passage of time—in reading—does not work. The thoughts and memories intrude on the wings of birds, or wind gusts, or rustles. And escape to Granny memories—although providing some relief—is not a solution, either. Whatever the strength that comes from those memories, they do not move time along and she ultimately has to return to the present with its emotional baggage. What appears to take a long time (the memories) in reality only occupies a few minutes of story time. But when the protagonist mobilizes by physical action, time and space move, and we get a sense of relief at entering the combat. Although she does not win every battle, the protagonist has some hope of eventually winning the war.

REFERENCES

Adams, M. J., & Collins, A. (1979). A schema–theoretic view of reading. In R. O. Freedle (Ed.), *New directions in discourse processing* (Vol. 2, pp. 1–22). Norwood, NJ: Ablex.

Adler, C. S. *The magic of the glits.* New York: MacMillan.

Allaire, E. B. (1963). Bare particulars. *Philosophical Studies, 14,* 1–8.

Allaire, E. B. (1965). Another look at bare particulars. *Philosophical Studies, 16,* 16–21.

Allen, J. F. (1981). *Maintaining knowledge about temporal intervals* (Tech. Rep. No. 86). Rochester: University of Rochester, Computer Science Department.

Allen, J. F. (1984). Towards a general theory of action and time. *Artificial Intelligence, 23,* 123–154.

Allen, J. F. (1987). *Natural language understanding.* Menlo Park, CA: Benjamin/Cummings.

Almeida, M. J. (1987). *Reasoning about the temporal structure of narratives* (Tech. Rep. No. 87–10). Buffalo: State University of New York at Buffalo, Department of Computer Science.

Almeida, M. (1989). A theory of the aspectual progressive. In *Proceedings of the 11th Annual Conference of the Cognitive Science Society* (pp. 244–251). Hillsdale, NJ: Lawrence Erlbaum Associates.

Almeida, M. J. (1992). An approach to the representation of iterative situations. *Proceedings of the 10th Annual Conference of the American Association for Artificial Intelligence, 291–295.* Menlo Park, CA: AAAI Press/MIT Press.

Almeida, M. J., & Shapiro, S. C. (1983). Reasoning about the temporal structure of narrative texts. *Proceedings of the 5th Annual Conference of the Cognitive Science Society.* Hillsdale, NJ: Lawrence Erlbaum Associates.

Ameka, F. (1987). A comparative analysis of linguistic routines in two languages: English and Ewe. *Journal of Pragmatics, 11,* 299–326.

Ameka, F. (1992a). Interjections [Special issue]. *Journal of Pragmatics, 18*(2/3).

Ameka, F. (1992b). Interjections: The universal yet neglected part of speech. In F. Ameka (Ed.), Interjections (pp. 101–118) [Special issue]. *Journal of Pragmatics, 18*(2/3).

Ameka, F. (1992c). The meaning of phatic and conative interjections. In F. Ameka (Ed.), Interjections (pp. 245–271) [Special issue] *Journal of Pragmatics, 18*(2/3).

Anderson, A., Garrod, S. C., & Sanford, A. J. (1983). The accessibility of pronominal antecedents as a function of episode shifts in narrative text. *Quarterly Journal of Experimental Psychology, 35A*, 427–440.

Anthony, P. (1982). *Ogre, ogre.* New York: Ballantine.

Apel, K-O. (1980). *Towards a transformation of philosophy.* B. Adey & D. Frisby (Trans.). London: Routledge & Kegan Paul.

Aristotle (1965). On the art of poetry. In T. S. Dorsch (Trans.), *Aristotle/Horace/Longinus: Classical literary criticism* (pp. 29–75). New York: Viking. (original work circa 325 BCE)

Asher, N. (1986). Belief in discourse representation theory. *Journal of Philosophical Logic, 15,* 127–189.

Atkinson, M. (1979). Prerequisites for reference. In E. Ochs & B. Schieffelin (Eds.), *Developmental pragmatics.* New York: Academic Press.

Auerbach, E. (1953). *Mimesis.* Princeton: Princeton University Press.

Austen, J. (1966). *Pride and prejudice.* New York: Norton.

Austen, J. (1980). In B. Southam (Ed. & Trans.). *Jane Austen's 'Sir Charles Grandison.'* New York: Oxford University Press.

Austin, J. L. (1962). *How to do things with words.* Cambridge, MA: Harvard University Press.

Bakhtin, M. (1981). *The dialogic imagination.* C. Emerson and M. Holquist (Trans.). Austin: University of Texas Press.

Bakhtin, M. (1984). *Problems of Dostoevsky's poetics.* C. Emerson (Ed. & Trans.). Minneapolis: University of Minnesota Press.

Bal, M. (1985). *Narratology: Introduction to the theory of narrative.* Toronto: University of Toronto Press.

Ballim, A., Wilks, Y., & Barnden, J. (1991). Belief ascription, metaphor, and intensional identification. *Cognitive Science, 15,* 133–171.

Balzac, H. (1967). *Eugenie Grandet.* London: Oxford University Press. (Original work published 1833)

Bamberg, M., & Damrad-Frye, R. (1991). On the ability to provide evaluative comments: Further explorations of children's narrative competencies. *Journal of Child Language, 18,* 689–710.

Banfield, A. (1982). *Unspeakable sentences: Narration and representation in the language of fiction.* Boston: Routledge & Kegan Paul.

Banfield, A. (1987). Describing the unobserved: Events grouped around an empty centre. In N. Fabb, D. Attridge, A. Durant, and C. MacCabe (Eds.), *The Linguistics of writing* (pp. 265–285). New York: Methuen.

Bartlett, F. C. (1932). *Remembering.* Cambridge, England: Cambridge University Press.

Barwise, J., & Perry, J. (1983). *Situations and attitudes.* Cambridge, MA: MIT Press.

Bennett, M., & Partee, B. (1972). *Toward the logic of tense and aspect in English.* Santa Monica, CA: System Development Corporation.

Benveniste, E. (1971). *Problems in general linguistics.* M. E. Meek (Trans.). Miami: University of Miami Press.

Black, J. B., Turner, T. J., & Bower, G. H. (1979). Point of view in narrative comprehension, memory, and production. *Journal of Verbal Learning and Verbal Behavior, 18,* 187–198.

Bloomfield, L. (1933). *Language.* London: George, Allen, & Unwin.

Bobrow, D. G. (1975). Dimensions of representation. In D. G. Bobrow & A. Collins (Eds.), *Representation and understanding: Studies in Cognitive Science* (pp. 1–34). New York: Academic Press.

Bobrow, D. G., & Winograd, T. (1977). An overview of KRL, a knowledge representation language. *Cognitive Science, 1,* 3–46.

Booth, W. (1983). *The Rhetoric of fiction.* Chicago: University of Chicago Press. (Original work published 1961)

Boring, E. G. (1950). *History of experimental psychology.* New York: Appleton-Century-Crofts.

Bower, G. H., & Morrow, D. G. (1990). Mental models in narrative comprehension. *Science, 247,* 44–48.

Brachman, R. J., & Levesque, H. J. (Eds.). (1985). *Readings in knowledge representation.* San Mateo, CA: Kaufmann.

Bransford, J. D., & Johnson, M. K. (1972). Contextual prerequisites for understanding: Some investigations of comprehension and recall. *Journal of Verbal Learning and Verbal Behavior, 11,* 717–726.

Bransford, J. D., & McCarrell, N. S. (1974). A sketch of a cognitive approach to comprehension: Some thoughts about what it means to comprehend. In W. B. Wiemer & D. S. Palermo (Eds.), *Cognition and the symbolic process* (pp. 189–229). Hillsdale, NJ: Lawrence Erlbaum Associates.

Breal, M. (1924). *Essai de se' manticquie: science des significations* (6th ed.). Paris: Librairie Hachette.

Brewer, W. F. (1977). Memory for the pragmatic implications of sentences. *Memory & Cognition, 5,* 673–678.

Brewer, W. F., & Lichtenstein, E. H. (1982). Stories are to entertain: A structural–affect theory of stories. *Journal of Pragmatics, 6,* 473–486.

Bridgers, S. E. (1979). *All together now.* New York: Knopf.

Brinton, L. (1980). "Represented perception": A study in narrative style. *Poetics, 9,* 363–381.

Bronte, C. (1973). *Jane Eyre.* New York: Pocket Books. (Original work published 1847)

Brown, G., & Yule, G. (1983). *Discourse analysis.* New York: Cambridge University Press.

Brown, R. (1958). How shall a thing be called? *Psychological Review, 65,* 14–21.

Bruder, G. (1988). The deictic center and sentence interpretation in natural narrative. Paper presented at the meeting of the Psychonomic Society, Chicago, IL.

Bruder, G., Duchan, J., Rapaport, W., Segal, E., Shapiro, S., & Zubin, D. (1986). *Deictic Center in narrative: An interdisciplinary cognitive science project* (Tech. Rep. No. 86–20). Buffalo: State University of New York at Buffalo, Department of Computer Science.

Bruder, G., Engl, L., & Schultz, J. (1985). Preposed adverbials signal change in the narrative deictic center. Paper presented at the meeting of the Psychonomic Society, Boston, MA.

Bruder, G. A., & Scott, P. (1989). *Exploring the roles of deictic verbs in narrative understanding.* Unpublished manuscript.

Bruder, G. A., & Wiebe, J. M. (1990a). *Paragraph breaks and continuity of subjective point of view in narrative.* Paper presented at the meeting of the Psychonomic Society, New Orleans, LA.

Bruder, G. A., & Wiebe, J. M. (1990b). Psychological test of an algorithm for recognizing subjectivity in narrative text. *Proceedings of the 12th Annual Conference of the Cognitive Science Society* (pp. 947–953). Hillsdale, NJ: Lawrence Erlbaum Associates.

Bruner, J. (1986). *Actual minds, possible worlds.* Cambridge, MA: Harvard University Press.

Bruner, J. (1990). *Acts of meaning.* Cambridge, MA: Harvard University Press.

Buchler, J. (Ed.). (1955). *Philosophical writings of Peirce.* New York: Dover.

Buhler, C. (1982). The deictic field of language and deictic words. In R. Jarvella & W. Klein (Eds.), *Speech, place and action: Studies in deixis and related topics* (pp. 9–30). New York: Wiley.

Burke, K. (1969). *A grammar of motives.* Berkeley: University of California Press.

Burroway, J. (1982). *Writing fiction: A guide to narrative craft.* Boston: Little, Brown.

Caldwell, T. (1966). *No one hears but him.* Garden City, NY: Doubleday.

Canadian Automobile Association. (1977). *How to drive.* Ottawa: Author.

Capote, T. (1965). *In cold blood.* New York: Random House.

Carroll, D. (1982). *The subject in question.* Chicago: University of Chicago Press.

Carroll, L. (1971). In D. J. Gray (Ed.), *Alice in Wonderland.* New York: Norton.

Castañeda, H-N. (1972/1974). Thinking and the structure of the world. *Philosophia, 4,* 3–40. (Original work in 1972)

Castañeda, H-N. (1975a). Identity and sameness. *Philosophia, 5,* 121–150.

Castañeda, H-N. (1975b). *Thinking and doing: The philosophical foundations of institutions.* Dordrecht, Holland: D. Reidel.

Castañeda, H-N. (1977a). On the philosophical foundations of the theory of communication: Reference. *Midwest Studies in Philosophy, 2,* 165–186. (Original work published 1970)

Castañeda, H-N. (1977b). Perception, belief, and the structure of physical objects and consciousness. *Synthese, 35*, 285–351.

Castañeda, H-N. (1979). Fiction and reality: Their basic connections. *Poetics, 8*, 31–62.

Castañeda, H-N. (1980). Reference, reality, and perceptual fields. *Proceedings and Addresses of the American Philosophical Association, 53*, 763–823.

Castañeda, H-N. (1989). Fiction and reality: Ontological questions about literary experience. In H-N. Castaneda (Ed.), *Thinking, language, and experience* (pp. 176–205). Minneapolis: University of Minnesota Press.

Chatman, S. (1978). *Story and discourse: Narrative structure in fiction and film.* Ithaca, NY: Cornell University Press.

Chatman, S. (1986). Characters and narrators: Filter, center, slant, and interest-focus. *Poetics Today, 7*(2), 189–204.

Chen, P. (1986). Referent introducing and tracking in Chinese narratives. (Doctoral dissertation, University of California, Los Angeles.) *Dissertation Abstracts International, 47-06*, 2143A.

Cherryh, C. J. (1987). *Cuckoo's egg.* London: Methuen.

Cherryh, C. J. (1988a). *Cyteen.* New York: Popular Library.

Cherryh, C. J. (1988b). *Exile's gate.* New York: DAW Books.

Chomsky, N. (1965). *Aspects of a theory of syntax.* Cambridge, MA: MIT Press.

Chomsky, N. (1970). Remarks on nominalization. In R. Jacobs & P. Rosenbaum (Eds.), *Readings in English transformational grammar* (pp. 184–221). Lexington, MA: Ginn.

Christie, A. (1939). *The murder of Roger Ackroyd.* New York: Pocket Books. (Original work published 1926)

Christie, A. (1941). *The A.B.C. murders.* New York: Pocket Books. (Original work published 1936)

Christie, A. (1984a). *Partners in crime.* New York: Berkley Publishing. (Original work published 1929)

Christie, A. (1984b). *Poirot loses a client.* New York: Berkley Publishing. (Original work published 1937)

Chun, S. A., & Zubin, D. A. (1990). Experiential vs. agentive constructions in Korean narrative. *Proceedings of the 16th annual meeting of the Berkeley Linguistics Society, 16*, 81–93.

Clark, H. H. (1973). Space, time, semantics, and the child. In T. E. Moore (Ed.), *Cognitive development and the acquisition of language* (pp. 27–63). New York: Academic Press.

Clark, H. H., & Carlson, T. B. (1982). Speech acts and hearer's beliefs. In N. V. Smith (Ed.), *Mutual knowledge* (pp. 1–36). New York: Academic Press.

Clark, H. H., & Clark, E. V. (1977). *Psychology and language.* New York: Harcourt Brace.

Clark, H. H., & Marshall, C. R. (1981). Definite reference and mutual knowledge. In A. Joshi, B. Webber, & I. Sag (Eds.), *Elements of discourse understanding* (pp.10–63). Cambridge, England: Cambridge University Press.

Clarke, M. (1986). Conversational narratives as altered states of consciousness. In D. Tannen & J. Alatis (Eds.), *Georgetown University round table on language and linguistics 1985* (pp. 320–336). Washington, DC: Georgetown University Press.

Cleary, B. (1973). *Socks.* New York: Dell.

Clifford, W. K. (1955). *The common sense of the exact sciences.* In J. R. Newman (Ed.). New York: Dover.

Cohen, P. R. (1978). On knowing what to say: Planning speech acts (Tech. Rep. No. 118). Toronto: University of Toronto, Department of Computer Science.

Cohen, P. R., Perrault, C. R., & Allen, J. F. (1982). Beyond question answering. In W. Lehnert & M. Ringle (Eds.), *Strategies for natural language processing* (pp. 245–274). Hillsdale, NJ: Lawrence Erlbaum Associates.

Cohn, D. (1978). *Transparent minds: Narrative modes for representing consciousness in fiction.* Princeton: Princeton University Press.

Cohn, D. (1989). Fictional versus historical lives: Borderlines and borderline cases. *Journal of Narrative Technique, 19* (1), 3–24.

Cole, P. (Ed.). (1981). *Radical pragmatics*. New York: Academic Press.

Comrie, B. (1976). *Aspect*. Cambridge, England: Cambridge University Press.

Connor, U. (1987). Argumentative patterns in student essays: Cross-cultural differences. In U. Connor & R. Kaplan (Eds.), *Writing across languages* (pp. 57–72). Reading, MA: Addison-Wesley.

Connor, U., & Lauer, J. (1988). Cross-cultural variation in persuasive student writing. In A. Purves (Ed.), *Writing across languages and cultures* (pp. 138–159). Newbury Park, CA: Sage.

Coulmas, F. (1986b). Reported speech: Some general issues. In F. Coulmas (Ed.), *Direct and indirect speech* (pp. 1–28). Berlin: Mouton.

Cowan, N. (1988). Evolving conceptions of memory storage, selective attention, and their mutual constraints within the human information-processing system. *Psychological Bulletin, 104*, 163–191.

Cresswell, M. J. (1985). Prepositions and points of view. In M. J. Cresswell (Ed.), *Adverbial modification* (pp. 97–141). Boston: Reidel.

Crichton, M. (1990). *Jurassic park*. New York: Knopf.

Crimmins, M. (1989). Having ideas and having the concept. *Mind and Language, 4*, 280–294.

Crimmins, M., & Perry, J. (1989). The prince and the phone book: Reporting puzzling beliefs. *Journal of Philosophy, 86*, 685–711.

Cukor, G. (Director). (1954). *A star is born*.

Daniels, J. (1986). A psychological investigation into the deictic center. *Proceedings of the 8th Annual Conference of the Cognitive Science Society* (pp. 621–626). Hillsdale, NJ: Lawrence Erlbaum Associates.

Davidson, D. (1967). The logical form of action sentences. In N. Rescher (Ed.), *The Logic of decision and action* (pp. 81–95). Pittsburgh: University of Pittsburgh Press.

de Beaugrande, R., & Dressler, W. (1981). *Introduction to text linguistics*. London: Longman.

Dell, G. S., McKoon, G., & Ratcliff, R. (1983). The activation of antecedent information during the processing of anaphoric reference in reading. *Journal of Verbal Learning and Verbal Behavior, 22*, 121–132.

Dickens, C. (1859/1980). *A tale of two cities*. New York: New American Library.

Dijk, T. A. van, & Kintsch, W. (1983). *Strategies of discourse comprehension*. New York: Academic Press.

Dilthey, W. (1977). *Descriptive psychology and historical undestanding*. Netherlands: Kluwer.

Dolezel, L. (1973). *Narrative modes in Czech literature*. Toronto: University of Toronto Press.

Donnellan, K. S. (1966). Reference and definite descriptions. *Philosophical Review, 60*, 281–304.

Dooling, D. J., & Lachman, R. (1971). Effects of comprehension on retention of prose. *Journal of Experimental Psychology, 88*, 216–222.

Dos Passos, J. (1937). *USA: 1. The 42nd parallel 2. Nineteen nineteen 3. The big money*. New York: Harcourt Brace.

Doubrovsky, S. (1966). *Pourquoi la Nouvelle Critique?* Paris: Mercure de France.

Dowty, D. R. (1977). Toward a semantic analysis of verb aspect and the English imperfective progressive. *Linguistics and Philosophy, 1*, 45–77.

Dowty, D. R. (1979). *Word meaning and Montague grammar*. Boston: Reidel.

Duchan, J., Meth, M., & Waltzman, D. (1992). Then as a marker of focal shift in the oral discourse of normal adults. *Journal of Speech and Hearing Research, 35*, 1367–1375.

Elliot, D. (1974). Toward a grammar of exclamations. *Foundations of Language, 11*, 231–246.

Epson. (1982). *EPSON MX printer manual with Graftrax-plus*. San Diego, CA: Compusoft, Inc.

Erman, B. (1987). *Pragmatic expresions in English: A study of* you know, you see *and* I mean *in face-to-face conversation*. Stockholm: Almqvist & Wiksell International.

ETS. (1990). *Test of written English (TWE)*. Princeton, NJ: Educational Testing Service.

Evans, N. (1992). "Wanjh! Bonj! Nja!;:Sequential organization and social deixis in Mayali interjections. In F. Ameka (Ed.), Interjections (pp. 225–244) [Special issue]. *Journal of Pragmatics, 18*(2/3).

Fauconnier, G. (1985). *Mental spaces: Aspects of meaning construction in natural language*. Cambridge, MA: MIT Press.

Fillmore, C. (1968). The case for case. In E. Bach & R. T. Harms (Eds.), *Universals in linguistic theory* (pp. 1–89). Chicago: Holt, Rinehart & Winston.

Fillmore, C. (1972). Subjects, speakers, and roles. In D. Davidson & G. Harman (Eds.), *Semantics of Natural Language* (pp. 1–24). Dordrecht, Holland: Reidel.

Fillmore, C. (1974). Pragmatics and the description of discourse. In C. Fillmore, G. Lakoff, & R. Lakoff (Eds.), *Berkeley studies in syntax and semantics I: Vol. 1–21*. Berkeley: University of California at Berkeley, Department of Linguistics and Institute of Human Learning.

Fillmore, C. (1975). *Santa Cruz lectures on deixis*. Bloomington: Indiana University Linguistics Club.

Fillmore, C. J. (1978). On the organization of semantic information in lexicon. In D. Farkas, W. M. Jacobsen, and K. W. Todrys (Eds.), *Papers from the parasession on the lexicon* (pp. 148–173). Chicago: Chicago Linguistic Society.

Fillmore, C. J. (1981). Pragmatics and the description of discourse. In P. Cole (Ed.), *Radical Pragmatics*. New York: Academic Press.

Fleischer, R. (Director). (1966). *Fantastic Voyage*.

Fodor, J. A. (1975). *The language of thought*. New York: Crowell.

Fodor, J. A. (1983). *The modularity of mind*. Cambridge, MA: MIT Press.

Fodor, J. D. (1979). *The linguistic description of opaque contexts*. New York: Garland Publishing.

Folman, S., & Sarig, G. (1990). Intercultural rhetorical differences in meaning construction. *Communication and Cognition, 23*, 45–92.

Fonagy, I. (1986). Reported speech in French and Hungarian. In F. Coulmas (Ed.), *Direct and indirect speech* (pp. 255–309). Berlin: Mouton.

Fox, B. A. (1987). *Discourse structures and anaphora*. Cambridge, England: Cambridge University Press.

Franchere, R. (1964). *Hannah herself*. New York: Crowell.

Francis, D. (1978). *In the frame*. New York: Pocket Books. (Original work published 1976)

Francis, D. (1985). *The danger*. New York: Ballantine. (Original work published 1984)

Freedle, R. O. (Ed.). (1977). *Advances in discourse processes: Vol. 1: Discourse production and comprehension*. Norwood, NJ: Ablex.

Freedle, R. O. (Ed.). (1979). *Advances in discourse processes: Vol. 2: New directions in discourse processing*. Norwood, NJ: Ablex.

Freedle, R. O., & Hale, G. (1979). Acquisition of new comprehension schemata for expository prose by transfer of a narrative schema. In R. O. Freedle (Ed.), *New directions in discourse processing* (pp. 121–135). Norwood, NJ: Ablex.

Frege, G. (1892). On sense and reference. M. Black (Trans.). In P. Geach & M. Black (Eds.), *Translations from the philosophical writings of Gottlob Frege* (pp. 56–78). Oxford, England: Basil Blackwell.

Galbraith, M. (1990). Subjectivity in the novel. (Doctoral dissertation, State University of New York at Buffalo.) *Dissertation Abstracts International, 51-03*, 0841A.

Gale, R. (1967). Indexical signs, egocentric particulars, and token-reflexive words. In P. Edwards (Ed.), *The encyclopedia of philosophy: Vol. 4*. New York: Macmillan.

Garling, T., & Golledge, R. (1993). *Behavior and environment: Psychological and geographical approaches*. Amsterdam: North–Holland.

Garnham, A. (1984). Effects of specificity on the interpretation of anaphoric noun phrases. *Quarterly Journal of Experimental Psychology, 36A*, 1–12.

Gee, J. (1991). Memory and myth: A perspective on narrative. In A. McCabe & C. Peterson (Eds.), *Developing narrative structure* (pp. 1–25). Hillsdale, NJ: Lawrence Erlbaum Associates.

Gee, J. P. (1986). Units in the production of narrative discourse. *Discourse Processes, 9*, 391–422.

Geis, M. (1985). *On the superiority of monostratal to multistratal accounts of adverb preposing*. Paper presented at the Eastern States Conference on Linguistics.

Gendlin, E. (1980). Experiential explication. In R. C. Solomon (Ed.), *Phenomenology and existentialism*. Lanham, MD: University Press of America.

Genette, G. (1980). *Narrative discourse: An essay in method*. J. E. Lewin (Trans.). Ithaca, NY: Cornell University Press.

Genette, G. (1988). *Narrative discourse revisited*. J. E. Lewin (Trans.). Ithaca, NY: Cornell University Press.

Gerts, D. B., & Youn, C. (1988). Korean Psych constructions: Advancement or retreat. *Chicago Linguistics Society, 24*, 155–175.

Gibson, J. J. (1966). *The senses considered as perceptual systems*. Boston: Houghton Mifflin.

Gilbert, M. (1983). *End-Game*. Harmondsworth, England: Penguin. (Original work published 1982)

Givon, T. (1979). *On understanding grammar*. New York: Academic Press.

Givon, T. (Ed.). (1983). *Topic continuity in discourse*. Amsterdam: Benjamins.

Givon, T. (1984). *Syntax: A functional–typological introduction: Vol. 1*. Amsterdam: Benjamins.

Goddard, C. (1983). *A semantically–oriented grammar of Yankunytjatjara*. Unpublished doctoral dissertation, Australian National University, Canberra.

Goddard, C. (1987). *A basic Pitjantjatjara/Yankunytjatjara to English dictionary*. Alice Springs, Australia: Institute for Aboriginal Development.

Goddard, C. (1989). Issues in natural semantic metalanguage. *Quaderni di Semantica, 10*(1), 51–64.

Goffman, E. (1974). *Frame analysis*. New York: Harper & Row.

Goffman, E. (1981). Response cries. In E. Goffman, (Ed.), *Forms of talk* (pp. 78–123). Oxford, England: Basil Blackwell.

Gould, M. D. (1989). Considering individual cognitive ability in the provision of usable navigational assistance. *Proceedings, 1st Vehicle Navigation & Information Systems Conference (VNIS '89)*, (pp. 443–447). Toronto: IEEE Vehicular Technology Division.

Graesser, A. C. (Ed.). (1993). Inference generation during text comprehension [Special issue]. *Discourse Processes, 16*, 1–202.

Greenspan, S. L., & Segal, E. M. (1984). Reference and comprehension: A topic-comment analysis of sentence–picture verification. *Cognitive Psychology, 16*, 556–606.

Grice, H. P. (1975). Logic and conversation. In P. Cole & J. C. Morgan (Eds.), *Syntax and semantics: Vol. 3* (pp. 41–58). New York: Academic Press.

Grice, H. P. (1989). *Studies in the ways of words*. Cambridge, MA: Harvard University Press.

Grimes, J. E. (1975). *The thread of discourse*. The Hague, Netherlands: Mouton.

Grisham, J. (1991). *The firm*. New York: Bantam.

Grosz, B. J. (1977). The representation and use of focus in a system for understanding dialogs. *Proceedings of the 5th International Joint Conference on Artificial Intelligence (IJCAI–77, MIT)*, (pp. 67–76). Los Altos, CA: Morgan Kaufmann.

Grosz, B. J., & Sidner, C. L. (1986). Attention, intentions, and the structure of discourse. *Computational Linguistics, 12*, 175–204.

Haberland, H. (1986). Reported speech in Danish. In F. Coulmas (Ed.), *Direct and indirect speech* (pp. 219–253). Berlin: Mouton.

Haiman, J. (1985). *Natural syntax: Iconicity and erosion*. Cambridge, England: Cambridge University Press.

Haiman, J., & Munro, P. (Eds.). (1983). *Switch-reference and universal grammar*. Amsterdam: Benjamins.

Halliday, M., & Hasan, R. (1976). *Cohesion in English*. New York: Longman.

Hamburger, K. (1957). *Die Logik der Dichtung*. Stuttgart: Ernst Klett Verlag.

Hamburger, K. (1973). *The logic of literature*. M. J. Rose (Trans.). Bloomington: Indiana University Press.

Hammett, D. (1980a). The Dain curse. In *Dashiell Hammett—Five complete novels*. New York: Avenel. (Original work published 1929)

Hammett, D. (1980b). The thin man. In *Dashiell Hammett—Five complete novels*. New York: Avenel. (Original work published 1934)

Hammett, D. (1984). *The Maltese Falcon*. New York: Vintage Books. (Original work published 1930)

Han, S. [Han Soosan]. (1980). *Haepingki-uy achim: Vol. 2*. Seoul.

Harper, M. P., & Charniak, E. (1986). Time and tense in English. *Proceedings of the 24th Annual Meeting of the Association for Computational Linguistics* (pp. 3–9). Morristown, NJ: Association for Computational Linguistics.

Has, W. J. (Director). (1965). *Rekopis Znaliziony W Saragossie (The Saragossa Manuscript)*. Polski State Film.

Heath, S. (1983). *Ways with words*. New York: Cambridge University Press.

Hemingway, E. (1938/1953). The killers. In *The short stories of Ernest Hemingway* (pp. 279–289). New York: Scribner's.

Henry, O. (1903). A retrieved reformation. In *Roads of Destiny* (pp. 134–143). Garden City, NY: Doubleday.

Hermstein-Smith, B. (1980). Narrative versions, narrative theories. *Critical Inquiry, 7* (1), 213–236.

Herskovits, A. (1986). *Language and spatial congition: An interdisciplinary study of the prepositions in English*. Cambridge University Press.

Hewitt, L., & Duchan, J. (in press). Subjectivity in children's fictional stories. In *Topics in language disorders*.

Hill, J. (1991, October). *The production of self in narrative*. Paper presented at the 2nd Bi-annual Conference on Current Thinking and Research of the Society for Psychological Anthropology. Chicago, IL.

Hillerman, T. (1990). *Coyote waits*. New York: Harper Paperbacks.

Hinrichs, E. (1986). Temporal anaphora in discourses of English. *Linguistics and Philosophy, 9* (1), 63–82. (Original work published 1982)

Hintikka, J., & Hintikka, M. B. (1983). Sherlock Holmes confronts modern logic. In U. Eco & T. A. Sebeok (Eds.), *The sign of three* (pp. 154–169). Bloomington: Indiana University Press.

Hirschman, L., & Story, G. (1981). Representing implicit and explicit time relations in narrative. *Proceedings of the 7th International Joint Conference on Artificial Intelligence* (IJCAI-81) (pp. 289–295). Los Altos, CA: Morgan Kaufman.

Hirst, G. (1981). *Anaphora in natural language understanding: A survey*. Berlin: Springer-Verlag.

Hobbs, J. R., Stickel, M., Martin, P., & Edwards, D. (1988). Interpretation as abduction. *Proceedings of the 26th Annual Meeting of the Association for Computational Linguistics (SUNY Buffalo)* (pp. 131–138). Morristown, NJ: Association for Computational Linguistics.

Hockett, C. F. (1963). The problem of universals in language. In J. H. Greenberg (Ed.), *Universals of language* (pp. 1–22). Cambridge, MA: MIT Press.

Hoffman, A. (1992). *Turtle moon*. New York: Berkley.

Hopper, P. (1979). Aspect and foregrounding in discourse. In T. Givon (Ed.), *Syntax and semantics 12: Discourse and syntax* (pp. 213–241). New York: Academic Press.

Hopper, P. (1982). *Tense-aspect: Between semantics and pragmatics*. Amsterdam: J. Benjamins.

Hopper, P., & Thompson, S. A. (1980). Transitivity in grammar and discourse. *Language, 56*, 251–299.

Hornby, A. S. (1974). *Oxford advanced learner's dictionary of current English* (3rd ed.). London: Oxford University Press.

Hornstein, N. (1977). Towards a theory of tense. *Linguistic Inquiry, 8* (3), 521–557.

Hosenfeld, C., & Segal, E. (in press). *Expert and novice problem solving in an ill defined task: Revising an announcement*.

Hottenroth, P-M. (1982). The system of local deixis in Spanish. In J. Weissenborn & W. Klein (Eds.), *Here and there: Cross-linguistic studies on deixis and demonstration* (pp. 133–153). Amsterdam: Benjamins.

Hughes, G. E., & Cresswell, M. J. (1968). *An introduction to modal logic*. London: Methuen.

Hutchins, E. (1991). The social organization of distributed cognition. In L. B. Resnick, J. M. Levine, & S. D. Teasley (Eds.), *Perspectives on socially shared cognition* (pp. 283–307). Washington, DC: American Psychological Assocation.

Hyde, T. S., & Jenkins, J. J. (1973). Recall for words as a function of semantic, graphic, and syntactic orienting tasks. *Journal of Verbal Learning and Verbal Behavior, 12,* 471–480.

Jakobson, R. (1960). Closing statement: Linguistics and poetics. In T. Sebeok (Ed.), *Style in language* (pp. 350–377). New York: Wiley.

Jakobson, R. (1971). *Selected writings II, word and language.* The Hague, Netherlands: Mouton.

James, D. (1973a). Another look at, say, some gramatical constraints on oh, interjections and hesitations. *Proceedings of the Chicago Linguistic Society, 9,* 242–251.

James, D. (1973b). *The syntax and semantics of some English interjections.* (Doctoral dissertation, University of Michigan, Ann Arbor.) *Dissertation Abstracts International, 35-03,* 1642A.

James, H. (1954). *What Maisie knew.* Garden City, NY: Doubleday.

Jarvella, R. J., & Klein, W. (1982). *Speech, place and action: Studies in deixis and related topics.* Chichester: John Wiley & Sons Ltd.

Johnson, M. (1987). *The body in the mind: The bodily basis of meaning, imagination, and reason.* Chicago: University of Chicago Press.

Johnson-Laird, P. N. (1983). *Mental models: Towards a cogntive science of language, inference, and consciousness.* Cambridge, MA: Harvard University Press.

Joyce, J. (1976). *Portrait of the artist as a young man.* Harmondsworth: Penguin.

Just, M., & Carpenter, P. (1987). *The psychology of reading and language comprehension.* Boston: Allyn & Bacon.

Kafka, F. (1936). The metamorphosis. In W. Muir & E. Muir (Trans.), *Selected short stories of Franz Kafka* (pp. 19–89). New York: Random House.

Kahane, C. (1994). *The passions of the voice: Hysteria and the figure of the speaking woman in British narrative, 1850–1915.* Unpublished manuscript.

Kamp, H. (1984). A theory of truth and semantic representation. In J. Groenendijk, T. M. V. Janssen, & M. Stokhof (Eds.), *Truth, interpretation and information* (pp. 1–41). Dordrecht: Foris.

Karmiloff-Smith, A. (1980). Psychological processes underlying pronominalisation and nonpronominalisation in children's connected discourse. In J. Kreiman & A. E. Ojeda (Eds.), *Papers from the Parasessions on Pronouns and Anaphora.* Chicago: Chicago Linguistic Society.

Katz, J. J., & Fodor, J. A. (1963). The structure of a semantic theory. *Language, 39,* 170–216.

Ke, Y. (1986). *Ye ye Zhou.* Beijing: Renmin Wenxue.

Keillor, G. (1985). *Lake Wobegon days.* New York: Viking.

Keillor, G. (1987). *Leaving home.* New York: Viking.

Kiefer, F. (1986). Some semantic aspects of indirect speech in Hungarian. In F. Coumas (Ed.), *Direct and indirect speech* (pp. 201–217). Berlin: Mouton.

Kintsch, W., & Dijk, T. A. van (1978). Toward a model of text comprehension and production. *Psychological Review, 85,* 363–394.

Konolige, K. (1986). *A deductive model of belief.* Los Altos, CA: Morgan Kaufman.

Kumar, D. (Ed.). (1990). *Current trends in SNePS-Semantic Network Processing System: Lecture notes in artificial intelligence, no. 437.* Berlin: Springer-Verlag.

Kuno, S. (1987). *Functional syntax.* Chicago: University of Chicago Press.

Kuroda, S.-Y. (1973). Where epistemology, style and grammar meet: A case study from the Japanese. In P. Kiparsky & S. Anderson (Eds.), *A festschrift for Morris Halle* (pp. 377–391). New York: Holt, Rinehart & Winston.

Kuroda, S.-Y. (1976). Reflections on the foundations of narrative theory—from a linguistic point of view. In T. A. van Dijk (Ed.), *Pragmatics of language and literature* (pp. 107–140). Amsterdam: North-Holland.

Labov, W., & Waletsky, J. (1967). Narrative analysis: Oral versions of personal experience. In J. Helm (Ed.), *Essays on the verbal and visual arts* (pp. 12–44). Seattle: University of Washington Press.

Lakoff, G. (1987). *Women, fire, and dangerous things: What categories reveal about the mind.* Chicago: University of Chicago Press.

Lakoff, G., & Johnson, M. (1980). *Metaphors we live by.* Chicago: University of Chicago Press.

Landman, F. (1986). Pegs and alecs. In J. Y. Halpern (Ed.), *Theoretical aspects of reasoning about knowledge* (pp. 45–61). San Mateo, CA: Morgan Kaufmann.

Langacker, R. (1985). Observations and speculations on subjectivity. In J. Haiman (Ed.), *Iconicity in syntax.* Philadelphia: Benjamins.

Lashley, K. S. (1951). The problem of serial order in behavior. In L. A. Jeffress (Ed.), *Cerebral mechanisms in behavior: The Hixon symposium* (pp. 112–136). New York: Wiley.

Laughren, M. (1982). A preliminary description of propositional particles in Warlpiri. In S. Swartz (Ed.). *Papers in Warlpiri grammar: In memory of Lothar Jagst* (pp. 129–163). Darwin, Australia: Summer Institute of Linguistics.

Lawrence, D. H. (1976). Sun. In *The complete short stories* (Vol. 2, pp. 528–545). Harmondsworth, England: Penguin.

Lawrence, D. H. (1978). *The first Lady Chatterley.* Harmondsworth, England: Penguin.

Leech, G. (1981). *Semantics: The study of meaning* (2nd ed.). Middlesex, England: Pelican.

Leggett, G., Mead, C., Kramer, M., & Beal, R. (1988). *Handbook for writers.* Englewood Cliffs, NJ: Prentice-Hall.

Lehmann, F. (Ed.). (1992). *Semantic networks in artificial intelligence.* Oxford, England: Pergamon.

L'Engle, M. (1986). *Many waters.* New York: Dell Publishing.

Levinson, S. (1983). *Pragmatics.* Cambridge, England: Cambridge University Press.

Lewis, D. (1975). Languages and language. In K. Gunderson (Ed.), *Language, mind and knowledge* (pp. 3–35). Minneapolis: University of Minnesota Press.

Lewis, D. (1978). Truth in fiction. *American Philosophical Quarterly, 15,* 37–46.

Lewis, S., & O'Kun, L. (1982). The sorcerer's apprentice. In *One-minute bedtime stories.* Garden City, NY: Doubleday.

Li, N. (1986). *Pronoun resolution in SNePS* (SNeRG Tech. Note No. 18). Buffalo: State University of New York at Buffalo, Department of Computer Science, SNePS Research Group.

Li, N. (1990). *Coding the experiencer: A study of perspective taking in Mandarin discourse.* Paper presented at NECCL 2, Philadelphia, PA.

Li, N. (1991). *Perspective taking in Mandarin discourse.* (Doctoral dissertation, Department of Linguistics, State University of New York at Buffalo, Buffalo, NY.) *Dissertation Abstracts International, 52-11,* 3907A.

Li, N., & Zubin, D. A. (1986). Anaphora resolution in Mandarin. *ESCOL, 3,* 335–349.

Li, N., & Zubin, D. (1990). Discourse continuity and perspective-taking. *Proceedings of the Chicago Linguistics Society, 26.*

Linde, C. (1979). Focus of attention and the choice of pronouns in discourse. In T. Givon (Ed.), *Syntax and semantics: Vol. 12.* New York: Academic Press.

Linde, C. (1993). *Life stories: The creation of coherence.* New York: Oxford University Press.

London, J. (1915). *The call of the wild.* New York: Grosset & Dunlap.

Longacre, R. E. (1983). *The grammar of discourse.* New York: Plenum.

Lu, T. (1986). *Nabian shilai yi tiao chuan.* Shouhou Series. Beijing: China Youth Publishing House.

Lucariello, J. (1990). Canonicality and consciousness in child narrative. In B. K. Britton & A. D. Pellegrini (Eds.), *Narrative thought and narrative language* (pp. 131–149). Hillsdale, NJ: Lawrence Erlbaum Associates.

Ludlum, R. (1982). *The Parsifal mosaic.* New York: Random House.

Lyons, J. (1968). *Introduction to theoretical linguistics.* New York: Cambridge University Press.

Lyons, J. (1975). Deixis as the source of reference. In E. L. Deenan (Ed.), *Formal semantics of natural language* (pp. 61–83). Cambridge, England: Cambridge University Press.

Lyons, J. (1977). *Semantics: Vol. 2.* London: Cambridge University Press.

Magliola, R. (1973). Parisian structuralism confronts phenomenology: The ongoing debate. *Language and Style, 6* (4), 237–248.

Maida, A. S. (1991). Maintaining mental models of agents who have existential misconceptions. *Artificial Intelligence, 50,* 331–383.

Maida, A. S., & Shapiro, S. C. (1982). Intensional concepts in propositional semantic networks. *Cognitive Science, 6,* 291–330.

Mailer, N. (1968). *Armies of the night.* New York: New American Library.

Mandler, J., & Johnson, N. (1977). Remembrance of things parsed: Story structure and recall. *Cognitve Psychology, 9,* 111–151.

Mann, P. (1973). *My dad lives in a downtown hotel.* Garden City, NY: Doubleday.

Mann, W., & Thompson, S. A. (1985). *Assertions from discourse structure* (Tech. Report RS–85–155). Los Angeles: USC Information Science Institute.

Mansfield, K. (1992). The garden party. In *The short stories of Katherine Mansfield.* New York: Knopf. (Original work published 1937)

Mark, D. M. (1985). Finding simple routes: "Ease of description" as an objective function in automated route selection. *Proceedings, 2nd Symposium on Artificial Intelligence Applications, Institute of Electrical and Electronic Engineers* (pp. 577–581). Piscataway, NJ: Institute of Electrical and Electronic Engineers, Inc.

Mark, D. M. (Ed.). (1988). *Cognitive and linguistic aspects of geographic space: Report on a workshop.* Santa Barbara, CA: National Center for Geographic Information and Analysis.

Mark, D. M. (1989). A conceptual model for vehicle navigation systems. *Proceedings, First Vehicle Navigation & Information Systems Conference (VNIS '89),* (pp. 448–453). Toronto: IEEE Vehicular Technology Division.

Mark, D. M., Gould, M. D., & McGranaghan, M. (1987). Computerized navigation assistance for drivers. *The Professional Geographer, 39,* 215–220.

Mark, D. M., & McGranaghan, M. (1986, September). Effective provision of navigation assistance for drivers: A cognitive science approach. *Proceedings, Auto-Carto London, 2,* 399–408.

Mark, D. M., Svorou, S., & Zubin, D. (1987). Spatial terms and spatial concepts: Geographic, cognitive, and linguistic perspectives. *Proceedings, International Symposium on Geographic Information Systems: The Research Agenda* (pp. 101–112). Crystal City, VA: NASA.

Marr, D. (1982). *Vision: A computational investigation into the human representation and processing of visual information.* San Francisco: Freeman.

Marslen-Wilson, W., Levy, E., & Tyler, L. (1982). Producing interpretable discourse: The establishment and maintenance of reference. In R. J. Jarvella & W. Klein (Eds.), *Speech, place and action* (pp. 339–378). Chichester: Wiley.

Martins, J., & Shapiro, S. C. (1988). A model for belief revision. *Artificial Intelligence, 35,* 25–79.

McCabe, A. (1991). Structure as a way of understanding. In A. McCabe & C. Peterson (Eds.), *Developing narrative structure* (pp. ix–xvii). Hillsdale, NJ: Lawrence Erlbaum Associates.

McCarthy, J. (1979). First-order theories of individual concepts and propositions. In J. Hayes, D. Michie, & L. Mikulich (Eds.), *Machine Intelligence: Vol. 9* (pp. 129–147). New York: Halsted.

McCawley, N. A. (1975). What strikes me about psych-movement. In P. Reich (Ed.), *LACUS, 2,* 320–328.

McCullers, C. (1952). The Jockey. In M. Crane (Ed.), *50 great short stories.* New York: Bantam. (Original work published 1931)

McDermott, D. (1982). A temporal logic for reasoning about processes and plans. *Cognitive Science, 6,* 101–155.

McHale, B. (1978). Free indirect discourse: A survey of recent accounts. *PTL, 3,* 249–287.

McHale, B. (1983). Unspeakable sentences, unnatural acts: Linguistics and poetics revisited. *Poetics Today, 4* (1), 17–45.

McKoon, G., & Ratcliff, R. (1980). The comprehension processes and memory structure involved in anaphoric reference. *Journal of Verbal Learning and Verbal Behavior, 19,* 668–682.

McKoon, G., & Ratcliff, R. (1992). Inference during reading. *Psychological Review, 99,* 440–466.

McMurtry, L. (1985). *Lonesome Dove.* New York: Simon & Schuster.

Meinong, A. (1904). The theory of objects. I. Levi, D. B. Terrell, & R. M. Chisholm (Trans.), in R. M. Chisholm (Ed.), *Realism and the Background of Phenomenology* (pp. 76–117). New York: The Free Press, 1960.

Melville, H. (1967). *Moby Dick*. New York: Bantam. (Original work published 1851)

Merleau-Ponty, M. (1962). Phenomenology of perception. C. Smith (Trans.). London: Routledge & Kegan Paul.

Meyer, N. (1974). *The seven-per-cent solution*. New York: Dutton.

Miller, P., & Sperry, L. (1988). Early talk about the past: The origins of conversation stories of personal experience. *Journal of Child Language, 15,* 293–315.

Minsky, M. (1981). A framework for representing knowledge. In J. H. Haugeland (Ed.), *Mind design* (pp. 95–128). Cambridge, MA: MIT Press.

Mitchell, M. (1936). *Gone with the wind*. New York: Macmillan.

Moore, R. C. (1980). *Reasoning about knowledge and action* (Tech. Rep. No. 191). Menlo Park, CA: SRI International.

Morrow, D. G. (1985a). Prepositions and verb aspect in narrative understanding. *Journal of Memory and Language, 24,* 390–404.

Morrow, D. G. (1985b). Prominent characters and events organize narrative understanding. *Journal of Memory and Language, 24,* 304–319.

Morrow, D. G., Greenspan, S. L., & Bower, G. H. (1987). Accessibility and situation models in narrative comprehension. *Journal of Memory and Language, 26,* 165–187.

Mourelatos, A. P. D. (1981). Events, processes, and states. In P.J. Tedeschi & A. Zaenen (Eds.), *Tense and aspect* (pp. 191–212). New York: Academic Press.

Müller, M. (1862). *Lectures on the science of language*. New York: Scribner's.

Murdock, I. (1965). *The red and the green*. London: Chatto & Windus.

Murphy, G. L. (1985). Processes of understanding anaphora. *Journal of Memory and Language, 24,* 290–303.

Murphy, G. L., & Wisniewski, E. J. (1989). Categorizing objects in isolation and in scenes: What a superordinate is good for. *Journal of Experimental Psychology: Learning, Memory, and Cognition, 15,* 572–586.

Nakhimovsky, A. (1988). Aspect, aspectual class, and the temporal structure of narrative. *Computational Linguistics, 14,* 29–43.

Nakhimovsky, A., & Rapaport, W. J. (1988). Discontinuities in narratives. *Proceedings of the 12th International Conference on Computational Linguistics (COLING–88, Budapest)* (pp. 465–470). Morristown, NJ: Association for Computational Linguistics.

Neumann, A. W. (1988). *Free indirect discourse in the eighteenth-century English novel: Speakable or unspeakable? The example of Sir Charles Grandison*. Paper presented at the meeting of the Modern Language Society, New Orleans, LA.

No, W. [No Won]. (1980). *Paesin-uy kyaycel*. Seoul: Minyaysa.

O'Brien, E. J., Duffy, S. A., & Myers, J. L. (1986). Anaphoric inference during reading. *Journal of Experimental Psychology: Learning, Memory, and Cognition, 12,* 346–352.

Oneal, A. (1971). *War work*. New York: Viking.

Parsons, T. (1975). A Meinongian analysis of fictional objects. *Grazer Philosophische Studien, 1,* 73–86.

Parsons, T. (1980). *Nonexistent objects*. New Haven: Yale University Press.

Partee, B. H. (1984). Nominal and temporal anaphora. *Linguistics and Philosophy, 7* (3), 243–286.

Pascal, R. (1977). *The dual voice: Free indirect speech and its functions in the nineteenth century novel*. Manchester: Manchester University Press.

Pavel, T. (1986). *Fictional worlds*. Cambridge, MA: Harvard University Press.

Peirce, C. S. (1931–1958). *The collected papers of Charles Sanders Peirce* (Vols. 1–6 edited by C. Hartshorne & P. Weiss; Vols. 7–8 edited by A. W. Burks). Cambridge, MA: Harvard University Press.

Perrault, C. R., & Cohen, P. R. (1981). It's for your own good: A note on inaccurate reference. In A. Joshi, B. Webber, & I. Sag (Eds.), *Elements of discourse understanding* (pp. 217–230). Cambridge, England: Cambridge University Press.

Peters, S. L., & Shapiro, S. C. (1987a). A representation for natural category systems: I. *Proceedings of the 9th Annual Conference of the Cognitive Science Society (Seattle)* (pp. 379–390). Hillsdale, NJ: Lawrence Erlbaum Associates.

Peters, S. L., & Shapiro, S. C. (1987b). A representation for natural category systems: II. *Proceedings of the 10th International Joint Conference on Artificial Intelligence (Milan)* (pp. 140–146). Los Altos, CA: Morgan Kaufmann.

Peters, S. L., Shapiro, S. C., & Rapaport, W. J. (1988). Flexible natural language processing and Roschian category theory. *Proceedings of the 10th Annual Conference of the Cognitive Science Society (Montreal)* (pp. 125–131). Hillsdale, NJ: Lawrence Erlbaum Associates.

Peterson, C., & McCabe, A. (1983). *Developmental psycholinguistics*. New York: Plenum.

Peterson, C., & McCabe, A. (1991). Linking children's connective use and narrative macrostructure. In A. McCabe & C. Peterson (Eds.), *Developing narrative structure* (pp. 29–53). Hillsdale, NJ: Lawrence Erlbaum Associates.

Pierson, F. (Director). (1976). *A star is born.*

Pinker, S. (1984). *Language learnability and language development.* Cambridge, MA: Harvard University Press.

Plato (c 375 BCE/1987). *The republic.* H. D. P. Lee (Trans.). New York: Viking. (Original work circa 375 BCE)

Polanyi, L., & Scha, R. (1984). A syntactic approach to discourse semantics. In *Proceedings of the 10th International Conference in Computational Linguistics* (pp. 413–419). Morristown, NJ: Association for Computational Linguistics.

Pollack, M. E. (1986). *Inferring domain plans in question-answering.* (Tech. Note No. 403). Menlo Park, CA: SRI International.

Pompi, K. F., & Lachman, R. (1967). Surrogate processes in the short-term retention of connected discourse. *Journal of Experimental Psychology, 75,* 143–150.

Postal, P. (1970). On the surface verb "remind". *Linguistic Inquiry, 1,* 37–120.

Postal, P. M. (1974). On certain ambiguities. *Linguistic Inquiry, 5,* 367–424. (Original work 1967)

Prince, G. (1982). *Narratology: The form and functioning of narrative.* Berlin: Mouton.

Quine, W. V. (1976). Quantifiers and propositional attitudes. In *The ways of paradox and other essays* (pp. 185–196). Cambridge, MA: Harvard University Press.

Quirk, R., Greenbaum, S., Leech, G., & Svartvik, J. (1972). *A grammar of contemporary English.* New York: Longman.

Quirk, R., Greenbaum, S., Leech, G., & Svartvik, J. (1985). *A comprehensive grammar of the English language.* New York: Longman.

Rapaport, W. J. (1976). *Intentionality and the structure of existence.* (Doctoral dissertation, Department of Philosophy. Bloomington: Indiana University). *Dissertation Abstracts International, 37-08,* 5187A.

Rapaport, W. J. (1978). Meinongian theories and a Russellian paradox. *Nous, 12,* 153–180 (errata, *Nous, 13,* 125).

Rapaport, W. J. (1985a). Meinongian semantics for propositional semantic networks. *Proceedings of the 23rd Annual Meeting of the Association for Computational Linguistics (University of Chicago)* (pp. 43–48). Morristown, NJ: Association for Computational Linguistics.

Rapaport, W. J. (1985b). To be and not to be. *Nous, 19,* 255–271.

Rapaport, W. J. (1985/1986). Non-existent objects and epistemological ontology. *Grazer Philosophische Studien, 25/26,* 61–95.

Rapaport, W. J. (1986a). Logical foundations for belief representation. *Cognitive Science, 10,* 371–422.

Rapaport, W. J. (1986b). Searle's experiments with thought. *Philosophy of Science, 53,* 271–279.

Rapaport, W. J. (1988a). Syntactic semantics: Foundations of computational natural language understanding. In J. H. Fetzer (Ed.), *Aspects of Artificial Intelligence* (pp. 81–131). Dordrecht, Holland: Kluwer Academic Publishers.

Rapaport, W. J. (1988b). To think or not to think. *Nous, 22,* 585–609.

Rapaport, W. J. (1989). Representing fiction in SNePS. In D. Kumar (Ed.), *Proceedings of the 1st Annual SNePS Workshop* (Tech. Rep. No. 89–14). Buffalo: State University of New York at Buffalo, Department of Computer Science.

Rapaport, W. J. (1991). Predication, fiction, and artificial intelligence. *Topoi, 10,* 79–111.

Rapaport, W. J. (1992). Belief representation systems. In S. C. Shapiro (Ed.), *Encyclopedia of Artificial Intelligence* (pp. 98–110) (2nd. ed.). New York: Wiley.

Rapaport, W. J. (in press). Meinongian semantics and artificial intelligence. In P. Simons (Ed.), *Essays on Meinong.* Munich: Philosophia Verlag.

Rapaport, W., Segal, E., Shapiro, S., Zubin, D., Bruder, G., Duchan, J., Almeida, M., Daniels, J., Galbraith, M., & Yuhan, A. (1989). *Deictic centers and the cognitive structure of narrative comprehension* (Tech. Rep. No. 89–01). Buffalo: State University of New York at Buffalo, Department of Computer Science.

Rapaport, W., Segal, E., Shapiro, S., Zubin, D., Bruder, G., Duchan, J., & Mark, D. (1989). *Cognitive and computer systems for understanding narrative text* (Tech. Rep. No. 89–07). Buffalo: State University of New York at Buffalo, Department of Computer Science.

Rapaport, W. J., Shapiro, S. C., & Wiebe, J. M. (1986). *Quasiindicators, knowledge reports, and discourse* (Tech. Rep. No. 86–15). Buffalo: State University of New York at Buffalo, Department of Computer Science.

Reddy, M. (1979). The conduit metaphor. In A. Ortony (Ed.), *Metaphor and thought* (pp. 284–324). Cambridge, England: Cambridge University Press.

Reichenbach, H. (1947). *Elements of symbolic logic.* New York: Macmillan.

Reichman, R. (1978). Conversational coherence. *Cognitive Science, 2,* 283–327.

Reichman, R. (1985). *Getting computers to talk like you and me.* Cambridge, MA: MIT Press.

Reid, W. H. (1977). The quantitative validation of a grammatical hypothesis. *NELS, 7,* 315–333.

Revzin, I. (1974). From animal communciation to human speech. In C. Cherry (Ed.), *Pragmatic aspects of human communication.* Boston: Reidel.

Ricoeur, P. (1969). *Le Conflit des Interpretations.* Paris: Editions du Seuil.

Ricoeur, P. (1974). *The conflict of interpretations.* Evanston: Northwestern University Press.

Rimmon-Kenan, S. (1983). *Narrative fiction: Contemporary poetics.* London: Methuen.

Rosch, E. (1978). Principles of categorization. In E. Rosch & B. B. Lloyd (Eds.), *Cognition and categorization* (pp. 27–48). Hillsdale, NJ: Lawrence Erlbaum Associates.

Rosch, E., & Lloyd, B. B. (1978). *Cognition and categorization.* Hillsdale, NJ: Lawrence Erlbaum Associates.

Roth, P. (1969). *Portnoy's complaint.* New York: Random House.

Routley, R. (1979). *Exploring Meinong's jungle and beyond.* Canberra: Australian National University, Research School of Social Sciences, Department of Philosophy.

Rule, S. (1989, November 5). Sherlock Holmes's mail: Not too mysterious. *New York Times,* p. 20.

Rumelhart, D. E. (1975). Notes on a schema for stories. In D. G. Bobrow & A. Collins (Eds.), *Representation and understanding: Studies in cognitive science* (pp. 211–236). New York: Academic Press.

Rumsey, A. (1990). Wording, meaning, and linguistic ideology. *American Anthropologist, 92.1,* 346–361.

Russell, B. (1905). On denoting. *Mind, 14,* 479–493.

Sadock, J. M., & Zwicky, A. M. (1985). Speech act distinctions in syntax. In T. Shopen (Ed.), *Language typology and syntactic description: Vol. I* (pp. 155–196). Cambridge, England: Cambridge University Press.

Sandor, A. (1986). Metaphor and belief. *Journal of Anthropological Research, 42* (2), 101–122.

Sapir, E. (1921). *Language.* New York: Harcourt Brace.

Sarte, J-P. (1965). *What is literature?* B. Frechtman (Trans.). New York: Harper & Row.

Schachter, P. (1976). A nontranformational account of gerundive nominals in English. *Lingusitic Inquiry, 7* (2), 205–241.

Schank, R. C., & Abelson, R. P. (1977). *Scripts, plans, goals and understanding.* Hillsdale, NJ: Lawrence Erlbaum Associates.

Schiffrin, D. (1987). *Discourse markers.* New York: Cambridge University Press.

Scholes, R. (1968). *Elements of fiction.* New York: Oxford University Press.

Searle, J. (1969). *Speech acts.* Cambridge, England: Cambridge University Press.

Searle, J. R. (1975a). Indirect speech acts. In P. Cole & J. R. Morgan (Eds.), *Syntax and semantics, Vol. 3: Speech acts.* New York: Academic Press.

Searle, J. R. (1975b). The logical status of fictional discourse. *New Literary History, 6,* 319–332.

Searle, J. R. (1975c). A taxonomy of illocutionary acts. In K. Gunderson (Ed.), *Language, mind, and knowledge: Minnesota studies in the philosophy of science: Vol. VII* (pp. 344–369). Minneapolis: University of Minnesota Press.

Segal, E. M. (1990). Fictional narrative comprehension. *Proceedings of the 12th Annual Conference of the Cognitive Science Society* (pp. 526–533). Hillsdale, NJ: Lawrence Erlbaum Associates.

Segal, E. M. (in press). Deixis in short fiction: The contribution of deictic shift theory to reader experience of literary fiction. Paper given at the 2nd International Conference on the Short Story in English, Iowa City, Iowa.

Segal, E. M., Bruder, G. A., & Daniels, J. (1984, November). *Deictic centers in narrative comprehension.* Paper presented by Daniels at the meeting of the Psychonomic Society, San Antonio, TX.

Segal, E., Duchan, J., & Scott, P. (1991). The role of interclausal connectives in narrative structuring: Evidence from adults' interpretations of simple stories. *Discourse Processes, 14,* 27–54.

Shannon, C., & Weaver, W. (1949). *The mathematical theory of information.* Urbana, IL: University of Illinois Press.

Shapiro, S. C. (1971). A net structure for semantic information storage, deduction and retrieval. *Proceedings of the 2nd International Joint Conference on Artificial Intelligence (IJCAI–71; Imperial College, London: Vol. 2* (pp. 512–523). San Mateo, CA: Morgan Kaufmann.

Shapiro, S. C. (1978). Path-based and node-based inference in semantic networks. In D. Waltz (Ed.), *Tinlap-2: Theoretical issues in natural language processing* (pp. 219–225). New York: Association for Computing Machinery.

Shapiro, S. C. (1979). The SNePS semantic network processing system. In N. V. Findler (Ed.), *Associative networks: The representation and use of knowledge by computers* (pp. 179–203). New York: Academic Press.

Shapiro, S. C. (1982). Generalized augmented transition network grammars for generation from semantic networks. *American Journal of Computational Lingusitics, 8,* 12–25.

Shapiro, S. C. (1991). Cables, paths and "subconscious" reasoning in propositional semantic networks. In J. Sowa (Ed.), *Principles of semantic networks: Explorations in the representation of knowledge* (pp. 137–156). San Mateo, CA: Morgan Kaufmann.

Shapiro, S. C. (1993). Belief spaces as sets of propositions. *Journal of Experimental and Theoretical Artificial Intelligence, 5,* 225–235.

Shapiro, S. C., McKay, D. P., Martins, J., & Morgado, E. (1981). *SnePSLOG: A "higher order" logic programming language* (SNeRG Tech. Note No. 8). Buffalo: State University of New York at Buffalo, Department of Computer Science.

Shapiro, S. C., & Rapaport, W. J. (1987). SNePS considered as a fully intensional propositional semantic network. In N. Cercone & G. McCalla (Eds.), *The knowledge frontier: Essays in the representation of knowledge* (pp. 262–315). New York: Springer-Verlag.

Shapiro, S. C., & Rapaport, W. J. (1991). Models and minds: Knowledge representation for natural-language competence. In R. Cummins & J. Pollock (Eds.), *Philosophy and AI: Essays at the interface* (pp. 215–259). Cambridge, MA: MIT Press.

Shapiro, S. C., & Rapaport, W. J. (1992). The SNePS family. *Computers and mathematics with applications, 23,* 243–275.

Shapiro, S. C., & The SNePS Implementation Group (1989). *SNePS–2 User's manual.* Buffalo: State University of New York at Buffalo, Department of Computer Science.

Shapiro, S. C., & The SNePS Implementation Group (1991). *SNePS–2.1 User's manual.* Buffalo: State University of New York at Buffalo, Department of Computer Science.

Sidner, C. L. (1983). Focusing in the comprehension of definite anaphora. In M. Brady & R. Berwick (Eds.), *Computational models of discourse* (pp. 267–330). Cambridge, MA: MIT Press.

Sissons, M. (1981). Race, sex and helping behaviour. *British Journal of Social Psychology, 20,* 285–292.

Smith, N. V. (1982). *Mutual knowledge.* London: Academic Press.

Sondheimer, N. (1976). Spatial inference and natural-language machine control. *International Journal of Man–Machine Studies, 8,* 329–336.

Sowa, J. (Ed.). (1991). *Principles of semantic networks: Explorations in the representation of knowledge.* San Mateo, CA: Morgan Kaufmann.

Sowa, J. (1992). Semantic networks. In S. C. Shapiro (Ed.), *Encyclopedia of artificial intelligence* (2nd ed.) (pp. 1493–1511). New York: Wiley.

Spielberg, S. (Producer). (1993). *Schindler's list.*

Srihari, R. K. (1981). *Combining path-based and node-based inference in SNePS* (Tech. Rep. No. 183). Buffalo: State University of New York at Buffalo, Department of Computer Science.

Stark, H. A. (1987). *Keeping track of characters in narrative.* (Doctoral dissertation, Stanford University, Palo Alto, CA). *Dissertation Abstracts International, 47-12,* 5080B.

Steedman, M. J. (1977). Verbs, time, and modality. *Cognitive Science, 1,* 216–234.

Stein, N., & Glenn, C. (1979). An analysis of story comprehension in elementary school children. In R. Freedle (Ed.), *New directions in discourse processing* (pp. 53–120). Norwood, NJ: Ablex.

Steinbeck, J. (1966). *The grapes of wrath.* New York: Bantam.

Steinbeck, J. (1975). *The pearl.* New York: Bantam. (Original work published 1954)

Strawson, P. F. (1950). On referring. *Mind, 59,* 320–344.

Streeter, L., & Vitello, D. (1986). A profile of driver's map-reading abilities. *Human Factors, 28* (2), 223–239.

Streeter, L., Vitello, D., & Wonciewicz, S. A. (1985). How to tell people where to go: Comparing navigational aids. *International Journal of Man/Machine Interaction, 22,* 549–562.

Sturtevant, E. H. (1961). *Linguistic change: An introduction to the historical study of language.* Chicago: University of Chicago Press. (Original work published 1917)

Sutton-Smith, B. (1981). *The folkstories of children.* Philadelphia: University of Pennsylvania Press.

Talmy, L. (1975). Semantics and syntax of motion. In J. P. Kimball (Ed.), *Syntax and semantics: Vol. 4* (pp. 181–238). New York: Academic Press.

Talmy, L. (1976). Semantic causative types. In M. Shibatani (Ed.), *Syntax and semantics: Vol. 6* (pp. 43–116). New York: Academic Press.

Talmy, L. (1978). Figure and ground in complex sentences. In J. Greenberg, C. Ferguson, & E. Moravcsik (Eds.), *Universals of human language* (pp. 625–649). Stanford, CA: Stanford University Press.

Talmy, L. (1983). How language structures space. In H. Pick & L. Acredolo (Eds.), *Spatial orientation: Theory, research and application* (pp. 225–282). New York: Plenum.

Talmy, L. (1985). Lexicalization patterns: semantic structure in lexical forms. In T. Shopen (Ed.), *Language typology and syntactic description, Vol. 3: Grammatical categories and the lexicon* (pp. 57–149). Cambridge, England: Cambridge University Press.

Talmy, L. (1988a). Force dynamics in language and cognition. *Cognitive Science, 12,* 49–100.

Talmy, L. (1988b). The relation of grammar to cognition. In B. Rudzka-Ostyn (Ed.), *Topics in cognitive linguistics* (pp. 165–205). Amsterdam: Benjamins.

Talmy, L. (1990, January). *Fictive motion in language and perception.* Paper presented at the Department of Geography Colloquium, State University of New York at Buffalo.

Talmy, L. (1994). The windowing of attention in language. In M. Shibatani & S. Thompson (Eds.), *Grammatical constructions: Their form and meaning*. New York: Oxford University Press.

Talmy, L. (in press). *The conceptual structuring system of language*. Cambridge, MA: Bradford Books/MIT Press.

Todorov, T. (1966). Les categories du recit Litteraire. *Communications, 8*, 125–151.

Todorov, T. (1977). *The poetics of prose*. R. Howard (Trans.). Ithaca, NY: Cornell University Press.

Tolkien, J. R. R. (1965). *The lord of the rings, Vol. 1: The fellowship of the ring, and Vol. 2: The two towers*. (2nd ed.). Boston: Houghton Mifflin.

Tomlin, S. S., & Pu, M. (1991). The management of reference in Mandarin discourse. *Cognitive Linguistics, 2*, 65–95.

Toolan, M. (1988). *Narrative: A critical linguistic introduction*. New York: Routledge & Kegan Paul.

Trabasso, T., & Sperry, L. L. (1985). Causal relatedness and importance of story events. *Journal of Memory and Language, 24*, 595–611.

Trabasso, T., & van den Broek, P. (1985). Causal thinking and the representation of narrative events. *Journal of Memory and Language, 24*, 612–630.

Twain, M. (1981). *The adventures of Huckleberry Finn*. New York: Bantam.

Uspensky, B. (1973). *A poetics of composition*. Berkeley: University of California Press.

Van Inwagen, P. (1977). Creatures of fiction. *American Philosophical Quarterly, 14*, 299–308.

Vendler, A. (1957). Verbs and times. *The Philosophical Review, 66*, 143–160.

Verkuyl, H. J. (1972). *On the compositional nature of the aspects*. Dordrecht, Holland: Reidel.

Verschueren, J. (Ed.). (1987). Concluding Round Table 1987 International Pragmatics Conference (Antwerp, Belgium). *IPrA Working Document No. 2*, 1–54.

Villaume, S. (1988). Creating context within text: An investigation of primary-grade children's character introductions in original stories. *Research in the Teaching of English, 22*, 161–182.

Vlach, F. (1981). The semantics of the progressive. In P. J. Tedeschi & A. Zaenen (Eds.), *Tense and aspect* (pp. 271–292). New York: Academic Press.

Wales, R. (1986). Deixis. In P. Fletcher & M. Garman (Eds.), *Language acquisition* (pp. 241–260). New York: Cambridge University Press.

Walton, K. L. (1990). *Mimesis as make-believe*. Cambridge, MA: Harvard University Press.

Warhol, A. (Director). (1964). *Empire*.

Warhol, A. (Director). (1969). *Blue Movie*.

Watanabe, N. (1989). The cognitive functions of "wa" and "ga" in sentences in discourse. Unpublished master's thesis. State University of New York at Buffalo.

Webber, B. L. (1978). On deriving aspectual sense. *Cognitive Science, 2* (4), 385–390.

Webber, B. L. (1983). So what can we talk about now? In M. Brady & R. Berwick (Eds.), *Computational models of discourse* (pp. 331–371). Cambridge, MA: MIT Press.

Weinreich, U. (1980) On the semantic structure of language. In W. Labov & B. S. Weinreich (Eds.), *Uriel Weinreich: On semantics* (pp. 37–97). Philadelphia, PA: University of Pennsylvania Press.

Wellman, W. A. (Director). (1937). *A star is born*.

Wiebe, J. M. (1990a). Identifying subjective characters in narrative. *Papers Presented to the 13th International Conference on Computational Linguistics (COLING–90, Helsinki)* (pp. 401–408). Morristown, NJ: Association of Computational Linguistics.

Wiebe, J. M. (1990b). *Recognizing subjective sentences: A computational investigation of narrative text* (Tech. Rep. No. 90–03). Buffalo: State University of New York at Buffalo, Department of Computer Science.

Wiebe, J. M. (1994). Tracking point of view in narrative. *Computational Linguistics, 20*(2).

Wiebe, J. M., & Rapaport, W. J. (1986). Representing De Re and De Dicto belief reports in discourse and narrative. *Proceedings of the IEEE, 74*, 1405–1413.

Wiebe, J. M., & Rapaport, W. J. (1988). A computational theory of perspective and reference in narrative. *Proceedings of the 26th Annual Meeting of the Association for Computational Linguistics* (pp. 131–138). Morristown, NJ: Association for Computational Linguistics.

Wierzbicka, A. (1980). *Lingua Mentalis: The semantics of natural language.* Sydney: Academic Press.

Wierzbicka, A. (1987a). Boys will be boys: "Radical semantics" vs. "radical pragmatics." *Language, 63* (1), 95–114.

Wierzbicka, A. (1987b). *English speech act verbs: A semantic dictionary.* Sydney: Academic Press.

Wierzbicka, A. (1988). *The semantics of grammar.* Amsterdam: Benjamins.

Wierzbicka, A. (1989). Semantic primitives—The expanding set. *Quaderni di Semantica, 10* (2), 133–157.

Wierzbicka, A. (1991). Lexical universals and universals of grammar. In M. Kefer & J. van der Auwera (Eds.), *Meaning and grammar.* Berlin: Mouton.

Wierzbicka, A. (1992). The semantics of interjection. In In F. Ameka (Ed.), Interjections (pp. 159–192) [Special issue]. *Journal of Pragmatics, 18*(2/3).

Wilkins, D. P. (1986). Particle/clitics for criticism and complaint in Mparntwe Arremte (Aranda). *Journal of Pragmatics, 10,* 575–596.

Wilkins, D. P. (1989). *Mparntwe Arrernte (Aranda): Studies in the structure and semantics of grammar.* Unpublished doctoral dissertation, Australian National University, Canberra.

Wilkins, D. P. (1992). Interjections as deictics. *Journal of Pragmatics, 18,* 119–158.

Wilks, Y., & Ballim, A. (1987). Multiple agents and the heuristic ascription of belief. *Proceedings of the 10th International Joint Conference on Artificial Intelligence (NCAI–87, Milan)* (pp. 118–124). Los Altos, CA: Morgan Kaufmann.

Wilks, Y., & Bien, J. (1983). Beliefs, points of view, and multiple environments. *Cognitive Science, 7,* 95–119.

Wilson, S. G., Rinck, M., McNamara, T. P., Bower, G. H., & Morrow, D. G. (1993). Mental models and narrative comprehension: Some qualifications. *Journal of Memory and Language, 32,* 141–154.

Wittgenstein, L. (1958). *Philosophical Investigations.* G. E. M. Anscombe (Trans.). New York: Macmillan.

Woods, A. Fletcher, P., & Hughes, A. (1986). *Statistics in language studies.* Cambridge: Cambridge University Press.

Woolf, V. (1944). The haunted house. In *The haunted house and other short stories.* New York: Harcourt Brace.

Woolf, V. (1948). *The voyage out.* New York: Harcourt Brace.

Woolf, V. (1955). *To the lighthouse.* New York: Harcourt Brace.

Woolf, V. (1963). *Mrs. Dalloway.* London: Hogarth.

Wyatt, R. (1989). *The representation of opaque contexts* (Tech. Rep. No. 89–13). Buffalo: State University of New York at Buffalo, Department of Computer Science.

Wyatt, R. (1990). Kinds of opacity and their representations. In D. Kumar (Ed.), *Current trends in SNePS–Semantic network processing system, Lecture Notes in Artificial Intelligence, No. 437* (pp. 123–144). Berlin: Springer-Verlag.

Wyatt, R. (1993). Reference and intensions. *Journal of Experimental and Theoretical Artificial Intelligence, 5,* 263–271.

Xu Xiaoyu. (1982). *Gu mu.* Beijing: Shouhuo, no. 5.

Yordy, J. (1990–1991). Teaching Hal to read: Algorithmic approaches. *Scientiae: Magazine of the [SUNY Buffalo] faculty of natural sciences and mathematics, 4.2,* 2–3.

Young, K. G. (1987). *Taleworlds and storyrealms: The phenomenology of narrative.* Hingham, MA: Kluwer.

Young, R., Becker, A., & Pike, K. (1970). *Rhetoric: discovery and change.* New York: Harcourt Brace.

Yuhan, A. H. (1991). *Dynamic computation of spatial reference frames in narrative understanding* (Tech. Rep. No. 91–03). State University of New York at Buffalo, Department of Computer Science.

Zelazny, R. (1971). Divine madness. In *The doors of his face, the lamps of his mouth, and other stories* (pp. 199–205). Garden City, NY: Doubleday.

Zubin, D. (1979). Discourse function of morphology, In T. Givon (Ed.), *Syntax and semantics 12: Discourse and syntax* (pp. 469–504). New York: Academic Press.

Zubin, D. (1989). Deictic devices in natural text. In W. J. Rapaport, E. M. Segal, S. C. Shapiro, D. A. Zubin, G. A. Bruder, J. F. Duchan, M. J. Almeida, J. H. Daniels, M. Galbraith, J. M. Wiebe, & A. H. Yuhan (Eds.), *Deictic centers and the cognitive structure of narrative comprehension* (pp. 12–21). (Tech. Rep. No. 89–09). Buffalo: State University of New York at Buffalo, Department of Computer Science.

Zubin, D. A., & Choi, S. (1984). Orientation and gestalt: Conceptual organizing principles in the lexicalization of space. In *Papers from the Parasessions* (pp. 333–345). Chicago: Chicago Linguistics Society.

Zubin, D. A., Chun, S. A., & Li, N. (1990). Misbehaving reflexives in Korean and Mandarin. *Proceedings of the 16th Annual Meeting of the Berkeley Linguistics Society, 16*, 338–354.

AUTHOR INDEX

A

Abelson, R. P., 7, 8, 9, 10, *487*
Adams, M. J., 8, *487*
Adler, C., 349, *487*
Allaire, E. B., 88, *487*
Allen, J. F., 161, 162, 164, 266, 274, 276, *487*
Almeida, M. J., 17, 46, 160, 162, 164, 170, 179, 189, 197, *487, 500*
Ameka, F., 360, 364, 372, 376, 377, 379, 384, *487*
Anderson, A., 326, 327, 331, *488*
Anthony, P., 77, *488*
Apel, K.-O., 23, *488*
Asher, N., 271, *488*
Atkinson, M., 22, *488*
Auerbach, E., 14, 67, *488*
Austen, J., 56, 143, *488*
Austin, J. L., 12, 64, *488*

B

Bakhtin, M., 43, 51, 53, *488*
Bal, M., 62, *488*
Ballim, A., 285, *488, 504*
Balzac, H., 65, *488*

Bamberg, M., 325, *488*
Banfield, A., 13, 14, 27, 35, 36, 46, 47, 55, 57, 67, 68, 69, 131, 133, 236, 264, 265, 268, 269, 284, 292, 293, 294, 315, 325, 326, 329, 342, 347, *488*
Barnden, J., 285, *488*
Bartlett, F. C., 8, *488*
Barwise, J., 10, 14, *488*
Beal, R., 408, *496*
Becker, A., 408, *504*
Bennett, M., 162, 163, 179, *488*
Benveniste, E., 23, 28, *488*
Bien, J., 285, *504*
Black, J. B., 244, 259, 342, 345, *488*
Bloomfield, L., 364, 365, 366, *488*
Bobrow, D. G., 8, 65, *488*
Booth, W., 43, 45, 69, *488*
Bower, G. H., 243, 244, 245, 258, 259, 327, 342, 345, 346, *488, 498, 504*
Brachman, R. J., 80, *489, 504*
Bransford, J. D., 7, 11, *489*
Breal, M., 196, *489*
Brewer, W. F., 7, *489*
Bridgers, S. E., 265, 275, *489*
Bronte, C., 48, 65, *489*
Brown, G., 145, *489*
Brown, R., 287, *489*

Bruder, G. A., 23, 46, 66, 76, 197, 227, 228, 229, 231, 247, 248, 252, 256, 341, 349, 350, 388, *489, 500, 501*
Bruner, J., 13, 14, 67, 68, 70, 116, *489*
Buchler, J., 21, 22, 23, *489*
Buhler, C., 14, 24, 73, 130, *489*
Burke, K., 10, *489*
Burroway, J., 65, *489*

C

Caldwell, T., 349, *489*
Canadian Automobile Association, 199, *489*
Capote, T., 26, *489*
Carlson, T. B. 13, *490*
Carpenter, P., 243, *495*
Carroll, D., 20, *489*
Carroll, L., 448, *489*
Castaneda, H.-N., 34, 86, 109, 263, 269, 280, *489, 490*
Charniak, E., 169, *494*
Chatman, S., 13, 14, 38, 62, 69, 264, *490*
Chen, P., 288, 289, 290, 299, *490*
Cherryh, C. J., 142, 265, 269, 270, 326, 329, 331, 336, 337, 338, 339, *490*
Choi, S., 292, *505*
Chomsky, N., 6, 7, 170, *490*
Christie, A., 172, 173, 180, 182, *490*
Chun, S. A., 293, 295, 297, 318, *490, 505*
Clark, H. H., 13, 142, 192, 194, 196, 266, 281, 282, 288, *490*
Clark, E. V., 142, 288, *490*
Clarke, M., 54, 55, 236, *490*
Cleary, B., 53, *490*
Cohen, P. R., 266, 281, 282, *490, 499*
Cohn, D., 14, 26, 34, 43, 50, 67, 68, 265, 267, 292, 315, 342, *490*
Cole, P., 362, *490 , 491*
Collins, A., 8, *487*
Comrie, B., 162, 166, *491*
Connor, U., 408, *491*
Coulmas, F., 384, *491*
Cowan, N., 288, *491*
Cresswell, M. J., 73, 197, *491, 494*
Crichton, M., 63, *491*
Crimmins, M., 83, *491*
Cukor, G., 63, *491*

D

Damrad-Fry, R., 325, *488*
Daniels, J., 46, 197, 247, 258, *491, 500, 501*
Davidson, D., 6, 80, 160, *491*
deBeaugrande, R., 144, *491*
Dell, G. S., 326, *491*
Dickens, C., 73, *491*
Dilthey, W., 39, *491*
Dolezel, L., 265, *491*
Donnellan, K. S., 266, 280, *491*
Dooling, D. J., 7, 11, *491*
Dos Passos, J., 55, *491*
Doubrovsky, S., 32, *491*
Dowty, D. R., 162, 164, *491*
Dressler, W., 144, *491*
Duchan, J., 23, 46, 66, 76, 197, 227, 228, 229, 231, 233, 236, 237, 341, 388, *491, 498, 494, 500, 501*

E

Edwards, D., 272, *494*
Elliot, D., 379, *491*
Engl, L., 256, *489*
Epson, 202, *491*
Erman, B., 360, *491*
ETS, 414, *491*
Evans, N., 372, *491*

F

Fauconnier, G., 62, 75, 144, 145, 270, *492*
Fillmore, C. J., 11, 29, 46, 67, 129, 135, 145, 197, 273, 276, 291, 292, 299, 306, 315, 382, *492*
Fleischer, R., 448, *492*
Fletcher, P., 335, *504*
Fodor, J. D., 263, 279, 280, 281, 282, *492*
Fodor, J. A., 6, 7, *492, 495*
Folman, S., 408, *492*
Fonagy, I., 360, 384, *492*
Fox, B. A., 289, 326, *492*
Franchere, R., 273, 278, *492*
Francis, D., 173, 183, *492*
Freedle, R. O., 7, 62, *492*
Frege, G., 86, *492*

G

Galbraith, M., 46, 69, 197, 292, *492*, *500*
Gale, R., 22, 23, *492*
Garling, T., 137, *492*
Garrod, S. C., 326, 327, 331, *488*
Garnham, A., 326, *492*
Gee, J., 227, 326, *492*
Gee, J. P., 325, *492*
Geis, M., 145, *492*
Gendlin, E., 50, *493*
Genette, G., 13, 14, 17, 28, 43, 48, 62, 65, 67, 69, 75, 423, *493*
Gerts, D. B., 320, *493*
Gibson, J. J., 13, *493*
Gilbert, M., 183, *493*
Givon, T., 141, 287, 288, 326, 328, 329, 367, 379, *493*
Glenn, C., 9, 227, 325, *502*
Goddard, C., 368, 372, *493*
Goffman, E., 74, 379, 383, *493*
Golledge, R., 137, *492*
Gould, M. D., 388, *493*, *497*
Graesser, A. C., 14, 243, *493*
Greenbaum, S., 264, 362, *499*
Greenspan, S. L., 11, 245, 258, 345, 346, *493*, *498*
Grice, H. P., 11, 12, 64, 72, 142, 367, 373, 379, *493*
Grimes, J. E., 141, *493*
Grisham, J., 69, *493*
Grosz, B. J., 275, 288, *493*

H

Haberland, H., 360, *493*
Haiman, J., 148, 367, *493*
Hale, G., 62, *492*
Halliday, M., 144, *493*
Hamburger, K., 25, 26, 30, 47, 68, 236, 268, *493*
Hammett, D., 173, 174, 176, 182, 183, *493*, *494*
Han, S., 315, *494*
Harper, M. P., 169, *494*
Has, W. J., 433, *494*
Hasan, R., 144, *493*
Heath, S., 227, *494*
Hemingway, E., 9, 62, *494*
Henry, O., 448, *494*
Herrnstein-Smith, B., 42, *494*

Herskovits, A., 447, *494*
Hewitt, L., 227, *494*
Hill, J., 437, 455, *494*
Hillerman, T., 384, *494*
Hinrichs, E., 170, 171, 175, *494*
Hintikka, J., 113, *494*
Hintikka, M. B., 113, *494*
Hirschman, L., 171, *494*
Hirst, G., 274, *494*
Hobbs, J. R., 272, *494*
Hockett, C. F., 21, *494*
Hoffman, A., 75, *494*
Hopper, P., 141, 145, 152, 325, 327, *494*
Hornby, A. S., 201, *494*
Hornstein, N., 169, *494*
Hosenfeld, C., 407, *494*
Hottenroth, P.-M., 395, 396, *494*
Hughes, A., 335, *504*
Hughes, G. E., 73, *494*
Hutchins, E., 451, *495*
Hyde, T. S., 14, *495*

J

Jakobson, R., 30, 129, *495*
James, D., 365, *495*
James, H., 50, *495*
Jarvella, R. J., 21, 24, 129, 130, *495*
Jenkins, J. J., 14, *495*
Johnson, M., 154, 387, 404, *495*, *496*
Johnson, M. K., 7, 11, *489*
Johnson, N., 9, 130, 227, 325, *497*
Johnson-Laird, P. N. 244, *495*
Joyce, J., 37, 38, 45, 50, *495*
Just, M., 243, *495*

K

Kafka, F., 456, *495*
Kahane, C., 452, *495*
Kamp, H., 269, *495*
Karmiloff-Smith, A., 328, *495*
Katz, J. J., 6, *495*
Ke, Y., 292, 296, 297, 300, 302, 303, 305, 306, *495*
Keillor, G., 252, 253, *495*
Kiefer, F., 360, *495*
Kintsch, W., 130, 197, 243, *491*, *495*
Klein, W., 21, 24, 129, 130, *495*
Konolige, K., 271, *495*

Kramer, M., 408, *496*
Kumar, D., 105, 128, *495*
Kuno, S., 130, 132, 133, 315, *495*
Kuroda, S.-Y., 26, 29, 30, 31, 133, 265, 268, 269, 292, 314, 315, *495*

L

Labov, W., 130, 325, 327, *495*
Lachman, R., 7, 11, *491*, *499*
Lakoff, G., 66, 154, 292, 322, 387, *496*
Landman, F., 88, *496*
Langacker, R., 292, 295, *496*
Lashley, K. S., 6, *496*
Lauer, J., 408, *491*
Laughren, M., 365, *496*
Lawrence, D. H., 36, 52, *496*
Leech, G., 264, 360, 362, *496*, *499*
Leggett, G., 408, *496*
Lehmann, F., 80, *496*
L'Engle, M., 265, *496*
Levesque, H. J., 80, *489*
Levinson, S., 360, 362, *496*
Levy, E., 288, 326, *497*
Lewis, D., 110, 379, *496*
Lewis, S., 198, *496*
Li, N., 14, 96, 288, 296, 297, 318, *496*, *505*
Lichtenstein, E. H., 13, *489*
Linde, C., 275, 457, *496*
London, J., 7, 319, *496*
Lloyd, B. B., 278, *500*
Longacre, R. E., 141, 202, *496*
Lu, T., 296, *496*
Lucariello, J., 10, 270, *496*
Lyons, J., 22, 129, 202, *496*

M

Magliola, R., 19, 25, 32, *496*
Maida, A. S., 79, 85, 86, 271, *497*
Mailor, N., 35, *497*
Mandler, J., 9, 130, 227, 325, *497*
Mann, P., 199, *497*
Mann, W., 289, *497*
Mansfield, K., 68, *497*
Mark, D. M., 66, 76, 227, 228, 229, 231, 388, 396, *497*, *500*
Marr, D., 14, *497*
Marshall, C. R., 266, 281, 282
Marslen-Wilson, W., 288, 326, *497*

Martin, P., 272, *494*
Martins, J., 80, 114, 118, 119, *497*, *501*
McCabe, A., 227, 325, *497*, *499*
McCarrell, N. S., 11, *489*
McCawley, N. A., 310, *497*
McCullers, C., 273, *497*
McDermott, D., 162, 164, *497*
McGranaghan, M., 388, *497*
McKay, D. P., 118, *501*
McHale, B., 13, 35, 36, 37, 38, 40, 43, 45, 50, 55, 67, *497*
McKoon, G., 243, 326, *491*, *497*
McMurtry, L., 349, 350, 352, 353, 354, 355, *497*
McNamara, T. P., 245, *504*
Mead, C., 408, *496*
Meinong, A., 86, 271, *498*
Melville, H., 70, *498*
Merleau-Ponty, M., 22, 23, 24, *498*
Meth, M., 229, 233, *491*
Meyer, N., 112, *498*
Miller, P., 227, *498*
Minsky, M., 7, 8, *498*
Mitchell, M., 62, *498*
Moore, R. C., 271, *498*
Morgado, E., 118, *501*
Morrow, D. G., 244, 245, 254, 258, 327, 345, 346, *488*, *498*, *504*
Mourelatos, A. P. D., 162, *498*
Muller, M., 383, *498*
Munro, P., 148, *493*
Murdoch, I., 33, *498*
Murphy, G. L., 278, *498*

N, O

Nakhimovsky, A., 276, 342, *498*
Neumann, A. W., 55, *498*
No, W., 319, *498*
O'Kun, L., 198, *496*
Oneal, A., 265, *498*

P

Parsons, T., 112, *498*
Partee, B., 162, 163, 179, *488*
Partee, B. H., 170, 175, 177, *498*
Pascal, R., 42, *498*
Pavel, T., 13, 64, 70, 71, *498*
Peirce, C. S., 21, 369, *498*

Perrault, C. R., 266, 281, 282, *499*
Perry, J., 10, 14, 83, *488*
Peters, S. L., 91, 278, *499*
Peterson, C., 227, *499*
Pierson, F., 63, *499*
Pike, K., 408, *504*
Pinker, S., 6, *499*
Polanyi, L., 74, *499*
Pollack, M. E., 286, *499*
Pompi, K. F., 7, *499*
Postal, P. M., 282, 310, *499*
Prince, G., 13, 71, 197, 198, *499*
Pu, M., 290, *503*

Q, R

Quine, W. V., 280, *499*
Quirk, R., 264, 362, *499*
Rapaport, W. J., 23, 36, 46, 66, 76, 79, 81,
    82, 83, 85, 86, 89, 90, 91, 105, 107,
    108, 109, 110, 112, 113, 114, 128,
    197, 206, 227, 228, 229, 231, 263,
    269, 270, 271, 276, 278, 341, 342,
    388, *489, 498, 499, 500, 501, 502, 503*
Ratcliff, R., 243, 326, *491, 497*
Reddy, M., 5, *500*
Reichenbach, H., 64, 71, 166, *500*
Reichman, R., 275, 288, *500*
Reid, W. H., 152, *500*
Revzin, I., 22, *500*
Ricoeur, P., 20, 23, 32, *500*
Rimmon-Kenan, S., 42, 47, 62, 69, *500*
Rinck, M., 245, 278, *504*
Rosch, E., 91, *500*
Roth, P., 48, *500*
Routley, R., 86, *500*
Rule, S., 111, *500*
Rumelhart, D. E., 7, 8, 9, 13, 130, 227, 325,
    500
Rumsey, A., 360, *500*
Russell, B., 202, *500*

S

Sadock, J. M., 367, *500*
Sandor, A., 403, *500*
Sanford, A. J., 325, 327, 331, *488*
Sapir, E., 360, 365, *500*
Sarig, G., 408, *492*
Sartre, J.-P., 57, *501*

Scha, R., 74, *499*
Schachter, P., 160, *501*
Schank, R. C., 7, 8, 9, 10, *501*
Schiffrin, D., 229, 233, *501*
Scholes, R., 109, *501*
Schultz, J., 256, *489*
Scott, P., 227, 228, 229, 233, 236, 237, 252,
    489, 501
Searle, J. R., 12, 13, 33, 66, 69, *501*
Segal, E. M., 11, 13, 17, 23, 46, 64, 66, 68,
    73, 76, 137, 197, 227, 228, 229, 231,
    233, 236, 237, 247, 341, 388, 407,
    489, 493, 494, 501
Shannon, C. E., 5, *501*
Shapiro, S. C., 23, 46, 66, 76, 79, 80, 81, 82,
    83, 85, 86, 89, 90, 91, 107, 109, 114,
    118, 119, 152, 162, 164, 170, 197,
    206, 227, 228, 229, 231, 270, 271,
    278, 341, *489, 497, 499, 500, 501, 502*
Sidner, C. L., 274, 275, 288, 327, *493, 502*
Sissons, M., 388, *502*
Smith, N. V., 142, *502*
The SNePS Implementation Group, 118, 206,
    502
Sondheimer, N., 192, *502*
Sowa, J., 80, *502*
Sperry, L. L., 243, *503*
Sperry, L., 227, *498*
Spielberg, S., 439, *502*
Srihari, R. K., 80, *502*
Stark, H. A., 244, 246, *502*
Steedman, M. J., 162, *502*
Stein, N., 9, 227, 325, *502*
Steinbeck, J., 57, 135, 136, 144, 146, 246,
    247, 248, 250, 256, 329, 337, *502*
Stickel, M., 272, *494*
Story, G., 171, *494*
Strawson, P. F., 202, *502*
Streeter, L., 388, 404, *502*
Sturtevant, E. H., 196, *502*
Sutton-Smith, B., 228, 230, 237, *502*
Svartvik, J., 264, 362, *499*
Svorou, S., 396, *497*

T

Talmy, L., 191, 292, 394, 402, 422, 423, 438,
    447, *502, 503*
Thompson, S. A., 195, 289, *494, 497*
Todorov, T., 13, 46, 71, 72, *503*

Tolkien, J. R. R., 135, 136, 137, 138, 140, 143, 278, *503*
Tomlin, S. S., 290, *503*
Toolan, M., 43, 46, 62, *503*
Trabasso, T., 243, *503*
Turner, T. J., 244, 259, 342, 345, *488*
Twain, M., 52, *503*
Tyler, L., 288, 326, *497*

U, V

Uspensky, B., 38, 265, 342, *503*
van denBroek, P., 243, *503*
van Dijk, T. A., 130, 197, 243, *491*, *495*
Van Inwagen, P., 112, *503*
Vendler, A., 151, 152, 162, *503*
Verkuyl, H. J., 162, *503*
Verschueren, J., 362, 382, *503*
Villaume, S., 229, 231, 234, *503*
Vitello, D., 388, 404, *502*
Vlach, F., 162, *503*

W

Wales, R., 23, *503*
Waletsky, J., 130, 325, 327, *495*
Walton, K. L., 14, 64, 67, 74, *503*
Waltzman, D., 229, 233, *491*
Warhol, A., 444, 445, *503*
Watanabe, N., 299, *503*
Weaver, W., 5, *501*
Webber, B. L., 162, 269, 274, *503*
Weinreich, U., 366, *503*
Wellman, W. A., 63, *503*
Wiebe, J. M., 17, 36, 40, 46, 67, 68, 76, 83, 90, 109, 114, 227, 264, 270, 279, 284, 292, 299, 315, 326, 329, 332, 342, 343, 345, 346, 348, 349, 350, 479, *489*, *500*, *503*
Wierzbicka, A., 318, 362, 364, 372, 373, 379, 384, *504*
Wilkins, D. P., 359, 372, *504*
Wilks, Y., 285, *488*, *504*
Wilson, S. G., 245, *504*
Winograd, T., 8, *488*
Wisniewski, E. J., 278, *498*
Wittgenstein, L., 12, *504*
Wonciewicz, S. A., 388, 404, *502*
Woods, A., 335, *504*
Woolf, V., 40, 48, 57, 438, *504*
Wyatt, R., 88, *504*

X, Y

Xu Xiaoyu, 298, *504*
Yordy, J., 108
Youn, X. 320, *493*
Young, K. G., 64, 74, *504*
Young, R., 408, *504*
Yuhan, A. H., 46, 191, 197, 200, 500, *504*
Yule, G., 145, *489*

Z

Zelazny, R., 446, *505*
Zubin, D. A., 23, 46, 66, 76, 144, 147, 197, 227, 228, 229, 231, 246, 248, 260, 288, 292, 293, 295, 297, 318, 328, 388, 396, *489*, *490*, *496*, *497*, *500*, *505*
Zwicky, A. M., 367, *500*

SUBJECT INDEX

A

Accomplishment, 163, 168, 169, 173, 186–187
  events, 172
  network representation of sentences, 184–187
  nonprogressive, 171
  progressive, 163, 175
Achievement, 168, 171–172, 175
  complete and imcomplete, 166
  event, 169, 172
  examples in narrative, 172–173
  examples of, 165, 172
  network representation of sentences, 187–188
Activity, 171–174
  events, 163–172
  examples in narrative, 173
  imperfective paradox, 164
  network representation of sentences, 186
  subinterval property of, 163
Adjacency pair, 374
Adverbials
  frame, 179–184
  nonnarrative, 179, 183
  time, 171, 179, 216
Affective structure of narratives, 470, 472,
    476–485
  affect tones, 481

  anchors, 479
  contrasts, 479–480
  suspense, 481
  tracking variations in, 481
Agentive contruction, 309, 311, 315, 318
  coherence, 316
  force-dynamic basis, 320
  interactional discourse, 313
  Korean, 309, 312, 313
  in narrative, 314–315
American Sign Language (ASL), 371, 376,
    377
Anaphor, 325–326, 333, *see also* Anaphora
Anaphor resolution
  text-based approach, 328
Anaphora, 24, 287–288
Anaphoric evocation
  of minor character, 327
  of protagonist, 327
Anaphoric reference, 134, 335–337, *see also*
    References, Anaphora
  theories of, 326
Argument from Fine Grained Representation,
    87
Argument from Displacement, 87
Argumentative texts, *see* Persuasive texts
Ascription, 113

Aspect, 166–171
  imperfective, 167
  perfective, 166, 222
Assertion, 17
Audience
  foregrounding of, 418
  in persuasive texts, 411, 417, 419
Australian languages, 360
  Mparntwe Arrernte, 359, 367, 370–375
  Pitjantjantjara, 368
  Warlmanpa, 370
  Warlpiri, 370

B

Basic level category, 91, 93
Background knowledge, 118
Beliefs, *see also* Belief space
  background, see real-world beliefs
  real world, 116, 120
  story world, 116
  representing, 82
Belief reports
  De Dicto, 83
  De Re, 83
Belief space, 83, 118–119, 271
  of characters, 271
  current, 271
  of hearers, 266
  mutual, 266
  of reader, 270–271
  of speakers, 266
Bilinguals
  written texts produced by, 407–420
Boundaries (*see also* Edgework)
  between real and story worlds, 74, 77
  within story world, 76–77

C

Caki, 315, 318, *see also* Reflexive, Korean
Canonical encounter, 196
Case frame, 81–83
  for representing nonstative proposition,
    160–161
  for representing stative proposition, 161
CASSIE, 88–105, 107–108, 110, 113,
    114–127, 191, 200, 206–211, 213–216,
    218–200, 221–223, 225

Children's narratives, 227–237
  analyses of, 227
    story grammar approach, 227, 237, *see
      also* Story grammar
  cultural differences, 227
  deictic organization in, 236–237
  language forms in, 227
  settings in, 237
  subjectivity in, 228
Cognitive agent, 88–89, 200
Cognitive modeling, 88–89, 107
Cognitive science, 3
  disciplines contained in, 4
Cognitive stance, 15
Cognitive systems, 422–423
  used for narrative, 422–423
Cohesive devices, 144
Communication theory, 5
  mathematical theory of communication, 5
Comprehension,
  reader's, 142
Computational philosophy, 107
Conduit metaphor, 5, 7, 9
Connectivity systems
  causality, 435
  import, 458–459
  plot structure, 458
  psychological, 454
  subsystems of
    continuity of identity, 456
    epistemic, 455
    motivational, 455
    sequiturity, 456
  viewpoint, 453
Consciousness, 52, 54, *see also* Subjectivity
  nonreflective, 53, *see also* Objective context
Consociation, 110
Consubstantiation, 109–110
Cultural variability and deixis
  North American vs. Spanish comparisons,
    387–404

D

DeDicto, 279
  reports, 281
De Re, 279
  reports, 280–281
Deictic center, 15–16, 17, 66, 108, 129, 142,
    197, 203, 206–207, 216
  children's stories, 227–237

components of, 133
current (active), 258
organization of, 133
principles of
  cumulative perspective, 144
  deictic synchronism, *see* Deictic synchronism
  extraposition, 144
  inertia, 142
  scope, 144
  textual economy, 142
  transparency, 143
psychological component, *see* WHO
spatial component, *see* WHERE
stable dissynchromism, 154–155
theory of, 63
tracking of (CASSIE), 210, 212–216, 218, 221–225
window of, 132
Deictic coordinate system, 24
Deictic devices, 140–141
  agreement and conflict among, 150–152
  anti-shifting, 147, 149, 151, 153
  introducing, 146, 149–150
  maintenance, 145, 149, 151
  shifting, 148, 150
  voiding, 151
Deictic field, 21, 23–24
  in narrative, 46
Deictic function
  of language, 22, 32
Deictic gestures, 368, 371, 373
Deictic operations
  introducing, 141
  maintaining, 141
  shifting, 141
  voiding, 141
Deictic shift, 70, 74, 228, 466, 469
  comparisons between persuasive and narrative, 418
  in persuasive texts, 408, 410, 411
Deictic shift model
  of fictional language, 26, 32–33, 46, 52–55, 57–59
Deictic shift theory, 13, 14–17, 130, 384–386, *see also* Deictic shift model
  properties of approach, 16
Deictic synchronism, 142–143
Deictic window, 143
Deictic terms, 10, 15
  departure verbs, 233, 235
  repetition as marker for distance, 398

spatial terms, 388, 392–396
verbs describing directional turns, 399–401
Deictic verbs, 244, 246, 248–249, 251
Deixis, 20–22
  linguistic marking of, 130
  in narrative, 243
  role in narrative, 23
  shifted, 131
  and subjectivity, 23
Demonstratives, 372
Directional relations, 195–200
  object-inherent, *see* Inherent directionality
  perspectivally imposed, *see* Perspectivally imposed directionality
Discourse, 62, 159, 170
  as distinct from story, 62–64, 67
  coherence, 203–205
  elements of, 63
Discourse continuity, 287
Discourse discontinuity, 233, 237
Domains in narrative structure, 426
  addressee, 430–431
  author, 431
  the work, 427–429
Dummy agents, 202

E

Edgework, 74, *see* Boundaries
Ellipsis, 366–367
Emotive interjections, 379–380
Empathy, 130
Epistemological ontology, 108–109
Epistemology
  fictional, 34–35, 43–44
  nonfictional, 34–35
Experiential construction, 309, 311, 315, 318–320
  coherence, 316
  interactional discourse, 313
  in Korean, 309, 312–313
  locative basis of, 320
  in narrative, 314–315
Expert system, 84
Event, 159–160, 162, 164, 166–167, 176–178, 187, 191–192
  imperfective, 175–177
  perfective, 175
  type, 171
  typology, 311

Event affair, 193
Event place, 193
Event time, 193, 209
Experience
  objects of, 296–297
Experiencer
  suppressed coding of, 295
Extensional entity, 88
External sentence contextualization, 11
Extranuclear properties, 112

F

Faded metaphor, *see* Semantic irradiation
Feigned reality statement, *see* Reality statement
Fiction, 25, 107, 109
  approaches to, 19–20
  ontological theories of
    Castaneda's theory, 109–110
    Lewis' theory, 110–112
    Parson's theory, 112
    Van Inwagen's theory, 112–113
  popular, 326
  SNePS approach to, 113–117
Fictional entity, 110
Fictional language
  models of, *see also* Deictic shift model
    dual voice view, 35–46
    "no difference" view, 33–35
Fictional narration, 25–32
Fictional narrator
  model of narrative, 69
Fictional narrative, 14, 17
  example of, 462–465
  temporal structure of, 468–473
  writing fiction, 467
Fictional objects, 108–109
  immigrant, 112
  native, 112
  surrogate, 112–113
Fictive motion, 402
Figure object, 192, 204, 209
Focal character, 199
Focal WHO, 342, 346
Focalized perspective, 132, *see also* Perspective
Focalizing perspective, 131–132, *see also*
    Perspective
Focalizing WHO, 134, 342, 346, 476, 479
Focus stack, 288
Frame, 8, 292
Frame adverbials, 179–184

Frame blending, 305
Frame embedding, 303–305
Frame interval, 179
Frame semantics, 292
Frame shifting, 299
Free indirect discourse, 27, 56, *see also*
    Represented speech, Represented thought

G

Generative grammar, 6
Giving verbal directions, *see* wayfinding
Ground object, 192, 195, 205–206
Guises, 109, *see also* Objects of thought,
    intensional

H, I

Heteroglossia, 39, 51
"I" pointer, 90
Identifying characters
  in relation to deixis, 245
Imperative sentences, 367
Inferencing, 326
Inherent directionalty, 195–197, 205
  front/back, 196
  left/right, 197
  up/down, 196
Inheritance, 90
  of information in networks, 80
Intensional entities, 86–87, *see also*
    Meinongian objects
Intentional entities, 87–88
Intentionality, 19
  continuum, 138–140
Interjections, 359–360, 362
  conative, 376
  as deictics, *see* as indexical
  deictic nature of, 370–371
  definition of, 363–364
  and direct quotations, 360–361
  felicity conditions, 372
  identification of, 363
  illocutionary purpose, 379
  imperative form, 368
  as indexical, 369
  and narrative, 383–386
  as particles, 365
  as phonologically aberrant, 372
  semantic content, 361
  as utterances, 365–369

Internal monologue, 305, 329
Internal property, 109
Internal sentence contextualization, 11
Interval types of the time-line
    covering, 181, 183
    noncovering, 181
Italian, 375, 377–378

K, L

Knowledge representation, 79, 107
    intensional, 86–88
Korean, 309–314, 316–321, 323
Language
    deictic functions of, 22
    in narrative
        multiconsciousness theory, 27
    nonreportive mode, 27
    phenomenology of, 19–20
    referentiality in, 19–20
    reportive mode, 27
Lexicon, 362
Linear continuity, 288–289, 299
Linear continuity hypothesis, 297–298, 300

M

Mandarin, 287–306
Mathematical theory of communication, 5
Meaning extraction theories, 5–7
Meinongian objects, 86, 89
Memory
    mental spaces in, 476
    of story characters, 469
        unbidden, 469
        voluntary, 469
Mental model, 17, 107–108, 131, 327
    of narrative, 244, 246
    of story, 65
Mental representation
    author, 130
    reader, 130
Mental space, 144
Metonymy, 322
Mimesis, 14, *see also* Narrative, as mimetic act
Minor sentence types, 366
Morpho-syntax
    and encoding of subjectivity, 311–313
Mparntwe Arrernte, *see* Australian languages
Multiconsciousness theory, *see* Language, in
    narrative

N

Narration
    first-person, 133
    language of, 49–50
    rules of, 170–178
    third-person, 133
Narrative, 65, 79, 108, 113, 170–171, 191, 206
    affect in, 461, *see also* Affective structure
        of narrative
    analysis of, 166
    Australian, 360
    background in, 327
    communication model of, 69
    comprehension, 3–17
        approaches to, 5–14
        difficulty and deixis, 255–258
    context, 211
    creative function of, 29
    events, 13, 17
    existents, 13, 17
    foreground in, 327
    global aspects, 461
    interpretation, 327
    language of, 14, 49
    as mimetic act, 67
    models of, 31–33
    now-point, 159, 170, *see also* Now-point
    object structure, 135
    participant structure, 134
    prototype, 427–430
    role in society, 61–62, 77
    SELF in, *see* SELF, WHO
    spatial relations and affect, 484
    SPEAKER in, *see* Speaker, WHO
    structural analysis of, 421
        cognitive approach to, 423–424
    structure of, 425, *see also* Affective
        structure of narrative
        across history/culture, 424
        basic factors in, *see* Domains in narrative
            structure, Parameters in narrative struc-
            ture, Strata in narrative structure
    temporal and affect relations, 483
    temporal and spatial relations, 481
    temporal, spatial, and affect relations, 481,
        484–485
    temporal structure, 137–138, 159, 468–473
    theoretical approaches to, 3–17
        communication theory, 5
        cooperative principle, 11–12
        meaning extraction theories, 5–7

Narrative *(Cont.)*
  theoretical approaches to *(Cont.)*
    relation theory of meaning, 10
    sentence contextualization, 11
    situational semantics, 10–11
    speech act theory, 12–13
    structures representation theories, 7–11
  time in, 159–189
  voice in, *see* Voice
Narrative convention, 171
Narrative discourse, 314–315
Narrative genre, 13
Narrative-line, 170–171, 179
  basic, 170
Narrative perspective taking, 287
Narrative production, 3–17
  approaches to, 5–14
Narrative space, 193–200
Narrative time progression, 171
Narrative theory, 13–14
Narrator, 45, 51
  necessity of, 43
  omnipresent, 45
  omniscient, 43, 57
  overt, 46
Nativism, 6
Natural language competence, 79, 107
Natural Semantic Metalanguage (NSM), 372,
  381
Nonexistent objects, 87
Nonfictional entity, 110
Nonreflective consciousness, *see* Consciousness
Nonsubjective character, 335
Now-point, 172–173, 175–181, 183, 186, 188
"Now" pointer, 90
Nuclear properties, 112

O

Objective context, 36, 52–54, 264, 315–316,
  see also Objective sentence
Objective sentences, 36, 53–54, 267, 342
Objects of thought
  intensional, 109
Occasion-meaning, 373
Omniscient narration, 27,
Open text, 16

P

Paragraph breaks and subjectivity
  psychological studies of, 348–352
Parameters in narrative structure
  degree of differentiation
    clarity, 439
    concentration, 437
    continuity, 437
    elaboration, 440
    explicitness, 440
    plexity, 438
    precision, 439
    prototypicality, 441
    veridicality, 441
  interrelations among, 442–443
  relative quantity (density, granularity,
    scope), 435–437
  structural relations (abstraction, alternation,
    concurrence, correlation, embedding),
    432–435
Participant
  tracking of, 328
Participant continuity, measures of
  referential competition, 329, *see also*
    Referential competition
  referential distance, 329, *see also*
    Referential distance
  referential persistence, 329, *see also*
    Referential persistence
Path image schema, 387, 404
Person deixis, 411, 413
  use of "you," 415–416
Perspectively imposed directionality, 197–200
Perspective
  content, 132
  encountering, 198–199
  expressive framing, 290, 296, 305, *see also*
    Expressive frame
  origin, 132
  projecting, 198–199
  reportive framing, 290, 296, 298, 305, *see
    also* Reportive frame
Perspective ego, 197–198
Perspective framing, 292
Perspective taking, 291, *see also* subjectivity
Perspective viewpoint, 199
Persuasive text, 407–420
  definition of, 407–408
  deixis in, 408–411
  formatting of, 414
  function of, 408

narrative comparison, 417, 418
Persuasive writing, 407–420
Place deixis
   presupposed home as center, 235–236
Plot, 325
Poetics of involvement in fiction, 19–20
Point of view, psychological, 341–342, *see also* WHO
   indicators of, 346, *see also* Paragraph breaks and subjectivity, Subjective elements
POP, 47–49
   POPping out of fiction, 51–52
Pragmatic checking, 334, 337
Pragmatics and semantics
   boundary between, 362
   relation between, 382
Predicate, 162
   classes of
      accomplishment, 163, *see also* Accomplishment
      achievement, *see* Achievement
      activities, 162, 175, *see also* Activity - events
      State, *see* State event, Stative sentence
Predication, 107, 109
   fictional, 107–116
   narrative, 116
Preposed adverbials
   as deictic indicators, 246–248
Private-state, 264, 347
   report, 265, 347
   sentences, 347
Procedure, 164
Production system, 84
Progressive, 176–177
Projective ego, 296
Pronominalization, 327–328, 338–339
Pronouns
   free reflexive, 134
   logophoric, 134
Proposition, 84–85, 193
   nonstative predicate (act), 160
   representing, 81–82
   spatial, 221
   stative predicate (property), 160
Protagonist, 331
Psycholinguistics, 326
Psychological predicates, 313
   Korean, 313
Psychonarration, 306, 339–330
PUSH, 47

Q, R

Quoted speech, 172
Rating scale
   for evaluating written text, 409, 414–417, 419
Real world, 121, 127
   context, 127
Reality statement, 25, *see also* Objective sentences
   feigned, 26, 49
Reasoning
   belief revision, 80
   node-based, 80, 84
   path-based, 80, 90
Reference
   anaphoric, 134, 274–276, *see also* Anaphor, Anaphora
   in conversation, 266
   indefinite, 276–279
   nonanaphoric definite, 272–274
   in objective sentences, 267–286
   propositional content of, 263
   resolution of, 271
   in subjective sentences, 269
Reference frame, 191–192, 195–200, 204–205, 218, 220–223, *see also* Spatial reference frame
   default resolution of, 205–205
   resolution, 203
Reference object, 194
Referent
   accessibility of, 287–288
Referential competition, 299, 330
Referential continuity, 294, 306
Referential distance, 329
Referential hierarchy, 326, 328
Referential persistence, 329
Referentiality in language, *see* Language
Referring expressions, 17
Reflexive
   in Korean, 315–316, *see also* Caki
   long-distance, 318, *see also* Caki
Reflexive pronoun, 297
Relation theory of meaning, 10
Reportive frame, 293, 299–301, 303
Representation
   of belief spaces, 271
   of proper names, 270
Represented perception, 264–265, 315, 330, 347
Represented speech, 55–56

Represented thought, 27, 56, 264–265, 306, 315–316, 317, 330, 347
Rhetorical continuity hypothesis, 299
Rhetorical structure, 289–296

S

Schema, 8, 192
Scripts, 8, 90
SELF, 36–39, 54–56, *see also* WHO
Self-world relations, 19
Semantic decomposition
    approaches to, 381, *see also* Natural
        Semantic Metalanguage
    of interjections, 370
Semantic irradiation, 196
Semantic network, 79, 159
    intensional, 79
    propositional, 80–86
Semantics, *see* Pragmatics and semantics
Sentence contextualization, 11
Shifters, 129–130
Situation models, 345, *see also* Mental models
SNePS, 79–105, 107, 109–110, 113–118, 159, 161, 163, 184, 206–208, 211, 223
    implementation of fiction representation and reasoning, 118–127
SNePS Belief Revision system (SNeBR), 114, 116, 118–121, 126
SNePSLOG, 118
Space
    computational representation of, 191–225
Spatial case relations, 194
Spatial deixis
    in persuasive texts, 410–411, 417
Spatial destination, 388, 393
Spatial distance, 397–399
Spatial direction, 397
Spatial events, 193–195
Spatial information, 191–193
Spatial landmarks, 393–395
Spatial metaphors, 402–403
Spatial proximity functions, 194–195
Spatial proximity relations, 195
Spatial relations, 194
Spatial reference frame, 213, 396, *see also*
        Reference frame
    problem of, 191–193
        strategies to resolve, 200–206
Spatial structure in narratives, 473–476
    affect relation to, 477–478

density, 475
location, 474
motion, 475
scale, 475
tracking variations in, 475–476
Spatial tracking
    in narrative, 243, 244–245
Spatially associated activity, 194
Spatially associated act, 194
SPEAKER, 36–43, 54–55, 58, *see also*
        Narrator
Speech acts, 33–34, 365
Speech act theory, 12–13
    illocutionary act, 12
    locutionary act, 12
    perlocutionary act, 12
    taxonomy of acts, 12
Situational semantics, 10–11
State, 176–177, *see also* Stative sentences
    events, 165
    network representation of stative sentence, 185
    subinterval property of, 165
Statives, 167
Stative sentences, 185
Story, 62, 159, *see also* Discourse
    as distinct from discourse, 62–64, 67
    events, 71
    relation with story world, 130
Story characters
    clauses containing introductions, 231
        rules for identifying, 238–241
    introductory devices, 229
        deictic term co-occurence, 234–235
        deictic term frequency, 233
        deictic term location, 233–236
Story context, 116
Story grammar, 8, 9, 13, 227, 237
Story operator, 109–110, 112–114, 116
Story space, 114, 116, *see also* Belief space
Story world, 30, 64, 70, 76, 108, 111, 114, 121–125, 130–131, 384
    logic of, 72–73, *see also* Verisimilitude
    mental model of, 108
    relation to real world, 73–76
Story world context, 120
Story world operator, 120
Story world time, 469–473
Storytelling
    oral, 131
Strata in narrative structure
    connectivity, *see* Connectivity systems

psychological structure, 448–452
spatial structure, 447–448
temporal structure, 443–447
Structures representation theories, 7–11
criticisms, 9–10
Subjective character, 264, 315, 319–320, 338, 342
expected, 344
Subjective context, 36, 54, 265, 315, 329, *see also* Subjective sentence
boundary of, 330
indication by referencing, 331
Subjective elements
psychological studies of, 353–355
Subjective experience, 296
Subjective sentence, 36, 53–54, 76, 264, 284, 342, *see also* Represented Perception, Represented Thought
Subjectivity, 23, 40, 58, 292, 310–311, 325–326, 386, 461, 466
indicators of, 330
in persuasive texts, 417
relation to deixis, 23
role in language-act, 19
role in narrative, 19–20
Syntactic theory, 362

T

Temporal deixis
hypothetical time vs., 410
individual differences in use, 412
in persuasive texts, 409–410, 417
time shift, 468
Temporal logic, 161
Temporal reference points, 166
Attachment time (AT), 167–169, 171–175, 177, 179, 184
Event time (ET), 167–169, 171–175, 179
Reference time (RT), 169, 171–172, 177, 180
Speech time (ST), 169, 172, 179, 183
Temporal shifts, 461, 468
Temporal structure in narratives, 468–473
continuous time, 469
density, 473
embeddedness, 473
granularity, 473
scale, 473
temporal jumps, 469
vagueness, 473

Tense, 166–170
Tests of Written English, 414
Text
situations, 343–344
theories of comprehension, 341
Text linguistics, 325
Theoretical entity of literary criticism, 113
Time, ontology of, 161
Time adverbials, 171, 179
Time of narration, *see* Temporal reference points, Speech time
Topic continuity, 287
Transivity devices, 145

U, V

Uniqueness principles, 85
Verbs, *see also* Deictic verbs
time schemata of, 162
Verisimilitude, 71–73, *see also* Story world logic
Verticality, see Fictional language models, dual voice view
Deictic shift model and, 46
Vividness
deixis and, 412, 415
in persuasive texts, 409, 411–412
Voice, 36–39, 49, 54, 57

W

Wayfinding, 387–404
grammatical style in directions, 401–402
instructions to turn, 399–401
WHAT
content, 135
history, 135
WHEN, 137, 150–152, *see also* Now-point
focalizing, 137
history, 138
WHERE, 148–150, 152–155, *see also* Deictic center - spatial component
content, 135
contraction, 136
disambiguation of, 251–252, 254
expansion, 136
history, 136
introduction of
maintenance, 246–249, 251–252
origin, 136

WHERE *(Cont.)*
    relation to perspective taking, 252, 254
    shifting, 246–249, 251–252, 254
WHO, 134, 146–148, 152–155, 342, *see also*
        Point of view
    content, 134
    focal, *see* Focal WHO
    focalized, 134, *see also* Focal WHO
    focalizing, *see* Focalizing WHO

    history, 134
    scope, 134

Z

Zero anaphor, 328
Ziji, 297, 306, *see also* Mandarin; Reflexive
    pronoun